Provence &
the Côte d'Azur

Nicola Williams

LONELY PLANET PUBLICATIONS
Melbourne • Oakland • London • Paris

PROVENCE & THE CÔTE D'AZUR

Vaucluse
Avignon's Palais des Papes & theatre festival; Mont Ventoux; Roman relics; Carpentras and Richerenches markets

Châteauneuf-du-Pape
Wine fit for a pope

The Camargue
Flamingo - pink wetlands: walking, cycling & bird-watching

Marseille
Art museums; morning fish market at the Vieux Port; bouillabaisse; boat trips to Château d'If & around Les Calanques

La Voulte
Privas
Loriol
Crest
Die
Vals-les-Bains
Aubenas
Aspres
Veyne
Villeneuve
Montélimar
La Bégude
Valréas
Nyons
Bollène
Vaison-la-Romaine
Pont-St-Esprit
Dentelles de Montmirail
MONT VENTOUX
1909m
Bagnols
Orange
Châteauneuf-du-Pape
Carpentras
Forcalquier
Moussac
Uzès
Pont du Gard
Villeneuve
AVIGNON
Apt
Manosque
Parc Regional
NÎMES
Cavaillon
MONTAGNE DU LUBÉRON
Beaucaire
Tarascon
St-Rémy-de-Provence
Les Alpilles
Cadenet
Mirabeau
Fontvieille
Les-Baux-des-Provence
Pertuis
Rians
Aimargues
Vauvert
St Gilles
ARLES
Eygulières
Lambesc
Montagne Ste Victoire
Aigues-Mortes
Salon-de-Provence
AIX-EN-PROVENCE
Etang de Vaccarès
Berre
St Maximin-la-Sainte Baume
Etang de Berre
Stes-Maries-de-la-Mer
Golfe de Beauduc
Port St Louis
Golfe de Fos
Rade de Marseille
MARSEILLE
Île Ratonneau
Île Pomègues
Le Beauss
Les Calanques
La Ciotat
Ollou
Bandol
Sanary
Cap Sic

0   10   20 km

MEDITERRANEAN SEA

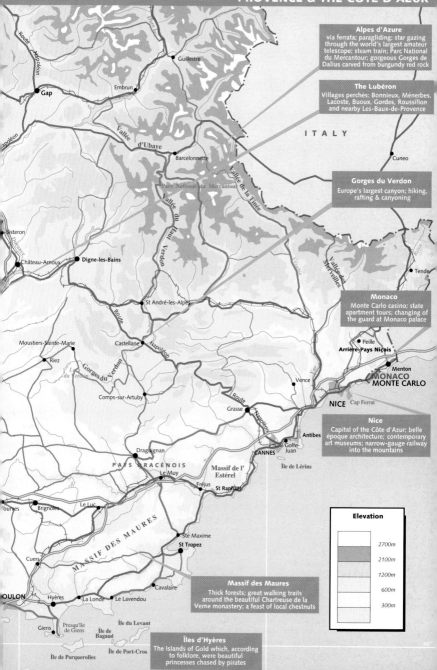

PROVENCE & THE CÔTE D'AZUR

Alpes d'Azure
via ferrata; paragliding; star gazing through the world's largest amateur telescope; steam train; Parc National du Mercantour; gorgeous Gorges de Dalius carved from burgundy red rock

The Lubéron
Villages perchés: Bonnieux, Ménerbes, Lacoste, Buoux, Gordes, Roussillon and nearby Les-Baux-de-Provence

Gorges du Verdon
Europe's largest canyon; hiking, rafting & canyoning

Monaco
Monte Carlo casino; state apartment tours; changing of the guard at Monaco palace

Nice
Capital of the Côte d'Azur; belle époque architecture; contemporary art museums; narrow-gauge railway into the mountains

Massif des Maures
Thick forests; great walking trails around the beautiful Chartreuse de la Verne monastery; a feast of local chestnuts

Îles d'Hyères
The Islands of Gold which, according to folklore, were beautiful princesses chased by pirates

Elevation

	2700m
	2100m
	1200m
	600m
	300m

ITALY

Cuneo

Tende

Guillestre

Embrun

Gap

Barcelonnette

Vallée d'Ubaye

Parc National du Mercantour

Vallée de la Tinée

Vallée du Haut Verdon

Sisteron

Château-Arnoux

Digne-les-Bains

St André-les-Alpes

Vallée Merveilles

Peille

Arrière-Pays Niçois

Menton

MONACO
MONTE CARLO

Moustiers-Sainte-Marie

Castellane

Napoléon

Route

Riez

Lac du Verdon

Gorges du Verdon

Comps-sur-Artuby

Vence

NICE

Cap Ferrat

Grasse

Route

Napoléon

Antibes

CANNES

Golfe-Juan

Île de Lérins

Draguignan

PAYS DRACÉNOIS

Le Muy

Massif de l' Estérel

Fréjus

St Raphaël

ourges

Brignoles

Le Luc

Le Lavandou

Cuers

MASSIF DES MAURES

Ste Maxime

St Tropez

Cavalaire

OULON

Hyères

La Londe

Giens

Presqu'île de Giens

Île du Levant

Île de Bagaud

Île de Port-Cros

Île de Porquerolles

Provence & the Côte d'Azur
1st edition – June 1999

Published by
Lonely Planet Publications Pty Ltd A.C.N. 005 607 983
192 Burwood Rd, Hawthorn, Victoria 3122, Australia

Lonely Planet Offices
Australia PO Box 617, Hawthorn, Victoria 3122
USA 150 Linden St, Oakland, CA 94607
UK 10a Spring Place, London NW5 3BH
France 1 rue du Dahomey, 75011 Paris

Photographs
Many of the images in this guide are available for licensing from
Lonely Planet Images.
email: lpi@lonelyplanet.com.au

Front cover photograph
Traditional Provençal dress (Mark Buscail, The Image Bank)

ISBN 0 86442 625 9

text & maps © Lonely Planet 1999
photos © photographers as indicated 1999

Digne-les-Bains climate chart compiled from information supplied by
Patrick J Tyson, © Patrick J Tyson, 1999

Printed by The Bookmaker Pty Ltd
Printed in China

Contents – Text

Contents – Maps

MAP INDEX

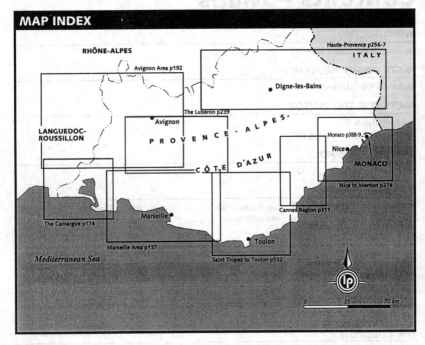

RHÔNE-ALPES

Avignon Area p192

Haute-Provence p256-7

ITALY

Digne-les-Bains

The Lubéron p239

LANGUEDOC-ROUSSILLON

Avignon

P R O V E N C E - A L P E S -

C Ô T E   D ' A Z U R

Monaco p388-9

Nice

MONACO

Nice to Menton p274

Cannes Region p311

The Camargue p174

Marseille

Marseille Area p137

Toulon

Saint Tropez to Toulon p532

Mediterranean Sea

0   35   70 km

The Author

Nicola Williams

Nicola lives in Lyon, at the crossroads to the Alps and France's hot south. A journalist by training, she first hit the road in 1990 when she bussed and boated it from Jakarta to East Timor and back again. Following a two year stint at the *North Wales Weekly News*, she moved to Latvia to bus it round the Baltics as Features Editor of the English-language *Baltic Times* newspaper. Following a happy 12 months exploring the Baltic region as Editor-in-chief of the *In Your Pocket* city-guide series, she traded in Lithuanian *cepelinai* for Lyonnaise *andouillette*.

Nicola graduated from Kent and completed an MA in Islamic Societies & Cultures at London's School of Oriental & African Studies. She updated Lonely Planet's *Estonia, Latvia & Lithuania* guide, authored *Romania & Moldova*, worked on part of *France* and – having spent far too many months in the sun – is currently bracing herself for a chilly trip back east to Ukraine.

FROM THE AUTHOR

Un grand merci to French chefs Alain Ducasse and Roger Vergé for kindly contributing recipes to this book; and to their right-hand women, Madame Sylvie Charbit from Le Moulin de Mougins, and Madame Céline Martin from Le Louis XV in Monaco, for organising the paperwork and illustrative slides. Equally sincere thanks to Patricia Wells for insider tips on Provence's truffle trade and divulging what makes a true tapenade; and to Deborah Orrill for putting me in touch.

Out of the kitchen, thanks to Peter Mayle for more than just *A Year in Provence*; Catherine Jeanicot and Laurence Puyot from the Comité Interprofessionnel des Vins Côtes de Provence in Les Arcs; Marc Rolley of the Syndicat des Vins Côtes de Provence; and Pascal Goyard from the Fédération des Syndicats de Producteurs de Châteauneuf-du-Pape who happily helped in unveiling the pleasures of Provence's papal wine.

Viticulture apart, thank you to Olivier Balderiotti from the Société des Joutes Raphaëloises in Saint Raphaël; Catherine Gentil of Côte d'Azur Développement (CAD); Félibrige in Aix-en-Provence; Sœur Miriam, Sœur Jacques-Marie and all the Dominican nuns at Matisse's Chapelle du Rosaire; Joëlle Diarra, guardian of Matisse's Villa Le Rêve in Vence; Bernaud Devaux and David Stubbs in the Village des Tortues for enlightening me about the Massif des Maures' threatened shelled creatures; the staff at the Parc National Port-Cros office in Hyères and their 'island of gold' colleagues on Porquerolles, Port-Cros and Le Levant. In Nice, thanks to the good-humoured proprietors of the Hôtel Le

6 The Authors

Petit Louvre and to Marc from the Hôtel Les Orangers (highly recommended). In Saint Tropez, thank you Dany Lartigue from the Maison des Papillons; Anne Van der Linden for expert local knowledge and a fabulous home; and to Reine & George Ortiz for that nifty little, one-off wedding number, *Saint Tropez In Your Pocket*!

In Melbourne, Oz, particular thanks to Jocelyn Harewood, Lisa Borg, Jane Fitzpatrick, Katie Cody and Darren Elder for their enthusiasm, patience, advice and painstaking work on this book; Sacha Pearson (LP-US); and fellow authors Steve Fallon and Daniel Robinson whose France texts formed an invaluable basis for parts of this book. In Germany, sincere gratitude to Christa and Karl Otto Lüfkens, and Peter and Marianne Rosiny for their top tips and photographs.

Closer to home, a sweet thank you to the men in my life: brother Neil Williams for driving me through ice ball storms and round the bends (literally) in the Vallée de la Roya; father Paul Williams for an endless supply of travel articles and much more; and husband Matthias Lüfkens for his *joie de vivre*, relentless proofreading, love of France, and gracious tolerance of a temperamental, workaholic wife.

This Book

Material from the Provence, Côte d'Azur and Monaco chapters of Lonely Planet's France guide was used for this book. These chapters were first written by Leanne Logan, updated for the 2nd edition by Steve Fallon and for the 3rd edition by Nicola Williams.

FROM THE PUBLISHER

This first edition was coordinated by Jocelyn Harewood (editor) and Lisa Borg (designer) at Lonely Planet's Melbourne office. Jocelyn was assisted with editing and proofing by Ada Cheung, Tom Smallman and Wendy Owen. Mapping assistance was provided by Paul Dawson, Adrian Persoglia, Paul Piaia, Maree Styles, Piotr Czajkowski, Sarah Sloane and Joelene Kowalski. Thanks to Katie Cody, Rachel Black and Tamsin Wilson for their advice and patience. The language section was developed by Quentin Frayne. Matt King advised on illustrations and Tim Uden on layout. Illustrations were drawn by Sarah Jolly, Picasso by Mick Weldon. Guillaume Roux designed the cover.

Foreword

ABOUT LONELY PLANET GUIDEBOOKS

The story begins with a classic travel adventure: Tony and Maureen Wheeler's 1972 journey across Europe and Asia to Australia. Useful information about the overland trail did not exist at that time, so Tony and Maureen published the first Lonely Planet guidebook to meet a growing need.

From a kitchen table, then from a tiny office in Melbourne (Australia), Lonely Planet has become the largest independent travel publisher in the world, an international company with offices in Melbourne, Oakland (USA), London (UK) and Paris (France).

Today Lonely Planet guidebooks cover the globe. There is an ever-growing list of books and there's information in a variety of forms and media. Some things haven't changed. The main aim is still to help make it possible for adventurous travellers to get out there – to explore and better understand the world.

At Lonely Planet we believe travellers can make a positive contribution to the countries they visit – if they respect their host communities and spend their money wisely. Since 1986 a percentage of the income from each book has been donated to aid projects and human rights campaigns.

Updates Lonely Planet thoroughly updates each guidebook as often as possible. This usually means there are around two years between editions, although for more unusual or more stable destinations the gap can be longer. Check the imprint page (following the colour map at the beginning of the book) for publication dates.

Between editions up-to-date information is available in two free newsletters – the paper *Planet Talk* and email *Comet* (to subscribe, contact any Lonely Planet office) – and on our Web site at www.lonelyplanet.com. The *Upgrades* section of the Web site covers a number of important and volatile destinations and is regularly updated by Lonely Planet authors. *Scoop* covers news and current affairs relevant to travellers. And, lastly, the *Thorn Tree* bulletin board and *Postcards* section of the site carry unverified, but fascinating, reports from travellers.

Correspondence The process of creating new editions begins with the letters, postcards and emails received from travellers. This correspondence often includes suggestions, criticisms and comments about the current editions. Interesting excerpts are immediately passed on via newsletters and the Web site, and everything goes to our authors to be verified when they're researching on the road. We're keen to get more feedback from organisations or individuals who represent communities visited by travellers.

> Lonely Planet gathers information for everyone who's curious about the planet – and especially for those who explore it first-hand. Through guidebooks, phrasebooks, activity guides, maps, literature, newsletters, image library, TV series and Web site we act as an information exchange for a worldwide community of travellers.

Research Authors aim to gather sufficient practical information to enable travellers to make informed choices and to make the mechanics of a journey run smoothly. They also research historical and cultural background to help enrich the travel experience and allow travellers to understand and respond appropriately to cultural and environmental issues.

Authors don't stay in every hotel because that would mean spending a couple of months in each medium-sized city and, no, they don't eat at every restaurant because that would mean stretching belts beyond capacity. They do visit hotels and restaurants to check standards and prices, but feedback based on readers' direct experiences can be very helpful.

Many of our authors work undercover, others aren't so secretive. None of them accept freebies in exchange for positive write-ups. And none of our guidebooks contain any advertising.

Production Authors submit their raw manuscripts and maps to offices in Australia, USA, UK or France. Editors and cartographers – all experienced travellers themselves – then begin the process of assembling the pieces. When the book finally hits the shops, some things are already out of date, we start getting feedback from readers and the process begins again ...

WARNING & REQUEST

Things change – prices go up, schedules change, good places go bad and bad places go bankrupt – nothing stays the same. So, if you find things better or worse, recently opened or long since closed, please tell us and help make the next edition even more accurate and useful. We genuinely value all the feedback we receive. Julie Young coordinates a well travelled team that reads and acknowledges every letter, postcard and email and ensures that every morsel of information finds its way to the appropriate authors, editors and cartographers for verification.

Everyone who writes to us will find their name in the next edition of the appropriate guidebook. They will also receive the latest issue of *Planet Talk*, our quarterly printed newsletter, or *Comet*, our monthly email newsletter. Subscriptions to both newsletters are free. The very best contributions will be rewarded with a free guidebook.

Excerpts from your correspondence may appear in new editions of Lonely Planet guidebooks, the Lonely Planet Web site, *Planet Talk* or *Comet*, so please let us know if you *don't* want your letter published or your name acknowledged.

Send all correspondence to the Lonely Planet office closest to you:

Australia: PO Box 617, Hawthorn, Victoria 3122
USA: 150 Linden St, Oakland, CA 94607
UK: 10A Spring Place, London NW5 3BH
France: 1 rue du Dahomey, 75011 Paris

Or email us at: talk2us@lonelyplanet.com.au

For news, views and updates see our Web site: www.lonelyplanet.com

HOW TO USE A LONELY PLANET GUIDEBOOK

The best way to use a Lonely Planet guidebook is any way you choose. At Lonely Planet we believe the most memorable travel experiences are often those that are unexpected, and the finest discoveries are those you make yourself. Guidebooks are not intended to be used as if they provide a detailed set of infallible instructions!

Contents All Lonely Planet guidebooks follow roughly the same format. The Facts about the Destination chapters or sections give background information ranging from history to weather. Facts for the Visitor gives practical information on issues like visas and health. Getting There & Away gives a brief starting point for researching travel to and from the destination. Getting Around gives an overview of the transport options when you arrive.

The peculiar demands of each destination determine how subsequent chapters are broken up, but some things remain constant. We always start with background, then proceed to sights, places to stay, places to eat, entertainment, getting there and away, and getting around information – in that order.

Heading Hierarchy Lonely Planet headings are used in a strict hierarchical structure that can be visualised as a set of Russian dolls. Each heading (and its following text) is encompassed by any preceding heading that is higher on the hierarchical ladder.

Entry Points We do not assume guidebooks will be read from beginning to end, but that people will dip into them. The traditional entry points are the list of contents and the index. In addition, however, some books have a complete list of maps and an index map illustrating map coverage.

There may also be a colour map that shows highlights. These highlights are dealt with in greater detail in the Facts for the Visitor chapter, along with planning questions and suggested itineraries. Each chapter covering a geographical region usually begins with a locator map and another list of highlights. Once you find something of interest in a list of highlights, turn to the index.

Maps Maps play a crucial role in Lonely Planet guidebooks and include a huge amount of information. A legend is printed on the back page. We seek to have complete consistency between maps and text, and to have every important place in the text captured on a map. Map key numbers usually start in the top left corner.

Although inclusion in a guidebook usually implies a recommendation we cannot list every good place. Exclusion does not necessarily imply criticism. In fact there are a number of reasons why we might exclude a place – sometimes it is simply inappropriate to encourage an influx of travellers.

Introduction

It is remarkable how many faces Provence really has.

The rough-cut diamond of cosmopolitan Marseille with its busy port, noisy streets and raucous fish market is a world away from the quaint medieval villages which gaze wearily down on sun-drenched plains from hilltop perches.

Blink again and the Camargue appears before you; an untamed land of cattle-herding cowboys, clouds of pink flamingos and silver salt marshes, where bulls fight in rings and gypsies dance wild flamenco. Lubéron, a manicured garden of gnarled vines and cherry trees is speckled with *mas* which have been splendidly restored as *résidences secondaires*, making another stunning contrast.

In Avignon, Papal Provence resides in a resplendent, 14th century palace. Around his feet, the Vaucluse region fans out into a sensual orgy of bright hues and scents: lavender, wild herbs, vines, olive trees. The turn of each season brings a new gift: blossoming almond and cherry trees in early spring; green fields sprinkled with buttons of scarlet poppies; asparagus, red cherries, and strawberries; pink chestnut tree blossoms; summer melons, pumpkins, and fields of bright yellow sunflowers. Come winter, truffles sprout underground for pigs to snout.

A world apart is the ancient legacy bequeathed by the Romans. Triumphal arches and amphitheatres attest to their grand architectural monuments. After defeating the Celto-Ligurians at Greek Massilia in 125 BC

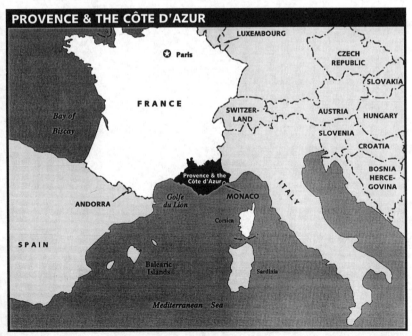

PROVENCE & THE CÔTE D'AZUR

they created Provincia Gallia, from which contemporary Provence takes its name.

The glamour queen of 20th century Provence races into gear along the coast – the alluring Côte d'Azur, immortalised on the silver screen by Grace Kelly, Brigitte Bardot *et al* and on canvas by Renoir, Matisse, Picasso and the host of other celebrated artists who helped make this place the legend it is today. Their works, displayed in museums in and around Nice, Cannes and Saint Tropez, attract millions of tourists each year – as do the nearby Massif des Maures, l'Estérel, and Alpine foothills that plummet precipitously into the Mediterranean east of Nice. No one leaves without visiting Monaco and its glittering capital, Monte Carlo. Offshore from this crowded coastal strip is a cluster of islands which, out of season, are among the glamour queen's prized treasures.

A far cry from all this pandemonium are the lush, green, scarcely inhabited valleys of the Alpes d'Azur which can languish for days without a tourist passing by. Here, in Haute-Provence, the land of sun and olives meets the Alps and their trusted terrain of snow and melted cheese. Clear Alpine lakes, torrential canyons, and a national park with a rich archaeological heritage are sheltered in this mountainous region that stretches north from Nice and west to the Gorges du Verdon and beyond.

Then there is the great hulk of Mont Ventoux, the indisputable king and guardian of Provence who – with the sun and the mistral – commands this kingdom from the top of his barren sun-baked slopes in northwestern Provence. The blow of the mistral adds a bitter bite to the air – ensuring tourists don't stay all year – while the sun for the vast majority of the year bathes Provence in the most glorious southern sunshine, with a warmth and intensity of light absolutely unknown in any other part of Europe.

Facts about Provence

HISTORY
Early Inhabitants
Provence was inhabited from an exceptionally early age. Prehistoric rock scratchings in the Grottes de l'Observatoire in Monaco, carved one million years ago, are among the world's oldest. Traces of fire discovered in the Grotte de l'Escale at Saint-Estève-Janson show prehistoric people to have used fire from 600,000 BC. The Terra Amata site in Nice was inhabited as early as 400,000 BC.

During the Middle Palaeolithic period (about 90,000 to 40,000 BC), Neanderthal hunters occupied the coast. Modern man followed in 30,000 BC. The ornate wall paintings of bisons, seals, ibex and other animals inside the decorated Grotte Cosquer (named after the Cassis diver who discovered it in 1991) in the Calanque de Sormiou, south of Marseille, date from 20,000 BC. Many more undiscovered examples of prehistoric art are believed to exist in the region in cave dwellings like this.

The Neolithic period (about 6000 to 4500 years ago), also known as the New Stone Age, witnessed the earliest domestication of sheep in Châteauneuf-lès-Martigues, followed by the cultivation of lands by the Ligurians. The first dwellings to be built (around 3500 BC) were *bories*, evident in Gordes. These one or two-storey beehive-shaped huts, constructed without mortar using thin wedges of limestone, were lived in until as late as the 18th century. The collection of 30,000 Bronze Age petroglyphs (1800 and 1500 BC) at the foot of Mont Bégo in the Vallée des Merveilles remain among the world's most spectacular.

Ancient Provence
The eastern part of the Mediterranean coast was colonised around 600 BC by Greeks, from Phocaea in Asia Minor, who settled in Massilia (Marseille). The Greeks were the first to develop the region, establishing trading posts at other coastal points from the 4th century BC: at Antipolis (Antibes), Olbia (Hyères), Athenopolis (Saint Tropez), Nikaia (Nice), Monoïkos (Monaco) and Glanum (near Saint-Rémy-de-Provence). The Greeks brought with them olives and grape vines.

At the same time as Hellenic civilisation was developing on the coast, the Celts were penetrating the northern part of the region. They mingled with ancient Ligurians to create a Celto-Ligurian stronghold around Entremont. Its influence extended as far south as Draguignan.

In 125 BC, the Romans were called in by the Greeks to help Massilia against the threat of invasion by Celto-Ligurians from Entremont. The Romans were victorious, and this marked the start of the Gallo-Roman era and the creation of Provincia Gallia Transalpina, the first Roman provincia (province), from which the name Provence is derived.

The Gallo-Roman Era
Provincia Gallia Transalpina, which quickly became Provincia Narbonensis, was much larger than modern-day Provence. It embraced all of southern France, from the Alps to the Mediterranean and as far west as the Pyrenees. Narbonne was its capital. In 122 BC the Romans destroyed the Ligurian capital of Entremont and established the Roman stronghold of Aquae Sextiae Salluviorum (Aix-en-Provence) at its foot.

During this period the Romans started building roads to secure the route between Italy and Spain. The via Aurelia linked Rome to Arles and Nîmes; the northbound via Agrippa followed the Rhône from Arles to Avignon, Orange and Lyon; and the via Domitia led from Nîmes westwards to the Pyrenees and beyond. Vestiges of these roads, such as the Pont Julien (dating from 3 BC), near Bonnieux in the Lubéron, still remain.

The Roman influence on Provence was tremendous, although it was only after Julius Caesar's conquest of Gaul in 58-51 BC and its consequent integration into the Roman Empire that the region really began to flourish. Massilia, which had retained its independence following the creation of Provincia, was incorporated by Caesar in 49 BC. In 14 BC, the still rebellious Ligurians were defeated by Augustus who built a trophy monument at La Turbie (6 BC) to celebrate his victory. Arelate (Arles) became the chosen Roman regional capital.

Under Augustus, grandiose amphitheatres seating 10,000 spectators, were built to host gladiator combats at Arelate, Nemausus (Nîmes), Forum Julii (Fréjus) and Vasio Vocontiorum (Vaison-la-Romaine). Triumphal arches were raised at Arausio (Orange), Cabelio (Cavaillon), Carpentorate (Carpentras) and Glanum; and a series of aqueducts were constructed. The mammoth Pont du Gard – 275m in length – was part of a 50km-long system of canals built around 19 BC by Agrippa, Augustus' deputy, to bring water from Uzès to Nîmes. Many of these ancient public buildings remain exceptionally well preserved.

The end of the third century saw the reorganisation of the Roman empire. Provincia Narbonensis was split into two provinces in 284 AD. The land on the right bank of the Rhône (Languedoc-Roussillon today) remained Narbonensis and the land on the left bank (today's Provence) became Provincia Viennoise. Christianity penetrated the region and was adopted by the Romans. Provençal legend says it was brought to the region by Mary Magdalene, Mary Jacob and Mary Salome who sailed into Saintes-Maries-de-la-Mer in 40 AD. Saint Honorat founded the Lérins monastical order on the Îles de Lérins at this time.

Medieval Provence

After the collapse of the Roman empire in 476 AD, Provence suffered invasions by the Visigoths, Burgundians and the Ostrogoths. It was ceded to the Franks at the start of the 6th century. Rebellions in Marseille, Arles and Avignon (732-39) against the Frankish rule were brutally squashed.

In the early 9th century, the Muslim Saracens emerged as a warrior force to be reckoned with. Attacks along the Maures coast, Niçois hinterland and more northern Alps, persuaded villagers to take refuge in the hills. Many of Provence's perched, hilltop villages date from this chaotic period. But the Saracens did teach the local population what could be done with the bark of cork oak. In 974 the Saracen fortress at La Garde Freinet was defeated by Guillaume Le Libérateur, Count of Arles, who consequently extended his feudal control over the entire region, marking a return of peace and unity to Provence which became a marquisat. In 1032 it became part of the Holy Roman Empire.

At the start of the 12th century, the Marquisat of Provence was split in two: the north fell into the hands of the Counts of Toulouse from 1125 and retained the title of marquisat while the Catalan Counts of Barcelona gained control of the southern part, which stretched from the Rhône to the Durance and from the Alps to the sea. This was called the Comté de Provence (County of Provence). Raymond Bérenger V (1209-45) was the first Catalan count to reside permanently in Aix (the capital since 1186). In 1229 he conquered Nice to gain better control of eastern Provence and the southern Alps and, in 1232, he founded Barcelonnette. In 1246, after Bérenger's death, the Comté de Provence passed to the House of Anjou under which it enjoyed great prosperity.

Troubadour literature composed in *langue d'oc* (Occitan, of which Provençal is a dialect) and Romanesque architecture – the grandiose 12th century abbeys at Sénanque, Silvacane and Le Thoronet – blossomed in medieval Provence.

The Popes

In 1274 Comtat Venaissin, situated in Provence's northern realm – namely Carpentras and its Vaucluse hinterland – was ceded to Pope Gregory X in Rome. In 1309, French-born Clement V (1305-14) moved the papal headquarters from feud-riven Rome to Avignon, thus beginning the most resplendent period in that city's history.

Between 1309 and 1376, nine pontiffs headed the Roman Catholic church from Avignon. Under the reign of Avignon's third pope, Benoît XII (1334-42), work started on the resplendent Palais des Papes (Popes' Palace) which was enlarged to monumental status during the reign of his successor, Clement VI (1342-52). In 1348 Pope Clement VI purchased the city of Avignon (not within the boundaries of Comtat Venaissin) from the reigning Countess of Provence, Queen Jeanne of Naples (1343-82). Accused of murdering her husband, she fled to Avignon where she sold the city for 80,000 florins – in exchange for a papal pardon. Clement VI had Avignon bridge built in 1350.

Cultural life in Provence flourished inside and outside the papal sphere during the 14th century. A university was established in Avignon as early as 1303, followed by a university in Aix, Provence's capital, a century later. In 1327, the Italian poet Petrarch (1304-74), exiled in Avignon, first encountered his muse, Laura. In 1336 he became the first person to climb to the top of Mont Ventoux. The Anjou reign of good King Réné, King of Naples (1434-80) further enhanced this period of relative peace and prosperity. French became the courtly language and a castle was built at Tarascon.

The papacy returned to Rome in 1403, although Avignon and Comtat Venaissin remained under papal control until 1792.

French Provence

In 1481, Réné's successor, his nephew Charles III, died heirless and Provence was ceded to Louis XI of France. In 1486 the state of Aix ratified Provence's union with France and the centralist policies of the French kings saw the region's autonomy greatly reduced. Aix Parliament, a French administrative body, was created in 1501.

This new addition to the French kingdom did not include Nice, Barcelonnette, Puget

Théniers and the hinterlands of these towns which, in 1388, had become incorporated into the lands of the House of Savoy. The Comté de Nice (County of Nice; essentially today's Alpes-Maritimes *département*), with Nice as its capital did not become part of French Provence until 1860.

A period of instability ensued. Jews living in Provençal France fled to ghettos in Carpentras, Pernes-lès-Fontaines, L'Isle-sur-Sorgue, Cavaillon or Avignon – all part of the pontifical enclave of Comtat Venaissin where papal protection remained assured until 1570. Following the French conquest of Milan during the Italian wars in the 1520s, Charles V invaded Provence. This was followed by another attack and further bloodshed in 1536. The Villers-Cotterêts statute approved in 1539 made French, rather than Provençal, the official administrative language in Provence.

An early victim of the Reformation sweeping Europe in the 1530s and the consequent Wars of Religion (1562-98) was the Lubéron. In April 1545, the population of eleven Vaudois villages in the Lubéron was massacred in six days. Numerous clashes followed between the staunchly Catholic stronghold of Comtat Venaissin and its Huguenot (Protestant) neighbours to the north around Orange. In 1580 the plague temporarily immobilised the otherwise volatile region. Treatments first used by the prophetic Nostradamus (1503-66) in Saint-Rémy-de-Provence were administered to plague victims. The Edict of Nantes in 1598, which recognised Protestant control of certain areas including Lourmarin in the Lubéron, brought an uneasy peace to the region – until its revocation by Louis XIV in 1685. A full-scale persecution of Protestants in Provence ensued, with leading Huguenots being killed or imprisoned. Many were jailed in the Tour de Constance in Aigues-Mortes and the Château d'If off the shores of Marseille.

The plague in 1720 killed half of Marseille's population. The close of the century was marked by the French Revolution (1789). As the *Féderés* (National Guard)

from Marseille marched northward to defend the Revolution, a merry little tune composed in Strasbourg several months earlier for the war against Prussia – *Chant de Guerre de l'Armée du Rhin* (War Song of the Rhine Army) – sprung from their lips. France's stirring national anthem, *La Marseillaise,* was born.

La Route Napoléon

Provence was divided into three départements in 1790: Var, Bouches-du-Rhône and the Basse-Alpes (Lower Alps). Two years later papal Avignon and Comtat Venaissin were annexed by France, making way for the creation of a fourth administrative department, Vaucluse.

In 1793, the Armée du Midi marched into Nice, captured the town, and declared it French territory on 31 January. France also captured Monaco, which until now had been a recognised independent state ruled by the Grimaldi family. When Toulon was besieged by the English, it was thanks to the efforts of a dashing young Corsican general named Napoléon Bonaparte (Napoléon I) that France recaptured it.

The Reign of Terror that swept through France between September 1793 and July 1794 saw religious freedoms revoked, churches desecrated and cathedrals turned into 'Temples of Reason'. In the secrecy of their homes, people in Provence handcrafted thumb nail-sized, biblical figurines, hence the rather inglorious creation of the Provençal *santon* (see the boxed text in the Marseille Area chapter).

In 1814, France lost the territories it had seized in 1793. The Comté of Nice was ceded to Victor Emmanuel I, King of Sardinia. It remained under Sardinian protectorship until 1860 when an agreement between Napoléon III and the House of Savoy helped drive the Austrians from northern Italy, prompting France to repossess Savoy and the area around Nice. In Monaco, meanwhile, the Treaty of Paris restored the rights of the Grimaldi royal family; from 1817 until 1860 the

principality also fell under the protection of the Sardinian king.

Meanwhile, the Allied restoration of the House of Bourbon to the French throne at the Congress of Vienna (1814-15) following Napoléon I's abdication and exile to Elba, was rudely interrupted by the return of the emperor. Following his escape from Elba in 1815, Napoléon I landed at Golfe-Juan on 1 March with a 1200-strong army. He proceeded northwards, passing through Cannes, Grasse, Castellane, Digne-les-Bains and Sisteron en route to his triumphal return to Paris on 20 May. Unfortunately, Napoleon's glorious 'Hundred Days' back in power ended with the Battle of Waterloo and his return to exile. He died in 1821.

During the revolutions of 1848, French revolutionaries adopted as their own the red, white and blue tricolour of Martigues, a small town near Marseille. This became France's national flag.

The Belle Époque

The Second Empire (1852-70) brought to the region a revival in all things Provençal, a movement spearheaded by poet Frédéric Mistral (see Literature later in this chapter). Rapid economic growth was the era's other hallmark: Nice, which had finally become part of France in 1860, was among Europe's first cities to have a purely tourist-based economy. Between 1860 and 1911 it was also Europe's fastest growing city. The city became particularly popular with the English aristocracy in the Victorian period. They followed their queen's example of wintering in Nice to indulge in its mild winter. European royalty followed soon after. The rail line reached Toulon in 1856, followed by Nice and Draguignan, and in 1864 work started on a coastal road from Nice to Monaco. The same year exotic palm trees, mimosas and eucalyptus plants were imported from Australia. In fine Second Empire architectural style, the Nice opera house and neoclassical Palais de Justice (Justice Palace) were built.

In neighbouring Monaco, the Grimaldi family had given up its claim over its former territories of Menton and Roquebrune in 1861 (under Monégasque rule until 1848) in exchange for France's recognition of its status as an independent principality. When Monte Carlo casino opened four years later, Monaco leapt from being Europe's poorest state to one of its richest.

The Third Republic ushered in the glittering *belle époque* (literally 'beautiful age'), with art nouveau architecture, a whole field of artistic 'isms' such as impressionism, and advances in science and engineering. Wealthy French, English, American and Russian tourists discovered the coast, attracted by its beauty and temperate climate in winter. The intensity and clarity of the region's colours and light appealed to many painters including Cézanne, Van Gogh and Matisse. Writers and other celebrities were also attracted to the region and contributed to its fame. Little fishing ports like Saint Tropez became exclusive resorts with lavish, castle-like villas hugged by manicured gardens, tennis courts and golf courses. In 1887 the first guidebook to the French coast was published, following which the coast finally had a name it could call its own – the Côte d'Azur (azure coast).

The Sky Blue Coast

The Côte d'Azur (literally 'Azure Coast') gained its name from an early, 19th century guidebook.

La Côte d'Azur, published in 1887 in picture-book size, was the work of Stéphane Liégeard (1830-1925), a lawyer-cum-aspiring poet from Bourgogne (Burgundy) who lived in Cannes. The guide covered the coast from Menton to Hyères and was an instant hit.

Its title, a reflection of the coast's clear blue cloudless skies, became the hottest buzz word to hit town. And it never tired. The Côte d'Azur is also known as the French Riviera by some Anglophones today.

WWI & the Inter-War Period

No blood was spilled on southern French soil during WWI although large areas of north-eastern France were devastated by trench warfare. Soldiers were conscripted from the region, however, and the human losses included two out of every 10 Frenchmen between 20 and 45 years of age. With its primarily tourist-based economy, the Côte d'Azur recovered quickly from the post-war financial crisis that lingered in the more industrial north.

The 1920s and 30s saw France – and the Côte d'Azur in particular – flourish as a centre of the avant-garde, with artists pushing into the new fields of cubism and surrealism, Le Corbusier rewriting the architectural textbook and foreign writers like Ernest Hemingway and F Scott Fitzgerald attracted by the coast's liberal atmosphere. Nightlife gained a reputation for being at the cutting edge with everything from jazz clubs to striptease. Rail and road access to the south improved: the railway line between Digne-les-Bains and Nice was completed and in 1922 the luxurious *Train Bleu* (Blue Train) made its first run from Calais, via Paris, to the coast. The train only had first-class carriages and was quickly dubbed the 'train to paradise'.

The glorious 1920s hailed the start of the summer season on the Côte d'Azur. Outdoor swimming pools were built and sunbathing sprang into fashion after Coco Chanel made her first appearance on the coast in 1923, draped over the arm of the Duke of Westminster. The ban on gambling in France was lifted, prompting the coast's first casino to open in the Palais de la Méditerranée on Nice's Promenade des Anglais in 1927. The first Formula One Grand Prix took to the streets of Monaco in 1929 while the early 1930s saw wide pyjama-style beach trousers and the opening of a nudist colony on Île du Levant. With the advent of paid holidays for all French workers in 1936, even more tourists flocked to the region. Second and third-class seating was added to the Train Bleu which, since 1929, had been running daily, year round.

WWII

With the onset of war, the Côte d'Azur's glory days turned grey. Depression set in and on 3 September 1939 France and Britain declared war on Germany. But again, Provence and the Côte d'Azur remained relatively unscathed. Following the armistice treaty agreed with Hitler on 22 June 1940, southern France fell into the 'free' Vichy France zone, although Menton and its northern Vallée de Roya (around Sospel) were occupied by the Italians. The Côte d'Azur – particularly Nice – immediately became a safe haven from war-torn occupied France; by 1942 some 43,000 Jews had descended on the coast to seek refuge. Monaco was neutral for the duration of the war.

On 11 November 1942, Nazi Germany invaded Vichy France. Provence was at war. At Toulon port, 73 ships, cruisers, destroyers and submarines – the major part of the French fleet and under the command of Admiral Jean-Baptiste Laborde – were scuttled by their crews to prevent the Germans seizing them. Almost immediately, Toulon was overcome by the Germans and Nice was occupied by the Italians. In January 1943 the Marseille quarter of Le Panier was completely razed, its 40,000 inhabitants being given less than a day's notice to pack up and leave. Those who didn't were sent to Nazi concentration camps. The Resistance movement was particularly strong in Provence where it became known as *maquis* after the Provençal scrub in which it hid.

Among the war casualties was French novelist and pilot, Antoine de Saint-Exupéry – author of *Le Petit Prince* – whose Lightning P38 went down during an Allied forces reconnaissance mission on 31 July 1944. The reason behind the crash remains a mystery.

Two months after D-day, Allied forces landed on the southern coast, on 15 August 1944. They landed at various beaches along the Côte d'Azur, including at Le Dramont near Saint Raphaël, Cavalaire, Pampelonne and the Saint Tropez peninsula. Saint Tropez and Provence's hinterland was almost immediately liberated, but it was not until after five days of heavy fighting that Allied troops, led by the French Général de Montsabert, freed Marseille on 28 August (three days after the liberation of Paris). Toulon was liberated on 26 August, one week after French troops under Général de Lattre de Tassigny first attacked the port.

The Italian occupied areas in the Vallée de Roya were not returned to France until 1947.

Modern Provence

The first international film festival at Cannes in 1946 heralded the return to 'normal life' on the Côte d'Azur: party madness was resumed. Noël Coward, Somerset Maugham and the rest of the coast's intellectual set returned to their abandoned seaside villas while Picasso set up a studio in Golfe-Juan. The 1950s and 60s saw a staccato succession of glamorous society 'events': the fairytale marriage of a Grimaldi prince to a Hollywood film legend in 1956; Vadim's filming of *Et Dieu Créa La Femme* with Brigitte Bardot in Saint Tropez the same year; the emergence of the bikini and the Nice new realists in the late 1950s; the advent of topless sunbathing (and consequent nipple-covering with bottle tops to prevent arrest for indecent exposure); Miles Davis, Ella Fitzgerald and Ray Charles appearing at the 1961 Juan-les-Pins jazz festival.

In 1962 the troubled French colony of Algeria negotiated its independence with President Charles de Gaulle. Some 750,000 *pieds noirs* (literally, 'black feet' – as Algerian-born French people are known in France) flooded into France. A substantial number settled in Provence (particularly in the large urban centres of Marseille, Nice and Toulon), as did immigrants from other French colonies and protectorates in North Africa.

Rapid industrialisation marked the 1960s. Five hydroelectric plants were constructed in 1962 on the banks of the Durance and in 1964 the Electricité de France (EDF, the French electricity company) started digging a canal from north of Manosque all the way south to the Étang de Berre, west of Marseille. The following year construction work began on a 10,000 hectare petrochemical zone and industrial port at Fos-sur-Mer, the most important in southern Europe. Eyesore tanker terminals and oil refineries were raised at the site soon after. 1969 saw the inauguration of a technological park – to become Europe's largest – at Sophia-Antipolis, just north of Antibes (dubbed the California of Europe by many). The first metro line opened in Marseille in 1977 and TGV high-speed trains reached the city in 1981. In the 1970s Provence's first purpose-built ski resort emerged at ugly Isola 2000 (1972) and a monumental, concrete marina was built at Villeneuve-Lourbet-Plage, west of Nice.

Corruption cast a shady cloud over France's hot south in the 1980s and early 1990s. Nice's mayor, the corrupt right-wing Jacques Médecin (son of another former mayor, Jean Médecin, who ruled Nice for 38 years) was twice found guilty of income tax evasion during his 24-year mayorship (1966-90). In 1990, King Jacques – as the flamboyant mayor was known – fled to Uruguay, following which he was convicted (*in absentia*) of misuse of public funds in 1992. Charges included accepting four million FF in bribes and stealing two million FF from the Nice opera. Médecin was extradited in 1994 and imprisoned in Grenoble where he served two years of a 3½ year sentence. The ex-mayor – who sold hand-painted T-shirts in Uruguay when he returned there after his prison release – died of a heart attack, aged 70, in November 1998.

Médecin's counterpart in Toulon, Maurice Arreckx, was an equally shady character and was also arrested and imprisoned on fraud charges. In June 1998 six people were convicted (two with life imprisonment) for the murder of French *député* Yann Piat, shot in 1994 in her Hyères constituency following her public denouncement of the Riviera mafia. Piat is the only member of France's National Assembly (parliament) since WWII to have been assassinated while in office. The press dubbed her assassins – local mafia kingpins barely in their 20s at the time – the 'baby killers'.

This blatant corruption, coupled with economic recession and growing unemployment, fuelled the rapid rise of the extreme-right *Front National* (FN, National Front) in Provence in the mid-1990s. Nowhere else in France has the xenophobic party gained such a fierce stronghold.

The Front National stormed to victory at the 1995 municipal elections in three cities in Provence: Toulon, Orange and Marignane. In neighbouring Vitrolles, voting was declared void and the FN candidate, Bruno Mégret, declared ineligible – only for his wife Catherine to be elected instead when elections were reheld in February 1997. A fourth conquest for the FN.

Despite such victories in local politics, the FN has yet to make any real headway in the national arena. Party support for the FN rose from 1% in 1981 to 15% in the 1995 presidential elections, yet the FN no longer holds any seats in the National Assembly. Regional elections in March 1998 saw the FN gain 15.5% of the nationwide vote, but its leader Jean Marie Le Pen was defeated in his bid to become chairman of the Provence-Alpes-Côte d'Azur regional council. In October 1998, the FN lost the by-election for the parliamentary seat of Toulon.

In December 1998, following a bitter power dispute, Le Pen sacked Bruno Mégret, his second-in-command. But Mégret called an extraordinary party conference in Marignane in January 1999, where party members voted him president of a rebel breakaway FN, leaving France with two FN parties. Both will run in the June 1999 European parliamentary elections. Opinion polls suggest that Le Pen has the upper edge. As this book was going to press, the two were squabbling over who had the legal right to the party name, Front National.

Life Under the FN

Life under the Front National, a party led by a man who sees the Holocaust as a mere detail of history, is not a bed of roses. Ridding the region of immigrants, terrorising foreigners, and favouring native-born citizens on the job and social benefit front, are just some of the racist-reeking policies of Jean-Marie Le Pen, Bruno Mégret and their xenophobic followers.

Extreme-right mayors front Toulon, Orange, Marignane and Vitrolles. In Toulon, Jean-Marie Le Chevallier celebrated three years as FN mayor in 1998 with a billboard campaign featuring a birthday cake decorated with a blue, a white and a red candle. The nationalistic posters did little to endear local Senegalese market vendors who, in early 1997, were all but barred from the market after Chevallier decreed no more than three Senegalese traders per market '... to give the public a better choice of products and assure more competition between vendors.' The director of an avant garde theatre sacked by the city was no doubt equally unmoved.

In Orange, FN mayor Edmond Bonpard has withdrawn city funding for a music festival and banned the distribution of flyers, slammed by the party as destroying the 'aesthetics of historical and touristic sites'. This decision was consequently annulled by the administrative court – the independent departmental watchdog. In Marignane, the city library head was fired and book orders are now censored to ensure works by leftist writers do not infiltrate the library.

Vitrolles was the next city to fall under the far right knife after Catherine Mégret – pliable wife of Bruno Mégret who later became rebel faction leader – landed 52.48% of votes in February 1997. The mayor's first move was to sack 150 municipal workers and give their jobs to loyal FN members. She then fired the municipal cinema director for screening a film about homosexuality and AIDS.

The immensely popular, city-funded café-theatre, Le Sous-Marin (The Submarine), was Vitrolles' next casualty. Its forced closure prompted public demonstrations in the town square, squashed by Mégret's municipal police force. Street names have also suffered: ave François Mitterand is now ave de Marseille and place Nelson Mandela has been renamed place de Provence.

In early 1998, the administrative court stepped in after Catherine Mégret announced a 5000FF bonus for each child born in Vitrolles to a family of European descent, blatantly excluded children of non-European descent. It was overturned by the court. The mayor continues to insist however that 'differences between races' exist – despite being fined 50,000FF and given a suspended three month prison sentence in January 1998 for inciting racial hatred over an interview with the German newspaper *Berliner Zeitung* the previous year.

Life under the FN allows little room for opposition. The Ras l'Front is a anti-fascist pressure group that campaigns *pour les Blacks-Blancs-Beurs et contre la fête des blue-blanc-rouge* (for Blacks-Whites-North African immigrants and against the party of blue-white-red). But it has little clout in Front-run towns in southern France.

GEOGRAPHY

Provence and the Côte d'Azur cover an area of 25,851 sq km in the extreme south-eastern corner of France. The area is shaped like an elongated oval, bordered by the Alpes du Sud (Southern Alps) to the north-east which form a natural frontier with neighbouring Italy. Its western border – just north of Orange down to Arles and the Camargue west of Marseille – is delineated by the Rhône river which separates Provence from the Gard department in Languedoc-Roussillon.

The Camargue – a wetland of salt marshes – is actually the delta of the Rhône River, a triangular alluvial plain (1400 sq km) formed by the Grand Rhône to the east and the Petit Rhône to the west. The three points of the triangle are marked by the town of Arles (north), Aigues-Mortes (west) and the Fos petro-chemical terminal (east). The barren Crau plain which straddles the north-east side of the triangle is the ancient delta of the Durance river, an affluent of the Rhône which it meets just south of Avignon.

The Mediterranean's sky-blue waters swirl around the entire length of Provence's southern boundary. The 70km stretch of coastline from Marseille to Menton on the French-Italian border, is called the Côte d'Azur or the French Riviera. Beaches are predominantly pebbly and several groups of islands dot the shores: the Îles du Frioul (Marseille), the Îles des Embiez (Toulon) and the Îles de Lérins (Cannes). The Îles d'Hyères, offshore from Hyères, are the region's southernmost point.

Heading inland, the coastal strip is cut off from the region's vast interior by three mountain ranges: the Massif de l'Estérel formed from red volcanic rock, the limestone Massif des Maures, and the foothills of the Alps that kiss the arrière-pays Niçois (Niçois hinterland) immediately north of Nice. The coastline around Marseille is formed from a chain of calcareous rocks, known as Les Calanques, with France's highest cliff (406m) on Cap Canaille.

The interior of Provence east of the Rhône is dominated by hills and mountains which become higher the farther north you climb, peaking with Mont Ventoux (1901m) in the north-west and the southern Alps – part of which form the Parc National du Mercantour – in the north-east. Lower-lying ranges from west to east include the little Alpilles, Mont Sainte-Victoire and Mont Sainte-Baume, the Vaucluse hills, and the rugged Lubéron range.

Farther east are the Gorges du Verdon, with Europe's largest most spectacular canyon. North-west of here on the right bank of the Durance is the Plateau de Valensole, Provence's lavender kingdom. On the left bank of the Durance, is the Plateau d'Albion, a vast and uninhabited *causse* (bare limestone plateau).

CLIMATE

If you like hot summers and mild winters, the Mediterranean climate is for you: frost is rare, spring and autumn downpours are sudden but brief and summer has virtually no rain. The region is blessed with 2500 to 2800 hours of sunshine a year – accounting for the extraordinary light which was

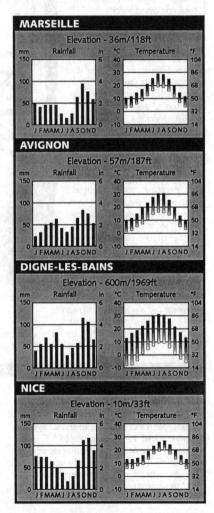

What a Menace

Folklore claims it drives people crazy. Its namesake, Provençal poet Frédéric Mistral, cursed it; while peasants in their dried-out fields dubbed the damaging wind *mange fange* (*manjo fango* in Provençal), meaning 'mud eater'.

The mistral (*mistrau* in Provençal) is a cold, dry north-westerly wind that whips across Provence for several days at a time. Its furious gusts, reaching over 100km/h, destroy crops, rip off roofs, dry the land and drive tempers round the bend. It chills the bones for 100 days a year and is at its fiercest in winter and spring.

The mistral's relentless rage is caused by high atmospheric pressure over central France, between the Alps and the Pyrénées, which is then blown southward through the funnel of the narrow Rhône valley to an area of low-pressure over the Mediterranean.

On the upside, skies are blue and clear of clouds when the mistral is in town. A soaking of rain in July followed by a healthy dose of sun and

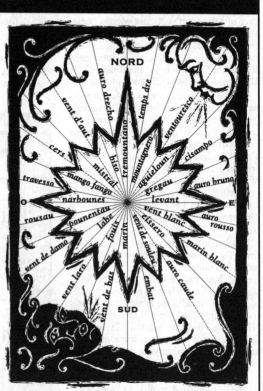

Les Vents de Provence – the mistral and 31 other winds.

mistral in August, followed by more showers and more mistral in early September works wonders for the grape harvest. The mistral has 31 siblings.

such a vital inspiration for painters like Van Gogh, Cézanne and Picasso.

The Côte d'Azur enjoys an annual average temperature of 15°C, dropping to 5°C in the higher-altitude north-east. Temperatures can reach 40°C on the coast in July and August. The sea water temperature (surface) is 20-25°C in summer, dropping to a toe-numbing 12-13°C during the winter months. Annual

precipitation is low: 250mm in the Marseille region, 1100mm in the Alpes-Maritimes department and 1500mm in the southern Alps, which are usually snow-covered from December to March at least. The Camargue delta is one of Europe's most humid zones.

Storms are frequent in the mountains from as early as August onwards. Check the weather forecast:

Alpes-de-Haute-Provence	☎ 08 36 68 02 04
Alpes Maritimes	☎ 08 36 68 02 06
Bouches-du-Rhône	☎ 08 36 68 02 13
Var	☎ 08 36 68 02 83
Vaucluse	☎ 08 36 68 02 84
Marine forecast (national)	☎ 08 36 68 08 08
Marine forecast (departmental)	☎ 08 36 68 08

plus the two-digit departmental number (eg ☎ 08 36 68 08 06 for Alpes-Maritimes).

All reports are in French and cost 2.23FF/minute.

Provence can experience sudden bouts of cold – extreme cold – particularly in early spring, winter and late autumn. In February 1985, the temperature dropped 20°C in the space of a few hours. The much-cursed, menacing Mistral is usually the reason for these dramatic, unexpected and utterly miserable weather changes.

ECOLOGY & ENVIRONMENT
Ecology
Since the late 1980s, the state-owned electricity company, Electricité de France (EDF), has produced about three-quarters of France's electricity using nuclear power. EDF also controls France's hydroelectric program. By damming rivers to produce electricity it has created huge recreational lakes such as Lac de Sainte Croix, southwest of the Gorges du Verdon, Lac de Castillon and the adjoining Lac de Chaudanne north-east of the gorges. This has destroyed the habitats of many animals.

Despite fierce opposition locally, a proposed high voltage line (400,000 volts) threatens to blight the countryside in the protected Parc Naturel du Verdon. In June 1997 the Ministry of Environment withdrew the authorisation it had granted five months earlier for the EDF to build the line through the park. The EDF says the 225,000 volt line currently linking Nice with power plants in the Rhône valley is insufficient to meet the city's power demands in emergency situations. In March 1998 the Ministry of Environment opened a public inquiry into the matter. High voltage lines electrocute at least 1000 birds of prey each year.

The French government took a positive step in February 1996 when President Jacques Chirac announced the decommissioning of France's land-based nuclear missile force which has been deployed at the Plateau d'Albion airforce base, 11km south of Sault in eastern Vaucluse, since the 1960s. Southern France's 18 operational, silo-based S-3D strategic missiles formed one leg of the country's nuclear triad. Chirac agreed to its disarmament one month after conducting a further round of controversial nuclear tests in the South Pacific. The Plateau d'Albion was de-nuclearised in February 1998. By July 1999 the 1er Groupement de Missiles Strategic will be dissolved and replaced by 450 Foreign Legionaries; a further 450 will follow in 2000.

Environment
Forest Fires Provence's 1.2 million hectares of forest – just 8.5% of which are protected –are managed by the Office National des Forêts (ONF; www.onf.fr) which has its regional office in Aix-en-Provence.

Summer forest fires pose the greatest annual hazard to these forests, with great tracts of land being burned each year. In June 1997 a two day inferno destroyed 3450 hectares of forest around Marseille, while a quarter of the Massif des Maures was destroyed by fire in 1990. Between 1993 and 1995 around 2500 hectares of forest were destroyed annually throughout the region. These fires are often caused by careless day-trippers but some are deliberately lit in the Maures and Estérel ranges to get licences to build on the damaged lands.

Reforestation – which costs a hefty 40,000FF (US$6500) per hectare or 30FF per tree – is tackled by the Fondation pour La Protection de la Forêt Méditerranéenne (www.fondation-pour-la-foret.enprovence.com).

The association replants around 16,000 trees a year in the region. It hopes to replant one tenth of the burnt Marseille forests. Preventive fire measures include replanting burnt areas with less flammable flora such as olive trees, vineyards or plants with a naturally high water content. In summer, forests are patrolled by wardens on horseback.

Tourism The 8.3 million tourists that descend on the region are an annual environmental hazard. The Côte d'Azur – a concrete minefield already – continues to be developed to cater for the increasing number of tourists. In summer 1998, a staggering 44 million vehicles – an increase of 4% on the 1997 figure – were recorded on the *autoroute* (highway) that crosses the region.

In February 1998 protesters in Marseille called for the creation of a national park to protect Les Calanques, a 20km stretch of coastline between Marseille and Cassis. Plans to construct several landing platforms for tourist boats to dock along Les Calanques prompted the protest march. Tourist boats, complete with loud commentaries and trash-happy tourists, run every three to four minutes along the coast between June and October. Port-Cros's fragile ecosystem is threatened not only by fire but by marine pollution caused mainly by the boats which bring 120,000 tourists annually to the island.

Bathing Water The quality of *eau de baignade* (bathing water) along the Côte d'Azur is surprisingly good. Of the 359 beaches in the region monitored during 1995, just 23 beaches (6%) did not conform to European standards. The rest were of medium or good quality.

Beaches awarded the European blue flag in 1998 included 10 beaches around Cannes, 21 around Antibes, two on Cap d'Ail, six in the Menton commune, La Ciotat, Martigues, the Port Gardian beach at Saintes-Maries-de-la-Mer and most beaches at Bandol, Hyères, Le Lavandou, Cogolin, Grimaud and Fréjus.

Industrial Development Industrial development menaces the region. North-west of Marseille, a large area of the Crau plain – France's last remaining steppe – has been devoured by the eyesore industrial complex and port at Fos, on the south-western shores of the Étang de Berre. Numerous oil refineries and the busy Marseille-Provence airport dominate the southern and eastern shores of the lagoon. Fishing has been banned in its heavily-polluted waters since 1957.

The opening of Europe's largest technological park (2300 hectares) at Sophia-Antipolis, 9km north-east of Cannes, has led to massive development in the immediate area. As part of a 180 million FF (US$30 million) upgrade of the park's infrastructure, a new four-lane highway (D535) linking Super Antibes with Sophia-Antipolis opened in 1997. Construction work started in 1998 on a second new road, intended to further relieve traffic congestion.

In 1993 the French and Italian governments gave their blessing to the construction of a highway tunnel that will cut beneath the Parc National du Mercantour, linking the southern Alps with Italy, to create a direct route from Barcelona to Milan. The project is estimated to cost 10 billion FF and will be completed around 2013.

Plans to construct a second inland road (55km) from Mandelieu-la-Napoule, just south of Cannes, to La Turbie, just north of Monaco, were suspended in July 1997. The A58 project – fiercely opposed by the local residents – skims Saint-Paul-de-Vence by 500m. Steps have to be taken, however, to relieve the intense traffic load between Nice and Italy. Options being considered in 1998 included widening the existing autoroute (A8). The A58, if approved, would open in 2015.

FLORA & FAUNA
Provence is blessed with a rich variety of flora and fauna: 2000 of the 4200 flora species known to France are found in the Parc National du Mercantour alone. Urbanisation, the encroachment of industries and an ever-expanding tourism infrastructure threaten the future of many fragile species outside protected areas.

Flora
About 1.2 million hectares of forest – 101,000 hectares of which is protected – covers 38% of the Provence and Côte d'Azur region. The most heavily-forested areas – predominantly *chêne* (oak) and *pin* (pine) – are in north-eastern Provence and the Var (57% of which is forested).

Chêne liège (cork oak) and *châtaignier* (chestnut) trees are dominant in the Massif des Maures. Its coastal counterpart is sprinkled with the tall, upright *pin maritime* and, on its less sandy-soiled capes, the distinctive umbrella-shaped *pin parasol* and *pin Aleppo*. The *platane* (plane tree), which can be found on most village squares, is Provence's best known tree, closely followed by the age-old *olivier* (olive tree) which the Greeks brought in the 4th century BC. The *palmier* (palm tree) arrived with the English in the 19th century, as did the sweet-smelling mimosas, eucalyptus and other succulents that were imported from Australia. Lemon and orange trees, typical only to the hot coast, have been grown since the Middle Ages.

Maquis is a form of vegetation whose low, dense shrubs provide many of the spices used in Provençal cooking. Rosemary, cistus (rock roses), laurel, thyme, myrtle, heather and strawberry bushes are among its floral patchwork. *Garrigue* grows on predominantly chalky soil and is also typified by aromatic Mediterranean plants such as juniper, broom and fern.

Fauna

The Camargue is home to over 400 land and waterbirds, including the kingfisher, bee-eater, stork, shelduck, white egret, purple heron and more than 160 migratory species. The Camargue's most spectacular resident is the greater or pink flamingo (*flamant rose*). The low-lying delta is the only flamingo breeding site in France and is home to an estimated 10% of the world's greater flamingo population. Its native white horses and large bull population are the Camargue's other famed fauna.

Some 150 pairs of the *ganga cata* (pin-tailed sand grouse) typically a desert bird, have been recorded in neighbouring Crau. Farther east in Les Calanques, the endangered Bonnelli eagle (see later) can be occasionally seen. Southern Port-Cros is home to 114 bird species and is an important stopover for migratory birds in autumn; seabirds include the puffin, ash-grey shearwater and yelkouan shearwater. The Parc

The marmot is a member of the squirrel family.

National du Mercantour is likewise home to a dazzling array of bird species, including the golden and short-toed eagles and the buzzard. Its more northern, higher-altitude plains in the southern Alps shelter marmots, mouflons and chamois (a mountain antelope), as well as the *bouquetin* (Alpine ibex) which was reintroduced into the region between 1987 and 1994. In lower-altitude wooded areas, the red and roe deer are common. Wild boar roam the entire park.

In all, France's 113 species of mammals (more than any other country in Europe), 30 kinds of amphibians, 36 varieties of reptiles and 72 kinds of fish are well represented in the region.

Endangered Species

Forest fires pose a great threat. The Hermann tortoise, once indigenous to the whole of Mediterranean Europe, is now found only in the maquis of the Massif des Maures (and Corsica). Its population in Les Calanques has already been wiped out by fires, while that of the Maures was severely reduced in 1990.

Fears that the flamingo was no longer breeding in the Camargue prompted ornithologists at the reserve, with the assistance of the World Wildlife Fund (WWF) and a local salt producer, to construct an artificial island in 1970 as a breeding safe haven for its flamingos. Erosion has led to restoration work on Fangassier Island in 1985, 1988 and most recently in 1995.

Many birds, including vultures and storks, have all but disappeared from the skies and the number of Bonnelli eagles is down to about two dozen pairs (in the whole of France) from 670 only 20 years ago. A growing black rat population threatens endemic bird species in the Port-Cros national park.

Some animals still live in the wild thanks to a re-introduction program based in certain national and regional parks. As part of an international program instigated by the WWF, the vulture, extinct in the Alps in the 19th century, was reintroduced into the

Bouquetin – a sturdy member of the goat family with elaborate horns for ritualised combat

Parc National du Mercantour in 1993; its wing span extends to 2.90m. The first vulture is expected to reproduce in 2003. Alpine creatures such as the chamois and the larger bouquetin were widely hunted until national parks such as Mercantour were established. The wolf, which disappeared from France in 1930, was spotted in the Parc National du Mercantour in 1992. Observations in 1995 confirmed that eight wolves had returned to the park from central Italy where there are over 500.

National & Regional Parks

There are two national parks. The largest is the Parc National du Mercantour, created in 1979 to protect 68,500 hectares in northeastern Provence. Part of its eastern boundary adjoins Italy's Parco Naturale delle Alpi Marittime. The park – uninhabited – embraces seven valleys in the Alpes-Maritimes and Alpes-de-Haute-Provence departments: the Roya, Tinée, Verdon and Ubaye valleys are the most spectacular. At its heart lies the Vallée des Merveilles (Valley of Marvels), an archaeological zone (12 sq km) at the foot of Mont Bégo (2873m) which protects Europe's most important collection of Bronze Age stone carvings. A 146,500 hectare peripheral zone – inhabited – surrounds the park. Mont Gélas (3143m) is the highest peak in the park. At 2802m, the Col de Restefond la Bonette is the highest *col* (mountain pass) in Europe.

The Parc National de Port-Cros – in 1963, the first marine park in Europe – protects Provence's southernmost territory: Île de Port-Cros (650 hectares) and its surrounding waters (1800 hectares). Since 1979, neighbouring Île de Porquerolles has also been protected, following the park's creation of the Conservatoire Botanique National Méditerranéen (1254 hectares). The Port-Cros National Park also manages the Conservatoire du Littoral, a 300 hectare slither of land on Cap Lardier, on the southern tip of the Saint Tropez peninsula.

Large areas of the Lubéron (147,600 hectares) and the Camargue (85,000 hectares) have embraced *parcs naturel régionaux* (regional nature parks) since the 1970s. The Parc Naturel du Verdon (146,000 hectares) around the Gorges du Verdon was set up in 1997. In addition, Provence has two marine parks – the Parc Marin de la Ciotat (70 hectares), near Marseille; and the Parc Régional Marin de la Côte Bleue (60 hectares) around Cap Couronne, west of Carry-le-Rouet. Numerous other areas, both inland (such as the Crau plain which constitutes France's last steppe) and coastal (such as Les Calanques on the Marseille coast) are preserved areas.

The Réserve Géologique de Haute-Provence (Haute-Provence Geological Reserve) covers an area of 190,000 hectares around Digne-les-Bains and is the largest protected area of its type in Europe. Its geological wonders include the fossilised skeleton of an ichthyosaurus dating from 185 million years ago and fossils from the tropical forests of 300 million years ago.

GOVERNMENT & POLITICS

Provence-Alpes-Côte d'Azur is one of 22 *régions* (regions) in France. It has an elected *conseil régional* (regional council) based in Marseille, but its powers are limited.

The region is split into six *départements* (departments). This book covers five of them: Alpes-de-Haute-Provence (04), Alpes-Maritimes (06), Bouches-du-Rhône (13), Var (83) and Vaucluse (84). The town of Nîmes on the western banks of the Rhône falls into the Gard department in the neighbouring Languedoc-Roussillon region. Departments are known by their two-digit code, included in postcodes and on the number plates of cars registered there. Metropolitan France (including Corsica) has 96 departments.

Each department has a *préfet* (prefect) – based in a *préfecture* (prefecture) – who represents the national government, and an elected *conseil général* (general council).

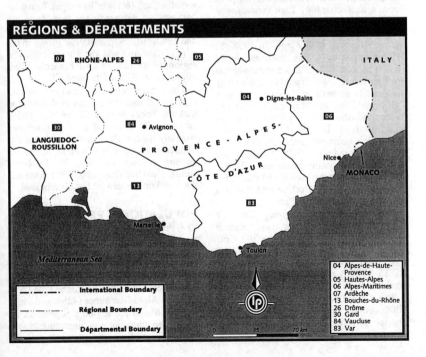

RÉGIONS & DÉPARTEMENTS

International Boundary

Régional Boundary

Départemental Boundary

04 Alpes-de-Haute-
   Provence
05 Hautes-Alpes
06 Alpes-Maritimes
07 Ardèche
13 Bouches-du-Rhône
26 Drôme
30 Gard
84 Vaucluse
83 Var

There is a prefecture in Digne-les-Bains (04), Nice (06), Marseille (13), Toulon (83) and Avignon (84).

ECONOMY

Provence is among France's wealthiest regions, thanks to its Mediterranean coastline and mild climate which generates its primary income – tourism. In 1997, an overwhelming 8.5 million tourists (out of France's 67 million) visited the region. Almost half (46%) were foreign tourists, mainly from Italy, the UK, Germany, Eastern Europe, the USA or Scandinavia. Summer 1998 was estimated to be a record year with hotels notching up a 74% occupancy rate in July and 90% in August. Not surprisingly, 78% of the region's workforce is employed in the service industry.

The region's secondary income is generated by its booming technology sector, the stronghold of which is the Sophia Antipolis Science & Technology Park (www.saem-sopia-antipolis), established in 1969 by France Telecom as a launch pad for pilot testing advanced technology. In 1998 the 1132 companies at the park employed 18,000 people: 40% of those at managerial level are foreign, which partly explains why the park is sometimes dubbed 'Europe's California'. The annual revenue in 1997 of hi-tech industries on the Côte d'Azur was 36.8 billion FF. Despite the region's relatively high unemployment rate (15.7% in 1996, compared with 12.3% for the whole of France), continuing expansion at Sophia Antipolis ensures the region will stay at the cutting edge of job creation and business growth – second only to Paris.

The region ranks among Europe's leading centres in oceanographic research and product development. The 300 Côte d'Azur companies which work in this sector have total annual sales of 30 billion FF (US$5 billion) and represent 1.5% of the world market.

The Grasse perfume industry employs 3000 people and has a three billion FF annual turnover, representing 50% of country turnover and 7% of world turnover in the industry. Exports (mainly to Germany, the USA, the UK and Switzerland) account for 70% of trade.

Exports overall for the Provence-Côte d'Azur region rose, for the third consecutive year, to a record 67.7 billion FF in 1996 – 14% higher than in 1995. Annual imports in 1996 totalled 73 billion FF (including 27 billion FF of crude oil in to Fos). Among the region's largest employers, mainly in industrial Bouches-du-Rhône, are Eurocopter France at Marignane; the Sollac metallurgic works at Fos-sur-Mer; and Naphtachimie chemical plant, Elf and BP at Martigues. The Arsenal (military shipyard) at Toulon employs over 5000.

Despite Provence's abundance of fresh fruit and vegetables, only 2.9% of its workforce is employed in agriculture. Almost 70% of France's rice production comes from Bouches-du-Rhône alone, while the region produces 30.5% of all France's tomatoes and 46.1% of its grapes. Provence harvests an extraordinary wealth of cut flowers – 106.4 million *oeillets* (carnations) and 194.8 million roses a year, grown in the Alpes-Maritimes and Var departments. The region grows just 56% of France's olives but produces 73% of its olive oil.

The general economic trend in traditional, age-old industries such as bottle-stop making bodes less well. In the 1960s around 5000 tonnes of bark was stripped annually from cork oaks in the Massif des Maures, assuring a livelihood for local *bouchonniers* (cork makers). By 1994 the annual yield had dropped to 500 tonnes and the bouchonnier had all but disappeared.

POPULATION & PEOPLE

The Provence-Côte d'Azur region has a population of 4,257,907, 40% of which lives in crowded Bouches-du-Rhône which has Marseille at the helm. Almost 70% of the population is packed in the two coastal departments, Bouches-du-Rhône (5087.5 sq km) and Alpes-Maritimes (4298.6 sq km).

Just 16% of the region's population inhabits the three interior departments, the most rural and mountainous being Alpes-de-Haute-Provence where 3.2% of people live. The rural population is on the rise however – increasing by 25% since the 1970s. Between 1982 and 1990 an average of 11,000 people a year moved into Alpes-de-Haute-Provence. Nonetheless, its population density remains refreshingly low – 10 people per sq km (compared to 352 per sq km in Bouches-du-Rhône).

Approximately 5% of the region's population is foreign, the exception being in Alpes-Maritimes where foreigners account for 12%. Of this foreign population, 31% are European, 23% are Algerian, 16.5% are Moroccan, 15.9% are Tunisian and 1% are Turkish. Unlike in the late 1980s which saw some 55,000 foreigners settle in Provence-Côte d'Azur, the foreign population remained static in the 1990s.

The south's Algerian community originates from the 1950s and early 60s when, as the French colonial empire collapsed, over one million French settlers returned to metropolitan France from Algeria, other parts of Africa and Indochina. At the same time, millions of Non-French immigrants from these places were welcomed as much needed manpower during France's '30 glorious years' of fast economic growth. Such large-scale immigration was stopped by a 1974 law banning all new foreign workers.

In recent years there has been a racist backlash against the country's non-white immigrant communities. The extreme-right Front National party has fanned these racist feelings in a bid to win more votes. In January 1997 the National Assembly approved (by a large margin) legislation legitimising the status of some illegal immigrants but implementing measures that made it easier to repatriate others.

Almost 60% of the region's population is aged 20 to 64 years; 17.5% are over 65.

ARTS
Dance
The *farandole* is a Provençal dance, particularly popular in and around Arles today. Dating from the Middle Ages, it is traditionally danced at the close of a village *fête*

(festival or party). Young men and women take their partner by the hand or remain linked with a cord or handkerchief. The brisk jig is accompanied by a tambourine and a *galoubet* (small, shrill flute with three holes).

In the realm of classical ballet, France was in the forefront until the 19th century when the Russian Imperial Ballet became the centre for innovation. France's leading talent, Marius Petipa (1818-1910), a native of Marseille, moved to Saint Petersburg in 1847 where he created masterpieces such as *La Bayadère* (1877) and *Le Lac des Cygnes* (Swan Lake, 1895). Petipa mixed French dance tradition with Slavic sensibilities. He choreographed more than 50 full-length ballets.

Literature
Middle Ages Lyric poems of courtly love composed by troubadours dominated medieval Provençal literature. This troubadour literature was written solely in *langue d'oc* (Occitan), from which Provençal evolved. Occitan was the language spoken in the court of the popes in Avignon and legend has it that Dante (1265-1321) almost wrote his *Divine Comedy* in Occitan.

Provençal life featured in the works of Italian poet, Petrarch (1304-74) who was exiled to Avignon in 1327. Here he met the beautiful and elusive Laura to whom he dedicated his entire life's works. Petrarch lived in Fontaine de Vaucluse between 1337 and 1353 where he composed his song book *canzoniere* and wrote numerous poems and letters about local shepherds, fishermen he met on the banks of the Sorgue, and his pioneering ascent up Mont Ventoux.

Renaissance The great landmark in Provençal literature is the work of Bellaud de la Bellaudière (1533-88), a native of Grasse who wrote *Œuvres et Rimes* in Occitan, a book of 160 sonnets drawing on influences by Petrarch and the French epic writer, Rabelais. In 1555, the philosopher/writer Nostradamus (1503-66), a native of Saint-Rémy-de-Provence, published (in Latin) his prophetic *Centuries* in Salon-de-Provence where he lived with his wife. The papal authorities immediately banned the blasphemous work.

Classicism The 17th *grand siècle* (grand century) was the century of the French classical writers. In Provence it yielded the *Noëls Provençaux*, a series of poems encapsulating a nativity scene, by Nicolas Saboly. Their pious tone, very occasionally humorous, was representative of the strait-laced fervour that dominated baroque Provençal literature.

19th Century Revival The 19th century witnessed a massive revival in Provençal literature, largely due to one man, Frédéric Mistral (1830-1914), the only minority-language writer to be awarded a Noble Prize for Literature (1904). A native of Maillane, Mistral's passion for Provence, its culture, history and language, was first awakened by Avignon tutor Joseph Roumanille (1818-91) who published *Li Margarideto* in 1847. In 1851 Mistral started work on what would become his most momentous work, *Mirèio*. Three years later Le Félibrige was founded by seven young Provençal poets who pledged to revive the Provençal language and codify its orthography. They published *L'Armana Prouvençau* (1859), the first journal to appear in Provençal.

Mistral's epic poem *Mirèio* – which tells the story of a beautiful girl who flees to Saintes-Maries-de-la-Mer in the Camargue when her parents forbid her to marry her true love, only to die of a broken heart on the beach – was published in 1859. A succession of poems followed, all written in Provençal and depicting a facet of Provence: *Les Îles d'Or* (1875), *Nerte* (1884), *La Reine Jeanne* (1896) and *Le poème du Rhône* (1896). Between 1878 and 1886, Mistral's most influential work on Provençal culture was published, the monumental *Trésor du Félibrige*. This encyclopaedia-style work utilised parts of the first Provençal-French dictionary, published as early as 1840 in Digne-les-Bains.

The 1890s saw Le Félibrige adopt a more popularist approach with the opening of a museum in Arles (Musée Arletan) devoted to all things Provençal, and the publication of the less academic *L'Aïoli* journal.

Dumas, Daudet et al In the 19th century, French writers turned to sun-soaked Provence for inspiration. Alexandre Dumas (1802-70) set two of his most outstanding novels in the region, namely *Le Comte de Monte Cristo* (The Count of Monte Cristo, 1845) which is partly set in Marseille and the Château d'If off its shores, and the adventurous *Les Trois Mousquetaires* (The Three Musketeers, 1844). Marseille served as a backdrop for the opening of Charles Dickens' *Little Dorrit* (1857) while Victor Hugo (1802-1885), the key figure of French romanticism, looked to the region to set a small part of his epic *Les Misérables* (1862). In 1887 a syphilis-ridden Guy de Maupassant sailed into the small fishing village of Saint Tropez where he was inspired to write *Sur l'eau*. Edmond Rostand (1868-1918), author of the novel *Cyrano de Bergerac* (1897) was a native of Marseille.

Born in Nîmes, Alphonse Daudet (1849-97) lived in Lyon then Paris but spent a considerable amount of time with Mistral in Maillane and in Fontvieille, near Arles, where he wrote *Lettres de mon moulin* (Letters from my windmill, 1869). He is best remembered for his novels which evoke the small Provençal town of Tarascon through the eyes of his anti-hero Tartarin. The *Tartarin de Tarascon* trilogy was published between 1872 and 1890.

Parisian novelist Émile Zola (1840-1902) grew up in Aix-en-Provence where he befriended Cézanne. The aim of Zola, who claimed literary peer Flaubert as a precursor of his school of naturalism, was to convert novel writing from an art to a science by application of experimentation. His theory may seem naive but his work (especially his *Les Rougon-Macquart* series) was powerful and innovative. He evokes Aix in *La Conquête de Plassans* (1874).

The year 1895 marked the birth of two of Provence's best known writers who both remained true to their homeland, dedicating their life's work to depicting Provence and scarcely setting foot outside the region. Jean Giono (1895-1970), a native of Manosque, blended myth with reality in his novels which remain a celebration of the Provençal Alps and the people who survive in this harsh landscape. Writer/film maker Marcel Pagnol (1895-1974) spent his life in Aubagne where he wrote numerous novels and screen adaptations (including Giono's *La Femme du Boulanger* in 1938). His realistic portraits of characters in rural Provence won him international acclaim. *L'Eau des Collines* (The Water of the Hills, 1963), a novel set in the inter-war period and comprising *Jean de Florette* and *Manon des Sources*, is the best known.

20th Century The Côte d'Azur sparkled as a centre of the avant-garde in the 1920s and 30s, luring numerous foreign writers into its net. Ernest Hemingway, F Scott Fitzgerald, Aldous Huxley, Katherine Mansfield, DH Lawrence and Thomas Mann were among the scores to seek solace in the sun. Guests at Somerset Maugham's villa on Cap Ferrat included just about every literary name, from TS Eliot and Arnold Bennet to Noël Coward, Evelyn Waugh and Ian Fleming. WB Yeats died here.

In 1919 Ezra Pound (1885-1972), leader of the imagist school of poetry that emerged at this time, published *Cantos*. Preceded by *Provença* in 1910, these two collections of poems included modern adaptations of Provençal songs and Troubadour ballads.

The surrealism that played a vital force in French literature until WWII is evident in the works of Jean Cocteau (1889-1963), poet, dramatist and film maker. Cocteau ran away from home to the French coast at the age of 15, but it was not until the end of his life that he became part of the Riviera set. His work, both in his prose and on the cinematic set (including the allegorical *Orphée*, 1950) capture the spirit of the surrealist movement: the fascination with dreams, divination and all manifestations of 'the marvellous'. His best known novel *Les Enfants Terribles* (1955) portrays the intellectual rebellion of the post-war era.

During WWII, Roussillon in the Vaucluse served as a refuge to playwright Samuel Beckett who arrived in the village in 1942 after fleeing Paris. He stayed until April 1945 and wrote *Watt* (not published until after *Waiting for Godot* in 1953) while he was here.

Colette (1873-1954), who thoroughly enjoyed tweaking the nose of conventional readers with titillating novels that detailed the amorous exploits of such heroines as the schoolgirl Claudine, lived in Saint Tropez from 1927 until 1938. *La Naissance du Jour* evokes an unspoilt Saint Tropez before tourism took over.

After WWII, existentialism, a significant literary movement, developed around Jean-Paul Sartre (1905-80), Simone de Beauvoir (1908-86) and Albert Camus (1913-60). The latter moved to Lourmarin in the Lubéron (where he is buried) in 1957 to write his autobiography. The same year, British novelist and travel writer Lawrence Durrell (1912-90) settled in Somières, near Nîmes, and dedicated the last 33 years of his literary career to writing about Provençal life. Other notable figures who settled in the region in the latter part of their careers include James Baldwin, Dirk Bogarde and Anthony Burgess.

Architecture

Prehistoric The earliest monuments in France were stone megaliths erected during the Neolithic period from about 4000 to 2400 BC. Although these prehistoric monuments are mainly found in northern France, dismantled remnants can be seen at Musée d'Archéologie Méditerranée in Marseille; Monaco's Musée d'Anthropologie Préhistorique, from where it is possible to visit the Grottes de l'Observatoire; and the Musée de Digne at Digne-les-Bains. Numerous menhirs are evident in the Vallée des Merveilles and examples of the region's earliest habitats (bories) can be visited in the Villages des Bories near Gordes.

Gallo-Roman Southern France – particularly Provence – is *the* place to go in search of France's Gallo-Roman legacy. The Romans constructed an incredible number of public works all over Roman Provincia from the 1st century BC: aqueducts, fortifications, marketplaces, temples, amphitheatres, triumphal arches and bathhouses. They also established regular street grids at many settlements.

Testimony to Roman architectural brilliance includes the Pont du Gard aqueduct between Nîmes and Avignon; the colossal amphitheatres at Nîmes and Arles; the theatres at Orange and Fréjus; the Maison Carrée (literally 'square house') in Nîmes; the public buildings in Vaison-la-Romaine; the excavated temples at Glanum; and triumphal arches at Orange, Carpentras and Cavaillon. See the regional chapters for details.

Dark Ages Although quite a few churches were built during the Merovingian and Carolingian periods (5th to 10th century), very little remains of them. However, fine traces of churches from this period are reflected in the octagonal, 5th century baptistry at Fréjus. The earliest Christian relics, dating from the 2nd to 4th centuries, can be seen at the Musée du Pays Brignolais in Brignoles, Fréjus' Musée Archéologique and the Musée d'Archéologique d'Arles.

The region has numerous examples of *villages perchés* (hilltop villages), which first took root in Provence in the 10th century. Villagers from the plains built new villages on top of rocky crags as a defence against Saracen attacks. Economics forced many to move back to the plains in the 19th and 20th centuries.

Romanesque A religious revival in the 11th century led to the construction of a large number of Romanesque churches, so-called because their architects adopted many architectural elements (eg vaulting) from Gallo-Roman buildings. Romanesque buildings typically have round arches, heavy walls whose few windows let in very little light, and a lack of ornamentation that

borders on the austere. The most famous examples of this era, considered typical of the high Romanesque period, are the trio of abbeys built by the Cistercian order at Sénanque (1148), Le Thoronet (1160) and Silvacane (1175).

The majestic but sober La Chartreuse de la Verne (1170), the older monastery (1073) on Île Saint Honorat, and the church at Saintes-Maries-de-la-Mer are examples of the fortress-like sacred buildings that also characterised this era. Chateaux – such as the Château Grimaldi in Antibes – likewise tended to be sturdy, heavily fortified structures that afforded few luxuries to their inhabitants. The Romanesque style remained popular until as late as the 14th century in Provence: the exceptional dimensions of the cathedral at Digne-les-Bains (1200-1330) is typical of late Provençal Romanesque.

Gothic Gothic structures are characterised by ribbed vaults carved with great precision, pointed arches, slender verticals, chapels (often built by rich people or guilds) along the nave and chancel, refined decoration and large stained-glass windows. The Gothic style, which emerged in the mid-12th century in northern France, only made its mark on Provençal architecture in the 14th and 15th centuries. The most important examples of Gothic architecture in Provence are the Palais des Papes (Pope's Palace) in Avignon, the adjoining basilica and convent in Saint-Maximin-La-Sainte Baume, the Val de Bénédiction Charterhouse in Villeneuve-lès-Avignon, and the Église Saint Siffrein in Carpentras.

Frescoes emerged at the end of the Gothic era as an important means of rich interior decoration. Although frescoes are evident in churches like Nice's Église Saint Martin-Saint Augustin and the Musée Franciscain in Cimiez, it was small churches tucked in the Niçois hinterland and as far north as the southern Alps that benefited the most from these treasured adornments. The interior of the Chapelle Notre Dame des Fontaines in the Vallée de la Roya is a classic example (see later under Painting).

Provence was scarcely touched by the French Renaissance period – an architectural style that began in France in the late 15th century and set out to realise a 'rebirth' of classical Greek and Roman culture. The 16th century saw the emergence of citadel architect, Sébastien Le Prestre de Vauban (1633-1707), as a force to be reckoned with. His works in Provence included the enlargement of the Fort Carré in Antibes with his signature star-shaped walls, the fortification of the hilltop village of Entrevaux, and constructions at Toulon port and Sisteron.

Baroque During the baroque period, which lasted from the end of the 16th century to the late 18th century, painting, sculpture and classical architecture were integrated to create structures and interiors of great subtlety, refinement and elegance. The Chapelle de la Miséricorde in Nice and Menton's Italianate Église Saint Michel are considered southern France's grandest baroque churches. Marseille's Centre de la Vielle Charité (1671-1749) is built around a beautiful baroque-domed chapel designed by Pierre Puget (see later under Sculpture).

Neoclassical Neoclassical architecture emerged around 1740 and remained popular until well into the 19th century. It grew out of a renewed interest in classical forms; more profoundly, a search for order, reason and serenity through the adoption of the forms and conventions of Graeco-Roman antiquity: columns, simple geometric forms and traditional ornamentation.

Neoclassicism really came into its own under Napoléon III, who used it extensively for monumental architecture intended to embody the grandeur of imperial France. Nice's imposing Palais de Justice and Palais Masséna, and Toulon's Église Saint Louis are examples. The true showcase of this era, however, is the Monte Carlo Casino (1878) in Monaco and adjoining opera house (1879), both designed by French architect Charles Garnier (1825-98) and ranked among the Second Empire's finest achievements. Garnier, together with Gustave

Eiffel (1832-1923), who lived in Beaulieu-sur-Mer, designed the Observatoire de Nice (1887).

Aix-en-Provence's public fountains and *hôtels particuliers* (large and elegant private residences) also date from this period; as do Provence's ornate wrought-iron *campaniles* – originally a feature of rural Provençal architecture – that top most church bell towers in towns and cities.

Eclecticism Alongside neoclassicism, the *belle époque* heralded a more fantastical eclecticism that would last into the early 20th century. Trademarks included anything and everything from decorative stucco friezes, trompe l'oeil paintings and glittering wall mosaics, to brightly-coloured domed roofs, Moorish minarets and Turkish towers. In short, anything went. Nice is exceptionally well endowed with these chocolate-box creations: the Hôtel Négresco (1906), the Crédit Lyonnais Bank (1882) and the very pink Château de L'Anglais (1859) are all buoyant reflections of this beautiful age. In Barcelonnette, the Château des Magnans is Mexican inspired.

The stark, concrete and glass Villa Noailles (1923) in Hyères is an expression of the cubism movement that gained momentum in the inter-war period.

Contemporary Architecture France's most celebrated architect this century, Le Corbusier (1887-1965), was born in Switzerland but settled in Paris in 1917 at the age of 30. He had a villa and studio on Cap Martin where, in 1965, he suffered a fatal heart attack while swimming in the sea. He is buried in the Roquebrune-Cap Martin cemetery. A radical modernist, Le Corbusier tried to adapt buildings to their functions in industrialised society without ignoring the human element. His most influential achievement was his creation of the Cité Radieuse development – a low-cost housing project for 1600 inhabitants – in Marseille, built between 1946 and 1952. Le Corbusier arranged buildings with related functions in a circular formation and constructed them in standard sizes based on the proportions of the human form. The resultant Unité d'Habitation was considered a coup by architects worldwide who flocked to Marseille to see the apartment block on stilts.

Steel meets glass with the modern Carrée d'Art (1993) in Nîmes. The reflective 'Square of Art' was designed by British architect Sir Norman Foster (1935-), responsible for the seminal Hong Kong and Shanghai Bank building in Hong Kong. Nîmes. which prides itself as the pioneer of modern design in southern France, also sports a marble *abribus* (bus stop) on Ave Carnot designed by Philippe Starck (1949-), a French designer best known for his furniture designs. Starck also redesigned the city's coat of arms.

Other bold examples of modern architecture include Nice's Musée d'Art Moderne et d'Art Contemporain (1990), marketed as the Louvre of the south; and Matisse's Chapelle du Rosaire in Vence which reflects a traditional Provençal cottage from the exterior. Port Grimaud (1969) was the conception of Francis Spoerry who went on to design Port Liberty in New York. The truly outstanding Fondation Maeght (1964) in Saint-Paul-de-Vence is considered the epitome of contemporary Provençal architecture.

Painting

To the 16th Century Sculpture and stained glass rather than paintings were the main adornments of the medieval Gothic churches, in part because the many windows left little wall space. The Sienese, French and Spanish artists working at the papal court in Avignon in the 14th century, however, created an influential style of mural painting, examples of which can be seen in the city's Palais des Papes.

While the rest of France found itself preoccupied with the Hundred Years' War, art flourished in the Comté de Nice (County of Nice) where the School of Nice emerged, led by Louis Bréa. Bréa, exalted as the 'Fra Angelico Provençal', created the burgundy colour known as *rouge bréa*. His works can be seen in Cimiez (Nice) and Menton's

Palais Carnolès. This school of primitive painters worked notably for the Penitent Brotherhoods which explains why their works are in rural chapels once used as a place of pilgrimage. Exceptional are the Gothic-inspired frescoes in the Chapelle Notre-Dame-des-Fontaines, painted around 1451 by Giovanni Baleison and Giovanni Canavesio, two Piedmontese painters who decorated many chapels in the Vésubie, Tinée and Roya valleys. The 16th century saw the movement shift from Gothic to Italian Renaissance influences.

17th & 18th Centuries Blindman's bluff, stolen kisses and other such courtly frivolities were the subject matter of the French school of artists that emerged in the late 17th and early 18th centuries during the Enlightenment. Avignon-born Joseph Vernet (1714-89) was among the most influential, leaving behind him a series of 15 landscapes depicting French ports. The series, commissioned by Louis XV, included *La Ville et la Rade de Toulon* (1756). Rococo influences played on the landscapes of Jean-Honoré Fragonard (1732-1806) whose playful scenes immortalised his native Grasse and captured the frivolity of the rococo spirit. The more elevated works of Nice-born Carle van Loo (1705-65) represented rococo's more serious 'grand style'. Works by these artists are displayed in the Musée des Beaux-Arts Jules Chéret in Nice; the Musée des Beaux Arts, Marseille; Avignon's Musée Calvet; Grasse's Musée Fragonard; and the Musée Granet, Aix-en-Provence.

Jacques Louis David (1748-1825) was undoubtedly the most influential artist to emerge at the end of the 18th century, stunning the public in 1785 with two large paintings touting clear republican messages, *Oath of the Horatii* and *Brutus Condemning His Son*. David became one of the leaders of the Revolution, and a virtual dictator in matters of art, where he advocated a precise, severe classicism. David's *Saint Roch* (1780) is in the Musée des Beaux Arts, Marseille. The Musée Granet, Aix-en-Provence, also has some of his works.

19th Century David's most gifted pupil, Jean Auguste Dominique Ingres (1780-1867), continued in the neoclassical tradition. The historical pictures to which he devoted most of his life are now generally regarded as inferior to his portraits. Another pupil was François Marius Granet (1775-1849) from Aix-en-Provence, who, though less celebrated, displayed a strong empathy with nature in his watercolours, which would became the trademark of Provençal painters at this time. Works by both are in the Musée Granet, Aix-en-Provence.

Landscape painting evolved further under the Barbizon School. Jean-François Millet took many of his subjects from peasant life and had a strong influence on Van Gogh. Millet anticipated the realist program of Gustave Courbet (1819-77), a prominent member of the Paris Commune, who made frequent trips to southern France. Among his most fervent pupils was Provençal realist Paul Guigou (1834-71), a native of Villars in the Vaucluse who painted numerous canvases of the Durance plains over-drenched in bright sunlight. *Deux Lavandières devant la Sainte-Victoire* (Two Washing Women in front of Mont Sainte Victoire) painted by Guigou near Aix-en-Provence in 1986, is in the Musée Grobet-Labadié, Marseille.

It was Provence's astonishing clarity and intensity of light that drew the impressionists to the region. Impressionism, initially a term of derision, was taken from the title of an experimental painting by Claude Monet in 1874, *Impression: Soleil Levant* (Impression: Sunrise). Monet was the leading figure of the school, which counted among its members Alfred Sisley, Camille Pissarro, Berthe Morisot and Pierre-Auguste Renoir (1841-1919). Renoir lived in Cagnes-sur-Mer on the French Riviera from 1903 until his death. Although he broke with the movement in his later career, as an impressionist his main aim was to capture fleeting light effects, and light came to dominate the content of his painting. Many are displayed in the Musée Renoir (his former home and studio) in Cagnes-sur-Mer. Monet painted the same subjects –

cathedrals, haystacks, trees, water lilies – many times to show the transient effect of light at different times of day.

Paul Cézanne (1839-1906) is Provence's best known artist. He was born and died in Aix-en-Provence, and is celebrated for his still life and landscape works which depict his native land. Cézanne painted numerous canvases in and around Aix, particularly of Mont Saint Victoire. *Les Baigneuses* (The Bathers) is in Aix's Musée Granet. Southern France was also immortalised on canvas by Paul Gauguin (1848-1904), who, despite being best known for his images of the South Pacific and his studies of Tahitian women, spent much time during the late 19th century in Arles. Both he and Cézanne are usually referred to as post-impressionists, something of a catch-all word for the diverse styles that flowed from impressionism.

When in Arles, Gauguin worked for a time with the Dutch artist Vincent van Gogh (1854-90), who spent most of his painting life in Paris and Arles. A brilliant and innovative artist, Van Gogh produced haunting self-portraits and landscapes in which colour assumes an expressive and emotive quality. Unfortunately, Van Gogh's talent was largely unrecognised during his lifetime. He was confined to an asylum in Saint-Rémy-de-Provence and eventually committed suicide. He painted his most famous works – *Sunflowers* and *Van Gogh's Chair* (1888) – in Arles. Van Gogh's later technique, exhibited in works dating from his Saint Rémy period such as *Starry Night* and *Olive Trees* (1889), foreshadowed pointillism.

Pointillism was developed by Georges Seurat (1859-91), who applied paint in small dots or with uniform brush strokes of unmixed colour, producing fine mosaics of warm and cool tones. His most devout pupil was Paul Signac (1863-1935) who settled in Saint Tropez from 1892 onwards. Among his many guests to the small fishing village were Pierre Bonnard (1867-1947) who lived in neighbouring Le Cannet, Henri Manguin (1874-1949) and Henri Matisse. Part of the Musée de l'Annonciade in Saint Tropez is devoted to pointillist works and includes *Étude pour le Chenal de Grave-lines* (Study for the Channel at Gravelines) painted by Seurat in 1890 as well as numerous works by Signac, most of which depict Saint Tropez or Marseille.

20th Century French painting in the 20th century has a bewildering diversity of styles, two of which are particularly significant: fauvism and cubism.

Fauvism took its name from the slur of a critic who compared the exhibitors at the 1905 Salon d'Automme in Paris with *fauves* (wildcats) because of their radical use of intensely bright colours. Among these 'wild' painters were Henri Matisse, André Derain and Maurice de Vlaminck. It was the young Matisse – who also sought the sunlight and vivacity of the Provençal coast – who paved the way for fauvism. While in Saint Tropez with Signac, he started preliminary sketches that would produce *Luxe, Calme et Volupté* (Luxury, Calm and Tranquillity). The signature uniform brush strokes of pointillism were still evident, but were intermingled with irregular splashes of violent colour. Matisse's consequent painting, *La Gitane* (1906) is considered the embodiment of fauvist principles. It is displayed in Saint Tropez's Musée de l'Annonciade, along with works by staunch fauvist Raoul Dufy (1877-1963) and George Braque (1882-1963) who flirted briefly with the movement.

Cubism was effectively launched in 1907 by the Spanish prodigy Pablo Picasso (1881-1973) with his pioneering *Les Demoiselles d'Avignon*. Cubism, as developed by Picasso, Georges Braque and Juan Gris, deconstructed the subject into a system of intersecting planes and presented various aspects of it simultaneously. The collage, incorporating bits of cloth, wood, string, newspaper and any thing lying around, was a cubist speciality. Picasso went on to experiment (and succeed) with other mediums and concepts, but his cubist works remain highly popular.

After WWI, the School of Paris was formed by a group of expressionists, mostly foreign-born, such as Russian-born Marc Chagall (1887-1985) who moved to France in 1922. His pictures combine fantasy and folklore, many of these from the Old Testament. Chagall spent the last few years of his life in Saint-Paul-de-Vence where he is buried. The largest collection of his works is in Nice. Many of Chagall's later works were influenced by the surrealists, most active in the inter-war period. Surrealism attempted to reunite the conscious and unconscious realms, to permeate everyday life with fantasies and dreams. Naive art, common to the 1930s and sometimes known as primitive art, offered a simple but precise presentation of ordinary scenes that very occasionally veered towards surrealism.

With the onset of WWII many artists left France's sunny south, and although some returned after the war, the region never regained its old magnetism. Picasso moved permanently to the Côte d'Azur, settling first in Golfe-Juan, then Vallauris and finally Mougins, where he died. In 1946 he set up his studio in Antibes' Château Grimaldi, the works which he completed here being exhibited in the Musée Picasso inside the chateau. Among his other accomplishments was the interior decoration of the chapel in Vallauris (also a museum today).

The other great artist of this period was undoubtedly Matisse (1869-1954) who lived in Nice from 1917 until his death – with the exception of the WWII period when he took refuge in nearby Vence. He also decorated a chapel after WWII. His bold and colourful works culminated in his familiar blue and white cut-out montages which he completed in the early 1950s prior to his death. Works representing his whole career can be seen at the Musée Matisse, Nice.

In the wake of Matisse came the French new realism movement (all represented in the Musée d'Art Moderne et d'Art Contemporain, Nice). The 1960s new realists – led by Arman, Yves Klein and César (see Sculpture) – rejected the abstraction of the post-war years and turned their attentions instead to 'modern nature'. Art was generated from recycled trash, used crockery, crushed cars and scrap metal. In 1960, Nice-born Klein (1928-1962) produced *Anthropométries*, a series of blue imprints made by sweetly persuading three naked women (covered from head to toe in blue paint) to roll around on a white canvas. Arman, also born in Nice in 1928, became known for his trash-can portraits, made by framing the litter found in the subject's trash bin. Another influential realist from the School of Nice was Martial Rayasse, born in Golfe-Juan in 1936, and renowned for pioneering the use of neon in contemporary art. Most notable is his 1964 portrait of *Nissa Bella* (Beautiful Nice) which incorporates a flashing blue heart on a human face.

The supports-surfaces movement that took root in the 1970s focused on deconstructing the traditional concept of a painting and transforming one of its structural components – such as the frame or canvas – into a work of art instead. The Groupe 70, specific to Nice, expressed an intellectual agitation, typical to Vivien Isnard's 1987 *Sans Titre* (Without Title) and Louis Chacallis' *Tension* (1978). Urban culture was the energising force behind free figuration in the 1980s.

Sculpture

At the end of the 11th century, sculptors decorated the portals, capitals, altars and fonts of Romanesque churches, illustrating Bible stories and the lives of the saints for the illiterate. Two centuries later, when the cathedral became the centre of monumental building, sculpture spread from the central portal to the whole façade, whose brightly painted and carved surface offered a symbolic summary of Christian doctrine. In the 17th century Provençal sculptor, Marseille-born Pierre Puget (1620-94), made his mark in France. He introduced the idea of adorning ship sterns with elaborate ornamentation, and was among the first to experiment with atlantes – the use of figures of men instead of columns to support an entablature. The anguished figures that support the balcony of honour at the old city hall on Quai Stalingrad in Toulon is a celebrated example. The Musée des Beaux Arts in Marseille has a large collection of his works.

Marseille also produced César Baldaccini (known as César), one of the most important French sculptors of the 20th century. César (1921-98) was greatly inspired by Michelangelo (a replica of his David stands in Marseille today) and Picasso (one of the first to use scrap metal as a medium). His work after WWII used wrought-iron and scrap metal to create a series of imaginary insects and animals. Later he graduated to pliable plastics. In 1960 he became the first artist to use motorised vehicles (notably, crushed cars) as an artistic medium. Between 1960 and 1989 he compressed 23 cars, some of which are displayed in the Musée d'Art Moderne et d'Art Contemporain, Nice. His work can be seen also in Marseille. Arguably his best known work is the little statue handed to actors at the Césars (named after him), the French cinema awards that date from 1976 and are equivalent to Hollywood's Oscars. César died, aged 77, in December 1998.

Cinema

Beginnings to WWII With its spectacular light and subtle shadows, it is not surprising that Provence was as inspirational to cinema as it was to art. Cinematographic pioneers, the Lumière brothers – who invented 'moving pictures' – made their earliest films on the Côte d'Azur. The world's first motion picture – a series of two-minute reels – was shown for the first time in the Château Lumière, a property owned by their father in La Ciotat, in September 1895. The film, entitled *L'Arrivée d'un train en gare de La Ciotat* (The arrival of a train at La Ciotat station), made the audience jump out of their seats as the steam train rocketed towards them. It only made its debut in Paris three months later. The Eden Théâtre in La Ciotat is the world's oldest movie house. Auguste and Louis Lumière went on to discover colour photography.

Nice was catapulted to stardom in the 1920s. The Victorine film studios, which Serge Sandberg had established in 1920, were sold for US$5 million to Hollywood director Rex Ingram in 1925. He transformed the studios almost overnight into the hub of European film making, welcoming avant-garde directors like René Clair, Marcel Carné and the intensely productive Jean Renoir, son of the famous artist, to his studios. These were innovative times for film in France. Clair created a world of fantasy in his films giving himself free rein to his penchant for invention. Carné's films, such as *Les Visiteurs du soir* (filmed in Tourettes-sur-Loup and at the Victorine studios) and *Les Enfants du paradis* – though visually stunning – presented a pessimistic world in which violence and poverty dominate. Jean Renoir's work was marked by poetic realism, strong narrative, and a strong sense of social satire.

Another big name at this time was the Aubagne-born, Provençal writer Marcel Pagnol whose film career kicked off in 1931 with *Marius*, the first part of his legendary *Fanny* trilogy starring Raimu (see Silver Screen Heroes) and portraying pre-war Marseille. Pagnol filmed *La Femme du Boulanger* (The Baker's Wife, 1938) in the hilltop village of Castellet. Throughout his career, he stuck to depicting what he knew best – Provence and its ordinary people.

New Wave Nice's film industry stagnated after WWII until the 1950s when a large group of new directors burst onto the scene with a new genre: *nouvelle vague* (new wave). With small budgets, sometimes self-financed, no extravagant sets or big-name stars, they made films like *Et Dieu Créa la Femme* (And God Created Woman, 1956), which brought sudden stardom to Brigitte Bardot, the little fishing village of Saint Tropez and the young director Roger Vadim. The film, which examined the amorality of modern youth, received international acclaim.

Many films followed, among them François Truffaut's *Les Mistons* (1958) filmed exclusively in Nîmes; Jacques Démy's *La Baie des Anges* (The Bay of Angels, 1962); Henri Decoin's *Masque de fer* (Iron Mask, 1962), parts of which were filmed in Sospel; Rohmer's *La Collectionneuse* (The Collectors, 1966) which was shot in Saint Tropez; and the first in the series of Jean Girault's celebrated *Gendarme de Saint Tropez* (1964). In 1972 François Truffaut filmed part of *La Nuit Américaine* (The American Night, 1972) in the Victorine studios, the Niçois hinterland and the Vésubie valley.

The region also featured in foreign films, most notably Hitchcock's suspense thriller, *La Main au Collet* (To Catch a Thief, 1956), starring Cary Grant and Grace Kelly; John Frankenheimer's *French Connection N° 2*; and Disney's lovable *Herbie goes to Monte Carlo* (1977) starring Herbie the Volkswagen.

The new wave lost its experimental edge in the mid-1970s: just two films were made at the Victorine studios in 1976, followed by a paltry three in 1977. The studios have since produced television commercials.

Contemporary Cinema Modern French cinema has seen a renewed interest in Pagnol's great classics of Provence. In 1986 Claude Berri came up with *Jean de Florette* followed by *Manon des Sources*, modern versions of Pagnol's original works, which proved enormously popular both in France and abroad. Parts of the films were shot in the Plan-d'Aups-Sainte-Baume and starred France's favourite contemporary actor Gérard Depardieu. In 1990 Yves Robert directed *La Gloire de mon père* (My Father's Glory) and *Le Château de ma mère* (My Mother's Castle), Pagnol's autobiographical novels.

The 1998 Hollywood box office hit, *The Man in the Iron Mask*, directed by screenwriter Randall Wallace, starred Gérard Depardieu alongside Leonardo DiCaprio and Jeremy Irons. The film was a modern adaptation of the 'iron mask' mystery which occurred on the Île Sainte Marguerite near Cannes in the late 17th century and was consequently immortalised by Alexandre Dumas in his novel *Le Vicomte de Bragelonne* (the final novel in the Musketeers trilogy).

The first novel in the Dumas trilogy, *Le Comte de Monte Cristo* (The Count of Monte

Cristo) – which opens with the lead character's dramatic escape from the Château d'If near Marseille – has been adapted for cinema/television 29 times since 1907. The most recent version was Josée Dayan's TV-series adaptation (1998) starring Gérard Depardieu as the revengeful Dantès.

Silver Screen Heroes Film stars congregate on the Côte d'Azur once a year for an orgy of glitz and glamour at the Cannes Film Festival (*Festival International du Film*), the French film industry's main annual event (see the boxed text Starring at Cannes).

Provence produced one of France's earliest screen heroes – Raimu (honoured at the Espace Raimu in Cogolin). The great comic actor was born in Toulon as Jules Auguste César Muraire (1883-1946). He is best remembered for his colourful portrayal of Provençal characters, most notably in Pagnol's early *Fanny* trilogy, *La Femme du Boulanger* and later *La Fille du Puisatier* (1940). In the latter, Raimu starred with Fernandel (1903-71), France's other legendary comic known as 'Horseface' because of his inimitable grin. Horseface was an honorary citizen of Carry-le-Rouet where he spent most summers.

The 1930s and 40s saw a rash of stars flock to Ingram's studios in Nice, including two of France's best loved actors, Jean Gabin and Arletty, who had leading roles, respectively in Jean Renoir's *La Grande Illusion* (1937) and Carné's *Les Enfants du Paradis* (1945). The indisputable star of the 1950s and 60s was the sexy Brigitte Bardot who made her first appearance at Cannes in 1953, aged 18 and already married to film director Roger Vadim who would later make her a star on screen. Bardot set up home in Saint Tropez. She was the first in a long long line of cinema celebrities to grace the southern French coast with their presence.

Stars galore gathered in Vallauris in October 1998 to mourn the death of French silver screen hero Jean Marais (1914-98) who lived near Cannes most of his life. The beautiful, blonde-haired actor was best known for his lead role in Jean Cocteau's *La Belle et la Bête* (Beauty and the Beast, 1946) and *Orphée* (Orpheus, 1950), and more recently as Prospero in the 1990s adaptation of Shakespeare's *The Tempest*. Marais and Cocteau (see Literature – 20th century earlier) met in 1937 and were lovers until Cocteau's death in 1963.

SOCIETY & CONDUCT

While Parisians systematically slam every city other than their own, so people in Provence perceive the rest of France – cold northern capital included – as far less attractive than their own sun-lit Provence. Provence, through their rose-coloured spectacles, is bathed in a golden glow year round. Come the big chill of the mistral in autumn and winter, true Provençaux are barely bitten by the unbearable cold, unlike their foreign neighbours who slam shut the shutters, curl up by the fire – and still shiver in their sleep. Unless you're born and bred in Provence, you have little hope of ever adjusting to the mistral's menacing climes, as any true Provençal will very proudly point out.

Provençaux are staunchly proud of their natural treasures and rich cultural heritage. Most have an equally staunch loyalty to the hamlet, village, town or city where they live. The rough and tumble Marseillais are famed throughout France for their blatant exaggerations and imaginative fancies – like the tale about the sardine that blocked Marseille port. The Niçois by contrast are more Latin in outlook and temperament, sharing a common zest for the good life with their Italian neighbours. Flash Monagésques in Monaco tend to drip with gold and hair cream, while Saint Tropez's colourful community is clearly split between glamour queens and reborn hippies – both ageless. Wild gesticulations, passionate cheek kissing and fervent hand-shaking are an integral part of Provençal daily life regardless of geographical location.

Food is an extremely serious matter. Many people live, dream and sleep food – a topic that miraculously wangles its way in to the most unrelated of conversations. Offences warranting social ostracism include expressing even a mild dislike for a traditional culinary dish such as *pieds et paquets* (sheep tripe) or *testicules de mouton* (sheep testicles); declining a *dégustation* (wine-tasting) session, regardless of time, day or circumstance; or failing to show as enthusiastic an interest in food as your next door neighbour.

Definite dining dos and don'ts include never *ever* asking for ice cubes to drop into warm wine, or ketchup/mayonnaise to douse over food. When tasting wine, don't just sniff, sip, swallow or spit (common to a true dégustation), but mimic the series of facial contortions required. If invited to lunch, don't make plans for the afternoon; lunch will last at least three hours and leave you feeling so blissfully full afterwards that it is doubtful you will be able to move. Skipping lunch (or indeed any meal) is seen as the ultimate sin, while a quick snack standing up is severely frowned upon.

Handy little tricks to make friends quickly include always saying 'Bonjour, monsieur/madame/ mademoiselle' with a smile when you sail into a shop/café/restaurant – or saying it with flowers when visiting someone's home. Never buy/offer chrysanthemums unless you intend laying them on a gravestone. Money, time and Le Pen are all taboo subjects.

When travelling in Monaco, don't mention the revolution – and never refer to Monaco as part of France. Most Monagésques will explain that their principality is a distinctly separate country to France with its own strong history, culture and traditions. Listen to what they have to say and respect their patch of land.

Nude bathing has theoretically been forbidden on Saint Tropez's municipal beaches since 1990 (bathers strip off anyway). Since 1994, fines have been imposed in Saint Raphaël and Sainte Maxime on tourists who walk round town barechested or bikini-clad. Bikinis on the streets are also forbidden in Monaco. Rules of the forest include sticking to marked tracks and paths, not littering, not camping, not smoking, and not lighting camp fires.

RELIGION

Countrywide, 80% of people identify themselves as Catholic, although few ever attend church. Catholicism is the official state religion in neighbouring Monaco which marks a number of religious feasts with public holidays (see Facts for the Visitor – Public Holidays & Special Events). Protestants account for less than 2% of today's population.

Many of France's 4 to 5 million nominally Muslim residents live in the south of France, comprising the second-largest religious group. France's Jewish community numbers 650,000 – the largest in Europe. There are synagogues in Avignon, Marseille, Cavaillon and Carpentras, a traditional Jewish stronghold with just 100 Jewish families today. The anti-Semitic desecration of its Jewish cemetery in the early 1990s sent shock waves through the international Jewish community.

Facts for the Visitor

HIGHLIGHTS

There is a wealth of wonderful places to go to and things to see in Provence and the Côte d'Azur. Highlights on the trampled tourist trail include Avignon's beautiful Palais des Papes; Mont Ventoux' barren summit; the 12th century abbeys of Sénanque, Silvacane and Thoronet; the *villages perchés* (perched villages) of Les-Baux-de-Provence, Gordes, Bonnieux, Ménerbes, Lacoste and Èze; the Roman treasures at Pont du Gard, Orange, Arles, Nîmes and Saint-Rémy-de-Provence; Monaco; Saint Tropez; and star-struck Cannes. Nice's fantastical mansions and Cap d'Antibes' plush villas dating from the Riviera's finest hour – the *belle époque* – are truly a sight to behold.

Away from the camera-happy crowds, activities to set the heart racing include canyoning through the Gorges du Verdon, exploring Les Calanques by boat or foot, climbing France's highest cliff on Cap Canaille near Cassis, scaling rock faces in La Colmiane, parasailing in Saint-André and star gazing through the world's largest amateur telescope at Puimichel.

Awe-inspiring natural wonders include the Gorges de Dalius, a fabulous gorge carved from burgundy red rock in the Haute Vallée du Var; and the Pénitents des Mées, a line up of larger-than-life stone figurines in the Vallée de la Moyenne Durance. The forested Massif des Maures, the red-rocked Massif de l'Estérel and the flamingo-pink wetlands of the Camargue are among the region's most dramatic landscapes. The fragile beauty and isolation of the protected Parc National du Mercantour in north-eastern Provence remains unrivalled. The pinprick island of Port-Cros and its snorkelling shores – Europe's first marine national park – ranks second.

Culinary thrill seekers should shop at a Provençal market; watch a harvest (lavender in July, rice in August, grapes in September, olives from November to January); sniff out some truffles (November to March); sip red wine in Châteauneuf-du-Pape; and sample bouillabaisse in Marseille.

Body-packed beaches, traffic-jammed roads and booked-up hotels are definitive lowlights in July and August.

PLANNING
When to Go

In short, not in July and August.

May and June are by far the best times to visit, followed by September and October. Spring in Provence is a cocktail of flowering poppy fields, blossoming almond trees and colourful wild flowers. Age-old vines turn heavy with plump red grapes in early September, pumpkin fields turn deliciously orange and the first olives turn black in Van Gogh's silver-branched olive groves. The *vendanges* (grape harvests) start around 15 September, followed by the *cueillette des olives* (olive harvest) from 15 November through to early January.

Stone-capped Mont Ventoux – Provence's highest elevation – stays snow-capped until as late as mid-May. The southern Alps in mountainous Haute-Provence are snow-covered most years from late November until early April; the ski season starts just before Christmas and lasts until March. Elsewhere, the legendary Mistral chills the bones all winter long.

On the coast, sun worshippers bare their bodies from April to early October. Easter to September sees the beach resorts on the Côte d'Azur buzz with activity around the clock. July and August are notoriously hot and generally unbearable for those unfortunate enough not to be within dipping distance of a pool (or the sea). Discomfort brought on by the sweltering heat is further exacerbated by the hordes of tourists and French holiday-makers who descend on the region, clogging up the roads, hotels and camping grounds and generally making life hell for anyone visiting the region to 'get away from it all'. Dream on.

Inland, sweet-smelling lavender fields carpet the region with a purple blaze for just a few precious weeks from June to mid-July when the little lilac flower is harvested. In August and September the days shorten and sudden storms and rainshowers are frequent, both on the coast and inland.

The region's rich pageant of festivals can also be a deciding factor when you are considering when to go (or not go). For details on what festival falls when, see the boxed text Feasts & Festivals.

Maps

Quality regional maps are widely available outside France and are invaluable in planning a trip to the region. City maps are easily found in-country, at Maisons de la Presse (large newsagencies found in most towns and cities), tourist offices, bookshops and some newspaper kiosks.

Regional Road Maps A variety of *cartes routières* (road maps) are available. Indisputably the best, particularly if you intend driving a lot, is Michelin's yellow-jacketed *Provence Côte d'Azur* (Map No 245; 28.50FF) which maps out the entire region covered in this book in a 1:200,000 scale (1cm = 2km); or *Provence Côte d'Azur* (Map No 115, TOP 250 series; 29FF) published in a 1:250,000 scale (1cm = 2.5km) by the Institut Géographique National (IGN). Both fold out.

Michelin (www.michelin-travel.com) and IGN (www.ign.fr) have Internet boutiques where you can purchase maps. Locally, a good selection of their maps is sold in FNAC stores in Marseille and Nice, and in smaller book shops.

Hiking & Cycling Maps Didier-Richard publishes an excellent set of 1:50,000-scale trail maps (1cm = 500m) in its *tracés grand air* hiking series, based on IGN mapping. Each map costs about 71FF and is perfect for hoofing it or cycling. The Provence-Côte d'Azur region is covered by eight maps in the series.

Southern France is also covered by IGN's *seriés verte* (green series), published in a scale of 1:100,000 (1cm = 1km). Each map costs 29FF and is geared mainly towards cyclists. Tops for serious hikers is IGN's recent Top 25 series (58FF). Maps are published in a 1:25,000 scale (1cm = 250m). Map No 3741OT (OT is short for *ouest*, ie west) covers an area slightly west of that covered by Map No 3741ET (short for *est*, ie east).

Nature trails and fishing, hiking and bathing spots are featured in IGN's *série plein-air* (outdoor series). The 1:50,000-scale maps (1cm = 500m) cover Provence with three maps: *Parc Naturel Régional de Camargue* (Map No 82004), *Provence – Le Pays d'Aix* (Map No 82052) and *Provence – De Calanques en Collines* (Map No 82051). Each costs 58FF.

IGN's 1:1,000,000-scale, grey-jacketed Map No 903 (29FF), entitled *France – Grande Randonnée*, shows the region's long-distance GR trails and is useful for strategic planning of a cross-country trek through Provence and the Côte d'Azur. Map No 906 (29FF), in the same series, called *France – VTT & Randonnées Cyclos*, indicates dozens of suggested bicycle tours around rural France. Map No 905 (29FF) entitled *France – Canoë-Kayak et Sports d'Eau Vive*, is useful for water sports enthusiasts.

City Maps The *plans* (street maps) distributed free by tourist offices range from the superb to the virtually useless. Michelin's *Guide Rouge* (Red Guide; see Guidebooks later in this chapter) includes maps for the south's larger cities, towns and resorts that show one-way streets and have numbered town entry points that are coordinated with Michelin's yellow-jacketed 1:200,000 road maps.

Blay-Foldex (www.geoshop.com/Blay-foldex) publishes *plans-guides* city maps/guides for Marseille, Toulon, Hyères, Cannes/Antibes, Grasse, Cagnes-sur-Mer, Nice, Monaco, Menton, Aix-en-Provence,

Arles, Avignon and Nîmes. The orange-jacketed street maps cost between 19 and 31FF.

What to Bring

As little as possible: forgotten items can be picked up practically anywhere in the region. If you intend travelling around or doing any walking with your gear – even from the train station to your hotel – a backpack is the way to go. Most useful is the type which has an exterior pouch that zips off to become a daypack.

Hostellers have to provide their own towel and soap. Bedding is almost always provided or available for hire; sheets cost around 17FF a night. Bring a padlock to secure your backpack by day and your storage locker (provided by most hostels) at night.

Other handy little numbers include a torch (flashlight), a Swiss army knife, an adaptor plug for electrical appliances, a universal bath/sink plug (a plastic film canister sometimes works) and several clothes pegs. Essential items for surviving the heat in July and August include a water bottle, pre-moistened towelettes or a large cotton handkerchief (to soak in fountains and cool off), sunglasses, a sun hat, plenty of sunscreen (including sunblock), and after-sun lotion (for when you burn).

A warm sweater can be useful on early and late summer evenings. If you intend venturing in to the mountains in August, bring a light, waterproof garment with you. Those heading into the Camargue need to pack a pair of binoculars and an excess of mosquito repellent.

TOURIST OFFICES
Local Tourist Offices

Every city, town, village and hamlet seems to have an *office de tourisme* (tourist office run by some unit of local government) or a *syndicat d'initiative* (tourist office run by an organisation of local merchants). Both are an excellent resource and can almost always provide a local map and information on accommodation possibilities. Some change foreign currency. Many make local hotel reservations.

Tourist information for the entire Provence-Côte d'Azur region is provided by the Comité Régional de Tourisme Provence-Alpes-Côte d'Azur (☎ 04 91 39 38 00, fax 04 91 56 66 61), Espace Colbert, 14 rue Sainte Barbe, 13231 Marseille.

Within the region, there are five departmental tourist offices known as a *comité départemental du tourisme*:

Alpes-de-Haute-Provence
(☎ 04 92 31 57 29, fax 04 92 32 24 94)
Maison des Alpes-de-Haute-Provence,
19 rue du Docteur Honnorat, 04005
Digne-les-Bains
Alpes-Maritimes
(☎ 04 93 37 78 78, fax 04 93 86 01 06,
crt06@nicematin.fr, www.crt-riviera.fr)
55 promenade des Anglais, 06011 Nice
Bouches-du-Rhône
(☎ 04 91 13 84 13, fax 04 91 33 01 82,
www.visitprovence.com)
13 rue Roux de Brignoles, 13006 Marseille
Var
(☎ 04 94 50 55 50, fax 04 94 50 55 51)
Conseil Général, 1 blvd Foch, BP 99, 83003
Draguignan
(☎ 04 94 18 59 60, fax 04 94 18 59 61)
1 blvd de Strasbourg, 83093 Toulon
Vaucluse
(☎ 04 90 80 47 00, fax 04 90 86 86 08,
info@provenceguide.com, www.Provence
Guide.com)
12 rue Collège de la Croix, BP 147, 84008
Avignon

Tourist information on the principality of Monaco is handled by its national tourist office in Monte Carlo (see the Monaco chapter).

French Tourist Offices Abroad

Information on Provence and the Côte d'Azur is available from French government tourist offices abroad:

Australia
(☎ 02-9231 5244, fax 02-9221 8682,
frencht@ozemail.com.au)
25 Bligh St, 22nd floor, Sydney, NSW 2000
Belgium
(☎ 09-02 88 025, fax 09-02 502 0410,
maisondelafrance@pophost.eunet.be)
21 ave de la Toison d'Or, 1050 Brussels

Canada
(☎ 514-288 4264, fax 514-845 4868,
mfrance@mtl.net)
1981 Ave McGill College, Suite 490, Montreal, Que H3A 2W9;
(☎ 416-593 4723, fax 416-979 7587,
french.tourist@sympatico.ca)
30 Saint Patrick St, Suite 700, Toronto, Ont
M5T 3A3

Germany
(☎ 069-758 021, fax 069-745 556,
maison_de_la_France@t-online.de)
Westendstrasse 47, 60325 Frankfurt;
(☎ 030-218 2064, fax 030-214 1238)
Keithstrasse 2-4, 10787 Berlin

Ireland
(☎ 01-703 4046, fax 01-874 7324)
35 Lower Abbey St, Dublin 1

Italy
(☎ 02-58 48 61, fax 02-58 48 62 22,
entf@enter.it)
Via Larga 7, 20122 Milano

Netherlands
(☎ 0900-112 2332, fax 020-620 3339,
fra_vvv@euronet.nl)
Prinsengracht 670, 1017 KX Amsterdam

South Africa
(☎ 011-880 8062, fax 011-880 7722,
mdfsa@frenchdoor.co.za)
Oxford Manor, 1st floor, 196 Oxford Road,
Illovo 2196

Spain
(☎ 91-541 8808, fax 91-541 2412,
maisondelafrance@mad.sericom.es)
Alcalá 63, 28014 Madrid

Switzerland
(☎ 01-211 3085, fax 01-212 1644)
Löwenstrasse 59, 8023 Zürich;
(☎ 022-732 8610, fax 731 5873)
2 rue Thalberg, 1201 Geneva

UK
(☎ 0891-244 123, fax 020-7493 6594,
piccadilly@mdlf.demon.co.uk,
www.franceguide.com)
178 Piccadilly, London W1V 0AL

USA
(☎ 212-838 7800, fax 212-838 7855;
info@francetourism.com,
www.francetourism.com)
444 Madison Ave, 16th floor, New York, NY
10022-6903;
(☎ 310-271 6665, fax 310-276 2835,
fgtola@ juno.com)
9454 Wiltshire Blvd, Suite 715, Beverly
Hills, CA 90212-2967

Monégasque Tourist Offices Abroad

Monaco has its own string of tourist offices
abroad:

France
(☎ 01 42 96 12 23, fax 01 42 61 31 52)
Office du Tourisme et des Congrès de la
Principauté de Monaco, 9 rue de la Paix,
75002 Paris

Germany
(☎ 211-323 7844, fax 211-323 7846)
Monaco Informations Centrum, WZ Center,
Königsallee 27-31, 40212 Düsseldorf

Italy
(☎ 02-86 45 84 80, fax 02-86 45 84 69)
Ufficio del Turismo e dei Congressi del
Principato di Monaco, Via Dante 12, 20121
Milano

Japan
(☎ 3-5798 7403, fax 3-3280 2655)
Monaco-Seifu-Kanko-Kyoku, Uhnex Twaindle 101, Shirogane-dai 5-15-5, Minato-Ku,
Tokyo 108

Spain
(☎ 91-578 16 97, fax 91-578 19 34)
Oficina de Turismo y Congresos de Monaco,
Calle Villanueva 19, 28001 Madrid

UK
(☎ 020-7352 9962, fax 020-7352 2103)
Monaco Government Tourist & Convention
Office, The Chambers, Chelsea Harbour,
London SW10 0XE

USA
(☎ 800-753 9696 or 212-286 3330, fax 212-
286 9890, mgto@monaco1.org,
www.monaco.mc/usa)
Monaco Government Tourist & Convention
Bureau 565 Fifth Avenue, New York, NY
10017

VISAS & DOCUMENTS

A visa for France is good for Monaco too.
Despite having its own diplomatic missions
abroad, the principality of Monaco does not
issue a visa of its own; rather it directs visa
applicants to the nearest French consulate.

Passport

By law, everyone in France and Monaco,
including tourists, must carry ID on them at
all times. For foreign visitors, this means a
passport or national ID card.

Visas

Tourist There are no entry requirements or restrictions on EU nationals and citizens of Australia, the USA, Canada, New Zealand and Israel who do not need visas to visit France or Monaco as tourists for up to three months. Except for people from a handful of other European countries, everyone else needs a visa.

A transit visa generally costs about US$12, a visa valid for 30 days around US$31 and a single/multiple entry visa of up to three months US$37/43.70. You need your passport (valid for three months beyond the date of your departure from France), a ticket in and out of France, proof of money and possibly of accommodation, two passport-size photos and the visa fee in cash. Visas are usually issued on the spot.

Tourist visas cannot be extended except in emergencies (eg medical problems). If you're in Nice or Marseille and have an urgent problem, you should consult with your consulate for guidance or call the *préfecture* (see Carte de Séjour below).

Long-Stay, Student & Au Pair If you'd like to work or study in France or stay for over three months, apply to the French embassy or consulate for the appropriate sort of *séjour* (long-stay) visa. Unless you are an EU citizen, it is difficult to get a visa allowing you to work in France. For any sort of long-stay visa, begin the paperwork in your home country several months before you plan to leave. People with student visas can apply for permission to work part time (inquire at your place of study).

Au pair visas (see Work section later) also have to be arranged before you leave home (unless you're an EU citizen).

Carte de Séjour If you are issued a long-stay visa valid for six or more months you'll probably have to apply for a *carte de séjour* (residence permit) within eight days of arrival in France. For details, inquire at your place of study or the local *préfecture* (prefecture), *sous-préfecture* (subprefecture),

hôtel de ville (city hall), *mairie* (town hall) or *commissariat* (police station).

The prefecture in Nice (☎ 04 93 72 20 00), cours Saleya; and in Marseille (☎ 04 91 15 60 00, metro Estrangin-Préfecture), place Félix Baret, both have special visa sections (Nice ☎ 04 93 72 26 75; Marseille ☎ 04 91 15 66 27) which also tackle cartes de séjour.

Travel Insurance

Travel insurance covers you for medical expenses, luggage theft or loss (vital if you intend visiting the coast in the high season), as well as for cancellation or delays in your travel arrangements. Cover depends on your insurance and sometimes on your type of airline ticket, so be sure to ask your insurer and ticket-issuing agency where you stand.

Driving Licence & Permits

Many non-European driving licences are valid in France, but it's still a good idea to bring along an International Driving Permit. It is a multilingual translation of the vehicle class and personal details noted on your local driving licence and is not valid unless accompanied by your original. An IDP can be obtained for a small fee from your local automobile association – bring along a passport photo and a valid licence.

Hostel Card

A Hostelling International (HI) card is only necessary at official *auberges de jeunesse* (youth hostels). You can buy one at most official French hostels for 70/100FF if you're under/over 26 years of age. One-night membership (where available) costs between 10 and 19FF, and a family card is 100FF.

Student, Youth, Teachers & Journalists' Cards

An International Student Identity Card (ISIC) can pay for itself through half-price admissions, discounted air and ferry tickets, and cheap meals in student cafeterias. Many places stipulate a maximum age, usually 24 or 25. ISIC cards are issued by student travel agencies such as Accueil des Jeunes en France (AJF) for 60FF.

If you're under 26 but not a student you can apply for a GO25 card issued by the Federation of International Youth Travel Organisations (FIYTO; 60FF), which entitles you to much the same discounts as an ISIC. It is also issued by student unions or student travel agencies.

A Carte Jeunes (120FF for one year) is available to anyone under 26 who has been in France for six months. It gets you discount air tickets, car rental, sports events, concerts, movies etc. Discount details are available online (info@cartejeunes.fr, www.cartejeunes.fr), or in France (☎ 08 03 00 12 26).

Teachers, professional artists, museum conservators, journalists and certain categories of students are admitted to some museums free. Bring along proof of affiliation, eg an International Teacher Identity Card (ITIC; 60FF).

Seniors' Card

Reductions are available for people over 60 at most cultural centres, including museums, galleries and public theatres. SNCF issues the Carte Senior to those over 60 which gives reductions of 20-50% on train tickets. It costs 140FF for a card valid to purchase four train tickets or 285FF for a card valid for one year.

Camping Card International

The Camping Card International (CCI) is a camping ground ID that can be used instead of a passport when checking into a camp site and includes third-party insurance for damage you may cause. As a result, many camping grounds offer a small discount if you sign in with one. CCIs are issued by automobile associations, camping federations and, sometimes, on the spot at camping grounds. In the UK, the AA issues them to its members for £4.

Carte Musée Côte d'Azur

The Carte Musée Côte d'Azur (Côte d'Azur Museum Card) gives card holders unlimited entry to about 60 museums along the coast. Better still, card bearers can jump the queues. A three/seven day pass costs 70/140FF and is sold at participating museums, tourist offices, FNAC stores and Thomas Cook exchange bureaux. There is no reduced rate for students or senior travellers. In Nice, details are available from the Inter-Musées-Monuments des Alpes-Maritimes (☎ 04 93 52 33 25, fax 04 93 52 92 57), Villa Arson, 20 ave Stéphane Liégeard (same building as the Centre National d'Art Contemporain), 06105 Nice.

La Clé des Temps

La Clé des Temps costs 100FF and gives key holders entry to 10 national monuments in Provence-Côte d'Azur.

Passes are sold at participating monuments (Glanum near Saint-Rémy-de-Provence, the Abbaye de Thoronet, La Turbie or the Groupe Épiscopal in Fréjus) or from FNAC stores in Nice and Marseille. Further information is available from the Caisse Nationale des Monuments Historiques et des Sites (☎ 01 44 61 21 50), Hôtel de Sully, 62 rue Saint-Antoine, 75186 Paris.

Photocopies

The hassle of losing your passport can be considerably reduced if you have a record of its number and issue date, or even better, photocopies of the relevant data pages. A photocopy of your birth certificate can also be useful.

Also keep the serial numbers of your travellers cheques (cross them off as you cash them) and photocopies of your credit cards, airline ticket and other travel documents. Keep all this emergency material separate from your passport, cheques and cash, and leave extra copies with someone back home. Add some emergency money, say US$50 in cash, to this separate stash. If you do lose your passport, notify the police immediately to get a statement, and contact your nearest consulate.

EMBASSIES & CONSULATES
French Embassies & Consulates

France's diplomatic and consular representatives abroad include:

Australia
Embassy:
(☎ 02-6216 0100, fax 02-6273 3193)
6 Perth Ave, Yarralumla, ACT 2600
Consulates:
(☎ 03-9820 0944/0921, fax 03-9820 9363)
492 St Kilda Rd, Level 4, Melbourne, Vic 3004;
(☎ 02-9262 5779, fax 02-9283 1210)
St Martin's Tower, 20th floor, 31 Market St, Sydney, NSW 2000
Belgium
Embassy:
(☎ 02-548 8711, fax 02-513 6871)
65 rue Ducale, 1000 Brussels
Consulate:
(☎ 02-229 8500, fax 02-229 8510)
12A place de Louvain, 1000 Brussels
Canada
Embassy:
(☎ 613-789 1795, fax 613-562 3704)
42 Sussex Drive, Ottawa, Ont K1M 2C9
Consulates:
4S3 (☎ 514-878 4385, fax 514-878 3981)
1 Place Ville Marie, 26th floor, Montreal, Que H3B;
(☎ 416-925 8041, fax 416-925 3076)
130 Bloor St West, Suite 400, Toronto, Ont M5S 1N5
Germany
Embassy:
(☎ 0228-955 6000, fax 0228-955 6055)
An der Marienkapelle 3, 53179 Bonn
Consulates:
(☎ 030-885 90243, fax 030-885 5295)
Kurfürstendamm 211, 10719 Berlin;
(☎ 089-419 4110, fax 089-419 41141)
Möhlstrasse 5, 81675 München
Ireland
(☎ 01-260 1666, fax 01-283 0178)
36 Ailesbury Rd, Ballsbridge, Dublin 4
Italy
Embassy:
(☎ 06-68 60 11, fax 06-860 13 60)
Piazza Farnese 67, 00186 Rome
Consulate:
(☎ 06-68 80 64 37, fax 06-68 60 12 60)
Via Giulia 251, 00186 Rome
Netherlands
Embassy:
(☎ 070-312 5800, fax 070-312 5854)

Smidsplein 1, 2514 BT Den Haag
Consulate:
(☎ 020-624 8346, fax 020-626 0841)
Vijzelgracht 2, 1000 HA Amsterdam
New Zealand
(☎ 04-472 0200, fax 04-472 5887)
1-3 Willeston St, Wellington
Spain
Embassy:
(☎ 91-435 5560, fax 91-435 6655)
Calle de Salustiano Olozaga 9, 28001 Madrid
Consulates:
(☎ 91-319 7188, fax 91-308 6273)
Calle Marques de la Enseñada 10, 28004 Madrid;
(☎ 93-317 8150, fax 93-412 4282)
Ronda Universitat 22, 08007 Barcelona
Switzerland
Embassy:
(☎ 031-359 2111, fax 031-352 2191)
Schosshaldenstrasse 46, 3006 Bern
Consulates:
(☎ 022-311 3441, fax 022-310 8339)
11 rue Imbert Galloix, 1205 Geneva;
(☎ 01-268 8585, fax 268 8500)
Mühlebachstrasse 7, 8008 Zürich
UK
Embassy:
(☎ 020-7201 1000, fax 020-7201 1004, www.embafrance.org.uk)
58 Knightsbridge, London SW1X 7JT
Consulate:
(☎ 020-7838 2000, fax 020-7838 2001)
21 Cromwell Rd, London SW7 2DQ;
Visa section:
(☎ 020-7838 2051, fax 020-7838 2001)
6A Cromwell Place, London SW7 2EW
☎ 0891-887 733 for general information on visa requirements.
USA
Embassy & Consulate:
(embassy ☎ 202-944 6000, fax 202-944 6166;
consulate ☎ 202-944 6195, fax 202-944 6148; direct fax for visa section 202-944 6212)
4101 Reservoir Rd NW, Washington, DC 20007
Consulates:
(☎ 212-606 3688, fax 212-606 3620)
934 Fifth Ave, New York, NY 10021;
(☎ 415-397 4330, fax 415-433 8357)
540 Bush St, San Francisco, CA 94108;
Other consulates are in Atlanta, Boston, Chicago, Houston, Los Angeles, Miami and New Orleans.

Monégasque Embassies

Monaco has the following diplomatic missions abroad:

Belgium
  (☎ 02-347 4987, fax 02-343 4920)
  17 place Guv-d'Arezzo, 1180 Brussels
France
  (☎ 01 45 04 74 54, fax 01 45 04 45 16)
  22 blvd Suchet, 75016 Paris
Germany
  (☎ 0228-232 007 or 0228-232 008, fax 0228-236 282)
  Zitelmannstrasse 16, 53113 Bonn
Italy
  (☎ 06-808 33 61 or 06-807 76 92, fax 06-807 76 92)
  Via Bertolom 36, 00197 Rome
Spain
  (☎ 91-578 2048, fax 91-435 7132)
  Calle Villanueva 12, 28001 Madrid
Switzerland
  (☎ 031-356 2858, fax 031-356 2855)
  34 Hallwylstrasse, 3006 Bern, CP 3000 Bern 6

Embassies & Consulates in Provence & Monaco

Foreign embassies are in Paris but most countries have a consulate in Nice, Marseille and/or Monaco:

Algeria
  (☎ 04 91 13 99 50) 363 rue Paradis, 13008 Marseille
  (☎ 04 93 88 79 86) 20bis ave Mont Rabeau, 06200 Nice
Belgium
  (☎ 04 93 87 79 56) Bureaux du Ruhl, 5 rue Gabriel Fauré, 06406 Nice
  (☎ 377-93 50 59 89) 26bis blvd Princesse Charlotte, Monaco
Canada
  (☎ 04 93 92 93 22) 64 ave Jean Médecin, 06000 Nice
France
  (☎ 377-93 50 99 66) 1 rue du Ténao, Monaco
Germany
  (☎ 04 91 16 75 20) 338 ave du Prado, 13008 Marseille
  (☎ 04 93 83 55 25) Le Minotaure, 34 ave Henri Matisse, 06200 Nice
Italy
  (☎ 04 91 18 49 18) 56 rue d'Alger, 13005 Marseille
  (☎ 04 93 88 79 86) 72 blvd Gambetta, 06048

Nice
  (☎ 377-93 50 22 71) 17 ave de l'Annonciade, Monaco
Monaco
  (☎ 04 91 33 30 21) 3 place aux Huîles, 13001 Marseille
  (☎ 04 93 80 00 22) Villa Printemps, 12 montée Désambrois, 06000 Nice
Netherlands
  (☎ 04 91 25 66 64) 137 ave de Toulon, 13005 Marseille
  (☎ 04 93 87 52 94) 14 rue Rossini, 06000 Nice
  (☎ 377-92 05 15 02) 24 ave de Fontvieille, Monaco
Switzerland
  (☎ 04 91 53 36 65) 7 rue d'Arcole, 13006 Marseille
  (☎ 04 93 88 85 09) Le Louvre, 13 rue Alphonse Karr, BP 1279, 06005 Nice
UK
  (☎ 04 91 15 72 10) 24 ave du Prado, 13006 Marseille
  (☎ 04 93 82 32 04) 8 rue Alphonse Kerr, 06000 Nice
  (☎ 377-93 25 76 55, insure@monaco.mc) 33 blvd Princesse Charlotte, Monaco
USA
  (☎ 04 91 54 92 00, fax 04 91 55 09 97, amcongenmars@calva.net)
  12 blvd Paul Peytral, 13006 Marseille
  (☎ 04 93 88 89 55)
  31 rue Maréchal Joffre, 06000 Nice

CUSTOMS

The usual allowances apply to duty-free goods purchased at airports or on ferries outside the EU: tobacco (200 cigarettes, 50 cigars, or 250g of loose tobacco), alcohol (1L of strong liquor or 2L of less than 22% alcohol by volume; 2L of wine), coffee (500g or 200g of extracts) and perfume (50g of perfume and 0.25L of toilet water).

Do not confuse these with duty-paid items (including alcohol and tobacco) bought at normal shops and supermarkets in another EU country and brought into France, where certain goods might be more expensive. Then the allowances are more than generous: 800 cigarettes, 200 cigars or 1kg of loose tobacco; 10L of spirits (more than 22% alcohol by volume), 20L of fortified wine or aperitif, 90L of wine or 110L of beer.

MONEY
Currency
The French franc (FF) remains the national currency in France and Monaco until January 2002 when it will be exchanged for the euro (€). The franc will cease to be legal tender from July 2002. Monégasque franc coins currently in circulation in Monaco will simply be replaced by 'Monégasque' euros, ie. euros bearing the national emblem of Monaco on the reverse side. See the boxed text Euroland for more euro details.

One franc is divided into 100 centimes. French coins come in denominations of 5, 10, 20 and 50 centimes (0.5FF) and 1, 2, 5, 10 and 20FF; the two highest denominations have silvery centres and brass edges. French franc banknotes are issued in denominations of 20FF (Claude Debussy), 50FF (the Little Prince and his creator, Antoine de Saint Exupéry), 100FF (Provence's very own Paul Cézanne), 200FF (Gustave Eiffel) and 500FF (Marie and Pierre Curie).

Exchange Rates

country	unit	€	FF
Australia	A$1	0.56	3.70
Canada	C$1	0.60	3.96
euro	€1		6.56
Germany	DM1	0.51	3.35
Japan	¥100	0.76	5.0
New Zealand	NZ$1	0.48	3.12
United Kingdom	UK£1	1.46	9.54
United States	US$1	0.91	5.97

Exchanging Money
Cash Cash is not a safe way to carry money; the Banque de France pays about 2.5% more for travellers cheques, easily compensating for the 1% commission usually involved in buying them.

Bring the equivalent of about US$100 in low-denomination notes for when you need small sums of money. Counterfeiting can make it difficult to change US$100 notes; most Banque de France branches don't accept them.

Euroland

Since 1 January 1999, the franc and the euro – Europe's new currency for 11 European Union (EU) countries – have both been legal tender in France. Euro coins and banknotes have not been issued yet but you can already get billed in euros and opt to pay in euros by credit card. Essentially, if there's no hard cash involved, you can deal in euros. Travellers should check bills carefully to make sure that any conversion has been calculated correctly. Luckily, the euro should make everything easier. One of the main benefits will be that prices in the 11 countries will be immediately comparable.

The whole idea behind this paperless currency is to give euro-fearing punters a chance to limber up arithmetically before euro coins and banknotes are issued on 1 January 2002. The same euro coins (one to 50 cents, €1 and €2) and bridge-adorned bills (€5 to €500) can be happily used in Euroland's 11 countries: France, Ireland, Austria, Italy, Spain, Germany, Belgium and Luxembourg, Finland, the Netherlands and Portugal. The French and Monégasque franc will remain legal tender alongside the euro until 1 July 2002, when the franc will be hurled on the scrapheap of history.

Until then, one euro is 6.56FF, 1936ITL, 166.4ESP, 1.96DEM, 40.3BEF, 0.788IEP, 200PTE, 2.20NLG, 5.95FIM, 37.5LUF and 13.77ATS. The Banque de France changes these currencies into francs at the official rate without charging any commission. You can log into Euroland on the Net at europa.eu.int/euro/html/entry.html. The Lonely Planet Web site at www.lonelyplanet.com has a link to a currency converter and up-to-date news on the integration process.

Travellers Cheques Except at exchange bureaux and the Banque de France you have to pay to cash travellers cheques: at banks, expect a charge of 22-30FF per transaction. A percentage fee may apply for large sums. American Express offices do not charge a commission on their own travellers cheques but holders of other brands must pay 3% on top (minimum charge 40FF).

Travellers cheques issued by American Express and Visa offer the greatest flexibility.

Eurcheques Eurocheques, available if you have a European bank account, are guaranteed up to a certain limit. When cashing them (eg at post offices or banks), you will be asked to show your Eurocheque card bearing your signature and registration number, and perhaps a passport or ID card. Many hotels and merchants refuse to accept Eurocheques because of the relatively large commissions.

Lost or Stolen Travellers Cheques If travellers cheques issued by American Express (www.americanexpress.com) are lost or stolen in France, call ☎ 08 00 90 86 00. Reimbursement can be made at the American Express offices in Aix-en-Provence (☎ 04 42 26 84 77, 15 cours Mirabeau); Cannes (☎ 04 93 38 15 87, 8 rue des Belges); Marseille (☎ 04 91 13 71 21, 39 La Canebière); Nice (☎ 04 93 16 53 53, 11 promenade des Anglais); and Monaco (☎ 377-93 25 74 45, 35 blvd Princesse Charlotte). Opening hours are listed in the Money section of the relevant chapters.

If you lose your Thomas Cook cheques (www.thomascook.com), contact any Thomas Cook bureau – eg at Nice train station, in Cannes or Saint Tropez – for replacements. The company's customer service bureau can be contacted toll-free (☎ 08 00 90 83 30).

ATMs In French, ATMs are *distributeurs automatiques de billets* or *points d'argent*. ATM cards can give you direct access to your cash reserves back home at a superior exchange rate. Most ATMs give a cash advance through Visa or MasterCard.

There are plenty of ATMs in Provence and the Côte d'Azur linked to the international Cirrus and Maestro networks. If you remember your PIN code as a string of letters, translate it back into numbers, as keyboards may not show letters.

Credit Cards This is the cheapest way to pay for things and to get cash advances. Visa (Carte Bleue) is the most widely accepted, followed by MasterCard (Access or Eurocard). American Express cards are not very useful except at upmarket establishments but they do allow you to get cash at certain ATMs and at American Express offices (see Lost or Stolen Travellers Cheques earlier).

Taking along two different credit cards (stashed in different wallets) is safer than taking one, as it may be impossible to replace a lost Visa or MasterCard until you get home (American Express and Diners Club International offer on-the-spot replacement cards).

Lost or Stolen Cards If your Visa card is lost or stolen, call Carte Bleue (☎ 02 54 42 12 12). To replace a lost card you have to deal with the issuer.

Report a lost MasterCard, Access or Eurocard to Eurocard France (☎ 01 45 67 53 53) and, if you can, to your credit card issuer back home. For cards from the USA, call ☎ 314-275 6690.

If your American Express card is lost or stolen, call ☎ 01 47 77 70 00 or 01 47 77 72 00; both are staffed 24 hours a day. In an emergency, American Express card holders from the USA can call collect ☎ 202-783 7474 or 202-677 2442. Replacements can be arranged at any American Express office (see Lost or Stolen Travellers Cheques earlier).

Report a lost Diners Club card on ☎ 01 47 62 75 75.

International Transfers Telegraphic transfers are not very expensive but can be quite slow. It's quicker and easier to have money wired via American Express (US$50 for US$1000). Western Union's Money Transfer system (☎ 01 43 54 46 12) and Thomas Cook's MoneyGram service (☎ 08 00 00 90 83 30) are popular.

Banque de France France's central bank offers the best exchange rates. It does not accept Eurocheques or provide credit card cash advances. Most do not accept US$100 notes due to the preponderance of counterfeit ones.

Post Offices Many post offices perform exchange transactions for a middling rate. The commission for travellers cheques is 1.2% (minimum 16FF).

Post offices accept banknotes in a variety of currencies as well as travellers cheques issued by American Express (in US dollars or French francs) or Visa (in French francs).

Commercial Banks Commercial banks usually charge between 22 and 50FF per foreign currency transaction. The rates offered vary, so it pays to compare.

Exchange Bureaux In cities, eg Nice and Marseille, *bureaux de change* are faster, easier, open longer hours and give better rates than the banks.

When using bureaux de change, shop around. Familiarise yourself with rates offered by banks and compare them with those offered at exchange bureaux (generally not allowed to charge commissions). On relatively small transactions, even exchange places with less than optimal rates may leave you with more francs in your pocket.

Costs

The bad news: Provence and the Côte d'Azur are the most expensive spots in France. Worse still for those planning a trip in July or August, prices soar sky high at this time. The good news: there are ways to save the odd centime.

If you stay in a camping ground, hostel, or showerless/toiletless room in a budget

hotel and have picnics rather than dining out, it's possible to travel around Provence-Côte d'Azur for about US$35 a day per person (US$45 in July/August).

Travelling with someone else immediately cuts costs: few hotels in the region offer single rooms. Those that do charge the same price (or only marginally less) for singles and doubles. Triples and quads (often with only two beds) are the cheapest per person and can offer an amazing price/comfort ratio. If visiting the Côte d'Azur, consider staying in Nice where accommodation is cheaper, and from where day trips can easily be made along the coast.

Dining wise, hearty picnics of baguette and cheese on the beach will cut costs dramatically. Carrying a water bottle instead of forking out an outrageous 15-25FF for a poxy canned drink is another massive money saver. In restaurants, sod the calorie count and opt for the *menu* – guaranteed to leave you stuffed and offering far better value than dining à la carte. Drinks-wise, ask for *une carafe d'eau* instead of bottled water, and order the house wine instead of beer (see Food & Drink section).

Discounts Museums, cinemas, the SNCF, ferry companies and other institutions offer all sorts of price breaks to people under 25 or 26; students with ISIC cards; le *troisième age* (people over 60 or 65). Look for the words *demi-tarif* or *tarif réduit* (half-price tariff or reduced rate) on rate charts and ask if you qualify.

Those under 18 get an even wider range of discounts, including free or reduced entry to most museums. For information on the Carte Musée Côte d'Azur and Le Clé des Temps – two cards offering a cheaper way to visit the sights, see Visas & Documents.

Look out for freebies too – eg entry to Nice museums is free on the first Sunday of the month. Throughout the region, numerous galleries, palaces, museums, gardens and other historic or cultural places which usually demand an entrance fee are free for two days in mid-September during France's *Journées du Patrimoine* (Days of Patrimony).

For information on the SNCF's Carte Is-abelle – a one day travel card allowing unlimited rail travel along the coast – see the Rail Pass section in the Getting Around chapter.

Tipping & Bargaining

French law requires that restaurant, café and hotel bills include the service charge (usually 10-15%), so a *pourboire* (tip) is neither necessary nor expected. However, most people – dire service apart – usually leave a few francs in restaurants.

Little bargaining goes on at Provençal markets.

Taxes & Refunds

France's Value Added Tax (TVA in French) is 20.6% on most goods except food, medicine and books, for which it's 5.5%; it goes as high as 33% on such items as watches, cameras and video cassettes. Prices are rarely given without VAT.

If you are not an EU resident, you can get a refund of most of the VAT provided that: you're over 15; you'll be spending less than six months in France; you purchase goods (not more than 10 of the same item) worth at least 1200FF (tax included) at a single shop; and the shop offers *vente en détaxe* (duty-free sales).

Present your passport at the time of purchase and ask for a *bordereau de détaxe* (export sales invoice). Some shops refund 14% of the purchase price rather than the full 17.1% you are entitled to in order to cover the time and expense involved in the refund procedure. When you leave France or another EU country, ensure that the country's customs officials validate all three pages of the bordereau; the green sheet is your receipt. You will receive a *virement* (transfer of funds) in your home country.

Instant Refunds If you are flying out of Nice-Côte d'Azur or Marseille-Provence airport, certain stores can arrange for you to receive your refund as you're leaving the country. You must make such arrangements at the time of purchase.

When you arrive at the airport, you have to get your bordereau validated at the *douane* (customs) office, where you will be told which customs refund window *(douane de détaxe)* or exchange bureau to go to for your VAT refund.

POST & COMMUNICATIONS
Post

Postal services in France are fast (next-day delivery for most domestic letters), reliable, bureaucratic and expensive. Post offices are signposted *La Poste*; older branches may be marked with the letters PTT (Postes, Télégraphes, Téléphones).

To mail things, go to a postal window marked *toutes opérations*.

Postal Rates From France and Monaco, domestic letters up to 20g cost 3FF. Postcards and letters up to 20g cost 3FF within the EU; 3.80FF to most of the rest of Europe and Africa; 4.40FF to the USA, Canada and the Middle East; and 5.20FF to Australasia. Aerograms cost 5FF to all destinations. France's worldwide express mail delivery service, Chronopost, costs a fortune.

Sending & Receiving Mail Most shops which sell postcards sell *timbres* (stamps) too. Stamps bought from coin-operated machines inside post offices come out as an uninspiring, blue-coloured sticker. French stamps can be used in Monaco; Monégasque stamps are only valid in Monaco.

When addressing mail to your truffle supplier in Provence, do it the French way: write the *nom de famille* (surname or family name) in capital letters first, followed by the *prénom* (first name) in lower case letters. Insert a comma after the street number and don't capitalise 'rue', 'ave', 'blvd'. CEDEX after the city or town name means mail sent to that address is collected at the post office rather than delivered to the door.

Poste restante is available at all post offices.

Telephone

France has one of the most modern and sophisticated telecommunications systems in the world. Monaco has a separate telephone system to France. Neither uses area codes. Most public telephones require a *télécarte* (40.60 or 97.50FF), sold at post offices, tabacs (tobacco shops), supermarket checkout counters and SNCF ticket windows.

French telephone numbers have 10 digits. To call anywhere in Provence-Côte d'Azur from Monaco and abroad, dial your country's international access code, followed by 33 (France's country code) and the 10-digit number, dropping the first 0. To call abroad from France, dial ☎ 00 (France's international access code), followed by the country code, area code (dropping the initial zero if there is one) and local number.

Telephone numbers in Monaco only have eight digits. To call Monaco from France and abroad, dial the international access code, followed by 377 (Monaco's country code) and the eight-digit number. To call abroad from Monaco, dial ☎ 00, followed by the country code, area code (dropping the initial zero) and local number. To call France from Monaco, dial ☎ 00-33, plus the 10-digit number.

Collect Calls & Inquiries To make a reverse-charge (collect) call (*en PCV*) or a person-to-person call (*avec préavis*), dial ☎ 00-33, then the country code of the place you're calling (dial 11 instead of 1 for the USA and Canada). If you're using a public phone, you must insert a télécarte (phonecard) or, in the case of public coin telephones, a 1FF coin, to place operator-assisted calls through the international operator.

To find out a country code (*indicatif pays*), call directory inquiries (☎ 12). To find out a subscriber's telephone number abroad, call international directory inquiries (☎ 00-3312 plus relevant country code). In public phones, you can access this service without paying; from private phones it costs 7.30FF per inquiry.

International Rates The cheapest time to call home is during reduced tariff periods – generally on weekday evenings from 9.30 pm to 8 am, weekends and public holidays.

The rate for a phone call to Europe is 2.47-4.45FF/minute; reduced tariffs are 1.98-3.46FF. Calls to continental USA and Canada cost 2.97FF/minute (reduced tariff 2.35FF), while to telephone Australia, New Zealand, Japan, Hong Kong or Singapore costs 6.55FF/minute (reduced tariff 5.20FF).

Calls to other parts of Asia, non-Francophone Africa and South America are 6.55-9.77FF/minute (reduced tariffs 5.20-7.79FF).

Domestic Tariffs Local calls are quite cheap. The regular, 1.39FF/minute rate – *tarif rouge* (red tariff) – applies Monday to Saturday from 8 am to 12.30 pm and Monday to Friday from 1.30 to 6 pm. The 1.02FF *tarif blanc* (white tariff) applies Monday to Saturday from 12.30 to 1.30 pm and Monday to Friday from 6 to 9.30 pm. The 0.56FF *tarif bleu nuit* (blue night tariff) is from 10.30 pm to 6 am; at other times the 0.74FF blue tariff applies.

Numbers starting with '08 36' are more expensive than other domestic calls: those starting '08 36 67' are billed at 1.49FF/minute. Numbers kicking off with '08 36 64/5' cost a flat 3.71FF, irrespective of time. The SNCF's national information number costs 2.23FF/minute. Avoid '08 36 70' numbers which command an 8.91FF connection fee as well as the 2.23FF/minute charge.

A 10-digit number which starts with '06' indicates a pricey-to-call mobile phone.

Toll-Free Numbers Two-digit emergency numbers (see Health – Emergency in this chapter), Country Direct numbers and *numéros verts* (toll-free numbers – literally, 'green numbers' – which have 10 digits and start '08 00'), can be dialled from public phones without a télécarte or coins.

Minitel

Minitel is a telephone-connected, comput-erised information service – expensive to use and being given a good run for its money by the Internet. Numbers consist of four digits (eg 3611, 3614, 3615 etc) and a string of letters. We have not included Minitel addresses in this book. However, France Telecom has an electronic directory which you can access in some post offices. 3611 is used for general address and tele-phone inquiries. 3615 SNCF and 3615 TER give train information – see the boxed text SNCF Regional Hot Lines in the Getting Around chapter.

Fax

Virtually all town post offices can send and receive domestic and international faxes (télécopies or téléfaxes), telexes and telegrams. It costs about 20FF to send a one page fax.

Email & Internet Access

There are cybercafés where you can send emails and access the Internet in Aix-en-Provence, Avignon, Cannes, Carpentras, Isola 2000, Marseille, Monaco, Nice, Nîmes, Orange, Saint Raphaël, Salon-de-Provence and Toulon. The region's premier cyber restaurant is in Avignon.

INTERNET RESOURCES

Provence-related Web sites are plentiful. Regularly updated, in English, and so prac-tical they almost compete with this guide, are the qualities which distinguish the fol-lowing:

Côte d'Azur Web News
  www.cad.fr
  Weekly Riviera news updates hot off the press from the Côte d'Azur Agency for Economic Development at Sophia-Antipolis technology park.
France Holiday Store
  www.fr-holidaystore.co.uk
  The one stop holiday shop for holidays to France from the UK; everything from the latest Eurostar deals to package breaks, property search and online bookings.

French Riviera
  www.french-riviera.fr
  Accommodation, arts & museums, tourism & leisure, real estate and shopping on the coast.
Provence Beyond
  www.beyond.fr
  Fabulously comprehensive site with insightful information on everything from gastronomy and astronomy to hotel/restaurant/museum/ perched village listings.
Provence Web
  www.provenceweb.com
  Department by department, town by town, village by village.
Serveur Provence
  www.enprovence.com
  Impressively comprehensive information and an exhaustive set of hot links.

BOOKS

Most books are published in different edit-ions by different publishers in different countries. So a book might be a hardcover rarity in one country while it's readily avail-able in paperback in another. Fortunately, bookshops and libraries search by title or author, so your local bookshop or library is best able to advise you on the availability of the books recommended here. The follow-ing list is limited to works still in print and generally available in paperback. The year in brackets is the original publication date.

Lonely Planet

Lonely Planet publishes guides to France, Western Europe and Mediterranean Europe which include chapters on Provence-Côte d'Azur. It also publishes a handy French phrasebook.

Guidebooks

Large travel bookshops carry hundreds of titles on virtually every aspect of Provence.

Michelin, the huge rubber conglomerate which has published travel guides since the earliest days of motorcar touring, covers Provence and the Côte d'Azur in its *guide vert* (green guide) series (as two separate guides, each available in English). Haute-Provence is included in its *Alpes du Sud guide vert*. Upside of Michelin: masses of historical information. Downside: conservative editorial approach.

Many people swear by Michelin's red-jacketed *guide rouge* to France (150FF), published each March, which has reams of information on mid and upper-range hotels and restaurants in Provence. Accompanied by city maps, it is best known for rating France's great restaurants with one, two or three stars. The *Guide Gault Millau France* (175FF), also published annually, awards up to four *toques rouges* (red chefs' caps) to restaurants with exceptional creative cuisine; *toques blanches* (white chefs' caps) to places with superb modern or traditional cuisine. Gault Millau is said to be quicker at picking up-and-coming restaurants than the Guide Rouge. An English edition is available.

Roman Remains of Southern France by James Bromwich is one of the few guides to unearth just what its title suggests.

General

The French National Front: The Extremist Challenge to Democracy by Simmons Harvey tackles the rise of the *Front National*.

The National Front And French Politics: The Resistible Rise Of Jean-Marie Le Pen by Jonathan Marcus.

J'Accuse: The Dark Side of Nice is a highly emotive essay by Grahame Greene (1982) in which he expounds local government corruption and organised crime in Nice.

Côte d'Azur: Inventing the French Riviera by Mary Blume looks at the glamorous rise and fall of the Côte d'Azur.

Hollywood on the Riviera: The Inside Story of the Cannes Film Festival (1992) by Cari Beauchamp & Henri Béhar. A history of the festival and its stars, laced with celebrity names.

Taurine Provence by 1930s matador Roy Campbell, unravels the history of the Provençal bullfight (re-published in 1994 by Alyscamps Provençal Library).

The Man Behind the Iron Mask (1988) by John Noone. An academic study on the identity of the enigmatic man behind the iron mask, immortalised by Dumas in his Three Musketeers trilogy (see Literature in the Facts About Provence chapter).

Aromatherapy from Provence by Nelly Grosjean (translated into English by Margaret Gray) reveals the secret behind a good old lavender bath soak.

Provençal Literature

For suggested reading by Provençal writers see Literature, in the Facts about Provence chapter.

Foreign Literature

Provence-Côte d'Azur has been immortalised in foreign literature since the 18th century when the first European writers ventured here. By the early 20th century it had blossomed into a bohemia for artists seeking sunlight and social freedom.

Jigsaw (1989) by Sybille Bedford. An autobiographical novel inspired by her years in Toulon during the 1920s and 30s. Bedford's earlier novel, *A Compass Error* (1968), uses the coast as a backdrop for a love triangle of lesbian and heterosexual encounters.

Jericho (1992) by Dirk Bogarde. A sleuth novel set in rural Provence where Bogarde lived for more than 20 years.

A Period of Adjustment (1994), Bogarde's sequel to *Jericho*, equally evokes the smells and seasons of Provence, as does the actor's hefty, six-volume autobiography.

To Die in Provence by Norman Bogner (1998). Thriller set in Aix-en-Provence.

The Rover (1923) by Joseph Conrad. Set in and around Toulon.

Perfume (1985) by Patrick Süskind. Evocation of the horrors of the 18th century perfume industry. Much of the action – a quest to create the perfect perfume from the scent of murdered virgins – takes place in steamy Grasse.

Little Dorrit (1857) by Charles Dickens. Classic novel which opens with Marseille 'burning in the sun'.

The Avignon Quartet (1992) by Lawrence Durrell. A one-volume, awesome 1367 page edition of five Durrell novels, written 1974-85, kicks off on a train to Avignon.

Tender is the Night (1934) by F Scott Fitzgerald. Vivid account of life during the decadent 1920s Jazz Age; set on Cap d'Antibes with day trips to Cannes.

Loser Takes All (1955) by Grahame Greene. Short novel written in 1955 in which a young couple are manipulated into honeymooning at the Hôtel de Paris in Monte Carlo.

Garden of Eden (1987) by Ernest Hemingway. Posthumous novel set in 1920s Le-Grau-du-Roi, near Aigues-Mortes in the Camargue. Two honeymooners pursue a hedonistic life in the sun.

Dying on the Vine – A Further Adventure of the Gourmet Detective (1998) by Peter King. A murder-mystery, set in Provence, geared to what the protagonist eats next.

The Bull that Thought (1924) by Rudyard Kipling. Short story with a twist by the 1907 Nobel Prize for literature winner about bull fighting in Arles.

The Doves' Nest & Other Stories (1923) by Katherine Mansfield. The lives of lonely women living in a villa on the Riviera.

Collected Short Stories (1990) by Somerset Maugham. Includes a short story, *The Facts of Life*, about a tennis player taking to the gambling tables at Monte Carlo; and *Three Fat Women from Antibes*, inspired by the years Maugham lived on Cap Ferrat.

Travelogues

Paradise & Pestilence – Aspects of Provence (1997) by Suzanne St Albans. Autobiography of the duchess of St Albans who moved to Vence in 1977 to restore her parents' home.

A Spell in Wild France (1992) by Bill & Laurel Cooper. A vivid portrait of the highs and lows of life on a boat moored near Aigues-Mortes in Camargue cowboy land. The couple's canal journey to Provence is recorded in *Watersteps to France*.

Cesar's Vast Ghosts: Aspects of Provence (1990) by Lawrence Durrell. Philosophical reflections on Provençal history & culture, published just days before the author's death in Somières, near Nîmes. Highlights include the poem *Statue of Lovers: Aix*; the travelogue on Roman Provence; and the look at 'bull mania of the extreme south'.

Two Weeks in the Midday Sun – A Cannes Notebook (1987) by Roger Ebert. 'Disneyland for adults' (Cannes' International Film Festival) seen through the backdoor by a festival hack.

Two Towns in Provence (1964) by MFK Fisher. A street-by-street, fountain-by-fountain celebration of Aix-en-Provence and Marseille. Particularly colourful accounts of women from Marseille.

Perfume from Provence (1935), *Sunset House & Trampled Lilies* by Lady Fortescue. A record of a lady's life, from the purchase of a house outside Grasse to her final flight back to the UK at the start of WWII.

A Little Tour in France (1885). Henry James vividly portrays Van Gogh's 19th century Arles, first visited by James in 1882.

A Year in Provence (1989) and *Toujours Provence* (1991) by Peter Mayle. Best-selling accounts of life in the Lubéron that take a witty look at the Provençal through English eyes.

A Dog's Life (1995), *Anything Considered* (1996) & *Chasing Cézanne* (1997) by Peter Mayle. A look at Lubéron life through the eyes of a dog; the adventures of a flat-sitter in Monaco; the hunt for a stolen Cézanne. Beach-reading.

Encore Provence (1999) by Peter Mayle. A non-fiction collection of pieces about people and other curiosities in the area.

Travels with Virginia Woolf (1993) by Jan Morris. Entertaining extracts from the playwright's journals, including observations made during visits to her sister's home in Cassis.

Travels through France & Italy (1766) by Tobias Smollett. The Scottish author's ruthless candour caused outrage amongst local Niçois when this book was published in the late 18th century.

Food & Wine

A banquet of books pertaining to Provençal food and wine exists. In the UK, specialist cook book shop, Books for Cooks (☎ 020-7221 1992, fax 020-7221 1517, info@booksforcooks.com), 4 Blenheim Crescent, London W11 1NN, stocks a superb range.

Ducasse Flavors of France (1998) published by Artisan/USA. Provence's six-starred chef reveals some of his secrets.

Roger Vergé's Vegetables (1994) published by Mitchell Beazley and *Roger Vergé's Cooking with Fruits* (1998) published by Harry N Abrams/New York. Two summery cookery books crammed with tasty recipes from one of the region's top chefs (see the special section Food & Wine of Provence).

The Cuisine of the Sun by Roger Vergé. A recipe book by the Provençal chef.

The Food of France. A timeless classic by Waverley Root.

Food Lovers' Guide to France. Another classic by Patricia Wells (nice truffle section).

Patricia Wells at Home in Provence. One of the few foreign cooks to find the soul of Provençal cooking (see the special section Food & Wine of Provence).

Pedalling Through Provence Cookbook. Sarah Leah Chase's softback book is quirky and colourful, bursting with quick and easy recipes which have the added bite of being written around a cycling tour.

Markets of Provence. Dip into the region's markets with Martin & Laurence Toulemonde and Jan & Christina Gabrius.

Hugh Johnson's Atlas of Wine. Solid wine reference.

Oxford Companion to Wine edited by Jancis Robinson.

Touring in Wine Country: Provence. Hubrecht Duijker's listings of chateaux where you can taste and buy wine.

Oz Clarke's Wine Companion: South of France.

Art, Artists & Architecture

Artists (Cézanne, Chagall, Matisse, Picasso etc) and movements (impressionism, fauvism etc) are covered by various titles in the World of Art series by Thames and Hudson (☎ 020-7636 5488, fax 020-7636 4799, sales@thbooks.demon.co.uk, www .thesaurus.co.uk/thamesandhudson), 30-34 Bloomsbury Street, London WC1B 3QP.

Artists and their Museums on the Riviera (1998) by Barbara Freed.

Lartigue's Riviera (essay by Mary Blume, picture selection by Martine D'Astier). Stunning B&W photographs of the coast taken by Jacques Lartigue from the 1920s to 60s.

Spoerry: A Gentle Architecture from Port Grimaud to Port Liberté (1991), published by Phoon books, on modern architecture.

Provence Interiors edited by Angelika Muthesius & Lisa Lovatt-Smith (1997).

Provence des Campaniles (1996). Hungarian-born photographer Étienne Sved captures the region's ornate wrought-iron bell towers and church toppings.

NEWSPAPERS & MAGAZINES

The leading regional, daily newspapers are *Nice Matin* (www.nicematin.fr), which has a separate Toulon-based Var edition, *Var-Matin*; and *La Provence* (www.laprovence.fr) which is the result of a merger between former *Le Provençal* and right-wing *Le Méridional*.

The *Riviera Reporter* (www.webstore .fr/riviera-reporter) is a free, A4 news-magazine 'for Riviera residents', published every two months and including handy job and property listings. *The News* is another English language publication, covering all of France but with a strong southern bias (10FF). Reams of fantastically expensive dream properties to buy/rent are featured in the glossy, *New Riviera-Côte d'Azur*. The

quarterly, 100-plus page magazine (45FF) markets itself as the 'international magazine' of the Côte d'Azur and runs a social diary and hotel/restaurant reviews.

English-language newspapers of the day – the *International Herald Tribune*, the *Washington Post*, *USA Today*, and London's *Guardian* or *The Times* – are easy to pick up in Nice, Marseille and most coastal resorts. They are practically impossible to find in Haute-Provence and other rural spots.

RADIO & TV

Monte Carlo-based Riviera Radio (riviera@monaco.com) is an English-language radio station that is broadcast 24 hours a day (BBC World Service news every hour). It can be picked up on 106.3 MHz FM in Monaco, and on 106.5 MHz FM and 98.8 MHz FM along the rest of the Côte d'Azur. It also has Internet relay (www.riviera-radio.com). The BBC World Service can be picked up on 6195, 9410, 11955, 12095 (a good daytime frequency) and 15575kHz, depending on the time of day.

VIDEO SYSTEMS

SECAM is used in France and Monaco (unlike the rest of Western Europe and Australia which uses PAL). French videotapes can't be played on video recorders and TVs that lack a SECAM capability.

PHOTOGRAPHY & VIDEO

Colour-print and slide *(diapositive)* film is widely available in supermarkets, photo shops and FNAC stores, as are replacement video cartridges for your camcorder.

Sunlight is extreme in Provence-Côte d'Azur; avoid snapping at midday when the glare is strongest. Photography is rarely forbidden, except in museums, art galleries and some churches (such as the Matisse chapel in Vence). Snapshots of military installations are not really appreciated. When photographing people, ask permission (basic courtesy). If you don't know any French, smile while pointing at your camera and they'll get the picture – as you probably will.

TIME

French and Monégasque time is GMT/UTC plus one hour, except during daylight-saving time (last Sunday in March to the last Sunday in October) when it is GMT/UTC plus two hours. The UK and France are always one hour apart – when it's 6 pm in London, it's 7 pm in Nice. New York is six hours behind Nice.

France uses the 24-hour clock and writes time like this: 15h30 (ie 3.30 pm). Time has no meaning for many people in Provence.

ELECTRICITY

France and Monaco run on 220V at 50Hz AC. Old-type wall sockets take two round prongs. New kinds of sockets take fatter prongs and have a protruding earth (ground) prong. Adaptors to make new plugs fit into the old sockets are said to be illegal but are available at electrical shops.

WEIGHTS & MEASURES

France uses the metric system. When writing numbers with four or more digits, the French use full stops (periods) or spaces (as opposed to commas): one million is 1.000.000 or 1 000 000. Decimals, on the other hand, are written with commas, so 1.75 becomes 1,75.

LAUNDRY

Doing laundry while on the road is a straightforward affair. There is a *laverie libre-service* (unstaffed, self-service laundrette) in most towns.

Laundrettes are expensive along the coast (18-30FF for a six or 7kg machine and 2/5FF for five/12 minutes of drying).

TOILETS
Public toilets

Public toilets, signposted *toilettes* or WC are surprisingly few and far between, meaning you can be left in a very desperate situation. Towns which have public toilets generally tout them near the *mairie* (town hall) or – in the case of Cannes, Saint Tropez and other port towns – in the port area. Expect to pay 2 to 5FF in exchange for a wad of toilet paper (soft variety). Other towns have coin-operated, self-flushing toilet booths – usually in car parks and public squares – which cost 2FF to enter: highly disconcerting contraptions should the automatic mechanism fail with you inside. Some places sport flushless, kerbside *urinoirs* (urinals) reeking with generations of urine. Failing that, there's always McDonalds.

Restaurants, cafés and bars are often woefully under-equipped with such amenities, so start queuing ahead of time. Bashful males be warned: some toilets are semi-coed; the urinals and washbasins are in a common area through which all and sundry pass to get to the closed toilet stalls. Older establishments often sport Turkish-style *toilettes à la turque* – a squat toilet with a high-pressure flushing mechanism that can soak your feet if you don't step back in time.

Hall toilets in cheap hotels can be in an impossibly small room, with the nearest washbasin absolutely nowhere to be found.

Bidets

A bidet is a porcelain fixture that looks like a shallow toilet with a pop-up stopper in the base. Originally conceived to improve the personal hygiene of aristocratic women, it's primary purpose is for washing the genitals and anal area, though its uses have expanded to include everything from hand-washing laundry to soaking your feet.

Bidets are to be found in many hotel rooms. Cheap hotels often serve rooms with a bidet and *lavabo* (washbasin).

HEALTH

Provence and the Côte d'Azur are healthy places. Your main risks are sunburn, foot blisters, insect bites and an upset stomach from eating and drinking too much.

Predeparture Planning

Immunisations No jabs are required to travel to France. However, there are a few routine vaccinations that are recommended whether you're travelling or not: polio (usually administered during childhood), tetanus and diphtheria (usually administered together during childhood, with a booster shot every 10 years), and sometimes measles.

All vaccinations should be recorded on an International Health Certificate, available from your doctor or government health department.

Health Insurance Make sure you have adequate health insurance. See under Documents in this chapter.

Other Preparations Ensure you're healthy before you start travelling. If you are going on a long trip make sure your teeth are OK. If you wear glasses take a spare pair and your prescription.

If you require a particular medication take an adequate supply, as it may not be available locally. Take part of the packaging showing the generic name, rather than the brand, which will make getting replacements easier. It's a good idea to have a legible prescription or letter from your doctor to show that you legally use the medication to avoid any problems.

Medical Treatment in France

Major hospitals are indicated on the maps in this book, and their addresses and phone numbers are mentioned in the text. Tourist offices and hotels can put you on to a doctor or dentist, and your embassy or consulate will probably know one who speaks your language.

Public Health System Anyone (including foreigners) who is sick can receive treatment in the *service des urgences* (casualty ward or emergency room) of any public hospital. Hospitals try to have people who speak English in casualty wards, but this is not done systematically. If necessary, the hospital will call in an interpreter. It's an excellent idea to ask for a copy of the diagnosis – in English, if possible – for your doctor back home.

Treatment for illness or injury in a public hospital costs less in France than in many

Medical Kit Check List

Following is a list of items you should consider including in your medical kit – consult your pharmacist for brands available in your country.

☐ **Aspirin** or **paracetamol** (acetaminophen in the US) – for pain or fever.
☐ **Antihistamine** – for allergies, eg hay fever; to ease the itch from insect bites or stings; and to prevent motion sickness.
☐ **Insect repellent, sunscreen, lip balm** and **eye drops.**
☐ **Calamine lotion, sting relief spray** or **aloe vera** – to ease irritation from sunburn and insect bites or stings.
☐ **Antifungal cream** or **powder** – for fungal skin infections and thrush.
☐ **Antiseptic** (such as povidone-iodine) – for cuts and grazes.
☐ **Bandages, Band-Aids (plasters)** and other wound dressings.
☐ **Cold** and **flu tablets, throat lozenges** and **nasal decongestant.**

other western countries: a consultation costs about 170FF (more on Sunday, public holidays and at night). Blood tests and other procedures each have a standard fee. Full hospitalisation costs from 3000FF a day. Hospitals usually ask that visitors from abroad settle accounts immediately after receiving treatment.

Dental Care Most major hospitals offer dental services. In Nice, SOS Dentaire (☎ 04 93 76 53 53) is a dental care nightline.

Pharmacies French pharmacies are usually marked by a green cross, the neon components of which are lit when it's open. *Pharmaciens* (pharmacists) can often suggest treatments for minor ailments.

If you are prescribed medication, make sure you understand the dosage, and how often and when you should take it. Ask for a copy of the prescription *(ordonnance)* for your records. During the mushroom picking season (autumn), pharmacies act as a mushroom identifying service.

Pharmacies coordinate their closure so that a town isn't left without a place to buy medication. Details on the nearest *pharmacie de garde* (pharmacy on weekend/night duty) are posted on any pharmacy door. There are 24-hour pharmacies in Nice and Marseille.

Emergency
The following numbers are toll-free:

SAMU medical treatment/ambulance	☎ 15
Police	☎ 17
Fire Brigade	☎ 18
Rape Crisis Hotline	☎ 08 00 05 95 95

SAMU When you ring ☎ 15, the 24-hour dispatchers of the Service d'Aide Médicale d'Urgence (Emergency Medical Aid Service) take down details of your problem and send out a private ambulance with a driver (250-300FF) or, if necessary, a mobile intensive care unit. For less serious problems, SAMU can dispatch a doctor for a house call. If you prefer to be taken to a particular hospital, mention this to the ambulance crew, as the usual procedure is to take you to the nearest one. In emergency cases (ie those requiring intensive care units), billing will be taken care of later. Otherwise, you need to pay in cash at the time.

24-Hour Doctor Service If your problem is not sufficiently serious to call SAMU, but you still need to consult a doctor at night, call the *médecin de garde*, a 24-hour doctor service, operational in most towns in the region, including:

Nice	☎ 04 93 52 42 42
Aix-en-Provence	☎ 04 42 26 24 00
Avignon	☎ 04 90 87 75 00 or
	☎ 04 90 87 76 00.

The hospitals in all three cities also operate a 24-hour emergency service.

Basic Rules
Everyday Health Normal body temperature is 37°C (98.6°F); more than 2°C (4°F) higher indicates a high fever. The normal adult pulse rate is 60-100 beats per minute (children 80-100, babies 100-140). As a general rule the pulse increases about 20 beats per minute for each 1°C (2°F) rise in fever. Respiration (breathing) rate is also an indicator of illness. Count the number of breaths per minute: between 12 and 20 is normal for adults and older children (up to 30 for younger children, 40 for babies). People with a high fever or serious respiratory illness breathe more quickly than normal. More than 40 shallow breaths a minute may indicate pneumonia.

Water Tap water all over France is safe to drink. Despite Provence's sheer abundance of fountains, the water spouting out of them is not always drinkable: *eau non potable* means 'undrinkable water'. Most fountains are signposted accordingly.

It's very easy to not drink enough liquids, particularly in summer on hot days or at high altitude. Don't rely on thirst to indicate when you should drink. Not needing to urinate or very dark-yellow urine is a danger sign. Carrying your own water bottle is a good idea.

In Haute-Provence, beware of natural sources of water. Its burbling Alpine stream may appear crystal clear, but it's inadvisable to drink untreated water unless you're at the source and can see it coming out of the rocks.

The simplest way of purifying water is to boil it thoroughly. At high altitude water boils at a lower temperature, so germs are less likely to be killed. Boil it for longer in these environments.

Environmental Hazards
Fungal Infections Fungal infections occur more commonly in hot weather and are usually found on the scalp, between the

toes or fingers, in the groin and on the body (ringworm). You get ringworm (which is a fungal infection, not a worm) from infected animals or other people. Moisture encourages these infections.

To prevent fungal infections wear loose, comfortable clothes, avoid artificial fibres, wash frequently and dry carefully. If you do get an infection, wash the infected area at least daily with a disinfectant or medicated soap and water, and rinse and dry well. Apply an antifungal cream or powder like tolnifate (Tinaderm). Try to expose the infected area to air or sunlight as much as possible and wash all towels and underwear in hot water, change them often and let them dry in the sun.

Heat Exhaustion Dehydration and salt deficiency can cause heat exhaustion. Take time to acclimatise to the high temperatures, drink sufficient liquids and do not do anything too physically demanding.

Salt deficiency is characterised by fatigue, lethargy, headaches, giddiness and muscle cramps; salt tablets may help, but adding extra salt to your food is better.

Motion Sickness Eating lightly before and during a trip will reduce the chances of motion sickness. If you are prone to motion sickness try to find a place that minimises movement – near the wing on aircraft, close to midships on boats, near the centre on buses. Fresh air usually helps; reading and cigarette smoke don't. Commercial motion sickness preparations, which can cause drowsiness, have to be taken before the trip commences. Ginger (available as capsules) and peppermint (including mint-flavoured sweets) are natural preventatives.

Prickly Heat This is an itchy rash caused by excessive perspiration trapped under the skin. It usually strikes people who have just arrived in a hot climate. Keeping cool, bathing often, drying the skin and using a mild talcum or prickly heat powder or resorting to air-conditioning may help.

Sunburn You can get sunburnt surprisingly quickly, even through cloud. Use a sunscreen, hat, and barrier cream for your nose and lips. Calamine lotion or Stingose are good for mild sunburn. Protect your eyes with good quality sunglasses, particularly if you will be near water, sand or snow.

Hay Fever Hay fever sufferers can look forward to sneezing their way round rural Provence in May and June when the pollen count is highest.

Infectious Diseases

Diarrhoea Simple things like a change of water, food or climate can all cause a mild bout of diarrhoea, but a few rushed toilet trips with no other symptoms is not indicative of a major problem.

Dehydration is the main danger with any diarrhoea, particularly in children or the elderly, as it can occur quickly. Fluid replacement (at least equal to the volume being lost) is most important. Weak black tea with a little sugar, soda water, or soft drinks allowed to go flat and diluted 50% with clean water are all good. Keep drinking small amounts often. Stick to a bland diet as you recover.

Hepatitis There are almost 300 million carriers of Hepatitis B in the world. It is spread through contact with infected blood, blood products or body fluids, for example through sexual contact, unsterilised needles and blood transfusions, or contact with blood via small breaks in the skin. Other risk situations include having a shave, tattoo, or having your body pierced with contaminated equipment. You should seek medical advice, but there is not much you can do apart from resting, drinking lots of fluids and eating lightly.

AIDS & HIV The Human Immuno-deficiency Virus (VIH in French), develops into AIDS, Acquired Immune Deficiency Syndrome (SIDA in French), which is a fatal disease. HIV is a major problem in many countries. Any exposure to blood, blood products or body fluids may put an individual at risk. The disease is often transmitted through sexual contact or dirty needles – vaccinations, acupuncture, tattooing and body piercing can be potentially as dangerous as intravenous drug use. HIV/AIDS can also be spread through infected blood transfusions; some developing countries cannot afford to screen blood used for transfusions.

If you do need an injection, ask to see the syringe unwrapped in front of you, or take a needle and syringe pack with you.

Fear of HIV infection should never preclude treatment for serious medical conditions.

AIDS & HIV Information For information on free and anonymous HIV-testing centres *(centres de dépistage)* in France, ring the SIDA Info Service toll-free, 24 hours a day (☎ 08 00 84 08 00). Information is available in Nice at the Centre de Dépistage du VIH (☎ 04 93 85 12 62), 2 rue Édouard Béri (corner of Hôpital Saint Roch); at the Centre de Dépistage in Marseille (☎ 04 91 78 43 43), 10 rue Saint Adrien, 13008 Marseille; or its counterpart in Aix-en-Provence (☎ 04 42 33 51 36), Centre Hospitalier, ave des Tamaris.

CRIPS PACA (Centre Régional d'Info-Prévention contre le SIDA; ☎ 04 91 38 16 00, fax 04 91 38 12 24), 6 place Daviel, 13224 Marseille, is an information centre offering practical advice and help.

AIDES (Association de Prévention, Information, Lutte contre le SIDA) is a national organisation that works for the prevention of AIDS and assists AIDS sufferers. AIDES Provence has its head office in Marseille (☎ 04 91 14 05 15, fax 04 91 14 05 16), 1 rue Gilbert Dru, and a *pôle* (centre) in Aix-en-Provence, Avignon (☎ 04 90 86 80 80), Digne-les-Bains, Draguignan, Fréjus, Marignane and Toulon.

Sexually Transmitted Diseases Gonorrhoea, herpes and syphilis are among these diseases; sores, blisters or rashes around the genitals, discharges or pain when urinating are common symptoms. In some STDs,

such as wart virus or chlamydia, symptoms may be less marked or not observed at all, especially in women. Syphilis symptoms eventually disappear completely but the disease continues and can cause severe problems in later years. While abstinence from sexual contact is the only 100% effective prevention, using condoms is also effective. The treatment of gonorrhoea and syphilis is with antibiotics. The different sexually transmitted diseases each require specific antibiotics. There is no cure for herpes or AIDS.

Condoms All pharmacies carry *préservatifs* (condoms) and many have 24-hour automatic condom dispensers outside the door. Some brasseries, discotheques, metro stations and WCs in cafés and petrol stations are also equipped with condom machines. Condoms that conform to French government standards are marked with the letters NF *(norme française)* in black on a white oval inside a red and blue rectangle.

Cuts, Bites & Stings

Rabies This is a fatal viral infection found in many countries. Animals can be infected and it is their saliva that is infectious. Any bite, scratch or even lick from a warm-blooded, furry animal should be cleaned immediately and thoroughly. Medical help should be sought promptly to receive a course of injections to prevent the onset of symptoms and death.

Insect Bites & Stings Bee and wasp stings are usually painful rather than dangerous. However, in people who are allergic to them severe breathing difficulties may occur and they may require urgent medical care. Calamine lotion or Stingose spray will give relief, and ice packs will reduce the pain and swelling.

Jellyfish Local advice will help prevent your coming into contact with *méduses* (jellyfish) and their stinging tentacles, often found along the Mediterranean. Dousing the wound in vinegar will de-activate any stingers that have not 'fired'. Calamine lotion, antihistamines and analgesics may reduce the reaction and relieve the pain. The sting of the Portuguese man-of-war, which has a sail-like float and long tentacles, is painful but rarely fatal.

Leeches & Ticks Check all over your body if you have been walking through a potentially tick-infested area, as ticks can cause skin infections and other more serious diseases. If a tick is found attached, press down around the tick's head with tweezers, grab the head and gently pull upwards. Avoid pulling the rear of the body as this may squeeze the tick's gut contents through the attached mouth parts into the skin, increasing the risk of infection and disease. Smearing chemicals on the tick will not make it let go and is not recommended.

Women's Health
Sexually transmitted diseases are a major cause of vaginal problems. Symptoms include a smelly discharge, painful intercourse and sometimes a burning sensation when urinating. Male sexual partners must also be treated. Medical attention should be sought and remember in addition to these diseases HIV or hepatitis B may also be acquired during exposure.

Antibiotic use, synthetic underwear, sweating and contraceptive pills can lead to fungal vaginal infections when travelling in hot climates. Maintaining good personal hygiene, and loose-fitting clothes and cotton underwear will help to prevent them.

Fungal infections, characterised by a rash, itch and discharge, can be treated with a vinegar or lemon juice douche, or with yoghurt. Nystatin, miconazole or clotrimazole pessaries or vaginal cream are the usual treatment.

WOMEN TRAVELLERS
French men have clearly given little thought to the concept of *harcèlement sexuel* (sexual harassment). Most still believe that staring suavely at a passing woman is paying her a compliment. Women need not walk round the region in fear however. Suave stares are about as adventurous as most French men get, with women rarely being physically assaulted on the street or touched up in bars at night.

Unfortunately, it's not just French men that women travellers have to concern themselves with. While women attract little unwanted attention in rural Provence, on the coast it's a different ball game. In the dizzying heat of the high season, the Côte d'Azur is rampant with men (and women) of *all* nationalities out on the pull. Apply the usual 'women traveller' rules and the chances are, you'll emerge from the circus unscathed. Remain conscious of your surroundings, avoid going to bars and clubs alone at night and be aware of potentially dangerous situations: deserted streets, lonely beaches, dark corners of large train stations, night buses in certain districts of Nice and Marseille.

Topless sunbathing is not generally interpreted as deliberately provocative.

Organisations
SOS Viol (☎ 04 91 56 04 10) is a voluntary women's group that staffs the national rape-crisis hotline (☎ 08 00 05 95 95). Its centre in Marseille is spearheaded by SOS Femmes (☎ 04 91 42 07 00), 14 blvd Théodore Thurner,

In Aix-en-Provence, the CIDF (Centre d'Information sur les Droits des Femmes; ☎ 04 42 63 18 92, fax 04 42 21 01 19), 24 rue Mignet, is an active women's information centre. It offers information, advice and practical support where possible. Its pocket-size booklet entitled *Informations Femmes Aix* contains a wealth of listings on everything from SOS services to family planning centres, crèches and baby sitters.

GAY & LESBIAN TRAVELLERS
France is one of Europe's most liberal countries when it comes to homosexuality, in part because of the long French tradition of public tolerance towards groups of people who have chosen not to live by conventional social codes. There are large gay and

lesbian communities in Aix-en-Provence, Cannes, Marseille – which hosts a colourful Gay Pride march in June – and Nice. The lesbian scene is less public than its gay counterpart.

The Maison des Associations (☎ 04 91 55 39 50), 93 La Canebière, 13001 Marseille, has contact details for gay and lesbian groups in the region. Leading lights in Marseille include the Collectif Gai et Lesbien (CGL; ☎ 04 91 42 07 48), 1 rue Ferrari; Act Up Marseille (☎ 04 91 94 08 43, actupp @compuserve.com, www.actupp.org), 40 rue Sénac; Centre Évolutif Lilith (☎ 04 91 55 08 61), 18 cours Pierre Puget, a lesbian group; and Marseille Arc-en-Ciel (☎ 04 91 91 01 17, maec@aix.pacwan.net, www .maec.net), BP 2081, 13203 Marseille, an active gay group which publishes *Le Chaperon Rouge*, a bi-monthly 'Gay Marseille' what's on listing.

On the Internet you can log into Gay Aix (www.angelfire.com/ok/gayaix), the homepage of lesbian students from the Université d'Aix; La Gaie Provence (mc13bri@aol.com, members.aol.com/Mc13Bri), a directory with lots of gay hotlinks; Gay & Lesbian (www.france.qrd.org), a queer resources directory; or *Guide Gai Pied* (www.gaipied .fr), a French and English-language annual guide (79FF) to France with bits on the Côte d'Azur.

In Nice, there is a gay hotel which offers 10% discount to homosexual travellers.

DISABLED TRAVELLERS

The region is not user-friendly for *handicapés* (disabled people): kerb ramps are few and far between, older public facilities and budget hotels lack lifts, and the cobblestone streets typical of Provence's numerous perched villages are a nightmare to navigate in a wheelchair.

But all is not lost. Many two or three-starred hotels are equipped with lifts; Michelin's *Guide Rouge* indicates hotels with lifts and facilities for disabled people.

Nice and Marseille airports both offer assistance to wheelchair travellers. At Aéroport International Nice-Côte d'Azur, contact the

Service Handicapés GIS (☎ 04 93 21 44 58) at Aéroport International Marseille-Provence, call the Société d'Assistance Midi-Provence (☎ 04 42 14 27 42). The SNCF's TGV and regular trains are also accessible to a passenger in a *fauteuil roulant* (wheelchair), provided they make a reservation by phone or at a train station at least a few hours before departure. Details are available in SNCF's booklet *Guide du Voyageur à Mobilité Réduite* (one page in English). Alternatively, contact SNCF Accessibilité (☎ 08 00 15 47 53).

In Nice, some museums have catalogues in braille while city transport and museum admission is free to blind people or those in need of assistance. The Aix-en-Provence based SOS Handicapés (☎ 04 42 26 26 20) is a telephone helpline for disabled people.

Particularly useful is *Gîtes Accessibles aux Personnes Handicapées*, an accommodation guide (60FF) listing *gîtes ruraux* and *chambres d'hôtes* with disabled access in the region. It's published by Gîtes de France (see Gîtes Ruraux & B&Bs under Accommodation in this chapter).

SENIOR TRAVELLERS

Senior citizens are entitled to discounts on public transport, museum admission fees etc, provided they show proof of their age. In some cases they might need a special pass (see Seniors' Card in the Visas & Documents section).

At mainline train stations, SOS Voyageurs (☎ 04 93 82 62 11 in Nice or 04 91 62 12 80 in Marseille) – a voluntary group usually run by retirees – offers help to elderly train travellers.

TRAVEL WITH CHILDREN

Successful travel with young children requires planning and effort. Don't overdo things; trying to see too much can cause problems. Include the kids in the trip planning. Balance a day traipsing round perched villages or the coast's art museums with time on the beach or an outing to Marineland. Many places along the coast offer special children's activities; the Parc

National du Mercantour in north-east Provence organises nature trails for kids.

Most car-rental firms have children's safety seats for hire at a nominal cost; book in advance. The same goes for highchairs and cots (cribs); they're standard in most restaurants and hotels but numbers are limited. The choice of baby food, infant formulas, soy and cow's milk, disposable nappies (diapers) and the like is as great in French supermarkets as it is back home, but the opening hours may be quite different. Run out of nappies on Saturday afternoon and you're facing a very long and messy weekend.

Most tourist offices have a list of *gardes d'enfants* (baby-sitting services) and crèches. Lonely Planet's *Travel with Children* is a good source of information.

DANGERS & ANNOYANCES
Theft
Theft *(vol)* – from backpacks, pockets, cars, trains, laundrettes, beaches – is a serious problem, particularly along the Côte d'Azur. Keep an eagle eye on your bags, especially at train and bus stations, on overnight train rides, in tourist offices in fast-food restaurants and on beaches.

Always keep your money, credit cards, tickets, passport, driver's licence and other important documents in a money belt worn inside your trousers or skirt. Keep enough money for the day in a separate wallet. Theft from hotel rooms is less common but it's still not a great idea to leave your life belongings in your room. In hostels, lock your non-valuables in a locker provided and cart your valuables along. Upmarket hotels have *coffres* (safes).

When swimming on the beach or by the pool, have members of your party take turns sitting with everyone's packs and clothes.

At the train station, if you leave your bags at a left-luggage office or in a luggage locker (where available), treat your claim chit (or locker code) like cash. Daypack snatchers have taken stolen chits to the train station and taken possession of the rest of their victims' belongings.

Racism
Racism is a big problem, big enough to prompt one reader (who lives in Nice) to write with the warning '… if you're black, Jewish, oriental or hispanic, rather go to another country for vacationing.' The rise in support for the extreme right-wing National Front in Provence and the Côte d'Azur in recent years further reflects a growing racial intolerance against North African Muslims and, to a lesser extent, blacks from sub-Saharan Africa and France's former colonies and territories in the Caribbean.

Places of entertainment (bars, discotheques etc) have been known, for all intents, to be segregated: owners and their ferocious bouncers make it abundantly clear what sort of people are 'invited' to use their nominally private facilities.

Forest Fires
Fires are common in heavily forested areas in July and August when the sun is hot and the land is dry. Between 1 July and 15 September, the forest authorities close high-risk areas. Never walk in a closed zone. Tourist offices in the region can tell you if a hiking trail is open or not; alternatively, call ☎ 04 94 47 35 45 for information on the Massif des Maures and Massif de l'Estérel.

All forested areas are criss-crossed with road tracks enabling fire crews to penetrate the forest. These roads – signposted DFCI (défense forestière contre l'incendie) – are closed to private vehicles but you can follow them on foot.

Lighting a camp fire anywhere in the region is forbidden.

Do not enter a forest where you see this sign which indicates a closed zone.

Rivers & Lakes

The major rivers in Provence are connected to hydroelectric power stations operated by the national electricity company, Electricité de France (EDF). Water levels can rise dramatically if the EDF decides to open a dam. White water sports on the Verdon river downstream of the Chaudanne dam *(barrage)* are forbidden when the water flow is less than 5 cubic metres/second. For information on water levels and dam releases, call ☎ 04 92 83 62 68.

Swimming is prohibited in lakes (ie Lac de Sainte Croix south-west of the Gorges du Verdon; Lac de Castillon and the adjoining Lac de Chaudanne north-east of the gorges) which are artificial and have steep, unstable banks. Sailing, windsurfing and canoeing are restricted to flagged areas.

Poisonous Mushrooms

Wild mushroom picking is a national pastime in Provence. Pick by all means but don't eat anything until it has been positively identified as safe by a pharmacist. Most pharmacies (see the Health section) in the region offer a mushroom-identifying service.

Mistral

During the balmy days of May/June and the steamy days of July/August, it is hard to believe that the region can be freezing cold if and when the Mistral strikes (see the boxed text in the Facts about Provence chapter).

Thunderstorms in the mountains and hot southern plains can be extremely sudden, violent and dangerous. Check the weather report before you set out on a long hike; even then, be prepared for a sudden weather change. Storms are extremely common in August and September.

Smoking

Non-smokers with a vehement dislike for sitting in smoke-filled restaurants should maybe holiday elsewhere. Even in places (very few) where smoking is supposedly prohibited, people still light up.

LEGAL MATTERS

The police are allowed to search anyone at any time, regardless of whether there is an obvious reason to do so or not. As elsewhere in the EU, laws are tough when it comes to drinking and driving. The acceptable blood-alcohol limit is 0.05%, with drivers who exceed this amount facing fines of up to 30,000FF (two years in jail maximum). Licences can be immediately suspended.

Importing or exporting drugs can lead to a 10-30 year jail sentence. The fine for possession of drugs for personal use can be as high as 500,000FF. If you litter, you risk a 1000FF fine.

Nude bathing is theoretically forbidden on Saint Tropez's municipal beaches (bathers still strip off). Since 1994 fines have been imposed in Saint Raphaël and Sainte Maxime on tourists who walk in town bare-chested or clad in a bikini.

BUSINESS HOURS

Museums and shops (but not cinemas, restaurants or *boulangeries*) are closed on public holidays. On Sunday, a boulangerie is usually about all that is open (morning only) and public transport services are less frequent. In villages, shops (including the boulangerie) close for a long lunch between 2 and 4 pm. In Provence, hotels, restaurants, cinemas, cultural institutions and shops close for their *congé annuel* (annual closure) in winter. Commercial banks are generally open Monday to Friday from 8 or 9 am to sometime between 11.30 and 1 pm and from 1.30 or 2 pm to 4.30 or 5 pm.

PUBLIC HOLIDAYS & SPECIAL EVENTS

In Provence, *fêtes* (festivals) and *foires* (fairs) are very much a way of life, with every city/town/village/hamlet throwing a street party at least once a year (usually more often) to celebrate everything from a good lavender or olive crop to the feast of their patron saint. An unimaginable abundance of food (monstrous-sized *aïolis*, paellas and the like), a pétanque championship and dancing late into the night are guaranteed to stir the soul of any traveller lucky enough to witness such a joyous occasion.

A *défilé* is a street procession and a *corso* is a procession of floral-decorated floats; a fleet of flower-adorned boats is a *corso nautique*. A *joute Provençale* is a jousting tournament on water (see Spectator Sports) and a *bravade* (literally 'act of bravado') is a festival with cannons and gun fire originating in Saint Tropez. *Féria* is the name given to a bullfighting festival (see Spectator Sports).

French National Holidays

Jours fériés (national public holidays) are often a cue for festivities to spill into the streets.

1 January
  Jour de l'An (New Year's Day)
Late March/April
  Pâques (Easter Sunday) & *lundi de Pâques* (Easter Monday)
1 May
  Fête du Travail (May Day) – buy a *muguet* (lily of the valley) from a street vendor for good luck
8 May
  Victoire 1945 – celebrates the Allied victory in Europe that ended WWII
May
  L'Ascension (Ascension Thursday) – celebrated on the 40th day after Easter
Mid-May to mid-June
  Pentecôte (Pentecost/Whit Sunday) & *lundi de Pentecôte* (Whit Monday) – celebrated on the 7th Sunday after Easter
14 July
  Fête Nationale (Bastille Day/National Day)
15 August
  L'Assomption (Assumption Day)
1 November
  La Toussaint (All Saints' Day)
11 November
  Le onze novembre (Remembrance Day) – celebrates the armistice of WWI
25 December
  Noël (Christmas)

Though not official public holidays, numerous Provençal fêtes fall on Shrove Tuesday (Mardi Gras), Maundy (or Holy) Thursday and Good Friday before Easter, and Boxing Day (26 December).

Monégasque National Holidays

Monaco shares the same holidays with France *except* those on 8 May, 14 July and 11 November. In addition it enjoys as public holidays:

27 January
  Feast of Sainte Dévote – patron saint of Monaco
June
  Corpus Christi – three weeks after Ascension
19 November
  Fête Nationale (National Day)
8 December
  Immaculate Conception

Feasts & Festivals

Provence has a spicy cultural calendar. Most festivals celebrate a historical or folklore tradition, a performing art or, failing that, the region's most beloved pastime – food.

Indispensable is *Terre de Festivals*, a festival-listing guide for the entire region. It's free and published annually by the Office Régional de la Culture (☎ 04 91 57 54 32, fax 04 91 57 54 40), 3 place Pierre Bertas, 13001 Marseille. Its entire contents are online (www.festival.cr-paca.fr).

January
Messe de la Truffe
  Truffle Mass, Richerenches, Sunday nearest to 17 January
Fête des Boudins
  Sausage festival, Cabrières d'Avignon, 22 January
Foire à Truffe
  Truffle Fair, Uzès, third Sunday of January

February
Fête des Citrons
  Lemon festival with street sculptures constructed from lemons, Menton
Féria Primavera
  Three day bullfighting Spring Festival, Nîmes
Carnaval de Nice
  The region's most celebrated two week carnival with floats, masks, fireworks and flower battles, Nice, Mardi Gras

March
Printemps du Jazz
  A week long, spring jazz festival, Nîmes

April

Les Rencontres Internationales d'Arts
Baroques en Provence
Three week baroque music festival with concerts all over the Vaucluse

Festival du Tambourin
Two day Tambourine Festival, Aix-en-Provence, mid-April.

Fête de Saint Marc
Two day wine-tasting festival when the best wines of the last *millésime* (vintage) are opened, Châteauneuf-du-Pape, 24-25 April

May

Fête des Gardians
The day of the Camargue cowboys, Arles, 1 May

Fêtes de la Vigne et du Vin
One or two-day wine festivals in Beaumes-de-Venise and neighbouring Sablet

Cannes International Film Festival
Ten day International Film Festival, Cannes, mid-May

Bravade
Saint Tropez honours its patron saint with a traditional bravade, 16 May

Festival de Jazz en Pays d'Apt
Five day jazz festival with concerts in different venues in the Lubéron

Pélerinage des Gitans
Three day international gypsy pilgrimage Saintes-Maries-de-la-Mer, 24-26 May

June

Fête de la Cerise
Cherry Festival, Apt, Pentecost weekend

Féria de la Pentecôte
Five day Pentecost Festival, marked in Nîmes with bullfights

Fête de la Transhumance
Traditional pastoral festival when shepherds lead their flocks (some 3000 sheep) to pastures anew, Saint Rémy de Provence, Pentecost Monday

Fête au Château
Two day, open-air music festival with performances in Nice's hilltop Parc du Château

Festival de Musique Sacrée
Two week sacred music festival, churches in Vieux Nice (Old Nice)

Bravades des Espagnols
Saint Tropez celebrates its victory over a fleet of Spanish galleons, 15 June

International Festival of Music
Classical musical festival, Toulon, June to early July

Les Nuits du Théâtre Antique
In June (and again in August), Orange's ancient Théâtre Antique is lit up with concerts, cinema screenings and other musical events.

Fête de la Tarasque
Traditional festival – the folkloric Tarasque dragon and five days of bonfires, fireworks, street processions and carnival, Tarascon, around 24 June (Midsummer's Night)

Fêtes d'Arles
Two week dance, theatre, music and poetry festival in Arles, end of June

July

Fête de la Mer et des Pêcheurs
Two days honouring Saint Peter, patron saint of fishermen. In La Ciotat, there's a Provençal Mass, folk music, and benediction of fishing boats; in Saint Raphaël local fishermen don traditional dress and joust Provençal-style from boats; in Martigues a fleet of traditional fishing boats process through the waters

Festival Provençal d'Aix et du Pays d'Aix
One week classical music, opera and ballet festival (tickets sell fast), Aix-en-Provence

Les Rencontres Internationales de la
Photographie
International photography festival, Arles, early July

Nice Jazz Festival
One week jazz festival with main venue an ancient olive grove in Cimiez, Nice

Jazz à Juan
Celebrated jazz festival in and around Juan-les-Pins, from mid-July

Aix Jazz Festival
Jazz, Aix-en-Provence, five days in mid-July

Festival d'Avignon
Among Europe's best known theatre festivals dating from 1947; tickets (available from mid-June) snapped up in seconds, Avignon, mid-July to early August

Festival Off
The funkier, fringe side to the official Festival d'Avignon

Les Nuits Musicales de Nice
Three weeks of open-air, classical music concerts in the cloisters of Cimiez Monastery, its olive grove, and in town around the Musée d'Art Moderne et d'Art Contemporain, Nice, from mid-July

Les Nuits d'Été de Lourmarin
Musical concerts in the grounds of Lourmarin chateau between July and September; runs alongside Les Rencontres Méditerranéenes Albert Camus, another music festival, July and August

International Folkloric Festival
Two day festival, Juan-les-Pins, end of July
Les Chorégies d'Orange
A two week classical and choral music festival held in Orange's Roman amphitheatre. Tickets are like gold dust and have to be reserved months in advance.
Éstivales de Carpentras
A two week music, dance and theatre festival, Carpentras.
Festival Mosaïque Gitane
Gypsy culture celebrations, Arles & Marseille's Plage du Prado in Marseille, mid-July
Festival Melon en Fêtes
Three day melon festival to honour the town's prized fruit, Cavaillon, mid-July

August
Danse à Aix
Dance, Aix-en-Provence, five days in early August
Musicales d'Oppède
Classical music festival, Oppède, first two weeks of August
Fête du Blé et de la Lavande
Wheat & lavender festival, Peille, first weekend in August.
Corso de La Lavande
Five day festival to celebrate the lavender harvest, Digne-les-Bains, first weekend in August
Festival d'Été au Théâtre Antique
Dance and jazz, Orange's Roman amphitheatre, three weeks in August
Festival de Ramatuelle
Two weeks of live jazz and theatre in the cobbled streets of medieval Ramatuelle

September
Fête Mistralienne
The birthday of literary hero Frédéric Mistral is celebrated on 12/13 September throughout Provence; Aix-en-Provence hosts particularly large celebrations
Féria des Vendanges
The start of the grape harvest is celebrated with a three day, bullfighting festival in Nîmes' Roman amphitheatre, third weekend in September
Fête des Prémices du Riz
Week long festival celebrating the start of the rice harvest with crowning of a rice ambassadress, Arles, mid-September

October
Fête de la Châtaigne
Chestnut Festival, Collobrières, last three Sundays of October

Pélerinage des Gitans
Gypsy pilgrimage Saintes-Maries-de-la-Mer, 22 October

November
Fête des Côtes du Rhône Primeurs
Celebration of Côtes du Rhône wines, Avignon, mid-November
Journées Gourmandes
Feast of the region's gastronomic pleasures, and soup *dégustation* (tasting) during the preceding Festival des Soupes (Soup Festival), Vaison-la-Romaine and surrounding villages

December
Noël
Almost every village in Provence celebrates Christmas with a *messe de minuit* (midnight Mass) with traditional chants in Provençal and a *pastrage* ceremony in which shepherds offer a new-born lamb. Séguret is one of the few places still to celebrate Christmas with Mass and a *crèche vivant* (living crèche) at 10 pm on 24 December; you must book (☎ 04 90 46 91 08 or 04 90 36 02 11).

ACTIVITIES
The region lives up to its reputation as a land of sea and mountains, offering a wealth of outdoor pursuits guaranteed to fulfil the most adventurous – or lazy – of travellers.

Numerous travel agencies abroad arrange thematic tours (golfing, cycling, hiking etc).

Astronomy
The world's largest telescope built for amateur use is in Puimichel, north-east of Manosque. Other *observatoires* (observatories) that welcome star gazers include the Observatoire de Haute-Provence in Saint Michel l'Observatoire, west of Manosque; the Observatoire des Vallons in Bauduen, on the southern shores of Lac de Sainte Croix; and the Observatoire de Nice, in La Trinité, east of Nice.

Bird-Watching
The spectacular Camargue delta – where clouds of pink flamingos are a common sight – and the Parc National du Mercantour lure ornithologists. The spotters' guide, *Where to Watch Birds in France* (1989), written by the French League for the Protection of Birds,

includes maps and marked itineraries cross-referenced to the text.

Cycling

Pedalling Provence is tremendously popular. Bar the barren slopes of Mont Ventoux in the Vaucluse, the region has few killing hills to climb, making it an ideal region to two-wheel for a couple of weeks or months. The country roads in the Lubéron which saunter through vineyards and fruit orchards are popular with cyclists (see the boxed text in The Lubéron chapter), as are the handful of roads that traverse the Massif des Maures. Bicycles are forbidden in the Mercantour and Port-Cros national parks.

Cycling is less tranquil on the coast where the noisy *autoroute* (highway) is never far away. Two-wheelers on a budget often base themselves in Nice, from where they take a train along the coast each morning with their bicycles, to avoid the trauma of cycling out of the city.

You can hire a *vélo tout-terrain* (VTT; mountain bike) in most towns. Some GR and GRP trails (see Hiking) are open to mountain bikes. A *piste cyclable* is a cycling path.

Didier-Richard publishes *Les Guides VTT*, a series of cyclists' topoguides (in French). Each department publishes excellent guides for cyclotourists, detailing numerous trails (in French). Many tourist offices sell cycling itineraries (some in English) compiled by the local cycling club. Useful cycling maps are listed under Maps earlier in this chapter.

Rollerblading

Rollerblading has taken off in a big way in recent years with blades being a tip-top way to cruise around town. A set can easily be hired in any of the larger cities as well as most resorts on the Côte d'Azur. Rates are around 30/50/80FF for half a day/day/two days.

Chic blading venues include Nice's promenade des Anglais, La Croisette in Cannes and La Canebière in Marseille.

Diving & Snorkelling

The coastline and its offshore islands – Porquerolles and Embiez particularly – offer enticing diving opportunities. Experienced divers enjoy the waters around Hyères where the seabeds are graced with numerous shipwrecks. Military WWII wrecks can be explored from Saint Raphaël.

Marseille's calanques offer some of the region's most spectacular diving. Henri Cosquer, known for his discovery of prehistoric paintings in a cave around the Calanques, has his own diving school in Cassis (see the Marseille Area chapter). The Institut National de Plongée Professionnelle (INPP, National Institute of Professional Divers; ☎ 04 91 73 34 62) is at 3 Port Pointe-Rouge, Entrée 3, 13008 Marseille.

If you stumble upon a wreck or want to know more about the region's underwater archaeological treasures, contact DRASM (Direction des Recherches Archéologiques Sous-Marines; ☎ 04 91 91 06 55), headquarters Fort Saint Jean, Marseille.

Diving shops and clubs where you can hire equipment, take a diving course etc, are listed in the relevant regional chapters. There are underwater nature trails designed for amateur snorkellers at the Domain du Rayol on the Corniche des Maures (see the Saint Tropez to Toulon chapter) and on the island of Port-Cros (see the Cannes Region chapter).

Golf

Golf hit the Riviera in the 1890s. Among France's oldest golf courses – dubbed *béton vert* (green concrete) – is the Golf Club de Cannes-Mandelieu, established by the Grand Duke Michael of Russia in 1891; the modern Riviera Golf Club built on a former polo pitch; and the Saint Raphaël-Valescure green which dates from 1895. The Saint Raphaël tourist office (see that city listing) sells two/three day golf passes for 440/670FF, entitling golfers to unlimited access to the area's four golf courses. It also offers weekend golf packages.

Complete details on the region's 40-plus manicured greens are listed in the *Golf in France* guide, published by the Maison de la France and available (free) at tourist offices abroad. Alternatively, contact the Fédération Française de Golf (☎ 01 41 49 77 00, fax 01 41 49 77 01), 68 rue Anatole France, 92309 Levallois-Peret.

Naturism

The region's numerous *naturiste* (nudist) camps are listed in the *Naturism in France* brochure, available at most tourist offices. Sites range from small rural camping grounds to large chalet villages with cinemas, tennis courts and shops where you can wander round in the nude. Most are open from April to October and visitors have to have a membership card from a naturist club or an International Naturist Federation (INF) *passeport naturiste* (naturist passport).

The coastline between Le Lavandou and the Saint Tropez peninsula is well endowed with *naturiste* (nudist) beaches. Héliopolis, on oddball Île du Levant – an island off the coast between Le Lavandou and Hyères, 90% of which is occupied by the French military – is the region's only genuine nudist colony. It dates from the 1930s and can be easily visited on a day trip by boat.

The Fédération Française de Naturisme (☎ 01 47 64 32 82, fax 01 47 64 32 63), Maison du Naturisme, 65 rue de Tocqueville, 75017 Paris, is a good source.

Rafting, Canoeing & Canyoning

Haute-Provence offers some exquisite white-water rafting, canoeing, kayaking and canyoning terrain. The Verdon, Vésubie, Roya and Ubaye rivers are the region's most dramatic waters. Leading centres where you can sign up for expeditions include Castellane (for the Gorges du Verdon), Saint-Martin-Vésubie (for the Vésubie descent), Breil-sur-Roya (for the Vallée de la Roya) and Barcelonnette (for the Vallée de l'Ubaye).

The Comité Départemental de Canoë-Kayak des Alpes-de-Haute-Provence (☎/fax 04 92 83 38 09), 04240 Annot; and Ligue Alpes Provence de Canoë-Kayak (☎ 04 66 89 47 71), 14 ave Vincent Auriol, 30200 Bagnols-sur-Cèze, can supply information on clubs in the region.

Rock Climbing & Via Ferrata

The Gorges du Verdon, Les Calanques around Marseille, the lacy Dentelles de Montmirail in the Vaucluse, Buoux in the Lubéron and the Vallée des Merveilles in the Parc National du Mercantour are just a handful of the numerous *escalade* (climbing) spots in the region. Many more are listed in the brochure entitled *Climbing in the Sun: The Largest Places of Climbing in the South-east*, published by the Fédération Française de la Montagne et de l'Escalade (☎ 04 93 96 17 43), 45 blvd de la Madeleine, 06000 Nice. Most tourist offices and branches of the CAF (Club Alpin Français) also stock lists of *sites d'escalade*.

There are Via Ferrata courses – rigged at a dizzying height guaranteed to set your heart beating faster, and accessible to first-timers – at Tende in the Vallée de la Roya (Haute-Provence) and at La Colmiane, just west of Saint Martin Vésubie (Haute-Provence).

Skiing

Haute-Provence's few ski resorts are low-key with little of the glitz and the glamour attached to the Alp's better known resorts. They are best suited to beginners and intermediates and tend to be marginally cheaper than their northern neighbours.

Resorts include the larger Pra Loup (1500m) and La Foux d'Allos (1800m) which share 230km of downhill pistes and 110km of cross-country trails; the pin-prick sister resorts of Le Sauze (1400m) and Super-Sauze (1700m), in the Vallée de l'Ubaye (Ubaye Valley) which tend to attract domestic tourists; and Barcelonnette (1300m), a small town surrounded by a sprinkling of hillside villages. Isola 2000

(2450m) is the largest of the resorts – and the ugliest.

These resorts – all in the Parc National du Mercantour – are open for the ski season from December to March/April/May (depending on the snow conditions), and then for a short period in July and August for summer hikers.

Buying a package is the cheapest way to ski. Information is online (www.skifrance .com).

Paragliding

Saint André-des-Alps, at the northern tip of Lac de Castillon, some 20km north of Castellane in Haute-Provence, is considered to be the French capital of *parapente* (paragliding). The Paragliding World Championships were hosted here in 1991.

This relaxing sport requires participants to hurl themselves off the top of a mountain, dragging a rectangular parachute behind them. As it opens, the chute fills with air and, acting like an aircraft wing, lifts you up off the ground. If the thermals are good – as in Saint André – you can stay up for hours, peacefully circling the area and enjoying the breathtaking aerial views. A *baptême de l'air* (tandem introductory flight) costs 250-500FF.

Walking & Hiking

The region is criss-crossed by a maze of *sentiers balisés* (marked walking paths). No permits are needed for hiking but there are restrictions on where you can camp, especially in the Mercantour national park.

The best known trails are the *sentiers de grande randonnée*, long-distance footpaths whose alphanumeric names begin 'GR' and whose track indicators are red and white stripes on trees, rocks, walls, posts etc. Some are many hundreds of kilometres long, such as the GR5, which goes from the Netherlands through Belgium, Luxembourg and the spectacular Alpine scenery of eastern France, before ending up in Nice. The GR4, GR6 and GR9 (and their various diversions such as the GR99, GR98 etc) all traverse the region too.

From 1 July to 15 September when there is a high risk of forest fire, some hiking paths in heavily forested areas – such as the section of the GR98 which follows the Calanques between Cap Croisette (immediately south of Marseille) and Cassis – are closed. The GR51 crossing the Massif des Maures and numerous trails in Haute-Provence are also closed by the forest authorities depending on prevailing weather conditions (heat, drought and wind). See Dangers & Annoyances for details.

Numerous hiking guides cover the region – most in French. Essential reading for anyone intending to trek Provence's GRs is *Walks in Provence*, a topoguide written by the Fédération Française de Randonnée Pédestre (FFRP; French Ramblers' Association) and translated into English by UK publisher Robertson McCarta. It has information on trail conditions, flora, fauna, villages *en route*, camping grounds, refuges etc.

COURSES

French language courses and cookery courses are big business in Provence. Less flamboyantly marketed are the art courses offered by local artisans, ranging from painting and pottery to furniture restoration and decoration. Choice offerings include the imaginative paper dying, wall mural painting and wood craft workshops run by the Association Okira (☎/fax 04 90 05 66 69), Usine Mathieu, 84220 Roussillon. The workshops, focused solely on traditional techniques, use natural dyes and pigments extracted from the village's ochre earth. Courses start from 500FF a day.

In Vence, informal drawing and painting sessions are held in the dreamy Villa La Rêve, Henri Matisse's home/studio between 1943-49. A week's course costs 1000FF, plus 100FF per person for accommodation (in the villa). Information is available (French only) from Vence Station Touristique (☎ 04 93 58 40 10, fax 04 93 24 69 07), Villa Alexandrine, place du Grand Jardin, 06140 Vence.

Responsible Hiking

The popularity of hiking is placing pressure on the environment. Please consider the following tips and help preserve the ecology and beauty of Provence.

Rubbish Carry out all your rubbish. Don't overlook items such as silver paper, orange peel, cigarette butts and plastic wrappers. Make an effort to carry out any rubbish left by others.

Never bury your rubbish: digging disturbs soil and ground-cover and encourages erosion. Animals dig up buried rubbish and may be injured or poisoned by it. It may also take years to decompose, especially at high altitudes.

Take minimal packaging and no more food than you will need. Unpack small-portion packages and combine their contents in one container before your trip. Take reusable containers.

Don't rely on bought water in plastic bottles. Disposal of these bottles is creating a major problem.

Sanitary napkins, tampons and condoms should also be carried out despite the inconvenience. They burn and decompose poorly.

Human Waste Disposal Contamination of water sources by human faeces can lead to the transmission of hepatitis, typhoid and intestinal parasites such as *Giardia*, amoebas and roundworms.

Where there is no toilet, bury your waste at least 100m from any watercourse. Cover the waste with soil and a rock. Use toilet paper sparingly and bury it with the waste. In snow, dig down to the soil; otherwise your waste will be exposed when the snow melts.

Washing Don't use detergents or toothpaste in or near watercourses, even if they are biodegradable.

For personal washing, use biodegradable soap and a water container at least 50m away from the watercourse. Disperse the waste-water widely to allow the soil to filter it before it makes it back to the watercourse.

Wash cooking utensils 50m from watercourses using a scourer, sand or snow instead of detergent.

Erosion Hillsides and mountain slopes are prone to erosion. It is important to stick to existing tracks and avoid short cuts that bypass a switchback. If you blaze a new trail straight down a slope, it will turn into a watercourse and eventually cause soil loss and deep scarring.

If a well used track passes through a mud patch, walk through the mud: walking around the edge will increase the size of the patch.

Avoid removing the plant life that keeps topsoils in place.

Wildlife Conservation Don't assume animals in huts to be nonindigenous vermin and attempt to exterminate them. In wild places they are likely to be protected native animals.

Discourage the presence of wildlife by not leaving food scraps about. Place gear out of reach; tie packs to rafters or trees.

Do not feed the wildlife as this can lead to animals becoming dependent on hand-outs, to unbalanced populations and to diseases such as 'lumpy jaw'.

Camping & Walking on Private Property Seek permission to camp from landowners. They will usually be happy if asked but may be confrontational if not.

Park Regulations Take note of and observe any rules and regulations particular to the national or state reserve that you are visiting.

French Language

Reams of Riviera language schools exist. Courses are substantially more expensive in July and August and during other school holiday periods. Schools in the region include the following:

Aix-en-Provence
American University Center
(☎ 04 42 38 42 38, fax 04 42 38 95 66, www .americancenter.net)
409 ave Jean-Paul Coste. Courses of varying length and intensity cost 1970FF for 30 hours of instruction and 2470FF for 40 hours spread over two weeks.
Université d'Aix Marseille III, Institut d'Études Française pour Étudiants Étrangers
(☎ 04 42 21 70 90, fax 04 42 23 02 64)
23 rue Gaston de Saporta, 13625 Aix-en-Provence. Four-week intensive courses (4800FF) from July to September. Homestay accommodation (without meals) for 1700-2100FF a month.

Avignon
Centre d'Études Linguistiques d'Avignon
(CELA; ☎ 04 90 86 04 33, fax 04 90 85 92 01, acomi@avignon-et-provence.com, www.avig non-et-provence.com/cela)
16 rue Sainte Catherine. Courses from 1500FF a week (1800FF in July). B&B accommodation (85FF a night). Special courses on wine, cinema (history of Cannes and Avignon festivals etc).
Association de Langue Française d'Avignon
(ALFA; ☎ 04 90 85 86 24, fax 04 90 85 89 55, alfavignon@pacwan.fr, perso.pacwan.fr/alfa vignon)
4 Impasse Romagnoli. Courses from 1500FF a week (minimum course two weeks). Special Avignon Festival course (1870FF a week) in July and August, centred around the festival. B&B/hotel accommodation for 980/1200FF a week (including evening meal).

Cannes
Cannes UFCM
(☎ 04 92 19 40 40, fax 04 93 90 22 45, ufcm@ ufcm.com)
Les Balladines, 1 rue de la Verrerie, 06150 Cannes-la-Bocca. Two-week courses for 4780FF (15 hours weekly tuition) including homestay accommodation and meals. Thematic language classes on wine (includes visits to vineyards and wine tasting) and Provençal cuisine.

College International de Cannes
(☎ 04 93 47 39 29, fax 04 93 47 51 97, cic@ imaginet.fr)
1 ave du Docteur Pascal. Two/four-week summer courses (3250/4000FF) in July and August. Campus accommodation an extra 2150/3550FF.

Cap d'Ail
Centre Méditerranéen d'Études Françaises
(☎ 04 93 78 21 59, fax 04 93 41 83 96, centre med@monte-carlo.mc)
chemin des Oliviers. School dating from 1901 with an open-air amphitheatre designed by Cocteau. Two-week courses for US$1145, including 28 hours' weekly tuition, two daily meals and shared accommodation.

Haute-Provence
Centre International des Langues
(☎ 04 92 72 46 19, fax 04 92 87 82 81, cil@lac .gulliver.fr, www.chez.com/artlingua)
166 ave du Majoral Arnaud, 04100 Manosque. Weekly courses (20 hours group tuition) for 1850FF; minimum stay, two weeks.
Le Monastère de Ségriès
(☎ 04 92 77 74 58, fax 04 92 77 75 18, crea .langues.be@ibm.net, perso.wanadoo.fr/crea langues)
04360 Moustiers-Ste-Marie. All inclusive, 11-day courses cost 7100/7450FF in the low/high season.

Hyères
Institut d'Enseignement de la Langue Française sur la Côte d'Azur
(ELFCA; ☎ 04 94 65 03 31, fax 04 94 65 81 22, elfca@elfca.com, www.worldwide.edu)
66 ave de Toulon. Courses from 1500FF a week (22 hour group tuition); 'buy' a bicycle for 700FF and 'sell' it for 600FF on departure.

Marseille
Alliance Française
(☎ 04 91 33 28 19, fax 04 91 33 70 30)
55 rue Paradis (6e). Basic, 17-week courses (six hours a week) for 2950FF. Sister school in Nice (☎ 04 93 62 67 66, fax 04 93 85 28 06) at 2 rue de Paris.

Monaco
Regency School
(☎ 92 05 21 21, fax 92 05 27 29)
7 ave Prince Pierre. Individual tuition (280FF, hour) as well as one-week courses (2100FF) B&B/half-board with a local family for 1400, 2000FF a week.

Nice

Alpha-B Institut Linguistique
(☎ 04 93 53 11 10, fax 04 93 53 11 20,
alpha.b@webstore.fr)
7 blvd Prince de Galles. Two/three/four weeks
for 2350/3300/4000FF; homestay accommodation for 90FF a night.

Azurlingua
(☎ 04 93 62 01 11, fax 04 93 62 22 56, info@
azurlingua.com, www.azurlingua.com)
25 blvd Raimbaldi. Two-week courses for
2100FF, plus 700/1300FF a week for a
flat/half-board with a family.

École France Langue
(☎ 04 93 13 78 88, fax 04 93 13 78 89,
frlang_n@club-internet.fr, www.france-langue
.fr)
22 ave Notre-Dame. Weekly rate for 22-hour
group tuition is 1425FF; self-catering, B&B or
hotel accommodation on request.

International House
(☎ 04 93 62 60 62, fax 04 93 80 53 09, info@
ih-nice.com)
62 rue Gioffredo. Two-week courses (20 hours
weekly tuition) and homestay accommodation
for US$1011.

Provençal Cooking

Most culinary courses for globe-trotting
gourmets revolve around markets, vineyards, olive groves – and the kitchen table.
The annual *Guide to Cooking Schools*
(Shaw Guides, www.shawguides.com); and
the *Guide to Cookery Courses of the British
Isles & Beyond*, (1998) compiled by
London's Books for Cooks (see Books
section) have exhaustive listings.

Association Cuisine et Tradition (ACT)
(☎ 04 90 49 69 20, fax 04 90 49 69 20;
ACTVedel@Provnet.fr),
30 rue Pierre Euzeby, 13200 Arles, France. Run
by Arles-born chef, Erick Vedel, it offers everything from a one meal workshop (500FF) to a
one week culinary course (4500FF excluding
accommodation). A five day, wine-lovers
course is US$1325/1095 with/without accom-
modation in a two-star hotel.

**At Home with Patricia Wells: Cooking in
Provence**
(Fax 214-343 1227, DebOrrill@usa.net,
foodlovers@usa.net),
7830 Ridgemar Drive, Dallas, Texas 75231.
Program director Deborah Orrill. Summer,
five-day cookery courses (US$3000 excluding

accommodation) with the author of the best-
selling *Food Lover's Guide to France*. Courses
take place in Wells' 18th century farmhouse
near Vaison-la-Romaine. Book *at least* six
months in advance.

A Taste of Provence
(☎/fax 04 93 42 43 05)
Le Mas du Loup, 694 chemin de Saint Jean,
06620 Le Bar-sur-Loup, France;
(☎ 415-383 9439, fax 383 6186, info@tasteof
provence.com, www.tasteofprovence.com),
925 Vernal Ave, Mill Valley, CA 94941, USA.
Family-style cookery courses in a restored
Provençal farmhouse between Grasse and Vence.
Courses in May, June, September and October
cost US$1800 per person a week (includes ac-
commodation, drinks, wines, breakfasts, dinners
and a session at the Roger Vergé cooking school).
Mediterranean Diet courses too.

Cooking at the Abbey
(☎ 04 90 56 24 55, fax 04 90 56 31 12, sainte
croix@relaischateaux.fr, www.integra.fr/relais
chateaux/saintecroix)
L'Abbaye de Sainte-Croix, place du Val de
Cuech, 13300 Salon-de-Provence;
EMI International
(☎ 718-631 0096, fax 718-631 0316)
PO Box 640713, Oakland Gardens, New York,
NY-11364-0713. Three-day courses (3895FF
including accommodation in a former monk's
cell) hosted in a restored 12th century abbey
surrounded by lavender and rosemary gardens.

Cooking with Friends in France
(☎ 04 93 60 10 56, fax 04 93 60 05 56,
kcookfr@aol.com, www.cookingwithfriends
.com)
La Pitchoune, Domaine de Bramafam, 06740
Châteauneuf-de-Grasse;
(☎ 617-350 3837, fax 247 6149, suzanne@
jackson-co.com),
Jackson & Co, 20 Commonwealth Ave,
Boston, MA 02116. Six-day cookery sessions
with accommodation in a farmhouse or cottage
cost US$1850 (evening meal not included).
Courses in May, June, September, October,
November.

École de Cuisine du Soleil de Roger Vergé
(☎ 04 93 75 35 70, fax 04 93 90 18 55)
Restaurant L'Amandier, place du Lamy, 06250
Mougins. Individual morning or afternoon sessions (2½ hours) cost 300/1350FF for one/five
sessions; reserve at least 48 hours in advance.

The International Kitchen
(☎ 800-945 8606, toll free, or 847-295 5363,
fax 295 0945, info@intl-kitchen.com, www
.intl-kitchen.com),
1209 North Astor, #11-N, Chicago, IL 60610,

USA. Six-day Passport to Provence for US$1475 (includes farmhouse or chateau accommodation).

Le Marmiton
(☎ 04 90 85 93 93, fax 04 90 86 26 85)
Hôtel de la Mirande, 4 place de la Mirande, 84000 Avignon. Hotel cookery school tucked behind the Palais des Papes, with classes led by a variety of known Provençal chefs. A morning class costs 400-600FF, a five-class weekly package is 2400-3000FF, and a morning class with accommodation is 1345-1915FF.

WORK
To work legally you need a carte de séjour (see Visas & Documents). Work *au noir* (in the black) is possible in the Côte d'Azur's tourist industry and during Provence's *vendanges* (grape harvests).

Agricultural Work
To pick up a job in a field, ask around in areas where harvesting is taking place – trees heaving with almost-ripe fruit are a sure sign that pickers will soon be needed. Provence from mid-May to September sees a succession of apple, strawberry, cherry, peach, pear and pumpkin harvests.

The annual vendange happens from about mid-September to mid or late October. The sun-soaked fruits of the Côtes de Provence vineyards are ready for harvest before those of the more northern, Châteauneuf-du-Pape vineyards. Increasingly, vendange is being done by machine, though mechanical picking is forbidden in some places (such as Châteauneuf-du-Pape).

Once the vendange starts it lasts just a couple of weeks although in large appellation areas such as the Côtes de Provence appellation, which extends from Aix-en-Provence to the coast, harvests are staggered – meaning a vendange can always be happening somewhere for most of September and October. The vendange start date is announced up to one week before picking starts.

Food for *vendangeurs* (grape pickers) is usually supplied but accommodation is often not – which explains why most pickers tend to live locally. The most effective way of securing work is to approach the

different wine producing *domaines* (estates) directly from May onwards. Tourist offices in the region have a list of producers, as do the different Maisons des Vins (see the Food & Wine section).

Environmental
Each summer, the Station d'Observation et de Protection des Tortues des Maures (Maures Tortoise Observation and Protection Station; SOPTOM) in the Villages des Tortues, 20km north of Collobrières in the Massif des Maures, offers a limited number of placements to students aged 17 and over. The centre allows students to spend 15 days to a month working at the village between March and November. Free board and lodging is included: to apply call (☎ 04 94 78 26 41, fax 04 94 78 24 27, soptom@compuserve.com), BP 24, 83590 Gonfaron.

Au Pair
Under the au pair system, single young people (aged 18 to about 27) who are studying in France live with a French family and receive lodging, full board and a bit of pocket money in exchange for taking care of the kids, babysitting, doing light housework and perhaps teaching English to the children. Many families want au pairs who are native English speakers, but knowing at least some French may be a prerequisite.

Ski Resorts
Haute-Provence's ski resorts – Isola 2000, Pra-Loup and La Foux d'Allos among them – are fairly small and offer few work opportunities. If you contact the ski resort months in advance you might be able to pick up some hospitality work in a hotel or restaurant.

Crewing on a Yacht
Working on a yacht sure looks glamorous although the reality is far from cushy. Cannes, Antibes or any other yacht-filled port on the Côte d'Azur is the place to look. Most jobs are filled by mid-April. Yacht owners often take on newcomers for a trial period of day crewing before hiring them

for the full charter season. By late September, long-haul crews are in demand for winter voyages to the West Indies.

Beach Hawkers & Street Performers

Selling goods and services on the beach is one way to make a few francs, though you've got to sell an awful lot of *beignets* (donuts) and ice cream or wrap a lot of hair with coloured beads to make a living.

If you play an instrument or have some other talent in the performing arts, you could try busking as a street musician, actor, juggler, pavement artist etc. The best way to avoid hassles with the police or music-hating shop owners is to consult with other street artists before you start blasting out your favourite Iggy Pop number. One good place to busk is on the street of Avignon during its May theatre festival.

ACCOMMODATION

Accommodation is notorious for being among the most expensive in France. But it is by no means unaffordable. With a bit of planning and consideration of all the accommodation options you can stay here cheaply.

Local authorities impose a *taxe de séjour* (tourist tax) on each visitor in their jurisdiction. This is usually only enforced in the high season – Easter through to the end of September. At this time, prices charged at camping grounds, hotels etc will be 1-7FF per person higher than the posted rates.

Reservations

These are the key to *not* having to join the hordes of dispirited backpackers waiting in line at Nice train station's public telephone booths each morning, in a tired bid to find a bed for the night.

Advance Reservations In July and August, if you don't have a reservation, don't even contemplate arriving later than 11 am anywhere along the coast – unless you're prepared to pay a fortune for the few rooms that might still be available.

Calling just a couple of days before to reserve a room, or even early in the morning (8 or 9 am) on the day you intend to arrive, can save you a back-breaking hike round town upon arrival. Budget accommodation is generally snapped up by 11 am, but almost never booked up weeks in advance (unlike mid-range and top end accommodation).

Don't turn up in Cannes, Avignon or Aix-en-Provence at festival time unless you have made a reservation months (a year in the case of Cannes) in advance.

Tourist Offices Tourist offices usually help people who don't speak French make local hotel reservations, often for a small fee. In some cases, you pay a deposit that is deducted from the first night's bill. Staff have information on vacancies but are not allowed to make recommendations. You have to stop by the office to take advantage of reservation services.

Deposits Many hotels only accept reservations if they are accompanied by *des arrhes* (a deposit) in French francs. Some two or more-starred places ask for your credit card number instead, or for a confirmation of your plans by letter or fax in clear, simple English (receipt of which is rarely acknowledged by French hoteliers).

Deposits can easily be sent by postal money order *(mandat lettre)* made payable to the hotel (available from any post office).

Camping

The region has hundreds of camping grounds – many beautifully set on river banks, near lakes, up mountains or overlooking the azure-blue sea. Most sites are open from March or April to September or October, although in the Saint Tropez area many grounds are open year round. Some hostels (such as the Relais International de la Jeunesse on Cap d'Antibes) allow travellers to pitch tents in the back garden.

Camping grounds have stars to reflect their facilities and amenities which, along with location and seasonal demand, influence the nightly rate. Separate tariffs are usually charged for people, tents or caravans (the latter are charged extra for electricity), and cars or motorcycles. Some places have *forfaits* (fixed price deals) for two or three people, including tent and car. Children up to about age 12 enjoy significant discounts. Receptions for reservations are often closed during the day; the best time to call is early morning or evening.

Camping à la ferme (camping on the farm) is coordinated by Gîtes de France (see Gîtes Ruraux & B&Bs) which publishes the annual *Camping à la Ferme* guide (70FF).

Wild camping *(camping sauvage)* is illegal although it is tolerated to some degree in places (*never* ever in any of the national parks). Pitching your tent on the beach or in a meadow does make you an immediate – and easy – target for thieves.

The Comité Régional de Tourisme Provence-Alpes-Côte d'Azur (see Tourist Office earlier) publishes an annual booklet listing all the camping grounds in the region.

Refuges & Gîtes d'Étape

Refuges (a simple mountain shelter) and *gîtes d'étapes* (basic dorm rooms) are options in rural Provence – the Parc National de Mercantour and Haute-Provence – where undeveloped areas still exist.

Gîtes d'étapes tend to be located in towns or villages popular with hikers and mountain climbers – such as Sospel, Castellane, Digne-les-Bains etc – which serve as a gateway to these areas. Refuges are in isolated wildernesses, often accessible only by hiking trail and usually marked on hiking maps.

Both accommodations are basic. They're often equipped with bunks, mattresses and blankets, but not sheets (sometimes available to rent). Nightly rates start at 50-70FF a night per person. Meals, prepared by the *gardien* (attendant) are sometimes available. Most refuges are only open from June to September; some are equipped with a telephone, so you can call ahead to book.

For details (including reservations) on the 10 refuges in the Alpes-Maritimes department, contact the Club Alpin Français des Alpes-Maritimes (☎ 04 93 62 59 99), 14 ave Mirabeau, 06000 Nice. Details on Haute-Provence refuges are available from the Centre d'Information Montagne et Sentiers (CIMES; ☎ 04 76 42 45 90, fax 04 76 42 87 08, grande.traversee.des.alpes@wanadoo.fr, perso.wanadoo.fr/routes.des.grandes.alpes/), BO 227, 38019 Grenoble. The latter has information on the region's gîtes d'étapes. Alternatively, get the annual Gîtes de France *Alpes-de-Haute-Provence* guide (66FF).

Gîtes Ruraux & B&Bs

Provence's most sought after accommodation – charming, century-old *mas* (Provençal farmhouses), *châteaux* (castles) or *moulins* (mills) surrounded by olive and orange groves or blossoming almond and cherry tree orchards – is represented by Gîtes de France, a 'green' organisation that liases between owners and renters. These idyllic little nests are off the public transport track and are only suitable for travellers with a vehicle.

Amenities in a *gîte rural* (a self-catering holiday cottage in a village or on a farm) or a *gîte communal* (owned by the commune rather than an individual) include a kitchenette and bathroom facilities. In most cases there is a minimum rental period – usually one week.

A *chambre d'hôte* (a French-style B&B) is a room in a private house rented to travellers by the night; breakfast is always included in the price while a delicious homemade evening meal is often available for an extra fee (about 100FF).

Gîtes de France' annual guide, *Provence-Alpes-Côte d'Azur – Chambres d'hôtes*, is a listing (complete with a photograph of the property) of gîtes ruraux, chambres d'hôtes, gîtes d'étapes and camping grounds in all the areas covered by this book. Advance bookings and information is available directly from the property owner, or a Gîtes de France *antenne* (branch):

Alpes-de-Haute-Provence
(☎ 04 92 31 52 39, fax 04 92 32 32 63)
Maison du Tourisme, Rond Point du 11 Novembre, BP 201, 04001 Digne-les-Bains
Alpes-Maritimes
(☎ 04 92 15 21 30, fax 04 93 86 01 06, www.crt-riviera.fr/gites06)
55 promenade des Anglais, 06011 Nice
Bouches-du-Rhône
(☎ 04 90 59 49 27 or 04 90 59 49 40, fax 04 90 59 16 75, gitesdefrance@visitprovence.com)
Domaine du Vergon, 13370 Mallemort
Var
(☎ 04 94 50 93 93 or 04 94 22 65 70, fax 04 94 22 65 72)
Conseil Général, Rond-Point du 4 Decembre 1974, BP 215, 83006 Draguignan
Vaucluse
(☎ 04 90 85 45 00, fax 04 90 85 88 49)
BP 164, 84003 Avignon

During holiday periods, it is vital to reserve rural accommodation well in advance; most require a deposit.

Homestays

Students, young people and tourists can stay with French families under an arrangement known as *hôtes payants* (literally, 'paying guests') or *hébergement chez l'habitant* (lodging with the occupants of private homes). In general you rent a room and have access (sometimes limited) to the family's kitchen and telephone. Most language schools (see the previous Courses section) arrange homestays for their students. Students and tourists alike should count on paying at least 3000-5200FF a month, 1200-1500FF a week, or 130-300FF a day for a single room, including breakfast.

Hundreds upon hundreds of agencies in the US and Europe arrange homestay accommodation in Provence and the Côte d'Azur; the Comité Régional de Tourisme Provence-Alpes-Côte d'Azur in Marseille (see Tourist Office earlier) has a list, as do all French tourist offices abroad.

Hostels

There are official *auberges de jeunesse* on the coast at Cassis, Marseille, Fréjus-Saint Raphaël, Le Trayas, Menton and Nice; in the mountains at La Foux d'Allos, La Palud sur Verdon and Manosque; and to the west, in Aix-en-Provence, Arles, Tarascon and Fontaine-de-Vaucluse. Expect to pay about 66-70FF a night, which does not include a sometimes-optional continental breakfast (about 15FF). Privately-owned hostels charge more. FUAJ and LFAJ affiliates require Hostelling International or similar cards (see Visas & Documents).

Most hostels have some kitchen facilities. Most do not accept telephone reservations so turn up early, especially in July and August, if you want to ensure you get a bed for the night.

In some spots (eg Nice and Fréjus-Saint Raphaël) the hostels are a good hike out of town. If there are a couple of you it can be as cheap (or cheaper) to stay in a budget hotel in town. Other hostels (such as those on Cap d'Antibes and Cap d'Ail) enforce a curfew during the day, so you are obliged to be out by 10 am and stay out until around 5 pm.

Hotels

Hotels have between one and four stars. Few no-star hotels (ie that have not been rated) exist.

Petit déjeuner (breakfast) is almost never included in the room price. Count on paying an extra 25-35FF (up to 100FF in four-star joints) for the privilege. Breakfast at a nearby café can be cheaper and invariably more pleasant.

Many hotels in the region only operate, deplorably so, on a half-board basis in July and August, meaning you are obliged to fork out the hefty prices they set for breakfast and an evening meal in a stuffy, cramped hotel restaurant (invariably inside).

A room with a bath is usually more expensive than a room with a shower. Most places tout neck-aching *traversins* (hot dog shaped bolsters) rather than *oreillers* (pillows).

Budget Hotels Expect to pay about 170FF a night for a double with a washbasin (and often bidet) in your room, and a shared toilet and shower in the corridor. A shower in the hall bathroom is sometimes free but usually *payant* – 10-25FF per shower. Most places have more expensive rooms equipped with shower, toilet and other amenities. Prices stay the same year round at budget hotels.

Budget establishments often do not have single rooms. Rather, they sport rooms fit for one or two people (ie with one double bed) for which they charge the same price, regardless of whether it is let as a single or double. Places which do have singles (ie with one single bed), usually charge marginally less for it than for a double (with a double bed or two singles). Triples and quads normally tout one or two beds.

In Marseille, Nice and Toulon, you can find rock-bottom places to stay which are generally frequented by prostitutes. Many places have an hourly or half-day rate, advertised as a rate for punters waiting for a train or bus departure. These are the places most likely to have no shower facilities, lift or fire escape.

Most cheap hotels demand pre-payment for the room. Make sure you see the room before parting with any cash. Do not expect any refund if you pay first, only to discover the room is an uninhabitable hovel, prompting immediate departure.

There are postmodern, pressboard and plastic hotels on the outskirts of most towns in the region – run by a hotel chain and remarkably cheap (159FF for a room for up to three people). These ugly boxes (not listed in this guide) sport revolting views of busy roads and are only convenient for travellers with a car. Chains include Formule 1, Fimôtel and Campanile.

Hôtel Meublé A *hôtel meublé* (literally 'furnished hotel') – most common in Nice – is a small hotel which rents rooms with spartan cooking facilities (usually a small fridge and hotplate) on a weekly basis. Little or no service is provided.

Mid-Range Hotels Expect to pay 200-400FF for a room. Mid-range hotels usually tout three sets of seasonally adjusted prices. Low-season applies from October/November to February/March. The middle season is usually March/April/May and September/October. High season, when prices rocket out of control, is July and August (sometimes June and September too).

Hotels usually close for several weeks in winter for their *congé annuel* (annual closure). Some places close straight through from September/October to March/April. The exception is in Haute-Provence's skiing resorts where hotels only open for the winter ski season.

Some 350 family-run places in the region – often in the mountains or *au bord de la mer* (next to the sea) belong to Logis de France, an organisation whose affiliated establishments meet strict standards of service and amenities. The Fédération Régionale Provence-Côte d'Azur (☎ 04 91 14 42 00, fax 04 91 14 42 45, www.logis-de-france .com), 8 rue Neuve Saint Martin. BP 1880, 13222 Marseille, issues an annual guide with details of each hotel-restaurant in the Provence-Côte d'Azur region.

Mills & Monasteries

Provence-Côte d'Azur has a wealth of upmarket hotels and restaurants housed in traditional properties: mas, *moulins à huile* (oil mills), *chateaux* (castles), *monastères* (monasteries) and *prieurés* (priories). Lakes, rose gardens and olive groves usually pepper the vast grounds typical to these exclusive estates. See regional chapters for details.

Details of monasteries which accept guests are listed in the *Guide Saint Christophe* (120FF), published by La Procure (☎ 01 45 48 20 25), 3 rue de Mézières, 75006 Paris. The annual *Moulin Étape* guide includes old mills in France where you can stay. Contact the Moulin d'Hauterive (☎ 03 85 91 55 56, fax 03 85 91 89 65), 71350 Saint Gervais en Vallière, for details.

Châteaux

There are several working *châteaux* (wine growing estates) in the Côtes de Provence wine region where you can stay. The

Maison des Vins in Les Arcs (see the Saint Tropez to Toulon chapter) has a list. Some are listed in the regional chapters.

Renting & Buying

Every tourist office has a list of self-catering studios, apartments, seaside villas and rural farmhouses to rent on a short (one week) or long term (several months) basis. The most sought-after properties are booked up a year before.

An excellent source of information for anyone aspiring to buy a rambling old stable and convert it Mayle-style into a Provençal dream home is *Buying a Home in France* by David Hampshire (Survival Books, 1998). It includes step-by-step instructions on how to buy a property in France and has an exhaustive appendix of every possible, house-related French word you might need to know (chimney sweep, land registry, mains draining system etc).

Domaines viticoles (working chateaux with vineyards, olive groves and woods) are the speciality of real estate agent Emile Garcin (☎ 04 90 92 01 58, fax 04 90 92 39 57, provence@emilegarcin.fr, www.emile garcin.fr), 8 blvd Mirabeau, 13210 Saint-Rémy-de-Provence.

Provence has the largest *résidence secondaire* (second home) community in France (13.6% of tourists own a résidence secondaire, followed by 34.1% who stay with family or friends).

FOOD

La cuisine Provençale, with its abundance of fruit, vegetables and olive oil, is the healthiest cuisine in France. It is also the most desirable; a remarkable number of travellers visit the region simply to eat their way around it. Luckily, gastronomic orgasms are plentiful.

Provençal cuisine is simple. The secret of its success lies not in elaborate preparation techniques or state of the art presentation, but rather in the use of fresh ingredients produced locally. Dubbed the 'garden of France', sun-soaked Provence is endowed with a truly magnificent choice of fruit,

vegetables, spices and herbs. It is best savoured in a Provençal marketplace where the fiesta of colour, aroma and texture never fails to thrill the traveller accustomed to dining à la microwave back home.

People in Provence generally think, dream and live food; most people's working day is completely geared around satisfying their insatiable appetite for dining well.

Consumer Warning: Provençal cuisine oozes garlic. After consumption, munch on a sprig of parsley to avoid reeking breath.

Vegetarian Cuisine

While most locals will stare at you as if you are downright crazy if you admit to not eating juicy slabs of practically raw meat, vegetarians will not starve when dining out. Few *menus* feature vegetarian dishes, but there are usually a couple of vegetarian *entrées* (starters or first courses) to titillate the tastebuds. Salads alone are usually giant sized. Traditional *pain aux raisins* (raisin bread), *pain aux noix* (walnut bread) or *pain aux olives* (olive bread) add a bite to the blandest of meals.

Ethnic & Kosher Cuisine

Southern France's considerable immigrant population is reflected in the exceptional variety of reasonably-priced, ethnic dishes on offer in its major cities. In Marseille, particularly, you can feast on everything from North African couscous and lamb shish kebabs to Thai, Armenian, Lebanese and Tunisian fare. There are *cacher* (kosher) restaurants in Marseille and Cannes.

Once out of cosmopolitan Provence and in the hinterland, there is but one delicious choice: Provençal.

Restaurants

Dining à la Provençale can mean spending anything from 70FF (in a village bistro) to 400FF or more (in one of the region's multi-starred, gastronomic temples). Regardless of price, most places have a *carte* (menu) pinned up outside, allowing for a quick price and dish check for those not wanting to end up washing the dishes or dining on *pieds et paquets* (literally 'feet and packets', in reality sheep tripe).

The most authentic Provençal places to eat are in tiny hamlets off the beaten track – living proof that locals will drive any distance for a good meal. These places tout just one *menu* with *vin compris* (wine included). The *patron* (owner) of the place is often the chef who, at the end of your meal or during it, comes to your table – clad in kitchen whites – to inquire about your meal. Dogs snoozing under tables are a common sight.

No restaurant can call itself truly Provençal unless it serves you a continuous flow of chunkily-cut bread from the start to the very end of your meal (if it runs out, just ask for more – it's free). Except in the most expensive places, side plates are not provided. Don't attempt to balance your bread chunk on your main course plate – sprinkling the table with crumbs is perfectly acceptable.

In cheaper restaurants, you might be expected to use the one set of eating utensils for the duration of your meal. Upon finishing your entrée, replace your knife and fork (a subtle wipe clean with bread is allowed; licking – less cool) on the table either side of your dirty plate. If not, the waiter will do it for you. The waiter is also likely to add up the *addition* (bill) on your paper tablecloth.

Cafés & Bars

The café is an integral part of French society, and never more so than in the sun-filled south where the café is the hub of village life and a highly respected institution. Many double as the village bar and bistro too. Most serve simple baguettes filled with cheese (around 25FF) or *charcuterie* (cold meats). Others have select terraces hidden outback where you can dine in the shade of overhead vines.

In towns, a café on a grand boulevard (or chic place to be seen such as the Vieux Port in Saint Tropez), charges considerably more than a place fronting a quiet side street.

Les Deux Garçons in Aix-en-Provence is the region's most famous café. It sits on the shady side of cours Mirabeau – a street considered to be the finest in southern France. In fine café tradition, prices are hiked up after 10 pm.

Châteaux & Fermes Auberges

A *château* is the main house or building on a wine-producing estate, and a *ferme auberge* or *auberge de Provence* is a small, family-run inn attached to a working farm or chateau. They are two of the most delightful places to dine à la Provençale.

Typical Provençal cuisine is guaranteed at both. Dining is around shared tables with wooden benches. Portions are sufficiently hearty for those with the largest of appetites to leave in a merry state of stuffed bliss. A *menu*, comprising four courses and often wine too, can cost 100-180FF.

The Maison des Vins in Les Arcs has a list of Côtes de Provence chateaux where you can eat. The Domaine de la Maurette in La Motte, 5km east of Les Arcs, (see the Saint Tropez to Toulon chapter) is a prime example of a ferme auberge.

Salons de Thé & Crêperies

Salons de Thé (tearooms) are trendy and expensive establishments that offer quiches, salads, cakes, tarts, pies and pastries in addition to tea and coffee.

Crêperies serve ultra-thin pancakes with a variety of sweet or savoury fillings, except in Nice where socca – a hearty Niçois pancake comprising chick-pea flour and lashings of olive oil – is served.

Self-Catering

Provence's premier culinary delight is to stock up on breads, pastries, fruit, vegetables and prepared dishes and sit down for a gourmet *pique-nique*.

When shopping, do as the locals do: spurn the supermarket and buy fresh local products from the market, followed by a stroll to the local *boulangerie* for a baked-that-hour baguette (long stick of white bread) or some pain aux noix; then to the *pâtisserie* for *tartes Tropézienne*, *tartes aux fruits* (fruit tarts), pains au chocolat and

continued on page 103

FOOD & WINE
OF
PROVENCE

FOOD

Provençal cuisine has its own regional differences but certain traits are upheld everywhere – oodles of olive oil and an abundance of garlic. Tomatoes are another common ingredient, and you can safely assume that any culinary delight described as *à la Provençale* will be prepared with garlic-seasoned tomatoes.

Other vegetables that frequently appear on local menus are *aubergines* (eggplant), *courgettes* (summer squash or zucchini) and *oignons* (onions). Tomatoes, eggplant and squash, stewed together along with green peppers, garlic and various aromatic herbs, produce that perennial Provençal favourite, *ratatouille*. The *artichaut* (artichoke), often eaten very young, is another typical vegetable. They can all be filled with a salted pork, onion and herb mix, then baked, to become *légumes farcis* (stuffed vegetables). Stuffed courgette flowers are an exquisite variation of this basic Provençal dish. Tomatoes and black olives are the mainstay of traditional *daube provençale* (beef stew), and they both feature in a typical *tian* (vegetable and rice gratin).

Another favourite way to eat vegetables is as *crudités* (raw), generally served with an aperitif accompanied by two of Provence's most classic dishes: *anchoïade*, a strong, anchovy paste laced with garlic and olive oil; and its dark counterpart, *tapenade*, a sharp, black olive-based dip seasoned with garlic, capers, anchovies and olive oil. *Endive* (chicory) tastes particularly good dipped into the latter. *Brandade de morue* is a mix of crushed salt cod, olive oil and garlic.

Strong-tasting sauces are also served to compliment soups and fish dishes. *Soupe au pistou* is a hearty vegetable, three or four-bean and basil soup, always served with *pistou*, a spicy basil, garlic and olive oil sauce which you can stir into the soup to spice it up, or spread on small toasts. *Soupe de poisson* (fish soup) also comes with crisp toasts, as well as a small pot of *rouille* and a clove of fresh garlic. Rouille is mayonnaise combined with garlic, breadcrumbs and crushed red chilli peppers (hence, its salmon-pink colour). The garlic clove is there to rub over the toasts before dousing them with the already very garlicky rouille.

In sea-faring Marseille, rouille is used as a condiment for *bouillabaisse*, Provence's most famous – and most fishy dish. *Bourride* is a variation of bouillabaisse.

The many other fish dishes which characterise Marseillais cooking are almost always accompanied by *aïoli*, a garlicky sauce similar to rouille, but lacking the hot chilli peppers and yellow in colour. Aïoli is smeared over everything from fish to vegetables: *Aïoli Provençale complet* is a plate of vegetables (including artichokes), boiled potatoes, a boiled egg, and *coquillages* (small shellfish) to dunk in the giant-sized pot of aïoli that comes with it.

Title Page photo
Adrienne Costanzo

Niçois cooking is more Italianate in flavour, while the cuisine of the Camargue wetland – land of bulls and rice fields – is more meaty. *Truffes* (truffles) are a precious black fungi, treated as gold dust, and uncovered in modest amounts in the Vaucluse.

Cheese is typical only to the region's rural hinterland: *chèvre* is made from goat's milk and *brebis* is a sheep's milk product. *Banon*, available all year, is a nut-covered chèvre wrapped in a chestnut leaf.

The Essentials

Herbs The titillating array of aromatic herbs and plants used in Provençal cooking is a legacy of the heavily-scented garrigue that covers vast areas of the region. Its classic herbal mix of dried basil, thyme and rosemary is one used to season numerous dishes throughout Europe. In Provençal cooking, fresh *basilic* (basil) lends its pea green colour and strong fragance to pistou and is used dried to flavour soupe de pistou. *Sauge* (sage), traditionally an antiseptic, is another pistou ingredient. Aromatic *romarin* (rosemary), a common Mediterranean shrub, is used fresh or dried to flavour most meat dishes. In medieval Provence it was said to possess magical powers which, if eaten regularly, ensured eternal youth.

Fresh *cerfeuil* (chervil) is an annual plant, the leaves of which are predominantly used in omelettes and meat dishes, while the tender young shoots of *estragon* (tarragon) can be used to lightly flavour sauces accompanying seafood. The sensual aniseed scent of the bulbous *fenouil* (fennel) is rife in the region. Its leaves (picked in spring) are finely chopped and used in fish dishes and marinades, while its potent seeds (plucked at summer's end) form the basis of several herbal liqueurs, including pastis and the 50% alc/vol Lérina liqueur made by monks on Île Saint Honorat. Equally distinctive to Provençal cuisine is the use of *lavande* (lavender). While its lilac flower is used to sweetly scent rooms, clothes and cupboards, only its green leaves are used in the kitchen. Lavender flavours marmalades and is used to spice up classical milk-based dishes like *crème brûlée*.

Fruit Trees Lemons, *marrons* (chestnuts) and olives are just some of the bounty yielded from the region's vast tree collection. Lemons are grown in abundance in warmer climes along the Côte d'Azur; squeeze its juice across a fresh Marseillais *huître* (oyster) for a bite of the land and the sea.

The Greeks bequeathed to Provence what many call *l'arbre de vie* (the tree of life) or *l'arbre devin* (divine tree), the fruits of which are crushed to a pulp to extract the region's most precious commodity – *huile d'olive* (olive oil).

Oliviers (olive trees) have knotty trunks, shimmering silver branches, grow in groves between altitudes of 300 and 800m, and live for an absolute age; olives are born from the clusters of white flowers that blossom between May and June. Temperatures below zero kill olive trees, as happened in 1956 when half the region's trees froze to death.

Olive Oil Succulent, sun-baked black olives are harvested from 15 November to January during the olivades – the time of the *cueillette des olives* (olive harvest). Olives destined for the oil press are not picked until December; 5kg of olives produce one litre of oil.

In 1990, olive oil produced in northern Vaucluse around Nyons was granted its own recognised AOC (appellation d'origine contrôlée), followed in 1997 by the Vallée de la Baux AOC which was granted to seven communes around the Alpilles. *Oléiculteurs* (olive growers) in these regions have to comply to a rigid set of rules in order to have their bottles of oil stamped with the quality-guaranteed AOC mark.

The finest Provençal olive oil costs around 120FF a litre. Prior to purchasing, it should be tasted in the same way one samples wine. An olive oil can have various degrees of sweetness or acidity, and can be clear or slightly murky (which means the oil has not been filtered). A bottle of olive oil should be kept out of direct sunlight and consumed within six months of opening. Some cooks say it loses some of its taste when heated above 80°C. Some restaurants serve a pool of olive oil in a ramekin – *beurre du soleil* (butter of the sun) to spoon on your bread.

Bouillabaisse Bouillabaisse is the region's quintessential dish. It was originally brewed up by the seafaring Marseillais – said to still cook the fishiest, freshest and most authentic bouillabaisse.

Bouillabaisse is essentially a fish stew made with *at least* four kinds of fresh fish cooked in a rockfish stock (broth) with onions, tomatoes, garlic, saffron which colours it a pungent orange, and herbs like parsley, *laurel* (bay leaves) and thyme. Its name is derived from the Provençal word *bouï abaisso* (literally 'boil turn-down') which reflects the fast cooking method the dish requires. A true bouillabaisse is rapidly brought to the boil, left to bubble ferociously for some 15 minutes, the heat immediately reduced and the pot is ready to serve.

Hundreds of different recipes have evolved over the centuries with no two cooks ever cooking an identical bouillabaisse. There are endless debates about exactly which fresh fish constitute a true bouillabaisse (sometimes listed as *bouillabaisse du pêcheur* on menus) which, even in Marseille, differs dramatically. A general consensus says *rascasse* (scorpion fish) must be included. A *bouillabaisse royale* touts a lavish selection of shell fish including some pricey *langouste* (crayfish) or *langoustine* (small saltwater lobster). The Toulonnais meanwhile, throw potatoes into their *bouillabaisse Toulonnaise*. Bourride is a cheap variation of bouillabaisse which contains no saffron, features cheaper white fleshed fish, and is served with aïoli instead of rouille.

Bouillabaisse is an entire meal. The *bouillon* (broth) in which the fish is cooked, is served as a fish soup entrée, accompanied by bite-sized crisp toasts and spicy rouille. Following this, the fish flesh is served on a platter; the pot of bouillon remains on the table allowing you to spoon it over the fish or dunk the fish as desired.

Truffles Truffes are Provence's most highly-sought, expensive and blackest gastronomic treat, often known as black diamonds. The legendary fungi is, in fact, a type of mushroom (tuber melanosporum) that takes root underground at the foot of a tree, usually in symbiosis with the roots of an elm or oak tree. The tuber can vary dramatically in size, anything from nail to fist-sized. It is coloured a rich black and has a distinctively strong and potent aroma.

Truffles are harvested between November and March. *Rabassaïres* (truffle hunters) unearth the hidden mushrooms with the aid of a dog trained to detect the smelly fungi. Once a spot has been sniffed out, the hunter carefully scrapes the top soil away to unveil the heavenly black, gastronomic gem.

Apparently, truffles have the same alluring pong as a male pig, which is why, traditionally, sows were used to track them down. In true pig-like fashion however, sows not only instinctively uproot, but also scoff truffles. Sows used today are generally muzzled.

Black diamonds are mainly harvested around Carpentras and Vaison-la-Romaine in the Vaucluse. The region's leading wholesale market is held in Richerenches and the precious fungi is canned for consumption year-round in Puymeras (see the Avignon Area chapter for details). Conserved truffles are scorned by true Provençal chefs however who insist on using purely *truffes frais* (fresh truffles) to conjure up a celestial treat.

Provençal Dining

Breakfast *Petit déjeuner* is one of the most delightful (and coolest) times of day in Provence, best spent on a terrace watching the world go by or gazing out across a sea of vineyards and fruit orchards. Breakfast comprises a croissant and piece of crusty baguette (usually with butter and jam), accompanied by a strong black coffee or *café au lait* (coffee with lots of hot milk).

Lunch & Dinner For most Provençal, *déjeuner* (lunch) is the main meal of the day. It starts dot on noon, continues well into the afternoon, and entails eating and drinking a delightfully excessive amount which will leave you vowing never to eat that much again – until tomorrow.

If you turn up at a popular restaurant later than 1 pm, the chances are you will be turned away unless you have a reservation. Most places stop serving at 2.30 pm and open again for *dîner* (dinner) from 7 or 7.30 pm to sometime around 10 pm. There is *nowhere* open to eat between 3 and 7 pm.

Most places have a *plat du jour* (dish of the day) or *formule* (fixed main course plus starter or dessert) at lunchtime as well as the *menus* available in the evening. A *menu* offers better value than ordering à la carte (hand-picking a dish for each course). It usually includes an entrée, plat principal and fromage or dessert, with drinks and coffee costing extra.

The order of courses is:
1 *apéritif* (pre-dinner drink, often with olives or tapenade)
2 *entrée* (first course/starter)
3 *plat principal* (main course)
4 *salade* (simple dressed green salad)
5 *fromage* (cheese)
6 *dessert* (dessert)
7 *fruit* (fruit)
8 *café* (coffee)
9 *digestif* (after-dinner drink)

Chefs of Provence

While Provence's healthy 'n hearty, fruit 'n veg-inspired dishes are not always seen as la crème de la crème of French cuisine, its chefs most certainly are.

Height of Modernity

Alain Ducasse holds several firsts: the world's first (and only) chef since the 1930s to be honoured with six Michelin stars (1998), spread between his gastronomic temples in Monaco and Paris; the youngest chef ever to merit three stars at the age of 33 (1990); and the first chef of a restaurant attached to a hotel to be starred (1990).

With these distinctions, Ducasse – a former apprentice of Roger Vergé – has carved out a new-age definition of what being a chef means. In Provence, France's most modern chef heads Monaco's Le Louis XIV and rural La Bastide de Moustiers in Moustiers Sainte Marie where his 150-variety vegetable garden alone is tended by an army of 10 gardeners. Olive oil reigns supreme in Ducasse's Provençal kitchen.

Cuisine of the Sun

Roger Vergé is the king of Provençal cuisine. His creation of the celebrated 'cuisine du soleil' in the 1970s – in his own words '... an art where Nature's own savours prevailed with utter simplicity ...' – pioneered modern Provençal cooking. A startling use of fresh-from-the-earth ingredients sensually spiced with the sweet to tart tangs of plants and herbs remain his trademark today.

Vergé's 'cuisine of the sun' is served with a flourish at his two Mougins restaurants, Le Moulin de Mougins in a century-old oil mill and the simpler L'Amandier. He has published several recipe books (see the boxed text Books to Read in the Facts About Provence chapter) and has his own sun-inspired cooking school.

Provençal at Heart

Patricia Wells is one of the few foreign cooks considered to have embraced the soul of Provençal cooking. The American author has published seven cookbooks and, away from her farmhouse kitchen in Vaison-la-Romaine, is a restaurant critic for the International Herald Tribune.

Culinary Lexicon

Entrées & Appetisers

anchoïade – anchovy purée laced with garlic and olive oil
assiette Anglaise – plate of cold mixed meats and sausages
assiette de crudités – plate of raw vegetables with dressings
banon – nutty goat cheese wrapped in chestnut leaves
brandade de morue – mix of crushed salt cod, olive oil and garlic
brebis – sheep milk dairy product
fromage de chèvre – goat cheese
pissala – Niçois paste mixed from puréed anchovies.
tapenade – sharp, black olive-based dip
tomme Arlesienne – moulded goat cheese from Arles

Tapenade

*This classic spread combines all the favourite flavors of Provence:
the tang of the home-cured black olives in brine, the saltiness of
the tiny anchovy, the briny flavor of the caper, the vibrant sharp-
ness of garlic, the heady scent of thyme, the unifying quality of a
haunting olive oil.*

Patricia Wells

Makes 1½ cups (32.5 cl) tapenade

10 anchovy fillets
4 tablespoons milk
2 cups (300g) best-quality
French or Greek brine-cured black olives, pitted
1 tablespoon capers, drained
1 teaspoon Dijon mustard
1 plump, fresh clove garlic,
peeled, green germ removed, and minced
1/4 teaspoon fresh thyme, leaves only
Freshly ground black pepper to taste
6 tablespoons extra-virgin olive oil

In a small shallow bowl, combine the anchovies and milk. Set aside
for 15 minutes to rid the anchovies of their salt and to soften and
plump them. Drain and set aside.

In the bowl of a food processor combine the drained anchovies,
olives, capers, mustard, garlic, and thyme. Process to form a thick
paste. With the food processor running, add the oil in a steady
stream until it is thoroughly incorporated into the mixture. Season
with pepper. Taste for seasoning.

Soup

bourride – fish stew; often eaten as a main course
bouillon – broth or stock
croûtons – fried or roasted bread cubes, sprinkled on top of soups
potage – thick soup made with puréed vegetables
soupe au pistou – vegetable soup made with basil and garlic
soupe de poisson – fish soup

Meat, Chicken & Poultry

agneau – lamb
aiguillette – thin slice of duck fillet
bœuf – beef
bœuf haché – minced beef
brochette – kebab
canard – duck
caneton – duckling
cervelle – brains
chapon – capon
charcuterie – cooked or prepared meats
cheval – horse meat
chèvre – goat
chevreau – kid (baby goat)
chevreuil – venison
cuisses de grenouilles – frog legs
entrecôte – rib steak
daube de bœuf à la Provençale – beef stew
épaule d'agneau – shoulder of lamb
escargot – snail
estouffade de bœuf – Carmargais beef stew with tomatoes and olive
faisan – pheasant
faux-filet – sirloin steak
filet – tenderloin
foie – liver
foie gras de canard – duck liver pâté
gibier – game
gigot d'agneau – leg of lamb
jambon – ham
lapin – rabbit
lard – bacon
lardon – pieces of chopped bacon
lièvre – hare
mouton – mutton
pieds de porc – pig trotters
pieds et paquets – sheep tripe; literally 'feet and packets'
pigeonneau – squab (young pigeon)
pintade – guinea fowl
poulet – chicken

rognons – kidneys
sanglier – wild boar
saucisson – large sausage
saucisson d'Arles – sausage made from pork, beef, wine & spice
saucisson fumé – smoked sausage
taureau de Camargue – Camargais beef
tournedos – thick slices of fillet steak
tripes – tripe
veau – veal
viande – meat
volaille – poultry

Fish & Seafood

aïoli Provençale complet – shellfish, vegetables, boiled egg and aïoli
anchois – anchovy
anguille – eel
brème – bream
brochet – pike
cabillaud – fresh cod
calmar – squid
carrelet – plaice
chaudrée – fish stew
colin – hake
coquille saint-jacques – scallop
coquillage – shellfish
crabe – crab
crevette grise – shrimp
crevette rose – prawn
écrevisse – small, freshwater crayfish
fruits de mer – seafood
gambas – king prawns
goujon – gudgeon (small freshwater fish)
hareng – herring
homard – lobster
huître – oyster
langouste – crayfish
langoustine – very small salt-water 'lobster'
lotte – monkfish
loup – sea bass
maquereau – mackerel
merlan – whiting
morue – dried, salted cod
morue pochée – poached cod
moules – mussels
oursin – sea urchin
paella – rice dish with saffron, vegetables and shellfish
palourde – clam

Baked Summer Vegetables with Two Cheeses

Tian de Légumes d'Été aux Deux Fromages

When you cut into this rustic dish, it exudes the aromas of the Provençal countryside. For a complete summer meal, make it and serve it in a southern French tian – a glazed earthenware baking dish. It is flavourful to stand on its own, but is also delicious served with a few sautéed veal scallopini.

Roger Vergé

4 servings

Preparation: 45 minutes
Cooking: 90 minutes
2 large onions
5 tablespoons olive oil
1 large firm eggplant
3 medium zucchini
3 medium tomatoes
1/2 pound mozzarella cheese
2 garlic cloves
1 teaspoon oregano leaves
Salt and freshly ground pepper
3 tablespoons grated Parmesan cheese

Preheat the oven to 400°F. Peel the onions, cut them into thin slices, and cook them in a saucepan with 3 tablespoons of olive oil until they begin to turn lightly golden.

Peel the eggplant and cut into ¼ inch-thick slices. Grease a baking sheet with a little olive oil, sprinkle it with salt, and arrange the eggplant slices in a single layer. Bake for 5 or 10 minutes until the eggplant slices have softened but not browned. Reduce the oven temperature to 325°F.

With a vegetable peeler, remove strips of peel from the zuchinni, leaving alternate stripes of peeled and unpeeled flesh. Cut into rounds 3/16 inch thick.

Wash and dry the tomatoes, remove their stems, and cut into slices 3/16 inch thick.

Cut the mozzarella in half, then into slices of the same thickness as the vegetables. Peel and finely chop the garlic and mix it into the cooked onions; add the oregano leaves. Spread this onion mixture into a 30 sq cm baking dish.

Arrange the eggplant, zucchini, tomatoes, and mozzarella on top of the onions: 1 slice of eggplant, then 1 of zucchini, 1 of tomato, 1 of mozzarella and so forth. Stand the slices on their edges rather than laying them flat. Sprinkle with salt and pepper and with the remaining olive oil.

Bake for about 1 hour. The vegetable juices should have evaporated and the vegetables should have begun to caramelise. Press down the vegetables with a fork, sprinkle with grated Parmesan, and bake for another 15 minutes.

Serve in the baking dish, hot or cold; this dish reheats perfectly well.

poisson – fish
poulpe – octopus
raie – ray
rascasse – spiny scorpion fish
rouget – red mullet
saint pierre – a flat fish used in bouillabaisse
saumon – salmon
seiche – cuttlefish
sole – sole
stockfish (estocaficada in Niçois) – dried salt fish soaked in water for 4-5 days, stewed for two hours with onion, tomato and white wine, then laced with anchovies and black olives.
thon – tuna
truite – trout

Vegetables, Herbs & Spices

ail – garlic
aneth – dill
anis – aniseed
artichaut – artichoke
asperge – asparagus
aubergine – aubergine (eggplant)
avocat – avocado
basilic – basil
barbouillade – stuffed or stewed aubergine
betterave – beetroot
blette de Nice – white beet
cannelle – cinnamon
carotte – carrot
céleri – celery
cèpe – cepe (boletus mushroom)
champignon – mushroom
chou – cabbage
citrouille – pumpkin
concombre – cucumber
cornichon – gherkin (pickle)
courgette – courgette (zucchini)
échalotte – shallot
endive frisée – chicory
épice – spice
épinards – spinach
estragon – tarragon
fenouil – fennel
fève – broad bean
fleur de courgette – courgette flower
genièvre – juniper
gingembre – ginger

haricots – beans
haricots blancs – white beans
haricots rouge – kidney beans
haricots verts – French (string) beans
herbe – herb
laitue – lettuce
légume – vegetable
légumes farcis – stuffed vegetables
lentilles – lentils
maïs – sweet corn
marjolaine – sweet marjoram
menthe – mint
mesclun – Niçois mix of lettuce
navet – turnip
oignon – onion
olive – olive
origan – oregano
oseille – sorrel
panais – parsnip
persil – parsley
petit pois – pea
pissaladière – Niçois onion, anchovy and black olive tart
poireau – leek
poivron – green pepper
pomme de terre – potato
ratatouille – casserole of aubergines, tomatoes, peppers and garlic
riz – rice
riz de Camargue – Camargais rice
romarin – rosemary
salade Niçoise – green salad featuring tuna, egg and anchovy
sarrasin – buckwheat
sarriette – savory
seigle – rye
thym – thyme
tian – vegetable and rice gratin served in a dish called a tian
tomate – tomato
tourta de bléa – Niçois white beetroot and pine kernel pie
truffe – black truffle

Sauces & Accompaniments
aïoli – garlicky sauce to acccompany bouillabaisse
béchamel – basic white sauce
huile d'olive – olive oil
mornay – cheese sauce
moutarde – mustard
pistou – pesto (pounded mix of basil, hard cheese, olive oil and garlic)
Provençale – tomato, garlic, herb and olive oil dressing or sauce

Vegetables of Provence with Black Truffles

Légumes des Jardins de Provence mijotés à la truffe noire écrasée, un filet d'huile d'olive de Ligurie, aceto balsamico et gros sel gris

I cannot make the ingredients which play a primary role in my dishes. I can only exalt them.

Alain Ducasse

4 servings

16 small sweet carrots
2 fennel bulbs
8 baby spring onions
8 small leeks
8 Provençal artichokes
30g finely chopped truffles
5 dl olive oil
100g butter
White pepper, table salt and coarse salt
16 turnip pieces
8 red radishes
8 courgette flowers
8 little gem (*sucrine*) lettuce leaves
Poultry stock (*bouillon*)
Thickened poultry stock (*fond blanc*)

Trim the carrots, radishes, turnips and fennel bulbs.

Cook all the vegetable individually in olive oil and butter in frying pans. Heat them together with bouillon and fond blanc to glaze. Trim the artichokes and cook them separately in fond blanc seasoned with a splash of lemon.

Wash the other vegetables. Cook them separately in well-salted, very hot water. Once cooked, remove and chill the pan in ice to stop the cooking.

Once all the vegetables are cooked, divide them into two large frying pans. Add a little fond blanc and olive oil, stir in the crushed black truffles, season with table salt and pepper to taste and leave to simmer. When hot, coat lightly in butter and add a little aceto balsamico (*aged vinegar*).

Arrange the vegetables on four plates and spoon over the truffle butter and vinegar on top to coat. Sprinkle with coarse grey salt.

rouille – aïoli based sauce spiced with chilli pepper; served with bourride
tartare – mayonnaise with herbs
vinaigrette – salad dressing made with oil, vinegar, mustard and garlic

Aïoli

This marvellous sauce made of garlic, olive oil, and eggs evokes the sunshine. It lends its name to the famous Provençal dish of poached vegetables and fish, but it has many other uses as well, such as thickening the fish soup, bourride. If you stir some into a cream sauce at the last minute, it will add smoothness and a vivid perfume. I recommend it with any raw, poached or steamed vegetable, and also with snails, braised fennel, baked potatoes, or hard-boiled eggs.

If your breath smells too aggressively of garlic afterwards, crunch a few coffee beans or parsley stems – or better still, share the aïoli with your friends.

Roger Vergé

4 servings

Preparation: 25 minutes
1/2 medium potato
2 garlic cloves
2 egg yolks
Salt and freshly ground pepper
1 cup olive oil

Boil the half potato, unpeeled, starting it in cold, salted water. When it is tender, drain it and peel it, then mash it with a fork on a plate.

Peel the garlic and crush in a mortar. Add the egg yolks, mashed potato, and salt and pepper to taste. Work this mixture with the pestle until smooth. Gradually add the oil in a slow stream, mixing thoroughly with the pestle.

If you are not serving your aïoli immediately, keep it at room temperature, not in the refrigerator, lest the cold will congeal the oil and break the sauce. If this happens accidentally, put a tablespoon of hot water into a bowl and vigorously whisk in the aïoli little by little. Plenty of elbow grease will restore your sauce.

Fruit & Nuts

abricot – apricot
agrumes – citrus fruits
amande – almond
ananas – pineapple
banane – banana
blonde de Nice – variety of orange
cassis – blackcurrant
cerise – cherry

Roger Vergé, king of Provençal cuisine

Baked summer vegetables with two cheeses

Cured meats hanging in a charcuterie

Fresh fish at the market

Alain Ducasse, France's most modern chef

Vegetables of Provence with black truffles

FOOD HIGHLIGHTS & WINE REGIONS

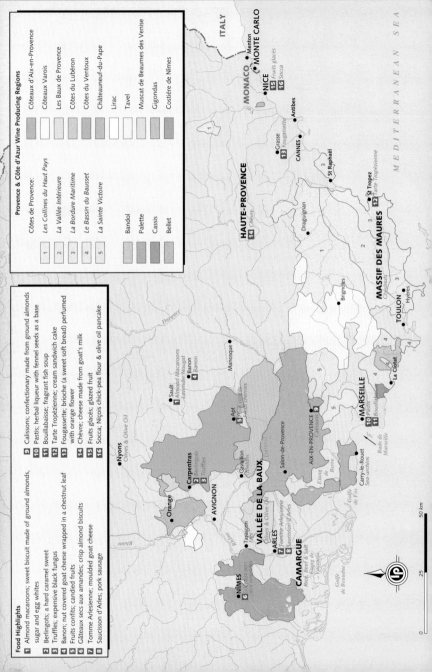

Food Highlights

1. Almond macaroons; sweet biscuit made of of ground almonds, sugar and egg whites
2. Berlingots; a hard caramel sweet
3. Truffles; expensive black fungus
4. Banon; nut covered goat cheese wrapped in a chestnut leaf
5. Fruits confits; candied fruits
6. Gâteaux secs aux amandes; crisp almond biscuits
7. Tomme Arlesienne; moulded goat cheese
8. Saucisson d'Arles; pork sausage
9. Calissons; confectionery made from ground almonds
10. Pastis; herbal liqueur with fennel seeds as a base
11. Bouillabaisse; fragrant fish soup
12. Tarte Tropézienne; cream sandwich cake
13. Fougassette; brioche (a sweet soft bread) perfumed with orange flower
14. Chèvre; cheese made from goat's milk
15. Fruits glacés; glazed fruit
16. Socca; Niçois chick-pea flour & olive oil pancake

Provence & Côte d'Azur Wine Producing Regions

Côtes de Provence:
1. Les Collines du Haut Pays
2. La Vallée Intérieure
3. La Bordure Maritime
4. Le Bassin du Bausset
5. La Sainte Victoire

- Bandol
- Palette
- Cassis
- Bellet

- Côteaux d'Aix-en-Provence
- Côteaux Varois
- Les Baux de Provence
- Côtes du Lubéron
- Côtes du Ventoux
- Châteauneuf-du-Pape
- Lirac
- Tavel
- Muscat de Beaumes des Venise
- Gigondas
- Costière de Nîmes

citron – lemon
datte – date
figue – fig
fraise – strawberry
framboise – raspberry
fruits confits – candied fruits
fruits glazée – glazed fruits
grenade – pomegranate
groseille – red currant or gooseberry
mangu – mango
marron – chestnut
melon – melon
melon canteloup – type of Cavaillon melon
mirabelle – type of plum
myrtille – bilberry (blueberry)
noisette – hazelnut
noix de cajou – cashew
pamplemousse – grapefruit
pastèque – watermelon
pêche – peach
pignon – pine kernel
pistache – pistachio
poire – pear
pomme – apple
prune – plum
pruneau – prune
raisin – grape

Desserts & Sweets

berlingots – hard caramel originating in Carpentras
calisson – Aixois almond sweet
crème caramel – caramel custard
crêpe – thin pancake
crêpes suzettes – orange-flavoured crêpes flambéed in liqueur
bergamotes – orange-flavoured confectionary
dragée – sugared almond
éclair – pastry filled with cream
flan – egg-custard dessert
gâteaux secs aux amandes – crisp almond biscuits
galette – wholemeal or buckwheat pancake; also a type of biscuit
gâteau – cake
gelée – jelly
glace – ice cream
île flottante – egg white cooked, floating on a creamy sauce: literally 'floating island'
macarons – macaroons (sweet biscuit made of ground almonds, sugar and egg whites)

Melon & Peach Zuppetta with Provençal Honey

Zuppetta de Melon au Miel de ma Provence

In Italian, zupetta means 'small soup'. Here we are reminded of the kinship between southern French and Italian cuisine, both of which reap the benefits of wonderful orchards. In the spring months, do what I do: garnish your zupetta with wild strawberries. If you cannot find lavender honey from Provence, you will enjoy rosemary honey or wildflower honey.

Roger Vergé

4 servings

Preparation: 25 minutes
2 ripe cantaloup melons
3 ripe peaches
1 vanilla bean
Juice of 1 lemon
2 tablespoons lavender honey
A few sprigs of mint

Halve the melons and remove their seeds. Using a melon ball spoon, scoop out most of the flesh into little balls. Set aside.

With a big spoon, scrape out the rest of the melon flesh and put it in a blender or food processor. Peel and pit the peaches. Slice two of them into wedges. Cut the third into large chunks and add to the melon. With a small knife, slice the vanilla bean lengthways. Scrape out the small seeds and add them to the melon and peach mixture. Purée.

In a small saucepan, heat the honey over a low flame just enough to liquefy it. Add it to the fruit purée. Stir in the lemon juice.

Divide the soup evenly among four shallow bowls. In each bowl, arrange the melon balls in the centre and the peach wedges around the outside. Garnish with a few sprigs of mint. Serve immediately.

sablé – shortbread biscuit
tarte – tart (pie)
tarte aux pommes – apple tart
tarte Tropézienne – cream sandwich cake from Saint Tropez
yaourt – yoghurt

Bread & Butter Basics

beurre – butter
brioche – sweet soft bread
chichi freggi – sugar-coated donuts from around Marseille
chocolat – chocolate
confiture – jam
crème fraîche – unsweetened cream
farine – flour
fougassette – brioche perfumed with orange flower
lait – milk
miel – honey
œufs – eggs
pan bagnat – Niçois bread soaked in olive oil and filled with anchovy, olives, green pepper
pain aux noix – walnut bread
pain aux olives – olive bread
pain aux raisins – raisin bread
panisses – chickpea flour cakes from around Marseille
poivre – pepper
sel – salt
socca – Niçois chick-pea flour & olive oil pancake
sucre – sugar
vinaigre – vinegar

WINE

Provençal wines are by no means the most sought after in France but, as with all good wines, their making and tasting is an art and a tradition which bears their own unique and tasty trademark. A remarkable variety of different AOC (appellation d'origine contrôlée) wines are produced in Provence but each is stamped by one common trait – an exceptionally cold mistral wind and an equally exceptional, hot ripening sun.

Regions

Côtes de Provence vineyards sprawl across 18,000 hectares stretching from Nice to Aix-en-Provence. The *terroir* ranges from the sandy coastal soils around Saint Tropez to the chalky soils of the subalpine slopes around Les Arcs, cooler due to mountains farther north. Its rich diversity is further marked by its 13 different *cépages* (grape varieties). Grenache, syrah (shiraz) and cabernet are the predominant red varieties; rolle, semillon and clairette are the whites.

The appellation, awarded in 1977, is the largest in Provence with an annual production of 100 million bottles: 75% are rosé wines, 20% red and a token 5% white wines. Côte de Provence rosé, Provence's quintessential summer aperitif, is always drunk young and is served at a crisp coldness of 8 to 10°C. Its luminous *robe* (colour) and delicate fruity taste is renowned for complimenting Provençal cuisine. Reds drunk young should be ideally served at 14 to 16°C, while older red *vins de garde*, the traditional accompaniment to game, sauced meats and cheese, are best drunk at 16 to 18°C. Côte de Provence whites, a golden friend to fish, have to be chilled to 8°C.

Six pocket-sized appellations are dotted in the Côtes de Provence wine growing area: Bandol, Cassis, Coteaux Varois, Coteaux d'Aix-en-Provence, Bellet and Palette. Of these, Bandol is the most respected appellation, best known for its deep flavoured reds produced from the dark-berried mourvèdre grape which needs oodles of sun to ripen, hence its rarity. The appellation demands that grapes be harvested by hand; watch out for reds from the Domaine Tempier vineyard in Le Plan du Castellet. In neighbouring Cassis, it is crisp whites (accounting for 75% of its production) that are drunk with great gusto.

Inland from Bandol is 1500 hectares of limestone terroir around Brignoles, mother of the Coteaux Varois appellation named after the Var department it sits in. Coteaux Varois dates from 1993 and is characterised by the vibrant mix of grapes (including mourvèdre) it uses in its reds and rosés.

Wine lovers who prefer a drier rosé should try Coteaux d'Aix-en-Provence. Vines were first planted in the Bellet area in 4 BC; wine yielded from its 45 hectares is almost impossible to find outside Nice. Palette, east of Aix-en-Provence is only 20 hectares in size, dates from 1948 and produces some well-structured reds from its appropriately old vines. Four out of every five bottles are Château Simone.

The centre of Provence is carpeted with vineyards of the Côtes de Ventoux appellation (6900 hectares established in 1973) and Côtes du Lubéron (3500 hectares dating from 1988).

Côtes du Rhône The southern vineyards of the highly respected Côtes du Rhône appellation dating from 1937 are synonymous with excellent red wine today. Châteauneuf-du-Pape, a legacy bequeathed on lucky Provence by the wealthy Avignon popes, is without a doubt the most sought after and prized southern Rhône vintage. Its strong, well-structured reds are considered masters in their field while the

Right: Tending Côtes de Provence vines.

sweeter reds that have sprung up in recent years afford a lighter alternative in the summer heat. White wine, traditionally only made by the *vignerons* (wine growers) for their private use, now accounts for 7% of total annual production. Both whites and reds can be drunk young (two to three years) or old (seven years or more). After five years a Châteauneuf-du-Pape white develops 'a rare aroma of honey, nuts and toast'. Regardless of age, whites should be served at 12°C; reds at 16 to 18°C.

Châteauneuf-du-Pape has a relatively high alcohol content of at least 12.5%. It was the first wine in France to be granted its own AOC in 1929, one rule being that grapes have to be harvested by hand. Within the 3200 hectare appellation area, there are five different soil types, 13 grape varieties (grenache being the dominant variety at 80 or 90%) and 320 producers, each using a different method. Exceptional Châteauneuf-du-Pape vintages are 1988-90, 1995 and 1997.

Some vignerons claim it is the *galets* (large smooth, yellowish stones which are very photogenic) covering their vineyards that distinguish Châteauneuf-du-Pape from other vineyards. Yet there is not a stone in sight on the sandy vineyards at Château Rayas, known for its incredibly strong, typically tannic, forceful reds which are sold to US buyers three years before production. A bottle of 1989 Château Rayas easily fetches 2000FF.

Wine Lexicon

appellation d'origine contrôlée (AOC) – wines which have met stringent government regulations governing where, how and under what conditions they are grown, fermented and bottled

cuvée – a limited vintage

dégustation – the fine art of tasting wine

domaine – the wine producing estate of a vigneron

grand cru – wine of recognised superior quality; literally 'great growth'

millésime – an exceptional wine produced in a year of optimum climatic conditions

négociant – a wine merchant

producteur – a wine producer or grower, also known as a **vigneron**

robe – a wine's colour

vendange – grape harvest

vin délimité de qualité supérieure (VDQS) – the second rank of quality control after AOC

vin de garde – a wine best drunk after several years in storage

vin de pays – literally 'country wine'

vintage – the year or growing season in which a wine was produced

continued from page 82
other yummy cakes and pastries. Margarine-based croissants can be identified by their almost touching tips; buttery ones have their tips facing outwards.

Purchase cheese in the *fromagerie*, and ask how to best preserve the cheeses you buy, which wines are best served with them etc. If you don't know a cheese type, ask to *goûter* (taste) it. Prewrapped cheese sold in supermarkets is unripe and utterly tasteless by comparison. Shop for slices of cold meats, seafood salads, tapenade, sweet peppers marinated in olive oil at a charcuterie – an equally colourful experience. The catch of the day is sold at a *poissonnerie* (fishmongers), general meat from a *boucherie* (butcher) and poultry from a *marchand de volaille* (poultry seller).

Any titbits you still need are probably sold at the local *épicerie* (literally 'spice shop' but actually a grocery store) or *alimentation générale*. Backpackers wanting to stock up on shedloads of beer, bottled water and the like, will – of course – find it cheaper to shop at a supermarket (Casino, Monoprix etc) in town or at one of the giant hypermarchés (Leclerc, Intermarché etc) on the outskirts of most Provençal towns.

Markets Every village, town and city in Provence has a weekly or daily market which sprawls across the central square and a nearby patchwork of streets. Farmers flock in to town from the outlying farms and villages to sell their fresh produce and chat with friends. No bargaining is allowed. Weighing is done with hand scales – or not at all.

The staple ingredients are fresh fruit and vegetables, *aïl* (garlic), olives, locally milled olive oil (see Oil Mills later), herbs and spices. Garlic is always sold in a bunch or woven plait. A wealth of green and black olives, marinated in every imaginable concoction, are displayed in plastic tubs or buckets. Herbs are dried, mixed, and displayed in stubby coarse sacks: the classic cocktail is *herbes de Provence*, a mix of *basilic* (basil), *romarin* (rosemary), *thym*

(thyme), *origan* (oregano), *sarriette* (savory) and *marjolaine* (marjoram). If you are in the Vaucluse (between November and March) you might also come across *truffes* (truffles) or, if in the Massif des Maures, *marrons* (chestnuts).

Everything from bread, cheese, charcuterie, *miel* (honey), marmalade and *confiture* (homemade jam) to enticing non-edibles (art and crafts, wicker baskets, clothing etc) are sold in most markets too.

Oil Mills The best place to buy Provence's most cherished nectar is from its source – the *moulin* (mill). Many, such as the one in Maussane-les-Alpilles, near Fontvieille, date from the 17th century. Moulins are not museums however: travellers wanting to buy are warmly welcomed by the region's busy mill owners; voyeurs are not.

Huile d'olive (olive oil) is sold by the litre, either in pretty glass bottles or in larger, plastic containers (cheaper). Expect to pay between 60 and 100FF a litre. *Dégustation* (tasting) is an integral part of selecting the right oil for your needs. Most mill owners will pour a tiny drop of the oil onto a spoon for you to taste; the taste is unique and incomparable to bottled oil sold in shops back home.

Moulins or *coopératives oléicoles* (olive oil cooperatives) are usually open on weekdays only between 9 am and noon and then from around 2 to 5 or 6 pm. The best time to visit is after the olive harvest, from January through to Easter. Depending on the year's crop, mills can sell out of the year's production as soon as August. Some moulins are listed in the regional chapters; most tourist offices stock comprehensive lists of mills in their area.

DRINKS

A drink in Provence invariably means a drink of the alcoholic variety – and indulging in an aperitif on a shaded terrace is among the region's great sensual delights. Pastis (see boxed text The Milk of Provence) is the quintessential Provençal drink, closely followed by a crisp, cold Côtes de Provence rosé. Both are wonderfully refreshing on hot and sunny days. Beaumes-de-Venise, a sweet muscat wine, is a popular aperitif in northern Vaucluse.

To ensure that appropriately 'plump and contented' feeling following a deliciously long and lazy meal, a digestif such as a *marc* or *eau de vie* (literally 'water of life') can be taken. Marc is a fiery spirit (similar to Italian *grappa*), distilled from grape skins and pulp left over from the winemaking process. Eaux de vie is the generic name for brandies distilled from the region's many fruits.

Ending a meal with a sweeter liqueur is considered more 'womanly'. Try Reverend Father Gaucher's Elixir, a yellow chartreuse from Tarascon elaborately blended from 30 different aromatic herbs.

Beer is not a Provençal drink and is priced accordingly.

Wine

Provence's wine-growing tradition dates back 2600 years. Its finest (and most renowned) vintage is Châteauneuf-du-Pape, a full-bodied red wine grown 10km south of Orange, which has an alcohol content of up to 15%. This is just one of the many diverse wines known under the name Côtes du Rhône, an appellation grown 200km along the Rhône River from Vienne to Avignon. The Tavel rosé is another popular Rhône valley *grand cru* (literally, 'great growth') in Provence. The vineyards around the Dentelles de Montmirail, some 15km east of Orange, produce notable red *(rouge)* and rosé Gigondas, and the sweet Muscat wine, Beaumes-de-Venise.

The area from Aix-en-Provence eastwards to the Var River valley produces red, rosé and white *(blanc)* Côtes de Provence, the sixth largest appellation in France. Rosé accounts

The Milk of Provence

When in Provence, do as the Provençaux do: drink pastis. The aniseed-flavoured, alcoholic drink is a classic aperitif in the region, although it can be drunk at any time of day.

Amber coloured in the bottle, it turns a milky white when mixed with water. Bars and cafés serve it straight, allowing you to decide how much water to add (roughly five parts water to one part pastis). It's best drunk in the sun and on the rocks.

A dash of *sirop de menthe* (mint cordial) transforms a regular pastis into a *perroquet* (literally 'a parrot'). A *tomate* (tomato) is tarted up with one part grenadine, while the sweet Mauresque is dressed with *orgeat*, a smooth orange and almond syrup.

Pastis was invented in 1932 in Marseille by Paul Ricard (1909-97). The earliest aniseed liqueur to hit the market was absinthe, a dangerous and potent liqueur distilled with wormwood oil which, from the early 1800s, was manufactured in France by Henri-Louis Pernod. The drink – which boasted an astonishing 72% alcohol content – was banned in 1915, paving the way for Ricard's 45% alc/vol pastis and other harmless (except for the alcohol) aniseed and liquorice liqueurs such as the modern day Pernod.

The leading pastis brands today are Pastis 51 (Pastis de Marseille) and Ricard, both owned by the Ricard empire (in addition to Pernod which was taken over by Ricard in 1974). In 1996, Ricard sales of 90 million bottles a year stood third on the world market after Bacardi rum and Smirnoff vodka. Berger, Casanis, Duval and Janot are among other pastis brands.

Despite the extraordinary wealth Paul Ricard amassed following his pastis success, the Marseillais industrialist's feet remained firmly on the ground. He invested in islands and oceanographic institutes, Formula One racetracks and bull-fighting rings, but never in grandiose palaces or limousines for his own use. The French press dubbed him *Le Citizen Kane Provençal*.

for 75% of overall production (5% white, 20% red). Among the better known of the eight other appellations grown in Provence are Cassis and Bandol, both found on the coast south-east of Marseille. The Cassis vineyards at the foot of France's highest cliff produce mainly white wines, best drunk young. Bandol is known for its full-bodied red wines. Coteaux d'Aix-en-Provence, Les-Baux-de-Provence and Palette are all red, full-flavoured *vins de garde*.

In Provence, wine is drunk with almost every meal – so much so that in many village bistros and more rustic restaurants, a bottle of the house wine greets you at your table when you sit down, the assumption being you will most certainly drink it. House wine – always drinkable but never startling – is the cheapest. It's served in a *carafe* (glass jug), *pichet* (a pottery jug) or *bouteille* (bottle).

Crisp, Côtes de Provence rosé is a classical summer drink, drunk in abundance from May to September regardless of the time of day. It is best served fridge cold on an outside terrace. Despite an unconvincing marketing campaign to the contrary, Côtes de Provence rosé remains a seasonal wine – unlike its red and white counterparts which are drunk year round.

Wine Tasting & Buying Wines of the region can be bought direct from the *domaine* (estate) of the *producteur* (wine producer) or *vigneron* (grower) – at a lower price than in shops. Most places offer *dégustation* (tasting) which allows you to sample two or three of their vintages, with no obligation to buy. Purchasing one or two bottles or one to 20 boxes (six or 12 bottles per box) is equally acceptable. A complete list of Côtes de Provence' *caves* (wine cellars) open to travellers is in the *Tourisme Vigneron en Côtes de Provence* brochure published by the Maisons des Vins in Les Arcs (see the Saint Tropez to Toulon chapter).

Tasting and buying the more sought-after wines of Châteauneuf-du-Pape, where the annual production of many estates is bought out years in advance, is more difficult. Few

producers have bottles to sell and those that do require that you make an appointment in advance (and buy a substantial amount of their wine). The Châteauneuf-du-Pape tourist office has a list of chateaux open to amateur wine tasters and buyers.

Nonalcoholic Drinks
Tap water in the hot south is safe to drink. Don't drink water spouting from fountains which tout a sign reading *eau non potable* (non-drinking water). In restaurants, it is perfectly acceptable to order *une carafe d'eau* (carafe of tap water) instead of a pricier soft drink, *eau de source* – *plate* or *gazeuse* (mineral water – flat or carbonated) or wine.

Soft drinks are generally 15-25FF a glass (wine can be cheaper). You don't get *des glaçons* (ice cubes) unless you ask.

The dazzling, pea-green drink you see people sipping through straws in cafés is *sirop de menthe* (mint syrup) diluted with water. Other cordials include *cassis* (blackberry), *grenadine* (pomegranate) and *citron* (lemon). The most expensive soft drink is a *citron* or *orange pressé* – freshly squeezed lemon or orange mixed with iced water and sugar.

Coffee costs about 7-10FF a cup. Unless you specify otherwise, you get a small, strong, black espresso. Those requiring a bigger caffeine fix should ask for *un grand café* (a double espresso). Milky versions include *un café crème* (espresso with steamed milk or cream) and *un café au lait* (hot milk with a dash of coffee). Coffee is never served with cold milk.

Thé (tea) and *chocolat chaud* (hot chocolate) are widely available. Most salons de thé serve a choice of *infusions* (herbal teas).

ENTERTAINMENT
Local tourist offices are the best source of information to find out what's on where. In addition, there is a host of regional entertainment journals and newspapers – most are free – which contain comprehensive cinema, theatre and festival listings.

FNAC (☎ 08 36 68 93 39, www.fnac.fr) is the leading hub for tickets and reservations for everything from theatre, opera and exhibitions to rock concerts, football matches and festivals. Most stores have a *billetterie* (ticket desk) where an upcoming calendar of events is posted, advance bookings made and tickets sold. There is an FNAC in Avignon, Nice and Marseille. The latter also has a Virgin Megastore with an entertainments desk.

Cinema
You can see films in their original language (with French sub titles) in selected cinemas in Marseille, Nice and Aix-en-Provence. Look for the letters VO *(version originale)* on cinema billboards. Some spots along the coast (such as Villefranche-sur-Mer and Monaco) have outside screenings in summer which are a joy to attend, regardless of language.

Discos & Clubs
Discos *(discothèque* or *boîte* in French) and clubs are few and far between once you escape the coast and penetrate rural Provence. Anything goes on the Côte d'Azur however, which is engulfed in party madness from mid-June until mid-September. Nice's party season sees discos on the beach and wild dancing on tables in many of its Anglophone music bars. Music (live or recorded) ranges from jazz and raï to Latino and techno. The crowd can be gay, lesbian, straight or mixed.

Tenue correcte exigée means 'appropriate dress required'. The action doesn't hot up in most places until at least midnight. Bouncers are invariably big and paid to indulge their megalomaniacal animalistic tendencies by keeping out 'undesirables', which, depending on the place, ranges from unaccompanied men who aren't dressed right to members of certain minority groups.

Music & Theatre
Provence is a land of music and theatre, playing host to some of the country's major festivals (see the Feasts & Festivals section) – including the celebrated Avignon Theatre Festival and concurrent Festival Off

(fringe). The Fête de la Musique brings live music to every corner of the region on 21 June.

SPECTATOR SPORTS
Bullfighting
Many consider it downright cruelty. Others see it as a sport, and never more so than in south-western Provence where bullfighting is regarded as a passionate celebration of Provençal tradition.

During a *mise à mort* bullfight *(corrida)*, a bull bred to be aggressive is killed in a colourful and bloody ceremony involving picadors, toreadors, matadors and horses. But not all bullfights end with a dead bull. In a *course Camarguaise* (Camargue-style bullfight), white-clad *razeteurs* try to remove ribbons tied to the bull's horns with hooks held between their fingers.

The season generally runs from Easter to September. Camarguaises and corridas can be seen in Aigues-Mortes (mid-October), Arles (last Sunday of April and 1 May, Easter weekend), Nîmes (February, June and mid-September), Pernes-les-Fontaines and Saintes-Maries-de-la-Mer. Fights at Arles and Nîmes sport magnificent settings – Roman amphitheatres. Tickets have to be reserved months in advance for most events (see the relevant city listings for details).

Cycling
The three-week Tour de France, which hits the road each year in July, rarely visits Provence and the Côte d'Azur (intense heat and horrendous traffic are big deterrents). But the early season, Paris-Nice stage – dubbed the 'race to the sun' and considered the official start to the professional cycling season – always does, as does the four-day Mediterranean Tour at the beginning of February.

Out of the 11 times (since 1951) the Tour de France has crossed Provence, it is 1967 that is remembered most by cycling fans: British cyclist Tommy Simpson suffered a fatal heart attack – triggered by the heat and a cocktail of amphetamines – on the climb up Mont Ventoux during the 211km Marseille-Carpentras stage. The 1965 world cycling champion, who had won the Paris-Nice stage that same year, was considered one of the greats of the sport at the time.

Numerous cyclists follow in Simpson's tracks up Ventoux's barren slopes today; they almost all stop at the roadside monument put up in his memory. A road which is immaculately tarmacked and graffitied with large-lettered slogans starting '*allez*' – such as the one up Ventoux – is a sure sign that a cycling race has recently passed by.

Football

Marseille has long been considered the heart of French football and never more so since France's victory in the 1998 World Cup which saw Marseille-born Zinedine Zidane score two of the side's three winning goals against reigning champions, Brazil. Overnight, *on est champions* (we are the champions) became the catch-phrase of the decade. Zidane – a mid-fielder of North African origin – was voted international footballer of 1998. His web site is www.zidane.net.

Politically, the strong multi-ethnic mix of the French side was hailed as a victory over the National Front's racist agenda and was a source of extreme pride to Marseille's large immigrant community. The early days of France 98 were marred by serious outbreaks of hooligan violence in Marseille when visiting English and local Tunisian supporters clashed.

At club level, in 1991 Marseille (Olympique de Marseille; OM) became the first French team to win the European Champions League. The team was national champion for five consecutive years between 1989 and 1992. Despite victory in 1993, the title was withdrawn following match-rigging allegations against OM chairman Bernard Tapie, later convicted for fraud. The club has won no major titles since. This is, in part, due to the 1995 Bosman decision to allow European clubs to field as many European players as they wish – resulting in a great exodus of French players to better-paid clubs abroad (including 'Zizou' Zidane who started off

with Cannes but plays for Juventus, Italy, today).

The region's other strong club is AS Monaco whose goalkeeper, Fabian Barthez, also stole the heart of a nation with his goal-saving heroics during France 98. Monaco won the French Cup in 1991 and the League championship in 1997.

Stadiums The home ground of Olympique de Marseille (OM; www.olympiquedemars eille.com) is Marseille's Stade Vélodrome (☎ 04 91 76 56 09 or 04 91 26 16 15, metro Rond Point du Prado), 3 blvd Michelet (8e). The stadium dates from 1937 and has a 60,000 seating capacity. Tickets (110-210FF) for matches are sold at the Boutique Officielles OM (☎ 04 91 81 54 54), 203 rue Paradis (6e), FNAC and the Virgin Megastore.

Motor Racing

The annual Monaco Grand Prix is the most glamorous race on the Formula 1 calender. It is also the only race which sees F1 mean machines tear round regular town streets rather than a track solely for motor sports. The Grand Prix takes place in May and attracts some 150,000 spectators. For details on the 78-lap circuit, ticket availability and prices, see the Monaco chapter.

Well known among motorcycle enthusiasts is the Circuit du Castellet Paul Ricard near Le Castellet. The 5.8km circuit hosts the Grand Prix de France Moto in July and the Bol d'Or in mid-September. Tickets to the Bol d'Or cost 290FF (under 12s free) and can be reserved through Réseau France Billet (☎ 01 42 31 31 31) or its agents (FNAC, Carrefour etc). See the Saint Tropez to Toulon chapter for more details.

Nautical Jousting

Joutes nautiques or *joutes Provençales* (Provençal jousting) is typical only to southern France. Spurred on by bands and a captive audience, the participants (usually male and traditionally dressed in white) try to knock each other into the water from rival boats with 2.60m-long lances. The jouster always stands balanced at the tip of a *tintaine*, a wooden gangplank protruding from the wooden boat where the rest of his team members spur him on.

The sport is particularly strong in Saint Raphaël where the joutes Provençales French championships were held in 1998. Contact the Société des Joutes Raphaëloises (☎ 06 09 77 89 67) BP 145, 83700 Saint Raphaël, for details. In the Vaucluse, Joutes Nautiques set the rivers of L'Isle-sur-la-Sorgue ablaze with colour on 14 and 26 July.

Pétanque

Pétanque (Provençal boules) is Provence's national pastime. Despite the game's humble appearance – a bunch of village men in work clothes throwing dusty balls on a gravel pitch scratched out wherever there's shade – it is a serious sport.

The Pétanque Open World Championships, won 19 times by France, including the 1998 championship in Spain, have been held annually since 1959. Provence hosted the competition in 1961 (Cannes), 1971 (Nice), 1976 and 1990 (Monaco). There have been separate pétanque world championships for women and youngsters since 1987.

The cool of late afternoon is the favoured hour for a casual game of pétanque, sometimes with a glass of pastis near to hand. In smaller towns and villages, you can almost always find a game being played, no matter what time of day. Spectators are welcomed.

To the untrained eye, pétanque is simply throwing your boules (polished steel balls) as close as possible to the *cochonnet* (jack), the small coloured ball thrown at the start of the match. But the painful look of concentration spilling across whoever's turn it is to aim makes you realise that there's more to pétanque than meets the eye (see the boxed text Boules and Bowled Out).

Pétanque was invented in La Ciotat, near Marseille in 1910, when arthritis-crippled Jules Le Noir could no longer take the running strides prior to aiming which was demanded by the *longue* boule game. The local champion opted to stand with his feet firmly on the ground instead – a style which became known as *pieds tanques* (Provençal for 'tied feet'). Pétanque is a slurred version of pieds tanques. Jeu Provençal – which uses heavier balls and requires a one-legged hop before throwing – is still played in parts of Provence.

SHOPPING

Those intent on sampling a different culinary item every day should follow the Food Highlights & Wine Regions map in the special Food & Wine section.

Before buying up an entire market stall as gifts for back home, consider the use-by date. Many edible products typical to Provence – such as *calissons* from Aix-en-Provence, *marrons au sirop* (chestnuts in syrup) from the Massif des Maures or rice from the Camargue – are easy to transport home. But many glass-jar products sold at markets are homemade and contain few (or no) preservatives. Lavender marmalade from Carpentras market for example lasts one month after being opened, while onion chutney from the Lubéron – mind-blowingly delicious as it is – will not survive outside a fridge. The same, sadly, goes for local breads, most cheeses and fresh truffles. But not wine!

Less tasty treats worth a shopping spree include perfumes from Grasse; leather sandals from Saint Tropez; colourful wicker baskets and carnations from Antibes; glassware from Biot; Picasso-inspired ceramics from Vallauris; or faïence from Moustiers-Sainte-Marie; pipes and carpets from Cogolin; soap and *santons* from Marseille or Salon-de-Provence; *courgourdons* (traditional ornaments made from dyed and hollowed marrows/squash) from Nice; lavender oil from the Lubéron; colourful Provençal fabrics from practically anywhere in Provence; antiques from L'Isle-sur-la-Sorgue; gallery art from Saint Paul de Vence or the latest haute couture designs from Monaco.

Boules & Bowled Out

Pétanque, Provençal *boules*, has a definitive set of rules that, despite the seemingly informal nature of the game, must be followed.

Two to six people, comprising two teams, can play. Each player has a triple set (twin set if there's six players) of solid metal boules. Each boule weighs 650-800g and must be stamped with the hallmark of a licensed boule maker. Personal initials, a name or family coat of arms can be crafted on to made-to-measure boules. The earliest boules, scrapped in 1930, comprised a wooden ball studded with hundreds of hammered-in steel nails. Antique shops still sell them.

Pétanque revolves around the *cochonnet* (jack), a small wooden ball 25-35mm in diameter. Each team takes it in turn to aim a boule at this marker, the idea being to land the boule as close as possible to the sneaky little cochonnet. The team with the closest boule wins the round; points are allocated by totting up how many boules the winner's team has closest to the marker (one point for each boule). The first to notch up 13 wins the match.

The team throwing the cochonnet (initially decided by a coin toss) has to throw it from a circle (30-50cm in diameter) scratched in the gravel. It must be hurled six to 10m away from the circle boundary. When boules are aimed, the player must likewise stand *pieds tanques* (literally 'feet tied') – that is, with both feet implanted firmly in this circle. At the end of a round, a new circle is drawn around the cochonnet, determining the spot where the next round will start.

Underarm throwing is compulsory. Beyond that, players can opt between rolling the boule in a dribble along the ground (known as *pointer*, literally 'to point'), or hurling it high in the air in the hope of it landing smack-bang on top of an opponent's boule, sending it flying out of position. This flamboyant tactic can turn an entire game around in a matter of seconds and is called *tirer* (literally 'to shoot').

Throughout matches, boules are lovingly polished with a soft white cloth. Players unable to stoop to pick up their boules can lift them up with a magnet attached to a piece of string.

A complete set of rules is available from the Fédération Internationale de Pétanque et Jeu Provençal, FIPJP (www.boulepetanque.se). Hot links to the 44 pétanque federations worldwide are available through the British Pétanque Association (www.compulink.co.uk/~atilio/BPA), 12 Ensign Business Centre, Westwood Park, Coventry CV4 8JA.

Getting There & Away

AIR

Air France, the national carrier, plus scores of other airlines link Marseille and Nice – the region's international airports – with most European cities as well as far-flung spots of the globe. While both airports are fiercely marketed as major international transport hubs, there are still many long-haul destinations that require a change of plane in Paris, London or another European capital. Only direct flights are mentioned below.

Airports & Airlines

Nice-Côte d'Azur airport (Aéroport International Nice-Côte d'Azur, www.nice .aeroport.fr) is the region's top airline hub, and France's largest outside Paris. A 1.1 billion FF extension program, to be completed by 2002, will raise the airport's passenger handling capacity to 11 million (16 million by 2015). Despite having direct flights to 86 destinations, Paris-bound flights account for 42% of its traffic. Marseille-Provence airport (Aéroport International Marseille-Provence, www .marseille.aeroport.fr) has an estimated 6 million passengers pass through each year.

Major airlines have an office at both airports. For details on how to travel to/from the town centres, see Getting Around in the relevant chapters.

Domestic routes are also served by smaller airports at Avignon (Aéroport d'Avignon), Nîmes (Aéroport de Nîmes-Arles-Camargue) and Toulon (Aéroport de Toulon-Hyères). Carriers with domestic networks include Air France, Air Liberté (owned by British Airways), AOM, Air Littoral, Corsair (run by the Nouvelles Frontières travel agency) and Corse Méditerranée. The government assigns routes and sets prices to avoid 'excessive competition', though the market is slowly being liberalised.

Buying Tickets

The only way to find the best deal is to shop around. Few discount travel agents are actually given access to a particular batch of discounted tickets. Always check the total fare, stopovers required (or allowed), the journey duration, the period of validity, cancellation penalties and any other restrictions. Better known travel agents where you may pay slightly more for security and peace of mind include: US-based Council Travel (www.counciltravel.com); France-based Nouvelles Frontières (www.newfrontiers .com); STA Travel (www.sta-travel.com); Canadian-based Travel CUTS (www.travel-cuts.com); and Irish-based USIT (www .usit.ie).

It sometimes pays to approach the airline direct, especially if you intend flying from Brussels or a UK airport to Nice. Easy Jet (www.easyjet.com) and Virgin Express (www.virgin-express.com) are among the no-frills, cut price airlines that have taken the market by storm in recent years. Both accept online bookings.

In France, any travel agent can make bookings for domestic flights and supply details on the complicated fare system. Inexpensive flights to destinations farther afield that are offered by charter clearing houses can also be booked through regular travel agents. Nouvelles Frontières (www.nouvelles-frontieres.com), which specialises in long-haul flights and has some cheap routings to Asia through Russia, eastern Europe and the Persian Gulf, has several bureaux in the region, including Nice (☎ 04 93 55 04 04) 4 quai Papacino and (☎ 04 93 88 32 84) 14 ave Verdun; Aix-en-Provence (☎ 04 92 26 47 22) 52 cours Sextius; Avignon (☎ 04 90 82 31 32) 14 rue Carnot and Toulon (☎ 04 94 46 37 02) 503 ave République.

Attractive youth fares are available from various student travel agencies.

Departure Taxes

Airport taxes – imposed by the country you are departing from and the country you are flying to – are added to the price of your airline ticket when you buy it. In mid-1998, the French government tax was 21FF plus 40/45FF for passengers departing from Marseille/Nice airport.

Metropolitan France & Corsica

Air France is the leading carrier on domestic routes in and out of Paris to Provence; AOM and Air Liberté run a handful. From Paris there are numerous (read: 37 to 50 a day) daily flights year round to/from Nice and Marseille – arrivals/departures every half an hour at peak times. Most use Paris Orly airport; a fraction use Roissy/Charles de Gaulle. From Paris there are five daily flights to/from Toulon; four to/from Nîmes; and three to/from Avignon.

To the rest of metropolitan France, there are daily flights from Marseille and Nice to most airports, including Bordeaux, Clermont-Ferrand, Lille, Lyon, Metz-Nancy, Mulhouse, Nantes, Pau, Strasbourg and Toulouse. From Toulon, there are weekly flights to Brest, Clermont-Ferrand and Lille.

Corse Méditerranée flies from Nice and Marseille to Ajaccio, Bastia, Calvi and Figari (four to six daily). There are weekly flights from Toulon to Ajaccio and Bastia too.

Passengers are generally allowed one carry-on bag and 23kg of checked luggage. Excess baggage, including bicycles and skis, costs just 10FF per kilogram.

Fares Fares vary dramatically depending on when you make the reservation and which days you intend staying in your chosen destination. Unless you are eligible for a cheaper youth or student fare, it is cheaper to train it from metropolitan France to Provence and the Côte d'Azur.

Air France (☎ 08 02 80 28 02, www.air-france.com) has four regular fare levels, ranging from full-fare with no restrictions, to reduced fares that require advance booking and have various restrictions. Senior travellers over 60, families, couples who are married or have proof of cohabitation (eg a French government-issued *certificat de concubinage*) are entitled to some discounts. A cheaper youth/student fare (with no restrictions or advance booking requirements) is available to under 25s and student card holders aged 26 or under.

The cheapest Paris-Nice return with Air France is 835FF (you have to reserve the ticket 14 days in advance and stay a weekend). The return fare leaps to 2300FF for those not staying a weekend. The student fare is 648FF return. Equivalent return fares from Paris to Marseille are 744FF (weekend rule), 2104FF (no weekend), 584FF (student).

The cheapest fares with Corse Méditerranée (☎ 08 36 67 95 20) require you to stay at least one night in your chosen destination. The cheapest Nice-Ajaccio fare is 1004FF return (reserve 14 days in advance, stay one night, no refund or change of ticket). It has a single/return youth fare of 347/706FF. Comparable fares from Marseille to Calvi are 743FF (with above restrictions) and 308/777FF (single/return youth fare).

The UK

With the advent of no-frills airlines such as Easy Jet and Virgin Express, airfares between London and Nice have been slashed considerably, while Paris-London tickets can sometimes be picked up for as little as 500FF return (making it cheaper to fly to/from the capital and train it down south).

In mid-1998, Easy Jet (☎ 0800 600 000, www.easyjet.com) was advertising single fares on its no-tickets-issued airline from Luton/Liverpool to Nice for as little as UK£49/39. Virgin Express (☎ 0800 528 528, www.virgin-express.com) meanwhile was offering London-Nice minimum-fare returns for UK£95 (maximum-fare UK£269) and Nice-London returns for 1697/2307FF (min/max). Virgin has seven different fare levels, calculated on the simple premise of how empty/full the plane is at the time of booking. Purchased tickets can't be changed or refunded. From Nice, there is one Virgin flight a day to/from London, via Brussels; Easy Jet operates several.

Air Travel Glossary

Baggage Allowance This will be written on your ticket and usually includes one 20kg item to go in the hold, plus one item of hand luggage.

Bucket Shops These are unbonded travel agencies specialising in discounted airline tickets.

Bumped Just because you have a confirmed seat doesn't mean you're going to get on the plane (see Overbooking).

Cancellation Penalties If you have to cancel or change a discounted ticket, there are often heavy penalties involved; insurance can sometimes be taken out against these penalties. Some airlines impose penalties on regular tickets as well, particularly against 'no-show' passengers.

Check-In Airlines ask you to check in a certain time ahead of the flight departure (usually one to two hours on international flights). If you fail to check in on time and the flight is overbooked, the airline can cancel your booking and give your seat to somebody else.

Confirmation Having a ticket written out with the flight and date you want doesn't mean you have a seat until the agent has checked with the airline that your status is 'OK' or confirmed. Meanwhile you could just be 'on request'.

Courier Fares Businesses often need to send urgent documents or freight securely and quickly. Courier companies hire people to accompany the package through customs and, in return, offer a discount ticket which is sometimes a phenomenal bargain. In effect, what the companies do is ship their freight as your luggage on regular commercial flights. This is a legitimate operation, but there are two shortcomings - the short turnaround time of the ticket (usually not longer than a month) and the limitation on your luggage allowance. You may have to surrender all your allowance and take only carry-on luggage.

Full Fares Airlines traditionally offer 1st class (coded F), business class (coded J) and economy class (coded Y) tickets. These days there are so many promotional and discounted fares available that few passengers pay full economy fare.

ITX An ITX, or 'independent inclusive tour excursion', is often available on tickets to popular holiday destinations. Officially it's a package deal combined with hotel accommodation, but many agents will sell you one of these for the flight only and give you phoney hotel vouchers in the unlikely event that you're challenged at the airport.

Lost Tickets If you lose your airline ticket an airline will usually treat it like a travellers cheque and, after inquiries, issue you with another one. Legally, however, an airline is entitled to treat it like cash and if you lose it then it's gone forever. Take good care of your tickets.

MCO An MCO, or 'miscellaneous charge order', is a voucher that looks like an airline ticket but carries no destination or date. It can be exchanged through any International Association of Travel Agents (IATA) airline for a ticket on a specific flight. It's a useful alternative to an onward ticket in those countries that demand one, and is more flexible than an ordinary ticket if you're unsure of your route.

No-Shows No-shows are passengers who fail to show up for their flight. Full-fare passengers who fail to turn up are sometimes entitled to travel on a later flight. The rest are penalised (see Cancellation Penalties).

On Request This is an unconfirmed booking for a flight.

Air Travel Glossary

Onward Tickets An entry requirement for many countries is that you have a ticket out of the country. If you're unsure of your next move, the easiest solution is to buy the cheapest onward ticket to a neighbouring country or a ticket from a reliable airline which can later be refunded if you do not use it.

Open Jaw Tickets These are return tickets where you fly out to one place but return from another. If available, this can save you backtracking to your arrival point.

Overbooking Airlines hate to fly empty seats and since every flight has some passengers who fail to show up, airlines often book more passengers than they have seats. Usually excess passengers make up for the no-shows, but occasionally somebody gets bumped. Guess who it is most likely to be? The passengers who check in late.

Point-to-Point Tickets These are discount tickets that can be bought on some routes in return for passengers waiving their rights to a stopover.

Promotional Fares These are officially discounted fares, available from travel agencies or direct from the airline.

Reconfirmation At least 72 hours prior to departure time of an onward or return flight, you must contact the airline and 'reconfirm' that you intend to be on the flight. If you don't do this the airline can delete your name from the passenger list and you could lose your seat.

Restrictions Discounted tickets often have various restrictions on them - such as needing to be paid for in advance and incurring a penalty to be altered. Others are restrictions on the minimum and maximum period you must be away, such as a minimum of 14 days or a maximum of one year.

Round-the-World Tickets RTW tickets give you a limited period (usually a year) in which to circumnavigate the globe. You can go anywhere the carrying airlines go, as long as you don't backtrack. The number of stopovers or total number of separate flights is decided before you set off and they usually cost a bit more than a basic return flight.

Stand-by This is a discounted ticket where you only fly if there is a seat free at the last moment. Stand-by fares are usually available only on domestic routes.

Travel Agencies Travel agencies vary widely and you should choose one that suits your needs. Some simply handle tours, while full-services agencies handle everything from tours and tickets to car rental and hotel bookings. If all you want is a ticket at the lowest possible price, then go to an agency specialising in discounted tickets.

Transferred Tickets Airline tickets cannot be transferred from one person to another. Travellers sometimes try to sell the return half of their ticket, but officials can ask you to prove that you are the person named on the ticket. This is less likely to happen on domestic flights, but on an international flight tickets are compared with passports.

Travel Periods Ticket prices vary with the time of year. There is a low (off-peak) season and a high (peak) season, and often a low-shoulder season and a high-shoulder season as well. Usually the fare depends on your outward flight - if you depart in the high season and return in the low season, you pay the high-season fare.

Both Nice and Marseille are served by regular daily British Airways flights to/from London. The cheapest London-Nice returns in mid-1998 were UK£122 (restricted to weekday travel), UK£142 (restricted to weekend travel) and UK£132 (weekend and weekday travel). Fares to Marseille are approximately UK£10-20 more. Air France offers a Nice-London youth/student fare (no restrictions) for 1000FF return. Sadly, this fare does not apply to London-Nice returns.

Europe

There are flights two or three times daily between Nice/Marseille and most other European cities. The cheapest fares are available in early spring and late autumn. Air France's youth fares often cost only marginally more than charters.

Sample return fares (with various restrictions) from Nice include Milan (1000FF) with Air Littoral; Rome (1300FF) with Air Littoral/Alitalia; Geneva, Brussels and Warsaw (2040FF) direct with LOT. Sample return fares from Marseille include Amsterdam (1943FF) and Barcelona (1550FF), both with Regional Airlines (www.regionalairlines.com); Zürich (1830FF with Swissair); Geneva (1570FF with Crossair); and Frankfurt (1746FF) with Air France.

Virgin Express (see The UK section earlier) has a daily flight to Brussels out of Nice airport. A return fare costs a min/maximum of 1110/1750FF. Single fares are 544-865FF.

Between Easter and September only, Crossair flies three times a week between Geneva and the private air strip at the Golfe de Saint Tropez airport in La Môle (see the Saint Tropez to Toulon chapter for details). It also operates a twice-weekly flight to Zürich. Lufthansa has tentative plans to operate a weekly La Môle-Munich flight in 1999.

The USA

The flight options across the North Atlantic, the world's busiest long-haul air corridor, are bewildering. The *New York Times*, *LA Times*, *Chicago Tribune* and *San Francisco Chronicle* all have weekly travel sections with any number of travel agents' ads. Council Travel (☎ 800-226 8624) and STA (☎ 800-777 0112) have offices in major cities.

Delta Airlines flies two or three times weekly direct from New York to Nice. Regular/youth return fares from Nice start at 2495/2281FF. Beyond that, any journey to France's sunny south entails a change of plane in Paris, London or another European transport hub. A New York-Paris round trip typically costs US$338/617 in the low/high season. Airhitch (☎ 212-864 2000, airhitch@ netcom.com, www.airhitch.org) specialises in cheap stand-by fares. In Paris 2000FF return fares are sometimes available, but 2500FF (3400FF in July and August) is more realistic.

Canada

Travel CUTS (☎ 888-835 2887) has offices in major Canadian cities. You might also scan the budget travel agents' ads in the *Toronto Globe & Mail*, the *Toronto Star* and the *Vancouver Province*. For courier flights from Canada contact FB on Board Courier Services (☎ 514-631 7925) in Montreal or in Vancouver (☎ 604-278 1266). A return courier flight to London will cost about C$590 from Vancouver and C$525 from Toronto.

Australia

STA Travel and Flight Centres International are major dealers in cheap airfares. Saturday's travel sections in the *Sydney Morning Herald* and the Melbourne *Age* have many ads offering cheap fares to Europe, but don't be surprised if they happen to be 'sold out' when you call. They're usually low-season fares on obscure airlines with conditions attached.

Airlines like Thai, Malaysian, Qantas and Singapore all have frequent promotional fares so it pays to check daily newspapers.

New Zealand

As in Australia, STA Travel and Flight Centres International are popular travel agents in New Zealand. The cheapest fares to Europe are routed through Asia. Fares (via Bangkok) in low season start at about NZ$1185 one way and NZ$2049 return. Via the USA, fares in low season start at NZ$1265/2299 one way/return. A RTW ticket will cost about NZ$2300.

Africa

Nairobi and Johannesburg are probably the best places in Africa to buy tickets to Europe, thanks to the many bucket shops and the lively competition between them. Several West African countries offer cheap charter flights to France.

There is one direct flight weekly from Nice and Marseille to Libreville (Gabon) with Air Gabon. Return fares start at 5700FF. Air Afrique operates flights from Marseille to Abidjan on the Ivory Coast (once weekly) and Senegal (twice weekly).

North Africa

Marseille is the leading airline hub for flights to North Africa. Nouvelles Frontières has a wide selection of destinations. Air Algérie operates one or two daily flights from here to Algiers, Annaba and Constantine in Algeria. It also has weekly flights to Bejaia, Oran and Tlemcen. The cheapest return fare to Algiers is 1965FF.

To Casablanca in Morocco, there are daily flights from Nice and Marseille with Royal Air Maroc/Air France. The cheapest, return discount fare is 1700FF. Royal Air Maroc also operates direct Marseille-Oujda flights three times a week.

The cheapest return (from Nice or Marseille) to Tunis or Monastir is 1467FF; Tunisair has twice daily flights to Tunis and weekly flights to Monastir from both airports.

East & South Asia

Singapore and Bangkok are the airfare capitals of the region. Their bucket shops are at least as unreliable as those of other cities, so shop around and ask the advice of other travellers before handing over any money. STA Travel has branches in Hong Kong, Tokyo, Singapore, Bangkok and Kuala Lumpur.

Mumbai and Delhi are the air transport hubs in India, but tickets may be slightly cheaper in Delhi. There are a number of bucket shops around Connaught Place in Delhi, but check with other travellers about their current trustworthiness.

Middle East

El Al operates four direct flights a week from Marseille to Tel Aviv; tickets are often cheaper if bought in Israel, eg from the student travel agency ISSTA (☎ 03-521 4444). Paris is well connected with the whole of the Middle East.

LAND
Metropolitan France

Bus Forget even attempting to catch a bus from Paris to Provence. French transport policy is completely biased in favour of its state-owned rail system; the inter-regional bus services are extremely limited. Take a train.

Train Thanks to the world-renowned TGV, travel between some cities can be faster and easier by rail than by air, particularly if you include the time and hassle involved in getting to/from airports.

The TGV (train à grande vitesse – 'high-speed train') is the pride and joy of the SNCF (Société Nationale des Chemins de Fer), the state-owned rail company that operates the country's top-notch rail network.

Rail links between Provence and the rest of France are good: the TGV Sud-Est links the south east (Nice, Marseille, Avignon and the Alps) with Dijon, Lyon and Paris' Gare de Lyon. On this service, only the stretch of track between Paris and Valence is currently served by super-fast TGV track, on which TGVs travel at a breathtaking 310km/h.

By June 2001 however, the super-fast TGV track will reach Marseille. The new high-speed service, the TGV Méditerranée, will link Valence with Avignon where the line will split – eastwards to Marseille and westwards to Montpellier in neighbouring Languedoc. The TGV Méditerranée, which has cost 24 billion FF to build, will cut travelling time between Paris and Marseille (782km) from 4¼ hours to a startling three hours. A 1st/2nd class single ticket will cost 558/367FF. SNCF authorities reckon the new service will boost annual traffic by 30%, upping the total number of passengers it handles between Paris to Marseille to six million a year.

Back to reality. There are direct daily TGV services from Paris to:

destination	FF	hours
Orange	356	3¼
Avignon	356	3½
Arles	366	3¾
Marseille	367	4¼
Toulon	393	5¼
Les Arcs-Draguignan	423	5½
Saint-Raphaël	438	5¾
Cannes	438	6¼
Antibes	438	6¼
Nice	438	6½
Monaco	440	6½
Menton	445	7

Most TGVs stop in Lyon en route. In summer 1998, there were 8-10 TGVs daily in each direction between Marseille and Paris, and a further 11 return trains between Marseille and Lyon.

Northern France is served by one direct night train between Calais and Menton (630FF; 15 hours), departing from Calais at 8.02 pm and arriving in Menton at 11.07 am the following morning. From Lille, there are two trains a day to Nice (583FF; 8½ hours) – one is an overnight (departing from Lille at 9.19 pm). Other northern destinations such as Roissy Charles de Gaulle airport require a change of train in Lyon or Paris, as do destinations in western France which are not linked by TGV with Provence.

Eastern France is served by two direct trains daily between Strasbourg and Nice (483FF; 12 hours) – one runs overnight, departing from Strasbourg at 8.54 pm. For Metz, Nancy and Dijon you have to change trains in Lyon. For destinations in

south-western France such as Bordeaux and Biarritz, change trains in Narbonne, Toulouse or Montpellier.

Smaller cities in Provence are linked to the TGV network by slower but equally efficient *trains express régionaux* (TER; regional express trains). See the Getting Around chapter.

Reservations & Tickets Most trains, including TGVs, have 1st and 2nd class sections. Most overnight trains are equipped with *couchettes* (sleeping berths) which have to be reserved. A couchette costs 90FF. Second class couchettes have six berths; 1st class have four. *Voitures-lits* (sleepers) have up to three beds and cost 259-907FF per person.

For 2nd class travel, count on paying 50-60FF per 100km for cross-country trips. Return tickets cost double the single ticket price. Travel in 1st class costs 50% more than 2nd class. Children under four travel free; those aged 4-11 are half-price.

A 20FF reservation fee is obligatory for TGV travellers (automatically included in the ticket price) and also applies on some trains that run busy holiday periods – such as July and August on coastal-bound trains which get absolutely jam-packed.

Reservations (☎ 08 36 35 35 35, www .sncf.com) can also be made at any SNCF ticketing office, or by using a ticket vending machine at any SNCF train station (tickets issued via machines are valid for two months). Advance reservations can be changed by telephone or, up to one hour before departure, at your departure station.

Tickets bought with cash can be reimbursed for cash (by you or a thief); keep them in a safe place. Alternatively, pay with a credit card at the ticket counter, at one of the automatic ticket vending machines found at every SNCF station (touch the screen to activate it and the UK flag for English), or online at the SNCF's Web site. Prohibitive tariffs apply for tickets bought direct from the conductor on board trains.

You risk an on-the-spot fine if you fail to validate your train ticket before boarding: time-stamp it in a *composteur*, a bizarre-looking orange post situated at the platform entrance. If you forget, find the conductor on board so he/she can punch it for you. Tickets are usually checked and punched by the conductor mid-way through a journey.

Tickets are valid for 24 hours after they have been time-stamped, meaning you can break your journey briefly mid-way providing you are not on a line (such as a TGV) requiring a reservation. Time-stamp your ticket again before reboarding.

Unused tickets (over 30FF) can be reimbursed (90% of the original ticket price) up to two months after the date of issue. Refunds are available from any train station ticket window.

SNCF Discounts Children under four travel free. Discounted fares (25% reduction) automatically apply to: travellers aged 12-25; seniors over 60; one to four adults travelling with a child aged 4-11; two people travelling on a return journey together.

Purchasing a travel pass (valid for 12 months) can yield a 50% discount (25% if the cheapest seats are sold out): a Carte 12/25 available to travellers aged 12-25 costs 270FF; the Carte Enfant Plus for one to four adults travelling with a child aged 4-11 costs 350FF; seniors 60-plus qualify for a 285FF Carte Sénior.

Anyone travelling at least 200km and spending a Saturday night in their final destination is eligible for a Découverte Séjour – an instant 25% reduction on a return ticket within France.

Auto Train Under Motorail's innovative Auto Train scheme you can travel with your car on a train. Cars are loaded on the train one hour before departure and are unloaded 30 minutes after arrival.

In 1998 this service was available at Avignon, Saint Raphaël, Marseille and Nice train stations. Auto Train is restricted to certain trains between stipulated destinations on certain days; so you cannot just hop on any train to anywhere at any time. In 1998 the overnight Calais-Avignon Auto

Train service, for example, was available 2-4 times weekly between May and October. Transporting a car shorter/longer than 3.81m cost 1250/1450FF and a motorcycle cost 500FF. Other available routings included Strasbourg to Avignon, Nice, Marseille and Saint Raphaël; Calais to Nice; Bordeaux to Marseille and Saint Raphaël; and Toulouse to Nice.

Information in the UK is available from Rail Europe UK (☎ 0990-848 848 or 0990-300 003), 179 Piccadilly, London W1V 0BA. In France, ticketing is handled by SNCF.

Transporting a Bicycle A bicycle can be taken free of charge as hand luggage on most trains in France, provided it is enclosed in a *housse* (cover) that measures no more than 120cm by 90cm. You are responsible for loading and unloading your bicycle from the luggage section of your train. The SNCF won't accept any responsibility for its condition. You can also register a boxed bicycle as checked baggage to any destination in Provence (and many places in Europe) for 135FF plus 15FF for an *emballage* (bicycle box). It will probably take three or four days to arrive.

Car & Motorcycle Number one rule when motoring to Provence: avoid it in July and August if at all possible. If impossible, be prepared to sit in some mighty long *bouchons* (traffic jams), both on and off the autoroute.

On the Road

Autoroute FM 107.7 MHz FM (traffic reports in English every 30 minutes at peak times)

Traffic Updates	☎ 08 36 68 10 77
or Autoroutel	☎ 08 36 68 09 79
Road Toll Info (ASF)	☎ 04 90 32 90 05
Plan your Itinerary	☎ 01 47 05 90 01

The main southbound route from Paris is along the A6 autoroute and its continuation from Lyon, the A7, which continues south through Orange and Avignon to Marseille. This road is poetically called the Autoroute du Soleil (literally the 'Road of the Sun'). From Marseille, the A8 – nicknamed La Provençale – bears east to Nice and eastwards still to Italy where it becomes the A10. The A9 bears west from just south of Orange to Nîmes, Montpellier, and farther south to Spain. The A51 is the main road into the interior of Provence, leading north-east from Aix-en-Provence to Sisteron from where Alpes-de-Haute-Provence can be accessed. Approaching Sisteron from the north, the N85 (Route Napoléon) follows the Napoléon Bonaparte trail from Grenoble, through Gap to Sisteron, Digne-les-Bains, Castellane and farther south to Grasse and Cannes on the coast.

Approximate road distances and average travelling times between cities in metropolitan France and Provence's main towns include:

cities	distance (km)	hours
Paris-Marseille	782	7¼
Bordeaux-Nice	804	8
Nîmes-Toulouse	281	2¾
Lyon-Marseille	320	3
Clermont-Ferrand-Orange	366	3¼
Calais-Marseille	1075	10

The speed limit is 130km/h (110km/h in the rain, 60km/h in icy conditions) on autoroutes, and 110km/h (100km/h in the rain) on dual carriageways (divided highways) or short sections of highway with a divider strip. A right-hand drive vehicle brought to France from the UK or Ireland must have deflectors fixed to the headlights

Road Distances (km)

	Aix/Marseille	Avignon	Cannes	Nice	Nîmes	Menton	Monaco	Orange	Toulon
Aix/Marseille	---								
Avignon	100	---							
Cannes	168	250	---						
Nice	196	278	28	---					
Nîmes	123	45	254	280	---				
Menton	223	306	55	27	307	---			
Monaco	215	305	48	20	300	10	---		
Orange	119	26	250	276	57	302	295	---	
Toulon	64	164	125	150	187	178	170	182	---
Bordeaux	655	585	776	804	538	832	825	589	718
Calais	1075	975	1206	1234	1013	1260	1253	962	1141
Lyon	320	220	445	473	251	500	493	200	379
Paris	782	682	908	935	710	965	958	516	837
Toulouse	408	326	538	565	281	592	585	342	471

to avoid dazzling oncoming traffic. France's famous yellow headlamps are being phased out in favour of the safer white ones. For a breakdown of the rules for driving in France, see the Getting Around chapter.

Road tolls are imposed on most stretches of autoroute, the exception being around major cities such as Nice. Count on paying about 40FF per 100km (see the Toll Table). Some parts of the autoroute have toll plazas every few dozen kilometres; most have a machine which issues a little ticket that you hand over at a *péage* (toll booth) when you exit. You can pay in French francs or by credit card. The toll plaza on the French side of the Italian Ventimiglia border crossing accepts French francs (11FF) or Italian lira (3000 lira).

Consider costs before instinctively leaping in the car. By autoroute, the drive from Paris to Nice (935km, 8½ hours) costs 380FF for petrol (at 16km a litre) and 356.50FF for autoroute tolls – a grand total of 736.50FF, not including wear and tear, depreciation, repairs, insurance or the risk of damage, theft or accident. By comparison, a regular, one-way, 2nd class train ticket for the six-hour Paris-Nice run costs 438FF.

Autoroutes in southern France are managed by the ASF (Autoroutes du Sud de la France; ☎ 04 90 32 90 05 or 01 47 53 37 00 in Paris, fax 01 47 53 36 40), 100 ave de Suffren, BP 533, 75725 Paris. The ASFA (Association des Sociétés Françaises d'Autoroutes; ☎ 01 47 53 39 41, asfa@ autoroutes.fr, www.autoroutes.fr) has an excellent Web site with oodles of traffic-related information. See the boxed text On the Road, earlier, for other ways to get information.

Road Tolls (FF)

	Aix/Marseille	Avignon	Cannes	Nice	Nîmes	Menton	Monaco	Orange	Toulon
Aix/Marseille	---								
Avignon	30	---							
Cannes	67.5	97.5	---						
Nice	89.5	119.5	22	---					
Nîmes	23	9	90.5	112.5	---				
Menton	99.5	129.5	32	10	122.5	---			
Monaco	102.5	132.5	35	13	125.5	0	---		
Orange	37	12	104.5	126.5	60	136.5	139.5	---	
Toulon	36.5	62.5	104	126	59.5	136	139	73.5	---
Bordeaux	240	268	307.5	329.5	209	239.5	342.5	277	276.5
Calais	366	344	433.5	455.5	371	465.5	468.5	330	402.5
Lyon	113	91	180.5	202.5	98	212.5	215.5	77	149.5
Paris	267	245	334.5	356.5	272	366.5	369.5	213	303.5
Toulouse	149	177	216.5	238.5	118	248.5	251.5	186	185.5

Hitching See the Getting Around chapter for advice about hitching. In metropolitan France, there are two organisations that put people looking for rides in touch with drivers going to the same destination. Allostop Provoya (☎ 01 53 20 42 42 in Paris, 01 53 20 42 43/44 from outside Paris and abroad, allostop@ecritel.fr, www.ecritel .fr/allostop) is based at 8 rue Rochambeau, 75009 Paris. Association Pouce (☎ /fax 02 99 08 67 02, allopouce@infonie.fr, www .idonline.net/pouce) is Brittany-based.

With Allostop, passengers pay 22 centimes a kilometre to the driver plus a fee to cover administrative expenses: 30/40/50/ 60FF for trips under 200/300/400/500km and 70FF for trips over 500km. Paris to Marseille/Nice is 239/257FF. Association Pouce has no cover charge.

The UK

The Channel Tunnel, inaugurated in 1994, is the first dry-land link between England and France since the Ice Age.

Buses Eurolines (euroline@imaginet.fr, www.eurolines.co.uk or www.eurolines.fr) has direct bus services year round (two to four times weekly) from London's Victoria Coach station via Dover and Calais to:

destination	UK£	hours
Avignon	58	20
Aix-en-Provence	59	21¼
Marseille	61	22¼
Toulon	66	23¼
Nîmes	58	15½

Between June and September there are additional buses to:

destination	UK£	hours
Fréjus	66	24¼
Saint Raphaël	66	24½
Cannes	66	25¼
Nice	66	25

The above fares are standard single fares; a return ticket is approximately UK£40 more;

a youth fare (available to under 26s) is just a few pounds cheaper than the standard fare.

Bookings can be made in London at the Eurolines office (☎ 0171-730 8235), 52 Grosvenor Gardens, London SW1W 0AU; by telephone through the main Eurolines office (☎ 01582-404 511) in Luton; or at any office of National Express, whose buses link London and other parts of the UK with the Channel ports of Dover and Folkestone. In Provence, ticket bookings can be made at the offices at:

Avignon bus station	☎ 04 90 85 27 60
Marseille bus station	☎ 04 91 50 57 55
Nîmes bus station	☎ 04 66 29 49 02

Eurostar There is no direct Eurostar – the much-heralded passenger train service through the Channel Tunnel – from London to Provence. However, a direct London-Marseille train is expected to follow soon after the inauguration of the TGV Méditer-année in 2001.

Until then, the journey from grey London to the sky-blue coast is possible with a change of train in Lille or Paris. In mid-1998, there was one Lille-connecting train daily, departing from London-Waterloo at 6.53 am and arriving in Avignon at 3.17 pm, Marseille at 4.20 pm, Toulon at 5.04 pm, Cannes at 6.21 pm and Nice at 6.48 pm.

From Paris there are plenty more southbound trains. The change of train is less convenient however, because you have to cross Paris on the RER (part of the metro system) from Gare du Nord to Gare de Lyon. London-Paris journey time is three hours.

Passport and customs checks are done in London, Lille and Paris prior to boarding – exactly as at an airport. The tunnel crossing takes 20 minutes. When the 109km of high-speed Channel Tunnel rail link between London and Folkestone is completed around 2007, travel on the English side will be reduced by 35 minutes.

Tickets & Fares The cheapest 2nd class fare from London to Avignon, Marseille, Nice,

Toulon, Saint Raphaël is UK£129. The ticket is non-refundable, non-reimbursable, includes a Saturday night stay in Provence, and has to be booked at least seven days in advance. A fully-flexible return ticket carrying no restrictions costs UK£270. A London-Provence youth fare for travellers under 26 is UK£119 return; the ticket can be changed but not reimbursed. A non-restrictive return fare for children aged four to 11 is UK£95. Eurostar tickets sold in the UK are marginally more expensive than those sold in France.

In London, Eurostar tickets (www.eurostar.com) are available from travel agents, mainline train stations, and the SNCF-owned Rail Europe (☎ 0990-300 003), 179 Piccadilly, London W1V 0BA. In France, ticketing is handled by SNCF. For schedule and ticket information call Eurostar UK (☎ 0990-186 186, ☎ 1233-617 575 from outside the UK). In France call ☎ 08 36 35 35 39. English is spoken.

Le Shuttle High-speed shuttle trains whisk passengers, cars, motorcycles, bicycles and coaches from Folkestone through the Channel Tunnel to Coquelles, 5km southwest of Calais, in air-conditioned and soundproofed comfort. Journey time is 35 minutes (open 24 hours, year round). For information and reservations, ask a travel agent or contact Le Shuttle (☎ 0990-353 535 in the UK, 03 21 00 61 00 in France, www.eurotunnel.com). A fully-flexible return ticket for a passenger car (and all passengers) is UK£179/220 in the low/high season. Motorcycles cost UK£95 return. Promotional fares for cars are often available; check the Internet.

When calculating costs, be sure to include hefty French road tolls from Calais to Provence in your budget (see the Road Toll table).

Bicycle European Bike Express (☎ 01642-251 440) facilitates independent cycling holidays by transporting cyclists and their bikes by bus and trailer from the UK to places all over France. Return fares start at

UK£140 (£10 less for members of the Cyclists' Touring Club).

Continental Europe

Intercars Buses Intercars (www.intercars.fr) operates buses to cities in southern and central Europe. Its main hub in Provence is at the bus station in Nice (☎ 04 93 80 08 70) although it has offices and buses depart from Marseille bus station (☎ 04 91 50 08 66), Nîmes bus station (☎ 04 66 29 84 22) and other stops en route. Typical fares from Nice include Bratislava (490FF), Budapest (550FF) and Warsaw (700FF). Intercars sells Eurolines tickets in some cities.

Eurolines Buses Eurolines (euroline@imaginet.fr, www.eurolines.co.uk or www.eurolines.fr), an association of companies that together form Europe's largest international bus network, links cities such as Nice, Marseille and Avignon with points all over Europe. Buses are slower and less comfortable than trains, but they are cheaper, especially if you qualify for the 10-20% discount available to people under 25 or over 60. Children aged 4-12 also get discounts.

Eurolines' direct buses link Nice, Marseille, Aix-en-Provence, Avignon and Nîmes with numerous destinations. Non-discounted, one-way adult fares include:

from	to	FF	hours
Nice	Amsterdam	660	23¼
	Brussels	560	21
	Rome	330	9½
	Florence	155	7
Nîmes	Barcelona	295	6¼
Avignon	Ventimiglia	305	4
	Rome	550	14
	Milan	395	10
	Venice	335/540	15
	Barcelona	295	7
Marseille	Prague	640	19½

Return tickets cost quite a bit less than two one-way tickets. In summer, it's not a bad idea to make reservations a few days in advance. Eurolines-affiliated companies can be found across Europe, including:

Amsterdam
☎ 020-560 87 87, www.eurolines.nl
Barcelona
☎ 93-490 4000, www.travelcom.es/juliavia
Berlin
☎ 030-86 0960, www.deutsche-touring.com
Brussels
☎ 02-203 0707
Göteborg
☎ 020-987377, www.eurolines.se
Madrid
☎ 91-528 1105
Prague
☎ 02-2421 3420, www.eurolines.cz
Rome
☎ 06-44 23 39 28, www.eurolines.it
Vienna
☎ 01-712 0435, www.eurolines.at

Eurolines offices in Provençal cities are all based at the central bus stations (see The UK section earlier).

Train Rail services link France with many countries in Europe; schedules are available from major train stations in France and abroad. Some people swear by the Thomas Cook European Timetable (118FF), to find out which domestic and international routings are feasible and use rail passes to their fullest. It is updated monthly and is available from Thomas Cook exchange bureaus. Different track gauges and electrification systems, mean you often change trains at the Spanish border. For details on SNCF, including telephone numbers, see the Getting Around chapter.

Provence is sandwiched between Spain and Italy, with an abundance of rail links to prove it. Nice is on the Barcelona-Rome rail line – a service which gets packed out (and heavily booked well in advance) by backpackers during the summer. From Nice, there are day and overnight trains in both directions. In mid-1998 a Nice-Barcelona single fare was 366FF (plus 90FF for a couchette on night trains). A Nice-Rome single ticket cost 226FF (plus 90FF for a couchette). The journey time from Nice to

Rome via Ventimiglia is around 10 hours; from Nice to Barcelona via Portbou (on the Spanish border) is approximately nine hours. There are many more trains with a change in Montpellier.

There are also direct train services from Nice to Milan (157FF; 4½ hours) and between Marseille and Ventimiglia (179FF; 3¼ hours). From Breil-sur-Roya and Tende in Haute-Provence there are regular daily TER trains to Cuneo (67FF; 1¾ hours) in Italy, with a further 1½ hour train ride to Turin (94FF from Breil). There are plenty of trains from Breil-sur-Roya to Ventimiglia (30FF; 30 minutes).

From Marseille there are three direct daily trains to Brussels (634FF; seven hours), one of which continues to Nice (715FF; 9¼ hours). There are also direct services from Menton (via Nice) to Frankfurt; Nice (via Milan) to Bale; and Nice (via Metz) to Luxembourg.

Fares quoted above are standard 2nd class single fares.

Eurail Youthpass If you are not a resident of Europe, are under 26 on your first day of travel, and anticipate doing more than 2400km around Provence, France and Europe, consider buying a Eurailpass which gives unlimited rail travel for 15/21 days or one/two/three months. One/two months

---

SNCF Hot Lines

SNCF information lines (www.sncf.com) are open daily from 7 am to 10 pm (calling from abroad dial 33 and drop the initial zero). Domestic calls are charged at 2.23FF a minute. The choice of languages includes:

English	☎ 08 36 35 35 39
French	☎ 08 36 35 35 35
German	☎ 08 36 35 35 36
Italian	☎ 08 36 35 35 38
Spanish	☎ 08 36 36 35 37

with the Eurail Youthpass costs US$605/857. In Provence, passes are sold at Nice and Marseille mainline train stations.

Europass The Europass, not available to European residents, lets you travel in certain European countries for 5-15 consecutive or non-consecutive days over two months. Regular adult fares, for 1st class passage within France, Germany, Italy, Spain and Switzerland, range from US$326 for five days to US$746 for 15 days (20% less for two adults travelling together). There is a cheaper Europass Youth, for people aged 25 and under.

Euro Domino France Euro Domino France – available only to residents of Europe outside of France – gives 3/5/10 consecutive or non-consecutive days of midnight-to-midnight 2nd class travel over one month. The pass also gives 25% discount (including on the Eurostar) from where you bought it to the French border. The youth version (people 25 and under) offers three/five/10 days of 2nd class travel for UK£85/115/185; the adult version costs UK£105/145/220. Euro Domino France is available from major train stations in most European countries, including France. In London it is sold by Rail Europe (☎ 0990-300 003) a subsidiary of the SNCF, with offices at 179 Piccadilly, London W1V 0BA and in Victoria Station.

Inter Rail Pass With the Inter Rail Pass, you can travel in 29 European countries organised into eight zones; France is in Zone E, with the Netherlands, Belgium and Luxembourg. For 22 days of unlimited 2nd class travel in one zone, the cost is 1836/1285FF over/under 25. One month of 2nd class travel in two/three/eight zones costs 2380/2720/3100FF (1700/1938/2210FF). Travel from your home country to your zone(s) and between non-adjacent zones is half-price.

Auto Train With Motorail (see the Auto Train section under Metropolitan France), you can transport your car by passenger train from Europe to certain destinations in Provence. In 1998, only Avignon and Saint Raphaël

train stations were open to international traffic. In France, the SNCF offices have information. In Germany, contact Rail Europe Deutschland (☎ 069-9758 4641), Lindenstrasse 5, 60325 Frankfurt; or in Belgium, try Rail Europe Benelux (☎ 02-534 4531), 113 ave Henri Jaspar, 1060 Brussels. For most European destinations you have to book at least two months in advance.

SEA

Provence is linked by ferry with Corsica, Italy and North Africa, with much of the passenger traffic run by the state-owned Société Nationale Maritime Corse Méditerranée (SNCM).

Ticket and schedule information is available for all SNCM ferries (☎ 08 36 67 95 00, www.sncm.fr) from the SNCM office in Marseille, Nice or Toulon (see the Getting There & Away section in those chapters).

Reservations and tickets for ferry travel are also available from travel agencies in France and the countries served. Prices listed below are for standard one-way tickets, unless stated otherwise. Return fares can be cheaper than two singles.

There are no direct ferries from the UK to Provence, however, you can take a ferry from Dover to Calais from where you can motor it south. Longer sea crossings include Folkestone-Boulogne, Newhaven-Dieppe, Poole-Cherbourg, and Portsmouth-Cherbourg/Le Havre/Ouistreham/Saint Malo.

Corsica

Almost all ferry services between Provence (Nice, Marseille and Toulon) and Corsica (Ajaccio, Bastia, Calvi, L'Ile-Rousse, Porto Vechio and Propriano) are handled by SNCM (www.sncm.fr). Schedules and fares are comprehensively listed in the SNCM pocket timetable, freely distributed at tourist offices, some hotels and SNCM offices. At the height of summer there are up to five ferries daily from Nice, three daily from Marseille and four times weekly from Toulon. In winter there are as few as one a day from Nice and Marseille.

Corsica-Toulon ferries do not run at all between October and April.

A one-way passage in a *fauteuil* (literally 'armchair' but in most cases a rather hard, straight-backed chair in a small cabin), is 210/240FF in winter/June to early September on sailings to/from Nice, and 256/292FF for sailings to/from Marseille or Toulon. Daytime crossings take about 6½ hours. For overnight trips, the cheapest couchette/most comfortable cabin costs 66/288FF per person.

People under 25 and seniors pay 184/210FF in winter/summer for all sailings to/from Nice and 224/256FF from Marseille and Toulon. Children under 12 pay 50% of the full adult fare. Transporting a small car costs between 214FF and 612FF, depending on the season. Motorcycles under/over 100cc cost 136/149 to 473FF. Bicycles cost 91FF and dogs in a kennel/vehicle are an additional 173/92FF.

From Nice, Corsica Ferries and the SNCM also run a 70km/h express NGV (Navire à Grande Vitesse) to Calvi (2¾ hours) and Bastia (3½ hours). Fares on these zippy NGVs, which carry 500 passengers and 148 vehicles, are similar to those charged on the regular ferries. The downside of the NGV is that it cannot sail in bad weather; last-minute cancellations are not unheard of. Updates are available on ☎ 08 36 64 00 95.

All Corsica-bound ferries get booked out in July and August; reservations for vehicles and couchettes should be made well in advance. In addition to the basic fares, a port tax is levied by the French government; it ranges from 19FF (Toulon-Calvi) to 44FF (Nice-Ajaccio) per person depending on which port you sail to and from, and from 35FF (Marseille-Porto Vecchio) to 64FF (Nice-Ajaccio) for a vehicle.

In Corsica, tickets are sold from the SNCM office in Ajaccio (☎ 04 95 29 66 69), 3 quai L'Herminier; in Bastia (☎ 04 95 54 66 99 or 04 95 54 66 81) at the new port; and in Calvi (☎ 04 95 65 01 38), quai Landry. In France, contact the SNCM office in Nice, Marseille or Toulon (see city listings for details).

Italy

From April to September, the SNCM has 4-8 car ferries a month from Marseille or Toulon to Porto Torres on the Italian island of Sardinia (Sardaigne in French). Sailing time is 15½ hours, with boats leaving Marseille or Toulon around 8 pm for arrival in Porto Torres around 11.30 am the next day.

In 1998, a *fauteuil* was 420FF per person (840FF return). A place in a cabin cost an additional 110FF each way. To transport a small car/bicycle cost 740/95FF.

Tickets and information are available from any SNCM office in Provence; in Sardinia tickets are sold by SNCF agent, Agenzia Paglietti Petertours (☎ 079-51 44 77), Corso Vittorio Emanuele in Porto Torres.

Spain

There is a weekly SNCM ferry from Marseille to Alicante in Spain (21 hours), from where the ferry continues to Oran in Algeria (see that section).

Tunisia

The SNCM and the Compagnie Tunisienne de Navigation (CTN) operate two weekly car ferries (almost daily services from late June to mid-September) between Marseille and Tunis (about 24 hours). The standard adult fare is 915FF (for an armchair) or 1570FF (in the cheapest cabin). If you're taking along a vehicle (1805/2880FF one way/return), it is important to book ahead, especially in summer. In Tunis, CTN's office (☎ 216-135 33 31) is at 122 rue de Yougoslavie. In Provence, ticketing is handled by SNCM.

Algeria

The regular SNCM ferry service from Marseille to Algiers (only resumed at the end of 1996) is aimed at the local North African community. Political troubles have prompted a state of emergency in Algeria since 1992 and travel is considered dangerous for foreign tourists.

SNCM operates three ferries weekly year round between Marseille and Algiers. The overnight sailing takes 24 hours. A return fare for two people with a car is 5570FF (7390FF for a cabin and including two meals). The equivalent for four people travelling in one car together is 6880FF (10,070FF). Fares increase in summer. There are also weekly ferries from Marseille to Oran and Bejaia.

RIVER
Canal Boat
Provence is well-connected with waterways thanks to the Rhône. Cruising along its sun-flooded channels on a canal boat is one of the most exciting, relaxing and romantic ways of getting to Provence – providing time is not of the essence of course. For a first-hand account see *Watersteps to France* listed under Books to Read in the Facts for the Visitor chapter.

The most popular canal route into Provence is via the beautiful Canal du Midi, a 240km waterway that runs from Toulouse to the Bassin de Thau between Agde and Sète, from where you continue north-east past Sète to Aigues-Mortes in the Camargue. From Toulouse, the Canal du Midi is connected with the Gardonne river leading west to the Atlantic Ocean at Bordeaux. The Midi affords great views over the sun-dried Languedoc plain and passes through more than 100 *écluses* (locks) – sometimes nine in a row, as is the case near Béziers.

Crown Blue Line (☎ 04 68 94 52 72, fax 04 68 94 52 73, boathols@crown-blue-line.com, www.crown-blueline.com), Le Grand Bassin, BP 21, 11401 Castelnaudary, is France's leading *tourisme fluvial* agency. It arranges a variety of one-week boat holidays on the Canal du Midi, ranging in length from 130km (26 hours navigation time and 44 locks) to 177km (36 hours navigation time and 98 locks). There are other house-boat rental agencies in Béziers (☎ 04 67 76 47 00 for the tourist office). Bookings for Crown Blue Line can also be made in the UK – see the detailed Canal Boat section in the Getting Around chapter.

Cruises
Many agencies offer luxury, four to seven-day river cruises into Provence – most

depart from Lyon. Year round, Alsace Croisières (☎ 03 88 76 40 66, fax 03 88 32 49 96), 12 rue de la Division Leclerc, 67000 Strasbourg, offers 3/4/7 day cruises from Lyon to the Camargue on the *MS Camargue*; seven-day cruises cost 3950FF per person.

Cruises on the four-star *MV Princesse de Provence* from Lyon to Arles and Avignon start at 9000FF/person for eight day (seven night) cruises with Peter Deilmann Cruises (www.deilmann-cruises.com). In France, book through Croisière Peter Deilmann (☎ 04 78 39 13 06), 5 rue Gentil, 69002 Lyon.

In the USA, contact Peter Deilmann EuropAmerica Cruises (☎ 800-348 8287 toll-free, or 703-549 1741, fax 549 7924, europe@cais.com), 1800 Diagonal Rd, Suite 170, Alexandria VA 22314.

There are also offices in: London (☎ 0171-436 29 31, fax 0171-436 26 07, gv13@dial.pipex.com), Albany House, Suite 404, 324-326 Regent St, London W1R 5AA; and Germany (☎ 0456-139 60, fax 0456-191 57), Am Hafensteig 17-19, 23730 Neustadt/H.

Warning
The information in this chapter is particularly vulnerable to change: prices for international travel are volatile, routes are introduced and cancelled, schedules change, special deals come and go, and rules and visa requirements are amended. Airlines and governments seem to take a perverse pleasure in making price structures and regulations as complicated as possible. You should check directly with the airline or a travel agent to make sure you understand how a fare (and any ticket you may buy) works. In addition, the travel industry is highly competitive and there are many lurks and perks.

The upshot of this is that you should get opinions, quotes and advice from as many airlines and travel agents as possible before you part with your hard-earned cash. The details given in this chapter should be regarded as pointers and are not a substitute for your own careful, up-to-date research.

Getting Around

AIR

Provence has six *aéroports* (airports) but there are only scheduled, inter-regional flights between two: Nice-Côte d'Azur airport (Aéroport International Nice-Côte d'Azur, www.nice.aeroport.fr) and Marseille-Provence airport (Aéroport International Marseille-Provence, www.marseille.aeroport.fr).

Flights between Nice and Marseille run three times daily (twice on weekends) and are operated by Air Littoral/Lufthansa. Flying time is 50 minutes and a return fare including a weekend stay is 596FF. A fully-flexible single is a hefty 799FF. Private jets tend to use the smaller airports at Avignon, Nîmes, La Môle and Toulon.

Billed as the 'airport of the stars', Cannes-Mandelieu airport (www.cannes-mandelieu.aeroport.fr) primarily serves as a helipad, handling some 90,000 helicopter passengers a year. An increasing number of high flyers are taking to the air to get from A to B in Provence because the road traffic is so damn atrocious.

From April to the end of October, Héli Air Monaco (☎ 92 05 00 50, fax 92 05 76 17) at Héliport de Monaco operates regular scheduled helicopter flights – Europe's busiest helicopter route – between Nice and Monaco (every 20 minutes from around 7 am to 9 pm). Charter flights run year round. A single/return fare is 380/700FF. Children aged 2-12 get 50% discount. Charters start at 1890/3780FF for up to five/10 people. Tickets in Monaco are sold at Héli Air Voyages (☎ 97 70 80 20, fax 97 77 80 21), Les Oliviers, 11 blvd du Jardin Exotique; and in Nice at the Héli Air Monaco desk at the international airport.

Héli-Inter (☎ 04 93 21 46 46, fax 04 93 21 46 47), Nice-Côte d'Azur airport, nips between Nice and Cannes in six minutes; a one-way/return ticket is 385/730FF. There is also a heliport in Saint Tropez (☎ 04 94 97 15 12).

To/From the Airport

Nice-Côte d'Azur airport is 6km from Nice centre. Marseille-Provence airport is equidistant (25km) between Marseille and Aix-en-Provence. Information on public transport links to/from the *centre ville* (city centre) is in the Getting Around section of the respective city listings.

From Nice, Marseille and Toulon-Hyères airports, there are longer-distance *navettes* (shuttle buses) to several other destinations in the region. From Marseille, COMETT (☎ 04 91 61 83 27 or 04 42 14 31 27 in Aix) operates buses every 30 minutes between 8 am and 10 or 11 pm (less frequent on Sunday) to Aix-en-Provence. A single fare is 43FF; journey time is 30 minutes.

Toulon-Hyères airport, 3km south of Hyères and 25km east of Toulon, has regular daily services – in summer only – along the coast to Saint Tropez (100FF; one hour) via Le Lavandou (53FF; 45 minutes). Buses are scheduled to coincide with flight arrivals and departures.

Buses from Nice airport (☎ 04 93 21 30 83 for bus information) serve countless destinations, including Avignon (165FF; 4¾ hours), Cannes via the coastal N7 (48.50FF; 1 hour) or via the A8 (70FF), Draguignan (86FF; 1 hour), Grasse (37FF; 1 hour), Isola 2000 (ski season only, 2 hours), Saint-Martin-Vésubie (47.50FF; 1½ hours) and Vence (21.50FF; 45 minutes).

Again, buses coincide with scheduled flights.

BUS

Buses are used for short-distance travel within departments, especially in rural areas such as Alpes-de-Haute-Provence where there are relatively few train lines. However, services and routes are extremely limiting – not to mention downright frustrating – for any traveller hoping to pack in as many perched villages in as short a time as possible. No more than one or two buses a day trundle their way from the coast to the handful of villages in the Niçois hinterland, for example. Bus services are more efficient between towns which are served by just a few trains (or no train at all). Between Marseille and Aix-en-Provence for example, there are several trains a day, but buses speed between the two towns approximately every 30 minutes.

Autocars (regional buses) are operated by a muddling host of different bus companies, most of whom usually have an office at the *gare routière* (bus station) of the cities they serve. One company usually sells tickets for all the bus companies operating from the same station.

Certain uneconomical SNCF rail lines have been replaced by SNCF buses in recent years. The main difference between these buses and regular regional ones is that travellers can often (but not always) take advantage of any rail pass they have on an SNCF service. Routes covered by SNCF buses (known as Autocars LER) include Marseille to Digne-les-Bains, Manosque and Sisteron; Nice, Toulon and Avignon to Aix-en-Provence;

Arles to Avignon; and Carpentras to Aix and Marseille via Cavaillon.

Few bus stations have left luggage facilities but some (eg Avignon or Marseille) have information desks that double as informal luggage rooms; leave your bag with the information clerk for around 10FF.

TRAIN

The SNCF's regional rail network in Provence, served by *trains express régionaux* (TER, regional express trains), is as equally efficient as its national network. It essentially comprises two routes – one which follows the coast and another which traverses the interior.

The Côte d'Azur between Saint Raphaël and Ventimiglia (Vintimille in French) past the Italian border is served by numerous daily TER trains that shuttle back and forth along the coast. From Saint Raphaël the train line cuts inland to Les Arcs-Draguignan then plunges back on to the coast at Toulon from where it continues its westwards journey along the coast to Marseille

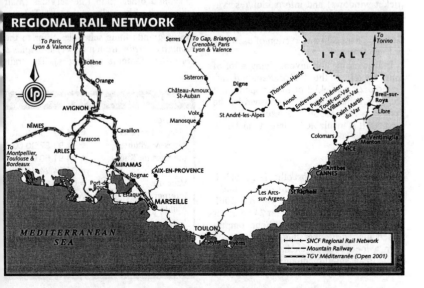

REGIONAL RAIL NETWORK

and a little beyond. At Miramas, the tracks bear inland to Arles and Avignon.

Inland, the Briançon-Marseille rail line slices through the western fringe of Alpes-de-Haute-Provence, linking the coast with the Provençal interior. *Gares* (train stations) from north to south include Sisteron, Château-Arnoux, Manosque and Aix-en-Provence.

In addition to these SNCF routes, a privately owned, narrow-gauge railway links Nice with Digne-les-Bains in Alpes-de-Haute-Provence. Known as *Les Chemins de Fer de la Provence*, the 150km track was constructed between 1890 and 1911 and is a great delight of Provence. It also serves a vital link between the Côte d'Azur and the ski resorts of Val d'Allos and the Gorges du Verdon. The train chugs from the sea to the mountains year round. Between May and October the *Train des Pignes*, a steam train dating from 1909, puffs along part of the track from Annot to Puget-Thèniers. Comprehensive details of both services are listed in the Haute-Provence chapter.

Information

Most train stations have separate *guichets* (ticket windows) and information/reservation offices; opening hours and phone numbers are listed under Train in the Getting There & Away section of each city or town listing.

Indispensable for anyone doing a lot of train travel, is the *Guide Régional des Transports*, a booklet of intra-regional rail and SNCF bus schedules published by the Provence-Alpes-Côte d'Azur regional council. It is available for free at most train stations.

Left-Luggage

Nice, Marseille and most other larger SNCF stations have either a *consigne manuelle* (left-luggage office), where you pay 30FF per bag or 35FF per bicycle for 24 hours; or a *consigne automatique*, a 72-hour computerised luggage locker that will issue you with a lock code in exchange for 15/20/30FF for a small/medium/large locker. At smaller stations you can usually check your

bag with the clerk at the ticket window (30FF). It's a good idea to find out when the left-luggage facilities close; some keep almost banking hours. Luggage lockers are often out of service due to security threats posed by terrorists.

Lost luggage is usually handled by SOS Voyageurs, an organisation of volunteers (mostly retirees) who attempt to help problem-plagued travellers. If your pack has been stolen or your ticket lost, or if you just need somewhere to change your baby, they may be able to help. The staff can be sweet and helpful, but they are not very good in a crisis.

Marseille train station has public showers (19/26FF for a 25/35 minute shower/bath).

Schedules

SNCF's pocket-size *horaires* (timetables), available free at stations, are not that complicated but have some French railway-speak, so we describe them here.

Printed train timetables come in two types – those for regional TER trains (a shiny azure-blue from top to toe) and those for the *grandes lignes* (big lines) covering TGV and other main line services (matt white with a blue stripe at the top). The two rows of boxed numbers that appear at the top of grande ligne schedules refer to the *numéro de train* (train number) and *notes à consulter* (footnote references). The train

SNCF Regional Hot Lines	
Alpes-de- Haute-Provence	☎ 04 92 51 50 50
Alpes-Maritimes	☎ 04 93 87 30 00
Bouches du Rhône	☎ 04 91 50 00 00
Var	☎ 04 94 24 30 00
Vaucluse	☎ 04 90 27 30 00
Internet	www.sncf.com
Minitel	3615 SNCF
	(1.29FF a minute)
or	3615 TER
	(1.01FF a minute)

Street entertainer in Miramas-le-Vieux, near Marseille

Gate into the walled town of Aigues-Mortes, The Camargue

Statue of Provençal poet, Frédéric Mistral, in Place du Forum, Arles

number is not listed in TER pocket timetables; CAR indicates a SNCF bus service (see preceding Bus section).

The footnotes at the bottom of both explain when a particular train *circule* (runs) – often Monday to Friday or Saturday or *jusqu'au* (only until) a certain date. Alternatively, it may operate *tous les jours* (every day) *sauf* (except) Saturday, Sunday and/or *fêtes* (holidays). Practically every ticket attendant at Nice station speaks English, as do most information desk operators at stations along the coast.

The SNCF generally issues two sets of timetables a year: a winter schedule valid from the end of September (or November on some toutes) to the end of May; and a summer schedule which runs from the end of May to the end of September (occasionally November).

There is also an excellent, multi-lingual 'how to read a timetable' section in the *Guide Régional des Transports* (see Information earlier).

Train Passes

Two *forfaits régionaux* (regional passes) exist, both available in summer to travellers of all ages.

The Carte Isabelle costs 60FF and is a one-day train pass entitling card holders to a day's unlimited rail travel along the coast between Théoule-sur-Mer and Ventimiglia. Inland, it covers the Nice-Tende rail line. The pass – ideal for Nice-based travellers wanting to explore the Côte d'Azur – cannot be used on TGVs and is only really cost-cutting if you intend visiting at least two or three different resorts before returning to your original destination. It also allows you to sit in 1st class for no extra supplement – a distinct advantage in July and August when the coastal trains are packed. In 1998 a Carte Isabelle could be purchased from 1 July to 30 September only.

The more restrictive, one-day pass called Carte Bermuda only covers trips from Marseille to Miramas via Port-de-Bouc on the Côte Bleue (Blue Coast). It costs 30FF, is only valid on weekends and holidays, and

(in 1998) was available between 14 June and 30 September.

Other country-wide SNCF discounts and rail passes (such as the Carte 12/25, Carte Enfant Plus, Carte Senior and Découverte Séjour) are all available on regional trains. Details are in the Getting There & Away chapter under Land – Metropolitan France.

Tickets

In most stations, you can buy your ticket at a regular ticket window or from an automatic vending machine. The latter cuts down queuing-time enormously, especially at busy stations like Nice where you usually have to wait *at least* 20 minutes in line in July and August.

Some stations have two types of vending machines: *billetterie automatique* (touch-screen machines) accept credit cards for tickets of 15FF or more and issue all ticket types (ie tickets for national and regional destinations). Other machines known as *billetterie régionale* only sell regional tickets and do not accept credit cards or banknotes – just coins. The red button marked *annulation* activates these machine, which then require you to twiddle a large knob to select your destination, *première* or *deuxième classe* (1st or 2nd class), and *aller-simple* or *aller retour* (single or return) ticket.

Return tickets are exactly twice the price of their single counterparts. Count on paying 70-100FF per 100km for short hops with 2nd class travel. For more details on costs see the Getting There & Away chapter. Train fares for specific routes are listed in the relevant city listings.

Reservations are not mandatory – or necessary – on most regional trains. If you intend travelling on a straight-through train, say, from Marseille to Avignon, it is advisable however to buy your ticket well in advance in summer. Tickets are valid for two months from the date of purchase; advance reservations (20FF) are also possible for many trains, meaning you will be assured a seat for the duration of the journey.

Tickets can be purchased on board, but unless the ticket window where you boarded was closed (quite often the case in smaller stations in Provence) *and* the station had no ticket machine (rarely the case), prohibitive tariffs apply: a flat 130FF for journeys under 75km, 90FF plus the price of a regular ticket for journeys of more than 75km. Finally, remember to time-stamp your ticket before boarding (see Validating Your Ticket in the Getting There & Away chapter) or you risk an on-the-spot fine.

CAR

If you're planning to drive along the coast in July or August, prepare for it to take hours to move a few kilometres, no doubt why the well-heeled travel by helicopter. Inland, year round, you can find idyllically quiet mountain roads laced with *lacets* (hairpins bends) and dimly-lit tunnels. The roads in Alpes-de-Haute-Provence have particularly dazzling scenery and breathtaking views.

In heavily forested areas such as the Massif des Maures, Massif de l'Estérel and Haute-Provence, unpaved roads wend off the main roads into the forest. These tracks are usually signposted 'DFCI' (défense forestière contre l'incendie) and are for fire crews to gain quick entry to the forest when there is a fire: they are strictly off-limits to private vehicles.

Except for the traffic-plagued high season, the Côte d'Azur is easy to get around by car. Fastest is the boring A8 autoroute which, travelling west to east, from near Aix-en-Provence, approaches the coast at Fréjus, skirts the Estérel range and runs more or less parallel to the coast from Cannes to Ventimiglia. Distances between towns and cities in the region include:

cities	distance (km)
Avignon-Marseille	100
Nice-Marseille	196
Orange-Nîmes	57
Aix-en-Provence-Manosque	53
Saint Raphaël-Toulon	190
Arles-Sisteron	186
Barcelonnette-Draguignan	201
Carpentras-Nice	250

Ultimately, having your own wheels is part of the secret to discovering the region's least touched backwaters; numerous treasures tucked in Haute-Provence's mountainous nooks and crannies are absolutely impossible to uncover by public transport. Moreover, a car allows you to avail yourself of cheaper camping grounds, hostels and hotels on city outskirts, as well as restored old farmhouses, delightfully rambling, old mills and chateaux in the countryside.

Documents

All drivers are required by French law to carry a national ID card or passport; a valid *permis de conduire* (driving permit or licence); car ownership papers, known as a *carte grise* (grey card); and proof of insurance, known as a *carte verte* (green card). If you're stopped by the police and don't have one or more of these documents, you can get a 900FF on-the-spot fine. Keep photocopies of all of them in a safe place. Never leave your car ownership or insurance papers in the vehicle.

Road Rules

In France, as throughout Continental Europe, people drive on the right side of the road and overtake on the left. Unless otherwise indicated, you must give way to cars coming from the right. North American drivers should remember that turning right on a red light is illegal in France.

There are three predominant types of roads in Provence, plus the autoroute which is handy for getting to/from the region (see Getting There & Away). *Routes nationales* are main highways whose names begin with N and are generally wide, well signposted and lavishly equipped with reflectors.

Routes départmentales – the most common in provincial Provence – are secondary and tertiary local roads whose names begin with D. *Chemins communaux*, which there are also a lot of, are minor (very minor in some cases) rural roads whose names sometimes begin with C and are maintained by the smallest unit of local government in rural areas, the commune.

Speed Limits Unless otherwise posted, a speed limit of 50km/h applies in all areas designated as built up, no matter how rural they may appear. On inter-city roads, you must slow to 50km/h the moment you pass a white sign with red borders on which a place name is written in black or blue letters. This limit remains in force until you arrive at the other edge of town, where you'll pass an identical sign with a red diagonal bar across the name.

Outside built-up areas, speed limits are 90km/h (80km/h if it's raining) on undivided N and D highways; and 110km/h (100km/h in the rain) on dual carriageways (divided highways) or short sections of highway with a divider strip. Speed limits are generally not posted unless they deviate from those mentioned above. Note that drivers in Provence are notoriously impatient, fast, and have no tolerance for drivers who do stick to the speed limit. Expect to have lots of cars coming to within a few metres of your rear bumper, flashing their lights, and overtaking at the first opportunity.

Alcohol French law is very tough on drunk drivers – a fact that seems to be of little deterrent to some Provençal who will drive 50km to their favourite village bistro, down a bottle of wine, and then drive home again.

To catch drivers whose blood-alcohol concentration (BAC) is over 0.05% (0.50 grams per litre of blood), the police sometimes conduct random breathalyser tests. Fines range from 500-8000FF, and licences can be suspended.

Fines You seldom see the police pulling anyone over for speeding – which may explain why Provençal drivers are so fearless. *Contraventions* (fines) for serious violations (eg driving through a red light) start at 1300FF.

Equipment A reflective warning triangle, to be used in the event of breakdown, must be carried in the car. Recommended accessories are a first-aid kit, a spare bulb kit and a fire extinguisher. In the UK, contact the RAC

(☎ 0990-275 600) or the AA (☎ 0990-500 600).

Road Signs

Sens unique means 'one way'. *Voie unique* means 'one-lane road' – common in Haute-Provence where there are numerous narrow bridges. Another handy one to know if you intend motoring along the famous, tunnel-clad corniches is *allumez vos feux*, meaning 'turn on your headlights'. *Éteignez vos feux* means 'turn off your headlights'. A sign reading *8 lacets* means there are eight consecutive hairpin bends coming up – a sign particularly favoured in the arrière-pays Niçois (Niçois hinterland) and the Roya and Vésubie valleys.

If you come to a *route barrée* (a closed road), you'll usually also find a yellow panel with instructions for a *déviation* (detour). Signs for *poids lourds* (heavyweights) are meant for lorries (trucks), not cars. The words *sauf riverains* on a no-entry sign mean 'except residents' – common at the foot of most *villages perchés* (perched villages). Road signs with the word *rappel* (remember) featured mean you should already know what the sign is telling you (eg the speed limit).

Petrol

Essence (petrol or gasoline), also known as *carburant* (fuel), is expensive in France, incredibly so if you're used to Australian or North American prices. In mid-1998, *sans plomb* (unleaded) petrol (98 octane) cost around 6.40FF a litre (US$4 per US gallon). *Gazole* (diesel fuel) is 4.60FF a litre (US$2.90 per US gallon). *Faire le plein* (filling up) is cheapest at stations on city outskirts and at supermarkets; the price can fluctuate by as much as 20% depending where you refuel.

Parking

Finding a place to park in Nice, Marseille and any largish town or touristy village, is likely to be the single greatest hassle you'll face. In city centres, your best bet is usually to ditch the car somewhere and walk or take public transport. Public parking facilities are marked by a white letter 'P' on a blue background – in Marseille many are underground. *Payant* written on the asphalt or on a nearby sign means you have to pay. Meters in above-ground car parks tend to swallow 5-10FF an hour. Most villages perchés have large, ugly purpose-built car parks at their foot where you park, pay 20FF to the attendant, then traipse uphill with the hordes of other tourists to the pedestrian village.

Rental

Even renting a car for just a couple of days to explore more remote spots will shed a different light on the way you view Provence – which, at its worst, can seem congested and packed with people. If you intend booking a hire car before you arrive, ring around first. All the major car rental companies have a desk at Nice and Marseille airports and in the city centres.

Multinational rental agencies such as Hertz, Avis, Budget and Europe's largest, Europcar, are outrageously expensive if you walk into one of their offices and hire on the spot – up to 900FF a day for a Twingo (Renault's smallest model) with unlimited kilometres. Their prebooked and prepaid promotional rates, by contrast, can be reasonable (weekly rates for Europe, as advertised in the USA, are as little as US$160). They sometimes have fly/drive combinations too, worth looking into.

Most rental companies require the driver to be over 21 (or, in some cases, over 23) and have had a driving licence for at least one year. The packet of documents you are given should include a 24 hour number to call in case of a breakdown or accident. Check how many 'free' kilometres are – or are not – included in the deal you're offered. *Kilométrage illimité* (unlimited mileage) means you can drive to your heart's desire. For rentals not arranged in advance, domestic companies such as Rent-a-Car Système and Century, as well as some student travel agencies (eg USIT) have the best rates. Companies are listed in city

chapters under Getting There & Away; few places are open on Sunday. Reserve at least a few days in advance in summer, especially with the cheaper companies.

All the major rental companies accept payment by credit card. They also require a deposit; some ask you to leave a signed credit card slip without a sum written on it as a deposit. If you don't like this arrangement, ask them to make out two credit card slips: one for the sum of the rental; the other for the sum of the excess. Make sure to have the latter destroyed when you return the car.

Insurance *Assurance* (insurance) for damage or injury you cause to other people is mandatory, but things like collision damage waivers vary greatly from company to company. The policies offered by some small, discount companies may leave you liable for up to 8000FF – when comparing rates, the most important thing to check is the *franchise* (excess/deductible). If you're in an accident where you are at fault, or the car is damaged and the party at fault is unknown (eg someone dents your car while it's parked), or the car is stolen, this is the amount you are liable for before the policy kicks in.

Purchase-Repurchase Plans

Non-EU residents who want a car in Europe for 17 days to six months will find that the cheapest option by far is to 'purchase' a brand new car from the manufacturer and then, at the end of your trip, 'sell' it back to them. In reality, you only pay for the number of days you use the vehicle, but the tax-free, *achat-rachat* (purchase-repurchase) aspect of the paperwork (none of which is your responsibility) makes this type of leasing much cheaper than renting, especially for longer periods. Eligibility is strictly restricted to people not resident in the EU (ie EU citizens are eligible provided they live outside the EU).

Payment must be made in advance. If you return the car earlier than planned, you usually get a refund for the unused time (seven days minimum). Cars have to be booked in advance (preferably two to four weeks at least), either in the US or in France. From the USA, a Twingo (the cheapest model available) costs around US$480 for the first 17 days and US$16 for each additional day. In Provence, Twingo prices are around 3780/52FF respectively. Rates include unlimited kilometres, 24 hour towing and breakdown service (☎ 08 00 05 15 15 in France), and comprehensive insurance with – incredibly – no excess (deductible). Cars with automatic transmission and diesel engines are also available. And, if you fall in love with your Twingo, you can buy it when your purchase-repurchase agreement comes to an end.

The Renault Eurodrive (☎ 212-532 1221 in the USA, ☎ 01 40 40 33 68 in Paris, www.eurodrive.renault.com) and Peugeot Vacation Plan (☎ 1-800 572 9655 in the USA, www.auto-france.com) programs get rave reviews. Renault allows you to pick up from and return cars to the TT Car-Autoservice (☎ 04 93 21 39 74, fax 04 93 21 41 25) in terminal 1 at Nice airport; or from Transcausse (☎ 04 91 13 15 56 or 04 91 13 15 55, fax 04 91 56 62 60) in terminal 1 at Marseille airport. With Peugeot, cars can be collected/returned at Nice, Marseille and Avignon airports; cars can also be picked up (but not returned) in Nîmes.

Minor problem: the red number plates announce to passing thieves that the car is being driven by a tourist. Be careful.

MOTORCYCLE

Provence is superb country for motorcycle touring, with winding roads of good quality and lots of stunning scenery. Make sure your wet-weather gear is up to scratch in spring and autumn. Riders of any type of two-wheel vehicle with a motor must wear a helmet – despite the abundance of bareheaded, motorised two-wheelers that tear around Nice and its coastal roads.

Easy riders caught bareheaded can legally be fined and have their bike confiscated. Bikes of more than 125cc must have their headlights on during the day. No special licence is required to ride a motorcycle of less than 50cc engine capacity. In Nice and along the coast there are ample places which rent scooters rated at 49.9cc as well as the bigger-engine mean machines.

To rent a *scooter* (scooter) or *moto* (motorcycle) you have to leave a *caution* (deposit) of several thousand francs, which you forfeit – up to the value of the damage – if you're in an accident and it's your fault. Since insurance companies won't cover theft, you'll also lose the deposit if the bike is stolen. Most places accept deposits made by credit card, travellers cheques or Eurocheques.

Provence Moto Évasion (☎/fax 04 93 24 81 36 or 04 93 58 77 58), 846 Chemin de la Sine, 06140 Vence, organises motorcycle tours of Provence from 110/1500FF for one/two people a day. Bikes and helmets are provided.

BICYCLE

Provence – particularly the Lubéron – is an eminently cyclable region, thanks in part to its extensive network of inland secondary and tertiary roads, which carry relatively light traffic (compared to the coast). These back roads, a good number of which date from the 19th century or earlier, are an ideal vantage point from which to view Provence's celebrated rural landscapes, be it lavender fields, vineyards or olive groves. One pitfall: they rarely have proper *verges* (shoulders). It is forbidden to cycle in national parks in Provence (Mercantour and Port-Cros).

French law mandates that bicycles must have two functioning brakes, a bell, a red reflector on the back and yellow reflectors on the pedals. After sunset and when visibility is poor, cyclists must turn on a white light in front and a red one in the rear. The name and address of the bike's owner are supposed to appear on a metal plate attached to the front of the bike. When being overtaken by a car or truck, cyclists are required to ride in single file. Bicycles are not allowed on most local and intercity buses; you can take them on regional trains.

See the Facts for the Visitor chapter (Activities, Maps, Books & Spectator Sports sections) for more cycling information and contacts. See the Air & Land sections in the

Getting There & Away chapter for details on transporting your bicycle to Provence by plane/train.

Rental

Most resorts have at least one shop that hires out *vélos tout-terrains* (mountain bikes), better known as VTTs (60-100FF a day). Most places require a 1000 or 2000FF deposit, which you forfeit if the bike is damaged or stolen. In general, deposits can be made in cash, with signed travellers cheques or by credit card (though a passport will often suffice). Rental shops are listed in the Getting Around sections of city and town listings.

Never leave your bicycle locked up outside overnight if you want to see it or most of its parts again. You can leave your bike in train station left-luggage offices for 35FF a day.

HITCHING

Hitching is never entirely safe anywhere in the world and we don't recommend it. Travellers who hitch should understand they are taking a small but potentially serious risk.

However, if you speak some French (few older people in rural areas know any English), thumbing it affords opportunities to meet Provençal people from all walks of life and many people still do it. So we offer the following advice.

Two women hitching should be safer than a woman hitching on her own, who faces a definite risk. Two men together may have a harder time getting picked up than a man travelling alone. The best (and safest) combination is a man and a woman. Never get in the car with someone you don't trust. Keep your belongings with you on the seat rather than in the boot (trunk). Dedicated hitchers may wish to invest in the *Hitch-Hikers Manual for Europe* by Simon Calder (Vacation Work; 1993).

BOAT
Yacht

Sailing the azure blue seas by yacht certainly has to be among the most pleasurable ways of getting to/from/around the Côte d'Azur. Among the largest marinas are those at Port Vauban (☎ 04 92 91 60 00) in Antibes, and Port Camargue (☎ 04 66 51 10 10 or 04 66 51 10 12) in La Grau du Roi which, with 4350 moorings, claims to be Europe's biggest. Antibes has attracted some of the world's grandest yachts in the past, including King Fahd of Saudi Arabia's *Prince Abdul Aziz* (which at 147m long is the world's largest).

Yachts can be hired at most marinas along the coast, including the less pompous sailing centres at Sainte Maxime and Le Lavandou. In Juan-les-Pins, yachts can be hired with/without a crew from Nautic 2000 (☎ 04 93 61 20 01) or Easy Yachting (☎ 04 93 67 75 91) in Port Gallice on Juan's southern fringe. In Antibes try Île Bleue (☎ 04 93 34 78 96), 2 blvd d'Aguillon, or At Your Service (☎ 04 93 34 09 96), 3 blvd d'Aguillon.

For marina or harbour master information contact the Comité Régional de Sailing Côte d'Azur (☎ 04 93 74 77 05, fax 04 93 74 68 87), Espace Antibes, 2208 route de Grasse, 06600 Antibes. See Climate in the Facts about Provence chapter for details on marine weather reports.

Ferry

A plethora of boats ply the waters from the shores of the Côte d'Azur to its various offshore islands. Daily ferries sail to the Îles de Lérins from Cannes (year round), Juan-les-Pins (April to September) and Vallauris-Golfe Juan (April to October).

To get to Port-Cros, the national park in the Îles d'Hyères archipelago, you can take a boat from Le Lavandou or Hyères (year round), Toulon or Saint Tropez (June to September), and Port Miramar, La Croix Valmer or Cavalaire (July and August). Its bare little sister, the Île du Levant, is accessible by boat from Le Lavandou and Hyères (year round), or Port Miramar, La Croix Valmer and Cavalaire (July and August). Porquerolles, the last in the Hyères trio, is served by regular passenger ferry from Le Lavandou and Hyères (year round), Toulon or Saint Tropez (June to September), or Port Miramar, La Croix Valmer and Cavalaire (July and August).

The Paul Ricard islands near Bandol and Toulon are equally well served by ferry. Boats to Île de Bendor depart year round from Bandol, while ferries to the larger Île des Embiez depart from Le Brusc (year round) and Sanary-sur-Mer (June to September). From Marseille, there are plenty of boats to the Îles du Frioul.

Between April and July, there are daily boats from Saint Tropez to Saint Raphaël, and weekly boats to Cannes and Nice. In July and August, speedy shuttleboats yoyo between Saint Tropez, Sainte Maxime and Port Grimaud.

In season, soulless boat excursions aimed solely at tourists, often with blaring music and always with loud recorded commentaries, service most hot spots along the Côte d'Azur.

Canal Boat

One of the most relaxing ways to see the most south-eastern corner of the region is to rent a houseboat for a leisurely cruise along the Camargue's canals and navigable rivers. At each *écluse* (lock), you can hop ashore to chat with the lock-keeper. Boats usually accommodate two to 12 passengers and are hired out on a weekly basis. Anyone over 18 can pilot a river boat without a licence (you do need a licence to fish). Learning the ropes takes about half an hour – the speed limit is 6km/h on canals and 10km/h on rivers. The tourist cruising season lasts from Easter to November.

To get a boat in July and August, reservations must be made at least several months ahead. You can hire a boat from abroad through Crown Blue Line (www.crownblueline.com) which has canal boat rental in the Camargue. You can hop aboard at Saint Gilles, 19km south of Nîmes, from where you can cruise along the Canal du Rhône to Aigues-Mortes and farther west along the Canal du Midi in to the Toulouse area. Eastbound, you can cruise in three or four hours as far as Beaucaire and Tarascon, south of Avignon. Boats can be booked through Blue Line Camargue (☎ 04 66 87 22 66, fax 04 66 87 15 20), 2 quai du Canal, 30800 Saint Gilles; or in the UK through Crown Travel (☎ 01603-630 513, fax 664 298, crowhols@ dial.pipex.com, www.crown-holidays.co .uk), 8 Ber Street, Norwich NR1 3EJ. Weekly rates for a boat for two/12 people start at UK£420/2110.

From Avignon, Beaucaire, Tarascon, Aigues-Mortes and Arles, there are plenty of river excursions organised along the Rhône (see the Organised Tours sections in regional chapters). You can only hire a boat for self-cruising however in Saint Gilles, or in Béziers in neighbouring Languedoc (see under River in the Getting There & Away chapter).

LOCAL TRANSPORT

Getting around cities and towns in Provence is a straightforward affair, thanks to excellent public transport systems. Marseille is the only city in the region to have a metro, while an ultra-modern tramway is planned for Nice and Toulon in the next century. Details on routes, fares, tourist passes etc are available at tourist offices and local bus company information counters; in this book see Getting Around at the end of each city and town listing.

Taxis are generally expensive. Most towns have a taxi rank in front of the train station. Count on paying between 3.50 and 10FF per kilometre depending on the time of day and the distance you are travelling. Rates to/from the city centre and Nice airport are criminally expensive – between 120-140FF for the 3km journey, plus of course an extra 10FF (per bag!) for the privilege of transporting your luggage in the boot (trunk).

Marseille Area

The urban geography and atmosphere of Marseille, utterly atypical of Provence, are a function of the diversity of its inhabitants, the majority of whom are immigrants (or their children and grandchildren) from Greece, Italy, Armenia, Spain, North Africa (Muslims, Jews, *pieds noirs*), West Africa and Indochina.

Marseille's southern tip is kissed by some of France's most dramatic coastline. From Callelongue on the city outskirts, a series of sharp-ridged, overhanging rocks – *Les Calanques* (literally 'rocky inlets') – plunge southwards to Cassis and La Ciotat.

West of Marseille is something of an eyesore. Rapid industrialisation has polluted the water and fast encroached on the land surrounding the Étang de Berre, a 15,530 hectare lagoon.

North of Marseille, Aix-en-Provence, which most people just call Aix (pronounced like the letter 'X'), is one of France's most graceful cities. Unfortunately it is among the most popular too, prompting one reader to slam it as '… a waste because it is too touristy' and another to say '… the nearest thing to traffic hell'. Either way, Aix's harmonious fusion of majestic public squares, shaded avenues and mossy fountains, many of which have gurgled since the 18th century, cannot be disputed.

Much loved by the Aixois, Montagne Sainte-Victoire flanks the eastern side of the fountain city.

Large Salon-de-Provence, 10km north of the Étang de Berre and 37km west of Aix-en-Provence, marks the boundary between the soft green and purple hues of Pays d'Aix (literally 'Aix Country') and the savage cut of the barren Crau plains in the lower Rhône valley.

- Rise at dawn to see Marseille fishermen set up shop at the Vieux Port; buy fresh fish

- Eat bouillabaisse

- Hike in Les Calanques

- Tour Aix-en-Provence's fountains followed by a pastis at Les Deux Garçons

- Discover what inspired Cézanne in Aix-en-Provence and its neighbouring Montagne Sainte Victoire

- Discover Cap Canaille and the route des Crètes

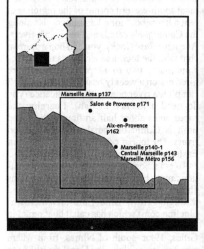

Marseille Area p137

Salon de Provence p171

Aix-en-Provence p162

Marseille p140-1
Central Marseille p143
Marseille Métro p156

Marseille

• pop 800,000

The cosmopolitan port of Marseille (Marseilles in English; Marsihès in Provençal), Provence's largest city (and France's second), is not in the least bit quaintified for the benefit of tourists.

It is notorious for organised crime, racial tensions and – since the 1998 World Cup – football hooliganism. The extreme-right polls about 25% citywide, and a member of the fascist *Front National* (FN; National Front) holds the mayoralty in neighbouring Marignane and Vitrolles.

Regardless of the city's dubious political leaning, visitors who enjoy exploring on foot will be rewarded with more sights, sounds, smells and big-city commotion than anywhere else in the region. Its seaport is the most important in France and the second-largest in Europe after Rotterdam, while super-speed rail tracks will put Marseille just a three hour train ride from Paris by 2001. In short, there really is no other French city quite like it; tell anyone in France you're off to La Canebière and they'll know instantly which city you mean. You'll either love it or hate it.

History

Massilia was founded by Greek mariners from Phocaea, a city in Asia Minor, around 600 BC. The city backed Pompey the Great in the 1st century BC, prompting Caesar's forces to capture the city in 49 BC and exact commercial revenge by confiscating its fleet and directing Roman trade elsewhere. Massilia retained its status as a free port and was, for a while, the last western centre of Greek learning. But the city soon declined and became little more than a collection of ruins. It was revived in the 10th century by the counts of Provence.

Marseille was pillaged by the Aragonese in 1423, but the greatest calamity in its history took place in 1720, when plague – carried by a merchant vessel from Syria – killed some 50,000 of the city's 90,000 inhabitants. Under French rule, the Marseillais quickly gained a rebel reputation. It is after

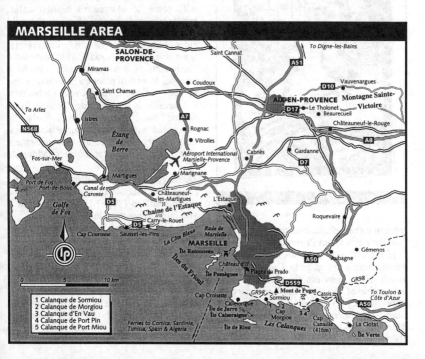

MARSEILLE AREA

1 Calanque de Sormiou
2 Calanque de Morgiou
3 Calanque d'En Vau
4 Calanque de Port Pin
5 Calanque de Port Miou

Passionate & Proud

Don't believe the yarns the Marseillais spin about how their city was created. Legend says it was built in a day from the passion of a hemp farmer's daughter and the pride of a dashing Greek sailor who, in their forbidden love, embraced in secret by the sea, out of which a city arose.

Which is maybe why, to this day, their rough-cut, seafaring ancestors are known far and wide as being hot blooded, passionate and proud, with tempers of fire, wills of iron and smouldering spirits. Resolutely stubborn, totally anti-establishment and prone to exaggeration are other rumoured traits.

them that France's national anthem is named (see the Facts about Provence chapter).

In the 19th century, Marseille grew prosperous from colonial trade. Commerce with North Africa grew rapidly after the French occupation of Algeria in 1830, and maritime opportunities expanded further when the Suez Canal opened in 1869. During WWII, Marseille was bombed by the Germans and Italians in 1940 and by the Allies in 1943-44.

Many literary figures in the 20th century turned to rough Marseille for inspiration, including Senegalese novelist Sembène Ousmane who portrayed his life as a black docker and African ghetto inhabitant in *Le Docker Noir* (The Black Docker, 1956). Provençal writer/film maker Marcel Pagnol was born in Aubagne, 16km east of Marseille. Marseille's best known contemporary products include World Cup super-hero Zinedine Zidane and pulsating rappers IAM.

Orientation

The city's main thoroughfare, the famed wide boulevard called La Canebière, stretches eastward from the Vieux Port (old port). The train station is north of La Canebière at the northern end of blvd d'Athènes. Just a few blocks south of La Canebière is bohemian cours Julien, a large pedestrian square dominated by a water garden, fountains and palm trees, and lined with some of Marseille's hippest cafés, restaurants and theatres. Not *all* the wild graffiti covering most building walls is considered street art. The city's commercial heart is around rue Paradis, which gets more fashionable as you move south. The ferry terminal is west of place de la Joliette, a few minutes walk from the Nouvelle Cathédrale.

Marseille is divided into 16 arrondissements; most travellers will only be concerned with three or four. Places mentioned in the text have the arrondissement (1er, 2e etc) listed after the street address.

Maps The tourist office distributes free city maps. The Blay-Foldex *Marseille et son agglomération* (30FF) is indispensable if you intend venturing into the suburbs.

The pocket-sized *Plan de Poche- Métro Bus Tramway* public transport map distributed free at the Espace Infos-RTM (see Getting Around later) is invaluable.

Information

Tourist Offices The tourist office (☎ 04 91 13 89 00, fax 04 91 13 89 20, www.mars eilles.com, metro Vieux Port), 4 La Canebière, 1er, is open from 9 am to 7 pm

(Sunday from 10 am to 5 pm). From mid-June to mid-September, it is open daily until 8 pm. Staff make hotel reservations.

The tourist office annexe (☎ 04 91 50 59 18, metro Gare Saint Charles), to the left through the main train station entrance, is open from 10 am to 1 pm and 1.30 to 6 pm (closed on weekends); during July and August, it's open from 9 am to 7 pm (closed Sunday).

Tourist information on the Bouches-du-Rhône department is available from the Comité Départemental du Tourisme (☎ 04 91 13 84 13, fax 04 91 33 01 82, www.visit provence.com, metro Estrangin-Préfecture), 13 rue Roux de Brignoles, 6e. For the region, go to the Comité Régional de Tourisme Provence-Alpes-Côte d'Azur (☎ 04 91 39 38 00, fax 04 91 56 66 61, metro Colbert), Espace Colbert, 14 rue Sainte Barbe, 2e.

The Club Alpin Français (CAF; ☎ 04 91 54 36 94, metro Vieux Port), 12 rue Fort Notre Dame, 1er, is open on Thursday between 6 and 8 pm.

Money The Banque de France (metro Estrangin Préfecture), place Estrangin Pastré, 6e, is open from 8.45 am to 12.30 pm and 1.30 to 3.30 pm (closed on weekends).

There are several banks and exchange bureaux west of the old port on La Canebière, 1er, (metro Vieux Port) including Barclays Bank at No 34. American Express (☎ 04 91 13 71 21, metro Vieux Port or Noailles) at No 39 is open from 8 am to 6 pm (Saturday until 5 pm; closed Sunday).

Post The main post office (metro Colbert), 1 place de l'Hôtel des Postes, 1er, is open from 8 am to 7 pm (Saturday until noon; closed Sunday). Exchange services are available.

Near the train station, the crowded branch post office (☎ 04 91 50 89 25, metro Gare Saint Charles), 11 rue Honnorat, 3e – which does not change money – is open from 8.30 am to 6.30 pm (Saturday until noon; closed Sunday). Hours at the post office (metro Notre Dame du Mont-Cours

Julien), place Jean Jaurès, 1er, are 8 am to 6.45 pm (Saturday until noon; closed Sunday).

Marseille's postcode is '130' plus the arrondissement number (postcode 13001 for addresses in the 1st arrondissement, 1er, etc).

Email & Internet Access The Internet Café (☎ 04 91 42 09 37, cafe@icr.internet cafe.fr, metro Estrangin Préfecture), 25 rue de Village, 6e, charges 30/50FF for 30 minutes/one hour access. It's open from 10 am to 8 pm (until 4.30 pm on Friday and from 2.30 pm on Sunday).

More 'in' is Le Rezo Cybercafé (☎ 04 91 42 70 02, rezo@wanadoo.fr, metro Notre Dame du Mont-Cours Julien), 68 cours Julien, 6e. It charges the same rates and is open from 10 am to 8 pm (midnight on Friday and Saturday).

Travel Agencies Voyages Wasteels (☎ 04 95 09 30 20, metro Noailles), 67 La Canebière, 1er, is open from 9 am to 12.30 pm and 2 to 6.15 pm (until 12.30 pm on Saturday; closed Sunday).

Bookshops The northern end of rue Paradis, 1er, is lined with bookshops including the Librairie Feuri Lamy (☎ 04 91 33 57 91, metro Vieux Port) at No 21, which has a good selection of English-language novels. It is open from 9 am to 12.30 pm and 1.45 to 6.45 pm (closed Sunday).

For the best range of maps, travel books and Lonely Planet guides, try the Librairie de la Bourse (☎ 04 91 33 63 06), 8 rue Paradis. English-language guides and books are also sold in FNAC (☎ 04 91 39 94 00), top floor of the Centre Bourse shopping centre (metro Vieux Port), off cours Belsunce, 1er.

Laundry The laundrette (metro Vieux Port), 5 rue Breteuil, 1er, is open from 6.30 am to 8 pm. The one at 15 allées Léon Gambetta, 1er, (metro Vieux Port) is open from 8 am to 9 pm. Strangely, there is a laundrette inside the Total petrol station (metro Vieux Port), 104 blvd Charles Livon, 7e.

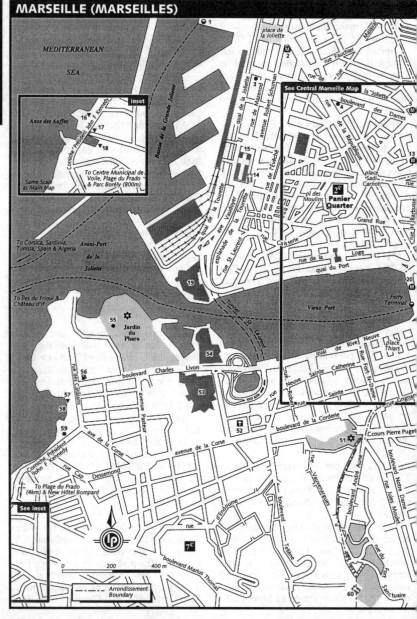

MARSEILLE (MARSEILLES)

MEDITERRANEAN
SEA

Inset

Anse des Auffes

16
17
18

Same Scale
as Main Map

To Centre Municipal de
Voile, Plage du Prado
& Parc Borély (800m)

To Corsica, Sardinia,
Tunisia, Spain & Algeria

To Îles du Frioul &
Château d'If

To Plage du Prado
(4km) & New Hôtel Bompard

See Inset

place de
la Joliette

rue Fauchier

rue de

M 2

quai de la Joliette

rue de Mazenod

avenue Robert Schuman

3

See Central Marseille Map

la Joliette

boulevard des Dames

4

rue de la République

13 M

place
Sadi-Carnot

rue

2ᵉ
Panier
Quarter

Grand Rue

rue H. Barbusse

15

rue de l'Évêché

14

rue Caisserie

pl des
Moulins

esplanade de la Tourette

rue St Laurent

rue de la Loge

Loge

quai du Port

Tunnel St Laurent

19

20

Vieux Port

Ferry
Terminal

Jardin
du
Pharo

55

54

quai de Rive Neuve

Rue Fort-N-Dame

place
Thiars

53

boulevard Charles Livon

avenue Pasteur

56

rue des Catalans

57
58
59

rue Robert

Neuve Sainte Catherine

Sainte

rue Grignan

52

boulevard de la Corderie

51

cours Pierre Puget

Corniche Président John F Kennedy

rue Cap Dessemond

ave de la Corse

avenue de la Corse

rue d'Endoume

rue Vacon

rue

rue Vauvenargues

boulevard André Aune

rue Notre Dame

rue Jules Moulet

boulevard

Teillane

rue du Fort

7ᵉ

boulevard Marius Thomas

Sanctuaire

60

0   200   400 m

- - - Arrondissement
      Boundary

MARSEILLE (MARSEILLES)

PLACES TO STAY
10 Hôtel Ibis Saint Charles
12 Hôtel Gambetta
22 Cheap Hotels
23 Hôtel Sphinx
26 Hôtel de Nice
28 Hôtel Ozea; Hôtel Pied-à-Terre
38 Hôtel Manon
39 Hôtel Massilia
40 Grand Hôtel Le Préfecture
41 Le Président
42 Hôtel Salvator
59 Hôtel Le Richelieu
61 Hôtel Béarn

PLACES TO EAT
16 Bistrot Plage &
   Restaurant de la Corniche
17 Chez Fonfon
18 Pizzeria Chez Jeannot
29 Restaurant Antillais
30 Rétro Julien & Eden Café Rock
31 Le Caucase
32 Le Resto Provençal
34 Le Sud du Haut
46 Café de la Banque
57 Pizzeria des Catalans

METRO STATIONS
2 Metro Joliette
5 Metro Jules Guesde
9 Metro Gare Saint Charles &
   Gare Saint Charles
11 Metro Canebière-Réformés
13 Metro Colbert
20 Metro Vieux Port
21 Metro Noailles
37 Metro Notre Dame du Mont-
   Cours Julien
49 Metro Estrangin Préfecture
63 Metro Castellane

ENTERTAINMENT
24 Drag Queen Café
25 New Can-Can Nightclub
35 Espace Julien
36 Chocolat Théâtre & Restaurant

OTHER
1 Passenger Ferry Terminal
3 SNCM Ferries Office
4 Algérie Ferries
6 Bus Station
7 Taxi Stand
8 Post Office
14 Ancienne Cathédrale de la Major
15 Nouvelle Cathédrale
19 Fort Saint Jean
27 Square Léon Blum
33 Le Rezo Cybercafé
43 Préfecture de Police
44 Préfecture
45 US Consulate
47 Place Estrangin Pastré
48 Banque de France
50 Fruit & Vegetable Morning Market
51 Jardin Pierre Puget
52 Abbaye Saint Victor
53 Fort d'Entrecasteaux &
   Fort St Nicholas
54 Bas Fort Saint Nicolas
55 Palais du Pharo
56 Total Petrol Station &
   Laundrette
58 Plage des Catalans
60 Basilique Notre Dame de la Garde
62 Internet Café

Map labels

To Airport (28km)
place Victor Hugo
ave du Général Leclerc
Autoroute Nord
rue Honnorat
boulevard National
place Jules Guesde
blvd Charles Nédélec
rue Bernard du Bois
boulevard Voltaire
To Palais de Longchamp & Jardin Zoologique (450m)
boulevard d'Athènes
rue des Dominicaines
ave Nationale
rue Nationale
cours Joseph Thierry
To Auberge de Jeunesse Château de Bois Luzy (3km)
Colbert
place des Capucins
Belsunce Area
Centre Bourse Shopping Mall
Allées L Gambetta
cours F Roosevelt
rue de Bir Hakeim
La Canebière
rue du Théâtre Français
rue Sénac de Meilhan
La Pleine Quarter
rue St Savournin
boulevard Garibaldi
place de Lycée
rue Curiol
rue Terrusse
rue des Trois Mages
Place Jean Jaurès
place du Général de Gaulle
rue St Ferréol
rue de Rome
rue d'Aubagne
cours Julien
rue des Trois Rois
rue Ferrari
rue Saint Pierre
To Hôpital de la Timone (1km)
rue Montgrand
place Félix
rue Auguste Blanqui
place Notre Dame du Mont
rue de la Loubière
rue de Lodi
place de la Préfecture
blvd Salvator
rue Sylvabelle
rue de Rome
rue d'Italie
cours Lieutaud
rue Marengo
rue du Dragon
rue de Village
rue Saint Suffren
place Castellane
boulevard Baille
avenue du Prado
rue de Rouet
rue Breteuil
boulevard Vauban
rue Paradis
To Plage du Prado (3.3km)
Parc Borély (3.3km), Seaquarium (3.3km),
UK Consulate & Auberge de Jeunesse de Bonneveine (4.3km)

Medical Services Hôpital de la Timone (☎ 04 91 38 60 00, metro La Timone) is at 264 rue Saint Pierre, 5e.

Emergency The Préfecture de Police (☎ 04 91 39 80 00, metro Estrangin Préfecture), place de la Préfecture, 1er, is open 24 hours.

Walking Tours

Old Port Area Marseille grew around the old port (metro Vieux Port) where ships have docked for at least 26 centuries. The main commercial docks were transferred to the Joliette area on the coast north of here in the 1840s, but the old port is still active as a harbour for fishing craft, pleasure yachts and ferries to Château d'If. The harbour entrance is guarded by **Bas Fort Saint Nicolas** (on the south side) and, across the water, **Fort Saint Jean**, founded in the 13th century by the Knights Hospitaller of St John of Jerusalem.

In 1943, the neighbourhood on the north side of quai du Port, which was a seedy area with a strong Resistance presence at the time, was systematically dynamited by the Germans. It was rebuilt after the war. There are two museums near the 17th century **Hôtel de Ville**: the Musée des Docks Romains and the Musée du Vieux Marseille. It adjoins to the north the **Panier** quarter, most of whose residents are North African immigrants. The Centre de la Vieille Charité and its museums sit at the top of the hill.

On the south side of the old port, large and lively **place Thiars** and **cours Honoré d'Estienne d'Orves**, with its late-night restaurants and cafés, stretches southward from quai de Rive Neuve.

The liveliest part of Marseille – always crowded with people of all ages, races and ethnic groups – is around the intersection of La Canebière (derived from the Provençal word '*canebe*' meaning hemp after Marseille's industrious rope industry) and cours Belsunce (metro Vieux Port or Noailles). The tourist office at the south end of La Canebière is housed in the former **Café Turc**, a major stopover for east-bound travellers in the 1950s.

The area bounded by La Canebière, cours Belsunce and rue d'Aix, rue Bernard du Bois and blvd d'Athènes is known as the **Belsunce** quarter of town (metro Noailles). Belsunce is a poor immigrant neighbourhood currently undergoing rehabilitation; future projects include a hi-tech district public library. Avoid walking alone here at night.

Aubagne-born Marcel Pagnol (1895-1974) grew up in **La Pleine** quarter of Marseille, immediately east of Belsunce around place Jean Jaurès. He lived at 52 rue Terrusse and went to the Lycée Thiers on place du Lycée. Ask the tourist office for the English-language brochure entitled *Le Marseille de Pagnol* which includes a short Pagnol city tour.

Worth a stroll is the fashionable **6th arrondissement**, especially the area between La Canebière and the **Préfecture building** (metro Estrangin Préfecture). Rue Saint Ferréol, half a block east of the Musée Cantini, is a pedestrian shopping street.

Along the Coast Another fine place for a stroll is along **Corniche Président John F Kennedy**, 7e, which follows the coast for 4.5km. It begins 200m west of **Jardin du Pharo**, a park with breathtaking views of the old port and new ferry terminal, and home to the **Palais du Pharo** built by Napoléon III at 58 blvd Charles Livon. The road continues southward past the small and busy **Plage des Catalans** (Catalan Beach) – which resembles a scene from *Baywatch* with its bronzed, bikini-clad volleyball players – to **Anse des Auffes**. This is a small cove, harbour and village presided over by a war memorial statue of a 'mother of liberty'. The sea-facing statue is framed by a giant archway. A narrow, appropriately crooked, *escalier* (staircase) leads from corniche Président John F Kennedy down to the harbour around which the village nestles.

Continuing farther south, past the landscaped **Centre Municipal de Voile** (☎ 04 91 76 31 60, fax 04 91 71 61 93) at 2 promenade Georges Pompidou, you come to **Plage du Prado** (also called Plage Gaston Defferre). This is Marseille's heavily built-up,

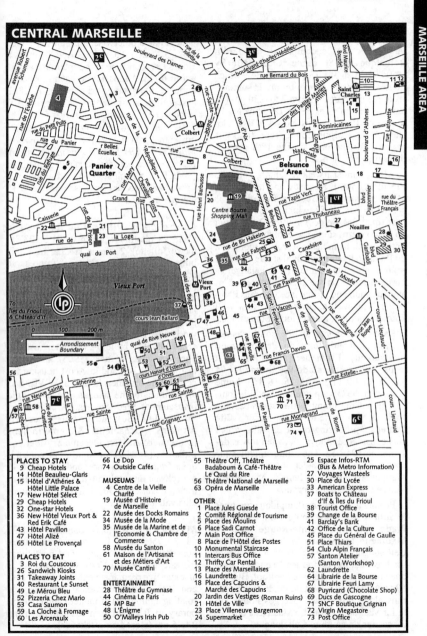

CENTRAL MARSEILLE

PLACES TO STAY
9 Cheap Hotels
14 Hôtel Beaulieu-Glaris
15 Hôtel d'Athènes &
   Hôtel Little Palace
17 New Hôtel Sélect
29 Cheap Hotels
32 One-star Hotels
36 New Hôtel Vieux Port &
   Red Erik Café
43 Hôtel Pavillon
47 Hôtel Alizé
65 Hôtel Le Provençal

PLACES TO EAT
3 Roi du Couscous
26 Sandwich Kiosks
31 Takeaway Joints
40 Restaurant Le Sunset
49 Le Mérou Bleu
52 Pizzeria Chez Mario
53 Casa Saumon
59 La Cloche à Fromage
60 Les Arcenaulx

66 Le Dop
74 Outside Cafés

MUSEUMS
4 Centre de la Vieille
   Charité
19 Musée d'Histoire
   de Marseille
22 Musée des Docks Romains
34 Musée de la Mode
35 Musée de la Marine et de
   l'Economie & Chambre de
   Commerce
58 Musée du Santon
61 Maison de l'Artisanat
   et des Métiers d'Art
70 Musée Cantini

ENTERTAINMENT
28 Théâtre du Gymnase
44 Cinéma Le Paris
46 MP Bar
48 L'Énigme
50 O'Malleys Irish Pub

55 Théâtre Off, Théâtre
   Badaboum & Café-Théâtre
   Le Quai du Rire
56 Théâtre National de Marseille
63 Opéra de Marseille

OTHER
1 Place Jules Guesde
2 Comité Régional de Tourisme
5 Place des Moulins
6 Place Sadi Carnot
7 Main Post Office
8 Place de l'Hôtel des Postes
10 Monumental Staircase
11 Intercars Bus Office
12 Thrifty Car Rental
13 Place des Marseillaises
16 Laundrette
18 Place des Capucins &
   Marché des Capucins
20 Jardin des Vestiges (Roman Ruins)
21 Hôtel de Ville
23 Place Villeneuve Bargemon
24 Supermarket

25 Espace Infos-RTM
   (Bus & Metro Information)
27 Voyages Wasteels
30 Place du Lycée
33 American Express
37 Boats to Château
   d'If & Îles du Frioul
38 Tourist Office
39 Change de la Bourse
41 Barclay's Bank
42 Office de la Culture
45 Place du Général de Gaulle
51 Place Thiars
54 Club Alpin Français
57 Santon Atelier
   (Santon Workshop)
62 Laundrette
64 Librairie de la Bourse
67 Librairie Feuri Lamy
68 Puyricard (Chocolate Shop)
69 Ducs de Gascogne
71 SNCF Boutique Grignan
72 Virgin Megastore
73 Post Office

modern beach resort. Overlooking the sandy, body-packed beach is **Parc Borély**, a large park that encompasses the **Jardin Botanique** and 18th century **Château Borély** (☎ 04 91 25 26 34), 134 ave Clot Bey, which houses temporary art exhibitions in summer. Its opening hours are from 2 to 6.30 pm (11 am to 6 pm on weekends). Take bus No 19 to ave du Prado or bus No 44 to ave Clot Bey. A new **hippodrome** (race track) is planned for the park; in the 18th century there was a track here.

Along almost its entire length, corniche Président John F Kennedy and its continuation, promenade Georges Pompidou, is served by bus No 83, which goes to the old port (quai des Belges) and the Rond Point du Prado metro stop on ave du Prado. To get to the beach from here, bear west along ave du Prado to the monumental statue of **David** – an impressive mimic of Michelangelo's masterpiece – on the busy intersection of ave du Prado and promenade Georges Pompidou. The well-endowed nude is a well known landmark among local Marseillais.

Parc Chanot sits on the south-eastern corner of Rond Point du Prado (Prado roundabout). From here, blvd Michelet leads south to the **stade vélodrome** (☎ 04 91 76 56 09 or 04 91 26 16 15), home ground of the Olympique de Marseille football club. Continuing further south past the stadium, you come to Le Corbusier's **Cité Radieuse**, a housing block on stilts which was considered innovative when it was designed in 1946-52. The estate straddles the corner of blvd Michelet and ave Guy de Maupassant. West of here is Marseille's Musée d'Art Contemporain.

Promenade Georges Pompidou continues to follow the coast south from **Plage du Prado**, past **La Pointe-Rouge** and **La Madrague** to the tiny harbour village of Callelongue on Cap Croisette, from where the breathtaking **calanques** (see Les Calanques later) can be accessed on foot. Bus No 19 from the Rond Point du Prado metro stop runs along promenade Georges Pompidou to La Madrague; from La Madrague bus No 20 carries on south to Callelongue.

Museums

Unless noted otherwise, museums are open from 10 am to 5 pm (closed Monday). Hours between June and September are 11 am to 6 pm. Admission to each museum's permanent/temporary exhibition is 12/18FF (exceptions are noted). Entrance is half-price/free for student/senior over 65.

If you intend visiting all Marseille's museums, invest in a *Passeport pour les Musées* (☎ 04 91 14 58 80 for information). It is available between June and September (50/25FF for adult/student) and allows unlimited entry to all city museums over a 15 day period.

Centre de la Vieille Charité The Old Charity Cultural Centre (☎ 04 91 56 28 38, metro Joliette), 2 rue de la Charité, 2e, is built around Provence's most impressive baroque churches, designed by Pierre Puget and located in the predominantly North African Panier quarter of town. The centre houses some superb permanent exhibits and imaginative temporary exhibitions in a workhouse and hospice built between 1671 and 1745. The building was later restored after serving as barracks (1905), a soldiers' rest home (WWI) and low-cost housing for people who lost their homes in WWII. It is also home to the **Musée d'Archéologie** (Museum of Mediterranean Archaeology; ☎ 04 91 14 58 80); and the **Musée des Arts Africains, Océaniens & Amérindiens** (Museum of African, Oceanic & American Indian Art; ☎ 04 91 14 58 38). The centre is open from 9 am to noon and 1.30 to 4.45 pm (closed on weekends). A combined entrance ticket costs 30FF; individual tickets are available too.

Musée Cantini Musée Cantini (☎ 04 91 54 77 75, metro Estrangin Préfecture), housed in a 17th century *hôtel particulier* (private mansion) at 19 rue Grignan, 6e, has an extensive permanent exhibit of both 17th and 18th century Provençal ceramics and rotating exhibitions of modern and contemporary art. It's open from 10 am to noon and 2 to 6 pm (closed on weekends).

Maison de l'Artisanat et des Métiers d'Art Contemporary photography, sculpture and calligraphy exhibitions among others are hosted at the House of Arts & Crafts (☎ 04 91 54 80 54, metro Vieux Port), 21 cours Honoré d'Estienne d'Orves, 1er. It is open from 1 to 6 pm; closed Sunday and Monday (free).

Musée d'Histoire de Marseille Roman history buffs should visit Marseille's Historical Museum (☎ 04 91 90 42 22, metro Vieux Port or Colbert), just north of La Canebière on the ground floor of the Centre Bourse shopping mall, 1er. Exhibits include the remains of a merchant vessel – discovered by chance in the old port in 1974 – that plied the waters of the Mediterranean in the early 3rd century AD. The 19m-long timbers, which include five different kinds of wood, show evidence of having been repaired repeatedly. To preserve the soaked

Little Saints

The custom of creating a *crèche* (Christmas crib) with figurines of Mary, Joseph, shepherds, kings, oxen, a donkey etc, dates from the Avignon papacy of John XII (1319-34). But it was only after the 1789 revolution and consequent Reign of Terror that these figures were cut down to size, marking the birth of the *santon* and the Provençal crèche.

Santons (from *santoùn*, Provençal for 'little saint') stand no higher than 2.5 to 15cm. The first colourfully-painted figures were created by Marseillais artisan Jean-Louis Lagnel (1764-1822) who came up with the idea of crafting clay miniatures in a plaster mould and allowing them to dry before firing the figures at 950°. *Santonniers* (santon makers) still stick to Lagnel's method today.

In a traditional Provençal crèche there are 55 santons ranging from the tambourine man, fishwife and gypsy, to the miller, tinsmith, scissors grinder, woman carrying garlic and a blowing angel. Since 1806 santonniers have flocked to Marseille each December to take part in the Foire aux Santonniers which sees the length of La Canebière transformed into one big santon fair.

Santons dating from the 18th and 19th centuries are displayed in Marseille's magical **Musée du Santon** (☎ 04 91 54 26 58; metro Vieux Port), 47 rue Neuve Sainte Catherine (7e). The museum houses the private collection of santonnier Marcel Carbonnel, who crafts santons in the adjoining *atelier* (workshop). The museum is open from 9.30 am to 12.30 pm and 2 to 6.30 pm (closed Monday). Carbonnel's workshop can be visited between 8.30 am and 1 pm and 2 to 5.30 pm (closed Friday afternoon and on weekends; guided tours in French on Tuesday and Thursday at 2.30 pm). Admission is free.

The Tinsmith

and decaying wood, the whole thing was freeze-dried right where it now sits – hidden behind glass in a dimly lit room. The museum is open from noon to 7 pm (closed Tuesday).

Roman buildings, uncovered during the construction of the Centre Bourse shopping centre, can be seen just outside the museum in the **Jardin des Vestiges** (Garden of Ruins), which fronts rue Henri Barbusse, 1er.

Musée des Docks Romains The Museum of Roman Warehouses (☎ 04 91 91 24 62, metro Vieux Port), on the north side of the old port in ugly place de Vivaux, 2e, displays in situ part of the 1st century Roman structures discovered in 1947 during post-war reconstruction. The huge jars on display could store 800-2000 litres of wine or oil.

Musée de la Mode Glitz and glamour is the name of the game at the Musée de la Mode (☎ 04 91 56 59 57, metro Vieux Port), 11 La Canebière, 1er. Housed in Marseille's Espace Mode Mediterranée (Mediterranean Fashion Centre), the museum follows French fashion trends over the past 30 years and displays some 2000 items of clothing and accessories. Temporary, contemporary art and photography exhibitions are held in the reception area. The museum is open from 2 to 6 pm (closed on weekends).

Chambre de Commerce A few doors along on La Canebière from the Fashion Museum is the colonnaded Chamber of Commerce building (also known as Palais de la Bourse), built from 1854 to 1860. It houses the **Musée de la Marine et de l'Écon omie** (Naval & Economic Museum; ☎ 04 91 39 33 33, metro Vieux Port). For about half the year, the ship models and engravings are replaced by an art exhibition (35FF). Both are open from 10 am to 6 pm (closed Tuesday).

Palais Longchamp Colonnaded Longchamp Palace (metro Cinq Avenues Longchamp), constructed in the 1860s, is at the eastern end of blvd Longchamp on blvd Philippon, 4e. It was designed in part to disguise a *château d'eau* (water tower) built at the terminus of an aqueduct from the Durance River. The two wings house the **Musée des Beaux-Arts** (☎ 04 91 14 59 30), Marseille's oldest museum whose speciality is 15th to 19th century paintings, and the **Musée d'Histoire Naturelle** (☎ 04 91 62 30 78).

Musée d'Art Contemporain Marseille's Museum of Contemporary Art (MAC; ☎ 04 91 25 01 07), 69 blvd de Haïfa, 8e, is north of the Prado beach area and Parc Borély. Works by Marseille's very own César (see later), as well as Christo, new realists like Ben and Klein, and pieces by pop artist Andy Warhol are displayed. Take bus No 44 from the Rond Point du Prado metro stop to the place Bonnefons stop, from where it is a short walk along ave de Hambourg to Rond Point Pierre Guerre – easily recognisable by a giant metal thumb (César's doing) that proudly sticks out of the middle of the roundabout.

One day a larger collection of works by Marseille born sculptor César Baldaccini (1921-98) will open in a new museum planned for the city (see the Facts about Provence chapter). Among other things César designed the little statue handed to actors and actresses at the Césars, the French cinema awards that bear his name. The museum should open on place du Mazeau; ask the tourist office for details.

Basilique Notre Dame de la Garde

Not to be missed, particularly if you like great panoramas or overwrought 19th century architecture, is a hike up to Basilique Notre Dame de la Garde (☎ 04 91 13 40 80), an enormous Romano-Byzantine basilica 1km south of the old port. It stands on a hilltop (162m) – the highest point in the city – and provides staggering views of sprawling Marseille.

The domed basilica, ornamented with all manner of coloured marble, intricate mosaics, murals and gilded objects, was erected between 1853 and 1864. The bell tower is topped by a 9.7m-tall gilded statue of the Virgin Mary on a 12m-high pedestal. The great bell inside is 2.5m tall and weighs a hefty 8.3 tonnes (the clapper alone is 387kg). Bullet marks from Marseille's Battle of Liberation on 15-25 August 1944 scar the cathedral's northern wall.

The basilica and the crypt are open daily from 7 am to 7 pm in winter and 7 am to 8 pm in summer; 7 am to 10 pm from mid-June to mid-August (free). Dress respectably. Bus No 60 links the old port (from cours Jean Ballard) with the basilica. Count on 30 minutes each way by foot.

Nouvelle Cathédrale

Marseille's Romano-Byzantine cathedral, also called Basilique de Sainte Marie Majeure (☎ 04 91 90 53 57, metro Joliette), just off quai de la Tourette, 2e, is topped with cupolas, towers and turrets of all shapes and sizes. The structure, built from 1852 to 1893 – a period not known for decorative or architectural understatement – is enormous: 140m long and 60m high. It dwarfs the nearby **Ancienne Cathédrale de la Major** (also called the Vieille Major), a mid-11th century Provençal Romanesque structure that stands on the site of what was once a temple to the goddess Diana. The Nouvelle Cathédrale is open from 9 am to noon and 2.30 to 5.30 pm (closed Monday). The Ancienne Cathédrale can be visited by appointment (☎ 04 91 90 53 57).

Abbaye Saint Victor

The twin tombs of 4th century martyrs and a 3rd century sarcophagus are among the sacred objects that rest in the imposing Romanesque 12th century Abbaye Saint Victor (☎ 04 91 05 84 48, metro Vieux Port), rue Neuve Sainte Catherine, 7e, set on a hill above the old port. Each year on 2 February the statue of the Black Virgin inside the abbey is carried through the streets in a candle lit procession; green candles are used to represent light and hope. Marseille's annual sacred music festival is held here. The abbey is open from 8.30 am to 6.30 pm.

Château d'If

The Château d'If (☎ 04 91 59 02 30), the 16th century fortress-turned-prison made famous by Alexandre Dumas' classic work of fiction, *Le Comte de Monte Cristo*, is on a 3 hectare island 3.5km west of the entrance to the old port. Among the people incarcerated here were all sorts of political prisoners, hundreds of Protestants (many perished in the dungeons), the revolutionary hero Mirabeau who served a stint here in 1774 for failing to pay debts, some 1848 revolutionaries and the Communards of 1871.

The fortress was built between 1524 and 1528. It can be visited between October and March from 9.15 am to 5.15 pm (closed Monday) and between April and September daily from 9 am to 7 pm (22FF).

Boats run by GACM (☎ 04 91 55 50 09, fax 04 91 55 60 23, metro Vieux Port), 1 quai des Belges, leave for the Château d'If from outside the GACM office in the old port. Hourly boats run between 9 am and 7 pm (20 minutes; 50FF return). There is a sailing at 6.45 am too. Return boats depart from Île d'If hourly between 9.30 am and 7.30 pm (early morning crossing at 7.15 am).

Îles du Frioul

The islands of Ratonneau and Pomègues, each of which is about 2.5km long, are a few hundred metres west of the Château d'If. They were linked by a dyke in the 1820s. From the 17th to 19th centuries the islands were used as a place of quarantine for people suspected of carrying plague or cholera. Today, the rather barren islands (total area about 200 hectares) shelter seabirds, rare plants and bathers, and are dotted with fortifications (used by German troops during WWII), the ruins of the old quarantine hospital, **Hôpital Caroline**, and Fort Ratonneau.

GACM boats to the Château d'If also serve the Îles du Frioul (50FF return; 80FF to stop at Château d'If too). In summer, boats also sail from Plage du David, immediately north of Plage du Prado. Boats depart from the jetty opposite the Hôtel Concorde hourly (on the half-hour) between 9.30 am and

6.30 pm; return boats leave the island hourly (on the hour) between 10 am and 7 pm. A return ticket costs 50FF.

Beaches

Marseille's main beach, 1km-long Plage du Prado is about 5km south of the city centre. Take bus No 19 or 72 from the Rond Point du Prado metro stop or bus No 83 (No 583 at night) from the old port (quai des Belges) and get off at either La Plage or Plage David stops. On foot, follow Corniche Président John F Kennedy, which runs along the coast, past short Plage des Catalans. The latter, open from 7 am to 7 pm, costs 15FF to access (walk down the steps signposted 'Bains des Catalans').

Five times a day in July and August (and on Wednesday, Saturday and Sunday in June) the local bus company RTM (☎ 04 91 91 92 10) runs a tourist train called *Via la Plage* – with a running commentary – from the Vieux Port to Prado beach. A single/return fare is 15/25FF.

Diving

The calanques (see Les Calanques later), islands and wrecks off the shores of Marseille offer spectacular diving. The Association Plongez Marseille (☎/fax 04 91 49 12 93), 5 rue de Valmy, 12e, has a list of diving schools in Marseille. The Institut National de Plongée Professionnelle (INPP; ☎ 04 91 73 34 62) has an office at 3 Port Pointe-Rouge, Entrée 3, 8e.

You can hire/buy equipment from Au Vieux Plongeur (☎ 04 91 48 79 48, metro Notre Dame du Mont), 116 cours Lieutard, 6e, open year round from 9 am to 8 pm (until 1 pm on Sunday). The Icard Maritime diving centre (☎/fax 04 91 48 37 83), 118 cours Lieutard, 6e, is next door.

To get to the No Limit diving school and Comptoir des Sports shop (☎ 04 91 72 56 56), 109 ave Madrague de Montredon, 8e, take bus No 19 to La Verrerie stop. Get off at the Pointe-Rouge stop for Évasion Sport (☎ 04 91 73 89 00, fax 04 91 73 88 90) which adjoins the Océan 4 diving centre (☎ 04 91 73 91 16), 83 ave de la Pointe-Rouge, 8e.

Organised Tours

The tourist office offers guided tours, including old town walking tours (40FF). Reservations (☎ 04 91 13 89 00) are recommended (obligatory for some). It also sells tickets for Marseille's Histobus Tour (three hours; 75/30FF for adult/child under 12), a city tour by coach that departs daily between June and September.

In summer, GACM (☎ 04 91 55 50 09) runs boat trips from the old port to Cassis and back (four hours; 120FF), which pass by stunning Les Calanques, dramatic coastal rock formations that attract a large amount of unusual wildlife (see Les Calanques later). On Saturday a glass-bottomed boat sails along the coast.

Places to Stay

Marseille has some of France's cheapest hotels – as cheap as 50FF a night! The bad news is many are filthy dives in dodgy areas whose main business is renting out rooms by the hour. Some don't even have any showers. Those we mention appeared, at the time, to be relatively clean and reputable. Map M refers you to the Marseille map; Map C to the Central Marseille map.

Details on the very reputable, family run hotels in the Logis de France chain throughout Provence are available from the Fédération Régionale Provence-Côte d'Azur (☎ 04 91 14 42 00, fax 04 91 14 42 45, www.logis-de-france.com), 8 rue Neuve Saint Martin, 1er.

Places to Stay – Budget

Camping Tents usually can be pitched on the grounds of the *Auberge de Jeunesse Château de Bois Luzy* (see Hostels) for 26FF per person.

Hostels The *Auberge de Jeunesse de Bonneveine* (☎ 04 91 73 21 81, fax 04 91 73 97 23, Impasse du Docteur Bonfils, 8e) is about 4.5km south of the centre and charges 72FF, including breakfast (closed in January). Take bus No 44 from the Rond Point du Prado metro stop and get off at the place Bonnefons stop. Alternatively take bus No 19 from the Castellane metro stop or bus No 47 from the Sainte Marguerite Dromel metro stop.

Auberge de Jeunesse Château de Bois Luzy (☎ 04 91 49 06 18, fax 04 91 49 06 18, *allées des Primevères, 12e)* is 4.5km east of the centre in the Montolivet neighbourhood. A bed/breakfast costs 44/17FF. A hostelling card is mandatory. Take bus No 6 from near the Réformés-Canebière metro stop or bus No 8 from La Canebière.

Hotels – Train Station Area The hotels around the train station are convenient if you arrive by train, but there is better value elsewhere. There's a cluster of small, extremely cheap hotels of less-than-stellar reputation along rue des Petites Maries, 1er.

The two-star *Hôtel d'Athènes* (Map C, ☎ 04 91 90 12 93, 37-39 blvd d'Athènes, *metro Gare Saint Charles, 1er)* is at the foot of the monumental staircase leading from the train station into town. Average but well-kept singles and doubles with shower and toilet cost 190-270FF. Rooms in its adjoining one-star annexe called the *Hôtel Little Palace* cost 120/140/220FF for singles/doubles/triples.

The one-star *Hôtel Beaulieu-Glaris* (Map C, ☎ 04 91 90 70 59, fax 04 91 56 14 04, 1-3 place des Marseillaises, metro Gare Saint Charles, 1er)* is also down the grand staircase. It has poorly maintained singles with washbasin from 126FF and similar doubles from 180FF. Hall showers are 15FF. Rooms overlooking the street are noisy.

Hotels – North of La Canebière Overlooking the bustling old port, the **New Hôtel Vieux Port** (Map C, ☎ 04 91 90 51 42, fax 04 91 90 76 24, info@new-hotel.com, 3bis rue Reine Elisabeth, metro Vieux Port, 1er)* is a large renovated complex with modern singles/doubles for 380/420FF. On weekends and from 7 July to 1 September, the rate for all rooms drops to 335FF, making it good value. Rooms at **New Hôtel Select** (Map C, ☎ 04 91 50 65 50, fax 04 91 50 45 56, 4 allées Léon Gambetta, metro Réformés-Canebière, 1er), run by the same

company, are marginally cheaper (275FF on weekends and in July/August).

Just a few blocks south-east of the old port, *Hôtel Le Provençal* (Map C, ☎ 04 91 33 11 15, 32 rue Paradis, metro Vieux Port, 1er)* has singles from 120FF and doubles/triples with TV and shower for 170/220FF.

Hôtel Gambetta (Map M, ☎ 04 91 62 07 88, fax 04 91 64 81 54, 49 allées Léon Gambetta, metro Réformés-Canebière, 1er)* has singles without shower for 95FF and singles/doubles with shower from 130/160FF. Hall showers cost 15FF.

Hôtel Ozea (Map M, ☎ 04 91 47 91 84, 12 rue Barbaroux, metro Réformés-Canebière, 1er)* is across square Léon Blum from the eastern end of allées Léon Gambetta. It welcomes new guests 24 hours a day (at night just ring the bell to wake up the night clerk). Clean, old-fashioned doubles without/with shower are 120/150FF. There are no hall showers. A couple of doors down at No 18 on the same street is the *Hôtel Pied-à-Terre* (Map M, ☎ 04 91 92 00 95) which has well-kept rooms for 120/150FF without/with shower. There are no hall showers. Reception is open until 1 am.

Hotels – South of La Canebière There are many rock-bottom, very sleazy hotels along rue Sénac de Meilhan, rue Mazagran and rue du Théâtre Français and around place du Lycée (all near metro Réformés-Canebière, 1er). Slightly to the west, rue des Feuillants (metro Noailles) has a number of one-star hotels.

A cut above its neighbours, *Hôtel Sphinx* (Map M, ☎ 04 91 48 70 59, 16 rue Sénac de Meilhan, metro Réformés-Canebière, 1er)* has well-kept rooms for one or two people with toilet for 70-120FF, with shower for 130-160FF. Hall showers are 17FF.

The *Hôtel de Nice* (Map M, ☎ 04 91 48 73 07, 11 rue Sénac de Meilhan, metro Réformés-Canebière, 1er)* is a small step up from other hotels in this area too. Unfortunately, the ladies in the house next door welcome more customers than a lemonade stand in the Sahara. Doubles without/with shower are 100/120FF; hall showers cost 20FF.

Good value is the nearby *Hôtel Pavillon* (Map C, ☎ 04 91 33 76 90, *27 rue Pavillon, metro Vieux Port, 1er)*. Rooms with shower/bath start at 139/149FF and rock-bottom singles with no perks cost from 99FF.

Hotels – Prefecture Area All the hotels in this section (metro Estrangin Préfecture, 6e) are on the Marseille map (Map M).

Blvd Louis Salvator, in a decent neighbourhood, has a number of renovated two-star hotels touting bright rooms with a modern decor. At No 9 is the *Grand Hôtel Le Préfecture (☎ 04 91 54 31 60, fax 04 91 54 24 95)* which has beautifully clean and modern rooms with shower, toilet and TV for 180FF and ones with a bath for 210FF. *Le Président (☎ 04 91 48 67 29, fax 04 91 94 24 44, 12 blvd Louis Salvator)* has rooms with a shower, toilet and TV for 190FF and ones with a bath for 240FF.

Continuing up the hill you come to the one-star *Hôtel Massilla (☎ 04 91 54 79 28, 25 blvd Louis Salvator)*, which has doubles with shower and toilet for 160FF, or singles/doubles with shower for 120/140FF. Guests have to punch in a code to enter this security-conscious hotel. Almost opposite at No 36 is the more upmarket *Hôtel Manon (☎ 04 91 48 67 01, fax 04 91 47 23 04)* which has bright singles/doubles with all mod cons from 170/230FF.

Half a block east of the Prefecture building, the *Hôtel Salvator (☎ 04 91 48 78 25, 6 rue Salvator)* has doubles with high ceilings and almost antique furniture for 120FF with shower.

Hôtel Béarn (☎ 04 91 37 75 83, 63 rue Sylvabelle) is quiet with colourfully decorated singles/doubles for 100/120FF with shower and from 180/210FF with shower and toilet. Guests can watch TV in the common room. Reception closes at 11 pm or midnight.

Places to Stay – Mid-Range & Top End

The clean, safe and large *Hôtel Ibis Saint Charles (Map M, ☎ 04 91 95 62 09, fax 04 91 50 68 42, 1 square Narvik, metro Gare Saint Charles, 1er)*, on the south side of the

train terminal building, has unexciting rooms for one or two people from 310FF.

The *Hôtel Alizé (Map C, ☎ 04 91 33 66 97, fax 04 91 54 80 06, 35 quai des Belges, metro Vieux Port, 1er)* is an elegant old pile overlooking the old port. It has pleasant singles/doubles with air-con and sound-proofed windows from 275/300FF.

Built into the rocks offering fantastic sea and beach views is the idyllic, two-star *Hôtel Le Richelieu (Map M, ☎ 04 91 31 01 92, 52 corniche Président John F Kennedy, 7e)* overlooking the Plage des Catalans. Rooms for one or two people cost 190FF with shower, 185-215FF with shower and toilet, and 220-240FF with TV too. Don't miss breakfast on the terrace.

The *New Hôtel Bompard (☎ 04 91 52 10 93, fax 04 91 31 02 14, 1 rue des Flots Bleues, 7e)* is just off corniche Président John F Kennedy and sports three stars thanks to its elegant sea views, swimming pool and extensive grounds. Singles/doubles with all the gadgets cost 400/440FF on weekdays (390/430FF on weekends and in July and August).

Places to Eat

Marseille's restaurants offer incredible variety. Unless noted otherwise, the places listed appear on the Central Marseille map.

Tasty tip: no trip to Marseille is complete without trying *bouillabaisse*, fishy as it may be (see the special Food & Wine section, pp 83-103).

Restaurants – French Fish is the predominant dish in Marseille, be it *soupe* (soup), *huîtres* (oysters), *moules* (mussels) or other *coquillages* (shellfish), all of which are plentiful in this lively port city. The length of quai de Rive Neuve, 1er, is plastered with outside cafés and touristy restaurants touting bouillabaisse on their menu boards; those along quai du Port on the northern side of the old port are pricier. To the south, the pedestrian streets around place Thiars to the south overflow with terrace cafés and restaurants in the warmer months.

The upmarket *Casa Saumon* (☎ 04 91 54 22 89, 22 rue de la Paix, metro Vieux Port, 1er) serves *saumon*, salmon and more salmon in a rustic but refined atmosphere. It's open from noon to 2.30 pm and 7.30 to 10.30 pm (closed Sunday).

Le Mérou Bleu (☎ 04 91 54 23 25, 32-36 rue Saint Saëns, metro Vieux Port, 1er) is a popular restaurant with a lovely terrace. It has bouillabaisse (89-135FF), other seafood dishes (72-125FF), hot first courses (38-78FF), pasta etc.

Pizzeria Chez Mario (☎ 04 91 54 48 54, 8 rue Euthymènes, metro Vieux Port, 1er) is more than just a pizzeria. Mario has fish and grilled meats (85-110FF) and pasta (from 50FF) too; open from noon to 2.30 pm and 7.30 to 11.30 pm.

La Cloche à Fromage (27 cours Honoré d'Estienne d'Orves, metro Vieux Port, 1er) has cheese, cheese and more cheese – 70 types in fact. Various *plateaux* (trays) are available from 93FF and there is a lunchtime *menu* for 59FF. Close by is the delightful restaurant-cum *salon de thé*, *Les Arcenaulx*, a beautifully restored complex wrapped around cours des Arcenaulx at 27 cours Honoré d'Estienne d'Orves, 1er. Advance bookings are recommended.

There is a colourful choice of French eateries on cours Julien (Map M, metro Notre Dame du Mont-Cours Julien, 6e). Particularly tasty places include *Le Resto Provençal* (☎ 04 91 48 85 12), at No 64, which has one of the most idyllic sky-topped terraces in the city. It has a *menu* offering (predominantly fishy) regional fare for 110FF, a *plat du jour* for 43FF and a good-value lunchtime *menu* for 65FF. *Le Sud du Haut* (☎ 04 91 92 66 64), at No 80, is painted bright blue and yellow on the outside and furnished with an eclectic collection of obscure items inside. Strictly Provençal dishes are served here too.

Restaurants – Ethnic Cuisine Couscous reigns supreme in certain parts of Marseille. *Roi du Couscous* (☎ 04 91 91 45 46, 63 rue de la République, metro Colbert or Joliette, 2e) is just a short distance north of the Panier quarter. This 'King of Couscous' dishes up the steamed semolina with meats and vegetables for 35 to 60FF, while a three-course lunchtime *menu* is just 50FF, including a quarter-litre of wine. The King holds court from noon to 2.30 or 3 pm and 7 to 10.30 pm (closed Monday).

For Vietnamese and Chinese fare, the many restaurants on, or just off, rue de la République (metro Vieux Port) are worth a nibble. Other than that, cours Julien – Marseille's trendy and bohemian patch of town – is lined with fun and funky restaurants offering a tantalising variety of other ethnic cuisines: Indian, Caribbean, Pakistani, Thai, Armenian, Lebanese, Tunisian, Italian and so on.

Noteworthy options include the upstairs Caribbean *Restaurant Antillais* (☎ 04 91 48 71 89) at No 10. It is run by a congenial couple from the West Indies who offer a 100FF *menu* (including a pichet of house wine), plus a colourful range of starters from 20FF, and main dishes from 40FF. The Armenian restaurant *Le Caucase* (☎ 04 91 48 36 30), at No 62, serves unpronounceable dishes that are as tasty as they are unrecognisable. The *menu* is 88FF. The Caucase is only open evenings.

Restaurants – Kosher *Restaurant Le Sunset* (☎ 04 91 33 27 77, 24 rue Pavillon, metro Vieux Port, 1er) has kosher Israeli food and a midday 59FF *menu*. It is open from noon to 2 pm (closed Saturday).

Restaurants – By the Beach Famed for its exquisite – and expensive – bouillabaisse is *Chez Fonfon* (☎ 04 91 52 14 38, 140 Vallon des Auffes, 7e), idyllically set overlooking the harbour of Anse des Auffes. Fish dishes are the house speciality with bouillabaisse du pêcheur costing 250FF per person and langoustine priced at 100FF per 100g. Reservations are advised at this chic, seaside spot.

Not quite so pricey but equally packed is the *Pizzeria Chez Jeannot* (☎ 04 91 52 11 28, 129 Vallon des Auffes, 7e) which despite its name, serves a good range of fresh salads, pastas, oysters and shellfish dishes as well as pizza. Its terrace restaurant is a great boat-watching spot.

Farther down the coast is *Pizzeria des Catalans* (☎ 04 91 52 37 82) with a terrace overlooking the courts of the volleyball club on Plage des Catalans. The *Bistrot Plage & Restaurant de la Corniche* (☎ 04 91 31 80 32 or 04 91 31 62 13), midway between Marseille's old port and Plage du Prado at 60 corniche Président John F Kennedy, has a wonderful terrace which juts out into the sea offering unbeatable views of the coast and Château d'If. It has a tasty 110FF *menu*. A beach mattress on the wooden sun terrace costs 45FF a day.

Cafés Cafés galore crowd quai de Rive Neuve and cours Honoré d'Estienne d'Orves, 1er, a long open square two blocks south of the quay. There is a less touristy cluster overlooking the fountain in place de la Préfecture at the south end of pedestrianised rue Saint Ferréol, 1er.

Fairly local is the large and pleasant *Café de la Banque (metro Estrangin Prefécture)*, just off place de la Préfecture on blvd Paul Reytal, 1er, which has outside seating on the sunny side of the street and attracts a young shades 'n attitude type of crowd. Ideal for a sedate and light lunch away from the crowds is *Red Erik Café (metro Vieux Port)*, next to the New Hôtel Vieux Port on rue Reine Elisabeth, 1er. Filled baguettes start at 15FF and simple salads from 40FF.

The *Salon de Thé* inside the Virgin Megastore (☎ 04 91 55 55 00, 75 rue Saint Ferréol, metro Estrangin Prefécture, 1er) is open from 10 am to 8 pm (until midnight on Saturday; closed Sunday). Equally chic is *Le Dop (metro Estrangin Prefécture)*, a small, clean and very green café specialising in pasta on rue Dumarsais (just off rue Paradis, 1er). Salads cost 35-42FF.

Dressed to kill? Then head for the elitist *Café de la Mode* (☎ 04 91 91 21 36, 11 La Canebière, metro Vieux Port, 1er) inside the Musée de la Mode, open from noon to 7 pm (closed Monday).

Cours Julien (Map M, metro Notre Dame du Mont-Cours Julien, 6e) has a cluster of great cafés at its north end, including the very retro *Rétro Julien* at No 22, touting bright yellow-brick walls and serving crêpes at, and the next-door *Eden Café Rock* (☎ 04 91 92 03 02), the walls of which are splashed with wild graffiti-style paintings.

Self-Catering Marseille is home to a wholesome array of markets, the most aromatic being the daily *fresh fish market (quai des Belges, metro Vieux Port, 1er)* between 8 am and 1 pm. Fresh fruit and vegetables are sold at the *Marché des Capucins (place des Capucins, metro Noailles, 1er)* and the fruit and vegetable *morning market (cours Pierre Puget, metro Estrangin Préfecture, 6e)*. Both are closed Sunday.

For foie gras (duck liver pâté) and Provençal wines, shop at *Ducs de Gascogne* (☎ 04 91 33 87 28, 39 rue Paradis, 1er). Chocolatier *Puyricard* (☎ 04 91 55 67 49, 25 rue Francis Davso, 1er) is suited to the sweeter-toothed shopper. Nearby, a rich array of coffee, tea and chocolate is sold at the *Maison Debout* (☎ 04 91 33 00 12, 46 rue Francis Davso, 1er).

Entertainment

Cultural event listings appear in the monthly *Vox Mag* and weekly *Taktik* and *Sortir*, all distributed free at the tourist office, cinemas and ticket offices mentioned later. Listings are also contained in the weekly *L'Officiel des Loisirs* (2FF in newspaper kiosks).

Tickets for most cultural events are sold at *billetteries* (ticket counters) in FNAC (☎ 04 91 39 94 00, metro Vieux Port) on the top floor of the Centre Bourse shopping mall, 1er; the Virgin Megastore (☎ 04 91 55 55 00, metro Estrangin Préfecture), 75 rue Saint Ferréol, 1er; Arcenaulx (☎ 04 91 59 80 37, metro Vieux Port), 25 cours Honoré d'Estienne d'Orves, 1er; and the Office de la Culture (☎ 04 91 33 33 79), 42 La Canebière, 1er.

The *Espace Julien* (☎ 04 91 24 34 14, 39 cours Julien, metro Notre Dame du Mont-Cours Julien, 6e) is a leading venue for rock concerts, opérock, alternative theatre, reggae festivals, hip hop, Afro-groove and other cutting-edge entertainment.

Bars & Clubs For a good selection of rock, reggae, country and other kinds of live music, try *La Maison Hantée (☎ 04 91 92 09 40, 10 rue Vian, metro Notre Dame du Mont-Cours Julien, 6e)*, on a hip street between cours Julien and rue des Trois Rois; or *La Machine à Coudre (☎ 04 91 55 62 65, 6 rue Jean Roque, 1er)*, tucked in a small street off the south end of blvd Garibaldi. Funk, blues and rap features here Tuesday to Saturday from 10 pm to 2 am.

Il Caffé (63 cours Julien, metro Notre Dame du Mont-Cours Julien, 6e), open until 10 pm (closed Sunday), is a pleasant watering hole. Marseille's Irish pub, *O'-Malleys (metro Vieux Port, 1er)*, overlooks the old port on the corner of rue de la Paix and quai de Rive Neuve.

You can play pétanque underground (for free) at *Le Trolley (☎ 04 91 54 30 45, 24 quai de Rive Neuve, metro Vieux Port, 7e)*, a nightclub with five different dance areas housed in an 18th century tunnel. It is open on Thursday, Friday and Saturday from 11 pm to 6 am (60FF on Saturday; free the other days).

Gay & Lesbian Venues Popular gay bars include *L'Énigme (☎ 04 91 33 79 20, 22 rue Beauvau, metro Vieux Port, 1er)* and the *MP Bar (☎ 04 91 33 64 79)* at No 10 on the same street. Camper than a row of tents and full of fun is the lively *Drag Queen Café (☎ 04 91 94 21 41, 2 rue Sénac de Meilhan, metro Noailles or Réformés-Canebière, 1er)* which hosts live bands and is open until 5.30 am at weekends. Opposite at No 3 is the equally hectic *New Can-Can* nightclub *(☎ 04 91 48 59 76)* which rocks until 6 am.

Cinema *Cinéma Le Paris (☎ 04 91 33 41 54 or 04 91 33 15 59, 31 rue Pavillon, metro Vieux Port, 1er)* shows nondubbed films in three halls. Screenings are daily between 2 pm and midnight. Tickets cost 33FF.

Theatre Marseille has a very active alternative theatre scene. Venues include the *Chocolat Théâtre (☎ 04 91 42 19 29, 59*

Planet Mars

Club music has struck dramatic new chords since the yéyé (imitative rock) of the 1960s sung by Johnny Hallyday – thanks in part to rappers *de la Planète MARS*.

IAM from Planet Mars (Mars being short for Marseille) – France's best known rap band – scored an instant hit, and a massive coup for Marseillais rap, with their first album entitled … *de la Planète MARS* released in 1991. It was followed by *Ombre est Lumière* (Shade is Light) in 1994 – which sent rappers reeling with the hit *Je Danse le Mia* – and by the more recent, triple vinyl *L'École du Micro d'Argent* in 1997. The six man band includes Philippe 'Chill' Fragoine (band leader), better known as Akhenaton to rap heads, Eric Mazel (DJ) whose band name is Khéops, Imhotep (sound engineer) and Shurik'n (lyricist). Log in at www.iam.tm.fr.

Other Marseillais rap bands to watch out for include Fonky Family, Soul Swing whose sound is a far cry from the name, Def Bond and Prodige Namor. *Rap a Cité*, released by Arsenal records (an independent French label), is a three-city compilation album featuring hip hop beats from Marseille, Paris and New York.

Marseille's other claim to fame over the past decade has been its contribution to sono mondial (world music) – notably Algerian raï. Acclaimed Marseillais voices include Cheb Khaled, Cheb Aïssa and Cheb Mami.

Ahmed Whaby, pioneer of Oran music and dubbed the world's most beautiful Arab voice, was born in Marseille in 1921. His mother was Spanish, his father Algerian.

cours Julien, metro Notre Dame du Mont-Cours Julien, 6e), which doubles as a restaurant, open from 11.30 to 2 am.

At the old port, the cobbled Passage des Arts off 16 quai de Rive Neuve, 7e, is home to the off-beat *Théâtre Off* (☎ 04 91 33 12 92) which has performances (60FF) every evening except Tuesday, at 8.30 pm; the *Théâtre Badaboum* (☎ 04 91 54 40 71); and the comic *Café-Théâtre Le Quai du Rire* (☎ 04 91 54 95 00, fax 04 91 74 35 80) where you can watch comedy shows while you eat (200FF including dinner).

Mainstream dramas are hosted at the nearby *Théâtre National de Marseille* (☎ 04 91 54 70 54, 30 quai de Rive Neuve, metro Vieux Port, 7e)* and the *Théâtre du Gymnase* (☎ 04 91 24 35 24, 4 rue de Théâtre Français, metro Noailles, 1er)*.

Opera The lovely *Opéra de Marseille* (☎ 04 91 55 00 70, 2 rue Molière, metro Vieux Port, 1er)* is a short distance south of the old port. The Art Deco building dates from 1921. A ticket to the opera costs 45 to 340FF.

Spectator Sports

Watching Marseille's football team, Olympique de Marseille (OM), play on their home ground is the city's top spectator sport. Stadium details and information on how/where to buy tickets are in the Facts for the Visitor chapter. During matches local supporters can be found staring agog at the TV screen in the OM Café (☎ 04 91 33 80 33), Vieux Port.

Shopping

Cours Julien (metro Notre Dame du Mont-Cours Julien, 6e) hosts a variety of morning markets: shop here for fresh flowers on Wednesday and Saturday, fruit and veg on Friday, antique books every second Saturday; and stamps or antique books on Sunday. Stalls laden with everything from second-hand clothing to pots and pans fill nearby place Jean Jaurès on Saturday from 8 am to 1 pm.

The best place to shop for traditional Provençal santons is the boutique inside the Musée du Santon (see the boxed text Little

Saints). Marseillais soap can be bought in any souvenir shop.

Getting There & Away

Air The Aéroport International Marseille-Provence (☎ 04 42 14 14 14, www .marseille.aeroport.fr), also known as Aéroport Marseille-Marignane, is 25km northwest of the city in Marignane.

Bus The *gare des autocars* (bus station; ☎ 04 91 08 16 40, metro Gare Saint Charles), place Victor Hugo, 3e, is 150m to the right as you exit the train station. The information counter (☎ 04 91 08 16 40) is open from 7 am to 6 pm (Sunday from 9 am to noon and 2 to 6 pm). It doubles as a left-luggage office (10FF per bag a day). Tickets are sold at company ticket counters (closed most of the time) or direct from the bus driver. Scrappy handwritten schedules are stuck on a noticeboard outside the bus station.

There are buses to Aix-en-Provence (26FF; 35 minutes via the autoroute/one hour via the N8), Avignon (91FF; 35 minutes; seven a day), Cannes (120FF; two hours), Carpentras (74FF), Cassis (23FF), Cavaillon (54FF), Digne-les-Bains (80FF; 2½ hours; four a day), Nice (133FF; 2¾ hours), Nice airport, Orange, Salon and other destinations. There is an infrequent service to Castellane in Haute-Provence (see that chapter).

Eurolines (☎ 04 91 50 57 55, fax 04 91 08 32 21) has a counter in the bus station, open from 8 am to noon and 2 to 6 pm (7.30 am to noon and 1 to 5 pm on Saturday; closed Sunday). Intercars (☎ 04 91 50 08 66, metro Gare Saint Charles), down the staircase from the train station at 14 place des Marseillaises, 1er, is open from 9 am to noon and 2 to 6 pm (until noon only Saturday; closed Sunday). See the Getting There & Away chapter for details.

Train Marseille's passenger train station, served by both metro lines, is called Gare Saint Charles (☎ 04 91 50 00 00 or 08 36 35 35 35, metro Gare Saint Charles). The information and ticket reservation office, one level below the tracks next to the metro entrance, is open from 9 am to 8 pm (closed Sunday). The luggage lockers are accessible between 8 am and 10 pm (15/20/30FF for a small/medium/large locker). They are in a hall next to the toilets (2.80FF) and showers (19/26FF for a 25/35 minute shower/bath; open from 6.30 am to 8 pm).

In town, train tickets can be bought in advance at the SNCF Boutique Grignan, 17 rue Grignan, 1er, which is open from 9 am to 4.30 pm (closed on weekends).

There are direct trains to Aix-en-Provence (38FF; 40 minutes; at least 18 a day), Arles (79FF; 40 minutes), Avignon (100FF; one hour), Cannes (150FF; two hours; over two dozen a day), Les Arcs-sur-Argens (119FF; 1½ hours), Nice (145FF; 1½ to two hours; over two dozen a day), Nîmes (114FF; 1¼ hours; 12 a day), Orange (107FF; 1½ hours; 10 a day) and many other destinations.

The Marseille-Hyères train (70FF; 1¼ hours; four daily) stops at Cassis, La Ciotat, Bandol, Ollioules-Sanary and Toulon (55FF; 40 minutes) en route.

Trains to other destinations in France and Europe are listed in the Getting There & Away chapter.

SOS Voyageurs office (☎ 04 91 62 12 80), across the corridor from the police post, helps problem-plagued passengers. It's open from 9 am to noon and 1 to 7 pm (closed Sunday).

Car & Motorcycle Rental agencies offering better rates include Thrifty (☎ 04 91 05 92 18, metro Gare Saint Charles), 8 blvd Voltaire, 1er, and Europcar (☎ 04 91 99 40 90, metro Gare Saint Charles), next to the train station at 7 blvd Maurice Bourdet, 1er.

Boat Marseille's giant passenger *gare maritime* (ferry terminal; ☎ 04 91 56 38 63, fax 04 91 56 38 70, metro Joliette) is 250m west of place de la Joliette, 2e.

SNCM ferries (☎ 08 36 67 21 00, fax 04 91 56 35 86) link Marseille with Corsica, Sardinia, Tunisia, Spain and Algeria. SNCM's office (metro Joliette), 61 blvd des Dames, 2e, is open from 8 am to 6 pm (Saturday from 8.30 am to noon and 2 to 5.30 pm; closed Sunday).

Algérie Ferries (☎ 04 91 90 64 70, metro Joliette), 29 blvd des Dames, 2e, is open from 8.15 to 11.45 am and 1 to 4.45 pm (closed on weekends). Ticketing and reservations for the Tunisian ferry company, Compagnie Tunisienne de Navigation (CTN) are handled by SNCM.

For more information see the Getting There & Away chapter under Sea.

Getting Around

To/From the Airport Shuttle buses operated by TRPA (☎ 04 91 50 59 34 in Marseille, ☎ 04 42 14 31 27 at the airport) link Aéroport International Marseille-Provence with Marseille train station (46/26FF for adult/child aged 6-10). Buses to the airport leave from outside the train station's main entrance every 20 minutes between 5.30 am and 9.50 pm; buses from the airport depart between 6.30 am and 10.50 pm.

Bus & Metro Marseille has two fast, well-maintained metro lines called Métro 1 and Métro 2, a tram line, and an extensive bus network.

The metro (which began operation in 1977), trams and most buses run from about 5 am to 9 pm. From 9.25 pm to 12.30 am, métro and tram routes are covered every 15 minutes by surface buses Nos M1 and M2 and Tramway No 68; stops are marked with fluorescent green signs reading *métro en bus* (metro by bus). Most of the 11 Fluobus night buses (☎ 04 91 91 92 10 for information) begin their runs in front of the Espace Infos-RTM office (metro Vieux Port), 6 rue des Fabres, 1er, which distributes route maps.

Bus/metro tickets (9FF) can be used on any combination of metro, bus and tram for one hour after they've been time-stamped (no return trips). A six day carnet costs 42FF, a day pass 25FF. Tram stops have modern blue ticket distributors to time-stamp your ticket before you board.

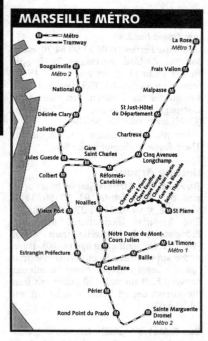

For information on Marseille's public transport system, drop into Espace Infos-RTM (☎ 04 91 91 92 10). It is open from 8.30 am to 6 pm (9 am to 5.30 pm on Saturday). Tickets can be purchased here from as early as 6.10 am until 7.50 pm.

Taxi There's a taxi stand to the right as you exit the train station through the main entrance. Marseille Taxi (☎ 04 91 02 20 20) and Taxis France (☎ 04 91 49 91 00) dispatch taxis 24 hours a day.

Boat To call a bateau taxi (boat taxi), call ☎ 06 09 95 89 26.

Les Calanques

Since 1975, this 20km strip of coast and inland Massif des Calanques covering 5000 hectares has been protected as a natural monument, although local residents want to see Les Calanques embraced by a national park.

Summer forest fires are a continual pest to the semi-arid flora that skirts the limestone coastline, and the Office National des Forêts closes the massif interior each year between July and September (see the Facts about Provence and Facts for the Visitor chapters). Despite its barren scape, the massif shelters an extraordinary wealth of flora and fauna – including 900 plant species of which 15 are protected, such as the dwarf red behen, Marseille astragalus and tartonraire sparrow wort. Myrtle and wild olive trees grow in the warmer valleys. The Bonnelli eagle is a frequent visitor to Les Calanques which, in their darker cracks and crevices give shelter to Europe's largest lizard and longest snake – the eyed lizard (60cm) and the Montpellier snake (2m).

Les Calanques offer ample hiking opportunities, including the coastal **GR98** which leads south from the Marseille suburb of **La Madrague** to Callelongue on **Cap Croisette**, and then eastwards along the coast to Cassis. Count on 11 to 12 hours at least to hike this 28km stretch. See Along the Coast in the Marseille Walking Tours section for bus information from Marseille to Callelongue.

Boat excursions in Les Calanques set sail from Marseille, Cassis and La Ciotat, as well as Bandol, Sanary-sur-Mer and Le Brusc (see the Saint Tropez to Toulon chapter).

Sormiou & Morgiou

There are plenty of shorter marked trails, the most popular being those that lead to **Calanque de Sormiou** and neighbouring Calanque de Morgiou.

Beach-clad Sormiou – the largest of the calanques – hit the headlines in October 1991 when Henri Cosquer, a diver from Cassis (see later) discovered an underwater cave here, the interior of which was adorned with prehistoric wall paintings dating from around 20,000 BC. The only access to the cave was a narrow, 150m-long passage, 36m deep underwater. The Grotte Cosquer is protected as a historical monument and closed to the public today. Many more are believed to exist here.

In October 1998, local fishermen caught a bracelet off the Sormiou coast belonging to French author Antoine de Saint-Exupéry, whose plane went down in 1944 during a reconnaissance mission. Marine salvage crews consequently combed the coastline in an attempt to uncover the wreckage, but the bracelet later proved to be a hoax.

To get to the calanque by car from place Louis Bonnefon (next to the Château Borély) in Marseille, follow the southbound ave de Hambourg past César's thumb on Rond Point Pierre Guerrefrom to chemin de Sormiou. From the end of this road, the route du Feu forest track (45 minutes) leads to Sormiou's small fishing port and beach in the calanque. By bus, take No 23 from the Rond Point du Prado metro stop to La Cayolle stop.

Sormiou and Morgiou are separated by Cap Morgiou. **Calanque de Morgiou** nestles on the east side of the cape. During the 17th century Louis XIII came to Marseille to fish for tuna in the bay here. From ave de Hambourg, follow the Morgiou road signs, past Marseille's infamous prison in Les Beaumettes. Morgiou beach is a one hour walk from the car park. By bus No 23, continue past La Cayolle and get off at the Morgiou-Beauvallon bus stop.

En Vau, Port Pin & Port Miou

Continuing east along the stone sculptured coast, you come to **Calanque d'En Vau** which – with its emerald waters encased by cliffs studded with dangling rope-clad climbers – is the most photographed calanque. Its entrance is guarded by **Doigt de Dieu**, a giant rock pinnacle. Its beach is pebbly. En Vau is accessible on foot. There is a marked trail (around three hours) starting from the car park on the Col de la Gardiole which is south off the D559, 5km from Cassis on a wiggly dirt road into the Forêt de la Gardiole. Approaching from the east, it is a good 1½ hour walk on the GR98 from Port Miou. En route you pass neighbouring **Calanque de Port Pin**, a 30 minute walk from Port Miou.

Calanque de Port Miou, immediately west of Cassis, is one of the few inlets accessible by car; the tourist office in Cassis distributes free maps featuring the three calanques plus the various walking trails leading to them.

Cassis
- **pop 8000**   ✉ 13260

Sweet little Cassis is best known for its white wines, of which Provençal poet Frédéric Mistral wrote 'the bee does not have a sweeter honey, it shines like an untroubled diamond ...' Quality aside, the picture-postcard appearance of Cassis' terraced vineyards that climb up the slopes in neat little steps against a magnificent backdrop of sea and cliffs can hardly be disputed.

Unfortunately, the fishing port – complete with a 14th century chateau, views of the Baie de Cassis and France's highest cliff – is a hub for boat trips along the calanques and gets overrun with camera-happy tourists in summer. An open-air market fills place du Marché on Wednesday and Friday morning. Local artisans set up stalls in the old town on September weekends.

Orientation & Information Cassis train station is 3km east of the centre on the D1. The old town surrounds the port, south of which sits its medieval chateau. Promenade Aristide Briand and its continuation, quai Saint Pierre, runs between the port and the beach, Plage de la Grande Mer.

From quai Saint Pierre, walk south along rue Barthélemy then cut through the Jardin Public (Public Garden) to get to place Baragnon, the central square home to the main tourist office (☎ 04 42 01 71 17, fax 04 42 01 28 31, omt-cassis@ enprovence .com, www.cassis.enprovence .com). It is open from 9 am to noon and 2.30 to 5.30 pm (until noon on Saturday; closed Sunday). In June, July and August a tourist office annexe operates on promenade Aristide Briand between 10 am and 1 pm and 3.30 to 10.30 pm.

Local hiking maps and guides are sold at the Librairie Préambule (☎ 04 42 01 30 83),

8 rue Pierre Eydin, an English language bookshop in a street behind the main tourist office.

Boat Excursions Year round, boats line up alongside quai des Baux at the port to take tourists on boat trips around Les Calanques: Moby Dick (☎ 04 42 01 03 31 or 06 09 34 95 96) and Le Napo (☎ 04 42 01 16 47 or 06 12 72 66 20) are among the host of companies clamouring for business; the tourist office has a complete list of operators. They all offer identical deals: a 45 minute trip to three calanques (Port Miou, Port Pin and En-Vau) costs 50FF; a 65 minute trip covering the latter plus Oule and Devanson calanques is 70FF; and a 1½ hour trip taking in seven calanques (including Morgiou) is 90FF.

Those aspiring to sail themselves can contact the École Municipale de Voile (☎ 04 42 01 16 65), quai du Moulin. The **sailing school** is open from 9 am to noon and 2 to 5 pm (closed on weekends); an initiation course on a catamaran (15 hours) is 530FF.

Diving expeditions in the calanques are organised by the Centre Cassidain de Plongée (☎ 04 42 01 89 16, fax 04 42 01 23 76, henri.cosquer@hol.fr), 3 rue Michel Arnaud, off quai des Baux. The school is run by Henri Cosquer (see Sormiou & Morgiou earlier). A baptism dive costs 300FF. Half/full day and night dives as well as shipwreck expeditions are also available.

Wine Tasting There is no better time to have a tipple of the local vino than at the annual Fête des Vendanges et du Vin Cassis, celebrated to mark the grape harvest on the first Sunday in September. Year round, you can visit any of the 13 *domaines* (wine producing estates) that produce the Cassis appellation (AOC), awarded to local wine growers in 1936. Just 168 hectares of land are carpeted with the distinctive terrace vineyards which yield an annual production of 600,000 to 700,000 bottles of whites, reds and rosés. Heading south-east out of Cassis towards route des Crètes (D141), you pass the **Domaine du Bagnol** (☎ 04 42

01 78 05, fax 04 42 01 11 22), 12 ave de Provence. There are more domaines on route de La Ciotat; the tourist office has a complete list.

The history of Cassis is unwoven in the **Musée Municipal d'Art et Traditions** (☎ 04 42 01 88 66), housed in a 17th century presbytery on place Baragnon (entrance on rue Xavier Dauthier). Its opening hours are Wednesday, Thursday and Saturday from 3.30 to 6.30 pm (from 2.30 to 5.30 pm between October and March).

Cassis wine is particularly tasty drunk with *oursins* (sea urchins). See the Carry-le-Rouet section.

Places to Stay The closest camp site to Cassis centre is *Camping Les Cigales* (☎ 04 42 01 07 34, ave de la Marne), 1km from the port off route de Marseille, open from March to November.

Beautifully isolated in the heart of the Massif des Calanques is the *Auberge de Jeunesse* (☎ 04 42 01 02 72), 3km west of Cassis centre. It has no *eau courante* (running water) and you have to bring your own food. The hostel is accessible by car (signposted off the D559 to/from Marseille). By foot, a trail – marked on the free city map available at the tourist office – leads from the end of ave des Calanques in Port Miou. Reception is open between 8 and 10 am and 5 to 11 pm; the hostel is open all year.

One-star hotels in town include: *Hôtel de France Maguy* (☎ 04 42 01 71 21, ave du Révestel), south of the centre near the stadium; and *Hôtel du Commerce* (☎ 04 42 01 09 10, fax 04 42 01 14 17), 1 rue Saint Clair, 20m north of the port. Nightly rates for a double are around 250FF at both. Midrange hotels include *Hôtel Le Liautaud* (☎ 04 42 01 75 37, fax 04 42 01 12 08, 2 rue Victor Hugo), overlooking the port, and pretty *Cassitel* (☎ 04 42 01 83 44, fax 04 42 01 96 31, place Clémenceau) which has 32 enchanting rooms from 300FF a double.

Getting There & Away Cassis is on the Marseille-Hyères rail line and has regular daily trains in both directions including to/from La Ciotat (13FF; 7 minutes), Bandol (25FF; 20 minutes), Toulon (39FF; 30 minutes) and Marseille (25FF; 22 minutes).

Cap Canaille & Route des Crêtes

The south-west side of the Baie de Cassis is dominated by the imposing Cap Canaille, a rocky limestone cape from which one of Europe's highest maritime cliffs (416m) rises. Its hollow peak hides the **Grotte des Espagnols** (Spaniard's Cave) which is filled with a magical assortment of stalactites and stalagmites. The cave cannot be visited. From the *falaise* (cliff) there are magnificent views of Cassis and Mont Puget (565m), the highest peak in the Massif des Calanques.

From Cassis the well maintained route des Crêtes (literally 'road of crests') wiggles its way along the top of the cliff-caked coastline to La Ciotat, 16km east. En route there are numerous spots to pull in, park up and partake in the awesome panorama that unfolds as you drive along. In summer, the road is sometimes closed because of fire; check with Cassis tourist office.

La Ciotat

The rusty old cranes cranked up over the shipyards of La Ciotat (pop 30,620; postcode 13600), 16km east of Cassis, lost their glean long ago. The *chantiers navals* (naval shipyards), which saw their heyday in the inter-war period, have since closed.

Facing the shipyards is La Ciotat's quaint Vieux Port, a favourite of Braque (1892-1963) who painted it several times. Behind the yards rises the imposing **Bec d'Aigle** (155m), a rocky massif on Cap de l'Aigle, the peak of which resembles the head of a bird of prey – hence its name (literally 'eagle's beak'). The ensemble – protected under the Parc Marin de la Ciotat – is best viewed from **Île Verte** (Green Island), a minuscule island offshore from the cape's south-eastern tip.

The world premier of the first ever movie was screened in La Ciotat in September 1895, courtesy of the pioneering Lumière brothers who filmed the motion picture at La Ciotat train station and then showed it for the first time at their father's chateau in the port-town. The film, entitled *L'Arrivée d'un train en gare de La Ciotat* (The arrival of a train at La Ciotat station), only made its debut in Paris three months later. La Ciotat remains home to the world's oldest picture house, the Eden Théâtre, overlooking the modern pleasure port from the corner of blvd Anatole France and blvd Jean Jaurès.

Pétanque – Provence's favourite game – was invented by local boules player Jules Lenoir in La Ciotat in 1907 (see the Facts for the Visitor chapter).

The tourist office (☎ 04 42 08 61 32 or 04 42 08 4 80, fax 04 42 08 17 88), blvd Anatole France, sits on the headland separating the old port from the Port de Plaisance (new pleasure port). Summer opening hours (shorter in winter) are 9 am to 8 pm (10 am to 1 pm on Sunday). The weekly market (Tuesday morning) is on place Evariste Gras, the square in front of the modern Cinéma Lumière. A nocturnal arts and crafts market (8 pm to 1 am) fills the quays around the old port in July and August.

Beaches & Boats The sandy beaches of **Plage Lumière** and **Grande Plage** are 1km east of La Ciotat centre. The sailing school, Club du Vieux Moulin (☎ 04 42 83 28 98), in Port de Saint Jean at the east end of Grande Plage, has sailboards/catamarans for 80/180FF an hour.

Between May and September, boats (☎ 04 42 71 53 32 or 04 42 83 11 44) depart daily from quai Ganteaume at the old port to Île Verte. Boats run hourly from 9 am to 8 pm (every 30 minutes between 9 am and 7.30 pm in July and August). Return tickets cost 30/15FF for adult/child. Les Amis des Calanques (☎ 04 42 83 54 50 or 06 09 35 25 68), also at the port, run boat excursions to Les Calanques in July and August (two hours; 95FF).

Getting There & Away The train station is a 5km trek from La Ciotat centre. La Ciotat is served by frequent trains on the Marseille-Hyères line (see Cassis earlier). Buses use the more convenient bus station

(☎ 04 42 08 90 90) adjoining the tourist office at the western end of blvd Anatole France. There are regular buses (☎ 04 42 08 41 05) to Marseille (29FF) and Aix-en-Provence (51FF).

La Ciotat is midway between Marseille and Toulon; from Cassis the most direct route is the inland D559 (bypassing route des Crètes).

Around the Étang de Berre

Oil refineries adorn the port area around the waters of Étang de Berre, while **Marignane**, on its south-eastern shore, is dominated by Marseille-Provence international airport. **Istres**, on the western shore of Étang de Berre, is best known for its military airport which has touched base here since 1914.

A horrifying view of this vast industrial scape can be scowled at from the ruins of an 11th century Saracen tower bizarrely perched on top of a rock in **Vitrolles**. The wall placards here informing residents that their streets are under 24-hour camera surveillance are the doing of the town's xenophobic National Front mayor (see the Facts about Provence chapter).

The Canal de Caronte links the reasonably attractive fishing port of **Martigues**, on the south-western corner of Étang de Berre, with Golfe de Fos in the Mediterranean. The national French flag comes from Martigues (tourist office ☎ 04 42 42 31 10, fax 04 42 42 31 11).

Pockets of crystal clear skies and blue waters still exist because of the **Chaine de l'Estaque**, a harsh, uninhabitable massif which forms a natural blockade between industrial Étang de Berre and the Mediterranean. The stretch of coast on the protected south side of the massif from Cap Couronne to Marseille is called La Côte Bleue (The Blue Coast).

Cap Couronne

From Martigues the D5 leads 10km south to Cap Couronne, a cape with a large sandy beach that draws a Marseillais crowd on weekends. The waters around it are protected by the Parc Régional Marin de la Côte Bleue, one of the region's first marine reserves aimed at safe-guarding and reviving marine life. The protected zone – which does not actually touch the coastline – is marked with yellow buoys topped with St Andrew's crosses. The park (☎ 04 42 45 45 07, fax 04 42 44 98 05) is headquartered at the Maison de la Mer, BP 37, 13960 Sausset-les-Pins.

The area is filled with camping grounds, including large *Le Cap* (☎ 04 42 80 73 02) located almost on the cape's tip in La Couronne and open year round. In Les Tamaris, midway between Sausset-les-Pins and Cap Couronne, *Camping Caravaning Lou Cigalon* (☎ 04 42 49 61 71) charges 90FF for two people with a car and tent, plus 24FF for each additional person. It is open from April to September.

Carry-le-Rouet

One of the region's most unique gastronomic delights can be sampled in this busy harbour town favoured by French comic actor Fernandel in the 1930s: *oursins*. These prickly little creatures – dubbed *châtaignes de mer* (sea chestnuts) – can only be caught between September and April (fishing for them is forbidden in summer when the urchins reproduce).

Each year, on the first three Sundays of February, Carry-le-Rouet celebrates **L'Oursinade** – an annual sea urchin fête which sees a giant open-air picnic spill across the quays of the Vieux Port. Restaurant proprietors and hoteliers set up stalls selling oursin platters, allowing everyone – tourists and locals alike – to indulge in a sea urchin *dégustation* (tasting) session around shared tables. The creatures are reportedly best served with chilled Cassis white wine.

Carry-le-Rouet tourist office (☎ 04 42 13 20 36, fax 04 42 44 52 03), ave Aristide Briand, is open from 10 am to noon and 2 to 5 pm (closed Sunday and Monday). Hours in July and August are 9 am to noon and 2 to 6 pm (closed Sunday). Carry has three hotels; the tourist office has details on *chambres d'hôtes*.

L'Estaque

East of Carry-le-Rouet by 17km is L'Estaque, a once-untouched fishing village adjoining Marseille's northern suburbs which, like Saint Tropez, lured artists from the impressionist, fauvist and cubist movements. Renoir, Cézanne, Dufy and Braque painted numerous canvases during their sojourns here. The only piece that remains in the region is Dufy's *L'Usine à L'Estaque* (Factory at L'Estaque), displayed in Marseille's Musée Cantini. Between 1870 and 1882, Cézanne stayed in a house overlooking the harbour on central place de l'Église.

Culinary snacks unique to L'Estaque and ideal for a munch while strolling the water's edge include *chichi freggi* (sugar-coated donuts) and *panisses* (chickpea flour cakes). Both are sold at kiosks around the harbour. The English-language brochure entitled *L'Estaque and the Painters*, distributed for free by Marseille tourist office, is handy for travellers interested in the artists' trail.

Getting There & Away

From Marseille, there are more than a dozen trains daily (less in winter) along La Côte Bleue as far as Port de Bouc, from where the train line heads inland to Miramas on the northern shore of the Étang de Berre. From Marseille trains stop at L'Estaque (13FF; 10 minutes), Carry-le-Rouet (26FF; 25 minutes), La Couronne (34FF; 40 minutes) and Miramas (48FF; 1¼ hours).

See the Getting Around chapter for information on day train passes.

Aix-en-Provence

• **pop 124,000**   ✉ **13100**

Aix was founded as a military camp under the name of Aquae Sextiae (the Waters of Sextius) in 123 BC on the site of thermal springs – which still flow. Fortunately for stuck-up Aix the settlement consequently became known as Aix – not Sex! The city reached its zenith as a centre of art and learning under the enlightened King René (1409-80), a brilliant polyglot who brought painters to his court from Europe. The city remains an academic centre today, thanks to its Universities of Aix-Marseille, whose forerunner was established in 1409, and which attract a student population of about 30,000. Many are foreigners in town on an intensive French-language course.

Some 200 elegant *hôtels particuliers* grace Aix's squares and avenues. Many, exhibiting the unmistakable influence of Italian baroque and coloured a distinctive Provençal yellow, date from the 17th and 18th centuries. Tree-covered cours Mirabeau is considered by many to be Provence's most beautiful street.

Orientation

Cours Mirabeau, Aix's main boulevard, stretches from La Rotonde, a roundabout with a huge fountain (dry at the time of research) on place du Général de Gaulle, eastward to place Forbin. The oldest part of the city, Vieil Aix, is north of cours Mirabeau; most of the streets, alleys and public squares in this part of town are closed to traffic. South of cours Mirabeau is the Quartier Mazarin, whose regular street grid was laid out in the 17th century. The entire city centre is ringed by a series of one-way boulevards.

Information

Tourist Offices Aix's busy tourist office (☎ 04 42 16 11 61, fax 04 42 16 11 62, aix tour@aix.pacwan.net, www.aix-en-provence .com/aixofftour), 2 place du Général de Gaulle, is open from 8.30 am to 8 pm (10 pm in July and August; Sunday year round from 10 am to 1 pm and 2 to 6 pm).

The Office National des Forêts (ONF; ☎ 04 42 17 57 00, fax 04 42 23 37 29) has its regional office for Provence-Alpes-Côte d'Azur at 46 ave Paul Cézanne.

Money Near graceful place des Quatre Dauphins, Banque de France, 18 rue du Quatre Septembre, is open from 9.15 am to

AIX-EN-PROVENCE

PLACES TO STAY
17 Hôtel du Globe
25 Hôtel des Arts-Le Sully
39 Hôtel du Casino
41 Hôtel de France
45 Grand Hôtel Nègre Coste
56 Hôtel Saint Christophe
63 Hôtel Cardinale
64 Hôtel Cardinale
   (Annexe)
68 Hôtel des Quatre
   Dauphins
69 Grand Hôtel Roi René

PLACES TO EAT
12 L'Arbre à Pain
19 Restaurant Nem d'Asie
20 La Fontaine
21 Le Platanos
23 University Restaurant
35 Les Bacchanales
36 L'Éclipse

40 Mondial Café
46 Les Deux Garçons
48 Gu et Fils
58 Yôji

MUSEUMS
3 Musée des Tapisseries
6 Musée du Vieil Aix
7 Galerie du Festival
43 Espace 13 Art Contemporain
61 Musée Paul Arbaud
66 Musée Granet

OTHER
1 Spar (Supermarket)
2 Cathédrale Saint
   Sauveur
4 Place des Martyrs de la
   Résistance
5 Université d'Aix-Marseilles III
   (Foreign Student Language
   Department)

8 Libre Service de l'Hôtel de Ville
9 La Boulangerie traditionnelle
10 Laundrette
11 Loc 2 Roues (Bicycle Rental)
13 Hublot Cybercafé
14 Place de l'Hôtel de Ville
15 Hôtel de Ville
16 Cave du Felibrige (Wine Shop)
18 Laundrette
22 Église de la Madeleine
24 Laundrette
26 Studio Keaton Cinema
27 Théâtre du Jeu de Paume
28 Rich Art (Chocolate Shop)
29 Place des Pêcheurs
30 Palais de Justice
31 Place Saint Honoré
32 Place d'Albertas
33 Change Nazareth
34 Fromagerie des Augustins
37 Council Travel
38 Laundrette

42 Change L'Agence
44 Monoprix Supermarket
47 Boulangerie
49 Bechard Fabrique de
   Calissons (Sweet Shop)
50 Banque Nationale de Paris
51 La Rotonde
52 Post Office
53 Bus Station
54 Car Go Car Rental
55 Citer Car Rental
57 Tourist Office
59 Le Cézanne
60 Cinéma Mazarin
62 Banque de France
65 Église Saint Jean de Malte
67 Paradox Librairie
   Internationale
70 Pétanque Court
71 Parc Jourdan &
   Bouldrome Municipal
72 Train Station

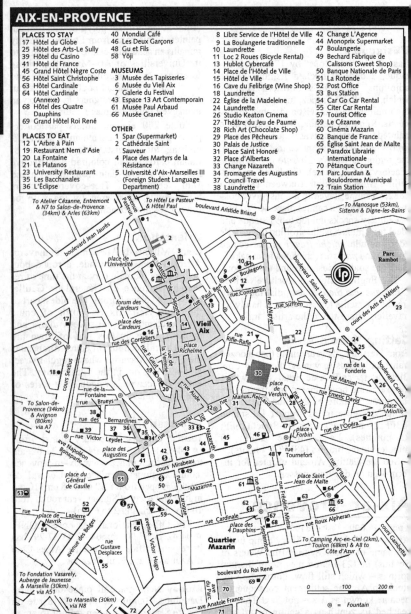

12.15 pm and 1.30 to 3 pm (closed on weekends).

Commercial banks mass along cours Mirabeau and cours Sextius which runs north-south to the west of La Rotonde. American Express agent, Change L'Agence (☎ 04 42 26 84 77), 15 cours Mirabeau, is open from 9 am to 6.30 pm (5.30 pm on Saturday; closed Sunday). Hours in July and August are 9 am to 9 pm. The Change Nazareth exchange bureau (☎ 04 42 38 28 28), 7 rue Nazareth, is open from 9 am to 7 pm (5 pm on Sunday) in July and August.

Post The post office on the corner of ave des Belges and rue Lapierre is open from 8.30 am to 7 pm (Saturday until noon; closed Sunday).

Email & Internet Access The hourly rate at the Hublot Cybercafé (☎ 04 42 21 37 31; hub1@mail.vif.fr), 15-27 rue Paul Bert, is 50FF.

Aixtravagames (☎ 04 42 16 00 16), 7 rue Frédéric Mistral, is a computer games outlet with Internet access too (40FF an hour). Its opening hours are 11 to 2 am.

Travel Agencies Council Travel (☎ 04 42 38 58 82, fax 04 42 38 94 00) has a branch at 12 rue Victor Leydet.

Bookshops Paradox Librairie Internationale (☎ 04 42 26 47 99), 15 rue du 4 Septembre, sells English-language novels and guidebooks, including Lonely Planet guides. It buys/sells second-hand books too; open from 9 am to 12.30 pm and 2 to 6.30 pm (closed Sunday).

Libraries The American Library in Aix (☎ 04 42 23 02 82), 2bis rue du Bon Pasteur, has a stock of more than 12,000 English and French-language books. It is open from 1 to 5 pm (closed on weekends).

Laundry Laundrettes abound: 3 rue de la Fontaine; 34 cours Sextius; 3 rue de la Fonderie; 15 rue Jacques de la Roque; 6 rue

Félibre Gaut; and 60 rue Boulegon. All are open from 7 or 8 am to 8 pm.

Walking Tour

Aix's social scene centres on shaded **cours Mirabeau**, laid out during the latter half of the 1600s and named after the heroic revolutionary Comte de Mirabeau. Trendy cafés adorned with young beauties basking in the shade of their sunglasses spill out onto the pavements on the sunny northern side of the street which is crowned by a leafy rooftop of green plane trees. The shady southern side shelters a string of Renaissance hôtels particuliers. The **Hôtel d'Espargnet** (1647) at No 38, which today houses the university's economics department, is among the most impressive. The Marquis of Entrecasteau murdered his wife in their family home, the **Hôtel d'Isoard de Vauvenargues** (1710), at No 10.

The large, cast-iron fountain at the west end of cours Mirabeau, **Fontaine de la Rotonde**, dates from 1860. The fountain at the avenue's eastern end on place Forbin is decorated with a 19th century statue of King René holding a bunch of Muscat grapes, a variety he is credited with introducing to the region. The moss-covered **Fontaine d'Eau Thermale** at the intersection of cours Mirabeau and rue Clemenceau spouts water at 34°C.

Other streets and squares lined with hôtels particuliers include **rue Mazarine**, one block south of cours Mirabeau; **place des Quatre Dauphins**, two blocks farther south, whose fountain dates from 1667; the eastern continuation of cours Mirabeau, **rue de l'Opéra** (at Nos 18, 24 and 26); and the pretty fountain-clad **place d'Albertas** just west of place St Honoré where live music is sometimes performed on summer evenings. Sunday strollers should not miss a jaunt to **place de Hôtel de Ville** where the city brass band trumpets out a host of jolly tunes most Sunday mornings to the delight of the smiling crowds. From place de Hôtel de Ville, rue Gaston de Saporta leads to the imposing **Cathédrale Saint Sauveur**. Opposite the city's cathedral is the old Université d'Aix dating from 1741 and the adjoining Institut d'Études Françaises pour Étudiants Étrangers (Institute of French Studies for Foreign Students) which belongs to the Université d'Aix-Marseille.

South of the historic centre lies the pleasing **Parc Jourdan**, a spacious green park dominated by Aix's largest fountain and home to the town's **Boulodrome Municipal** where men gather beneath the shade of the trees to play pétanque on sunny days. Pétanque is also the name of the game on the tree-studded court, opposite the park entrance on ave du Parc. Spectators are warmly welcomed.

Museums

The tourist office sells a Passeport Musées for 60FF that gets you into the Atelier Paul Cézanne, Musée Granet, Musée des Tapisseries, Musée d'Histoire Naturelle and the Pavillon de Vendôme.

Aix's finest is the **Musée Granet** (☎ 04 42 38 14 70), place Saint Jean de Malte, housed in a 17th century priory of the Knights of Malta. Exhibits include Celtic statues from Entremont and Roman artefacts, while the museum's collection of paintings boasts 16th to 19th century Italian, Dutch and French works and some of Aix-born Cézanne's lesser known paintings and watercolours. The museum is open from 10 am to noon and 2 to 6 pm; closed Tuesday (10FF; free for students under 25).

An unexceptional collection of artefacts and documents pertaining to the city's history is housed in the **Musée du Vieil Aix** (☎ 04 42 21 43 55), 17 rue Gaston de Saporta. It's open from 10 am to noon and 2 to 5 pm; 2.30 to 6 pm between April and October; closed Monday (15/10FF for adult/student). The **Musée des Tapisseries** (Tapestry Museum; ☎ 04 42 23 09 91), in the Ancien Archevêché (Former Archbishop's Palace), 28 place des Martyrs de la Résistance, is open from 10 am to noon and 2 to 5.45 pm; closed Sunday (15FF). The **Musée Paul Arbaud** (☎ 04 42 38 38 95), 2a rue du Quatre Septembre, displays books, manuscripts and a collection of Provençal

faïence (earthenware); it is open from 2 to 5 pm (closed Sunday).

Art lovers should not miss the **Petit Musée Cézanne** (☎ 04 42 23 42 53, fax 04 42 21 60 30), inside the Galerie du Festival straddling rue de Littera at 24 rue Gaston de Saporta. Next door at 22 rue Gaston de Saporta is the chic **Galerie Mosca** (☎ 04 42 21 07 51) which hosts interesting and unusual art exhibitions; as does the **Espace 13 Art Contemporain** (☎ 04 42 93 03 67), 21bis cours Mirabeau, open from 10.30 am to 6 pm (closed Sunday and Monday).

Cathédrale Saint Sauveur

Aix's cathedral incorporates architectural features representing every major period from the 5th to the 18th century. The main Gothic structure, built between 1285 and 1350, includes the Romanesque nave of a 12th century church as part of its south aisle. The chapels were added in the 14th and 15th centuries. There is a 5th century sarcophagus in the apse. The cathedral is open from 8 am to noon and 2 to 6 pm. Mass is held here at 8 am (Saturday at 6.30 pm, Sunday at 9, 10.30 am and 7 pm). Soulful Gregorian chants are sung at 4.30 pm on Sunday – a riveting experience not to be missed.

The 15th century *Triptyque du Buisson Ardent* (Triptych of the Burning Bush) in the nave is by Nicolas Froment. It is usually only opened for groups. Near it is a triptych panel illustrating Christ's passion. The tapestries encircling the choir date from the 18th century and the fabulous gilt organ is baroque. There's a *son et lumière* (sound and light) show at 9.30 pm most evenings in summer.

Fondation Vasarely

The Vasarely Foundation (☎ 04 42 20 01 09, fax 04 42 59 14 65, www.netprovence .com/fondationvasarely), 1 ave Marcel Pagnol, is about 4km west of town near the hostel. It is the creation of Hungarian-born artist Victor Vasarely who sought to brighten up grey urban areas with huge, colourful works that integrated art with architecture and earned him the title 'the father of Op

Art'. Vasarely's works are displayed here in several hexagonal spaces recognisable from afar by their black-and-white, geometrical designs.

The foundation is open from 10 am to 1 pm and 2 to 7 pm (35/20FF for adult/ student). Take bus No 12 to the Vasarely stop.

Paul Cézanne Trail

Cézanne (1839-1906), Aix's most celebrated son (at least after his death), did much of his painting in and around the city. If you're interested in the minute details of his day-to-day life – where he ate, drank, played and worked – just follow the **Circuit de Cézanne**, marked by round bronze markers in the pavement that begin at the tourist office. The markers are coordinated with a trilingual guide, *In the Footsteps of Paul Cézanne*, available free from the tourist office. Cézanne was a close friend of the French novelist Émile Zola (1840-1902) who, as a child and teenager, also lived in Aix.

Cézanne's last studio, now opened to the public as the **Atelier Paul Cézanne** (☎ 04 42 21 06 53), is atop a hill about 1.5km north of the tourist office at 9 ave Paul Cézanne. It has been left exactly as it was when he died and though none of his works are here, his tools are. It's open from 10 am to noon and 2 to 5 pm; 2.30 to 6 pm from June to September; daily except Tuesday (16/10FF for adult/student). Take bus No 1 to the Cézanne stop.

Organised Tours

The tourist office offers a variety of thematic walking tours around the city (50/25FF for adult/student). Between 1 April and 31 October it also runs a packed schedule of guided bus tours in the region (English and French). Ask at the tourist office for the brochure entitled *Excursions en Provence* or study the noticeboard outside.

Special Events

Aix has a sumptuous cultural calendar. The most sought-after tickets are for the week-long Festival Provençal d'Aix et du Pays d'Aix which each July brings classical music, opera and ballet to city venues such as Cathédrale Saint Sauveur. Practitioners of more casual musical expression – buskers – bring the festival spirit to cours Mirabeau.

Other festivals include the two-day Festival du Tambourin (Tambourine Festival) in mid-April, the Aix Jazz Festival in early July, and the Fête Mistralienne marking the birthday of Provençal hero Frédéric Mistral on 13 September. For detailed information contact the Comité Officiel des Fêtes (☎ 04 42 63 06 75) or the tourist office.

Places to Stay

Despite being a student town, Aix is not cheap. In July and August, when hotel prices rise precipitously, it may be possible to stay in the university dorms – the tourist office has details or you can call the student accommodation outfit CROUS (☎ 04 42 26 47 00), ave Jules Ferry, in the Cité des Gazelles.

The tourist office has comprehensive details on *chambres d'hôtes* and *gîtes ruraux* in and around Aix; and a list (updated weekly) of all types of accommodation, including studios and farmhouses, to rent on a longer-term basis.

Places to Stay – Budget
Camping *Camping Arc-en-Ciel* (☎ 04 42 26 14 28), open from April to September, is at Pont des Trois Sautets, 2km south-east of town on the route de Nice. A tent site costs 90FF per person. Take bus No 3 to Les Trois Sautets stop.

Hostel The *Auberge de Jeunesse du Jas de Bouffan* (☎ 04 42 20 15 99, fax 04 42 59 36 12, 3 ave Marcel Pagnol) is almost 2km west of the centre. B&B is 68FF and sheets cost 11FF a night. Rooms are locked between 10 am and 5 pm. Take bus No 12 from La Rotonde to the Vasarely stop.

Hotels On the city centre's eastern fringe, the laid-back and friendly *Hôtel des Arts-Le Sully* (☎ 04 42 38 11 77, fax 04 42 26 77 31, 69 blvd Carnot & 5 rue de la Fonderie) is away from the milling crowds. It has decent singles/doubles with shower and toilet for 149/175FF and doubles with TV for 195FF.

Just north of blvd Jean Jaurès, the *Hôtel Paul* (☎ 04 42 23 23 89, fax 04 42 63 17 80, 10 ave Pasteur) has rooms for one or two with shower and toilet for 197FF. The hotel is a 10 minute walk from the tourist office; alternatively, take minibus No 2 from La Rotonde or the bus station.

Places to Stay – Mid-Range

One of the best and most central places in this range is the cosy *Hôtel du Casino* (☎ 04 42 26 06 88, fax 04 42 27 76 58, 38 rue Victor Leydet) in the old city north-west of La Rotonde. It has one smallish single with shower for 200FF; the rest of the rooms are doubles with toilet/toilet and shower for 260/380FF. All prices include breakfast. Better still, the management is exceedingly friendly.

The *Hôtel Cardinale* (☎ 04 42 38 32 30, fax 04 42 26 39 05, 24 rue Cardinale) is a charming place in a charming street and has large rooms with shower, toilet and a mix of modern and period furniture. Year round, prices are 220-300FF for a single, 260-320FF for a double, and 350-420FF for a small self-catering suite in its annexe at 12 rue Cardinal. The similar *Hôtel de France* (☎ 04 42 27 90 15, fax 04 42 26 11 47, 63 rue Espariat) has serviceable singles/doubles with washbasin from 190/210FF; with shower for 300/350FF.

Just out of the pedestrianised area, the *Hôtel du Globe* (☎ 04 42 26 03 58, fax 04 42 26 13 68, 74 cours Sextius) has pleasant singles with toilet from 170FF and doubles/triples with shower and toilet from 260/320FF. Garage parking costs 45FF a night. Farther north, the two-star *Hôtel Le Pasteur* (☎ 04 42 21 11 76, 14 ave Pasteur) touts singles/doubles with washbasin and shower for 250/350FF.

Places to Stay – Top End

Aix is well endowed with three and four-star hotels, though many are on the outskirts of town. Those close to the centre include the very friendly, very recommended *Hôtel*

des Quatre Dauphins (☎ 04 42 38 16 39, fax 04 42 38 60 19, 54 rue Roux Alpheran) which charges 290/330/490FF for singles, doubles/triples with period furnishings and shower. The *Hôtel Saint Christophe* (☎ 04 42 26 01 24, fax 04 42 38 53 17), sporting a pleasant outside breakfast terrace at 2 ave Victor Hugo, has singles/doubles with shower for 350/390FF.

The elegant *Grand Hôtel Roi René* (☎ 04 42 37 61 00, fax 04 42 37 61 11, 24 blvd du Roi René) is a 'could-be-anywhere-in-the-world' type of place with all creature comforts including an outdoor pool and solarium. Singles/doubles start at 640/790FF.

In a prime location with a prime view of the goings-on on slick cours Mirabeau is the very grand, three-star *Grand Hôtel Nègre Coste* (☎ 04 42 27 74 22, fax 04 42 26 80 93 33 cours Mirabeau). Fanciful singles, doubles overlooking the beautiful main street cost around 350/700FF. Garage parking is available.

Places to Eat

Aix has lots of lovely places to dine, but the prices do little to moderate the town's upmarket gastronomic image. Fortunately cuisines brought from overseas are plentiful and of high quality. Aix's cheapest dining street is rue Van Loo which is lined with tiny restaurants offering Chinese, Thai, Italian and other oriental cuisines.

Aix's pastry speciality is the *calisson*, a sweet biscuit made with almond paste and fruit, comprising 40% almonds and 60% fruit syrup.

University Restaurant If it's a very cheap meal you're after, there's a *Restaurant Universitaire* (☎ 04 42 38 03 68, 10 cours des Arts et Métiers). You may have to buy a ticket from a student for about 15FF. It is generally open from 11.15 am to 1.15 pm and 6.30 to 7.30 pm.

Restaurants The area around rue de la Verrerie and rue Félibre Gaut offers various options, though Vietnamese-Chinese eateries predominate. The *Restaurant Nem d'Asie*

☎ 04 42 26 53 06, 22 rue Félibre Gaut) is one of the least expensive places with 45FF lunchtime *menus*.

Nearby is the very local *La Fontaine* ☎ 04 42 27 53 35), named after the pretty little fountain that tinkles away on its outside terrace at 5 rue Fontaine d'Argent. Strictly Provençal cuisine is cooked here, as at the upmarket *Les Bacchanales* (☎ 04 42 27 21 06, 10 rue de la Couronne) which offers a delectable *menu gourmand* for 295FF and a cheaper, less rich *menu* for 145/75FF adult/child.

Numerous cafés, brasseries and restaurants are in the city's heart on place des Cardeurs and place de l'Hôtel de Ville. For Greek food, *Le Platanos* (☎ 04 42 21 33 19, 13 rue Rifle-Rafle) offers a 55FF *menu* for lunch and an 85FF *menu* for dinner. *Yôji* (☎ 04 42 38 48 76, 7 ave Victor Hugo) is an upmarket joint specialising in Japanese cuisine and offering succulent *menus* for 119-198FF in the evening and from 75FF at lunchtime.

L'Arbre à Pain (☎ 04 42 96 99 95, 12 rue Constantin) is a vegetarian place which prides itself on its low calorie, full-flavoured dishes. Its homemade ice cream in such flavours as melon, violet and lavender is particularly enticing

If you're on the Mayle-trail, head straight for *Gu et Fils* (☎ 04 42 26 75 12, 3 rue Frédéric Mistral), or rather 'Chez Gu' as the author of *A Year in Provence* described the place before launching into verbal raptures about the patron's moustache and culinary skills. Distinctive features include purely Provençal dishes, a heavy scent of lavender in the air, photographs of Gu with stars on the walls, and aperitifs *à la composition secrète*. Expect to pay 65FF or more for an entrée, 75-150FF for a pasta dish and 150FF for a meat dish.

Cafés No visit to Aix is complete without a quick pose and peering session at Aix's most renowned café, *Les Deux Garçons* (☎ 04 42 26 00 51), on the sunny side of cours Mirabeau at No 53. Dating from 1792, this pricey café-cum-brasserie – a former intellectual hangout – is just one of many hot spots along cours Mirabeau designed purely for the sort of people-watching that is not free of pretension. In summer an astonishing number of people spend entire evenings simply strolling up and down the crowded street.

Not quite so conspicuous are the plentiful open-air cafés which sprawl across the back street squares: place des Cardeurs, forum des Cardeurs, place de Verdun and place de l'Hôtel de Ville are all safe bets. The *Mondial Café*, overlooking La Rotonde at the western end of cours Mirabeau, specialises in shellfish dishes and super-sized salads (from 48FF). *Cookies & Co (4 rue Peyresc)* is a nice salad and sandwich lunch spot.

Self-Catering Aix is among Provence's premier *market* towns. A mass of fruit and vegetable stands are set up each morning on place Richelme, just as they have been for centuries. Depending on the season, you can buy olives, goat's cheese, garlic, lavender, honey, peaches, melons and a whole host of other sun-kissed products. Another *marché d'alimentation* (grocery market) is set up on place des Pêcheurs on Tuesday, Thursday and Saturday mornings.

The next best thing after bread from the market is a warm loaf from *La Boulangerie traditionnelle (4 rue Boulegon)*. The *boulangerie* on rue Tournefort never closes.

A splendid array of local wines are sold at the *Cave du Felibrige (18 rue des Cordeliers)*. For cheeses of all shapes, sizes and pongs head for the *Fromagerie des Augustins* on rue Espariat.

And finally, what sweeter way to end that sunny summer picnic than with a couple of calissons from *Bechard Fabrique de Calissons*, a classy pâtisserie and confiseur at 12 cours Mirabeau. Aix's traditional almond candies are 17FF per 100g (50FF per 100g with ornate packaging). Designer chocolates are sold at *Rich Art*, 6 rue Thiers, open from 9.30 am to 12.30 pm and 3 to 7 pm.

Entertainment

Pick up a free copy of the monthly *Le Mois à Aix* at the tourist office to find out what's on where and when.

Cinema The Aixois are fond of *le septième art* (the seventh art), and two cinemas are dedicated solely to screening nondubbed films: *Ciné Mazarin (☎ 04 42 26 99 85, 6 rue Laroque)*; and the small *Studio Keaton (☎ 04 42 26 86 11, 45 rue Manuel)*. The massive 12-theatre *Le Cézanne (☎ 04 36 68 04 06, 3 rue Marcel Guillaume)* hosts dubbed and nondubbed films.

Classical Music & Theatre The curtain goes up at the *Théâtre du Jeu de Paume (☎ 04 42 38 07 39, 21 rue de l'Opéra)* at 8.30 pm. For alternative café-theatre go to *La Fontaine d'Argent (☎ 04 42 38 43 80, 5 rue Fontaine d'Argent)*. For live jazz head for *La Fonderie (☎ 04 42 63 10 11, 14 cours St Louis)*. Classical concerts are held in the *Chapelle du Sacre Cœon*, rue de la Cépede, and the *Cathédrale Saint Sauveur*.

Shopping

A flower market sets place des Prêcheurs ablaze with every colour of the rainbow on Sunday mornings. On Tuesday, Thursday and Saturday mornings there's a flower market on place de Hôtel de Ville and a *marché aux puces* (flea market) on place de Verdun.

Santons can be admired and bought at the santon workshop (☎ 04 42 26 33 38), dating from 1934, on 65 cours Gambetta, route de Nice, or at the Crèches et Santons de Provence (☎/fax 04 42 21 16 62), Villa Mireille, 32 ave Jean Moulin. The tourist office has a list of other *ateliers*.

Aix's chic shops (designer clothes, hats, accessories etc) are clustered along pedestrian rue Marius Reinaud which winds it way behind the Palais de Justice on place de Verdun.

Getting There & Away

Air Marseille-Provence airport is 25km from Aix-en-Provence. See the Marseille section for details.

Bus The small run-down bus station at the western end of rue Lapierre is served by numerous companies. The information office (☎ 04 42 27 17 91) is open from 7.30 am to 6.30 pm (closed Sunday). In July and August, it's also open on Sunday from 9 am to 5.30 pm.

There are buses to Marseille (26FF; 35 minutes via the autoroute/one hour via the N8; every 5-10 minutes), Arles (65FF; 1¾ hours; two a day); Avignon via the autoroute (85FF; one hour; six a day) Avignon via the national road (70FF; 1½ hours; four a day) and Toulon (82FF; one hour; four a day).

Sumian buses serve Apt, Castellane and the Gorges du Verdon via La Palud (see the Haute-Provence chapter).

Train Aix's tiny train station, at the southern end of ave Victor Hugo leading from La Rotonde, is open from 5.45 am to 10 pm The information office is open daily from 9 am to 7 pm. Luggage lockers (15-20FF) are accessible between 5 am and 10 pm. There are frequent services to Marseille (37FF; 35 minutes; at least 18 a day) from where there are connections to everywhere.

Car Rental agencies include Citer (☎ 04 42 93 10 14), 32 rue Gustave Desplaces; Ca Go (☎ 04 42 27 92 34), 5 rue Lapierre; and Le Système (☎ 04 42 38 58 29), 35 rue de la Molle.

Getting Around

To/From the Airport There is a regular shuttlebus between Aix bus station and Marseille-Provence airport; see the Getting Around chapter.

Bus The city's 14 bus and three minibus lines are operated by Aix en Bus (☎ 04 42 26 37 28), whose information desk inside the tourist office is open from 10 am to 6 pm (Saturday from 10 am to 12.30 pm; closed Sunday).

La Rotonde is the main bus hub. Most services run until 8 pm. A single/10-ticket carnet costs 7/41FF. Minibus No 1 links the train nd bus stations with La Rotonde and cours Mirabeau. Minibus No 2 starts at the bus station and then follows much the same route.

axi Taxis lurk outside the bus station. To order a cab, call Taxi Radio Aixois (☎ 04 42 27 71 11) or Taxi Mirabeau (☎ 04 42 21 61 01).

Bicycle Loc 2 Roues (☎ 04 42 21 37 40), 52 rue Boulegon, rents city bicycles for 50FF a day (deposit 1000FF). Mountain bikes cost 60/100FF for a half-day/day (deposit 1500FF). The shop is open from 9 am to noon and 2 to 5 pm (3 to 7 pm in summer; closed Sunday). Cycles Naddeo (☎ 04 42 21 06 93), 54 ave de Lattre de Tassigny, is another rental outlet.

MONTAGNE SAINTE-VICTOIRE

Among Cézanne's favourite haunts was Montagne Sainte-Victoire, a mountain ridge immortalised on canvas numerous times by artists over the centuries. Garrigue covers its dry slopes and its foot is carpeted with 4200 hectares of vineyards from which the local Coteaux d'Aix-en-Provence white, red and rosé wines originate. The mountain's southern face is scarred from forest fires that burnt 5000 hectares in 1989.

Contemporary art exhibitions are hosted in the **Moulin de Cézanne**, a restored mill in Le Tholonet, 5km east of Aix on the D17. In front of the gallery is a statue of Cézanne. The village is dominated by the 17th century **Château du Tholonet**, a green-shuttered mansion which cannot be visited. Continuing east on the D17, you pass local artists at their easels in the roadside pine forests trying to reproduce works painted by Cézanne along this stretch. *La Montagne Sainte-Victoire au Grand Pin* (1887) is one of his best known paintings.

About 10km south of Le Tholonet off the D6 in the **Arc valley** – the inspiration for Cézanne's Cubist *Les Baigneurs* and *Les Baigneuses* (The Bathers) – is **Gardanne**. Traditionally a mining town, just 900-odd miners remain employed in the mines which are slated for closure by 2005. The

Écomusée de la Forêt (☎ 04 42 65 42 10, fax 04 42 65 42 11, fondation-foret@en provence.com, www.fondation-pour-le-foret .enprovence.com), set in a 13 hectare park off chemin de Roman (D7), is run by the people responsible for reforestation in the Provence-Alpes-Côte d'Azur region and is well worth the 30FF entrance fee (15FF for children under 15).

Saint Antonin sur Bayon, 4km east of Le Tholonet, is home to the Maison de Sainte-Victoire (☎ 04 42 66 84 40, fax 04 42 66 85 15). The converted stables in the southern shadow of the limestone ridge shelter an **Écomusée**, restaurant (100FF *menu*) and terrace café, and shop which sells hiking guides and maps for the region. The centre is open from 10 am to 7 pm.

A further 8km east in Puyloubier (400m) oleiculture exhibitions are held in the village **moulin à huile** (oil mill; ☎ 04 42 66 30 28).

Returning to Aix-en-Provence via the westbound D10, you pass through the village of Vauvenargues. Picasso (1881-1973), who spent most of his creative life living on the Côte d'Azur, is buried on the estate of his 14th century **Château de Vauvenargues**. The red brick castle, purchased by the artist in 1958, still belongs to the Picasso family; a sign outside the main gate bluntly reads *Le château n'est pas à visiter. N'insistez pas, merci. Le musée est à Paris* (This castle cannot be visited. Do not insist. The museum is in Paris).

Places to Stay & Eat

There are camping grounds in Beaurecueil and Puyloubier. *Camping Sainte Victoire* (☎ 04 42 66 91 31, fax 04 42 66 96 43, quartier Le Paradou, 13100 Beaurecueil) is open all year. In Puyloubier, *Camping Le Cézanne* (☎ 06 80 32 11 10) is only open from April to November. The tourist office in Aix has details on *chambres d'hôtes* in the area.

In Le Tholonet, *Le Relais Cézanne* (☎ 04 42 66 91 91, ave Cézanne) is a pleasant family run hotel with comfortable doubles for 200FF. It has a restaurant and terrace too. At the 10-room *Relais Sainte Victoire* (☎ 04 42 66 94 98, fax 04 42 66 85 96) in

Beaurecueil, rooms cost 400/650FF in the low/high season. Vauvenargues' one-star *Moulin de Provence* (☎ *04 42 66 02 22, fax 04 42 66 01 21, 33 ave des Maquisards)* has 12 single/double rooms from 120/220FF.

A superb place to dine, be it for lunch or dinner, is *La Petite Auberge du Tholonet* (☎ *04 42 66 84 24)*, beautifully set at the end of a country lane overlooking fields and Montagne Sainte-Victoire. House specialities on its menu include *tarte aux olives et chèvre chaud* (olive and goat cheese tart), *rougets au beurre de basilic* (red mullet in basil butter) and *mignon de veau au citron vert confit* (veal with lime). The auberge has 85, 110, 170 and 260FF *menus*; it is closed Sunday evening and all day Monday. Book in advance to be sure of a table.

Salon-de-Provence

• pop 34,000   ✉ 13300

Salon-de-Provence is known for its olive oil production and *savon de Marseille* soap industry. Medieval Salon served as the residence of the Arles archbishops. The philosopher Nostradamus (1503-66) lived and died here.

Since 1936 France's military flying school, the École de l'Air et École Militaire de l'Air, has been stationed here. Tuesdays between noon to 2 pm is the practice slot of aerial acrobatic showmasters, the Patrouille Aérienne de France – France's equivalent of the UK's Red Arrows.

An open-air market fills place Morgan on Wednesday morning.

Orientation & Information

Salon-de-Provence is surprisingly small. Banks, the tourist office and most sights are centred in the Vieille Ville (old town) or on cours Grimon, cours Victor Hugo and cours Carnot which circle it. From place Crousillat, the train station is a straight 1km walk west along blvd de la République.

The tourist office (☎ 04 90 56 27 60, fax 04 90 56 77 09, www.salon-de-provence .org), cours Gimon, is open from 9 am to noon and 2 to 6.30 pm (closed Sunday).

Hours are longer from mid-June to mid-September (10 am to noon on Sunday).

The post office, on the corner of blvd Maréchal Foch and rue Massenet, is open from 9 am to 6.45 pm (8.30 am to noon on Saturday; closed Sunday). Log in with a coffee in hand at the Colisée Oriental Cyber Café (☎ 04 90 56 00 10), place Crousillat

Walking Tour

A giant, moss-covered mushroom of a fountain, known as **Fontaine Moussue**, dominates **place Crousillat**, Salon's prettiest square tucked just outside the walled Vieille Ville. Bear east through the *porte* (gate) of the 12th century **Tour d'Horloge** to enter the old city. Note the ornate wrought-iron campanile which crowns the bell tower.

Pedestrian rue de l'Horloge brings you to place de Ancienne Halle, a large open square from which rue Nostradamus leads to the **Maison de Nostradamus** (☎ 04 90 56 64 31) at No 11. From 1547 until his death in 1566, Nostradamus lived here. The family home has since been converted into a museum with 10 tableaux depicting scenes from the philosopher's life. Nostradamus wrote his famous prophecies, published in Lyon in 1555, here. His house is open from 9 am to noon and 2 to 6 pm, closed weekend mornings (20/15FF for adult/student).

Nostradamus is buried in the Chapelle Centrale de la Vierge inside the imposing **Collègiale Saint Laurent**, built in 1344 on place Saint Laurent. The side chapel dedicated to the Virgin Mary, where his tomb lies, is opposite the side entrance to the collegiate church.

From the south end of place de Ancienne Halle, steps lead to the **Château-Musée de L'Empéri**, one of the oldest remaining castles in Provence which served as the residence to the Archbishops of Arles from the 9th to 18th centuries. Some 30 of its spacious medieval halls are filled with over 10,000 exhibits dedicated to French military history up to WWI. Napoléon I steals the limelight. The **Musée d'Art et d'Histoire Militaires de L'Empéri** (☎ 04 90 56 22 36) is open from 1 am to noon and 2 to 6.30 pm (closed Tuesday). More local lore and legend is unravelled with 54 life-size waxworks at the **Musée Grévin de la Provence** (☎ 04 90 56 36 30), place des Centuries, open 9 am to noon and 2 to 6 pm (closed weekends).

The **Tour du Bourg Neuf** at the east end of rue du Bourg Neuf is part of the fortified ramparts that were built around the city in the 12th century. In the 13th century, young women wanting to conceive venerated the statue of the Black Virgin tucked in the gate, in the hope of bearing a child nine months

later. A rare treat are the solemn Gregorian chants sung at Sunday Mass (9 am) in the 13th century **Église Saint Michel**, place Saint Michel, every first and third Sunday of the month (except July and August).

One of Salon's two remaining *savonneries* (soap factories), the **Savonnerie Marius Fabre** (☎ 04 90 53 24 77), 148 ave Paul Borret, can be visited *sur rendez-vous* (by appointment only). Exit the train station, turn right along ave Émile Zola, left along blvd Maréchal Foch, then right on to ave Paul Borret. The soap boutique is open to

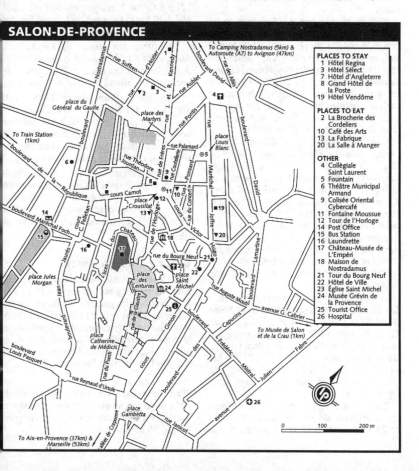

SALON-DE-PROVENCE

PLACES TO STAY
1 Hôtel Regina
3 Hôtel Sélect
7 Hôtel d'Angleterre
8 Grand Hôtel de la Poste
19 Hôtel Vendôme

PLACES TO EAT
2 La Brocherie des Cordeliers
10 Café des Arts
13 La Fabrique
20 La Salle à Manger

OTHER
4 Collègiale Saint Laurent
5 Fountain
6 Théâtre Municipal Armand
9 Colisée Oriental Cybercafé
11 Fontaine Moussue
12 Tour de l'Horloge
14 Post Office
15 Bus Station
16 Laundrette
17 Château-Musée de L'Empéri
18 Maison de Nostradamus
21 Tour du Bourg Neuf
22 Hôtel de Ville
23 Église Saint Michel
24 Musée Grévin de la Provence
25 Tourist Office
26 Hospital

all from 9 am to noon and 1.30 to 4.30 pm (closed weekends). The history of Salon's soap and olive industries, its popular arts and traditions are well explained in the **Musée de Salon et de la Crau** (☎ 04 90 56 28 37), 500m east of the centre on ave Roger Donnadieu.

Places to Stay

Accommodation in Salon is not expensive. The nearest camping ground is *Camping Nostradamus* (☎ 04 90 56 08 36, fax 04 90 56 65 05, route d'Eyguières), 5km north of Salon.

Near the train station, *Le Terminus* (☎ 04 90 56 00 92, 111 ave Émile Zola) has singles/doubles with shower for 130/160FF and rooms with shower and toilet for 160/180FF. Closer to the city's heart is *Hôtel Vendôme* (☎ 04 90 56 01 96, fax 04 90 56 48 78, 6 rue Maréchal Joffre) which markets itself as a 'garden in town'. Two-star doubles with washbasin are 200FF; doubles with toilet and shower cost 225 to 300FF.

Near the imposing Collègiale Saint Laurent, one-star *Hôtel Regina* (☎ 04 90 56 28 92, fax 04 90 56 77 43, 245 rue Kennedy) has bargain basement rooms starting at 110FF for ones with washbasin and bidet. Rooms with shower for one/two/three/four guests cost 120/130/170/190FF, and with a toilet too 130/160/180/210FF. It also has a five-person room for 260FF. Just round the corner, there are more upmarket rooms for 200FF at the two-star *Hôtel Sélect* (☎ 04 90 56 07 17, fax 04 90 56 42 48, 35 rue Suffren).

In the heart of town overlooking the Tour de l'Horloge is the *Grand Hôtel de la Poste* (☎ 04 90 56 01 94, fax 04 90 56 20 77, 1 rue Kennedy) which has rooms warranting no complaints from 190FF. A few doors down, *Hôtel d'Angleterre* (☎ 04 90 56 01 10, fax 04 90 56 71 75, 98 cours Carnot) has modern rooms off spacious landings starting at 195FF.

Top of the range is the exclusive, four-star *L'Abbaye de Sainte-Croix* (☎ 04 90 56 24 55, fax 04 90 56 31 12, saintecroix@ relaischateaux.fr, www.integra.fr/relais chat eaux/saintecroix, route du Val de Cuech), a sweet-smelling 12th century abbey amid lavender gardens.

Places to Eat

In a 13th century house, *La Brocherie des Cordeliers* (☎ 04 90 56 43 42, 20 rue d'Hozier) ranks as one of Salon's much-loved haunts. It is rustic, busy and has meats from 55FF, *menus* for 90, 100 or 120FF, and *pichets* (25 cl) of local wine for 12FF a throw. It is open at noon for lunch and 7.30 pm in the evening (closed Sunday evening and all Monday).

The other hot choice is *La Salle à Manger* (☎ 04 90 56 28 01, 6 rue Maréchal Joffre), open from noon to 2 pm and 7.30 until 10 pm (closed Sunday and Monday).

Bohemian *La Fabrique* (☎ 04 90 56 07 39, 75 rue de l'Horloge) is a really charming Italian place with brilliantly painted walls and delicious pasta dishes from 45FF. It is closed Sunday lunchtime. The adjoining shop sells homemade pasta to take away.

Elegant, refined and absolutely unbeatable in summer is the pleasing terrace of the small but chic *Café des Arts* which overlooks the moss-clad fountain on place Crousillat. Light snacks such as carpaccio start at 55FF.

Getting There & Away

Bus Inter-regional buses share Autobus Aréliens' intercity bus station (☎ 04 90 56 50 98) which adjoins place Jules Morgan, on the corner of blvd Maréchal Foch and blvd Victor Joly. There are more than a dozen daily buses to Aix-en-Provence, and a handful to Arles and Avignon. In summer, there are four buses a day to Les-Baux-de-Provence.

Train From the train station on ave Émile Zola there are some eight trains a day to Marseille (55FF; two hours) and Avignon (48FF; 50 minutes).

The Camargue

The sparsely populated, 780 sq km delta of the Rhône River known as the Camargue (La Camargo in Provençal), is famed for its desolate beauty and the incredibly varied bird life that its wetlands support. Over 400 species of land and waterbirds inhabit the region, including storks, bee-eaters and some 160 other migratory species. Most impressive of all are the huge flocks of *flamants roses* (pink flamingos) that come here to nest during the spring and summer; many set up house near the **Étang de Vaccarès** and **Étang du Fangassier**. In 1997, some 30,000 flamingos wintered in the Camargue and 15,000 to 20,000 couples hatched and raised their offspring in spring 1998.

The Camargue has been formed over the ages by sediment deposited by the Rhône *(Rose* in Provençal) River as it flows into the Mediterranean. In the southern Camargue, the areas between the *digues à la mer* (sea-wall embankments) that line water channels are taken up by shallow salt marshes, inland lakes and lagoons whose brackish waters positively shimmer in the Provençal sun. The northern part of the delta consists of dry land, and in the years following WWII huge tracts were desalinated as part of a costly drainage and irrigation program designed to make the area suitable for large-scale agriculture, especially the cultivation of rice. Rice production has dropped sharply since the 1960s, but is still a very important part of the Camarguais economy: 69.2% of France's annual rice yield is produced here.

At some places along the coast, the delta continues to grow, leaving one-time seaside towns many kilometres from the Mediterranean. Elsewhere, sea currents and storms have, in recent centuries, swept away land that had been around long enough for people to build things on. The course of the Rhône has changed repeatedly over the millennia, but the Grand Rhône (which carries 90% of the river's flow) and the Petit Rhône

HIGHLIGHTS

- Follow Vincent van Gogh's footsteps in Arles, see Picasso sketches in the Musée Réattu and watch a bullfight at the Roman amphitheatre

- Explore the Camargue on horseback while pink clouds of flamingos fly overhead

- Walk on top of the walled city of Aigues-Mortes

- Hike and bird-watch in the wetlands but watch out for the mosquitoes

- Join in the festive fun at a rice fête, a cowboy festival, or at a gypsy pilgrimage

THE CAMARGUE

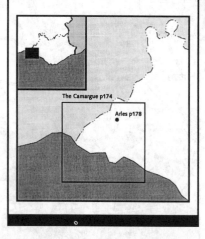

The Camargue p174

Arles p178

have followed their present channels for about 500 years.

Most of the Camargue wetlands are within the **Parc Naturel Régional de Camargue**, established in 1970 to preserve the area's fragile ecosystems by maintaining an equilibrium between ecological considerations and the region's economic mainstays:

173

agriculture, salt production, hunting, grazing and tourism. The central, 6000 hectare Étang de Vaccarès has been protected by the **Réserve Naturelle Zoologique et Botanique** – a 135 sq km nature reserve embracing the lagoon and its nearby peninsulas and islands – since 1927. A further 2000 hectares in the less habited eastern zone of the Camargue between Arles and Salin-de-Giraud is managed by the **Conservatoire du Littoral**.

The Camargue's famous herds of cream-coloured *cheveaux* (horses) and black *taureaux* (bulls) which roam free under the watchful eyes of the mounted *gardians* (Camarguaise cowboys) can still be seen. An equally likely sight is bulls grazing in fenced-in fields and horses saddled and tethered, waiting in rows under the blazing sun for tourists to pay for a ride. The *cheval de Camargue* – always grey-cream in colour, with a square-shaped head and about 13.1 hands in size – has been recognised as a breed in its own right since 1978. Most bulls are raised for bullfighting.

At least one traditional Camargue phenomenon is alive and well: the area's savage

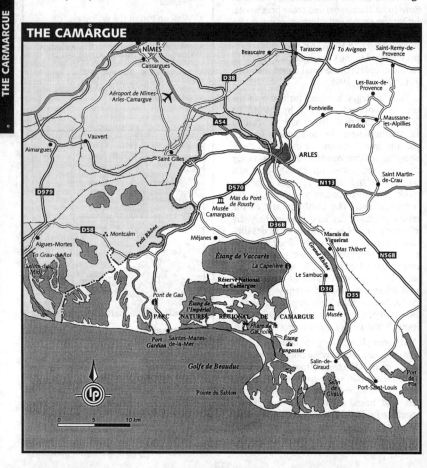

THE CAMARGUE

mosquitoes are flourishing, feeding on the blood of hapless passers-by just as they have for countless eons. Pack *plenty* of insect repellent – then pack more.

Camarguaise cuisine tends to be extremely meaty: *le guardianne de taureau* (literally, 'the bull's herdsman') is a heart warming beef stew.

Orientation

Shaped like a croissant, the 850 sq km Parc Naturel Régional de Camargue is enclosed by the Petit Rhône and Grand Rhône rivers. The protected Étang de Vaccarès is bang in its centre.

Rice is cultivated in the northern sections of the delta. There are enormous salt evaporation pools around Salin-de-Giraud, which is at the Camargue's south-eastern tip.

Inland, the old Roman town of Arles rides on the croissant's back and is the gateway to the park. The Camargue's other two towns are on the coast – the seaside resort of Saintes-Maries-de-la-Mer, 39km south-west and the walled town, Aigues-Mortes, 34km north-west.

Park Offices

The Parc Naturel Régional de Camargue has an information centre (☎ 04 90 97 86 32, fax 04 90 97 70 82, info@parcs-naturels-re gionaux.tm.fr, www.parcs-naturels-regionaux .tm.fr/lesparcs/camab.html) at Pont de Gau, 4km north of Saintes-Maries-de-la-Mer off the D570. Exhibits focus on environmental issues. From the glassed-in foyer you can watch birds – including flamingos – through powerful binoculars in the nearby marshes. The centre is open from 9 am to 6 pm (9.30 am to 5 pm from October to March; closed Friday).

The Réserve Nationale de Camargue has an information centre (☎ 04 90 97 00 97, fax 04 90 97 01 44) at La Capelière on the D36B. It has exhibits on the Camargue's ecosystems, flora and fauna, and many trails and paths fan out from the centre. It is open from 9 am to noon and 2 to 5 pm (closed Sunday).

Bird-watching & Hiking

The Parc Ornithologique (ornithological park; ☎ 04 90 97 82 62, fax 04 90 97 74 77), adjoining the information centre of the Parc Naturel Régional de Camargue Maison du Parc in Pont de Gau, should be the first port of call for anyone keen to peek at some of the area's winged creatures or hike in the wetland. Within the bird park several kilometres of marked hiking trails wend their way through reed beds and marshes, enabling you to experience the Camargue at its wildest and most wonderful – mosquitoes and all. The park, which also has some caged birds, is open daily from 9 am to sunset; from 10 am between October and April (33/18FF for adult/student).

There are numerous other walking paths and trails in the Parc Naturel Régional, the Réserve Nationale, on the embankments and along the coast. A 3.5km nature trail (two hours) starts from the Musée Camarguais, 10km south-west of Arles (see that section later).

The traditional Camargue cross, in which the cross symbolises faith, the heart symbolises charity and the anchor represents hope.

Pretty in Pink

The pink or greater flamingo (phoenicopterus ruber) in flight is a breathtaking sight. Equally majestic is the catwalk stance – neck high, breast out – adopted by this elegant, long-legged creature when strutting through shallow waters.

Flamingo courtship starts in January, with mating taking place from March to May. The single egg laid by the female in April or May is incubated in a mud-caked nest for one month by both parents. The young chicks shakily take to the skies when they are about three months old. By the time they reach adulthood (around five years old), their soft grey down has become a fine feather coat of brilliant white or pretty rose-pink.

This well-dressed bird lives to the grand old age of 34 (longer if kept in captivity). It stands between 1.5 to 2m tall and has an average wing span of 1.9m. When the flamingo feels threatened, its loud hiss is similar to the warning sound made by a goose. It feeds on plankton, sucking in water and draining it off with a disproportionately heavy, curved bill.

Some flamingos remain in the Rhône delta year round. Come September, several thousand take flight to Spain, Tunisia and Senegal where they winter in warmer climes, before returning to the Camargue in February in time for early spring.

Both park offices sell detailed hiking maps of the area including the 1:25,000 IGN Série Bleue maps, Nos 2944E and 2944O.

Bicycling

As long as you can put up with the insects and stiff sea breezes, bicycles are the finest way to independently explore the Camargue, which is, of course, very flat. East of Saintes Maries, areas along the seafront and farther inland are reserved for hikers and cyclists. For a list of cycling routes with detailed route explanations in English, head to Le Vélo Saintois (☎/fax 04 90 97 74 56), 19 ave de la République, Saintes Maries, which hires mountain bikes for 80/200FF for one/three days. It has tandems, can deliver bicycles to your hotel door, and is open year round. Other rental agencies in Saintes Maries, Aigues-Mortes and Arles are listed under Getting Around in those sections.

Horse Riding

There are numerous horse farms offering *promenade à cheval* (horse riding) along the D570 (route d'Arles) leading into Saintes Maries. Expect to pay 75/350FF an hour/day. You can also ride at the Auberge de Jeunesse near Saintes Maries. For more information on equestrian activities contact the Association Camarguaise de Tourisme Équestre (☎ 04 90 97 86 32, fax 04 90 97 70 82) in the Centre de Ginès at Pont de Gau.

Organised Tours

Boat excursions can be picked up in Aigues-Mortes and Saintes Maries. Les Guides du Terroir Camprolan (☎ 04 90 97 96 82, fax 04 90 97 96 79), 17 place des Gitans, Saintes Maries, organises all types of activities including three-hour fishing expeditions (195FF) and guided tours with a local ornithologist (95FF). Kayak Vert Camargue (☎ 06 09 56 06 47 or 04 90 97 88 89, fax 04 90 97 88 91, www.canoe .france.com), Mas des Baumelles, 8km north off the D38, arranges canoeing and kayaking on the Petit Rhône. La Maison du Guide (☎ 04 66 73 52 30 or 06 12 44 73 52, fax 04 66 88 71 25), in Montcalm, 10km west of Saintes Maries on the D58, organises guided tours by foot, boat and bicycle.

Numerous companies in Arles organise trips by jeep into the Camargue heartland, including: Provence Camargue Tours (☎ 04 90 49 85 58), 1 rue Émile Fassin; Havas Voyages (☎ 04 90 96 13 25), 4 blvd des Lices; and Destination Camargue (☎ 04 90 96 94 44), 29 rue Balechou. Rates start at 180/100FF for adult/child under 12 for a half day trip. Camargue-Safaris Photo-Loisirs (☎ 04 90 97 86 93 or 04 09 97 84 12), 22 ave Van Gogh, Saintes Maries, organises helicopter, horseback and jeep excursions.

ARLES
- pop 52,000   ✉ 13200

The attractive city of Arles at the northern tip of the Camargue alluvial plain, lies on the Grand Rhône River just south of where the Petit Rhône splits off from it. Avignon is 36km north-east and Nîmes is 31km north-west.

Arles began its ascent to prosperity and political importance in 49 BC, when the victorious Julius Caesar – to whom the city had given its support – captured and plundered Marseille, which had backed Caesar's rival, the general and statesman Pompey the Great. Arles soon replaced Marseille as the region's major port and became the sort of Roman provincial centre that, within a century and a half, needed a 20,000 seat amphitheatre and a 12,000 seat theatre to entertain its citizens. These days, the two imposing structures stage cultural events and Camarguaise bullfights.

The Arlésiens' most famous resident was Vincent van Gogh (1853-90) who settled in the town for a year in 1888, immortalising many of the city's most picturesque streets and surrounding rural areas on canvas.

Orientation

The centre of Arles is enclosed by the Grand Rhône River to the north-west, blvd Émile Combes to the east and, to the south, by blvd des Lices and blvd Georges Clémenceau. It is shaped like a foot, with the train station, place de la Libération and place Lamartine (where Van Gogh once lived) at the ankle, the Arènes at the anklebone and the tourist office squashed under the arch. It's a fairly small area, easily explored on foot.

Maps The Blay-Foldex *Arles Plan de Ville* (22FF) includes an alphabetical street listing and is sold at the Presse de l'Hôtel de Ville, 12 rue de l'Hôtel de Ville.

Information

Tourist Offices Arles' central tourist office (☎ 04 90 18 41 20, fax 04 90 18 41 29), on esplanade Charles de Gaulle, a short

ARLES

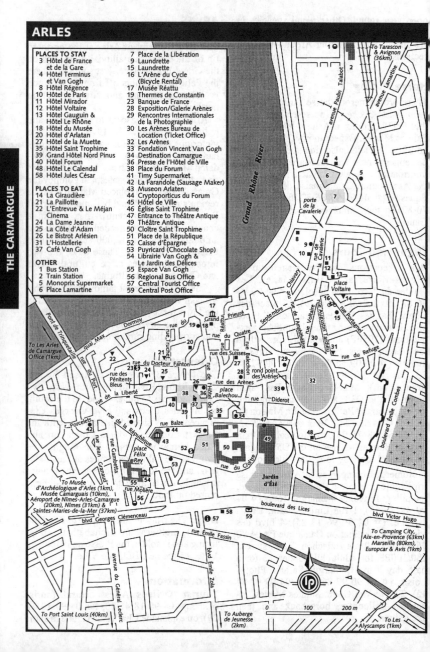

PLACES TO STAY
3   Hôtel de France
    et de la Gare
4   Hôtel Terminus
    et Van Gogh
8   Hôtel Régence
10 Hôtel de Paris
11 Hôtel Mirador
12 Hôtel Voltaire
13 Hôtel Gauguin &
    Hôtel Le Rhône
18 Hôtel du Musée
20 Hôtel d'Arlatan
27 Hôtel de la Muette
35 Hôtel Saint Trophime
39 Grand Hôtel Nord Pinus
40 Hôtel Forum
48 Hôtel Le Calendal
58 Hôtel Jules César

PLACES TO EAT
14 La Giraudière
21 La Paillotte
22 L'Entrevue & Le Méjan
    Cinema
24 La Dame Jeanne
25 La Côte d'Adam
26 Le Bistrot Arlésien
31 L'Hostellerie
37 Café Van Gogh

OTHER
1   Bus Station
2   Train Station
3   Monoprix Supermarket
6   Place Lamartine

7   Place de la Libération
9   Laundrette
15 Laundrette
16 L'Arène du Cycle
    (Bicycle Rental)
17 Musée Réattu
19 Thermes de Constantin
23 Banque de France
28 Exposition/Galerie Arènes
29 Rencontres Internationales
    de la Photographie
30 Les Arènes Bureau de
    Location (Ticket Office)
32 Les Arènes
33 Fondation Vincent Van Gogh
34 Destination Camargue
36 Presse de l'Hôtel de Ville
38 Place du Forum
41 Timy Supermarket
42 La Farandole (Sausage Maker)
43 Museon Arlaten
44 Cryptoporticus du Forum
45 Hôtel de Ville
46 Église Saint Trophime
47 Entrance to Théâtre Antique
49 Théâtre Antique
50 Cloître Saint Trophime
51 Place de la République
52 Caisse d'Épargne
53 Puyricard (Chocolate Shop)
54 Librairie Van Gogh &
    Le Jardin des Délices
55 Espace Van Gogh
56 Regional Bus Office
57 Central Tourist Office
59 Central Post Office

trip along blvd des Lices, is open from 9 am to 6 pm (7 pm from April to September). Sunday hours are 10 am to noon (9 am to 1 pm from April to September). The tourist office (☎ 04 90 49 36 90) next to the train station is open from 9 am to 1 pm and 1.30 to 5 pm (closed Sunday); from April to September hours are 9 am to 1 pm and 2 to 6 pm (closed Sunday).

Both offices make accommodation bookings (☎ 04 90 18 41 22, fax 04 90 18 41 29) and exchange foreign currency. They also sell a discounted combination ticket giving you entrance to all Arles' sights for 60/40FF adult/student; museums sell the pass too.

From mid-June to mid-September the tourist offices run thematic city tours, including a two hour 'In the Footsteps of Van Gogh' tour (20/10FF adult/student).

Money The Banque de France, 35ter rue du Docteur Fanton, is open from 8.30 am to 12.10 pm and 1.50 to 3.50 pm (closed on weekends). There are more banks on place de la République.

Post The post office, 5 blvd des Lices, is open from 8.30 am to 7 pm (Saturday until noon; closed Sunday).

Bookshops The Librairie Van Gogh (☎ 04 90 96 86 65), wrapped around the courtyard of the Espace Van Gogh at 1 place Félix Rey, has an extensive range of English-language art, history, culture and cookery books pertaining to Provence. It's open from 10 am to 12.30 pm and 2 to 6.30 pm (closed Sunday and Monday).

Laundry The laundrette, 6 rue de la Cavalerie, is open from 7 am to 7 pm. The one at 12 rue Portagnel is open from 7.45 am to noon and 1.45 to 6.30 pm (closed Wednesday and Sunday).

Les Arènes

Arles' Roman amphitheatre (☎ 04 90 96 03 70), built in the late 1st or early 2nd century AD, measures 136m by 107m, making it marginally larger than its counterpart in Nîmes. Like other such structures around the Roman empire, it was built to stage sporting contests, chariot races and the wildly popular and bloody spectacles so beloved by the Roman public. Wild animals were pitted against other animals or gladiators (usually slaves or criminals), who fought each other until one of them was either killed or surrendered (in the latter case his throat was usually then slit). Executions were carried out either by the executioner or by pushing the victim into the arena with a wild animal.

In the early medieval period, during the Arab invasions, the Arènes was transformed into a fortress; three of the four defensive towers can still be seen around the structure. These days, the Arènes has a capacity of over 12,000 and still draws a full house during the bullfighting season.

The Arènes is open daily – unless there's a performance on – from 10 am to 4.30 pm. From April to September, hours are 9 am to 7 pm (15/9FF for adult/student). The Arènes' *bureau de location* (ticket office; ☎ 04 90 96 03 70), on the north side of the amphitheatre on Rond Point des Arènes, is open from 9 am to noon and 2.30 to 6 pm (until 5 pm on Friday; closed on weekends).

Théâtre Antique

The Roman theatre (☎ 04 90 96 93 30), which dates from the end of the 1st century BC, was used for many hundreds of years as a convenient source of construction materials, so little of the original structure – measuring 102m in diameter – remains, except for two imposing columns. Entered through the **Jardin d'Été** (Summer Garden) on blvd des Lices, it hosts open-air dance, film and music festivals in summer. The Théâtre Antique is open the same hours as the Arènes and charges the same admission fee.

Église Saint Trophime

This austere Romanesque church, once a cathedral (Arles was an archbishopric from the 4th century until 1790), stands on the site of several earlier churches. It was built

Bulls & Cowboys

In *mise à mort* bullfighting *(corrida)*, which is popular in Spain, Latin America and parts of southern France, a bull bred to be aggressive is killed in a colourful and bloody ceremony involving picadors, toreadors, matadors and horses. But not all bullfighting ends with a dead bull.

In a *course Camarguaise* (Camargue-style bullfight), white-clad *raseteurs* try to remove ribbons or *attributs* (rosettes) tied to the bull's horns with hooks (known as *crochets*) held between their fingers. The origins of the course Camarguaise date to the 15th century when dogs, lions and bears were let loose in a ring to chase a bull. The merry circus was finally slammed as cruel in the 19th century and the other animals banished from the ring, leaving man alone to pit his wits against the *taureau*.

During a course Camarguaise, six bulls are chased around the arena. Each bull remains in the ring for just 15 minutes. A *course de tàu* is a fight with bulls that have not been castrated, a *course de vaches cocardières* is a fight against cows, while young bulls and novice raseteurs only take part in a *course de protection*.

Out of the limelight, bulls are bred, fed, loved and tended by *gardians*, Camargue cowboys who herd the region's cattle. These mounted herdsmen are honoured by the Fête des Gardians in Arles in May, during which they parade through town on horseback – clad in leather hats, chequered shirts and dusty boots. Traditionally, mounted gardians usher bulls from their paddocks to the bullfighting ring. Long ago, gardians lived in *cabanes de gardians*, white-washed cottages crowned with a thatched roof and sealed with a strip of mortar.

Courses Camarguaises are common in Arles but not so popular in Nîmes where *férias* (bullfighting festivals) sport corridas and novilladas in which young bulls less than four years old are thrown in the ring to fight. A bullfighting fan is known as an aficionado.

in the late 11th and 12th centuries – perhaps using stone cut from the Théâtre Antique – and was named after St Trophimus, a late 2nd or early 3rd century bishop of Arles.

Unlike the almost unadorned (save for a few tapestries) interior, the western portal facing place de la République is richly decorated in 12th century stone carvings that have been beautifully restored. Two lateral chapels were added in the 14th century. The choir and the ambulatory are from the 15th century, when the structure was significantly enlarged.

Across the courtyard is the serene **Cloître Saint Trophime** (☎ 04 90 49 36 36), a cloister surrounded by superbly sculptured columns. The church and cloister are open the same hours as the Arènes and Théâtre Antique (20/14FF).

Les Alyscamps

This large necropolis (☎ 04 90 49 36 36), 1km south-east of the Arènes, was founded by the Romans and taken over by Christians in the 4th century. Because of the presence of Christian martyrs among the dead, which was said to work miracles, Les Alyscamps became a popular last resting place.

The necropolis was treated badly during and after the Renaissance and today is a shadow of its former glorious self. Some of the original marble sarcophagi are preserved in the Musée d'Archéologique d'Arles. Both Van Gogh and Gauguin painted Les Alyscamps with great vividness. Les Alyscamps is open the same hours as the Arènes (15/9FF for adult/student).

Other Roman Sites

The **Thermes de Constantin**, Roman baths built in the 4th century near the river on rue du Grand Prieuré, are only partly preserved. When they open again following extensive renovations in 1998, hours should be 10 am to noon and 2 to 4.30 pm; 9 am to noon and 2 to 7 pm from April to September (15/9FF for adult/student).

The **Cryptoporticus du Forum**, underground storerooms most of which were carved out in the 1st century BC, can be accessed though a 17th century Jesuit chapel on rue Balze. It keeps the same hours as the Arénes (12/7FF).

Museums

The **Musée d'Archéologique d'Arles** which is also called the Musée de l'Arles Antique (☎ 04 90 18 88 88 or 04 90 18 88 89) brings together the rich collections of the former museums Musée d'Art Païen (Museum of Pagan Art) and the Musée d'Art Chrétien (Museum of Christian Art). Exhibits include Roman statues, artefacts, marble sarcophagi and a renowned assortment of early Christian sarcophagi from the 4th century. The archaeology museum is 1.5km south-west of the tourist office at ave de la Première Division Française Libre on the Presqu'île du Cirque Romain. It is open from 9.30 am to noon and 1.30 to 6 pm (closed Tuesday); hours from April to September are 9 am to 7 pm (35/25FF for adult/student).

The **Museon Arlaten** (☎ 04 90 96 08 23), 29 rue de la République, founded by Provençal poet Frédéric Mistral (see the Facts about Provence chapter), is dedicated to preserving and displaying everyday objects related to traditional Provençal life: furniture, crafts, costumes, ceramics, wigs, a model of the Tarasque (a human-eating amphibious monster of Provençal legend) etc. It occupies a 16th century townhouse constructed around Roman ruins and is open from 9.30 am to 12.30 pm and 2 to 5 pm (6 pm in April, May and September). Hours from June to August are 9.30 am to 1 pm and 2 to 6.30 pm. The museum is closed on Monday from October to June (20/15FF for adult/student).

The **Musée Réattu** (☎ 04 90 96 37 68), housed in a 15th century priory at 10 rue du Grand Prieuré, exhibits works by some of the world's finest photographers, modern and contemporary works of art, and paintings by 18th and 19th century Provençal artists. It also has 57 Picasso drawings, sketched by the eccentric artist between December 1970 and November 1971. The conventional portrait of his mother Maria, painted by Picasso in Côte d'Antibes in 1923 is particularly fine. The museum is open daily from 10.30 am to noon and 2 to 5.30 pm; 9 am to noon and 2 to 7 pm from April to September (15/9FF for adult/student).

Contemporary art exhibits can be viewed at the **Rencontres Internationales de la Photographie** (☎ 04 90 96 76 06), 10 Rond

Point des Arènes, open 9 am to noon and 2 to 6 pm (closed on weekends); and at the **Exposition Galerie Arènes** inside the École Nationale de la Photographie (National School of Photography; ☎ 04 90 99 33 33), 16 rue des Arènes.

Van Gogh

The **Fondation Vincent van Gogh** (☎ 04 90 49 94 04 or 04 90 93 08 08, fax 04 90 49 55 49), inside the Palais de Luppé at 24bis Rond Point des Arènes, displays paintings by other artists inspired by Arles' most famous resident. The centre is open from 9.30 am to noon and 2 to 5.40 pm; 10 am to 7 pm between April and October (30/20FF for adult/student).

The gallery, **La Rose des Vents** (☎ 04 90 96 15 85), 18 rue Diderot, displays various Van Gogh reproductions and letters written by him to his brother Theo. In 1888 Van Gogh wrote to his sister Willemien, 'nature in the south cannot be painted with the palette of a mauve for instance which belongs to the north ... now the palette is distinctly colourful, sky blue, orange, pink, vermilion, a very bright yellow, bright green, wine red and violet'. The gallery is open from 10.30 am to 12.30 pm and 3 to 7 pm (closed Sunday morning, Monday, and in winter).

Various art exhibitions take place at the modern **Espace Van Gogh** (☎ 04 90 49 39 39, fax 04 90 43 80 85), housed in the old Hôtel Dieu and former hospital on place Félix Rey where Van Gogh spent some time.

Musée Camarguais

Housed in a sheep shed built in 1812, the Camargue Museum (☎ 04 90 97 10 82) at Mas du Pont de Rousty (10km south-west of Arles on the D570 to Saintes Maries) is an excellent introduction to the history, ecosystems, flora and fauna of the Camargue river delta. Much attention is given to traditional life in the Camargue (sheep and cattle raising, salt production at Salin de Giraud, local arts). A 3.5km nature trail that ends at an observation tower leads from the museum. Count on two hours walking.

Vincent van Gogh

When Vincent van Gogh (1853-90) arrived in Provence in 1888, the quality of light and the colours were a great revelation to him. He spent an intensely productive year at Arles, during which he painted all sorts of local scenes, among them the Pont de Langlois, a little bridge that has been rebuilt 3km south of Arles (from town, take bus No 1 to the Pont van Gogh terminus). A famous painting of the bridge entitled *The Bridge at Arles* is on display in the Kröller-Müller National Museum in the Netherlands.

In 1888, Van Gogh's friend and fellow artist Gauguin came to stay with him for several months. But their different temperaments and approaches to art soon led to a quarrel after which Van Gogh, overcome with despair, chopped off part of his left ear. In May 1889, because of recurrent bouts of madness, he voluntarily retreated to an asylum in Saint Rémy (25km northeast of Arles over the Alpilles), staying there for a year during which he continued to be amazingly productive. In 1890, while staying in Auvers-sur-Oise (just north of Paris), Van Gogh, lonely to the point of desperation and afraid that his madness was incurable, shot and killed himself.

There are few tangible remains of Vincent van Gogh's stay in Arles. All traces of his rented yellow house and the nearby café on Place Lamartine, both of which appear in his paintings, were wiped out in WWII.

The museum is open October to March from 10.15 am to 4.45 pm (closed Tuesday). From April to October, hours are 9.15 am to 5.45 pm; until 6.45 pm in July and August (25/13FF for adult/student). The museum can be reached from Arles by bus. See Getting There & Away later for details.

Organised Tours

Jeep tour reservations can be made at La Boutique Provençal (☎ 04 90 49 84 31), 8

Rond Point des Arènes. Most companies only run trips between March and October.

Special Events
In early July, Les Rencontres Internationales de la Photographie (International Photography Festival) attract photographers and aficionados from around the world. The two week Fêtes d'Arles at the end of June brings dance, theatre, music and poetry readings to the city. For more information contact the Festiv'Arles office (☎ 04 9 96 47 00 or 04 90 96 81 18, fax 04 90 96 81 17), 35 place de la République.

Other fascinating events include the Festival Mosaïque Gitane in mid-July which celebrates Gypsy culture, and the week long Fête des Prémices du Riz in September marking the start of the rice harvest.

The bullfighting season at the Arènes starts around Easter and runs until September.

Places to Stay
Arles has plenty of reasonably priced accommodation. There are many *gîtes ruraux* (☎ 04 90 59 49 40 to book) in the surrounding Camargue. Ask the tourist office for the list.

Places to Stay – Budget
Camping Arles' nearest camping ground is the two-star *Camping City* (☎ 04 90 93 08 86, fax 04 90 93 91 07, 67 route de Crau), 1km south-east of Arles' centre on the road to Marseille. It's open from March to October and charges 21/15FF per adult/child plus 22FF for a tent and car. Take bus No 2 to the Hermite stop.

Hostel The 100 bed *Auberge de Jeunesse* (☎ 04 90 96 18 25, fax 04 90 96 31 26, 20 ave Maréchal Foch), which charges 75FF including breakfast, is 2km south of the centre. It is closed the first half of February. Take bus No 3 from blvd Georges Clémenceau or No 8 from place Lamartine to the Fournier stop.

Hotels The *Hôtel de France et de la Gare* (☎ 04 90 96 01 24, fax 04 90 96 90 87, 1 *place Lamartine)* has rooms for one or two people with shower and toilet for 185FF. Next door at No 5, the renovated *Hôtel Terminus et Van Gogh* (☎/fax 04 90 96 12 32) has similar rooms with washbasin, for one or two people, for 140FF. Doubles/triples/quads with shower are 180/270/320FF.

Heading into town you come to another couple of cheapies. The *Hôtel Régence* (☎ 04 90 96 39 85, fax 04 90 96 67 64, 5 rue Marius Jouveau)* overlooks the Rhône and has uninspiring singles/doubles from 140/175FF. The nearby *Hôtel de Paris* (☎ 04 90 96 05 88, 10 rue de la Cavalerie)* is above a café and has rooms for two for 160FF.

The *Hôtel Voltaire* (☎ 04 90 96 13 58, 1 *place Voltaire)* has serviceable rooms, some overlooking the pretty square, from 120/140FF with washbasin/shower. The old fashioned and cluttered *Hôtel Le Rhône* (☎ 04 90 96 43 70, fax 04 90 93 87 03, 11 *place Voltaire)* has rooms with washbasin/shower/shower and toilet for 130/170/210FF.

Simple, no-frill rooms at the *Hôtel de la Poste* (☎ 04 90 96 03 30, fax 04 90 49 80 28, 2 rue Molière)* start at 140FF.

Places to Stay – Mid-Range
The renovated, two-star *Hôtel Gauguin* (☎ 04 90 96 14 35, fax 04 90 18 98 87, 5 *place Voltaire)* has doubles with alarm clock and shower for 180FF. Doubles at the 15 room *Hôtel Mirador* (☎ 04 90 96 28 05, fax 04 90 96 59 89, 3 rue Voltaire)* cost 230/255FF with toilet and shower/bath. Cheaper rooms with no toilet – just shower – are 190FF.

The appealing, 20 room *Hôtel du Musée* (☎ 04 90 93 88 88, fax 04 90 49 98 15, 11 rue du Grand Prieuré)* occupies a 12th to 13th century building and is spacious, calm and has a terrace garden out the back. Doubles with shower/bath and toilet start at 220/320FF.

The family-run, two-star *Hôtel de la Muette* (☎ 04 90 96 15 39, fax 04 90 49 73 16, 15 rue des Suisses)* is part of the Logis de France chain and has prettily-furnished rooms with toilet and shower/bath for

220/300FF. Rooms with shower only (no toilet) cost 210FF.

A refined option is the *Hôtel Saint Trophime* (**☎** *04 90 96 88 38, fax 04 90 96 92 19, 16 rue de la Calade),* housed in a 17th century mansion. Singles/doubles with shower, toilet and TV cost 210/285FF, doubles with bath are 310FF, and triples/quads cost 385/430FF. Equally charming is the *Hôtel Le Calendal* (**☎** *04 90 96 11 89, fax 04 90 96 05 84, 22 place Pomme).* Rooms for one or two with shower/bath start at 250/320FF. A garden view costs more.

The *Hôtel Forum* (**☎** *04 90 93 48 95, fax 04 90 93 90 00, 10 place du Forum)* has rooms from 280-700FF. The elegant *Hôtel d'Arlatan* (**☎** *04 90 93 56 66, fax 04 90 49 68 45, info@hotel-arlatan.fr, 26 rue du Sauvage)* has lavish doubles from 298-465FF.

Places to Stay – Top End
If you've got money to burn, try the four-star *Hôtel Jules César* (**☎** *04 90 93 43 20, fax 04 90 93 33 47, julescesar@calva.net, www.hotel-julescesar.fr, 9 blvd des Lices).* Its grand, Roman style portico, private chapel and sumptuous Provençal-style rooms go for 650/1450FF.

Overlooking chic place du Forum at No 14 is the *Grand Hôtel Nord Pinus* (**☎** *04 90 93 44 94, fax 04 90 93 33 47)* where fancy singles/doubles start at 770/840FF.

Places to Eat
Blvd Georges Clémenceau and blvd des Lices are lined with plane trees and terraced brasseries. The latter are fine for a meal if you don't mind dining à la traffic fumes.

Restaurants Place du Forum, an intimate square shaded by eight large plane trees, becomes one big dining room at lunch and dinner times. Most restaurants are mid-range places, although *Le Bistrot Arlésien,* on the corner of rue des Arènes, has salads for 20-60FF and reasonably priced *plats du jour* for 55-60FF. *La Côte d'Adam* (**☎** *04 90 49 62 29, 12 rue de la Liberté)* is a cosy and

popular, slightly cheaper place than its counterparts on the square. *La Dame Jeanne* (**☎** *04 90 96 37 09, 4 rue des Pénitents Bleus)* is devoid of pretension and offers a three-course 72FF *menu.*

The calm and cool *L'Entrevue* (**☎** *04 90 93 37 28, 23 quai Max Dormoy)* is down by the riverfront in an artsy cinema and bookshop complex. It doesn't offer a view of the water, but is a stylish laidback place serving oriental and Caribbean cuisine, including a fantastic couscous royal (98FF) and wonderfully refreshing mint and pine kernel tea.

L'Hostellerie (**☎** *04 90 96 13 05, 62 rue du Refuge)* has a terrace with an excellent view up towards the amphitheatre. It offers a good selection of salads (18-52FF) and a *menu* for 75FF (closed Tuesday). Nearby *La Giraudière* (**☎** *04 90 93 27 52, 53-55 rue Condorcet)* is an attractive blue wooden-shutter place overlooking place Voltaire, with a tempting regional *menu* for 79FF.

La Paillotte (**☎** *04 90 96 33 15, 26 rue du Docteur Fanton)* dishes up great *aïoli Provençal* for 78FF and a bouillabaisse for 108FF.

Cafés Arles' most idyllic café, *Le Jardin des Délices* (**☎** *04 90 93 34 56, 1 place Félix Rey)* in the Espace Van Gogh, overlooks ornamental gardens inspired by Van Gogh's painting entitled *The Hospital Garden at Arles.* A variety of salads and light meals are served here; a set *formule* costs 40-50FF.

Also paying homage to the artist's Arlésien roots is the *Café Van Gogh* which spills out on place du Forum. Its very yellow façade mimics the canary yellow house on place Lamartine which Van Gogh chose as the subject for his canvas *Café de Nuit.* The Café Van Gogh, which doubles as a busy bar by night, has *menus* for 75 and 99FF.

Self-Catering On Wednesday, *market stalls* sprawl the length of blvd Émile Combe outside of the city walls. On Saturday morning, the market is on blvd des Lices and blvd Georges Clémenceau.

Local *saucisson d'Arles* (Arles sausage) is sold at sausage makers *La Farandole*

(☎ 04 90 96 01 12, 11 rue des Porcelets).
The sweeter-toothed can purchase exquisite
Provençal chocolates from *Puyricard* on
rue de la République.

Entertainment

Cinéma Le Méjan (☎ 04 90 93 33 56 or 08
36 68 47 07, 23 quai Max Dormoy), adjoining L'Entrevue restaurant, screens
nondubbed films.

Cargo de Nuit (☎ 04 90 49 55 99, 7 ave
Sadi Carnot) is a modern café-cum-club
which hosts live bands and alternative
music concerts. It's open from 8 pm to 5
am. The brasseries along blvd Georges Clémenceau are the liveliest spots in town for
a drink. There are more subdued bars
around place Voltaire and place du Forum.

Getting There & Away

Air Aéroport de Nîmes-Arles-Camargue
(also called Aéroport Garons; ☎ 04 66 70 49
49) is 20km north-west of the city on the
A54 to Nîmes.

Bus The inter-regional bus station is at the
end of ave Paulin Talabot, about 1km north
of the Arènes. Its information office (☎ 04
90 49 38 01) is open from 9 am to 4 pm
(Saturday until noon; closed Sunday and
Monday). The regional bus company, Les
Cars de Camargue (☎ 04 90 96 94 78), has
an office at 24 blvd Georges Clémenceau
(the bus stop for intercity buses – see
Getting Around) and at 4 rue Jean Mathieu
Artaud. It runs services to Nîmes (33FF; 50
minutes; six a day) and Marseille (82FF;
2½ hours; two a day) via Aix-en-Provence
(65FF; 1¾ hours).

Les Cars de Camargue buses link Arles
with other parts of the Camargue, including
Saintes-Maries-de-la-Mer (36.50FF; one
hour; two a day in winter and six to nine a
day in summer), Port Saint Louis (36FF; 65
minutes; six a day) and many places en
route such as Mas du Pont de Rousty, Pioch
Badet and Pont de Gau. If you are in the Camargue for a few days, consider purchasing
a Passe Camargue (140FF) which allows

three days of unlimited travel on the two
main bus routes.

Ceyte Tourisme Méditerranée (CTM;
☎ 04 90 93 74 90), 21 Chemin du Temple,
runs buses to Aix-en-Provence, Marseille
and Avignon (37.50FF; five daily).

Eurolines (☎ 04 90 96 94 78), the long
haul bus company, sells tickets at 24 blvd
Georges Clémenceau.

Train Arles train station is opposite the bus
station. The information office is open from
8 am to noon and 2 to 6 pm (closed Sunday).
Major rail destinations include Nîmes
(61FF; 30 minutes), Marseille (79FF; 40
minutes) and Avignon (35FF; 20 minutes).

Car & Motorcycle Car rental companies
with offices in Arles include Avis (☎ 04 90
96 82 42), ave Talabot; and Europcar (☎ 04
90 93 23 24) or Hertz (☎ 04 90 96 75 23),
both on blvd Victor Hugo.

Getting Around

To/From the Airport CTM (☎ 04 90 93
74 90) runs bus services to Nîmes-Arles-
Camargue Airport from 24 blvd Georges
Clémenceau.

Bus Local buses are run by STAR (☎ 04 90
96 87 47). The information office at 16 blvd
Georges Clémenceau, west of the tourist
office, is open from 8.30 am to 12.30 pm and
1.30 (2 in summer) to 6 pm (closed on weekends). Blvd Georges Clémenceau is the main
bus hub, though most buses stop at place
Lamartine, a short walk south of the train
station, too. In general, STAR buses run from
7 am to 7 pm (5 pm on Sunday). A single
ticket/10-ticket carnet costs 5/42FF. In addition to its 11 bus lines, STAR runs minibuses
called Starlets that circle most of the old city
every half hour from 7.15 am to 7.40 pm (not
Sunday). Best of all, they're free.

Bicycle Bicycles can be hired from
Peugeot (☎ 04 90 96 03 77), 15 rue du Pont,
or L'Arène du Cycle/Dall'Oppio (☎ 04 90
96 46 83), 10 rue Portagnel. The latter
charges 60/100FF per day plus deposit for

bicycles/mountain bikes and is open March to October only from 8 am to noon and 2 to 7 pm (until 6 pm on Saturday; closed Sunday and Monday).

SAINTES-MARIES-DE-LA-MER
• pop 2200   ✉ 13460

Saintes-Maries-de-la-Mer is no more than a seaside village, marooned between the Étang de l'Impérial and the sea in the Camarguaise outback. It is best known for its magnificent fortified Romanesque church which, for centuries, has served as a pilgrimage site for Europe's colourful *gitan* (gypsy) population. The coastline is lined with 30km of uninterrupted sandy beaches. Nudists frequent the patch near Phare de la Gacholle, a lighthouse 11km east of the village.

Orientation & Information
The Arènes, tourist office and Port Gardian are lined up between ave Van Gogh and the sea. From the bus stop on ave d'Arles (the southern end of the D570), bear south along ave Frédéric Mistral then east across place des Remparts and place Portalet to get to place de l'Église.

The tourist office (☎ 04 90 97 82 55, fax 04 90 97 71 15, saintes-maries@enprovence .com, www.saintes-maries-camargue.enprov ence.com), 5 ave Van Gogh, is open from 9 am to 6 pm (until 7 pm from Easter to September and until 8 pm in July and August).

Things to See & Do
The donjon style **Église des Saintes Maries** (☎ 04 90 97 80 25), built between the 12th and 15th centuries on place de l'Église, dominates the village. Its sober, dim interior shelters a beautiful elevated choir and a crypt where the statue of Saint Sarah is religiously kept. Year round, a sea of smoky candles burns at the foot of the over-dressed black statue which, at pilgrimage time, is showered with at least 40 or 50 brightly colourful dresses (see the boxed text The Gypsy Pilgrimage). Saint Sarah's relics – discovered in the crypt by King René in 1448 – are enshrined in a gaudy wooden chest, stashed away in a hole cut in the sturdy stone wall

above the choir. In summer, pay 10FF for a panoramic view of the Camargue wetlands from the roof terrace. The church can be visited between 8 am and 6 pm (until 7 pm in March, April and October).

Gypsy culture is unravelled at the **Musée des Gitanes** (Gypsy Museum; ☎ 04 90 97 52 85), next to the Auberge de Jeunesse in Pioch Badet, 8km north of Saintes Maries on the D570.

Back in Saintes Maries, the **Musée de Baroncelli** (☎ 04 90 97 87 60), housed in the old 19th century city hall on rue Victor Hugo, is dedicated to the Marquis of Baroncelli (1869-1943) – an authentic *manadier* who devoted his life to reviving local Carmarguaise culture when not herding in the *manades* (herds of bulls and horses). The museum is open from 10 am to noon and 2 to 6 pm (closed Tuesday between mid-September and mid-November). A combined ticket good for the museum and church terrace costs 15FF.

The **Arènes** (☎ 04 90 97 85 86), next to Port Gardian, can only be visited during bullfights. Tickets (60-160FF) are sold at the office in the outer walls of the Arènes on ave Van Gogh, open 3 and 7 pm (closed Sunday). Advance reservations can be made by telephone. Bullfights are also held at the **Arènes de Méjanes** (☎ 04 90 97 10 60), 30km north in Méjanes.

Several companies offer **boat excursions** (usually 1½ hours), including Camargue Bateau de Promenade (☎ 04 90 97 84 72), 5 rue des Launes, and Quatre Maries (☎ 04 90 97 70 10), 36 ave Théodore Aubanel. Both have boats departing between March and November from **Port Gardian**. *Le Tiki III* (☎ 04 90 97 81 68 or 04 90 97 81 22) plies the delta's shallow waters (60FF for a 1½-hour tour) and is docked at the mouth of the Petit Rhône 1.5km west of Saintes Maries.

For information on other tours and activities see Organised Tours at the start of this chapter.

Special Events
The village bursts with life during its annual Gypsy pilgrimages (24-25 May, 17-18

The Gypsy Pilgrimage

Europe's gypsy population has its roots in Camargue's shifting waters. Each May and October, *gitans* (gypsies) from all over Europe flock to the fishing village of Saintes-Maries-de-la-Mer to honour their patron saint, Sarah. According to Provençal legend, Sarah was the servant of Mary Jacob and Mary Salome who (along with other New Testament figures) fled the Holy Land by boat and drifted in the open sea until landing near the Rhône River in 40 AD.

Testimony to this legend, in 1448 skeletal remains believed to belong to Sarah, Mary Jacob and Mary Salome were uncovered in the church crypt at Saintes Maries. Analysis this century has only been able to identify the bones as part of female corpses of oriental origins, dating to the 1st century BC. Uncertainties raised by modern science as to the real identity of these relics however, remain of little concern to *pélerins* (pilgrims) for whom the *pélerinage* (pilgrimage) is as much an expression of traditional gypsy culture as of Christian faith. In May 1998, some 10,000 gypsies and 1819 caravans (most Mercedes-pulled) rolled into town.

A pilgrimage sets the streets of Saintes Maries ablaze with song, music and dance. The May festivities last for three days, the first two of which celebrate the feast day of Mary Jacob (25 May) and see gypsies party with great gusto. Many hit the road for the long journey home on the third day which honours the Marquis de Baroncelli-Jaron (1869-1943), a local herdsman responsible for reviving many Camarguais traditions in the 19th century such as *courses Camarguaises* and Provençal folkloric dances. Fewer gypsies travel to the autumn pilgrimage which falls on the Sunday nearest to Mary Salome's feast day (22 October).

In anticipation of a *pélerinage des gitans*, the wooden chest above the choir at Église des Saintes Maries in which the saintly relics are enshrined, is lowered to the altar so that pilgrims may touch the chest and silently pray by its side. After a solemn mass, the statue of black Sarah is joyfully carried from the church crypt through the streets to the sea to symbolise the arrival of the gypsy patron saint. The flamboyant procession is led by *gardians* (Camargue cowboys) on horseback who usher the statue of Sarah to the seashore where it is placed in a wooden fishing boat in the sea and blessed by a priest. The pilgrims pour into the sea fully clothed – to the great joy of the countless tourists, thigh-high in water, clad in nothing but bikinis, clutching their whirring camcorders. The same ritual is showered upon statues of Mary Jacob and Mary Salome on 25 May when, following the benediction of the sea, the sacred relics in the church are winched back up to their safe hidey-hole.

Religious ceremonies aside, the pilgrimage offers a rare glimpse of a culture absolutely impenetrable to non-gypsies. Its traditions, taboos and superstitions spring to life in lyrics sung by the colourful array of gypsy bands that perform on the streets. Around the musicians, clans form a tight circle, in the centre of which gypsy women – hair flowing, skirts of green and pink, crimson lips and stilettos (imagine a bad taste party) – dance Camargue flamenco.

Gypsy bands like Los Reyes, the Gypsy Kings, Chico & the Gypsies (founded by former Gypsy King, Chico Bouchikki) and Manitas de Plata have all sung on the streets of Saintes Maries.

THE CAMARGUE

October). Bullfights usually animate the Arènes every Sunday in May and June, during gypsy pilgrimages, in mid-June for the village's five day Fête Votive, and in mid-August at the Fete Biou y Toros. The tourist office has an updated schedule.

Places to Stay & Eat

Camping *Camping La Brise* (☎ 04 90 97 84 67, fax 04 90 97 72 01, ave Marcle Carrière) is north-east of the centre. It is open all year. *Camping Le Clos du Rhône* (☎ 04 90 97 85 99, fax 04 90 97 78 85, route *d'Aigues-Mortes)* is only open from April to September. Both have a swimming pool. Expect to pay 75FF a night.

Hostels There's an *Auberge de Jeunesse* (☎ 04 90 97 51 72, fax 04 90 97 54 88) in Pioch Badet, 8km north of Saintes Maries on the D570 to Arles. B&B is 65FF. Half/full board is 120/165FF and it costs 16FF to hire sheets. Reception is open from 7.30 to 10.30 am and 5 to 11 pm (5 pm to midnight in July and August). The hostel has bicycles to rent (60FF a day) and organises horse riding (65/300FF for an hour/full day).

Les Cars de Camargue buses from Arles to Saintes Maries (36.50FF; one hour; 6-9 a day) drop you at the door (see Getting There & Away in the Arles section).

Cabanes Aspiring cowboys can rent a traditional *cabane de gardian* (see the boxed text Bulls & Cowboys); the tourist office has details. Most cabanes sleep up to five people and are rented on a weekly basis from April to September. There is a cluster for hire on ave Riquette Aubanel, a narrow lane (D38) leading out of Saintes Maries past the port to Aigues-Mortes.

Farmhouses Numerous *mas* (farmhouses) surround Saintes Maries; many have rooms to let. Particularly good value is the *Mas de la Grenouillère* (☎ 04 90 97 90 22, fax 04 90 97 70 94, route d'Arles), 1.5km along a dirt track signposted off the D570 1km north of Saintes Maries. Small but comfortable rooms have a terrace overlooking open fields while a choir of frogs sing guests to sleep each night. Doubles/triples/quads start at 260/380/460FF. La Grenouillère (literally 'Frog Farm') has a swimming pool, stables and organises horse riding.

Even more idyllic – if you can afford it – is the nearby *Étrier Camarguais* (☎ 04 90 97 81 14, fax 04 90 97 88 11), a farmhouse-hotel made from 'a dream, flowers and the sun'. It is 500m before La Grenouillère along the same dirt track. Doubles cost 400/540FF in the low/high

season. The reception of the 'Camargue Stirrup' is in a cabane de gardian.

Hotels Heaps of hotels – mostly three or four-star and at least 300FF a night – line the D570, the main road (known as route d'Arles) from Arles into Saintes Maries. Hotels in the village are equally dear. The cheapest rooms can be had at *Les Vagues* (☎/fax 04 90 97 84 40, 12 ave Théodore Aubanel) on the road which runs along the port, west of the tourist office; or *Le Delta* (☎ 04 90 97 81 12, fax 04 90 97 72 85, 1 place Mireille) on the right as you enter Saintes Maries from the north. Doubles at Les Vagues start at 190FF. Le Delta has singles/doubles for 185/205FF; triples/quads for 245/275FF, all with showers. Both hotels have just seven rooms each.

If you want to be closer to the birds, the *Hostellerie du Pont de Gau* (☎ 04 90 97 81 53, fax 04 90 97 98 54), a Logis de France hotel with an excellent restaurant (*menus* from 95FF) next to the Parc Ornithologique on the D570, is for you. Doubles are 255FF. It is closed from January to mid-February.

Getting There & Away

Saintes Maries has no real bus station; buses use the shelter at the north entrance to town on ave d'Arles (continuation of route d'Arles and the D570).

For bus connections to/from Arles (via Pont du Gau and Mas du Pont de Rousty) and details about the three-day Passe Camargue ticket, see Getting There & Away in the Arles section. In summer there are two buses a day from Saintes Maries to Nîmes (1¼ hours) via Aigues-Mortes.

Getting Around

Saintes Maries is the best place to hire two wheels: try Vélo Saintois (☎/fax 04 90 97 74 56), 19 ave de la République; or Le Vélociste (☎ 04 90 97 83 26 or 04 90 97 86 44), place des Remparts. Both charge 80FF a day. The Pioch Badet hostel has wheels to rent (60FF a day).

AIGUES-MORTES
- pop 5000   ⊠ 30220

On the Camargue's western edge, 28km north-west of Saintes Maries in the Gard department, is the curiously named walled town of Aigues-Mortes (literally, 'Dead Waters'). Sleepy Aigues-Mortes was established on marshy flat land in the mid-13th century by Louis IX so the French crown would have a Mediterranean port under its direct control. At the time, the area's other ports were controlled by various rival powers, including the counts of Provence. In 1248, Louis IX's ships – all 1500 of them – gathered here before setting sail to the Holy Land for the Seventh Crusade.

Aigues-Mortes' sturdy, rectangular ramparts – the tops of which afford great views over the marshlands – can be easily circumambulated from **Tour de Constance** (☎ 04 66 53 61 55). Count on 30 minutes for the 1.6km wall-top walk. Inside the impregnable fortress whose walls are 6m thick, you can visit the 32m tall tower which served as a Huguenot women's prison following the revocation of the Edict of Nantes in 1685. The word *register* ('to resist', in old French) on the millstone in the centre of the prison was carved by heroine inmate Marie Durand, jailed here for 38 years. The Tour de Constance (named by Louis VII after his sister) is open from 9.30 am to 8 pm (until 5 pm in September) and 10 am to 5 pm from October to December (32/21FF for adult/student).

The tourist office (☎ 04 66 53 73 00, fax 04 66 53 65 94), inside the walled city at Porte de la Gardette, is open from 9 am to noon and 2 to 6 pm (until 8 pm with no break in July and August).

Salins du Midi
There are magnificent views of the pink-hued saltpans that stretch south from the top of Aigues-Mortes' southern ramparts. By road, the lone D979 follows the narrow land bar that cuts across the still pools. The salt manufacturing company, Salins du Midi – which also has *salins* (salt marshes) in **Salin-de-Giraud** (pop 3000), a marsh-village in the

south-east corner of the Camargue near Port Saint Louis – is France's leading salt producer. The checkered evaporation saltpans *(marais salants)* at Salin-de-Giraud cover 14,000 hectares and produce about 1,000,000 tonnes a year, making them among Europe's largest. *Sel* (salt), which takes three years to produce, is harvested each September then stored in giant mountains.

In July and August, it is possible to visit the salt marshes at Salins du Midi by guided tour. Book through Aigues-Mortes' tourist office.

Boat Excursions
Between March and November, boats line up at the port to take tourists on a 2½ hour *safari croisière* (safari cruise) around the wild waters of the Camargue (60/35FF for adult/child). In addition, you can **hire a boat** (170FF an hour for up to four people) to sail yourself; or imagine you're in Florida aboard a **hydroglisse** (☎ 06 11 36 06 72; 100FF for 30 minutes with driver).

A navette shuttle boat (☎ 06 03 91 44 63) plies the waters daily between Aigues-Mortes and the neighbouring resort of **Grau-du-Roi**, 4.5km farther west along the coast from where **Port Camargue**, Europe's largest pleasure port can be accessed. Journey time is 35 minutes (single/return is 13/20FF).

Places to Stay & Eat
The cheapest place to stay in Aigues-Mortes' historical centre is *Hôtel Carrière* *(☎ 04 66 53 73 07, fax 04 66 53 84 75, 18 rue Pasteur)*, with rooms from 200FF. A cut above is *Hôtel Le Saint Louis (☎ 04 66 53 72 68, fax 04 66 53 75 92, 10 rue Amiral Courbet)* which has rooms for 280-490FF. Saint Louis is closed from January to mid-March. Both hotels have good restaurants with *menus* from 79 and 98FF respectively.

The three-star *Hôtel des Ramparts (☎ 04 66 53 82 77, fax 04 66 53 73 77, 6 place France)* overlooks Tour de Constance. It charges 280/380FF for a double room with shower/bath. Next door, the rough and ready *Café de la Bourse* has a handful of

THE CARMARGUE

rooms above its bar, starting at 170/240FF for a double/triple with shower and toilet.

Getting There & Away

From Aigues-Mortes' tiny train station (☎ 04 66 53 74 74), route de Nîmes, there are a handful of trains to Grau-du-Roi (9FF; 10 minutes) and Nîmes (39FF; 45 minutes). Some scheduled trains are replaced by SNCF buses.

SOUTH-EASTERN CAMARGUE

The wetland is at its most savage around the eastern shores of the Étang de Vaccarès. Much of this area is protected and off limits to tourists. In **Le Sambuc**, a small hamlet some 20km south of Arles on the D35, is the **Station Biologique de la Tour du Valat** (☎ 04 90 97 20 13, fax 04 90 97 20 19). The research station, dating from 1954, covers an area of 2500 hectares and is open to the public one day a year (in January). In 1970 it instigated the construction of the artificial **Étang du Fangassier**. The 4000 sq metre island serves as a breeding colony for the flamingo which, a few years previously, had started to breed less in the region. Since 1974, some 50,000 flamingos have been born here.

About 6km south of Le Sambuc is the **Musée du Riz du Petit Manusclat** (☎ 04 90 97 20 29, fax 04 90 97 21 84) in Petit Manusclat. The history of the Camargue rice industry dating from the 13th century is explained. The wetland yields 8 million *quintaux* (400,000 tonnes) of rice a year.

On the east bank of the Grand Rhône is the Mas Thibert, from where the **Marais du Vigueirat**, an extensive marshland, can be explored with a local guide. Eight heron species frequent these dense swamps. Six-hour expeditions (four hours between April and September) have to be booked in advance through the tourist office in Arles.

Avignon Area

Avignon – the capital of the Vaucluse department – will enter the next millennium as the European Capital of Culture. It acquired its ramparts and its reputation as a city of art and culture during the 14th century, when Pope Clement V and his court, fleeing political turmoil in Rome, established themselves near Avignon. From 1309-77, the Holy See was based in Avignon under seven French-born popes, and huge sums of money were invested in building and decorating the papal palace and other important church edifices.

North of Avignon, fan-shaped Vaucluse – with Avignon at its hinge – spreads out into a multitude of contrasting landscapes.

The area south of Avignon has a colourful past. Many of the towns were settled by the Greeks followed by the Romans, leaving behind a treasure trove of archaeological treasures.

The fortified village of Les Baux de Provence pulls in 2.5 million tourists a year, making it one of France's biggest tourist attractions outside of Paris.

Avignon

- pop 87,000   ⊠ 84000

Avignon continues its traditional role as a patron of the arts, most notably through its annual performing arts festival. Avignon's other attractions include its fine Côtes du Rhône wines, its *pont d'Avignon* (Avignon bridge), a bustling (and touristy) walled city and a number of interesting museums, including several across the Rhône River in the town of Villeneuve-lès-Avignon.

Orientation

The main avenue inside the walled city *(intra-muros)* runs northward from the train station to place de l'Horloge; it's called cours Jean Jaurès south of the tourist office and rue de la République north of it.

Place de l'Horloge is 200m south of place du Palais, which abuts the Palais des

HIGHLIGHTS

- See how the popes lived at Avignon's Palais des Papes
- Follow in the footsteps of the Romans through Orange, Vaison-la-Romaine, Carpentras, Saint Rémy and Nîmes
- Climb Mont Ventoux or cycle around the Dentelles de Montmirail
- Shop for lavender marmalade and fresh truffles at Carpentras market
- Sample the strongest wine in France at Châteauneuf-du-Pape

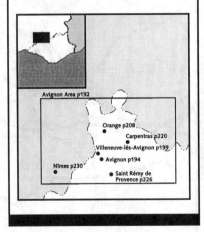

Avignon Area p192

Orange p208

Carpentras p220

Villeneuve-lès-Avignon p199

Avignon p194

Nîmes p230

Saint Rémy de Provence p226

AVIGNON AREA

Papes. The city gate nearest the train station is Porte de la République, and the one next to Pont Édouard Daladier, which leads to Villeneuve-lès-Avignon, is Porte de l'Oulle. The rehabilitated Quartier des Teinturiers (dyers' quarter), around rue des Teinturiers south-east of place Pie, is Avignon's bohemian, and trendy, part of town.

Villeneuve-lès-Avignon (sometimes written Villeneuve-lez-Avignon), the suburb on

191

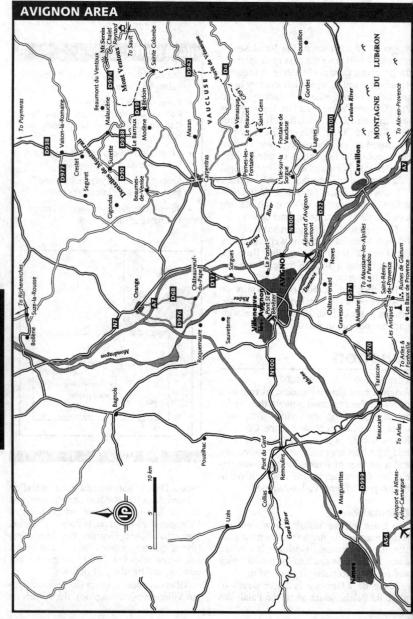

AVIGNON AREA

...olk in traditional costume celebrate authentic Carmarguaise culture in Saintes-Maries-de-la-Mer.

STEVE DAVEY

...ardians escort the procession of Saint Sarah into the sea during the Gypsy Festival, The Camargue.

STEVE DAVEY

STEVE DAVEY

Statues of the two Saintes Maries are carried to the sea during a Gypsy Festival, The Camargue.

the right (north-west) bank of the Rhône, is reached by crossing the two branches of the river and Île de la Barthelasse, the island that divides them. Rue de la République is Villeneuve-lès-Avignon's main street.

Information

Tourist Offices The tourist office (☎ 04 90 82 65 11, fax 04 90 82 95 03, information@ ot-avignon.fr, www.ot-avignon.fr), 41 cours Jean Jaurès, is 300m north of the train station. Staff arrange city tours in summer (in English and French; 50/30FF for adult/child). It's open from 9 am to 1 pm and 2 to 6 pm (5 pm on Saturday; closed Sunday). In July and August it's open weekdays from 10 am to 7 pm; and on Sunday from 10 am to 5 pm from mid-April to mid-August.

At Pont Saint Bénézet, Le Châtelet tourist office annexe (☎ 04 90 85 60 16), which doubles as a ticket booth for the bridge and adjoining museum, is open from 9 am to 1 pm and 2 to 7 pm (closed Monday).

In Villeneuve-lès-Avignon, the tourist office (☎ 04 90 25 61 33, fax 04 90 25 91 55), 1 place Charles David (also called place du Marché; foot access from the main car park), is open from 8.45 am to 12.30 pm and 2 to 6 pm (until 6.30 pm in July and August; closed Sunday).

The Club Alpin Français (CAF; ☎ 04 90 25 40 48) is at 7 rue St Michael. The Office National des Forêts (ONF; ☎ 04 90 89 32 39, www.onf.fr) is at 1175 chemin du Lavarin.

Money The Banque de France, place de l'Horloge, is open from 8.35 am to 12.05 pm and 1.35 to 3.35 pm (closed on weekends).

There are 24-hour banknote exchange machines outside the Lyonnais de Banque, 13 rue de la République, and the Caixa Bank, 67 rue Joseph Vernet (opposite the Musée Requien).

The Change Chaix Conseil (☎ 04 90 27 27 89), 43 cours Jean Jaurès, is open April to October from 10 am to 1 pm and 3 to 7 pm. In July and August hours are 8.30 am to 8.30 pm.

Post The main post office, cours Président Kennedy, is open from 8 am to 7 pm (Saturday until noon; closed Sunday). Currency exchange stops at 5 pm on weekdays; 11 am on Saturday.

Email & Internet Access Cyberdrôme (☎ 04 90 16 05 15, fax 04 90 16 05 14, cyberdrome@cyberdrome.fr), 68 rue Guillaume Puy, charges 25FF for 30 minutes access; it's open from 7 to 1 am.

Le Site (☎ 04 90 27 12 00, lesite@web office.fr), 25 rue Carnot, is France's only cyber restaurant. It charges 25FF for 30 minutes surfing and has *menus* for 79FF. It is open from noon to midnight (Saturday from 4 pm to midnight; closed Sunday). From rue Carnot, walk under the arch between Red Zone and the Piano Bar.

Bookshops The Maison de la Presse (☎ 04 90 86 57 42), opposite the tourist office at 34 cours Jean Jaurès, has a good selection of maps and French-language regional guides. Alternatively try Shakespeare (☎ 04 90 27 38 50), 155 rue Carreterie, an English bookshop and tearoom open from 9.30 am to 12.30 pm and 2 to 6.30 pm (closed Sunday and Monday).

Laundry The Lavmatic, 27 rue du Portail Magnanen, is open from 7 am to 7.30 pm; Laverie La Fontaine, 66 place des Corps Saints, from 7 am to 8 pm.

Medical Services The Centre Hospitalier (☎ 04 90 80 12 90), 2.5km south of the train station on rue Raoul Follereau, is at the southern terminus of bus line Nos 1 and 3 (marked on bus maps as Hôpital Sud).

Pont Saint Bénézet

St Bénézet's Bridge (☎ 04 90 85 60 16) – better known as Le Pont d'Avignon – was built between 1177 and 1185 to link Avignon with what later became Villeneuve-lès-Avignon across the Rhône. By tradition,

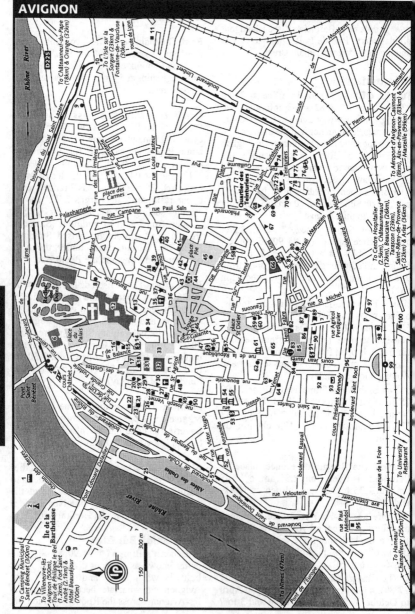

AVIGNON

the construction of the bridge began when Bénézet (Benedict the Bridge Builder), a pious lad from Savoy, was told in three visions to get the Rhône spanned at any cost. Yes ... this is the **Pont d'Avignon** mentioned in the French nursery rhyme. In actual fact, though, people did not dance *sur le pont d'Avignon* (on the bridge of Avignon) but *sous* (under) it in between the arches.

The 900m structure was repaired and rebuilt several times. It was originally made of wood in the 12th century and rebuilt in stone by Pope Clement VI around 1350. All but four of its 22 spans – over both channels of the Rhône and Île de la Barthelasse in the middle – were washed away by floods in 1669. To celebrate the millennium, the lost 18 arches of the bridge will be rebuilt – enabling

AVIGNON

PLACES TO STAY
- 2 Camping Bagatelle & Auberge Bagatelle
- 11 Avignon Squash Club (Hostel)
- 13 Hôtel de la Mirande
- 15 Hôtel du Palais des Papes
- 22 Hôtel L'Europe
- 26 Hôtel Mignon
- 28 Hôtel Le Provençal
- 38 Hôtel Médiéval
- 64 Hôtel Innova
- 65 Hôtel Central
- 79 Hotel Le Magnan
- 86 Hôtel du Parc
- 89 Hôtel Colbert
- 90 Hôtel Splendid
- 92 Cloître Saint Louis & Restaurant Le Saint Louis
- 95 Hôtel Saint Roch
- 100 Hôtel Monclar

PLACES TO EAT
- 19 Simple Simon Tea Lunch
- 29 Natural Café & La Fourchette
- 30 Le Brantes
- 37 Le Belgocargo
- 46 Tapalocas
- 60 Le Caveau du Théâtre & Les Caulisses
- 63 La Cuisine de Reine
- 67 Le Jujubier
- 68 Le Bistro Russe
- 72 Sindabad
- 75 Restaurant au 19ème
- 77 Café-Théâtre Tache d'Encre
- 78 Woolloomooloo
- 81 Le Petit Comptoir

MUSEUMS
- 6 Musée du Petit Palais
- 52 Musée Louis Vouland
- 54 Musée Calvet

- 55 Musée Requien
- 61 Musée Lapidaire

OTHER
- 1 Swimming Pool
- 3 La Barthelasse Bus Stop
- 4 Le Châtelet Tourist Office & Musée en Images
- 5 Tour de Châtelet & Entrance to Pont Saint Bénézet
- 7 Cathédrale Notre Dame des Doms
- 8 La Manutention & Cinéma Utopia, Le Grand Café, AJMI (Jazz Club)
- 9 Shakespeare (Bookshop)
- 10 Porte Saint Lazare
- 12 Palais des Papes
- 14 Banque de France
- 16 Conservatoire de Musique
- 17 Place Campana
- 18 Maison des Pays de Vaucluse
- 20 Le Val d'Arômes (Luxury Food Shop)
- 21 Galerie Ducastel (Art Gallery)
- 23 Place Crillon
- 24 Porte de l'Oulle
- 25 Mireio Embarcadère (Boat Excursions)
- 27 Casino Grocery
- 31 Opéra d'Avignon
- 32 Hôtel de Ville
- 33 Place de l'Horloge
- 34 Bureau du Festival
- 35 Église Saint Pierre
- 36 Place Carnot
- 39 Le Site (Cyber Restaurant), Red Zone & Le Blues Piano Bar
- 40 Post Office
- 41 Palais de Justice

- 42 TCRA Bus Information Kiosk
- 43 Place Jérusalem
- 44 Synagogue
- 45 Les Halles
- 47 Lyonnais de Banque
- 48 Boulangerie Pâtisserie
- 49 Puyricard (Chocolate Shop)
- 50 Université d'Avignon
- 51 Porte Sainte Dominique
- 53 Caixa Bank
- 56 FNAC
- 57 Codec (Supermarket)
- 58 Pub Z
- 59 Maison des Vins
- 62 Monoprix (Supermarket)
- 66 École des Beaux-Arts
- 69 Chapelle des Pénitents Gris
- 70 Caves Breysse (Wine Cellar)
- 71 Salle Benoît XII
- 73 Espace Gaillanne (Art Gallery)
- 74 Cyberdrome (Cybercafé)
- 76 Cycles Peugeot
- 80 Lavmatic (Laundrette)
- 82 Koala Bar
- 83 Tourist Office
- 84 Maison de la Presse
- 85 Square Agricol Perdiguier
- 87 Laverie La Fontaine (Laundrette)
- 88 Place des Corps Saints
- 91 Change Chaix Conseil
- 93 Main Post Office & Bus No 10 (to Villeneuve-lès-Avignon)
- 94 Porte Saint Roch
- 96 Porte de la République & Local Bus Information Office
- 97 Bus Station
- 98 Car Rental Agencies
- 99 Train Station

AVIGNON AREA

visitors to walk across to Île de la Barthelasse. Bizarrely, the authorities plan to pull down the reconstructed structure in 2001.

Entry to the bridge via cours Châtelet is 15/7FF for adult/student and senior. It's open from 9 am to 1 pm and 2 to 5 pm (closed Monday). Daily hours between April and September are 9 am to 6.30 pm. The distant view of the bridge from Rocher des Doms or Pont Édouard Daladier is free.

Walled City

Avignon's most interesting bits are within the roughly oval walled city, which is surrounded by almost 4.5km of ramparts built between 1359 and 1370. They were restored during the 19th century, but the original moats were not re-dug, leaving the crenellated fortifications looking rather purposeless and certainly less imposing than they once did. Even in the 14th century this defence system was hardly state-of-the-art: the towers were left open on the side facing the city and machicolations (openings in the parapets to drop things like boiling oil or to shoot arrows at attackers) are missing in many sections.

Palais des Papes The huge Gothic Palace of the Popes (☎ 04 90 27 50 74, rmg@palais-des-papes.com, www.palais-des-papes.com), place du Palais, was built in the 14th century as a fortified palace for the pontifical court. It is of interest in large part because of the dramatic events that took place here, since the undecorated stone halls, though impressive, are nearly empty except for occasional art exhibits. The best view of the Palais des Papes complex is from Villeneuve-lès-Avignon. The fabulous cours d'Honneur – the palace's main courtyard – has played host to the Avignon theatre festival since 1947.

The Palais des Papes is open from 9.30am to 5.45pm (9am to 7pm from April to November; until 8pm from 4 August to 30 September). Visiting the interior costs 40/32FF for adult/student and senior which includes a very userfriendly audioguide in English. One-hour guided tours are available

(in English) between April and October usually at 11.30am, 2.30 and 4.45pm. Occasionally special exhibits raise the entrance fees by 9FF or more.

Musée du Petit Palais This museum (☎ 04 90 86 44 58), which served as a bishop's and archbishop's palace during the 14th and 15th centuries, is at the far northern end of place du Palais. It houses an outstanding collection of 13th to 16th century Italian religious paintings. It is open from 9.30 am to noon and 2 to 6 pm (closed Tuesday). In July and August daily hours are 10 am to 6 pm (30/15FF for adult, student and senior).

Cathédrale Notre Dame des Doms This unexciting Romanesque cathedral, on the north side of the Palais des Papes, was built in the mid-12th century but repeatedly redecorated. The Baroque galleries, for instance, were added in the 17th century. Like Avignon's other church buildings, it was sacked during the Revolution.

Rocher des Doms Just up the hill from the cathedral is Rocher des Doms, a delightful bluff-top park that affords great views of the Rhône, Pont Saint Bénézet, Villeneuve-lès-Avignon, the Alpilles etc. A viewpoint indicator tells you what you're looking at.

Conservatoire de Musique Avignon's Conservatory of Music, across place du Palais from the Palais des Papes, occupies the former Hôtel des Monnaies (mint), which was built in 1619 to house a papal legation led by Cardinal Scipione Borghese. His enormous coat of arms decorates the ornate Baroque façade.

Musée Calvet The Musée Calvet (☎ 04 90 86 33 84), 65 rue Joseph Vernet, housed in the rather elegant Hôtel de Villeneuve-Martignan (1741-54), contains a large archaeological collection of artefacts from prehistory to Roman times and paintings from the 16th to 20th centuries. It is open from 10 am to 1 pm

The Avignon Popes

Nine popes held court in Avignon. The papal palace, admired at the time as the 'most handsome of houses and greatest of strongholds in the world', took 20 years to build and remains the greatest testimony to the extraordinary extravaganza lived out by Rome's exiled pontiffs.

Protocol demanded that guests invited to papal banquets only dined from dishes within reach, so the most precious were placed strategically for the pope and his favoured guests. Dishes selected by the pope were then scanned with a branch of coral mounted on a gold stand and adorned with glittering pendants, shark teeth and whale ivory – a highly sophisticated, poison detection device.

Banquets were of tremendous proportions. A feast held to celebrate the coronation of Clement VI (1342-52) comprised 7428 chickens, 3043 fowl, 1500 capons, 1195 geese, 1023 sheep, 914 kids, 180 oxen, 101 calves, 60 pigs, 3 tonnes of bacon, 5 tonnes of almonds and 10 tonnes of sugar, 50,000 sweet tarts, 39,980 eggs and 95,000 loaves of bread.

In 1348 Pope Clement VI bought the city of Avignon from the Queen of Naples.

Each year on the fourth Sunday in Lent, the Avignon papacy presented a golden rose, 305g of gold with a sapphire at its heart, to a sovereign it wished to honour. At Christmas, a prince was honoured with a sword, hat and belt studded with pearls. As an even greater reward for his regal achievements, the honoured prince was granted permission to kiss the pontiff's foot.

Opponents of the Avignon papacy, many of them Italian like the poet Petrarch who lived in Fontaine de Vaucluse at the time, slammed the Provençal city as 'the second Babylonian captivity' and charged that Avignon had become

Pope Clement VI

a den of criminals and brothel-goers unfit for papal habitation. In 1376, the city was given a break when Pope Gregory XI left Avignon. But his death two years later led to the Great Schism (1378-1417), during which rival popes – up to three at one time, each with his own College of Cardinals – resided at Rome and Avignon and spent most of their energies denouncing and excommunicating one another. They also went to great effort to gain control of church revenues, including the sale of indulgences.

Even after the schism was settled (1414-17) and a pope, Martin V, acceptable to all factions established himself in Rome, Avignon remained under papal rule until 1791.

and 2 to 6 pm; 10 am to 7 pm from June to September; closed Tuesday (30/15FF for adult/student and senior).

Musée Requien This museum (☎ 04 90 82 43 51), next door to the Musée Calvet at 67 rue Joseph Vernet, explores the city's natural history. Hours are 9 am to noon and 2 to 6 pm; closed Sunday and Monday (free).

Musée Lapidaire The Statuary Museum (☎ 04 90 85 75 38), 27 rue de la République, housed in the Baroque 17th century former chapel of a Jesuit college, is an annexe of the Musée Calvet. Displays include stone carvings from the Gallo-Roman, Romanesque and Gothic periods. It is open from 10 am to noon and 2 to 6 pm; closed Tuesday (10FF).

Musée Louis Vouland This small but interesting museum (☎ 04 90 86 03 79), 17 rue Victor Hugo, displays a fine collection of 17th and 18th century decorative arts, including *faïence* (earthenware) and some superb French furniture. It is open from 2 to 6 pm (closed Sunday and Monday). From June to September, it's also open from 10 am to noon (20/10FF for adult/student and senior).

Synagogue The synagogue (☎ 04 90 85 21 24), 2 place Jérusalem, was first built in 1221. A 13th century oven used to bake unleavened bread for Passover can still be seen, but the rest of the present round, domed, neoclassical structure dates from 1846. It can be visited from 10 am to noon and 3 to 5 pm (closed Friday afternoon and on weekends). Visitors should be modestly dressed, and men have to cover their heads as is the custom.

Quartier des Teinturiers Stone-paved rue des Teinturiers follows the course of the Sorgue river through Avignon's old dyers' district which was a hive of activity until the 19th century. Some of the water wheels can still be seen. Under the giant plane trees that line the narrow street is the 16th century **Chapelle des Pénitents Gris**, open from 8 am

to noon and 2.30 to 7 pm (closed Tuesday). Sunday Mass is at 9.30 am. From the north end of rue des Teinturiers, turn left along rue des Lices, right on to rue Noël Biret, then left on to rue Roi René. At No 22 on this street is **Chapelle Saint Clare**, the church where the poet Petrarch first cast eyes on Laura, his lifetime muse. Laura was buried in the **Couvent des Cordeliers** near the corner of rue des Lices and rue des Teinturiers.

Wine Tasting The Maison des Vins, run by the Comité Interprofessionnel des Vins d'AOC Côtes du Rhône (☎ 04 90 27 24 00, fax 04 27 24 13), is in the Hôtel du Marquis de Rochegude, 6 rue de Trois Faucons. Head here for information on where to taste Côte du Rhône wines, including the Avignon popes' favourite tipple, Châteauneuf-du-Pape (see that section later).

Villeneuve-lès-Avignon
• pop 11,500   ✉ 30400

Villeneuve-lès-Avignon, across the Rhône from Avignon (and in a different department), was founded in the late 13th century. It became known as the City of Cardinals because many primates affiliated with the papal court built large residences (known as *livrées)* in the town, despite the fact that it was in territory ruled by the French crown and not the pope.

The *Passeport pour l'Art* (45FF) gets you into the Chartreuse du Val de Bénédiction, Fort Saint André, Musée Pierre de Luxembourg, the Collégiale Notre Dame, cloître and Tour de Philippe le Bel. The last three are all open 10 am to 12.30 pm and 3 to 7 pm (10 am to noon and 2 to 5.30 pm from April to September; closed Monday and February).

Chartreuse du Val de Bénédiction The Val de Bénédiction Charterhouse (☎ 04 90 25 05 46 or 04 90 15 24 24), 60 rue de la République, was founded in 1356 by Pope Innocent VI and, with its 40 cells and three cloisters, was once the largest and most important Carthusian monastery in France. Today it houses the Centre National des

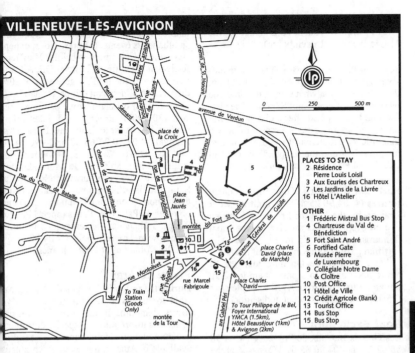

VILLENEUVE-LÈS-AVIGNON

0   250   500 m

PLACES TO STAY
2 Résidence
   Pierre Louis Loisil
3 Aux Ecuries des Chartreux
7 Les Jardins de la Livrée
16 Hôtel L'Atelier

OTHER
1 Frédéric Mistral Bus Stop
4 Chartreuse du Val de
   Bénédiction
5 Fort Saint André
6 Fortified Gate
8 Musée Pierre
   de Luxembourg
9 Collégiale Notre Dame
   & Cloître
10 Post Office
11 Hôtel de Ville
12 Crédit Agricole (Bank)
13 Tourist Office
14 Bus Stop
15 Bus Stop

To Train Station (Goods Only)

To Tour Philippe de le Bel,
Foyer International
YMCA (1.5km),
Hôtel Beauséjour (1km)
& Avignon (2km)

AVIGNON AREA

Écritures du Spectacle (National Centre of Playwrights) which offers shelter in the old monks' quarters to aspiring playwrights.

The largest cloister, **Cloître Saint Jean**, gives you an idea of the architecture and layout of the charterhouse. In the 14th century church, the delicately carved **mausoleum of Pope Innocent VI** (died 1362) is an extraordinary example of Gothic artisanship. It was removed during the Revolution and only returned in 1963.

The centre is open from 9.30 am to 5.30 pm; 9 am to 6.30 pm from April to September (32/21FF for adult/student and senior).

Musée Pierre de Luxembourg This museum (☎ 04 90 27 49 66), 3 rue de la République, inside Hôtel Pierre, has a fine collection of religious art taken from the Chartreuse during the Revolution, including paintings from the 15th to 17th centuries.

The museum's most exceptional objects include the *Vierge en Ivoire* (Ivory Virgin), a superb 14th century Virgin carved from an elephant's tusk; the nearby 15th century *Vierge Double Face*, a marble Virgin whose two faces point in opposite directions; and *Couronnement de la Vierge* (Coronation of the Virgin), painted by Enguerrand Quarton in 1453, which is displayed on the 1st floor. Entrance is 20/12FF and includes a visit to the cloister of the Collégiale Notre Dame et Cloître around the corner.

Collégiale Notre Dame et Cloître This former collegiate (and now parish) church on rue Montolivet just off rue de la République was established in 1333. To visit the rather empty, late 14th century **cloître** (part of which has been privately owned since church property was sold off during the Revolution) ring the bell of the sacristy, to the left of the 18th century altar (7/5FF; free if you have a ticket to the Musée Pierre de Luxembourg).

Tour de Philippe le Bel This 32m defensive tower (☎ 04 90 27 49 68) was built in the 14th century at what was, at the time, the western end of Pont Saint Bénézet. The platform on top, reached after a dizzying climb up 172 steps of spiral staircase, affords a magnificent panorama of Avignon's walled city, the river and the surrounding countryside (10/6FF for adult/student).

Fort Saint André This 14th century fortress (☎ 04 90 25 45 35), built on Mont Andaon by the king of France to keep an eye on events across the river in the papal domains, also affords lovely views. The **fortified gate** is a fine example of medieval military architecture. Opening hours are 10 am to noon and 2 to 5 pm; 10 am to 12.30 pm and 2 to 6 pm from April to September (25/15FF for adult/student and senior).

Boat Excursions

Les Grands Bateaux de Provence (☎ 04 90 85 62 25, fax 04 90 85 61 14), based at the Mireio Embacardère on allées de l'Oulle, opposite the Porte de l'Oulle, runs excursions from Avignon down the Rhône to Arles and the Camargue (4-7 hours; 160-345FF including a meal). Bateau Bus (same ☎ and address) makes less-ambitious trips seven times a day in July and August to Villeneuve-lès-Avignon (near the Tour de Philippe le Bel) and back (1½ hours; 35/18FF for adult/child).

From the embacardère in Villeneuve-lès-Avignon, Bateau Odyssée (☎ 04 90 49 86 08, fax 04 90 93 11 82), Berge du Rhône, Quartier du Moulin, runs cruises in July and August to Arles, Tarascon and Châteauneuf-du-Pape.

Special Events

The world famous Festival d'Avignon, founded in 1947, is held every year from early July to early August. It attracts hundreds of performance artists (actors, dancers, musicians, etc) who put on some 300 *spectacles* (shows) each day in every imaginable venue. There are, in fact, two simultaneous events: the prestigious, expensive and government-subsidised official festival, and the fringe Festival Off. A Carte Public Adhérent (65FF) gets you a 30% discount on all Festival Off performances.

Tickets for official festival performances cost 130-190FF. Program and ticket information is available from the Bureau du Festival (☎ 04 90 27 66 50 or 04 90 14 14 26, fax 04 90 27 66 83, www.festival avignon.com), 8bis rue de Mons. During the festival there is a bureau de location at Saint Louis d'Avignon, 20 rue Portail d'Avignon (open from 11 am to 7 pm) and on place du Palais des Papes (open 11 am to 9 pm). Tickets can be reserved from mid June onwards by telephone (☎ 04 90 14 14 14), by Minitel or at FNAC branches.

Places to Stay

During the festivals, it is practically impossible to find a hotel room unless you've reserved months in advance. The tourist office has information on special dormitory accommodation. Hotel rooms are readily available in August, however, when places in the rest of the Vaucluse are at a premium.

Places to Stay – Budget

Camping *Camping Bagatelle* (☎ 04 90 85 78 45) is an attractive, shaded camping ground north of Pont Édouard Daladier, 850m from the walled city on Île de la Barthelasse. Charges are 17.80/8.50/6.50FF per adult/tent/car. Reception is open from 8 am to 9 pm. Take bus No 10 from the main post office to La Barthelasse stop.

Camping Municipal Saint Bénézet (☎ 04 90 82 63 50, Île de la Barthelasse) is slightly farther north on chemin de la Barthelasse. It is open from March to October and charges 60/80FF in the low/high season for two people with a tent and car.

Hostels – Avignon The 210 bed *Auberge Bagatelle* (☎ 04 90 85 78 45, fax 04 90 27 16 23) is part of a large, park-like area on Île de la Barthelasse that includes Camping

Bagatelle (see earlier). A bed in a room for two, four, six or eight people is 59FF.

From April to September a bunk in a converted squash court in the *Avignon Squash Club* (☎ 04 90 85 27 78, 32 blvd Limbert) costs 58FF. Reception is open from 9 am and 10 pm (closed Sunday from September to June; open 8 to 11 am and 5 to 11 pm in July and August). Take bus No 7 from the train station and get off at the Université stop.

Hostels – Villeneuve-lès-Avignon The well managed *Résidence Pierre Louis Loisil* (☎ 04 90 25 07 92, fax 04 90 25 88 03, ave Pierre Sémard) accepts groups but welcomes individual travellers if there's room. A bed in a three or four-person room costs 68FF. There are facilities for disabled travellers. Take bus No 10 from Avignon train station to the Frédéric Mistral stop.

B&B at the *Foyer International YMCA* (☎ 04 90 25 46 20, fax 04 90 25 30 64, 7bis chemin de la Justice) is 96FF. Take bus No 10 to the Pont d'Avignon stop.

Hotels – Within the Walls The *Hôtel du Parc* (☎ 04 90 82 71 55, 18 rue Agricol Perdiguier) has singles/doubles without shower for 140/160FF and 180/195FF with shower. Hall showers are 5FF.

Friendly *Hôtel Splendid* (☎ 04 90 86 14 46, fax 04 90 85 38 55, 17 rue Agricol Perdiguier) has singles/doubles with shower for 130/200FF and rooms with shower and toilet for 170/280FF.

The third in the trio, *Hôtel Colbert* (☎ 04 90 86 20 20, fax 04 90 85 97 00, 7 rue Agricol Perdiguier), smells of disinfectant but has well-priced singles with shower for 150FF, and doubles/triples with shower and toilet for 250/300FF.

Busy *Hôtel Innova* (☎ 04 90 82 54 10, fax 04 90 82 52 39, 100 rue Joseph Vernet) has bright, comfortable and well sound-proofed doubles without/with shower for 140/150FF; rooms for two/three/four people with shower and toilet cost 200/240/260FF. Nearby, the less than friendly *Hôtel Central* (☎ 04 90 86 07 81, fax 04 90 27 99 54,

31-33 rue de la République) has uninspiring doubles from 160FF.

One-star *Hôtel Mignon* (☎ 04 90 82 17 30, fax 04 90 85 78 46, 12 rue Joseph Vernet) has spotless, well-kept and sound-proofed singles/doubles with shower for 150/185FF and doubles with shower and toilet for 220FF. Take bus No 10 from the post office to the Porte de l'Oulle stop.

The charming, two-star *Hotel Le Magnan* (☎ 04 90 86 36 51, fax 04 90 85 48 70, 63 rue Portail-Magnanen), over-looking the city walls, is part of the Logis de France chain and has doubles with TV, bath and toilet from 180FF.

Hotels – Outside the Walls The noisy, family run *Hôtel Monclar* (☎ 04 90 86 20 14, fax 04 90 85 94 94, 13 ave Monclar) is in an 18th century building across the tracks from the train station. Eminently service-able doubles start at 165FF with sink and bidet. The hotel has its own car park (20FF) and a pretty little back garden.

In Villeneuve-lès-Avignon, the *Hôtel Beauséjour* (☎ 04 90 25 20 56, 61 ave Gabriel Péri) has bargain-basement rooms for one or two without/with shower for 130/160FF.

Places to Stay – Mid-Range

Two-star *Hôtel Le Provençal* (☎ 04 90 85 25 24, fax 04 90 82 75 81, 13 rue Joseph Vernet) has singles/doubles with toilet for 180FF and rooms with shower, toilet and TV for 237FF. Take bus No 10 from the post office to the Porte de l'Oulle stop.

The very charming, old-worldly *Hôtel du Palais des Papes* (☎ 04 90 86 04 13 or 04 90 82 47 31, fax 04 90 27 91 17, 1 rue Gérard Philippe) has doubles with shower, TV and toilet for 280-480FF; pricier rooms sport a view of Palais des Papes. Triples start at 520FF and dogs cost an extra 50FF a night.

The splendid two-star *Hôtel Médiéval* (☎ 04 90 86 11 06, fax 04 90 82 08 64, 15 rue Petite Saunerie), housed in a restored 17th century mansion, has singles/doubles with all the perks from 195/240FF. It also has studios to rent on a weekly/monthly/long-term basis.

Outside the walls, *Hôtel Saint Roch* (☎ *04 90 82 18 63, fax 04 90 82 78 30, 9 rue Paul Mérindol)* has airy doubles with shower, toilet and TV for 250FF; triples and quads cost 330FF.

In Villeneuve-lès-Avignon, the beautifully located *Hôtel L'Atelier* (☎ *04 90 25 01 84)* has charming doubles with toilet from 250FF and ones with bath/toilet for 360FF. Equally idyllic is the small and select *Les Jardins de la Livrée* (☎ *04 90 26 05 05, 4bis rue Camp de Bataille)* which has a small stone terrace, swimming pool, Provençal kitchen and calm rooms for 250-370FF. Book in advance. The Gîte de France *Aux Écuries des Chartreux* (☎*/fax 04 90 25 79 93, 66 rue de la République)*, next to the Chartreuse monastery, has one to four people studios from 260FF a night.

Places to Stay – Top End

'A place of pilgrimage for men and women of taste' is how the French newspaper *Le Figaro* summed up *Hôtel de la Mirande* (☎ *04 90 85 93 93, fax 04 90 86 26 85, 4 place de le Mirande)*, Avignon's most exclusive hotel housed in a former 14th century cardinal's palace behind the Palais des Papes. Exquisitely furnished rooms start at 1700FF (1850FF from April to October). The hotel has its own cooking school.

Four-star *Hôtel L'Europe* (☎ *04 90 14 76 76, 12 place Crillon)* is cheap in comparison: rooms cost 630-2500FF, breakfast is 89FF, dogs are 50FF, and *menus* in its restaurant cost 210, 285 and 400FF. On Sunday it serves a good value 160FF brunch from 11.30 am.

Another fine place to languish away a few days is the elegant *Cloître Saint Louis* (☎ *04 90 27 55 55, fax 04 90 82 24 01, hotel@cloitre-saint-louis.com, www.cloitre-saint-louis.com, 20 rue du Portail Boquier)*. The four-star hotel is housed in a Jesuit school dating from 1589. The ultra-modern new wing – which touts a roof-top swimming pool – was designed in 1991 by French architect Jean Nouvel (best known

for his Institut du Monde Arabe in Paris). Room rates start at 450/575FF in the low/high season.

Places to Eat

University Restaurant The *restaurant universitaire* of the Faculté de Droit (Law Faculty), south-west of the train station on ave du Blanchissage, is open from October to June (closed during university holidays). Meals are served from 11.30 am to 1.30 pm and 6.30 to 7.30 pm (closed Saturday evening and Sunday). People with student cards can buy tickets (about 15 or 30FF) at the CROUS office (☎ 04 90 82 42 18), 29 blvd Limbert, open Monday, Tuesday, Wednesday and Friday from 10 30 am to 12.30 pm.

Around Place de l'Horloge For hearty and healthy fodder in a rustic setting (tree trunks for benches etc) look no further than the atmospheric *Natural Café* (☎ *04 90 85 90 82, 17 rue Racine)*, behind the opera house (closed Sunday and Monday). Adjoining it, is the more conventional *La Fourchette (The Fork,* ☎ *04 90 85 20 93)*, a Michelin-recommended place with *menus* for 150FF. La Fourchette is closed on weekends.

The nearby *Simple Simon Tea Lunch* (☎ *04 90 86 62 70, 26 rue Petite Fusterie)* is an endearing, *très anglais* place for an afternoon cuppa (20-23FF) with cake, pie, scones or cheesecake (27FF). Light meals (40-52FF) are available all afternoon. Simple Simon is closed on Sunday and in August. At No 22, *Le Brantes* (☎ *04 90 86 35 14)* is a large pizza-grill place which has excellent value 69FF *menus*. Pizzas/pasta dishes cost 42/33FF upwards and there is a kids' *menu* for 35FF. Don't miss the flower-filled courtyard out the back.

Extremely delicious cuisine is served in a magnificent setting at *Le Grand Café* (☎ *04 90 86 86 77, 4 rue des Escaliers Sainte Anne, La Manutention)*, tucked behind the Palais des Papes. Contemporary creations hang from the red-brick, former warehouse ceiling while tantalising *menus* cost 140FF. To get here follow the Promenade des Papes signs which lead through Le

Verger (literally 'The Orchard'), a garden behind the palace walls.

South of the square on rue des Trois Faucons is *Le Caveau du Théâtre* (☎ 04 90 82 60 91). It has a lunchtime *formule* comprising a *tarte salée* (savoury tart) and dessert for 65FF, and evening *menus* for 110FF. You can taste wine here too, as at the less formal *Les Caulisses* next door. Both are open from noon to 2 pm and 7.30 to 10.30 pm.

Spanish-inspired tapas – 12FF each – are dished up hot and cold at *Tapalocas* (☎ 04 90 82 56 84, 10 rue Galante, www.tapalocas.com). The tapas bar, whose ceiling is adorned with posters past and present from Festival Off, is open daily from 11.45 to 1.30 am. By night, it's a good drinking hole.

There is a Belgian place, *Le Belgocargo* (☎ 04 90 85 72 99, 7 rue Armand de Pontmartin), tucked behind the Église Saint Pierre. It serves mussels 16 different ways for 49-68FF and *waterzooi de volaille* (a creamy Belgian stew of chicken, leeks and herbs) for 58FF. Swill it down with a glass of cherry-flavoured kriek beer.

Quartier des Teinturiers & Around

Rue des Teinturiers is one of Avignon's most fun streets. Pleasant bohemian-style restaurants and bistros include the small *Sindabad* (☎ 04 90 14 69 45, 53 rue des Teinturiers) which offers good Tunisian, oriental and Provençal home cooking. It has a 50FF *plat du jour* and is open from noon and from 6 pm (closed Sunday).

At No 13 is *Le Bistro Russe* (☎ 04 90 85 64 35), a Russian bistro specialising in flaming, vodka-fuelled café Cosaques for 25FF and other vodka-inspired treats. Lunchtime/evening *menus* start at 60/80FF (closed Monday).

The highlight of the street is *Woolloomooloo* (☎ 04 90 85 28 44), next to the old paper mill at No 16. Each week the jumble of eclectic antique and contemporary furnishings is rearranged to create a 'new look' for this arty restaurant. During festival time Woolloomooloo really lets rip with its eccentric furniture antics spilling out onto the street. *Menus* are around 60FF

and it has vegetarian and Antillean dishes too; open from noon and from 7.30 pm (closed Sunday lunch and all day Monday).

On the western fringe of the dyers' quarter is *Le Petit Comptoir* (☎ 04 90 86 10 94, 52 rue des Lices), opposite the crumbling, four-storey arched façade of the *très belle* École des Beaux Arts. This tiny, eight table place offers the choice of a main course, and dessert or entrée for 40FF, or all three for 70FF. Its pork kebab marinated in lemon and ginger is particularly tasty.

At No 24 on the same street is the traditional Provençal *Le Jujubier* (☎ 04 90 86 64 08) which markets itself as 'anti fast food'. Dining here is a bit like dining in someone's home.

For a classical approach, try the refined *Restaurant Au 19ème* (☎ 04 90 27 16 00, 75 rue Guillaume Puy), housed in the 19th century townhouse where absinthe inventor, Jules Pernod, lived. It hosts live jazz on Saturday evenings, harp recitals on Friday evening, and has lunch/evening *menus* from 89/120FF (closed Saturday lunch and Monday evening).

Restaurants – the Ultimate Splurge *La Cuisine de Reine* (☎ 04 90 85 99 04, rue Joseph Vernet), opposite Hôtel Innova inside Le Cloître des Arts, is an elegant restaurant and *salon de thé* wrapped around an 18th century courtyard. *Menus* start at 110FF and include a *pique-nique à la maison* comprising smoked meats, olives and crusty bread. Calorie-killer cakes and pastries are served in its art café (closed Sunday and Monday).

Equally worth the cash are the gastronomic feasts served at the *Restaurant Le Saint Louis* (☎ 04 90 27 55 55, 20 rue du Portail Boquier), overlooking a 16th century cloister courtyard and huge moss-covered fountain. Lunch/dinner *menus* start at 99/140FF.

Self-Catering There is a food market open from 7 am to 1 pm in *Les Halles* on place Pie (closed Monday). Luxury foods in jars, tins and bottles are sold at upmarket *Le Val* *d'Arômes*, 28 rue Petite Fusterie. *Puyricard*, at 33 rue Joseph Vernet, sells designer chocolate.

Near place de l'Horloge, the *Boulangerie Pâtisserie*, 17 rue Saint Agricol, is open from 7.45 am to 7.30 pm (closed Sunday). There is a *Codec* supermarket across from 16 rue de la République. *Monoprix* is opposite the Musée Lapidaire on the same street.

Entertainment

Tickets for cultural events are sold at the tourist office and at FNAC (☎ 04 90 14 35 35), 19 rue de la République (open 10 am to 7 pm; closed Sunday). There are event listings in the free weekly *César* magazine and in the tourist office's fortnightly *Rendez-vous d'Avignon*.

Pubs & Bars Avignon is surprisingly light on pubs, bars and clubs. A cool hang-out is *Le Bistrot d'Utopia* (☎ 04 90 27 04 96, 4 rue des Escaliers Sainte Anne) inside La Manutention, a trendy entertainment and cultural centre with a jazz club, restaurant and cinema. The arty bar is open daily from noon to 1 am.

Le Blues Piano Bar (☎ 04 90 85 79 71) and *Red Zone* (☎ 04 90 27 02 44) are two good choices side by side at 25 rue Carnot. The *Koala Bar* (2 place des Corps Saints), founded and run by an Australian ex-rugby player, is another popular hang-out, particularly with Anglophones, including American university students and Aussie rugby league professionals brought in to play for Avignon. There is an Irish pub called *Gallagher's Temple Bar* (2 rue Portail Matheron).

Last in line is the striped *Pub Z* (58 rue Bonneterie), where a lifesize zebra greets you as you enter the black and white bar.

Classical Music, Opera & Ballet From October to June, the *Opéra Théâtre d'Avignon* (☎ 04 90 82 23 44, place de l'Horloge), housed in an imposing structure built in 1847, stages operas, operettas, plays, symphonic concerts, chamber music

concerts and ballet. The box office is open from 11 am to 6 pm. Its hours on Sundays and performance days are 11 am to 12.30 pm (closed in August).

Ticket prices range from 90/15FF for adult/student in the 4th gallery and from 340/60FF for adult/student in the orchestra.

Jazz La Manutention arts centre hosts *AJMI* (☎ 04 90 86 08 61, 4 rue des Escaliers Sainte Anne), an abbreviation for Association pour Le Jazz & La Musique Improvisée. This cool jazz club has concerts most Thursdays at 9 pm.

Cinema *Cinéma Utopia* (☎ 04 90 82 65 36, 4 rue des Escaliers Sainte Anne, La Manutention)* screens non-dubbed films, both old and new. Tickets are cheap at 30FF (250FF for 10 tickets). The program is listed in the free magazine *Utopia*, published each fortnight.

Theatre Avignon has numerous theatres, both mainstream and alternative. Venues include the *Théâtre du Chien qui Fume* (☎ 04 90 82 33 12, 75 rue des Teinturies, www.avignon-et-provence.com/theatre-cqf); the *Théâtre du Bourg-Neuf* (☎ 04 90 14 35 35, 5bis rue du Bourg-Neuf); and the *Théâtre des Halles* (☎ 04 90 85 52 57, 4 rue Noël Biret).

Avignon also has a lively café-theatre scene. Try the *Café-Théâtre Tache d'Encre* (☎ 04 90 85 97 13, 1 rue Tarasque or 22 rue des Teinturies) in the Teinturiers quarter.

Shopping

Avignon's classiest shopping streets, rue Saint Agricol and the northern part of rue Joseph Vernet, are just west of place de l'Horloge. There are art and antique shops on rue du Limas. Galerie Ducastel (☎ 04 90 82 04 54), 9 place Crillon, is a contemporary art gallery.

Sundials are sold at Cadrans Solaires (☎ 04 90 25 10 14), 26 ave Gabriel Péri. Shop at Caves Breysse, 41 rue des Teinturiers, for Côtes du Rhône wines.

Getting There & Away

Air Aéroport d'Avignon-Caumont (☎ 04 90 81 51 51) is 8km south-east of Avignon.

Bus The bus station (☎ 04 90 82 07 35) is in the basement of the building down the ramp to the right as you come out of the train station on blvd Saint Roch. The information window is open from 8 am to noon and 1.30 to 6 pm (Saturday until noon only; closed Sunday). You can leave luggage there (10FF). Tickets are sold on the buses, which are run by about 20 different companies.

Places you can get to by bus include:

destination	FF	hours	number/day
Aix-en-Provence			
(via highway)	86	1	2
(secondary roads)	79	1½	4-6
Apt	41	1¼	3-4
Arles	37.50	1½	4-5
Carpentras	20	¾	15
Cavaillon	19	½	
Fontaine de			
Vaucluse	25	1	2-3
Marseille	89	½	7
Nice	165	5½	1
Nîmes	40	1¼	5
Orange	28.50	¾	20
Pertuis	44.50	2	2-3
Pont du Gard	32	¾	3
Vaison-la-Romaine	36	1¼	3

Most lines operate on Sunday at a reduced frequency.

Long haul bus companies Linebus (☎ 04 90 85 30 48) and Eurolines (☎ 04 90 85 27 60) have offices at the far end of the bus platforms.

Train The train station is across blvd Saint Roch from Porte de la République. The information counters are open from 9 am to 6.15 pm (closed Sunday). The left luggage room, to the right as you exit the station, is open from 8 am to noon and 2 to 5.30 pm (20FF).

There are frequent trains to:

destination	FF	hours	number/day
Arles	35	¼	14-18
Marseille	89	1	12-14
Nice	201	2½	30
Nîmes	45	½	15
Orange	29	¼	17

Car & Motorcycle Most car rental agencies are signposted from the train station: Europcar (☎ 04 90 85 01 40) is in the Ibis building. Budget (☎ 04 90 27 34 95) is down the ramp to the right as you exit the station. Hertz (☎ 04 90 82 37 67) is at 4 blvd Saint-Michel.

Getting Around

Bus Local TCRA bus tickets cost 6.50FF each if bought from the driver; a carnet of five tickets (for 10 rides) costs 48FF at TCRA offices. Buses run from 7 am to about 7.40 pm (8 am to 6 pm and less frequently on Sunday). The two most important bus transfer points are the Poste stop at the post office and place Pie.

Carnets and free bus maps *(plan du réseau)* are available at the Point d'Accueil-Vente (☎ 04 90 82 68 19) in the tower wall (La Tourelle) of the old city at Porte de la République across from the train station, and from the Espace Bus kiosk (☎ 04 90 85 44 93), place Pie. Both are open from 8.15 am to noon and 1.45 to 6.30 pm (Saturday from 8.45 am to noon).

Villeneuve-lès-Avignon is linked with Avignon by bus No 10, which stops in front of the main Avignon post office and on the west side of the walled city near Porte de l'Oulle. Unless you want to take the grand tour of the Avignon suburb of Les Angles, take a bus marked 'Villeneuve puis Les Angles' (rather than 'Les Angles puis Villeneuve'). For the major sights in Villeneuve-lès-Avignon, get off at the Office du Tourisme or the Frédéric Mistral stops in Villeneuve.

Taxi Pick up a taxi from in front of the train station or call place Pie taxi stand (☎ 04 90 82 20 20), open 24 hours.

Bicycle Cycles Peugeot (☎ 04 90 86 32 49), 80 rue Guillaume Puy, has three-speeds and 10-speeds for 60/130/240FF for one/three/seven days (plus 1000FF deposit). It is open from 8 am to noon and 2 to 7 pm (closed Sunday and Monday).

Hôtel Splendid (☎ 04 90 23 96 08), 17 rue Agricol Perdiguier, has mountain bikes to rent for 100/180/650FF a day/weekend/week (plus 2500FF deposit).

North of Avignon

Vaucluse fans out northwards, from the lucrative vineyards of Châteauneuf-du-Pape and the Roman treasures of Orange, through to the rocky Dentelles de Montmirail, the slopes of Mont Ventoux and the harsh and uninhabitable Albion plain in the Vaucluse's easternmost corner.

If you don't have access to a car, it is possible to labour from town to town by local bus, but the frequency and pace of services are in keeping with the relaxed tempo of Provençal life.

CHÂTEAUNEUF-DU-PAPE
• pop 2000   ✉ 84230

Wealthy Châteauneuf-du-Pape, 18km north of Avignon, used to be a humble mining hamlet named Calcernier after its limestone quarries. Then in 1317, Pope John XXII (1316-34) had a pontifical residence built in the village, around which he established a papal vineyard. Today the village is renowned world-wide for its rich, full-bodied Châteauneuf-du-Pape red wines which boast a minimum alcoholic strength of 12.5% (the highest in France).

The wine produced was called *vin d'Avignon* in the 18th century and Château euf-du-Pape-Calcernier in the 19th century. In 1923 Baron Le Roy, a local *vigneron* (wine grower), compiled a set of rules on how to produce Châteauneuf-du-Pape wine – prompting the establishment of an *appellation d'origine contrôlée* (AOC) in France. Châteauneuf-du-Pape became a certified vintage in 1929, distinguishable by its

heavily embossed label bearing the pontifical coat of arms.

The Châteauneuf-du-Pape vineyards – usually covered with large smooth stones called *galets* – cover 3200 hectares between Avignon and Orange. They are tended by 350 vignerons, many of whose annual production is sold years in advance, making it impossible for tourists to taste, let alone buy, the region's top wines which command 2000FF a bottle. Count on paying from 79FF for a run-of-the-mill bottle of Châteauneuf-du-Pape 1997 white and 80/80/74FF for a 1996/95/94 red.

Information
The tourist office (☎ 04 90 83 71 08, www.chateauneuf-du-pape.enprovence.com), place du Portail on the central village square, distributes maps and a mind-boggling list of *domaines* (wine producing estates) where you can taste and buy wine. Don't bother asking the staff which are the best producers; they are not allowed to make recommendations. The office is open from 9 am to noon and 2 to 6 pm (closed Sunday and November).

The Maison des Vignerons – Comité de Promotion des Vins (☎ 04 90 83 72 21, fax 04 90 83 70 01) is at 12 ave Louis Pasteur.

Château des Papes
The Castle of the Popes, built between 1317 and 1333, stands on a hillock (118m) at the north end of the village. It was plundered and burnt during the Wars of Religion, and further destroyed by German troops on 20 August 1944. One ruined tower, partially restored, is all that remains of the pontifical palace.

From the foot of the castle there are sweeping views of Avignon, the Vaucluse plateau, the Lubéron, the Rhône river and beyond. From the car park next to the castle, steps lead down to the *vieille ville* (old town). The car park is also the starting point for a circular, 16km hike (four hours) through vineyards along the Rhône; the tourist office has the *Circuit Pédestre No 1* brochure with trail notes and a map.

AVIGNON AREA

Tasting & Buying Wine

A good place to start is the **Musée des Outils de Vignerons** (☎ 04 90 83 70 07), 100m south of the Maison des Vignerons opposite the Elf petrol station on ave Louis Pasteur. The Museum of Wine Producers' Tools is essentially a ploy to make you buy wines from the Caves Laurent Charles Brotte. However, you can soak up the pungent smell of wine, indulge in an informative *dégustation* (wine tasting) session, and happily ask 'beginner-level' questions without feeling completely stupid. The *caves* (wine cellars) are open from 9 am to noon and 2 to 6 pm.

Most producers allow *visites des caves* (wine cellar visits) and offer *dégustation gratuite* (free wine tasting). However, some only cater to groups while many can be visited *sur rendez-vous* (*sur RV*; by appointment only) and are closed on weekends. Visiting requirements and opening hours are detailed on the list of producers available at the tourist office.

Château Mont-Redon (☎ 04 90 83 72 75), 4km north of Châteauneuf-du-Pape on route d'Orange, is among the largest and oldest producers of Châteauneuf-du-Pape. A *circuit touristique* cuts through part of its 163 hectares of galet-crusted vineyards – each row flagged with a rose bush – to Châteauneuf-du-Pape village. This is a particularly beautiful bike ride.

Château de Beaucastel (☎ 04 90 11 12 00, fax 04 90 11 12 19; Vins.Perrin@wanadoo .fr; www.vinternet.fr/Perrin), chemin de Beaucastel; and Château de Vaudieu (☎ 04 90 83 70 31, fax 04 90 83 51 97) are two *domaines* worth visiting, simply for a peek at the grandiose château on each estate.

All known for producing good, typically strong, well-structured reds are: Domaine Chante Cigale (☎ 04 90 83 70 57, fax 04 90 83 58 70), ave Louis Pasteur; Domaine Font de Michelle (☎ 04 90 33 00 22, fax 04 90 33 20 27), 14 Impasse des Vignerons; Clos Mont Olivier (☎ 04 90 83 72 46, fax 04 90 83 50 51), 15 ave Saint Joseph; EARL du Clos des Papes (☎ 04 90 83 70 13), 13 ave Saint Pierre de Luxembourg; and Château

Fortia (☎ 04 90 83 72 25, fax 04 90 83 51 03), still in the hands of the AOC-founding Le Roy family on route de Bédarrides.

Less traditional, sweeter and lighter reds are produced by the Domaine de Bois de Boursan (☎ 04 90 83 73 60, fax 04 90 83 73 60), Quartier Saint Pierre; and Château de la Gardine (☎ 04 90 83 73 20, fax 04 90 83 77 24), route de Roquemaure. Exceptionally good whites can usually be found at the Domaine de la Charbonnière (☎ 04 90 83 74 59, fax 04 90 83 53 46), route de Courthézon.

Special Events

Not surprisingly, Châteauneuf-du-Pape celebrates a string of festivals related to wine. The Fête de la Saint Marc – the feast day of the patron saint of vignerons – is on 25 April; a Fête de la Véraison is held on the first weekend in August to mark the ripening of the grapes; and the Fête des Vendanges fills the streets with merry-making in mid-September to celebrate the start of the harvest.

Places to Stay & Eat

The tourist office has a list of *chambres d'hôtes*; the going rate for B&B is 200-250FF for a double. *Camping Caravaning de L'Isle Saint Luc* (☎ 04 90 83 56 36, fax 04 90 83 76 77) is open from June to October and charges 65/70FF a night for two people in the low/high season. The ground is 2km south of the village along route de Sel.

Excellent value and oozing charm is *La Mère Germaine* (☎ 04 90 83 54 37, fax 04 90 83 50 27, place du Portail) overlooking the main square. Its beautifully furnished eight rooms, with shower and toilet, cost 180-320FF depending on the view from the shuttered windows. *Hôtel La Garburie* (☎ 04 90 83 75 08, fax 04 90 83 52 34, 3 rue Joseph Ducos) has doubles with shower/ bath for 310/340FF.

South of the village amid sprawling vineyards off the Avignon-bound D17 is the dreamlike *Hostellerie du Château des Fines Roches* (☎ 04 90 83 70 23, fax 04 90

AVIGNON AREA

83 78 42, finesroches@enprovence.com). A
night's stay in this made-in-heaven, turreted castle is worth every centime if you
have the cash; doubles start at 750FF and *menus*
in its Michelin-recommended restaurant
begin at 210FF.

In the village, the best place to eat is on the
back-yard terrace at *La Mère Germaine* (see
earlier). It has a brasserie *menu* for 85FF, a
155FF *menu du marché*, an 185FF *menu à
carte* and an absolutely splendid *menu pontifical* – seven courses accompanied by seven
different Châteauneuf-du-Pape wines. It
costs 350/280FF with/without wine.

Shopping

Chocoholics can spend a fortune on chocolate at Bernard Castelain's Chocolaterie
Artisanale (Chocolate Factory; ☎ 04 90 83
54 71, fax 04 90 83 54 62), south of
Châteauneuf on route d'Avignon (D17).

Getting There & Away

You have one choice: your own wheels.

ORANGE

• pop 27,000   ✉ 84100

Through a 16th century marriage with the
German House of Nassau, the House of
Orange – the princely dynasty that had ruled
Orange since the 12th century – became
active in the history of the Netherlands and
later, through William III (William of
Orange), Britain and Ireland. Orange (Arenja
in Provençal), which had earlier been a
stronghold of the Reformation, was ceded to
France in 1713 by the Treaty of Utrecht, but
to this day many members of the royal house
of the Netherlands are known as the princes
and princesses of Orange-Nassau.

Orange is best known for its magnificent
Roman relics and less than magnificent National Front mayor. Thursday is market day.

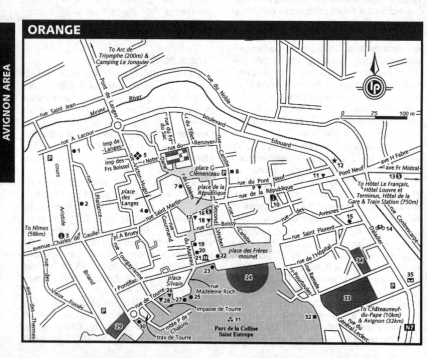

Orientation
The train station is about 1km east of place de la République, the city centre, along ave Frédéric Mistral and rue de la République. Rue Saint Martin links place de la République and nearby place Georges Clémenceau with the tourist office, 250m west. The Théâtre Antique – Orange's Roman theatre – is two blocks south of place de la République. The tiny Meyne River lies north of the city centre.

From the train station, bus No 2 from rue Jean Reboul (first left out of the station) goes to the Théâtre Antique stop.

Information
Tourist Offices The tourist office (☎ 04 90 34 70 88, fax 04 90 34 99 62, officetourisme @infonie.fr, www.provence-orange.com), 5 cours Aristide Briand, is open from 9 am to 6 pm. Sunday hours between April and September are 9 am to 7 pm and 10 am to 6 pm.

Money The Banque de France, 5 rue Frédéric Mistral, is open from 8.30 am to noon and 1.30 to 3.30 pm (closed on weekends).

Post The post office, opposite the bus station on blvd Édouard Daladier, is open from 8.30 am to 6.30 pm (until noon Saturday; closed Sunday).

Email & Internet Access The Cyber Station (☎ 04 90 34 27 27, cybersta@club-internet.fr), north of the tourist office at 2 cours Aristide Briand, charges 25/45FF for 30/60 minutes online. The station is open from 7.30 am to 7 pm (until 11 pm Friday; Saturday from 11 am to 11 pm; closed Sunday).

Laundry The laundrette, 5 rue Saint Florent, is open from 7 am to 8 pm.

Théâtre Antique
Orange's Roman theatre (☎ 04 90 51 17 60), designed to seat about 10,000 spectators, was probably built during the time of Augustus Caesar (ruled 27 BC to 14 AD). Its **stage wall** *(mur de scène)* – the only such Roman structure still standing in its entirety (minus a few mosaics and the roof) – is 103m wide and almost 37m high. Its plain exterior can be viewed from adjacent place des Frères Mounet to the north.

For a panoramic view of the Roman masterpiece, follow montée Philbert de Chalons or montée Lambert to the top of **Colline Saint Eutrope** (Saint Eutrope hill; alt 97m) where a viewing table explains what is what. En route you pass the **ruins of a 12th century château**, the former residence of the princes of Orange.

From April to early October, the theatre is open from 9 am to 6.30 pm (9 am to noon

ORANGE

PLACES TO STAY	OTHER	
8 Bar-Hôtel	1 Cyber Station (Cybercafé)	15 Laundrette
19 Hôtel Arcotel	2 Pêche Chasse Bourgeois	16 Banque de France
20 Hôtel Saint	(Fishing & Bowls Shop)	21 Musée Municipal
Florent	3 Tourist Office	22 Tourist Train
32 Hôtel Saint Jean	4 Imprimerie Martin-Peyre	23 Entrance to Théâtre Antique
	5 Casino (Supermarket)	24 Théâtre Antique
PLACES TO EAT	6 Cathédrale Notre Dame de	25 Service Culturel
9 Le Bambou	Nazareth	27 Location Théâtre Antique
11 Le Provençal	7 Hôtel de Ville	29 Municipal Theatre
17 Le Sangria	10 Maison des Vins	30 Europcar (Car Rental)
18 Chez Daniel	12 Police Municipale	31 Chateau Ruins
26 Le Yaca	13 Crédit Lyonnais	33 Bus Station
28 New Kasmir	14 MTS (Bicycle Rental)	34 Palais des Princes
		35 Post Office

AVIGNON AREA

and 1.30 to 5 pm the rest of the year). In the 17th century Hôtel can Cuyl opposite on rue Madeleine Roch is the unexciting **Musée Municipal** (☎ 04 90 51 18 24, fax 04 90 34 55 89). This museum – yawn – is known for its Roman cadastres (land survey registers). Hours from April to October are 9.30 am to 7 pm; 9 am to noon and 1.30 to 5.30 pm the rest of the year (30/25FF for adult/student).

Arc de Triomphe

Orange's Roman triumphal arch is at the northern end of plane tree lined ave de l'Arc de Triomphe about 450m from the centre. Probably built around 20 BC, it is 19m in height and width and 8m deep/thick. The exceptional friezes commemorate Julius Caesar's victories over the Gauls in 49 BC. The arch has been restored several times since 1825.

Overlooking the east side of the arch is the local **pétanque** court. Fancy a spin? Deck yourself out with balls from the Pêche Chasse Bourgeois shop, 20 cours Aristide Briand.

Wine Tasting

The Maison des Vins (☎ 04 90 34 44 44), 15 rue de la République, has information on Côtes du Rhône wines and offers wine tasting. It is open from 10 am to 6 pm (closed Sunday and Monday in winter).

Special Events

In June and August, the Théâtre Antique comes alive with all-night concerts, cinema screenings and various musical events during Les Nuits du Théâtre Antique. During the last fortnight in July, it plays host to Les Chorégies d'Orange (www.choregies .asso.fr), a series of weekend operas, classical concerts and choral performances. Seats (50-900FF) for this prestigious festival have to be reserved months beforehand; it is possible to catch a free glimpse of the action from the lookout atop Colline Saint Eutrope. Orange also plays host to a week-long jazz festival in June.

Tickets for events held in the Théâtre Antique can be reserved at the Location Théâtre Antique (☎ 04 90 34 24 24 or 04 90 34 15 52, fax 04 90 11 00 85), 14 place Silvain, open from 9 am to noon and 2 to 5 pm (closed on weekends). FNAC branches also sell tickets. For tickets to other cultural events (including those held at the modern Palais des Princes, cours Pourtoules), go next door to the Service Culturel (☎ 04 90 51 57 57, fax 04 90 51 60 51), open from 8.30 am to 5.30 pm (closed on weekends).

Places to Stay

Camping Three-star *Camping Le Jonquier* (☎ 04 90 34 19 83, fax 04 90 34 86 54, rue Alexis Carrel), near the Arc de Triomphe, is open from mid-March to October. It charges 28/30FF per person/tent. Take bus No 1 from the République stop (on ave Frédéric Mistral 600m from the train station) to the Arc de Triomphe. From here, walk 100m back, turn right onto rue des Phocéens and right again onto rue des Étudiants. The camping ground is across the football field.

Chambres d'Hôtes The tourist office publishes a list, updated weekly, of rooms and apartments to rent on a short and long-term basis.

Hotels The cheapest joint is the *Bar Hôtel* (☎ 04 90 34 13 31, 22 rue Caristie) which has very basic rooms for one or two people with shower/shower and toilet for 136/ 146FF. The reception is the downstairs bar. Also dirt cheap is *Hôtel de le Gare*, next to the train station on ave Frédéric Mistral. Rooms start at 160FF.

Close to the bus station, *Hôtel Saint Jean* (☎ 04 90 51 15 16, fax 04 90 11 05 45, 7 cours Pourtoules) has singles/doubles with washbasin and toilet from 180/260FF. There are also a couple of three-star hotels here: *Hôtel Le Français* (☎ 04 90 34 67 65, fax 04 90 51 89 50, place de la Gare) and *Hôtel Louvre et Terminus* (☎ 04 90 34 10 08, fax 04 90 34 68 71, 89 ave Frédéric Mistral) which has a swimming pool. Both charge around 260FF for a double with shower.

A block north of the Théâtre Antique, the welcoming *Hôtel Arcotel* (☎ *04 90 34 09 23, fax 04 90 51 61 12, 8 place aux Herbes)* has singles/doubles from 110/150FF and triples/quads from 160/300FF.

Around the corner, atmospheric *Hôtel Saint Florent* (☎ *04 90 34 18 53, fax 04 90 51 17 25, 4 rue du Mazeau)* has great rooms with wall murals and fantastic *belle époque* wooden beds adorned with crushed and studded velvet. Rooms cost 160/200FF with shower.

Out of Town Four kilometres north of Orange in the village of Piolenc is the laid-back *Auberge de l'Orangerie* (☎ *04 90 29 59 88, fax 04 90 29 67 74, 4 rue de l'Ormeau)*, housed in a converted 18th century inn and part of the Logis de France chain. Rooms cost 300-480FF and breakfast is 45FF.

Places to Eat

East of place Georges Clémenceau on rue du Pont Neuf, there are a number of moderately priced restaurants: *Le Bambou* (☎ *04 90 51 65 19)*, at No 17, is said to be particularly tasty.

La Sangria (☎ *04 90 34 31 96, 3 place de la République)* has a 50FF lunch *menu* and evening ones for 68 and 100FF. Close by, *Chez Daniel* (☎ *04 90 34 63 48)*, on the corner of rue Second Weber and rue Boissy, dishes out oysters, mussels and other shellfish by the dozen. Daniel also offers inspirational fish platters costing 120-180FF, to eat in or take away.

Indian fare is served at *New Kasmir* (☎ *04 90 34 90 09)*, just west of Théâtre Antique on rue de Tourre. Hot *menus* cost 79 and 95FF. Best known for its local fare is *Le Yaca* (☎ *04 90 34 70 03, 24 place Silvain)* which has a regional *menu* for 65FF. The locally inspired *soupe au pistou* at *Le Provençal* (☎ *04 90 34 01 89, 27 rue de la République)* is delicious.

For the ultimate splurge head for *Le Garden* (☎ *04 90 34 64 47, 6 place de Langes)*, a block west of place Georges Clémenceau. The restaurant is furnished 1930s-style and specialises in truffles. Its

brouillade aux truffes with salad (180FF) is a veritable feast of pricey black fungi.

Getting There & Away

Bus The bus station (☎ 04 90 34 15 59 or 04 90 34 13 39) is south-east of the centre of the city on cours Pourtoules. Buses from here go to Avignon, Carpentras, Marseille and Vaison-la-Romaine.

Train Orange train station (☎ 04 90 11 88 64), at the eastern end of ave Frédéric Mistral, is 1.5km east of the tourist office.

Trains go in two directions – northward to Lyon (134FF; 2¼ hours; 13 a day) and Paris' Gare de Lyon (365FF; 3¼ hours) and southward to Avignon (29FF; 15 minutes; 17 a day), Marseille (127FF; 1½ hours; 10 a day) and beyond.

Getting Around

Bicycle MTS (☎/fax 04 90 34 94 92), 571 blvd Édouard Daladier, rents mountain bikes/tandems for 120/350FF a day or 200/600FF a weekend. It is open from 8 am to noon and 3 to 8 pm (closed on weekends).

VAISON-LA-ROMAINE
• pop 5900   ✉ 84110

Vaison-la-Romaine, 23km and 47km northeast of Orange and Avignon respectively, is endowed with extensive Roman ruins, a picturesque medieval old city and too many tourists.

In the 2nd century BC, the Romans conquered an important Celtic city on this site and renamed it Vasio Vocontiorum. The Roman city flourished, in part because it was granted considerable autonomy, but around the 6th century the Great Migrations forced the population to move to the hill across the river, which was easier to defend. The counts of Toulouse built a castle on top of the hill in the 12th century. The resettlement of the original site began in the 17th century.

The Roman remains discovered at Vaison include mosaic-decorated villas, colonnaded streets, public baths, a theatre and aqueduct; the latter brought water down from Mont Ventoux.

Vaison – like Malaucène and Carpentras, 10km and 27km respectively to the south – serves as a good base for exploring the Dentelles de Montmirail and Mont Ventoux region. A *grand marché Provençal* fills place François Cevert on Tuesday morning; smaller markets are held on Thursday and Saturday mornings. In July and August there is a more touristy market every Sunday in the Haute Ville.

Orientation

Vaison is bisected by the ever-flooding Ouvèze River. The Roman city centre, on top of which the modern city centre has been built, is on the river's right (north) bank; the medieval Haute Ville is on the left (south) bank. In the modern city, pedestrianised Grand Rue heads north-westward from the Pont Romain bridge, changing its name near the Roman ruins to ave du Général de Gaulle.

To get from the bus station to the tourist office, exit the station and turn left, then left into rue Colonel Parazols, which leads past the Puymin excavations along rue Burrus to the tourist office.

Information

Tourist Office The tourist office (☎ 04 90 36 02 11, fax 04 90 28 76 04), inside the Maison du Tourisme et des Vins, is just off ave du Général de Gaulle on place du Chanoine Sautel. It's open from 9 am to noon and 2 to 5.45 pm. Sunday hours from Easter to September are 9 am to 1 pm. In July and August daily hours are 9 am to 6.45 pm.

Post The post office, which has an exchange service, is diagonally opposite place du 11 Novembre. It is open from 8.30 am to noon and 2 to 5 pm (until noon Saturday; closed Sunday).

Gallo-Roman Ruins

The Gallo-Roman ruins that have been unearthed in Vaison can be visited at two sites: **Fouilles de Puymin**, the excavations on the east side of ave du Général de Gaulle; and **Fouilles de la Villasse**, which are to the west of the same road.

Fouilles de Puymin, whose entrance is opposite the tourist office, is the more interesting of the pair. It includes houses, mosaics and a theatre (designed to accommodate 6000 people) built around 20 AD under the reign of Tiberius. The **Musée Archéologique** displays some of the artefacts found. Its collection of statues includes the silver bust of a 3rd century patrician and likenesses of Hadrian and his wife Sabina. At Fouilles de la Villasse, you can visit the mosaic and fresco-decorated house in which the bust was discovered.

Both sites are open November to February from 10 am to noon and 2 to 4.30 pm (closed Tuesday). From March to October, daily hours are 9 or 9.30 am to 12.30 pm and 2 to 6 or 7 pm (40/22/14FF for adult/student at both sites). From April to October, there are guided tours (10FF) in English; check the schedule at the tourist office.

Medieval Quarter

Across the much repaired **Pont Romain**, on the south bank of the Ouvèze, lies the **Haute Ville** which dates from the 13th and 14th centuries. Narrow, cobblestone alleys lead up hill past restored houses. At the summit is the imposing 12th century **château**, modernised in the 15th century only to be later abandoned.

Wine Tasting

Local wines and *produits du terroir* (local food products) can be tasted and bought at the Maison des Vins, in the basement of the Maison du Tourisme et des Vins.

Organised Tours

Rando Ventoux (☎ 04 90 46 42 76 or 04 75 45 65 66), place du Marché Saint Romain en Viennòis, organises motorcycling tours of the Ventoux region. A two-day trip costs 750FF including *gîte* accommodation.

Special Events

The two-week Choralies choral festival, held every three years in August in Vaison's old Roman theatre, is the largest of its kind in Europe. The next will take place in 2001.

A highlight of this *fête de la polyphonie* is the *chant commun*, during which some 3000 voices from all over Europe sing in unison. Program and ticket information is available from the Centre à Cœur Joie (see Hostels later) or from the Mouvement Choral à Cœur Joie (☎ 04 72 19 83 40, fax 04 78 43 43 98), 24 ave Joannès Masset BP 317, 69337 Lyon Cedex 09.

The latter also has details on the Festival des Chœurs Lauréats, a smaller-scale polyphonic festival held each year in the last week of July. Each summer various concerts are held in the Roman theatre; ask the tourist office what's on.

Places to Stay

Camping *Camping du Théâtre Romain* *(☎ 04 90 28 78 66, chemin de Brusquet)* is opposite the Théâtre Antique in the northern section of the Fouilles de Puymin. It is open from mid-March to October and charges 65/80FF for two people with a tent or caravan in the low/high season. Larger *Camping Carpe Diem (☎ 04 90 36 02 02)*, south-east of the centre on route de Saint Marcellin, is open from mid-March to November. Both have a swimming pool.

Hostels The quiet but expensive *Centre à Cœur Joie (☎ 04 90 36 00 78, fax 04 90 36 09 89)*, 500m south-east of town along the river at the end of ave César Geoffray, has great views of Mont Ventoux. Singles/doubles/triples with breakfast cost 220/280/345FF.

Hotels Hotels are few and far between. The 24 room *Hôtel Le Burrhus (☎ 04 90 36 00 11, fax 04 90 36 39 05, 2 place Montfort)* and the eight room *Hôtel des Lis (same ☎/fax, 20 cours Henri Fabre)*, practically next door and owned by the same people, charge from 240 and 350FF respectively for a double with shower and toilet. Both close from mid-November to 20 December and on Sunday in January and February.

Shopping

Wine (Villages des Côtes du Rhône, Gigondas, Châteauneuf-du-Pape), honey and *nougat au miel* (honey nougat) are all local specialities, but nothing can compare with the delectable black truffles harvested around Vaison-la-Romain. Sure, they don't come cheap, but just a few shavings will turn the most prosaic plate of pasta into a bite-sized helping of heaven itself.

Getting There & Away

Bus The bus station, where Lieutaud buses (☎ 04 90 36 09 90 in Vaison, ☎ 04 90 86 36 75 in Avignon) has an office, is east of the modern town on ave des Choralies. There are limited services from Vaison to Orange (45 minutes), Avignon (1¼ hours) and Carpentras (45 minutes).

Getting Around

Bicycle Hire a set of wheels from Ets Lacombe (☎ 04 90 36 03 29), ave Jules Ferry; or Sport House (☎ 04 90 36 23 60), 10 place Montfort.

DENTELLES DE MONTMIRAIL

Immediately south of Vaison-la-Romaine loom the pinnacles of the Dentelles de Montmirail, a series of limestone rocks which cut into the sky like needles. Vineyards cling to the lower parts of the rocky slopes while climbers dangle perilously from the south-facing rocks around Gigondas. This area, stretching as far west as Mont Ventoux, makes great hiking terrain.

Looping the lacy outcrop of the Dentelles by car or bicycle is a good day trip: from Vaison-la-Romaine, take the southbound D938 to Carpentras which snakes around the eastern side of the Dentelles to Le Barroux. Just south of here, follow the westbound D21 to Beaumes-de-Venise from where you can continue north to Gigondas, Sablet, Séguret and back to Vaison-la-Romaine.

Malaucène (pop 2000; postcode 84340; alt 333m), 10km south of Vaison-la-Romaine, is where many people begin their forays into the Dentelles and the surrounds of Mont Ventoux, 21km to the east. The

Black Diamonds

Provence's truffle trade is far from glamorous. In fact, the way these diamond dealers operate – out of a car trunk; cold hard cash – is a remarkably black business.

Unknown Richerenches, a deceptively wealthy, pinprick-sized village shielded within the thick walls of a medieval fortress built by the Templar Knights in the 12th and 13th centuries, is the congruous setting for a *marché aux truffes* (truffle market). The market is Provence's leading wholesale truffle market and affords a rare glimpse into the cloak and dagger trade. In January the village celebrates a *messe des truffes* (truffle Mass) when parishioners offer truffles instead of cash. The Mass (☎ 04 90 28 02 00 at the Mairie) always falls on the closest Sunday to 17 January, the feast day of Antoine, the patron saint of truffles and its harvesters.

Crisp cold Saturday mornings from November to March (10 am to noon) see Richerenches' main street resound with the furtive whisperings of local *rabassaïres* (truffle hunters) gearing up to sell their weekly harvest to a big-time dealer from Paris, Germany, Italy or beyond. No more than four or five cash-laden dealers attend the weekly market. Each sets up shop – the trunk of their car – on the street, from where they carefully inspect, weigh and invariably buy kilos of the precious black fungi. Their *courtiers* (brokers) mingle with the truffle hunters to scout out the best truffles and keep tabs on deals being cut by rival dealers.

Truffes (truffles) are a fungi hunted by dogs or pigs (see the special section Food & Wine of Provence). Truffle hunters, harvesters and dealers alike store the ugly, mud-caked truffles in grubby white plastic bags. Their rich, earthy, velvet aroma permeates the entire street.

In November 1998, truffles sold for 1100FF a kilogram, a price that rises to the peak in the third week in December. Essentially, the price depends on the quality – absolutely impossible to assess with the untrained eye, meaning that an amateur is guaranteed to get severely ripped off.

The average weekly turnover at Richerenches market is 160kg (176,000FF). In 1997, the record turnover for one trading session was reportedly a staggering 1.7 tonnes (1.87 million FF). Unless you speak fluent French with a heavy southern accent and have oodles of spare cash to blow, you have absolutely no chance of purchasing truffles at Richerenches market.

Individuals seeking black diamonds generally have their own dealer whom they telephone to place an order; the Tabac-Presse (☎ 04 90 28 00 91) in Richerenches has been known to take advance orders. Alternatively, the Café Le Provençal (☎ 04 90 28 00 59) at the south end of the main street cooks up truffle omelettes for 140FF a throw.

Neighbouring **Valréas** (☎ 04 90 35 04 71 for the tourist office) hosts a small truffle market on Wednesday morning. The tiny village of **Puymeras**, about 7km north-east of Vasion-la-Romaine, is home to the world's largest truffle cannery (☎ 04 90 46 41 44, fax 04 90 46 47 04) where the pricey lumps of fungi are conserved in a jar for consumption year-round. The cannery, signposted 'Plantin' just west of Puymeras village on the D46/D938 junction, can be visited from 8 am to noon and 1.30 to 5.30 pm (closed on weekends).

tourist office (☎/fax 04 90 65 22 59), cours des Isnards, is open from 10 am to noon and 3.30 to 5.30 pm (closed Sunday). Winter hours are 8.30 am to noon.

Crestet
• pop 25   ✉ 84110

Signposted west off the D938 is the superbly placed village of Crestet, 14km south of Vaison-la-Romaine. What must be the narrowest streets in Provence lead from the car park at the top of the village to the **Panoramic Café** which affords breathtaking views of the Dentelles and Mont Ventoux.

Art in nature and nature in art is the thematic leaning of contemporary works displayed at **Crestet Centre d'Art** (☎ 04 90 36 34 85, fax 04 90 36 36 20), signposted from the foot of the village along chemin de la Verrière. A one hour walking trail wends its way around 12 sculptures exhibited in the woods. Works by artists in residence are displayed in the centre, open from 10 am to noon and 2 to 5 pm.

Le Barroux
Yellow stone Le Barroux tumbles down the hillside around medieval **Château du Barroux** (☎ 04 90 62 35 21), the perched village's crowning glory. The castle was built as a watchtower to protect the plain from Saracen attacks in the 12th century. During WWII it was occupied by German troops who set fire to it when they left; the castle burnt for 10 days. The restored, 16th century *salle des gardes* (guards' hall) above the chapel hosts classical music concerts. The castle is open from Easter to October between 2 and 6 pm (15FF).

From the north end of the village, route de Suzette leads to the **Abbaye Sainte Madeleine** (☎ 04 90 62 56 31), a monastery built in traditional Romanesque style and surrounded by lavender gardens. Each morning at 9.30 am (10 am on Sunday and holidays) the *moines* (monks) meet in the chapel to sing Gregorian chants, followed by a sung Mass. The Benedictine monks, whose life revolves around hard work, poverty and prayer, rise at 3.15 am. Lights are out by 8.30 pm.

Beaumes de Venise
At the foot of the loop around the Dentelles sits Beaumes de Venise, 10km south-west of Le Barroux at the crossroads of the D21 and the D90 which leads northwards into the massif. The sweet little village is best known for its fruity and sweet, golden **Muscat wines** – best drunk young, chilled and as an aperitif or digestif. The tourist office (☎ 04 90 62 94 39, fax 04 90 65 00 24), cours Jean Jaurès, has a list of domaines where you can taste and buy the nectar. Count on paying around 50FF a bottle.

Séguret
• pop 900   ✉ 84110

Quaint old Séguret, 9km south of Vaison-la-Romaine, is considered one of the most beautiful villages in France. A sweeping view of the vineyards on the plain below can be had from the top of the rocky outcrop – tinged yellow. From the village, a cycling track leads north to Vaison along chemin de la Montagne.

Séguret is at its most beautiful on Christmas Eve when villagers gather in the church for *Li Bergie de Séguret* (*crèche vivant*) where the traditional Christmas nativity scene is brought to life with real-life shepherds, lambs and a newly born baby in a manger.

Places to Stay & Eat
Camping *Aire Naturelle La Saousse* (☎ 04 90 65 23 52), 4km north of Malaucène, offers lovely views in an unspoilt neck of the woods. To get here, head north from Malaucène on the D938, turn right on to the D13, then right again at the first crossroads.

In Beaumont du Ventoux, 15km north-east of Malaucène off the D974, is *Camping Le Mont Serein* (☎ 04 90 60 49 16, fax 04 90 65 23 10, route du Mont Ventoux), charmingly located at 1400m altitude. It costs 20/25FF per person/tent in summer. In winter, you can rent a chalet for 1800-2300FF a week.

Gîtes d'Étape In Gigondas, the *Gîte d'Étape des Dentelles de Montmirail* (☎ 04 90 65 80 85, fax 04 90 65 84 63) in the village centre has 11 rooms for two or three people plus dormitory beds. It charges 65FF for a dorm bed. The gîte is closed from mid-January to mid-February.

L'Oustalet (☎ 04 90 65 80 74, fax 04 90 65 80 29, place du Village) is a 12 bed place open from Easter to mid-November. A bed here is also 65FF.

Chambres d'Hôtes Many sleepy-eyed *mas* open their doors to B&B guests in summer. Particularly recommended is delightful *Le Mas de la Lause (☎ 04 90 62 32 77, chemin de Geysset)*, off route de Suzette in Le Barroux. Modern rooms in the renovated farmhouse dating from 1883 cost 280FF for two, or 400/460FF for a split-level, mezzanine suite for three/four. Prices include a breakfast of fresh bread, croissants and homemade jam. Evening meals at a shared table are 90FF per person. It is closed from November to March.

A handful of chambres d'hôtes line the D23 leading northwards to Séguret.

Hotels In Malaucène, *Hôtel Le Venaissin (☎ 04 90 65 20 31, fax 04 90 65 18 03, cours des Isnards)* has 18 comfortable rooms costing 210-260FF.

Les Géraniums (☎ 04 90 62 41 08, fax 04 90 62 56 48) in Le Barroux is a charming, yellow stone hotel with luxurious doubles furnished in a traditional Provençal style for 240FF. In summer half-board – 240FF per person in a double room or 380FF for a single – is obligatory (minimum three days).

Séguret has two upmarket hotels. Book both months in advance. The *Auberge de Cabasse (☎ 04 90 46 91 12, fax 04 90 46 94 01, route de Sablet)*, on the plain, has rooms from 250/600FF in the low/high season; while *La Table du Comtat (☎ 04 90 46 91 49, fax 04 90 46 94 27)* in the village up top charges from 460/600FF.

MONT VENTOUX

The 25km narrow ridge, dubbed the *désert de pierre* (stone desert) – immediately east of the Dentelles de Montmirail – is Mont Ventoux. It is Provence's most prominent

geographical feature thanks to its height (1909m) and supreme isolation. The mountain's stone-capped top gives it the appearance from afar of being snow-capped, which it is from December through to April. The radar and antenna-studded peak, accessible by road for just a few months in summer, affords spectacular views of Provence, the southern Alps and beyond.

Mont Ventoux is the boundary between the fauna and flora of northern France and those of southern France. Some species, including the snake eagle, numerous spiders and a variety of butterflies, are found only here. The mountain's forests were felled 400 years ago to build ships, but since 1860 some areas have been reforested with a variety of species, including the majestic cedar of Lebanon. The mix of deciduous trees makes the mountain especially colourful in autumn. The broken white stones that cover the top are known as *lauzes*.

Since the summit is considerably cooler than the surrounding plains – there can be a difference of up to 20°C – and receives twice as much precipitation, bring warm clothes and rain gear. Areas above 1300m are usually snow-covered from December to April.

Near the western end of the Mont Ventoux massif is the small agricultural village of **Bédoin** (pop 2215; postcode 84410; alt 295m) and, 4km farther east along route du Mont Ventoux (D974), neighbouring **Sainte Colombe**. Road signs here tell you if the *col* (mountain pass) over the summit is closed. At the eastern end of the Mont Ventoux massif is **Sault** (pop 1200; postcode 84390; alt 800m) which is surrounded in summer by a patchwork of purple lavender. Come winter, **Mont Serein** (1445m), 16km east of Malaucène and 5km west Mont Ventoux' summit on the D974, is transformed into a bustling ski station.

Maps

Didier-Richard's 1:50,000 scale map No 27, entitled *Massif du Ventoux*, includes Mont Ventoux, the Monts du Vaucluse and the Dentelles de Montmirail. More detailed is

IGN's Série Bleue 1:25,000 *Mont Ventoux* (No 3140ET; 58FF).

Information

Tourist Offices Malaucène tourist office (see the Dentelles de Montmirail section) has plenty of information on exploring Mont Ventoux by bicycle or on foot, including night climbs up the mountain. Its efficient and friendly counterpart in Bédoin (☎ 04 90 65 63 95, fax 04 90 12 81 55), Espace Marie-Louis Gravier, place du Marché, organises hikes up the mountain, as does Sault tourist office (☎ 04 90 64 01 21, fax 04 90 64 15 03), ave de la Promenade, which is open from 1 April to 30 September from 9 am to noon and 2 to 7 pm.

In Sault, the Maison de l'Environnement et de la Chasse (☎ 04 90 64 13 96, fax 04 90 64 15 64), ave de l'Oratoire, organises thematic tours (lavender, mushrooms, truffles, flora and fauna etc).

Hiking & Cycling

The GR4, running from the Ardèche to the west, crosses the Dentelles de Montmirail before climbing up the northern face of Mont Ventoux. It then joins the GR9, and both trails follow the bare, white ridge before parting ways, with the GR4 winding eastward to the Gorge du Verdon. The GR9, which takes you to most of the area's ranges (including the Monts du Vaucluse and Lubéron range) is arguably the most spectacular trail in Provence. The first person to climb to the top of Mont Ventoux was the exiled Italian poet Petrarch who scaled the mountain with a donkey in 1336, leaving everyone convinced he was mad.

In summer countless cyclists labour up the sun-baked slopes of Mont Ventoux (from Chalet Reynard on the westbound D974) to the summit. Many are clearly inspired by British world champion cyclist Tommy Simpson (1937-1967) who suffered a fatal heart attack here during the 1967 Tour de France. Most cyclists pedal to the top, then back track to add their water bottle to the cycling memorabilia surrounding the roadside **memorial to Tommy Simpson**, 1km east of the summit and 1km west of Chalet Reynard. The epitaph on the grey stone tablet reads *There is no mountain too high.*

The EgoBike Shop (☎ 04 90 65 22 15 or 04 90 60 90 08) in Malaucène rents mountain bikes. In Bédoin, try Le Passe Montagne (☎ 04 90 65 60 25), route de Carpentras. In Sault, Passion Vélo (☎ 04 90 64 09 32), route de la Lavande, rents bicycles.

Skiing

Between December and March locals flock up Mont Ventoux to ski down its slopes. **Chalet Reynard** (☎ 04 90 61 84 55), at the intersection of the D974 and the eastbound D164 to Sault, is a small ski station (1420m) on the southern slopes with two *téléskis* (drag lifts) to two blue runs – both about 900m long. You can hire a set of skis, boots and poles here for 100FF a day. Cross country skiing is popular too. Non-skiers can test the luge (50FF).

Mont Serein (1400m), 5km west of the summit on the colder northern side, is the main ski station served by six drag lifts. Skis, information on ski schools, piste maps etc are available from the Chalet d'Accueil, adjoining Ski Location (☎ 04 90 63 20 93). Chalet Liotard (☎ 04 90 60 68 38) is a mid-station restaurant-cum-bar for skiers, 100m further uphill.

Places to Stay & Eat

Places listed in the Dentelles de Montmirail also serve as a good base to explore Mont Ventoux. In Bédoin, *Camping La Garenne* (☎ *04 90 65 61 18*) is open from April to September and charges 17/10FF per adult/child plus a small tent/parking fee.

Sault has a couple of appealing choices, namely *Hôtel Le Louvre* (☎ *04 90 64 08 88, place du Marché*) which has rooms overlooking the village square for 250-300FF (450-500FF half-board) and has an excellent Provençal kitchen. In Sainte Colombe *Hôtel Le Justine* (☎ *04 90 65 63 10*), 18km from the Ventoux summit, has doubles for 180-250FF.

Don't leave Sault without indulging in a slab of its sweet, lavender-honey and almond flavour nougat or bitter-sweet macaroons.

AVIGNON AREA

Both are sold at *André Boyer (☎ 04 90 64 00 23, place de l'Europe)*, a *maître nougatier* (master nougat maker) featured in the *Guinness Book of Records* for cooking up the largest bar of nougat (12.45m long and 180kg in weight).

Getting There & Away

If you've got a car, the summit of Mont Ventoux can be reached from Sault via the tortuous D164 or, in summer, from Malaucène or Saint Estève via the switchback D974, built in the 1930s. This mountain

The Perfume of Provence

If there's one aroma associated with Provence, it's *lavande* (lavender). Lavender fields – once seen, never forgotten – include those at the Abbaye de Sénanque near Gordes and the Musée de la Lavande in Coustellet; around Digne-les-Bains and on the Plateau de Valensole in Haute-Provence; and those carpeting the arid Sault region, east of Mont Ventoux on the Vaucluse plateau.

The sweet purple flower is harvested when it is in full bloom between 15 July to 15 August. It is mechanically harvested on a hot dry day, following which the lorry-loads of cut lavender, known as *paille* (straw), are packed tight in a steam still and distilled to extract the sweet essential oils.

Authentic lavender farms, all the rage in Provence in the 1920s, are a dying breed today. Since the 1950s, *lavandine* (lavandin), a hybrid of *lavande fine* (fine lavender) and aspic cloned at the turn of the century, has been produced on a mass scale for industrial purposes. Both blaze the same vibrant purple when in flower, but lavandin yields five times more oil than fine lavender (which produces 1kg of oil from 130kg of cut straw).

Approximately 80% of Provence's lavender farms produce lavandin today. In 1997, the region yielded 1000 tonnes of lavandin essential oils compared to 20 tonnes of fine lavender oils. The few remaining traditional lavender farms tend to colour higher areas; wild lavender needs an altitude of 900 to 1300m to blossom, unlike its common sister which can grow anywhere above 800m.

Lavender farms, distilleries and ornamental gardens open to visitors are listed in the English language brochure *Les Routes de la Lavande* (The Lavender Roads), available free from tourist offices and published by the Association 'Les Routes de la Lavande' (☎ 04 75 26 65 91, fax 04 75 26 32 67, routes.lavande@edu cagai.fr), 2 ave de Venterol, BP 36, 26111 Nyons. Many farms and distilleries are open for a couple of months prior to the harvest. The Maison de l'Environnement et de la Chasse in Sault organises lavender tours.

Lavandin (left) and fine lavender (right)

road is snow-blocked most years until as late as April. For information on bus services in the area, see the Carpentras section.

CARPENTRAS

• pop 25,000   ✉ 84200   alt 102m

The drowsy, agricultural town of Carpentras, an important trading centre in Greek times and later a Gallo-Roman city, became the capital of the papal territory of the Comtat Venaissin in 1320. It flourished in the 14th century, when it was visited frequently by Pope Clement V (who preferred it to Avignon) and numerous cardinals. During the same period, Jews expelled from territory controlled by the French crown (especially in Provence and neighbouring Languedoc) sought refuge in the Comtat Venaissin, where they could live under the protection of the pope – subject to certain restrictions. Today, Carpentras' 14th century synagogue is the oldest such structure in France still in use. In March 1997, skinheads apologised in court for desecrating tombs in the Jewish cemetery years previously.

Carpentras is equidistant (25km) from Avignon (south-west) and Orange (north-west). The town is small, easy to navigate on foot, and best known for its bustling Friday markets which sell everything from truffles (November to March) to *berlingots* (hard-boiled sweets).

Orientation

In the 19th century, the city's 16th century fortifications and walls were replaced by a ring of boulevards: ave Jean Jaurès, blvd Alfred Rogier, blvd du Nord, blvd Maréchal Leclerc, blvd Gambetta and blvd Albin Durand. Inside these is the partly pedestrianised old city. Northern Porte d'Orange (1560) still stands.

If you arrive by bus, walk north-east to place Aristide Briand, a major traffic intersection at the southernmost point on the heart-shaped ring of boulevards. Ave Jean Jaurès leads to the tourist office, while the pedestrians-only rue de la République heads due north to the cathedral and Palais de Justice. The Hôtel de Ville is a few blocks north-east of the cathedral.

Information

Tourist Offices The tourist office (☎ 04 90 63 00 78 or 04 90 63 57 88, fax 04 90 60 41 02), 170 ave Jean Jaurès, sells maps, guides and organises city tours (25/10FF for adult/child). Ask for the English-language brochure, *The Discover Carpentras Tour*, if you prefer a do-it-yourself-job. The office is open from 9 am to 12.30 pm and 2 to 6.30 pm (6 pm on Saturday; closed Sunday). Hours in July and August are 9 am to 7 pm (Sunday from 9.30 am to 12.30 pm).

Money The Banque de France, 161 blvd Albin Durand, is open from 9 am to 12.15 pm and 1.30 to 3.30 pm (closed on weekends). Commercial banks line place Aristide Briand and blvd Albin Durand.

Post The post office, 65 rue d'Inguimbert, is open from 8 am to 7 pm (until noon on Saturday; closed Sunday).

Email & Internet Access Cyber Espace (☎ 04 90 63 43 08), above a crêperie on the corner of place Colonel Mouret and rue Raspail, is open from 11 am to 2 pm and 7 to 10 pm (Saturday from 3 to 10 pm; closed Sunday). One hour online is 50FF.

Laundry The laundrette, 118 rue Porte de Monteux, is open from 7 am to 8 pm. Hours at the Laverie du Nord, 10 blvd du Nord, outside Porte d'Orange, are 7 am to 9 pm.

Synagogue

Carpentras synagogue – inconspicuous as it is – was founded on this site in 1367, rebuilt in 1741-43 and restored in 1929 and 1954. The 1st-floor sanctuary is decorated with wood panelling and liturgical objects from the 18th century. Down below, there's an oven that was used until 1904 to bake matzo *(pain azyme* in French), the unleavened bread eaten at Passover.

The synagogue, opposite the Hôtel de Ville on place Juiverie, can be identified by a stone plaque positioned high on the wall, which is inscribed with Hebrew letters. It can be visited from 10 am to noon and 3 to 5 pm (4 pm on Friday; closed on weekends). The tourist office sells the informative English booklet entitled *The Road to Jewish Heritage in the South of France* (15FF). Some 100 families live in Carpentras today.

Cathedral

Carpentras' one-time cathedral, officially known as Église Saint Siffrein, place Charles de Gaulle, was built in the Méridional (southern French) Gothic style between 1405 and 1519. The doorway, whose design is classical, was added in the 17th century. The bell tower is modern. The **Trésor d'Art Sacré** (Treasury of Religious Art) displays various liturgical objects and reliquaries from the 14th to 19th century, including the **Saint Mors**, the Holy Bridle-bit supposedly made by St Helen for her son Constantine from a nail taken from the True Cross.

The cathedral is open from 10 am to noon and 2 to 4 pm (until 6 pm in summer; closed

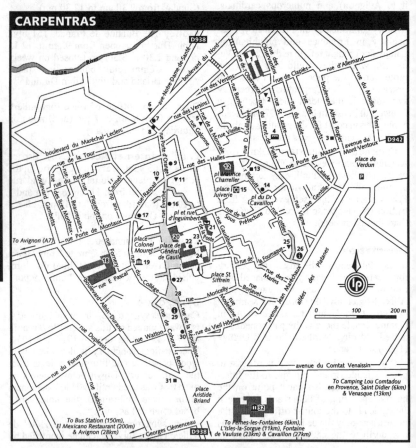

CARPENTRAS

Tuesday year round). Sunday Mass is celebrated at 9 and 10.30 am. Piano and organ recitals are held here in summer.

Arc de Triomphe

Hidden in a corner off rue d'Inguimbert – next to the cathedral and behind the **Palais de Justice** housed inside a palais épiscopal dating from 1801 – this triumphal arch (or what's left of it) is the town's only Roman relic. Built under Augustus in the 1st century AD, it has regrettably become little more than a convenient public urinal. One of the carvings on the east side depicts two Barbarian captives (note the beards and chains), their faces all but worn away by time and the weather.

Facing the arch on the opposite side of the square are the paltry remains of a 7th century **Cathédrale Romane**, most of which was destroyed in 1399.

Carpentras' northern outskirts are crossed by an equally impressive stone relic, the remains of a 10km **aqueduct** which brought water to the city between 1745 and 1893. It had 48 arches.

Museums

Carpentras' museums are open from 10 am to noon and 2 to 4 pm; until 6 pm in summer; closed Tuesday year round. The **Musée Comtadin**, which displays artefacts related to local history and folklore, and the **Musée Duplessis** which houses a bunch of paintings, are on the western side of the old city at 234 blvd Albin Durand. The same 18th century building houses the **Bibliothèque Inguimbertine**, a library with rare books, incunabula and manuscripts.

The **Musée Sobirats Arts Décoratifs**, one block west of the cathedral at 112 rue du Collège, is an 18th century private residence decorated and crammed with furniture, faïence and *objets d'art* in the Louis XV and Louis XVI styles. Hours are 10 am to noon and 2 to 4 pm; until 6 pm from April to September (a token 2FF; ring the bell).

The 18th century **Hôtel Dieu**, place Aristide Briand, has an old-time pharmacy, complete with pharmaceutical ceramics. It's open on Monday, Wednesday and Thursday from 9 am to 11.30 am (8FF).

Markets

Friday is market day. Place Aristide Briand and rue de la République have the usual knock-off jeans, generic T-shirts and junky doodads, but rue d'Inguimbert and most of ave Jean Jaurès are laden with tables covered with nougat, strong local cheese, orange and lavender marmalade, cauldrons of paella, buckets of olives, fresh fruit and

AVIGNON AREA

CARPENTRAS

PLACES TO STAY	4 Piscine Couverte Renovée	19 Musée Sobirats Arts Décoratifs
3 Hôtel La Lavande		20 Palais de Justice
13 Hôtel du Mont Ventoux; Le Malaga Restaurant	7 Laverie du Nord (Laundrette)	21 Post Office
31 Hôtel du Théâtre	8 Porte d'Orange	22 Arc de Triomphe
	9 Chocolats René Clavel (Chocolate Shop)	23 Remains of Cathédrale Romane
PLACES TO EAT	12 Hôtel de Ville	24 Église Saint Siffrein (Cathedral)
2 Le Vert Galant	14 Chapelle des Pénitents Blancs	26 Tourist Office
5 L'Oriental		27 Confiseur Chocolatier Sobirats (Sweet Shop)
6 Rives d'Auzon	15 Synagogue	
10 Le Marijo	16 Jouvard Pâtissier (Cake Shop)	28 Fountain
11 L'Atelier de Pierre		29 Maison des Vins des Côtes du Ventoux
25 La Garrigue - Chez Serge	17 Cyber Espace (Cybercafé)	
	18 Musée Comtadin & Musée Duplessis	30 Maison de la Presse
OTHER		32 Hôtel Dieu
1 Église Notre Dame de l'Observance		

veg. A *marché biologique* fills rue Raspail on Tuesday morning.

From November to March, truffles are sold on place Aristide Briand every Friday from 8 to 10 am. Carpentras' biggest fair is held on the Fête de Saint Siffrein (Feast of St Siffrein) on 27 November.

Wine Tasting

During July and August, free tastings of Côtes du Ventoux vintages are held around Carpentras. Drop in at the Maison des Vins des Côtes du Ventoux, 88 rue de la République.

Swimming

Art-deco fans who enjoy taking a plunge should head for the **Piscine Couverte Renovée 1930** (☎ 04 90 60 92 03), rue du Mont de Piété, a lovely covered swimming pool built by the Caisse d'Épargne almost seven decades ago and restored to its geometric glory. The water temperature is 20°C. Hours vary, but in general it is open between 3 and 5.15 pm and 6 to 8 pm (12.50/8.80FF for adult/child and senior).

Special Events

For information on the eclectic Éstivales de Carpentras – a two-week music, dance and theatre festival held each July, contact Bureau du Festival (☎ 04 90 60 46 00), La Charité, 77 rue Cottier.

Places to Stay

Camping Outside town on route de Saint Didier is *Camping Lou Comtadou en Provence* (☎ 04 90 67 03 16, ave Pierre de Coubertin), open from Easter to October. It charges 22/29FF per person/tent or car. *Camping Le Brégoux* (☎ 04 90 62 62 50, chemin du Vas), 8km north-west in Aubignan, is open from March to October.

Hotels Arguably the best place in town to stay for travellers watching their wallets is the one-star *Hôtel du Théâtre* (☎ 04 90 63 02 90, 7 blvd Albin Durand), a friendly establishment overlooking place Aristide

Briand. Large rooms for one or two start at 145FF; triples are 250FF.

At the northern end of town, eight room *Hôtel La Lavande* (☎ 04 90 63 13 49, 282 blvd Alfred Rogier) has doubles without/ with shower for 145/175FF.

Two-star *Hôtel du Mont Ventoux* (☎ 04 90 63 03 15, fax 04 90 60 49 73, 153 rue Vigne), above Le Malaga restaurant and piano bar, is also known as Hôtel du Fiacre. It has rooms for one or two with shower and toilet for 190-390FF; rooms with bath start at 295FF.

Places to Eat

Restaurants Regional fare rules at *Le Marijo* (☎ 04 90 60 42 65, 73 rue Raspail) which serves up superb three and four-course locally-inspired *menus* for 88 or 123FF. The pick of its entrées is local melon served with Muscat de Beames de Venise. For the cheese course, order the *chèvre* (goat's cheese) marinated for 15 days in herbs and olive oil and sprinkled with *marc*, a local eau de vie. This place is closed Sunday.

La Garrigue – Chez Serge (☎ 04 90 60 21 24), immediately behind the tourist office, has a flower-filled terrace. Despite its abundance of pizzas (from 62FF), Serge also concocts a wide variety of Provençal dishes which change daily.

Carpentras' finest terrace sits at the foot of a 16th century belfry topped by an ornate campanile dating from 1572: *L'Atelier de Pierre* (☎ 04 90 60 75 00, 30 place de l'Horloge) has a 110FF *menu* worth every centime for the setting alone.

Equally palatable are the *truffes* served in season at *Le Vert Galant* (☎ 04 90 67 15 50, 12 rue de Clapiès). Expect to pay at least 100FF a head, plus a lot more if you intend sampling the precious bits of black fungi (closed Saturday lunchtime, Sunday, and the last three weeks of August). Another prized restaurant is the colourful *Rives d'Auzon* (☎ 04 90 60 62 62, 47 blvd du Nord), outside the city wall opposite the Porte d'Orange. *Menus* are 130 or 190FF (closed Wednesday).

L'Oriental (☎ 04 90 63 19 57, 26 rue de la Monnaie) specialises in Moroccan couscous from 69FF. *El Mexicano (☎ 04 90 67 21 80, 34 ave Georges Clémenceau)*, north of the bus station, is a hybrid of an American-style steakhouse and a Tex-Mex joint with beef fondue, every conceivable cut of steak, tacos and chilli and the more exotic bison and *autruche* (ostrich).

Shopping
Chocolats René Clavel (☎ 04 90 63 07 59), 30 rue Porte d'Orange, is packed with fantastical sculptures carved from berlingot, a hard caramel candy typical to Carpentras. The largest weighs 56kg and is a *Guinness Book of Records* record-breaker.

Shop at Confiseur Chocolatier Sobirats, 25 rue de la République, for *calissons* and chocolate olives. Almond and pine kernel meringues are sold at Jouvard Pâtissier, 40 rue Éveche.

Getting There & Away
Bus The bus station, place Terradou, is 150m south-west of place Aristide Briand. Schedules are available from Cars Comtadins (☎ 04 90 67 20 25) across the square at 38 ave Wilson. It is open from 8 am to noon and 2 to 6 pm (closed on weekends).

There are hourly services to Avignon (45 minutes) and less frequent runs to Orange (40 minutes), Cavaillon (45 minutes) and L'Isle-sur-Sorgue (20 minutes). Even less frequent are buses (weekday only) to Vaison-la-Romaine via Malaucène (45 minutes), Bédoin (40 minutes) and Sault (1½ hours).

Train The train station is only served by goods trains.

AROUND CARPENTRAS
From Carpentras, a circular day trip takes travellers through a waterworld of fountains and water wheels, gushing springs and breathtaking gorges.

Pernes-les-Fontaines
• pop 8300   ✉ 84210
A former capital of Comtat Venaissin, Pernes-les-Fontaines, 5km south of Carpentras, is named after the 36 (some say 40)

fountains that spring from its stone walls and decorate its squares. Upon discovering the Font de Bouvery source in the 18th century, the town mayor graced the town's four quarters with a monumental mushroom of a fountain, extravagantly decorated and spouting from a 3.20m-wide base. The grandiose, moss-covered fountains – Fontaine du Cormoran, Fontaine Reboul (also known as La Grand Font) and Fontaine du Gigot – are the result.

The tourist office (☎ 04 90 61 31 04, fax 04 90 61 33 23), place du Comtat Venaissin, distributes city maps marked up with a fountain tour.

L'Isle-sur-la-Sorgue
• pop 15,550   ✉ 84800
A farther 11km south sits L'Isle-sur-la-Sorgue, a chic spot known for its antique shops, bustling markets and graceful waterways that encircle the town. L'Isle-sur-la-Sorgue dates from the 12th century when villagers built huts on stilts above what was then a swampy marshland. By the 18th century, it was a thriving silk weaving centre surrounded by canals, ploughed by water wheels that powered its paper mills and silk factories.

On Sunday the quays are swamped with book and antique sellers. A food market fills the streets on Thursday morning. **Le quai de la Gare** (☎ 04 90 20 73 42), near the train station at 4 ave Julien Guigue, is a fine old warehouse housing 35 antique dealers. Another 100 or so can be found in **Le Village des Antiquaires de la Gare** (☎ 04 90 38 04 57), an antique shopping mall fronted by an 18th century mill, 2bis ave de l'Egalité. Don't expect any bargains.

The tourist office (☎ 04 90 38 04 78, fax 04 90 38 35 43), place de l'Église, has information on **canoeing** the 8km along the Sorgue from neighbouring Fontaine de Vaucluse to L'Isle-sur-la-Sorgue. Between May and September, Canoë Évasion (☎ 04 90 38 26 22), next to Camping La Coutière on route de Fontaine de Vaucluse (D24), and Kayak Vert (☎ 04 90 20 35 44 in Fontaine de Vaucluse) both rent canoes (110/70FF for adult/child aged 7-14).

Fontaine de Vaucluse

• pop 580 ✉ 84800

The mighty spring which gives Fontaine de Vaucluse (Vau-Cluso La Font in Provençal) its name is the spot where the Sorgue River ends its subterranean course and gushes to the surface. At the end of winter and in early spring, up to 200 cubic metres of water per second spill forth from the base of the cliff, forming one of the world's most powerful springs. During drier periods, the reduced flow seeps through the rocks at various points downstream from the cliff and the spring becomes little more than a still, very deep pond. Following numerous unsuccessful human and robotic attempts to reach the bottom, an unmanned submarine touched the 315m-deep base in 1985.

Some 1.5 million visitors descend upon Fontaine de Vaucluse each year to stroll its streets and throw pebbles in its pond.

The tourist office (☎ 04 90 20 32 22, fax 04 90 20 21 37, officetourisme.vaucluse@ wanadoo.fr), chemin de la Fontaine, southeast of central place de la Colonne, is open from 10 am to 6 pm (closed Sunday).

Museums Three of Fontaine's museums (each 20FF) deal with: the Resistance movement, **Musée d'Histoire 1939-1945** (☎ 04 90 20 24 00) adjoining the tourist office; justice and punishment, **Musée Historique de la Justice et des Châtiments** (☎ 04 90 20 24 58), chemin de la Fontaine; and stalactites and speleology, **Le Monde Souterrain** (☎ 04 90 20 34 13), chemin de la Fontaine.

The **Moulin à Papier Vallis Clausa** (☎ 04 90 20 31 72), opposite the tourist office on chemin de la Fontaine, is a reconstruction of a paper mill, built where Fontaine de Vaucluse's old mill was from 1522 to 1968. Flower-encrusted paper, made as it was in the 16th century, is sold in the adjoining boutique and Galerie Vallis Clause (☎ 04 20 20 83) where there is a **Musée du Santon**.

The Italian Renaissance poet Petrarch (Pétrarque in French) lived in Fontaine de Vaucluse from 1337 to 1353 where he immortalised his true love, Laura, wife of Hugues de Sade, in verse. The **Musée Pétrarque** (☎ 04 90 20 37 20) on the left bank of the Sorgue is devoted to his work, sojourn and broken heart (10FF).

Pays de Venasque

The *villages perchés* sprinkled around Venasque are beautiful yet seldom explored. The area is crossed with parts of **Le Mur de la Peste** (literally, 'Wall of Plague'), a 1.5m-high, dry stone wall built under Papal orders in 1721 to prevent (unsuccessfully) the plague penetrating Comtat Venaissin.

The village baptistery in **Venasque** (pop 1010; alt 320m), 13km south-east of Carpentras, was built in the 5th century on the site of a Roman temple and is one of France's oldest edifices. The fortress village of **Le Beaucet** (pop 300; alt 300m), tumbles down the hillside 6km south via the winding D314. Two kilometres south along chemin des Oratoires (D39A) in the hamlet of **Saint-Gens** is a small Romanesque basilica, rebuilt in 1884. The hermit Gens, who lived with wolves and performed rain-making miracles, died here in 1127.

The **Forêt de Venasque**, crossed by the GR91 hiking trail, lies to the east of Venasque. From here the GR91 heads north to the foot of the magnificent **Gorges de la Nesque**, from where Sault and the eastern realms of the Ventoux can be accessed.

Venasque tourist office (☎ 04 90 66 11 66), Grande Rue, has information on Pays de Venasque.

Place to Stay

Camping In Fontaine de Vaucluse, *Camping Municipal Les Prés (☎ 04 90 20 32 38, route du Cavaillon)* is west of the village centre near the large public car park and the Sorgue. You can also camp in the hostel grounds (see later). Just south of Fontaine towards Lagnes on the D24 is *Camping La Coutière (☎ 04 90 20 33 97, route de Fontaine de Vaucluse)*, 300m from the Sorgue and open from April to October.

Hostel The *Auberge de Jeunesse (☎ 04 90 20 31 65, fax 04 90 20 26 20, chemin de la*

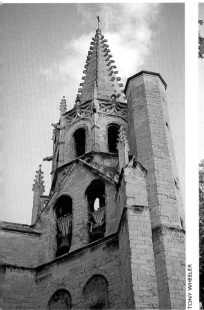

TONY WHEELER

lise St Pierre, Avignon

JON DAVISON

Les Antiques, St Remy de Provence

STEVE DAVEY

he 14th century Palais du Papes, Avignon

Field of poppies in early June, The Vaucluse

Vignasse) is 800m south of Fontaine de Vaucluse towards Lagnes (walk uphill from the bus stop). B&B is 63FF, sheet hire is 14FF, and an evening meal costs 48FF. Campers can pitch their tent here for 26FF per person. You can also hire a bicycle for 60FF a day. If you don't have an HI card, you need to buy a 19FF nightly stamp. Reception is open from 8 to 10 am and 5 to 10 pm.

Chambres d'Hôtes The respective tourist offices have a list of *chambres d'hôtes*. In Venasque, try the *Maison Provençale* (☎ 04 90 66 02 84, fax 04 90 66 61 32), home of Monsieur and Madame Gérard Ruel; B&B for two starts at 250FF.

Hotels Avoid L'Isle-sur-la-Sorgue; it's stupidly expensive. The most affordable of Fontaine de Vaucluse's three hotels is the 12 room *Hôtel Les Sources* (☎ 04 90 20 31 84, route de Cavaillon) which has doubles for 170FF. In Venasque *La Garrigue* (☎ 04 90 66 03 40, fax 04 90 66 61 43, route de Cavaillon), 200m from the old village, is an endearing place with terrace, garden, swimming pool and 15 rooms for 300-450FF.

Getting There & Away

Bus Fontaine de Vaucluse is 21km southeast of Carpentras and about 7km east of L'Isle-sur-Sorgue. From Avignon, Voyages Arnaud (☎ 04 90 38 15 58 L'Isle-sur-Sorgue) runs a bus to L'Isle-sur-Sorgue (40 minutes; 3-4 a day) and Fontaine de Vaucluse (one hour). There are also Arnaud buses from Carpentras to L'Isle-sur-Sorgue (20 minutes).

L'Isle-sur-Sorgue train station is not served by passenger trains.

South of Avignon

There are some wonderful day trips south of Avignon, notably the ancient Roman relics at Saint-Rémy, Nîmes and Pont du Gard. The Vallée des Baux, surveyed by the well-known perched village of Les Baux de Provence, safeguards its own culinary secret.

SAINT-RÉMY-DE-PROVENCE
• pop 9340 ✉ 13210

Saint-Rémy-de-Provence is a colourful place with a colourful past. The Greeks, then the Romans settled Glanum on the city's southern fringe. Philosopher Nostradamus was a Saint-Rémois by birth (1503-66), only later moving to Salon-de-Provence to compile his influential prophecies. Three centuries on, the tormented Vincent van Gogh (1853-90) sought refuge from his mental meanderings in Saint-Rémy. The artist painted many of his best known works here between 1889 and 1890.

Sheep, sheep and more *moutons* (sheep) fill the streets each year on Pentecost Monday during the annual Fête de la Transhumance, marking the movement of the flocks to pastures new.

Orientation & Information

Glanum is 2km south of the centre. From the ruins, ave Vincent van Gogh (D5) and its continuation, ave Pasteur, leads north to place Jean Jaurés and farther to blvd Victor Hugo, the street encircling the old town.

The tourist office (☎ 04 90 92 05 22, fax 04 90 92 38 52, www.visitprovence.com), place Jean Jaurès, has information on guided tours (35/20FF for adult/student), including one that follows in Van Gogh's footsteps. In summer it organises nature walks in the Alpilles. The office is open from 9 am to noon and 2 to 7 pm (closed Sunday afternoon).

Site Archéologique de Glanum

The Glanum archaeological site sits at the foot of Mont Gaussier. It was uncovered in 1921 and comprises excavated remains dating from the Gallo-Greek era (3rd to 1st centuries BC) to the Gallo-Roman era (1st century BC to 3rd century AD). The Celto-Ligurians first inhabited the site which they called Glaniques. Among the archaeological finds uncovered were parts of Glanum's temple, enabling archaeologists to partially reconstruct the columned edifice, complete with its decorative upper mouldings. Other Roman buildings clearly evident are the public baths dating from 50 BC and the forum. Smaller fragments of treasure dug up are displayed in the Renaissance **Hôtel de Sade** (☎ 04 90 92 64 04), rue du Parage, in the centre of Saint-Rémy. The *Taverne Romana* café on site serves light dishes dating from antiquity like *cicerona*, a chickpea and cumin purée.

Glanum archaeological site (☎ 04 90 92 23 79) is open from 9 am to 7 pm; 9 am to noon and 2 to 5 pm between October and 31 March (32/21FF for adult/student). A combined ticket for entry to Hôtel de Sade (open 10 am to noon and 2 to 5 or 6 pm) is 36/25FF.

The roadside opposite the archaeological site entrance is dominated by two of Provence's most spectacular Roman monuments: the **triumphal arch** and **Mausoleum**. **Les Antiques**, as the majestic pair is known, date from 20 AD and 30-20 BC respectively. No admission fee is required to stop and photograph the ancient relics.

Van Gogh

The Dutch born artist retreated to **Monastère de Saint-Paul-de-Mausole**, a monastery that served as an asylum in the 18th century. Van Gogh voluntarily admitted himself on 3 May 1889 and stayed here until 16 May 1890. During this time, he accomplished 100 drawings and about 150 paintings, including the well-known *Les Irises* (Still life with Iris, 1890) and *Le champ de blé au cyprès* (Yellow Cornfield, 1889). During WWI, the building was a prison camp. Today it is a hospital.

Van Gogh's former room and ground floor studio cannot be visited (this is expected to change in the near future). Only the small 11th century church and cloister which adjoins the main building are open to visitors. From the monastery entrance, coloured information boards mark the route of the *Promenade sur les lieux peints par Van Gogh*

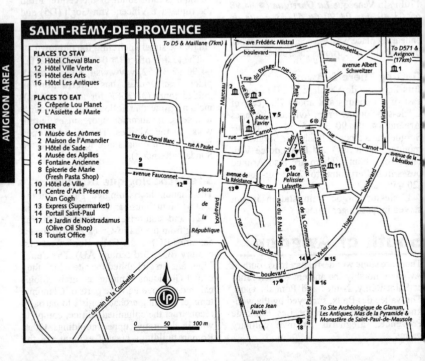

SAINT-RÉMY-DE-PROVENCE

PLACES TO STAY
9   Hôtel Cheval Blanc
12 Hôtel Ville Verte
15 Hôtel des Arts
16 Hôtel Les Antiques

PLACES TO EAT
5   Crêperie Lou Planet
7   L'Assiette de Marie

OTHER
1   Musée des Arômes
2   Maison de l'Amandier
3   Hôtel de Sade
4   Musée des Alpilles
6   Fontaine Ancienne
8   Épicerie de Marie
    (Fresh Pasta Shop)
10 Hôtel de Ville
11 Centre d'Art Présence
    Van Gogh
13 Express (Supermarket)
14 Portail Saint-Paul
17 Le Jardin de Nostradamus
    (Olive Oil Shop)
18 Tourist Office

AVIGNON AREA

– a trail which leads you to the places where Van Gogh painted some of his most famous works. Next to the Glanum archaeological site entrance, he painted *Les Oliviers* (Olive Trees) and *Montagnes de Saint Rémy* (Saint Rémy Mountains) in July 1889.

The life and works of Vincent van Gogh is unravelled at the **Centre d'Art Présence Van Gogh** (☎ 04 90 92 34 72), in the 18th century Hôtel Estrine at 8 rue Estrine. It is open from 10 am to 12.30 pm and 2.30 to 6.30 pm; closed Monday (20FF).

Frédéric Mistral

The Provençal poet and 1904 winner of the Noble Prize for Literature was a native of unmomentous **Maillane,** a small village 7km north-west of Saint-Rémy-de-Provence. Frédéric Mistral (1830-1914) was born in the Mas du Juge, a farmhouse on the village outskirts. After his father's death, he and his mother moved into the centre of the village. Upon marrying, the 46-year-old Mistral left home – moving with his new wife (aged 19) into a house directly opposite his mother's.

The house where he spent his married life (11 rue Lamartine) is a museum today. You can also see the lizard and short verse written in Provençal that he engraved on his mother's house opposite. Mistral is buried in Maillane village cemetery.

Tasting & Buying Olive Oil

The famed, smooth rich oils from the Vallée des Baux – credited with their own *appellation d'origine contrôlée* (AOC) since 1997 – can be tried and tasted (from a small plastic white spoon) at Le Jardin de Nostradamus (☎ 04 90 92 24 23), 18 blvd Victor Hugo.

The history of the region's olive industry is touched upon in the **Musée des Alpilles** (☎ 04 90 92 68 24), place Favier, a local history, geology, arts and popular tradition museum dating from 1919. More oleiculture details are included in the Food and Wine of Provence special section.

Places to Stay

The grand old four-star *Hôtel Les Antiques* (☎ 04 90 92 03 02, fax 04 90 92 50 40, 15 ave Pasteur) has equally grand doubles for 360-590FF. The hotel is closed from mid-October to mid-April.

Nearby, *Hôtel des Arts* (☎ 04 90 92 08 50, 30 blvd Victor Hugo) has good-value singles/doubles, above its popular Café des Arts, for 200/240FF.

The charming, pool-equipped *Hôtel Ville Verte* (☎ 04 90 92 06 14, fax 04 90 92 56 54, place de la République) has 37 two-star rooms. Doubles with shower/shower and toilet are 190/225FF and self-catering studios start from 1500/1800FF a week in the low/high season. Equally good value is *Hôtel Cheval Blanc* (☎ 04 90 92 09 28, fax 04 90 92 69 05, 6 ave Fauconnet). The large, green-shuttered building has 22 rooms costing 230/260FF for a single/double. The White Horse is closed from mid-November to mid-December.

Out of town is *Mas de Cornud* (☎ 04 90 92 39 32, fax 04 90 92 55 99, mascornud@compuserve.com, route de Mas Blanc) which has six rooms for two costing 720-1600FF a night (including breakfast). The farmhouse has its own cookery school.

Places to Eat

Crêperie Lou Planet (place Favier) is a pleasant spot to sit in the sun and munch on a sweet or savoury crêpe after museum visiting or old town strolling. Highly recommended for local cuisine in an old-worldly Provençal setting is *L'Assiette de Marie* (☎ 04 90 92 32 14, 1 rue Jaume Roux). The cluttered, old fashioned bistro has a 135FF lunch *menu* and an evening one for 179FF. Advance bookings are recommended. Around the corner, self-caterers can enjoy a hearty selection of Marie's treats at *L'Épicerie de Marie (1 place Isdores Gilles)*.

Getting There & Away

Buses to Tarascon and Nîmes operated by Cévennes Cars (☎ 04 66 29 27 29) depart from the bus stop on place de la République. Avignon-bound buses run by Sociétés Rapides du Sud Est (☎ 04 90 14 59

AVIGNON AREA

00) leave from in front of the École de la République on blvd Victor Hugo.

LES BAUX DE PROVENCE

• pop 468   ⊠ 13520   alt 185m

Some 10km south of Saint-Rémy-de-Provence is Les Baux de Provence – a perched village which takes its name from bauxite, the chief ore of aluminium first mined in the village in 1822. In Provençal *baou* means 'rocky spur'.

The most pleasant time to visit the Château des Baux (☎ 04 90 54 55 56), a former feudal home of Monaco's Grimaldi royal family, is early evening after the caterpillar of tourist coaches has evacuated the village for the day. The castle affords fine views of the surrounding **Chaîne des Alpilles** mountain range. Opening hours are 7 am to 7.30 pm; 8.30 pm in July and August (35/27FF for adult/student).

A dramatic portrait of Provence is projected on 3000 sq metres of rock at the **Cathédrale d'Images** (☎ 04 90 54 38 65, catimage@worldnet.fr), at the northern foot of Les Baux. The museum is in a redundant quarry and screens 2800 different images during its 30 minute sound and light show. The Image Cathedral is open from 10 am to 7 pm; until 6 pm in winter (43/38FF for adult/student).

Les Baux tourist office (☎ 04 90 54 34 39, fax 04 90 54 51 51) has information on Les Baux' limited (and expensive) accommodation options.

LES ALPILLES

The rocky limestone Alpilles, which sprawl between Saint Rémy and Les Baux from north to south, are wild, barren, carpeted with Provence's aromatic herbal *garrigue* in parts – and studded with century-old mills.

Maussane-les-Alpilles

• pop 1880   ⊠ 13520

Maussane-les-Alpilles, 3km south of Les Baux de Provence on the Alpilles southern fringe, shelters one of Provence's most renowned *moulins d'huile* (oil mills) where freshly harvested olives are pummelled and

pressed into smooth, golden olive oil. You cannot tour the mills here, but you can buy olive oil.

The **Coopérative Oléicole de la Vallée des Baux** (☎ 04 90 54 32 37 or 04 90 54 38 12) was established in 1924. It is housed in a 17th century mill and is sometimes called Moulin Oléicole or Moulin Jean Marie Cornille after the original mill owner. Its fine olive oil – just 120,000 litres of which are produced each year – costs 110FF a litre. Depending on the year's harvest, it often sells out by mid-August. New stock goes on sale from 15 December. From the village centre, bear north along ave Jean Marie Cornille. The mill is open from 8 am to noon and 2 to 6 pm (closed on weekends).

The **Moulin du Mas des Barres** (☎ 04 90 54 44 32), on the eastern edge of the village (signposted off the D78 which runs through the village), is another mill which sells oil. Complete the day – as Peter Mayle did in *A Year in Provence* – with lunch at *Le Bistrot du Paradou* (see boxed text The Mayle Trail in the Lubéron chapter) in neighbouring **Paradou**, 3km west along the D78.

Fontvieille

• pop 3640   ⊠ 13990

Sleepy Fontvieille, 10km west of Maussane-les-Alpilles along the D17, is famed for its windmill immortalised by Alphonse Daudet in his collection of short stories *Lettres de mon Moulin* (Letters from my Windmill), published in 1869. Despite the French author being born in Nîmes and spending most of his life in Paris, he shared a strong spiritual affinity with Provence and is regarded as a Provençal writer.

Contrary to popular belief, the *moulin de Daudet* (Daudet's windmill) dating from 1814 which houses the **Musée de Daudet** is not the windmill where the writer spent hours sunk deep in literary thought. The view from here extends across the Alpilles plain and as far south as the majestic **Abbaye de Montmajour**, 7km south-west and the restored chateaux of Tarascon and Beaucaire.

From the windmill-museum, a trail (signposted *sur les traces de Daudet*) leads past ruined **Moulin Ramet** to **Moulin Tissot** – Daudet's true haunt, defunct since 1905. The trail continues to **Château de Monfaubon** (☎ 04 90 54 75 12) – home to Daudet cousins with whom he stayed when in town. It hosts local history exhibitions and art shows. Admission to the Musée de Daudet and chateau is 10/5FF for adult/child.

In town, Fontvieille tourist office (☎ 04 90 54 67 49, fax 04 90 54 69 82), 5 rue Marcel Honorat, is open from 9 am to noon and 2 to 6.30 pm (closed on Sunday).

TARASCON & BEAUCAIRE

The mighty chateaux of right-bank Tarascon (pop 10,800) and left-bank Beaucaire (pop 13,400) stare at each other across the murky grey waters of the Rhône. Tarascon was immortalised by Daudet in his *Tartarin de Tarascon* stories. Each year during June's Fête de la Tarasque, a Chinese-style dragon parades through town to celebrate Saint Martha's slaying of Tarasque, a dragon that lurked in the Rhône according to Provençal legend.

Louis II had the **Château de Tarascon** (☎ 04 90 91 01 93) built in the 15th century to defend Provence's political frontier marked by the Rhône. The interior was richly decorated under King René, but later stripped and used as a mint, then, from the 18th century until 1926, as a prison. Inmates' wall scratchings are still evident in the king's salon: 'here is 3 Davids in a mess/prisoners we are in distress/by the French we was caught/and to this prison we was brought/taken in the xephyr strop of war (1778)'. The fortress is open from 9 am to noon and 2 to 5 pm; 9 am to 7 pm from April to September (32/21FF for adult/student).

The partly restored ruins of the 11th century **Château de Beaucaire** serve only as a setting for a falconry display (☎ 04 66 59 26 72); afternoon shows are held from mid-March to November. The rest of the year the castle grounds are inaccessible.

According to legend, shabby and dusty Beaucaire was also plagued by a dragon, Drac de Beaucaire, who slept in the Rhône but prowled the streets of Beaucaire by day disguised as a man. One day he snatched a washerwoman and took her back to his filthy hole where she tended Drac's baby son, Le Draconnet, for seven years. Years after her release, she spotted Drac in Beaucaire. Upon greeting him, Drac was so horrified to have his disguise blown that he poked out the woman's eyes. A sculpture of him can be seen on place de la République.

Accommodation in both towns is limited. Beaucaire tourist office (☎ 04 66 59 26 57, fax 04 44 59 68 51), 24 cours Gambetta, and its counterpart in Tarascon (☎ 04 90 91 03 52, fax 04 90 91 22 96), 59 rue des Halles, has details. *Camping Tartarin* (☎ 04 90 91 01 46, route de Vallebrègues), next to Château de Tarascon, charges 20/18FF per person/tent. The ground is open from April to October.

NÎMES

• **pop 133,000**   ✉ **30000**

Lazy, laid-back Nîmes, a little bit Provençal (Avignon is only 44km to the north-east) but with a soul as Languedocien as *cassoulet*, is graced by some of the best preserved Roman public buildings in Europe. Founded by Augustus, Roman Colonia Nemausensis reached its zenith during the 2nd century AD, receiving its water supply from a Roman aqueduct system that included the Pont du Gard, an awesome arched bridge 23km north-east. The sacking of the city by the Vandals in the early 5th century began a downward spiral from which Nîmes has never recovered.

The city is also known for its contemporary architectural creations, notably its Carrée d'Art. Nîmes' *armoires* (coat of arms), featuring a palm tree and a crocodile, was redesigned by Philippe Starck (1949-) in 1987. The French designer, best known for his furniture creations, went on to design an *abribus* – Provence's most attractive bus stop – on ave Carnot. Fountain-clad place d'Assas is the creation of new realist painter Martial Raysse, who designed the water-splashed square in 1989.

Nîmes becomes more Spanish than French during its *férias*, the city's bull-fighting festivals. The surrounding countryside is composed of vineyards and *garrigue* whose herbal vegetation gives off a powerful fragrance in spring and early summer.

Orientation

Everything, including traffic, revolves around the Arènes. Just north of the amphitheatre, the fan-shaped, largely pedestrianised old city is bounded by blvd Victor Hugo, blvd Amiral Courbet and blvd Gambetta. The main squares are place de la Maison Carrée, place du Marché and place aux Herbes. Just north of place aux Herbes lies the carefully preserved Îlot Littré, the old dyers' quarter where denim de Nîmes (see boxed text) was fabricated in the 18th century.

South-east of the Arènes is the esplanade Charles de Gaulle, a large open square, from where ave Feuchères leads south to the train and bus stations.

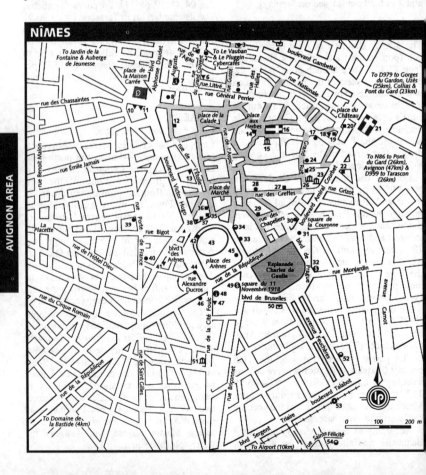

NÎMES

AVIGNON AREA

Information

Tourist Offices The main tourist office
(☎ 04 66 67 29 11, fax 04 66 21 81 04;
tourisme_nimes@compuserve.com; www
.nimes.mnet.fr), 6 rue Auguste, is open
from November to March from 8.30 am to
7 pm (closed on weekends). Summer hours
are 8 am to 7 pm (8 pm in July and August),
Saturday from 9 am to 7 pm, Sunday from
10 am to 6 pm.

The tourist office annexe (☎ 04 66 84 18
13), inside the train station, is open from 9.30
am to 12.30 pm and 2 to 6 pm (Sunday from
10 am to 3 pm; closed on weekends in winter).

Money Banque de France is on square du
11 Novembre 1918. Blvd Victor Hugo and
blvd Amiral Courbet are lined with commercial banks.

Mondial Change (☎ 04 66 21 93 94), 5
blvd de Prague, is open from 9 am to 7 pm
year round.

Post The post office, 1 blvd de Bruxelles,
is open from 8 am to 7 pm (Saturday until
noon; closed Sunday).

Email & Internet Access Nîmes sports
two cybercafés. Le Vauban (☎ 04 66 76 09
71; levauban@mnet.fr), 34ter rue Cléris-
seau, charges 30/50FF and is open from
8.30 am to 8 pm. Continue north from rue
du Grand Couvent for two blocks. Le
Pluggin (☎ 04 66 21 49 51; info@lepluggin
.com; www.lepluggin.com), 17 rue Porte
d'Alés, charges the same rates and is open
from 11 to 1 am (closed Sunday).

Laundry There are laundrettes at 20 rue de
l'Agau, 26 rue Porte de France and 14 rue
Nationale. Hours are 7 am to 9 pm.

Arènes

This superb Roman amphitheatre (☎ 04 66
76 72 77), reminiscent of the Colosseum in
Rome, was built around 100 AD on place des
Arènes to seat 24,000 spectators. It is better
preserved than any other such structure in
France, even retaining its upper storey –
unlike its Arles counterpart. The interior has
four tiers of seats and a system of exits and
passages designed so patricians attending the

AVIGNON AREA

NÎMES

	PLACES TO STAY		OTHER		
12	Hôtel de la Maison Carrée	2	Laundrette	28	Hôtel de Ville
19	Hôtel Temple	3	La Coupole des Halles	30	Prisunic (Supermarket)
20	Hôtel Central		(Shopping Centre)	31	TCN Bus Kiosk
22	Cat Hôtel		& FNAC	32	Mondial Change
25	Hôtel Dauphiné	4	Post Office	33	Palais de Justice
27	Hôtel La Mairie	5	Les Halles	34	Airport Buses
29	Hôtel Concorde	7	Main Tourist Office	39	Laundrette
35	Hôtel Le Lisita	8	Maison Carrée	40	Le Sémaphore
36	Hôtel Amphithéâtre	9	Carrée d'Art		Cinema
37	Hôtel Le France		& Musée d'Art	42	Boutique des Arènes
			Contrmporain	43	Arènes
	PLACES TO EAT	14	Cafés Nadal	44	Bureau de Locations
1	Loir dans la Théière	15	Musée du Vieux Nîmes		des Arènes
6	Côte Bleue	16	Cathédrale de	45	Matador Statue
10	Le Portofino Brasserie		Saint Castor	46	Europcar
	Italienne	17	Le Pétrin	48	Maison du Tourisme
11	L'Assiette		(Boulangerie)	49	Banque de France
13	Lakayna	21	Église Saint Baudille	50	Post Office
18	Le Menestrel	23	Musées d'Archéologie &	51	Musée des
38	Grand Café de la Bourse		d'Histoire Naturelle		Beaux-Arts
41	Les Olivades & Vinothéque	24	Boulangerie	52	TCN Bus Stops
47	Chez Edgar	26	Musée de Nîmes	53	Train Station
				54	Bus Station

Denim de Nîmes

During the 18th century, Nîmes' sizeable Protestant middle class, barred from government posts and various ways of earning a living, turned its energies to trade and manufacturing. Among the products made in Protestant-owned factories was a twilled fabric known as *serge*. The soft but durable fabric became very popular among workers and, stained blue, was the 'uniform' of the fishermen of Genoa.

When Levi Strauss (1829-1902), a Bavarian-Jewish immigrant to the USA, began producing trousers in California during and after the gold rush of 1849, he soon realised that miners needed garments that would last. After trying tent canvas, he began importing the *serge de Nîmes*, now better known as 'denim'.

animal and gladiator combats never had to rub shoulders with the plebeians.

Throughout the year the Arènes, which is covered by a high-tech removable roof from October to April, is used for theatre performances, music concerts and bullfights. Unless there's something on, it's open from 9 am to 12.30 pm and 2 to 6 pm; 9 am to 6.30 pm in summer (26/20FF for adult/student). Tickets, available until 30 minutes before it closes, are sold at the Boutique des Arènes (☎ 04 66 67 29 11), tucked in the amphitheatre's northern walls.

Maison Carrée

The rectangular, Greek-style temple known as the Maison Carrée (Square House; ☎ 04 66 36 26 76), place de la Maison Carrée, is one of the world's most remarkably preserved Roman temples. Built around 5 AD to honour Augustus' two nephews, it survived the centuries as a meeting hall (during the Middle Ages), a private residence, a stable (in the 17th century), a church and, after the Revolution, an archive.

The Maison Carrée, entered through six symmetrical Corinthian columns, sits at the end of rue Auguste. It is open from 9 am to noon or 12.30 pm and from 2.30 to 7 pm; until 6 pm in winter (free).

The striking glass and steel building to the west across the square completed in 1993 is the modern **Carrée d'Art** (Square of Art; ☎ 04 66 76 35 77, www.mns.fr/carreat), which contains the municipal library and Musée d'Art Contemporain (see Museums). It is the work of British architect Sir Norman Foster, who designed the seminal Hong Kong Bank building in Hong Kong. It perfectly reflects the Maison Carrée and is everything modern architecture should be: innovative, complementary and beautiful.

Jardin de la Fontaine

The Fountain Garden, home to Nîmes' other important Roman monuments, is laid out around the Source de la Fontaine (the site of a spring, temple and baths in Roman times). It retains an elegant air, with statue-adorned paths running around deep, slimy-green waterways. The **Temple de Diane** is to the left through the main entrance.

A 10 minute walk through the gardens takes you to the crumbly shell of the **Tour Magne** (☎ 04 66 67 65 56), the largest of the many towers that once ran along the city's 7km Roman ramparts. The tower is open from 9 am to 7 pm; until 5 pm in winter (12/10FF for adult/student). A combination ticket allowing entry to the Arènes as well costs 32/26FF.

The garden is almost 1km north-west of the amphitheatre. Bus No 2 from ave Feuchères or the esplanade Charles de Gaulle stops near the main entrance at the intersection of ave Jean Jaurès and quai de la Fontaine, the city's classiest thoroughfare. The grounds close at sunset.

Museums
Museums are open daily from 11 am to 6 pm (closed Monday) and each charge 26/20FF for adult/student. Museum buffs should buy a three day pass (60/30FF) from the tourist office which allows entry to most sights.

The **Musée du Vieux Nîmes** (☎ 04 66 36 00 64) is housed in the 17th century episcopal palace, south of the unimpressive **Cathédrale de Saint Castor** on place aux Herbes. Themes change annually but the emphasis is usually on Nîmes' history. The fusty **Musée de Nîmes** (☎ 04 66 67 39 14), 19 Grande Rue, hosts uninspiring temporary exhibitions.

The **Musée d'Archéologie** (☎ 04 66 67 25 57), 13 blvd Amiral Courbet, brings together columns, mosaics, sculptures and personal effects from the Roman and pre-Roman periods that have been unearthed around Nîmes. In the same building, the **Musée d'Histoire Naturelle** has a musty collection of stuffed animals and rows of bulls' horns.

The **Musée des Beaux-Arts** (☎ 04 66 67 38 21), on rue de la Cité Foulc between Nos 20 and 22, has an unsurprising collection of Flemish, Italian and French works and a Roman mosaic.

The ultra-modern **Musée d'Art Contemporain** (☎ 04 66 76 35 70) in the Carrée d'Art (see earlier) has rotating exhibits of modern art. It's worth a visit just to see the insides of this striking building and the view of the Roman temple across the square. It opens at 10 am (28/20FF).

Special Events
In March, Nîmes hosts a week-long Printemps du Jazz (Spring Jazz) festival. July and August bring forth an abundance of dances, theatre, rock, pop and jazz events. A yearly calendar is available at the tourist office.

Férias & Bullfights The three férias – the three-day Féria Primavera (Spring Festival) in February, the five-day Féria de Pentecôte (Pentecost Festival) in June, and the three-day Féria des Vendanges to mark the start of the grape harvest on the third weekend in September – revolve around a series of *corridas* (bullfights), one or two of which are held on each of the days. Tickets to a corrida cost 100-500FF; reservations have to be made months in advance through the Bureau de locations des Arènes (☎ 04 66 67 28 02), on the south-west side of the Arènes at 1 rue Alexandre Ducros. The bureau is open from 10 am to 12.30 pm and from 3 to 6.30 pm (without a break during férias). It accepts telephone bookings.

Courses Camarguaises (see the boxed text Bulls & Cowboys in the Camargue chapter) are held on the weekend before a féria and at other times during the bullfighting season. Tickets cost 50-100FF. The best bulls are rewarded with a couple of bars from the opera *Carmen* as they leave the arena.

Places to Stay – Budget
Camping *Domaine de la Bastide* (☎ 04 66 38 09 21, route de Générac) is about 4km south of town on the D13 heading toward Générac. Two people with tent pay about 60FF. From the train station, take bus No 1 in the Caremeau direction. At the Jean Jaurès stop, change to bus D and get off at La Bastide stop.

Hostel The *Auberge de Jeunesse* (☎ 04 66 23 25 04, fax 04 66 23 84 27, chemin de la Cigale) is 3.5km north-west of the train station. A bed is 47FF and sheets/breakfast is an extra 17/19FF. From the train station, take bus No 2 in the Alès or Villeverte direction and get off at the Stade stop.

Gîtes The *Gîtes de France* office (☎ *04 66 27 94 94, fax 04 66 27 94 95, place des Arènes)*, inside the Maison du Tourisme, arranges rural accommodation as well as B&B in town.

Hotels Nîmes has plenty of cheap, decent hotels, many conveniently situated in the old city.

For supposedly excellent views of the Arènes (if the wooden shutters covering the windows open), try *Hôtel Le France (☎ 04 66 67 23 05, fax 04 66 67 76 93, 4 blvd des Arènes)*. It has an assortment of dreary rooms and a pricing policy not unlike that used by the Romans at the amphitheatre: the higher up you go, the cheaper the room gets. Fourth-floor (no lift) singles with washbasin start at 120FF, 3rd-floor singles/doubles with shower at 140FF, and triples with bath at 250FF. Between September and Easter the hotel reception is closed from 3 to 6.30 pm. Next door at No 2, *Hôtel Le Lisita (☎ 04 66 67 66 20, fax 04 66 76 22 30)* is a bit cheaper, with singles/doubles with shower from 100/180FF.

The *Hôtel Concorde (☎ 04 66 67 91 03, 3 rue des Chapeliers)* has small but adequate singles/doubles from 110/115FF and ones with shower for 135/140FF.

The friendly *Hôtel de la Maison Carrée (☎ 04 66 67 32 89, fax 04 66 76 22 57, 14 rue de la Maison Carrée)* has poky rooms, most with shower, toilet and TV. Singles with washbasin start around 115FF; singles/doubles with shower are 125/180FF, triples/quads 270/330FF. Two-star *Hôtel La Mairie (☎ 04 66 67 65 91, 11 rue des Greffes)* has doubles with washbasin/ shower from 115/150FF. Triples/quads with shower cost 220/240FF.

Just south of the Église Saint Baudille is a cluster of bargain basements. Sparse *Hôtel Temple (☎ 04 66 67 54 61, fax 04 66 36 04 36, 1 rue Charles Dabut)* has singles/ doubles/quads with shower for 160/200/ 300FF. Equally sterile is the *Cat Hôtel*

(☎ 04 66 67 22 88, fax 04 66 21 57 51, 22 blvd Amiral Courbet), which has unrefined singles with toilet for 135FF and doubles with shower for 159FF. The most comical of the bunch is *Hôtel Dauphiné (12 Grande Rue)*, where old men cluster permanently in the reception playing cards. Rock-bottom rooms with no mod-cons cost 110/120FF for one/two people.

Places to Stay – Mid-Range

Just up from its namesake, the 17 room *Hôtel Amphithéâtre (☎ 04 66 67 28 51, fax 04 66 67 07 79, 4 rue des Arènes)* is one of the loveliest options. Rooms have eclectic furnishings, and most have a shower and toilet. Singles/doubles/triples start at 170/ 170/290FF.

Equally colourful is *Hôtel Central (☎ 04 66 67 27 75, fax 04 66 21 77 79, 2 place du Château)* which has creaky floorboards and wild flowers painted on the bedroom doors. Singles/doubles/triples with bath and TV are 210/230/250FF.

Places to Eat
Restaurants Just west of place des Arènes is packed *Les Olivades (☎ 04 66 21 71 78, 18 rue Jean Reboul)* which specialises in local wines. It has *menus* for 85 and 120FF.

Across rue de la République at 3 rue de la Cité Foulc, *Chez Edgar* has excellent regional *menus* from 86FF, a nippy express *menu* for 60FF, and a 36FF one for kids.

Le Portofino Brasserie Italienne (☎ 04 66 36 16 14, 3 rue Corneille) and *L'Assiette (☎ 04 66 21 03 03)*, next door, offer startling views of the Carrée d'Art. The Portofino serves good homemade pasta dishes; the carbonara topped with a raw egg (45FF) is particularly tasty. More upmarket The Plate has a lunch *menu* for 60FF.

Tucked close to Église Saint Baudille is *Le Menestrel (☎ 04 66 67 54 45, 6 rue le Bavarois Nîmois)*. The Minstrel conjures up *menus* for 60, 75 and 110FF (closed all day Sunday and Monday lunch).

Small and blue is *Côte Bleue* on the corner of rue Littré and rue du Grand Couvent. The Blue Coast serves local dishes inside and outside on a straw-covered terrace.

Lakayna (☎ *04 66 21 10 96, 18 rue de l'Étoile)* is an attractive North African cellar restaurant which has couscous and tangines prepared in the manner of the Kabyles of eastern Algeria. An overly generous couscous royal – one of 13 couscous variations – is 130FF.

Cafés Place aux Herbes is one big outside café in summer. Equally bustling with the clink of coffee cups beneath its huge palm tree is place du Marché. Young bohemians snub both. They hang out in the cafés around Maison Carrée, place de la Maison Carrée.

Aptly named is the minuscule *Loir dans la Théière* (☎ *04 66 67 23 07, 29 rue du Grand Couvent)*, an alternative *salon de thé* (tea salon) decorated in primary colours and serving a mouthwatering array of sweet and savoury crêpes. The Dormouse in the Teapot is closed Sunday.

Ideal for breakfast or a quick coffee inside or out is the *Grand Café de la Bourse* (☎ *04 66 67 21 91, 2 blvd des Arènes)*, opposite the Arènes ticket booth.

Self-Catering Nîmes plays host to colourful *street markets* in the old city on Thursday in July and August. *Les Halles*, the covered food market between rue Guizot and rue des Halles, is open daily until midday. There is a *Prisunic* supermarket at the south end of blvd Admiral Courbet.

For bread shaped like a bull's head shop at the *boulangerie* on Grande Rue. Traditional breads are also sold at *Le Pétrin* on rue de la Curaterie.

Local herbs, oils and spices are sold at the quaint *Cafés Nadal* overlooking place aux Herbes at 4 rue Marchands. Local wines sold by knowledgeable staff can be found at the *Vinothéque* adjoining Les Olivades (see Restaurants).

Getting There & Away
Air Aéroport de Nîmes-Arles-Camargue, also called Aéroport Garons (☎ 04 66 70 49 49) is 10km south-east of the city on the A54 to Arles.

Bus The bus station is behind the train station on rue Sainte Félicité. The information booths for regional operators like STD Gard (☎ 04 66 84 96 86), Cariane (☎ 04 66 38 13 98), Rapides de Camargue (☎ 04 66 29 52 57) and Cars de Camargue (☎ 04 90 96 36 25 in Arles) are at one end of the terminal, while Eurolines and Intercars are at the other. The general bus information counter (☎ 04 66 29 52 00) is open from 8 am to noon and 2 to 6 pm (closed on weekends).

Destinations served include five buses a day to Pont du Gard (32FF; 35 minutes), Avignon (41FF; 1¼ hours) and Arles (31FF; one hour). STD Gard organises day excursions to Nice, Menton and other coastal destinations in summer.

Train The train station is at the south-eastern end of ave Feuchères. The information office is open from 8 am to 6.30 pm (closed Sunday). Left luggage is open from 8 am to 8 pm.

Major destinations include Paris' Gare de Lyon by TGV (328FF; five hours), Arles (61FF; 30 minutes; nine a day), Avignon (65FF; 30 minutes; 15 a day) and Marseille (114FF; 1¼ hours; 12 a day). Some SNCF buses and trains head to Aigues-Mortes (39FF; one hour) in the Camargue.

Getting Around
To/From the Airport Airport buses (☎ 04 66 67 94 77) depart from the bus station four times daily to coincide with flights. En route, the bus (28FF; 30 minutes) stops at blvd des Arènes and blvd de Prague near the esplanade Charles de Gaulle, and blvd Gambetta.

Taxi Taxis hover around the esplanade Charles de Gaulle. To order one call ☎ 04 66 29 40 11.

Bicycle The Auberge de Jeunesse (see Places to Stay earlier) rents mountain bikes for 50FF a day.

MC Cycles (☎ 04 66 04 02 54), 116 blvd Sergent Triaire, charges 100/150FF a day/weekend, plus deposit.

PONT DU GARD

The exceptionally well preserved, three-tiered Roman aqueduct known as the Pont du Gard – photographs of which invariably appear in textbooks on western European history – was once part of a 50km system of canals which were built around 19 BC by Agrippa, Augustus' powerful deputy and son-in-law, to bring water from near Uzès in Languedoc to Nîmes. The 35 small arches of the 275m upper tier of the pont, 49m above the Gard River, contain a 1.2m by 1.75m watercourse that was designed to carry 20,000 cubic metres of water a day. The Romans built the aqueduct with stone from the nearby Vers quarry. The largest boulders weigh over five tonnes.

From car parks either side of the river, you can walk along the road bridge, built in 1743 alongside the top of the aqueduct's lower tier on the Gard's upstream side. Once extensive renovations (280 cubic metres of stone are to be replaced) are completed in the year 2000, visitors will be able to amble along the aqueduct's middle and (maybe) top tier too. The best view of the Pont du Gard is from the hill on the northern side (left bank) about 200m from the aqueduct (signposted 'Panorama'). On hot days you can swim in the river. The Pont du Gard – the fifth most-visited site in France – is frequented by two million people a year (averaging a horrendous 5000-plus visitors a day).

Information

The Maison de Tourisme (☎ 04 66 37 00 02) near the aqueduct on the southern side (right bank) is open from June to September from 9 am to 7 pm.

Plans for 1999 and 2000 include building a massive new tourist centre on the site of the present car park on the north side (left bank) of the river. A new car park will be built farther away (but still within walking distance) of the aqueduct.

Made by a Woman

It comes as no surprise to learn that the creation of the Pont du Gard was the doing of a woman.

Curious villagers, keen to cross the Gard river to lands unexplored, asked a stonemason to build them a bridge. So day upon day, week upon week, the village stonemason struggled in vain. With each stone laid, the ferocious Gard rose, snarled and smashed his stones to smithereens.

The day came when, out of sheer desperation, the mason struck a bargain with the devil: a bridge for eternity in exchange for a life. Shaking with fear, the sorrowful mason returned home to tell his wife the sad news.

At dawn the next day a magnificent bridge rose shimmering in the sunlight. The devil stood waiting. As the stone arches trembled with footsteps, he opened in his mouth to snap up his prey. SNAP!

It was a quivering hare who'd crossed the bridge first, courtesy of the stonemason's clever wife.

Canoeing

The beautiful and wild Gard River which descends from the Cévennes mountains, flows through the hills in a long gorge, passing under the Pont du Gard. You can hire canoes to paddle around beneath the aqueduct from Kayak Vert Gardon (☎ 04 66 22 84 83 or 04 66 22 80 76, fax 04 66 22 88 78) and Canoë Le Tourbillon (☎ 04 66 22 85 54), both based in the neighbouring village of **Collias**, 6km upstream, under the town's single bridge.

You can paddle from Collias to the Pont du Gard with a group in half a day (175/100FF for a canoe/kayak for two) or arrange to be dropped off 22km upstream at Russan, from where there's a great descent back. The latter is a full day trip and is usually available between March and May only. Canoes/kayaks rent for 50/35FF an hour and 145/90FF a day.

The region is known for its unpredictable weather. Torrential rains can rapidly raise the water level by 2-5 metres. In contrast, during long dry spells, the Gard can virtually disappear.

Places to Stay

There are a couple of camping grounds near Pont du Gard, including two-star **Camping International** (☎ 04 66 22 81 81, chemin Barque Vieille), 2km from the aqueduct's northern side. The tariff is around 65FF for two people with a tent. It's open from mid-March to mid-October. On the southern side (right bank), **Camping Municipal La Sousta** (ave du Pont du Gard), a five minute walk from the aqueduct, charges 64FF for two people with tent.

Near the car park on the northern side, **Le Vieux Moulin** (☎ 04 66 37 14 35, fax 04 66 37 26 48), an attractive inn with truly splendid views of the Pont du Gard, has rooms for one or two people with washbasin and bidet for 205FF, or with toilet and shower/bath for 310/460FF. It is open from mid-March to early November.

Getting There & Away

The Pont du Gard is 23km north-east of Nîmes and 26km west of Avignon. Buses from Avignon and Nîmes stop 1km north of the bridge. To get to Collias (33.50FF; one hour) take bus No 168 (two daily) from Nîmes' bus station – or hitch.

Motorists have to pay 22/17FF to park in one of the extensive car parks on the north/south side of the river.

The Lubéron

The Lubéron hills stretch from Cavaillon in the west to Manosque in the east, and from Apt southward to the Durance River and the Romanesque Abbaye de Silvacane. The area is named after the main range, a compact massif with the gentle, 1125m summit of Mourre Nègre. Its oak-covered northern face is steep and uneven, while its southern face is drier and more Mediterranean in both climate and flora. Fruit orchards and vineyards carpet the lower slopes. The Combe de Lourmarin divides the Petit Lubéron in the west with the Grand Lubéron in the east. The entire region is criss-crossed with great hiking trails and is an excellent region for bicycling.

Much of the Lubéron is protected by the Parc Naturel Régional du Lubéron. The 1200 sq km regional park created in 1977 encompasses 67 villages, desolate forests (some of them recently scarred by fire), unexpected gorges and abandoned *mas* (farmhouses) falling into ruin – or perhaps being restored by fans of Peter Mayle whose purchase and renovation of a traditional Provençal mas just outside the pretty village of Ménerbes in the late 1980s formed the basis of his witty, bestselling book *A Year in Provence*. Tourism in the region has not looked back since.

The Lubéron is greener, less densely populated and extremely affluent compared to the rest of the Vaucluse department of which it is a part. Unlike Haute-Provence, most of its lower lying land is farmed, forming a rich manicured patchwork of vineyards, olive groves and fruit farms as toy-like (and lucrative) as the perfectly-restored, golden-stone mas. The northern part of the region around Apt is dotted with *bories*, archaic dry stone huts.

APT

- **pop 11,500** ✉ **84400** alt 250m

Apt, an excellent base for exploring the Lubéron, is largely unexceptional beyond its grapes, cherries and *fleurions* (candied

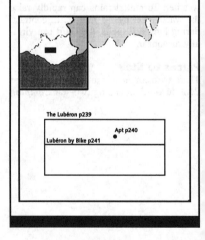

The Lubéron p239

Apt p240

Lubéron by Bike p241

or crystallised fruits), which are well worth a nibble. The town celebrates a Fête de la Cerise (Cherry Festival) in May.

Ticket details for the annual Festival de Jazz en Pays d'Apt (☎ 04 90 75 54 27, www.luberon.net/kiosk.html) are available at the Point Jazz du Festival, Bureau du Groupement Commercial, place de la Bouquerie.

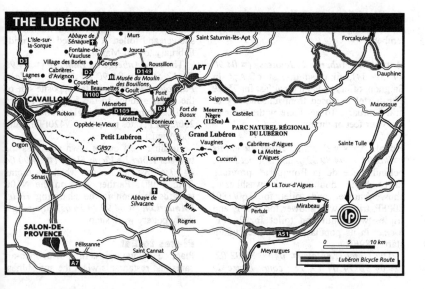

THE LUBÉRON

Orientation & Information

Tourist Office As you enter Apt from Cavaillon, the tourist office (☎ 04 90 74 03 18, fax 04 90 04 64 30, tourisme.apt@ avignon.pacwan.net) is just over the bridge at 20 ave Philippe de Girard, overlooking place de la Bouquerie. It's open from 9 am to noon and 2 to 6 pm (closed Sunday). In July and August hours are until 7 pm and on Sunday from 9 am to noon.

Park Office Information on the Parc Naturel Régional du Lubéron, including details about the park's two dozen *gîtes d'étape*, is available from the Maison du Parc (☎ 04 90 04 42 00, fax 04 90 04 81 15, pnr@wanadoo.fr), 60 place Jean Jaurès. The centre has information on hiking and cycling in the park too, and sells an excellent range of guides including the recommended topoguide *Le Parc naturel régional du Lubéron à pied* (75FF), which details 24 hikes including the GR9, GR92 and GR97 trails (available in English too). It also houses a **Musée de Paléontologie** (Palaeontology Museum) which focuses on

prehistoric history, flora and fauna. The centre is open from 8.30 am to noon and 1.30 to 7 pm (closed Sunday; open until 6 pm from October to March).

Maps are available from the bookshop at 16 rue des Marchands, the Librairie l'Héliotrope at 13 rue Saint Pierre, or the Maison de la Presse, 28 rue des Marchands.

Money Commercial banks frame the west side of place de la Bouquerie.

Post The post office, 105 rue Victor Hugo, is open from 9 am to noon and 2 to 7.30 pm (Saturday from 8.30 am to noon; closed Sunday).

Laundry Wash your whites at the laundrette at 63 rue Eugène Brunel.

Places to Stay

Camping *Camping Municipal Les Cèdres* (☎ 04 90 74 14 61), by the river out of town on route de Rustrel, is open from mid-February to mid-November. It charges 10.70FF per person and 7.70FF for a tent or car. *Camping Le Lubéron* (☎ 04 90 04 85 40, *fax 04 90 74 12 19)*, south-east of Apt on route de Saignon, is open from April to September.

Hostel The *Auberge de Jeunesse (☎ 04 90 74 39 34)*, 6km south-east of Apt in Saignon, offers bed and breakfast for 75FF. The hostel is closed from mid-January to mid-February. To get there without a car, use your feet or thumb.

Hotels Apt's welcoming *Hôtel du Palais (☎/fax 04 90 04 89 32, place Gabriel Péri)*, behind place de la Bouquerie, provides fairly basic doubles with washbasin/shower/shower and toilet for 160/180/200FF, triples with shower for 210FF, and triples with bath and toilet for 260FF. *Menus* in its popular streetside restaurant start at 89FF.

The *Hôtel L'Aptois (☎ 04 90 74 02 02, fax 04 90 74 64 79, 289 cours Lauze de Perret)*, on the eastern edge of town, has doubles from 170/320FF with washbasin/shower and toilet. It is closed from mid-February to mid-March.

The cosy *Auberge du Lubéron (☎ 04 90 74 12 50, fax 04 90 04 79 49, 8 place Faubourg du Ballet)*, on the opposite side of the river, belongs to the Logis de France chain. Comfortable singles/doubles are 250/290FF; rates jump to 290/420FF in July and August.

Heading west out of town you pass the two-star *Hôtel Le Victor Hugo (☎ 04 90 04 74 60, 67 ave Victor Hugo)* which has rooms from 150FF. Farther west on the N100 towards Avignon is the charming *Hôtel l'Aquarium (☎ 04 90 74 16 05)* adjoining a dusty pottery work shop.

Places to Eat
Place de la Bouquerie is filled with open-air cafés and restaurants when the sun shines.

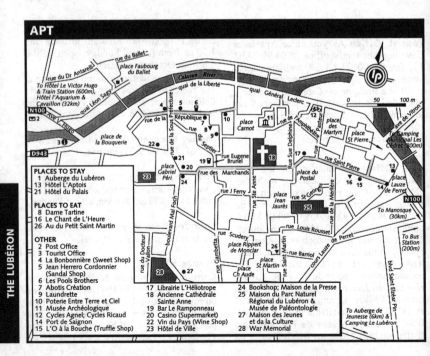

APT

PLACES TO STAY
1 Auberge du Lubéron
13 Hôtel L'Aptois
21 Hôtel du Palais

PLACES TO EAT
8 Dame Tartine
16 Le Chant de L'Heure
26 Au du Petit Saint Martin

OTHER
2 Post Office
3 Tourist Office
4 La Bonbonnière (Sweet Shop)
5 Jean Herrero Cordonnier (Sandal Shop)
6 Les Pools Brothers
7 Abotis Création
9 Laundrette
10 Poterie Entre Terre et Ciel
11 Musée Archéologique
12 Cycles Agnel; Cycles Ricaud
14 Port de Saignon
15 L'O à la Bouche (Truffle Shop)

17 Librairie L'Héliotrope
18 Ancienne Cathédrale Sainte Anne
19 Bar Le Ramponneau
20 Casino (Supermarket)
22 Vin du Pays (Wine Shop)
23 Hôtel de Ville

24 Bookshop; Maison de la Presse
25 Maison du Parc Naturel Régional du Lubéron & Musée de Paléontologie
27 Maison des Jeunes et da la Culture
28 War Memorial

THE LUBÉRON

Lubéron by Bike

Cyclists can cross the Parc Naturel du Lubéron from east to west by following a marked route which stretches for just over 100km. The itinery uses roads which have little traffic, except for fellow cyclists, and pass through many beautiful villages.

Vélo Loisir en Lubéron (☎ 04 92 79 05 82), BP 14, 04280 Céreste, assists cyclists keen to explore the Lubéron. It provides information on accommodation, bicycle rental and technical support to cyclists following the Lubéron cycle route.

White markers signpost the eastbound route from Cavaillon, through Ménerbes (20km), Lacoste (27km) and Bonnieux (31km) – Peter Mayle country – to Apt (42km) and farther on eastward to Forcalquier (100km). En route, cyclists pedal past vineyards and olive groves, lavender fields and fruit farms. Saddle-sore riders can take to the skies at the observatory in Saint Michel l'Observatoire (86km).

Orange-ochre signs mark the westbound route. Colourful information boards along the way provide details on accommodation, places to eat and sights in and around the 19 villages included in the two-wheel itinerary.

The Lubéron can be very hot, so it is important to take plenty of water, a hat, sunglasses and sun screen. There are many cafés with shady terraces on the way, where you can enjoy a refreshing drink.

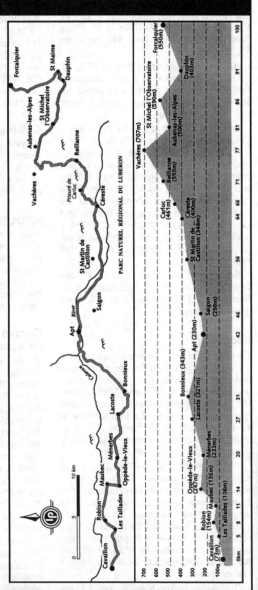

THE LUBÉRON

Rue Saint Pierre is another busy spot with plenty of shops, bars and places to eat. *Le Chant de l'Heure (☎ 04 90 74 08 38, 23 rue Saint Pierre)* is a crêpe place with *menus* for 65, 72 and 88FF.

Au Petit Saint Martin (☎ 04 90 74 10 13, 24 rue Saint Martin) is a cosy restaurant tucked in the back streets with *menus* for 50, 65 and 120FF. A large wooden spoon and fork hang outside.

One of the finest places for lunch in the shade is *Dame Tartine (☎ 04 90 74 27 97, 3 place du Septier)*, a chic but unpretentious *salon de thé* and *saladerie* in a quiet courtyard wrapped around a small fountain. It is open between 10.30 am and 7 pm (closed Sunday and Monday). *Bar Le Ramponneau* on rue Eugene Brunel; and *Les Pools Brothers (☎ 04 90 09 70 95)*, a pool hall almost opposite Abotis Création on rue de la République, are two fun evening spots.

Self-caterers can stock up at the *Casino* supermarket on rue des Marchands, open from 8 am to 12.30 pm and 3.30 to 7.30 pm (closed Sunday).

Shopping

Côtes du Lubéron wine is sold at the rustic Vin du Pays, 70 rue du Docteur Gros, open from 9 am to noon and 3 to 7 pm. Count on paying between 8.50FF and 10FF a litre. For locally-produced candies, fleurions and *miel* (honey), head for La Bonbonnière at 47 rue de la Sous Préfecture. L'O à la Bouche, 98 rue Saint Pierre, sells savoury treats, including truffles in season.

Abotis Création (☎ 06 07 14 62 92), 120 rue de la République, is a funky art gallery which touts all types of contemporary creations, from mirrors and teapots to magnificent wall hangings. Pottery is sold at the equally interesting Poterie entre Terre et Ciel, 144 rue de la République. Jean Herrero Cordonnier (☎ 04 90 74 09 17), 103 rue de la République, sells hand-made leather sandals.

Rue Saint Pierre hosts a *marché aux puces* (flea market) every Tuesday.

Getting There & Away

Bus Buses leave from the bus station (☎ 04 90 74 20 21) east of the centre at 250 ave de la Libération. There are two a day to/from Aix-en-Provence (45FF; 1½ hours), Digne-les-Bains (62FF; two hours), Cavaillon (26.50FF; 40 minutes), Manosque (one hour), Marseille (55FF; 2½ hours); and 3 or 4 a day to Avignon (41FF; 1¼ hours).

Getting Around

Bicycle Hire a mountain bike from Cycles Agnel VTT (☎ 04 90 74 17 16), 86 quai Général Leclerc; or Cycles Ricaud (☎ 04 90 74 16 43), 44 quai Général Leclerc. Rates are 80/400FF a day/week.

AROUND APT

From Apt a good day trip is to head northwest to red-rocked Roussillon, Gordes and the Abbaye de Sénanque – three of Provence's hottest tourist spots – and return via the pretty villages of **Murs** (from where there are marvellous views of the Apt region), **Joucas** and **Saint Saturnin-lès-Apt**.

Gordes

• pop 2000   ✉ 84220   alt 372m

On the white, rocky southern face of the Vaucluse plateau, the tiered village of Gordes, 20km west of Apt on the Lubéron slopes, forms an amphitheatre overlooking the Sorgue and Calavon rivers. The village is crowned by a sturdy château dating from 1025 and rebuilt in 1525. In summer, this once typical Provençal village is frighteningly overrun with tourists, but it's still worth a wander around if you've got the wheels to get you there. Gordes tourist office (☎ 04 90 72 02 75; fax 04 90 72 04 39), in the Salle des Gardes (Guards' Hall), place du Château, is open from 9 am to noon and 2 to 6 pm.

South of Gordes, 3.5km along route de Saint Pantaleon (D148), just west of Saint Pantaleon, is the **Musée du Moulin des Bouillons** (☎ 04 90 72 22 11), a preserved olive oil mill complete with a 10m-long press weighing seven tonnes. A **Musée de** l'Histoire du Verre et du Vitrail (Museum of Glass and Stained Glass) adjoins the mill.

Camping des Sources (☎ 04 90 72 12 48, fax 04 90 72 09 43, route de Murs) is a large ground open from March to October. Nightly rates are 25/31FF per person/tent in July and August (19/24FF the rest of the year). Buses run by Les Express de la Durance (☎ 04 90 71 03 00 in Cavaillon) link Gordes with Cavaillon twice a day except Sunday.

Village des Bories

The walled Village des Bories (☎ 04 90 72 03 48) is 4km south-west of Gordes off the D2 towards Cavaillon. *Bories* are one or two-storey beehive-shaped huts constructed without mortar using thin wedges of limestone. They were first built in the area in the Bronze Age and were continuously lived in, renovated and even built anew until as late as the 18th century. It is not known what purpose they first served but over the centuries they have been used as shelters, workshops, wine cellars and storage sheds. The 'village' contains about 20 such structures, restored to the way they were about 150 years ago. Some say that the bories remind them of Ireland's *clochán*. The site is open to visitors from 9 am to sunset (30/22FF adult/person under 17).

Abbaye de Sénanque

Some 4km north-west of Gordes off the D177 is the Cistercian Abbaye de Sénanque (☎ 04 90 72 05 72) which, in summer, is framed by fields of lilac lavender. The abbey, founded in 1148 and inhabited by five monks today, is open from 10 am to noon and 2 to 6 pm (2 to 5 pm only between November and March). Sunday hours year round are 2 to 6 pm (25/20FF for adult/student). Morning Mass is at 9 am.

Roussillon

- pop 1200   ✉ 84220   alt 360m

Some two millennia ago, the Romans used the distinctive ochre earth around Roussillon, situated in the valley between the Vaucluse plateau and the Lubéron range, for

producing pottery glazes. These days the whole village – even gravestones in the cemetery – is built of reddish local stone, making it a popular place for painters eager to try out the range of their palettes. The red and orange hues are especially striking given the yellow-white bareness of the surrounding area and the green conifers sprinkled around town.

A 1km **Sentier des Ocres** (Sentier trail) begins about 100m north of Roussillon centre and leads you through fairytale groves of chestnuts, maritime pines and scrub to the bizarre and beautiful ochre formations created by erosion and fierce winds over the centuries. It is steep at times, but there are lead ropes to hold on to. Don't wear white; you'll return rust-coloured.

Innovative work shops exploring the colouring properties of ochre, first realised in the 18th century, are held at the **Usine Mathieu** (☎/fax 04 90 05 66 69). Guided tours in English of the Conservatoire des Ocres et Pigments appliqués are available between March and November. The centre is open from 10 am to 7 pm.

Roussillon tourist office (☎/fax 04 90 05 60 25), place de la Poste, is open from 10 am to noon and 2 to 6.30 pm (closed Sunday in winter). It changes money and has a list of hotels, *chambres d'hôtes* and restaurants pinned outside. Roussillon, 9km east of Gordes in the direction of Apt, is inaccessible by public transport. The GR6 hiking trail passes through. Picnic goodies (cold meats etc) are sold in the *Boucherie des Ocres* (*☎ 04 90 05 64 26, place de la Poste*).

LE PETIT LUBÉRON

The rocky landscape of the 'little Lubéron' embraces the western part of the massif and is studded with a maze of *villages perchés*. These villages, perched aloft stony spurs, offer good views of the region's lower lying treasures, like its thick cedar forests.

Côtes du Lubéron vineyards – which cover just 3500 hectares – line the southbound route de Bonnieux (D3) from Apt to Bonnieux; *domaines* (wine producing estates) you pass en route include Château de L'Isolette (☎ 04 90 74 16 70) and the Domaine de Mayol (☎ 04 90 74 14 80) known for its great reds. Lubéron wine has had its own *appellation d'origine contrôlée* (AOC) since 1988.

Bonnieux

• pop 1420   ⊠ 84220   alt 425m

Bonnieux, 11km south-west of Apt and 26km east of Cavaillon, is Le Petit Lubéron's best known perched village. Its **Musée de la Boulangerie** (☎ 04 90 75 88 34) is housed in a century-old bakery and unravels the history of bread. Eighty-six steps lead from place de la Liberté and rue de la Mairie to the **Église Vieille** (old church).

Six kilometres north of the village on the D149 is **Pont Julien**, a three-arched Roman bridge built in the 3rd century BC. Five kilometres north towards Goult (D36) is **La Gare de Bonnieux**, home to the local wine cooperative, the old village train station and a contemporary art gallery (☎ 04 90 75 91 29). The adjoining Café-Restaurant de la Gare (see the boxed text The Mayle Trail) rents bicycles for 70/130FF a half/full day.

From Bonnieux, a route forestière leads south-west to the **Forêt des Cèdres** where a 2½ hour forest trail starts. Guided hikes (35FF) are arranged between July and September by the Office National des Forêts (☎ 04 90 89 32 39 in Avignon). Bonnieux tourist office (☎ 04 90 74 91 90, fax 04 90 75 92 94, www.provenceguide.com), place Carnot, also has details of guided hikes. It has accommodation lists for surrounding villages as well. It is open between April

---

Sadism

The Marquis de Sade (1740-1814) was a sadist, hence the word. His sexually-explicit novels – *120 Journées de Sodome* (120 Days of Sodom; 1785), *Justine* (1791) and *Juliette* (1798) – caused an outrage when published (and banned) in the late 18th century. Equally shocking were the sex scandals surrounding de Sade's own life, 27 years of which were spent in prison.

De Sade lived in Lacoste with his wife and three children from 1771, following his ostracism by Parisian society for accosting and flagellating a woman who consequently took him to court for rape. Although born in Paris, de Sade spent much of his childhood in Provence where his family had owned property, including Château de Lacoste, since 1627. Among the de Sade family members were Hugues de Sade and wife Laura, a radiant beauty and lifelong muse for the Italian poet Petrarch.

The Marquis de Sade wed at the age of 22 but never allowed his marriage to Parisian bourgeoisie, Renée Pélagie de Montreuil, tamper with his love of orgies. While in Lacoste he was brought to trial on charges of sodomy and attempted poison after indulging in a whipping session with four prostitutes and his manservant in Marseille. In between sexual pranks, de Sade doled out aniseed sweets which left all five sick for days.

In 1778 a *lettre de cachet* instigated by his mother-in-law prompted his arrest and eventual imprisonment for 14 years in the Bastille where he started work on *120 Journées de Sodome*. The revolution set him free in 1789, upon which his wife sensibly filed for a separation order. The chateau in Lacoste was stormed and looted by revolutionaries and in 1796, de Sade sold it. Five years later he was back behind bars, this time for his Gothic romance *Justine*, starring two sex-mad sisters who clearly enjoyed more than the odd thrashing.

De Sade spent the last 11 years of his life locked up in a mental asylum where he died, far from mad, aged 74. It was only after WWII with the onset of the surrealist movement that his works were freely published.

and September only, from 10.30 am to 12.30 pm and 2.30 to 6.30 pm.

Places to Stay & Eat *Camping Le Vallon (☎/fax 04 90 75 86 14, route de Ménerbes)* charges 12.50/10/8FF per adult/tent/car. The ground is outside Bonnieux on the westbound D3 to Lacoste.

Bonnieux's cheapest hotel is the six room *Le César (☎/fax 04 90 75 80 18, fax 04 90 75 89 35, place de la Liberté)* which charges 200-500FF for a double with bath. Count on paying around 600FF at least a night in season at the *Hostellerie du Prieuré (☎ 04 90 75 80 78, fax 04 90 75 96 00, rue Jean Baptiste Aurard)*.

A cut above an average village restaurant is *Le Fournil (☎ 04 90 75 83 62)* next to the tourist office on fountain-clad place Carnot. Its interior is cut around a rock face and its exterior around a trickling fountain. Delicious Provençal dishes served with a flourish include *gâteau de tomates aux herbes fraîches* (tomato gateau with fresh herbs) and *thon poêle* (panfried tuna) topped with *sabayon de l'estragon* (a creamy tarragon sauce). *Menus* at The Bakehouse cost 125, 170 or 185FF (children's 55FF). Book in advance (closed Monday).

Lacoste
• pop 400   ✉ 84220   alt 320m

It was to the 9th century **Château de Sade** atop Lacoste, 6.5km west of Bonnieux, that the notorious Marquis de Sade retreated in 1771 when his writings became too scandalous for the Parisians. His 45 room palace cared for by 20 servants is an eerie ruin today. The steep climb is rewarded with unbeatable views of the valley. The village visible from the sunny terrace of the *Café de France* (open 11 am to midnight) is Bonnieux. The adjoining, excellent value hotel (☎ 04 90 75 82 25) has six rooms, starting at 190FF for a double with shared bathroom. A double with shower overlooking the square is 240FF; one with shower and toilet overlooking Bonnieux is 290FF.

Ménerbes
• pop 1120   ✉ 84560   alt 230m

Continue 6km west on the D109 to Ménerbes, a pretty perched village marked on the tourist trail by British novelist Peter Mayle who lived in a *mas*, 2km from the village on the D3 to Bonnieux (second house on the right after the football pitch).

Cork has retained its traditional importance as a stopper for bottles of wine, and over the years corkscrews have been equally important. You can taste the local wine and stare agog at over 1000 different corkscrews at the **Musée Tire Bouchon** (☎ 04 90 72 41 58), in the chateau of the Domaine de la Citadelle at the village's western foot on the D3 to Cavaillon. The museum is the brain child of Yves Rousset-Rouard, village mayor and French MP who resides in the restored chateau at the top of Ménerbes village. In the 1970s he produced films, notably the soft porn *Emmanuelle* (1974).

The museum also houses César's *Compression de Tire-Bouchons*, a block of compressed corkscrews (entry 20/15FF).

La Bouche à Feu (☎ 04 90 72 30 17, rue Klébert Guendon) is an excellent little pizzeria which dishes out giant-sized salads with plenty of local Ménerbien flavour. There are a couple of expensive places to stay on route Beaumettes.

A decorative corkscrew from the Musée Tire Bouchon.

THE LUBÉRON

Oppède-le-Vieux
• pop 1130   ⊠ 84580   alt 300m

Large car parks designated for tourist traffic sit at the foot of Oppède-le-Vieux, 6km south-west of Ménerbes. This medieval village was abandoned in the 1900s by the villagers who moved down the valley to the cultivated plains. A steep rocky path leads to the **ruins** which cling to the hillside. The Romanesque church has been restored; Mass is celebrated here on 10 August (the village patron saint's day) and on Christmas Eve. The new village, Oppède les Poulivets, is 1km north of Oppède-le-Vieux.

Locally milled olive oil is sold at the **Moulin à Huile d'Olives** (☎ 04 90 76 90 66), between the two Oppèdes on route du Four Neuf. Mill tours are available between 15 November and Christmas when the freshly harvested olives are being pressed (closed Sunday).

Coustellet
Coustellet, on busy route de Gordes (N100) about 6km north of Oppède les Poulivets, is uninspiring beyond its **Musée de la Lavande** (☎ 04 90 76 91 23, fax 04 90 76 85 52, jack.lincele@wanadoo.fr). The museum has stills used to extract the sweet smelling scent, and a boutique selling lavender scented products, but the most informative part is a short video (in English) which explains how the lilac flower is harvested and distilled (see the boxed text in the Avignon

---

The Mayle Trail

British novelist Peter Mayle – former waiter, truck driver & advertising copywriter – is the single most influential writer on Provence this decade. No other book has had such an outstanding impact on the region as his bestseller *A Year in Provence* (1989).

Mayle's vivid description of life in Provence and its quirky, real-life characters (some unimpressed to find their names in print) captured the imagination of millions. Readers flocked to trail Mayle from his 'honey-hued' *mas* in Ménerbes where he lived between 1986-93, to the select handful of upmarket Provençal bistros and auberges he evoked so well.

Four million copies sold in 22 languages later, the Mayle trail thrives. The author's New Year haunt in Lacoste (Le Simiane) and the converted mill in Lambesc (now a private club) have closed. In Ménerbes, the Café du Progrès sells village maps to the incoming coachloads and doles out directions to Mayle's former mas.

Le Bistrot à Michel *(☎/fax 04 90 76 82 08, Cabrières-d'Avignon)*
Truffle omelettes are served here in season (November to March) to appease Mayle-hungry fans. Otherwise, Michel Bosc cooks up memorable meals served on a flower-filled terrace behind the simple village bar. There's a 90FF plat du jour, a 100FF lunch formule and a choice of five entrées and mains à la carte. The tomato and marinated salmon mousseline served with onion sorbet is heavenly, as are the tasty black olives and confiture d'onions (a sweet onion chutney) which accompany aperitifs. Closed on Tuesday in July and August (Monday and Tuesday from December to June) and all of January.

Auberge de la Loube *(☎/fax 04 90 74 19 58, Boux, 11km east of Lacoste)*
Chef and owner Maurice still collects horse-drawn carriages but lacks horse and man power to take tourists for a ride. La Loube has a 120FF lunch menu and a four course evening 165FF menu which includes hors d'œuvre Provençal de la Loube – a wicker tray filled with appetisers guaranteed to fill. Tapenade, anchoïade, quail eggs, melon slices, cherry tomatoes and fresh figs are some of the Provençal treats. Closed Thursday. Credit cards not accepted.

Area chapter). An 80 hectare lavender farm in Lagarde d'Apt can be visited prior to, and during, the July harvest; visits have to be arranged through the museum. Opening hours are from 10 am to noon and 2 to 6 pm; until 7 pm in summer (15FF).

Lagnes & Cabrières-d'Avignon

There is little to do in the yellow brick village of Lagnes (pop 1400; postcode 84220; alt 110m) beyond strolling its cobbled streets and visiting the temporary art exhibitions held in the **vieux lavoir** (old wash-house) off central place du Fontaine.

Cabrières-d'Avignon (pop 1140; postcode 84220; alt 167m), 5km east, was one of 11 Lubéron villages destroyed by troops under the terms of the Aix Parliament's *Arrêt de Mérindol* in 1545 which condemned Vaudois heretics to death. The Vaudois (Waldenses) were a minority group who sought refuge in the Lubéron hills following the excommunication of their leader, Valdès, from the church by Pope Lucius III in 1184. The Vaudois joined the reformation in 1532, leading to their eventual massacre on 15-20 April 1545 during which 3000 people were murdered and a further 600 sent to the galleys. In Cabrières-d'Avignon, troops stormed the 12th century **château** (1182). The castle, since restored, is private property and can't be visited.

The northern part of the village is shrouded with beautiful pine and cedar forests,

The Mayle Trail

Gu & Fils (☎ 04 42 26 75 12, 3 rue Frédéric Mistral, Aix-en-Provence)
Gu, with his handsome moustache, continues to enchant (see the Marseille Area chapter).

Café-Restaurant de la Gare (☎ 04 90 75 82 00, La Gare de la Bonnieux, 5km north of Bonnieux towards Goult)
A small and unassuming one-man show which touts a sunny terrace out back. Tables have to be booked so the chef knows how many guests to cook for. Menus cost 105 and 135FF and punters who drink too much can hire a bicycle to wobble home. Closed Sunday evening and all Monday.

Le Bistrot du Paradou (☎ 04 90 54 32 70, Le Paradou, 3km west of Maussane-les-Alpilles)
Every table is snapped up by 12.30 pm at this village bistro capturing authentic Provençal dining. It touts one fixed menu (170FF) which includes house wine, a choice of entrées and homemade desserts, a no-choice main course and a fantastic array of suitably ponging cheeses. Book ahead to guarantee a seat. Closed Sunday.

Mayle on Mayle

"... In the end our life wasn't our own, so we decided to sell the house and take a break from Provence. I once found two Italians with a video camera in our pool, and there was an afternoon when I came into the house to find a trio of English tourists in the living room inspecting the furniture. There was also a flying photographer who circled the house in a helicopter. Not the kind of visit you like on a summer afternoon.

The rhythm of daily life (in Provence) suits me very well, and there's the enormous pleasure of living in a beautiful part of the world. Also, I happen to like the French. The food, the wine, cafés, sunshine, clean air, tranquillity, lavender, village markets, boules – all these are wonderful and the combination is what makes Provence special for me.

We would like to buy another house in Provence. If we do, we won't be advertising the address ..."

THE LUBÉRON

criss-crossed with *promenades touristes* (walking paths), picnic tables and a small amphitheatre made from the same dry stone as the region's bories.

Le Bistrot à Michel (☎/fax 04 90 76 82 08) in the village centre (see the boxed text The Mayle Trail) has nine delightful rooms for 400-600FF. Book months in advance.

CAVAILLON

- **pop 23,470** ✉ **84300** **alt 75m**

The market town of Cavaillon, 28km southeast of Avignon, is the western gateway to the Lubéron. It is best known for its sweet melons, mountains of which are sold at the early morning Monday market in season between May and September. Melons abound during the Fête du Melon in August.

A **triumphal arch** built by the Romans in the 1st century BC adorns place François Tourel, a large square at the west end of cours Bournissac, one of Cavaillon's main streets. Three blocks north is the 12th century **Cathédrale Saint Véran** with its fine Roman **cloître** (cloister). Cavaillon's beautiful **synagogue** (1772) and adjoining **Musée Juif Comtadin** (Jewish Museum), rue Hébraïque, are worth a visit too.

Information

The tourist office (☎ 04 90 71 32 01, fax 04 90 71 42 99), place François Tourel, organises various guided tours (35FF) in July and August, including a three hour cycling tour in the countryside and a *dégustation* (tasting) session of melons, melon liqueur and melon-filled chocolates. The office is open from 9 am to 1 pm and 2 to 7 pm (closed Sunday afternoon). Winter hours are 9.30 am to 12.30 pm and 1.30 to 6.30 pm.

The post office, on place du Cros, the square adjoining place François Tourel, exchanges currency. Commercial banks dot cours Bournissac and cours Gambetta.

Places to Stay & Eat

The tourist office has details on *gîtes ruraux* and *chambres d'hôtes*. **Camping La Durance** (☎ 04 90 71 11 78, fax 04 90 71 98 77, digue des Grands Jardins), is open from April to October. There are sites in Robion (6km east) and Maubec (9km east) too.

Central hotels in Cavaillon that won't break the bank include *Hôtel Le Provence* (☎ 04 90 78 03 38, cours Bournissac) which has 10 rooms starting at 110FF; and *Hôtel Le Forum* (☎ 04 90 78 37 55, 60-68 place du Clos) which has 12 rooms costing 130-280FF. *Le Fin de Siècle* (☎ 04 90 71 28 85, 42 place du Clos) is a popular brasserie, dating from 1900, with a lovely people-watching pavement terrace and a 69FF menu.

Auzet Cavaillon (☎ 04 90 78 06 54, 61 cours Bournissac) is a master bakers which sells 21 types of bread (walnut, olive, anchovy etc) plus an additional 11 varieties (roquefort, thyme, onion etc) which have to be ordered in advance. Do what Mayle did and have a coffee in the boulangerie while perusing the bi-lingual, French-English *carte des pains* (ask at the counter for it).

Getting There & Away

Bus The bus station (☎ 04 90 78 32 39), ave Pierre Semard, is next to the train station. Voyages Arnaud (☎ 04 90 63 01 82 in Carpentras) runs four SNCF buses daily (except Sunday) from Cavaillon to L'Isle-sur-la-Sorgue (13FF; 15 minutes), Carpentras (32FF; 35 minutes), Aix-en-Provence (91FF; one hour) and Marseille (69FF; 1½ hours).

Train Cavaillon train station, place de la Gare, is at the east end of ave Maréchal Joffre. Walk to the end of this street, turn right on to ave Gabriel Péri, then left on to cours Bournissac to get to the centre. From Cavaillon there are trains to Marseille (69FF; 1¼ hours) and Avignon (32FF; 30 minutes).

Getting Around

Bicycle Hire two wheels from Cyclix Cavaillon (☎ 04 90 78 07 96, cyclix@ wanadoo.fr), 166 cours Gambetta, for 100/ 180/450FF a day/weekend/week. Cycles Rieu (☎ 04 90 71 45 55), 25 ave Maréchal Joffre, is another rental outlet.

LE GRAND LUBÉRON

The deep **Combe de Lourmarin** which cuts through the massif in an almost perfect perpendicular from Bonnieux to Lourmarin marks the great divide between the Petite and the Grand Lubéron. Dramatic gorges and grand fortresses are the trademarks of the 'Big' Lubéron.

Buoux

• pop 118   ⊠ 84480

Several kilometres north-east of Bonnieux and 8km south of Apt is Buoux, dominated by the splendid hilltop **ruins of Fort de Buoux**. A traditional Protestant stronghold, Buoux was destroyed in the 1545 Vardois massacres and again in 1660. The fort and old village ruins, perilous in places due to loose rocks etc, can be explored on foot. From the watchtower at the far end of the fort there are magnificent views of the valley. White arrows painted on rocks mark a return route (optional) via a magnificent 'hidden' spiralling staircase cut in the rock. Tickets (10/7FF for adult/child) are sold at the cottage below the ruins.

From Buoux, an invigorating cycling (or driving route) takes you north on the D113 to a set of crossroads straddled by lavender fields which, in June and July, are a blaze of blue. At the crossroads you can bear west to Bonnieux, or continue on the northbound lavender trail for a further 9km to Apt. After passing more lavender fields, the road climbs to **Les Agnes** where there are good views of stone-capped Mont Ventoux. In Les Agnes, visit **Distillerie Agnel** (☎ 04 90 74 14 43).

Buoux is popular with rock climbers; Amethyste (☎ 04 90 04 80 55), Quartier Seguins, Buoux, arranges climbing expeditions from 200FF per person a day.

The rambling **Auberge des Seguins** (☎ *04 90 74 16 37, fax 04 90 74 03 26*), signposted from Buoux village centre, is beautifully set in the middle of nowhere with half-board starting at 220FF per person. Hikers head for the neighbouring **gîte d'étape** (*☎/fax 04 90 74 47 82, Quartier de la Loube*) which has dormitory beds for 70FF, breakfast for 25FF, additional meals for 70FF, and half-board for 160FF.

The *gîte* is closed in January; book in advance.

Lourmarin

• pop 1100   ⊠ 84160   alt 230m

The little village of Lourmarin, also the site of a massacre in 1545, is 6.5km south of Bonnieux. Its main draw is its Renaissance **château** (☎ 04 90 68 15 23) which can be visited by guided tour (30/20FF for adult/student). The schedule (every half-hour between 10 am and 5.30 pm in July and August) is pinned outside the tourist office (☎/fax 04 90 68 10 77), across the field opposite the castle at 9 ave Philippe de Giraud.

Provençal writer Albert Camus (1913-60) and his wife are buried in the village **cimitière**; his tombstone is planted with rosemary, hers with lavender. Henri Bosco (1888-1976), best known for his children's books, is also buried here. From the chateau, continue along rue du Temple past a converted windmill, left on to the D27, then turn right down a narrow street that leads to the cemetery.

Freestyle (☎ 04 90 08 53 46), rue du Temple, rents bicycles for 100/450FF a day/week. Next door is the grandiose **Moulin de Lourmarin** (☎ 04 90 68 06 69, fax 04 90 68 31 76, lourmarin@francemarket.com), a four-star hotel in a restored 18th century oil mill. Doubles start at 700/850FF in the low/high season.

Vaugines & Cucoron

From Lourmarin the eastbound D56 follows the G97 hiking trail for 5km to **Vaugines**, a charming Provençal village where parts of Claude Berri's Pagnol films *Manon des Sources* and *Jean de Florette* (1986) were shot. Take one look at the giant horse chestnut tree and fabulous moss-covered fountain that fills central place de la Fontaine and you will understand why. Continuing east on route de Lourmarin (D56) towards Cucoron, you pass **Miel de Provence** (☎ 04 90 77 29 70) where you can buy lavender, rosemary and chestnut honey.

In **Cucoron**, olive oil is milled between mid-November and January at the **Moulin à**

Huile d'Olive Dauphin (☎ 04 90 77 26 17), rue du Moulin à Huile. Cucoron is the starting point for walks up Mourre Nègre. The tourist office (☎ 04 90 77 28 37, fax 04 90 77 17 00), rue Léonce Brieugne, stocks hiking maps and guides.

Cucoron has two camping grounds. *Le Moulin à Vent* (*☎ 04 90 77 25 77, fax 04 90 77 21 64*), open April to October, is southeast of the village on chemin de Gastoule. *Camping du Plan* (*☎ 04 90 77 20 99*) is on the D135 between Cadenet and Ansouis. In Vaugines, the friendly *Hostellerie du Lubéron* (*☎ 04 90 77 27 19, fax 04 90 77 13 08, cours Saint Louis*) is open from March to mid-November and has a handful of doubles for 320FF.

Abbaye de Silvacane

The lovely Silvacane abbey is the third in the trio of the Medieval Provence abbeys built in an austere Romanesque style in the 12th century. It sits south of the Durance river, 7km south of **Cadenet**. The Cistercian monks, responsible for the magnificent architectural creations, built Abbaye de Silvacane between 1175 and 1230. Work on the large refectory which adjoins the cloister's northern side, did not begin until 1420. The abbey (☎ 04 42 50 41 69) is open from 9 am to noon and 2 to 5 pm. It is closed Tuesday (32/21FF for adult/student).

Pays d'Aigues

Many consider rugged Pays d'Aigues (literally 'Aigues country') the last remaining stronghold in Lubéron not yet colonised by *residence secondaire* owners.

The **Château d'Ansouis** (☎ 04 90 09 82 70) in Ansious was built at various times between the 10th and 18th centuries. The castle is still inhabited by the original family and can be visited by guided tour at 2.30 pm (closed Tuesday). In July and August there is a tour at 11 am.

La Tour d'Aigues (pop 3400), 10km further east, is dominated by the Renaissance **Château de la Tour d'Aigues** (☎ 04 90 07 50 33), a substantial part of which (including its roof) was destroyed by fire in 1792. The 12th

to 15th century castle houses a **Musée des Faïences** in which 18th century earthenware made in La Tour is exhibited, a **Musée du Pays d'Aigues**, and a tourist office (☎ 04 90 07 50 29, fax 04 90 07 35 91). Open-air concerts are held here in summer (☎ 04 90 07 50 33 for ticket reservations). The southern Lubéron tourist office, Sud Lubéron Tourisme (☎ 04 90 07 59 72, fax 04 90 07 59 72, provence.luberon@wanadoo.fr) has an office in the castle too.

MANOSQUE

• pop 19,100   ⌷ 04100   alt 387m

Manosque (actually in the Alpes-de-Haute-Provence department) straddles the Lubéron's eastern fringe and is a perfect stepping stone between toy-town Lubéron and its wilder eastern neighbour. Accommodation is substantially cheaper here, making it a good base to explore the Lubéron.

The Provençal writer Jean Giono (1895-1970) was born and bred in Manosque. **Mont d'Or** (Mount d'Auro in Provençal meaning 'mount of the wind'), immediately north of the town, offers good views of Manosque's red roof tops and the Lubéron hills beyond. There are unparalleled, circular views from **Montforon** (600m), about 10km west of Manosque. The *moulin à vent* (windmill) can be visited by appointment only (☎ 04 92 76 41 65).

Manosque tourist office (☎ 04 92 72 16 00, fax 04 92 72 58 98), place du Docteur Joubert, is open from 9 am to 12.15 pm (11.45 am on Tuesday) and 1.30 to 6.30 pm (closed Sunday afternoon).

Giono & Carzou

Art exhibitions frequent the **Centre Jean Giono** (☎ 04 92 70 54 54), blvd Elémir Bourges, an arts centre dedicated to the Manosque born writer. The small cottage, on the corner of Grande Rue and rue Torte, where Giono lived his whole life still stands.

The frescoes covering 670 sq metres of wall inside the adjoining 19th century Chapelle de la Congrégation (1840), 7 blvd Elémir Bourges, are a shock. The serial paintings – entitled *L'Apocalypse* and intended to portray a frightening year 2000 – were painted by contemporary Armenian-born artist Jean Carzou between 1985 and 1991. Hitler, the Holocaust, Stalin and Pol Pot all feature on the chapel walls, as do the 'great whore' and 'lustful immoral couples'. The chapel, run by the **Fondation Carzou** (☎ 04 92 87 40 49, www.karatel.fr/carzou) is open on Friday, Saturday and Sunday from 10 am to noon and 2.30 to 6.30 pm (25/15FF for adult/student).

Places to Stay
Manosque has numerous camping grounds and an *Auberge de Jeunesse* (☎ 04 92 87 57 44, ave de l'Argile, Parc de la Rochette) which charges 65FF for bed and breakfast.

Somewhat dated (read: fusty) but friendly is the central *Hôtel François 1er* (☎ 04 92 72 07 99, fax 04 92 87 54 85, 18 rue Guilhempierre). Single/double rooms with washbasin and bidet cost 130/150FF, singles/doubles with shower are 180/210FF, and rooms with shower and toilet cost 220/270FF. Nearby, downtrodden *Hôtel du Terreau* (☎ 04 92 72 15 50, fax 04 92 80 42, 21 place du Terreau), above a noisy bar, has singles/doubles starting at 105/115FF. Rooms with shower are 160/190FF.

Two-star *Grand Hôtel de Versailles* (☎ 04 92 72 12 10, fax 04 92 72 62 57, 17 ave Jean Giono), has good-value rooms starting at 130/170FF for doubles with washbasin/shower. Dogs can stay for 20FF a night. *Hôtel Peyrache* (☎ 04 92 72 07 43, 37 rue Rousseau), is not picturesque but is dead in the town centre. Singles with washbasin and bidet cost 160FF; doubles/triples with shower are 220/260FF. This place does not accept credit cards.

Places to Eat
Le Lubéron (☎ 04 92 72 03 09, 21bis place du Terreau), next door to Hôtel du Terreau, is considered the top eating spot. Regional *menus* cost 135, 170 or 180FF and include a complimentary dip of *tapenade*. The chef tours the restaurant during coffee.

Renowned for its down-to-earth, hearty homemade cuisine is *Le Petit Pascal* (☎ 04 92 87 62 01, 17 promenade Aubert Millot). Its 60FF *menu* comprising a buffet of hors d'œvres, a main dish and choice of dessert or cheese is particularly good value.

The Irish *Pub Saint Patrick* (☎ 04 92 72 13 94, 2 rue Mont d'Or) and adjoining *Cantina Tex Mex* overlooking place de l'Hôtel de Ville are in the heart of the old town. Saint Patrick hosts occasional philosophy soirées while its Tex Mex sister specialises in Texan fondue and hearty slabs of beef.

Aux Mille Pâtes (43 Grande Rue) sells homemade pasta. Organically-grown fruit and veg are sold at *Le Blé en Herbe*, a biological product cooperative at 7-9 rue des Marchands.

Getting There & Away
Bus Manosque bus station (☎ 04 92 87 55 99 or 04 92 72 48 80), blvd Charles de Gaulle, is 500m from the centre. Exit the station, turn left along blvd Charles de Gaulle, then right on to ave Jean Giono. There are daily buses to Apt (one hour; twice daily), Forcalquier (35 minutes), Saint Maximin and Avignon.

Train The train station, place Frédéric Mistral, is 2km south of the centre. Walk or bus it along ave Maréchal de Lattre de Tassigny and its continuation, ave Jean Giono. There are about six daily trains to/from Marseille (101FF; 1½ hours), Aix-en-Provence (78FF; 1¼ hours), Sisteron (66FF; one hour) and Gap (114FF; 1¼ hours).

Haute-Provence

Haute-Provence is Provence at its rawest. Mass tourism has yet to touch these mountainous 'Alpes d'Azur' and peace, tranquillity and isolation are not hard to find. The splendid snow-capped peaks of the southern Alps dominate the north, while its south-eastern valleys are sprinkled with hilltop villages where the tempo of life has barely shifted gear since medieval times. South-west lies the land of lakes, gorges and Europe's grandest canyon.

A substantial part of the Alpes-de-Haute-Provence department (among France's largest and least populated) is protected by the **Parc National du Mercantour** (see National Parks in Facts about Provence). Spreadeagled in an arc along the French-Italian border, it is Provence's only national park and offers a rich variety of outdoor activities: hiking, mountain biking and white water rafting in summer; skiing in winter.

The Rallye Automobile Monte Carlo (Monte Carlo Rally) tears around Haute-Provence's overdose of *lacets* (hairpin bends) each year in January. Part of the region is also crossed by an enchanting narrow gauge railway; a steam train huffs and puffs along a small section of it. Exploring is tough without your own wheels and a sturdy set of hiking boots.

GORGES DU VERDON

The gorgeous 25km of Gorges du Verdon (also known as the Grand Canyon du Verdon), the largest canyon in Europe, slice through the limestone plateau midway between Avignon and Nice on the southernmost fringe of Haute-Provence. The green gorges begin at **Rougon** (near the confluence of the Verdon and Jabron rivers) until the river flows into **Lac de Sainte Croix**. The villages of **Castellane**, at the east end of the gorges, and **Moustiers Sainte Marie** at their west end, are the main gateways into what many consider the region's most fabulous sight.

HIGHLIGHTS

- Discover Europe's grandest gorges – on foot, by canoe or by bicycle
- Scale new heights at La Colmiane's via ferrata
- Steam it by train from the sea (Nice) to the mountains (Digne-les-Bains)
- Track down rock drawings made by prehistoric man in the geological reserve near Digne-les-Bains
- Sniff Provence's perfumes and pongs at Salagon priory
- Star gaze through the world's largest amateur telescope at Puimichel

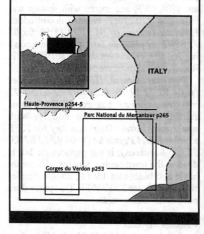

Since 1997 the Parc Naturel Régional du Verdon has protected the 250 to 700m deep gorges, carved by the greenish waters of the Verdon River. The gorges are from 8 to 90m wide at the bottom and the rims are 200 to 1500m apart. The unusually high fluorine content of the water gives the river its vibrant green colour.

Information

Tourist Offices The best information source is Castellane tourist office (☎ 04 92 83 61 14, fax 04 92 83 76 89), rue Nationale, or its counterpart in Moustiers Sainte Marie (☎ 04 92 74 67 84, fax 04 92 74 60 65, www.ville-moustiers-sainte-marie.fr), rue Bourgade. The Castellane office organises summer excursions into the gorges (115FF) and has an endless stream of information on outdoor activities. It is open from 9 am to 1 pm and 2 to 7 pm (closed Sunday afternoon).

The Moustiers office sells excellent English-language guides and stocks a wealth of information on the Parc Naturel Régional du Verdon (☎ 04 92 74 63 95, fax 04 92 74 63 94), BP 14, 04360 Moustiers Sainte Marie. Moustiers tourist office is open from 10 am to noon and 2 to 7 pm.

There's a small, seasonal tourist office in La Palud-sur-Verdon (☎ 04 92 77 38 02 or 04 92 77 32 02, fax 04 92 77 30 87), and a Syndicate d'Initiative (☎/fax 04 94 85 68 40 or ☎ 04 94 76 91 01) in Trigance.

The Canyon

The bottom of the gorges can be visited on foot or by raft. Motorists and cyclists can enjoy spectacular (if dizzying) views from two cliff-side roads which stretch from Moustiers Sainte Marie to Castellane.

La route des Crêtes (the D952 and D23) follows the northern rim and passes the **Point Sublime** viewpoint at the canyon's entrance, from where the GR4 trail leads to the bottom of the canyon.

La Corniche Sublime (the D19 to the D71) goes along the southern rim and takes you to such landmarks as **Balcons de la Mescla** (Mescla Terraces) and **Pont de l'Artuby** (Artuby Bridge), the highest bridge in Europe.

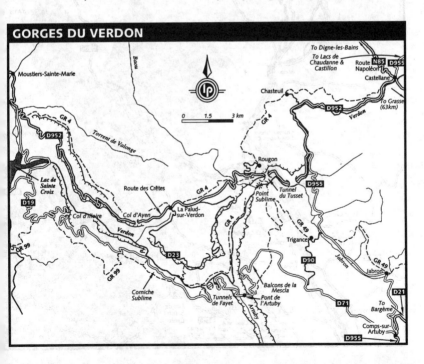

A complete circuit of the Gorges du Verdon involves about 140km of driving; the tourist office in Castellane has a good English language brochure with 11 itineraries entitled *Driving Tours*. The only real village en route is La Palud-sur-Verdon (930m), 2km north-east of the northern bank of the gorges. In summer, heavy traffic slows to a crawl.

The bottom of the canyon, first explored in its entirety in 1905, presents hikers and white water rafters with an overwhelming series of cliffs and narrows. You can walk most of it along the often difficult GR4, which is covered by Didier-Richard's 1:50,000-scale map No 19, entitled *Haute-Provence-Verdon* (70FF). It is also included in the excellent, *Canyon du Verdon – The Most Beautiful Hikes* (25FF at Castellane or Moustiers tourist office), which lists 28 shorter hikes in the gorges. The full GR4 takes two days, though short descents into the canyon are possible from a number of points. Bring a torch (flashlight) and drinking water. Camping rough on gravel beaches along the way is illegal, but people do it.

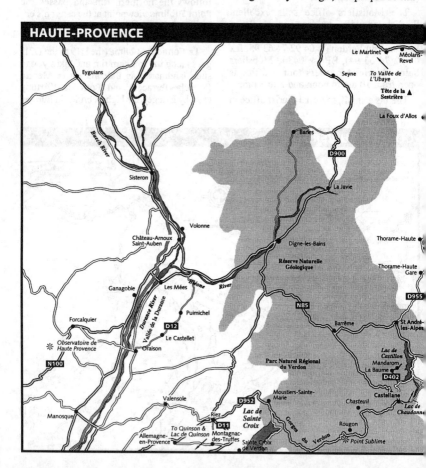

The water level of the river in the upper part of the canyon can rise suddenly if Electricité de France (EDF; France's electricity company) opens the hydroelectric dams upstream, making it difficult if not impossible to ford the river. Before setting out, call ☎ 04 92 83 62 68 to find out the Verdon's level and ☎ 08 36 68 02 04 for the weather report.

Castellane
- **pop 1349** ✉ **04120 alt 730m**

The small town of Castellane is unmomentous beyond its favoured status as the starting point for expeditions into the gorges. The post office, banks, most hotels and canoe/kayaking shops line central place Marcel Sauvaire and adjoining place de l'Église. On 3 March 1815, Napoléon I stopped off at the prefecture, 34 rue Nationale (north off place Marcel Sauvaire), today the **Conservatoire des Arts & Traditions Populaires** (☎ 04 92 83 71 80). It is open in July and August from 2 to 6 pm (9 am to noon on Wednesday).

Peering down on the square from an altitude of 903m is the **Chapelle Notre Dame**

du Roc (1703), a small chapel perched precariously on the 180m needle shaped rock. A hiking trail leads from place de l'Église to the rock top and chapel. Before embarking on the ascent (30 minutes), ask for the chapel key from Mrs Le Curé who lives opposite the sacristy at 35 rue de la Merci (off place de l'Église). Each year on 15 August (Assumption), pilgrims process up to the rock to celebrate Mass.

Four kilometres north of town is Lac de Chaudanne and, a further 4km north, Lac de Castillon (see Lacs du Verdon section later). About 10km south of Castellane on the picturesque D955 to Trigance, is the **Moulin des Soleils** (☎ 04 94 76 92 62), one of Provence's few remaining flour mills still in operation. You can visit in summer between 3 and 6 pm; don't leave without sampling freshly baked bread.

Moustiers Sainte Marie
• pop 580   ⊠ 04360   alt 634m

Pretty little Moustiers Sainte Marie comprises a quaint crop of houses which nestle on a rocky shelf beneath a backdrop of two towering cliffs. A 227m long gold chain bearing a star hangs between the rocks. The 12th century **Chapelle Notre Dame de Beauvoir** is perched on a ledge on the side of one of the limestone cliffs, past which a waterfall tumbles. Numerous stone bridges grace the village below, through which the **Ravin de Notre Dame** streams.

In the 17th century, Moustiers earned itself European recognition for its decorative Provençal *faïence* (earthenware) a tradition that is kept alive by a handful of potters who tend these days to turn out tourist souvenirs rather than works of art. The latter can be admired in the **Musée de la Faïence** (☎ 04 92 74 61 64), rue Bourgade, open from 9 am to noon and 2 to 6 pm; 7 pm in July and August; closed Tuesday (10FF).

A steep trail, with countless steps, leads from rue Bourgade to the Chapelle Notre Dame de Beauvoir, passing 14 stations of the cross en route. Count on at least one hour's walking to get to the top, from where there are breathtaking views.

Activities
Most outdoor activity places have a base in Castellane: Aboard Rafting (☎/fax 04 92 83 76 11), 8 place Marcel Sauvaire, runs white water rafting trips (180-440FF), canyoning expeditions (200-350FF), as well as hot-dogging (200FF), windsurfing, hang-gliding and mountain biking excursions. Trips have to be booked in advance; you must know how to swim, but no white water experience is necessary. Aboard Rafting is open from April to September. Montagne & Rivière (☎ 04 92 83 67 24 or 04 92 83 73 57), 20 rue Nationale, and Aqua Verdon Castellane (☎ 04 92 83 72 75), 9 rue Nationale, are two other outlets.

Four kilometres west of Castellane on route des Gorges du Verdon (D952) is Acti-Raft (☎ 04 92 83 76 64, fax 04 92 83 76 64), an activity centre that organises rafting (200FF for a 1½ hour initiation; 500FF for a one day expedition), hot-dogging (250FF), canyoning (200FF) and canoe-kayaking (180FF). In La Palud-sur-Verdon contact the Bureau des Guides (☎/fax 04 92 77 30 50).

Places to Stay & Eat
Camping *Camping de Bourbon* (☎ 04 92 77 38 17), just east of La Palud-sur-Verdon, charges about 14FF per person and 6FF for a tent. It is open May to September. Near Castellane, the river is lined with some 15 seasonal camping grounds – crowded and pricey. The *Domaine de Charteuil Provence* (☎ 04 92 83 79 39), just south of Castellane and open from June to mid-October, charges 58/71FF for two people with car and tent in the low/high season.

Hostels The *Auberge de Jeunesse Le Trait d'Union* (☎/fax 04 92 77 38 72, fax 04 92 77 30 48, route de la Maline), 500m south of La Palud-sur-Verdon at the start of route des Crêtes, is open from April to October. Bed and breakfast costs 66FF. Non HI-card holders can buy a one night stamp for 19FF. Sheets are 17FF.

Gîtes d'Étape The *Gîte d'Étape de Fontaine Basse* (☎ 04 94 85 68 36 or 04 94

ont Saint Bénézet, with the Palais du Papes and Cathedral Notre Dame des Doms, Avignon

bbaye de Sénanque, the Cistercian abbey near Gordes, founded in 1148

A Roman theatre, part of the extensive Roman ruins found in Vaison-la-Romaine

The Pont du Gard, a three-tiered Roman aqueduct near Avignon, built by Agrippa around 19 BC

85 68 60, fax 04 94 85 68 50), 16km south-east of Castellane in Trigance, charges 100FF for B&B. Sheets are 10FF. In Castellane, a bed at *L'Oustaou* (☎ *04 92 83 77 27, chemin des Listes)* is 60FF a night.

Chambres d'Hôtes Pays du Verdon offers ample B&B opportunities; ask at the tourist office. In the 16th century, hilltop village of Chasteuil (900m), 8km south-west of Castellane along the D952 and then 2.5km north on a narrow lane, is *Le Gîte de Chasteuil* (☎/*fax 04 92 83 72 45)* which offers B&B in the old village schoolhouse for 200/245FF for one/two people.

About 10km north-east of Comps-sur-Artuby off the D21 is the pinprick village of Bargème which, at 1097m, is one of the region's highest villages. Carefully restored as if it were a toy town, the village has one *chambre d'hôte* (☎ 04 94 84 20 86).

Hotels – Castellane If you're not looking for something expensive, Castellane is the place. Numerous hotels line place Marcel Sauvaire and place de l'Église. Particularly good value is the *Grand Hôtel du Levant* (☎ *04 92 83 60 05, fax 04 92 83 72 14, place Marcel Sauvaire),* an impressive pile which has singles/doubles with shower and toilet for 150/180FF.

Doubles with shower and toilet at *Hôtel La Forge* (☎ *04 92 83 62 61, place de l'Église)* start at 200FF. Next door, the *Hostellerie du Roc* (☎ *04 92 83 62 65)* has doubles/triples from 225/300FF.

On rue de la République, off place Marcel Sauvaire, *Hôtel du Verdon* (☎ *04 92 83 62 02, fax 04 92 83 73 80)* has doubles with washbasin/shower for 160/180FF. On the same street, *Ma Petite Auberge* (☎ *04 92 83 62 06, fax 04 92 83 68 49)* has doubles with shower for 190FF and ones with toilet too for 240FF.

A 10 minute walk from town is the excellent value *Stadi Hôtel* (☎ *04 92 83 76 47,* ☎ *04 94 70 34 67, fax 04 94 84 63 36)* on the N85 out of Castellane (direction Digne-les-Bains). It has a swimming pool, shows English-language films every

evening, and has doubles for 220FF. A week's stay in a two to four person studio is 2700FF.

Hotels – Moustiers Sainte Marie The village has three hotels which fill up fast: *La Bonne Auberge* (☎ *04 92 74 66 18, fax 04 92 74 65 11, route de Castellane); Le Belvédère* (☎ *04 92 74 66 04, fax 04 92 74 62 31, ave de Lérins); and Le Relais* (☎ *04 92 74 66 10, fax 04 92 74 60 47, place du Couvent).* All have rooms from around 250FF.

One of the region's most refined places to stay offering a rare glimpse of Provence at its most luxurious is less than 1km outside of Moustiers. *La Bastide de Moustiers* (☎ *04 92 70 47 47, fax 04 92 70 47 48, bastide@i2m.fr, www.bastidemous tiers.i2m.fr, chemin de Quinson),* run by acclaimed French chef Alain Ducasse, is a 17th century country house and a treat to stay at. It has seven rooms costing between 850 and 1480FF in the low season (950 and 1700FF between May and September). Chefs can pack guests a gourmet picnic hamper (150FF per person), and offer cooking lessons (450FF per person) upon request. A stroll around the Bastide's vegetable garden is sheer delight.

Hotels – Elsewhere About 10km south-east of the canyon in Comps-sur-Artuby, the *Grand Hôtel Bain* (☎ *04 94 76 90 06, fax 04 94 76 92 24),* run by the same family for eight generations since 1737, has fine rooms for 250-370FF.

Big spenders should head for the three star *Château de Trigance* (☎ *04 94 76 91 18, fax 04 94 85 68 99),* 16km south-east of Castellane in the hilltop village of Trigance. Rooms in the restored 10th century castle start at 600FF. Tables in the upmarket restaurant, which has delicious *menus* for 210 and 250FF, have to be booked in advance.

Getting There & Away

Bus Public transport is limited. Autocars Sumian (☎ 04 42 67 60 34 in Jouques) runs buses from Marseille to Castellane via Aix-en-Provence (109FF), La Palud and Moustiers. VFD (☎ 04 93 85 24 56 in Nice) runs a daily bus from Grenoble to Nice via Digne-les-Bains and Grasse, stopping in Castellane en route. The tourist offices have schedules.

Getting Around

Bus In July and August, Navettes Autocar (☎ 04 92 83 40 27) runs shuttle buses around the gorges daily except Sunday, linking Castellane with the Point Sublime, La Palud, La Maline, etc. Ask at the tourist office in Castellane or Moustiers for schedules and fares.

Bicycle The Stadi Hôtel (see Places to Stay) rents mountain bikes for 50/75FF a half/full day. L'Arc-en-Ciel (☎ 04 92 77 37 40), a restaurant and gîte near central place de l'Église in La Palud-sur-Verdon, rents bicycles too.

LACS DU VERDON

The Verdon lakes – all creations of the national electricity company – are coloured an appropriately spectacular, sparkling green.

Lac de Sainte Croix

Pretty little **Bauduen** sits on the southeastern banks of the Verdon's largest lake, Lac de Sainte Croix (2200 hectares) which stretches for 10km south of Moustiers Sainte Marie. The lake was created in 1974 and is the second largest of its kind in France. Numerous camping grounds are dotted along the lakeside D71 and D249 which lead to the village where you can hire sailboards and paddle boats. From the **Observatoire des Vallons** (☎ 04 94 84 39 19), on the lake's southern shore (D71) 2km west of Bauduen, you can star-gaze.

Sainte Croix de Verdon (pop 87; alt 525m) is the only village on the lake's western banks. From the village centre a road leads down to the Petit Port (☎ 04 92 77 77 23) where you can hire electric boats. Swimming is forbidden on the pebble beach. Sailboards and catamarans can be hired from the École Français de Voile (☎ 04 92 77 76 51).

Lac de Quinson

Quinson lake sits at the southernmost foot of the Basse (lower) Gorges du Verdon. The lake is crossed by the D11, the main road that cuts through **Quinson**. A major museum complex devoted to the gorges prehistoric past and archaeological treasures, the **Musée de la Préhistoire des Gorges du Verdon**, covering 4274 sq metres is currently being built on the D11 at the south end of the village; it should open in summer 1999.

The endearing village of **Montagnac**, 11km north of Quinson off the D11, is known for its abundance of *truffes frais* (fresh truffles) in season between November and March. Madame Fabre (☎ 04 92 77 52 47), who absolutely everyone in the village knows, is the local dealer (she has no shop; order by telephone).

Eight kilometres west of Montagnac on the D111 is **Allemagne-en-Provence** (pop 365). The village adopted its German influenced name during the Wars of Religion when the Baron d'Allemagne (Baron of Germany) besieged the place. Its centrepiece is the privately owned Château d'Allemagne (☎ 04 92 77 46 78), dating from the 12th to 16th centuries. The donjon style building, part fortress, part pretty palace, can be visited by guided tour between July and September at 4 and 5 pm (closed Monday and Tuesday). In April, June and October, there are tours on weekends only (see Places to Stay, Chambres d'Hôtes, later).

Lacs de Chaudanne & Castillon

The eastern end of the Gorges du Verdon is adorned with **Lac de Chaudanne**. At Chaudanne, it is possible to visit the EDF's Centrale Hydroéléctrique de Chaudane (central hydroelectric plant) in July and August. Guided tours (free), bookable through Castellane tourist office (☎ 04 92 83 61 14), depart from the **Barrage de Chaudanne** (Chaudanne dam) at 2, 3, 4 and 5 pm on Thursday afternoon.

Four kilometres north is **Lac de Castillon**, a steep banked lake with little opportunity for water sports. You can swim and hire paddle boats from the banks of the south-west tip of the lake only. From here, the single track D402 cuts into the mountains to the walled **Cité Sainte de Mandarom Shambhasalem** (Holy City of Mandarom Shambhasalem; ☎ 04 92 83 63 83, mandarom@aumisme.org, www.aumisme.org).

The oversized relics which glitter and sparkle from Castillon's western shores are worshipped by the Aumist cult. Founded in 1969, its burgundy robed, shaven-headed members adhere to a cocktail of all the world religions (considered drug induced by many locals) with a dash of other things thrown in. Since the death of their founder (who left them 22 books and 9000 pages of writings to study) in March 1998, the cult has been patiently waiting for a new leader to inspire them. The park is open to visitors on weekends between 10 and 11.15 am and 3 and 4.15 pm (daily during school holidays and in July and August).

Saint André les Alpes (pop 800; postcode 04170; alt 914m) is on the northern tip of Lac de Castillon. It is among France's leading *parapente* (hang-gliding) centres. Amateurs (1600FF for a five day initiation course) and experts alike can spread their wings at Aérogliss (☎ 04 92 89 11 30, fax 04 92 89 02 36, www.aerogliss.com) on chemin des Iscles, at the south end of the village overlooking the lake. Local culinary specialities sold at the Maison du Saucisson (☎ 04 92 89 03 16) on place du Verdun, the central village square, include *âne* (donkey) and *sanglier* (wild boar) sausage.

You can hire a mountain bike from Gazel Sports (☎ 04 92 89 07 91), place Charles-Bron, for 100FF a day. Saint André is linked with eastern Provence and Nice on the coast by the narrow gauge **Chemin de Fer railway** (see the Digne-les-Bains section and the boxed text Along the Mountain Railway).

Places to Stay & Eat

Camping There are numerous camping grounds in and around Sainte Croix de Verdon. The Castellane tourist office has details. Campers wanting to bare it all can try the **Centre Naturiste** (☎/fax 04 92 83 64 24, fax 04 92 83 68 79, La Grande Terre), signposted off the D402 in La Baume (see Gîte later). The nudist centre charges 38FF per person to pitch a tent or park a caravan (20/10% less in the low/middle season). It also has two/four-berth caravans to rent for 106/133FF a night. The ground is open from Easter to the end of September.

Camping Les Iscles (☎ 04 92 89 02 29, chemin des Iscles), in Saint André next to the hang-gliding school, charges 9/13FF per tent/car. It is open from April to September.

Gîte d'Étape In the hamlet of La Baume (1150m), 2km south of the 'Holy City' on the D402 and 9km north of Castellane, is **Au Soleil Gourmand** (☎/fax 04 92 83 70 82). The gîte, which affords lovely views of Lac de Castillon, has dorm beds for 60FF a night and double rooms for 180FF. Breakfast is 30FF, a picnic is 40FF per person and an evening meal costs 70FF.

Saint André has a lovely located gîte d'étape, **Les Cougnas** (☎ 04 92 89 18 78) from where you can watch the hang-gliders at Aérogliss plopping down from the sky. A bed for the night costs 65FF, breakfast is 25FF and half board is 155FF. The gîte is open year round.

Chambres d'Hôtes The **Château d'Alle-magne** (☎ 04 92 77 46 78, fax 04 92 77 73 84) in Allemagne-en-Provence is a *chambre d'hôte de prestige* and offers rooms inside a beautifully preserved 12th to 16th century chateau. Its three luxurious doubles cost 500-900FF and should be booked well in advance.

Hotels Bauduen and Sainte Croix du Verdon have a couple of hotels each. In Montagnac-des-Truffes, the **Relais de la Lavande** (☎ 04 92 77 53 68) has simple singles/doubles for 120/160FF. Opposite **La Colonne** (☎ 04 92 77 53 63) charges 170FF.

In Sainte André, head for **Hôtel de France** (☎ 04 92 89 02 09, place de l'Église) where doubles with shower are 150FF; or the lakeside **Hôtel Lac et Forêt**

(☎ 04 92 89 07 38), just south of the village. Doubles with/without salle de bain are 250/150FF.

Dine on wild boar at the *Auberge du Parc* (☎ 04 92 89 00 03), a highly recommended Provençal inn which also has rooms (160-280FF).

DIGNE-LES-BAINS

- pop 16,000   ⊠ 04000   alt 608m

The land of snow and melted cheese meets the land of sun and olives around Digne-les-Bains, 39km east of Sisteron, 106km north-east of Aix-en-Provence and 152km north-west of Nice. The town is named after its thermal springs, visited annually by 11,000 people seeking a water cure for rheumatism, respiratory ailments and other medical conditions.

Digne itself is unremarkable, although it was home to a remarkable woman, Alexandra David-Neel whose travels to Tibet brought her wide acclaim. The shale around Digne is rich in fossils and is protected by the Réserve Naturelle Géologique (150,000 hectares). The area is also known for its production of *lavande* (lavender), usually harvested in July or August and honoured in Digne with the five day Corso de la Lavande, starting the first weekend of August. Throughout the region the little purple flower is celebrated with Les Journées Lavande in mid-August. In spring, flowering poppies sprinkle the green fields with buttons of bright red.

The **Route Napoléon** (now the N85 in these parts), which Bonaparte followed in 1815 on his way to Paris after his escape from Elba, passes though Digne. The north-bound D900 takes you past the mountain village of **La Javie** to **Seyne** (pop 1230; alt 1200m), 42km north in the Vallée de la Blanche. In winter you can ski here.

Orientation

Digne-les-Bains is built on the eastern bank of the shallow Bléone River. The major roads into town converge at the Rond Point du 11 Novembre 1918, a roundabout 400m north-east of the train station. The main street is plane tree-lined blvd Gassendi which heads north-eastward from the Rond Point and passes large place du Général de Gaulle, the town's main public square.

Information

Tourist Office The tourist office (☎ 04 92 31 42 73, fax 04 92 32 27 24) inside the Maison du Tourisme, 11 Rond Point du 11 Novembre 1918, is open from 8.45 am to noon and 2 to 6 pm (closed Sunday). From May to October its hours are 8.45 am to 12.30 pm and 2 to 7 pm (Sunday from 10.30 am to noon and 3 to 7 pm). The office has information on guided tours in the region.

The Relais Départemental des Gîtes de France (☎ 04 92 31 52 39, fax 04 92 32 32 63), also in the Maison du Tourisme, books gîte accommodation. It is open from 8 am to noon and 2 to 6 pm (5 pm on Friday; closed on weekends). Bookings can be made between 9 and 11 am and 1 to 4 pm.

Money The Banque de France, 16 blvd Soustre, is open from 8.45 am to noon and 1.45 to 3.45 pm (closed on weekends).

Post & Communications The post office, 4 rue André Honnorat, is open from 8 am to 7 pm (Saturday until noon; closed Sunday).

Laundry There is a laundrette at 4 place du Marché and one at 99 blvd Gassendi, both open from 8 or 9 am to 7 pm.

Fondation Alexandra David-Neel

Paris-born writer and philosopher Alexandra David-Neel (1868-1969), who spent her last years in Digne (reaching the ripe old age of 101), is known for her incognito voyage early in this century to Tibet. Her memory and all-consuming passion for Tibet are kept alive by the Fondation Alexandra David-Neel (☎ 04 92 31 32 38), which occupies her erstwhile residence at 27 ave Maréchal Juin. The Journées Tibetaines, an annual celebration of Tibetan culture, is held in August. Fondation Alexandra David-Neel is just over 1km om town on the road to Nice. From tober to June, free tours (with headones for English speakers) start at 10.30 1, 2 pm and 4 pm; from July to September, tours begin at 10.30 am, 2 pm, 3.30 pm d 5 pm. To get there take TUD bus No 3 the Stade Rolland stop.

Museums

he **Musée de Digne** (☎ 04 92 31 45 29), blvd Gassendi, closed for renovation til 1999, has displays of art, archaeology d mineralogy. It is usually open from 1.30 5.30 pm (closed Monday). In July and ugust hours are 10.30 am to noon and 1.30 6.30 pm.

In the old city, the **Musée d'Art Religieux** ☎ 04 92 32 35 37), place des Récollets, uth-east of the 16th century **Cathédral aint Jérome** in the Chapelle des Pénitents, isplays liturgical objects and religious art. t is open from July to October from 10 am 6 pm. At other times, telephone (☎ 04 92 6 75 00) to arrange a visit.

Réserve Naturelle Géologique

Digne-les-Bains is in the middle of the Réserve Naturelle Géologique, whose spectacular fossil deposits include the footprints f prehistoric birds as well as ammonites, piral shells that look something like a ram's orn. You'll need a detailed regional map or a topoguide to the Digne and Sisteron areas sold at the tourist office) and your own ransport (or a patient thumb) to get to the 18 sites, most of which are around **Barles** (24km north of Digne) and **Barrême** (28km south-east of Digne). There's an impressive limestone slab with some 500 ammonites 3km north of Digne on the road to Barles (and 1km north of the Centre de Géologie).

The Réserve Naturelle's headquarters, the **Centre de Géologie** (☎ 04 92 36 70 70, fax 04 92 36 70 71, resgeol@calvanet.cal vacom.fr) at Saint Benoît, is 2km north of town off the road to Barles. Its exhibits on matters mineral and geological are open from 9 am to noon and 2 to 5.30 pm; 4.30 pm on Fridays. It's closed on weekends from November to March (25/18/15FF for

adult/student). Take TUD bus No 2, get off over the bridge at the Champourcin stop, then take the road to the left. Cars aren't allowed up, so it's a 15 minute walk along the rocky overhang above the river.

Thermal Spas

Take to the waters from mid-February to early December at the Établissement Thermal (☎ 04 92 32 32 92) 2km east of Digne's centre. A good soak costs 35FF but you may require a doctor's certificate. Voyeurs rather than *curistes* can join the weekly free tour on Thursday at 2 pm from March to August.

Places to Stay

Camping *Camping du Bourg* (☎ 04 92 31 04 87, route de Barcelonnette), almost 2km north-east, is open from April to October and costs 63FF for two people with a car and tent or caravan (58FF if you're taking a cure). Take bus No 2 towards Barcelonnette and get off at the Notre Dame du Bourg stop. From there it's a 600m walk.

Camping des Eaux Chaudes (☎ 04 92 32 31 04, route des Thermes) near the Établissement Thermal about 1.5km from Digne, is open from April to November and charges 73FF for two people with a car and tent or caravan (65FF for *curistes*).

Gîtes d'Étape Hikers can use the *Gîte du Château des Sièyes* (☎ 04 92 31 20 30, ave Georges Pompidou), nearly 2km north-west of the centre off the road to Sisteron. It costs 55FF for a dormitory bed. Take bus No 1 headed for Sisteron; get off at the Pompidou stop.

The peaceful *Centre de Géologie* (☎ 04 92 36 70 70) in Saint Benoît has beds in rooms for one, two and four people for 60FF per head.

Hotels The *Hôtel Petit Saint Jean* (☎ 04 92 31 30 04, fax 04 92 36 05 80, 14 cours des Arès), overlooking central place du Général de Gaulle, has good-value singles/doubles with washbasin and bidet for 120/140FF, ones with toilet for 130/150FF and ones

HAUTE-PROVENCE

with shower and toilet for 160/190FF. Triples with toilet cost 190FF. *Menus* in its terrace restaurant start at 67FF.

In the old city, *Hôtel L'Origan* (☎ 04 92 31 62 13, 6 rue Pied de Ville) is little with an upmarket restaurant (*menus* for 70, 98, 125 and 170FF) but affordable single rooms with washbasin from 90FF and doubles with shower from 140FF.

Two star *Hôtel Central* (☎ 04 92 31 31 91, fax 04 92 31 49 78, 26 blvd Gassendi) has doubles from 150FF. *Hôtel Le Coin Fleuri* (☎ 04 92 31 04 51, 9 blvd Victor Hugo) has functional rooms for one or two with washbasin/shower from 170/250FF and a great garden.

The *Hostellerie de L'Aiglon* (☎ 04 92 31 02 70, fax 04 92 32 45 83, 1 rue de Provence) has an entrance attached to the Chapelle Saint Esprit which leads to calm pastel rooms starting at 240FF. Its restaurant, *La Chapelle*, serves good regional fare.

Places to Eat

Restaurants One of the cheapest places for lunch is the *Restaurant-Cafétéria Le Victor Hugo* (☎ 04 92 31 57 23, 8-10 blvd Victor Hugo), with *plats du jour* from around 35FF. *Le Point Chaud* (☎ 04 92 31 30 71, 95 blvd Gassendi) is a dark, cheap and local haunt.

Away from the terraces on place du Général de Gaulle, *La Braisière* (☎ 04 92 31 59 63, 19 place de l'Évêché) has a good lunch *menu* for 68FF, a dinner one for 90FF and a fine view over the town. They do excellent *tartiflette* (85FF) and *raclette* (95FF) – two traditional, cheesy Alpine treats.

Self-Catering A *food market* spills across place du Général de Gaulle on Wednesday and Saturday mornings. Luxury local products are sold at *Saveurs et Couleurs* at 7 blvd Gassendi. There is a *Casino* at 42 blvd Gassendi.

Getting There & Away

Bus The bus station (☎ 04 92 31 50 00) is behind the tourist office on place du ...pinet. Some 11 regional companies

operate buses to Nice (144FF; 2¼ hours; 1.15 pm) via Castellane (62FF; 1¼ hours) well as Marseille (76FF; 2½ hours; fou day) and Apt (60FF; two hours; two a da The bus station is open from 8.40 am to 12. pm and 2.30 to 6.30 pm (closed Sunday).

Train The train station (☎ 04 92 31 00 6 is a 10 minute walk westward from t tourist office on ave Pierre Sémard. T ticket windows are open from 8.15 am 12.30 pm and 1 to 8 pm (Saturday fro 8.15 am to 12.30 pm and 1.45 to 4.45 pm There are four trains a day to Marseil (135FF; 2¼ hours).

In addition to SNCF trains, Digne-le Bains is served by two-car diesel trai operated by the privately-owned L Chemins de Fer de la Provence (☎ 04 92 3 01 58 in Digne; ☎ 04 93 82 10 72 in Nic which chug along a scenic and windin narrow gauge line from Digne to Nice Gare du Sud (☎ 04 93 82 10 17) stopping various very lovely villages en route (se the boxed text).

VALLÉE DE LA DURANCE

The Durance valley ploughs along th western fringes of Haute-Provence. Th **Durance river**, an affluent of the Rhôn follows a 324km course from its source i Montgenèvre in the southern Alps to th Camargue delta. Its impetuous waters slammed by Frédéric Mistral in the 19t century as one of Provence's great thre curses (along with the Aix Parliament an the mistral wind), were partly tamed by th EDF in the 1960s. Canals snake the length of the Vallée de la Durance, as does th noisy A51 *autoroute* (highway).

Manosque, on the eastern edge of the Lubéron (see that chapter) and **Sisteron**, 50km farther north on the confluence of the Durance and the Buéch rivers, are the two main towns along this 100km stretch. Sisteron (pop 6600; postcode 04200; alt 485m) is shabby and unstartling beyond its 13th to 16th century **Château de Sisteron**, perched on a rock above the *cluse* (transverse valley) in which sunken Sisteron sits. Open-

Along the Mountain Railway

The celebrated *Chemin de Fer* Digne-Nice railway chugs from the sea into the mountains, crossing five valleys en route and affording breathtaking views of dramatic landscapes scarcely navigable by road.

The 150km narrow gauge track was built between 1890-1911 and tunnels through kilometres of rock on its adventurous mountain journey. From May to October, passengers can enjoy a blast from the past along part of the route with the *Train des Pignes à Vapeur*, a steam locomotive dating from 1909. It used to be fuelled by pine cones, hence its pretty name.

Eastbound, the scenic journey takes you from Digne-les-Bains through **Saint André les Alpes** (50 minutes), stopping at a sprinkling of tiny villages on the way. In Saint André, you can hang-glide, hire a bicycle, hike around Lac de Castillon and feast on wild boar sausages (see the Lacs de Verdon section). The next stop is **Thorame-Haute** (11 minutes), a village (1012m) at the foot of the Vallée du Haut Verdon which, despite its pinprick size, serves as a vital link on bus routes between southern Provence and the Allos ski resorts. The bus stop is in front of the crumbling old train station on the D955; opposite is the Logis de France *Hôtel de la Gare* (☎ 04 92 89 02 54), open from April to October with *menus* for 68 and 136FF and rooms for two from 225FF. Upon leaving Thorame, the **Col de Saint Michel** (1431m) and the ancient shepherdry village at **Peyresq** flash past the train window.

Annot (pop 1050; alt 700m) is the next halt. The village is known for its *grès d'Annot*, a haphazard arrangement of bizarre rock formations, which can easily be explored on foot. Exploratory day hikes are in the free brochure entitled *Rando Train: Les Randonées des Chemins de Fer de Provence* which details walks in the Chemin de Fer region. Guided hikes are also organised (☎ 04 93 05 05 05). The Annot tourist office (☎ 04 92 83 23 03, fax 04 92 83 32 82) is a five minute walk from the station on blvd Saint Pierre.

Entrevaux (pop 785), 7km farther east, is an impressive *village perché* which tumbles down the steep hillside from the Vauban-built citadel. Across the drawbridge, outside the 17th century fortifications surrounding the village, is an oil and flour mill which can be visited. Ask at the tourist office (☎ 04 93 05 46 73, fax 04 93 05 43 91), inside the old city gate.

The elegant train à vapeur is stationed at **Puget-Théniers**, eight minutes east of Entrevaux and 25 minutes from Annot. Between May and October it shunts its way between Puget and Annot (110FF return; 50 minutes). Annot tourist office has details. In Puget, passengers seeking some hearty Haute-Provence fodder should head for the charming *Auberge des Acacias* (☎ 04 93 05 05 25), 1km from village on the N202. Equally memorable is the **Écomusée du Pays de la Radoule** (☎ 04 93 05 07 38, fax 04 93 05 13 25, ecomusee@ enprovence.com) in the quaint village of **Puget-Rostang**, 6km north of Puget-Théniers. The museum affords a valuable insight into traditional life in rural Haute-Provence a century ago. The area also offers good hiking opportunities.

Picking up the eastward trail again, you reach the mountain villages of **Touët-sur-Var** and **Villars-sur-Var** before plunging south along the Var through **Saint Martin du Var** and **Colomars** to Nice. The entire trip from Digne-les-Bains to Nice (109FF one way) takes 3¼ hours.

air concerts are held here during the Nuits de la Citadelle (☎ 04 92 61 06 00) in July and August.

Twenty kilometres south of Sisteron in Les Mées are the **Rocher des Mées**, a geological wonder comprising a row of rocky pinnacles that stand 100m high. According to legend, the rock formations, also known as Les Pénitents des Mées, were created from a gaggle of monks who were turned to stone for lusting after Saracen women. Hiking trails lead around the rocks, signposted from Les Mées village square. The 10th century **Monastère Notre Dame** (☎ 04 92 68 00 04) in Ganagobie, 10km south on the west bank of the Durance, is also worth visiting. The 12th century floor mosaic, the largest of its kind in France, that carpets the altar in the chapel of the Benedictine is absolutely exquisite. The monastery is open from 3 to 5 pm (until 5.30 pm in summer; closed Monday).

Forcalquier (pop 4000; postcode 04300; alt 550m) sits atop its rocky perch 20km south-west. Fields of sunflowers blossom at its feet. Steep steps lead to the citadel and octagonal shape chapel at the top of the village where carillon concerts are held in summer (Sunday at 11.30 am). The tourist office (☎ 04 92 75 10 02), place du Bourget, overlooks the Gothic Église Notre Dame. The town cemetery, sectioned off with 5m-high hedges, is 1km north of the centre on place du Souvenir Français. It is the only *cimitière classé* (listed cemetery) in France.

The **Prieuré de Salagon** (☎ 04 92 75 19 93), 4km south along the N100 in Mane, is a 13th century priory on a farm estate. It houses the Conservatoire Ethnologique de la Haute-Provence which works towards the preservation of the region's rich ethnographical heritage. Aromatic herbs used for traditional remedies grow in the Jardin Médiéval, while *senteurs* (perfumes) typical to Provence, lavender, mints, mugworts, sage, fill the Jardin de Senteurs. Numerous unique exhibitions are held in the priory. Salagon is open from 10 am to noon and 2 to 7 pm; 2 to 6 pm only from October to May (28/16FF for adult/student).

Observatories

The world's largest amateur telescope can be gazed through at the **Observatoire de Puimichel** in Puimichel, a hamlet 20km south-east of Les Mées via the northbound D4 and the southbound D12. The privately owned, domed observatory run by astrophotographer Dany Cardoen (☎ 04 92 78 79 22, fax 04 92 78 79 69) houses a 1.06m Newton telescope. It costs 100FF per

person (maximum six people) to use the telescope; visits (usually from 8 or 9 pm to midnight) have to be booked in advance.

Ten kilometres south-west of Forcalquier at the end of the D305 from Saint Michel l'Observatoire is the **Observatoire de Haute-Provence** (☎ 04 92 70 64 00, fax 04 92 76 62 95, www.obs-hp.fr), a national research centre that can be toured (15FF) on Wednesday (at 3 pm between October and March and from 2 to 4 pm from 1 April to 30 September).

Accommodation is available in Puimichel at *La Remise* (☎ *04 92 79 95 00, fax 04 92 79 62 41, 113760@compuserve.com),* a gîte d'étape which has beds in a converted barn for 90FF. Breakfast/lunch/dinner is available for 25/55/90FF and full board costs 250FF. It is open year round.

In Saint Michel l'Observatoire, try the six-room *Hôtel l'Observatoire (☎/fax 04 92 76 63 62).*

Getting There & Away

There are buses from Sisteron *halte routière* (☎ 04 92 61 22 18) to Marseille (two hours; four a day), Aix-en-Provence (2½ hours; four a day), and Nice (3¾ hours; one a day) via Digne-les-Bains (45 minutes).

From Forcalquier there are buses to Manosque, Aix-en-Provence and Marseille (☎ 04 92 75 16 32 for information), Sisteron (☎ 04 92 75 33 74) and Digne-les-Bains (☎ 04 92 75 33 74).

Parc National du Mercantour

The Mercantour national park is Provence at its most majestic. Its protected, uninhabited heart covers 68,500 hectares in the north-east of the region and embraces six *vallés* (valleys). The park kisses Italy's Parco Naturale delle Alpi Marittime to the east and is hugged by a 146,500 hectare peripheral zone.

Europe's highest *col* (mountain pass) strides through the Vallé de l'Ubaye, the park's most northern and wildest valley. Come winter's snows, the Ubaye, together with its southern sisters, the Haut Verdon and Tinée valleys, offers fine skiing. Farther south sit the Vésubie, Merveilles and Roya valleys – a heady mix of gorges, ageless rocks and white waters, all within easy reach of the Côte d'Azur.

The Park National du Mercantour has information offices open year round in Barcelonnette, Saint Martin-Vésubie and Tende, and summer bureaux in Saint Sauveur sur Tinée and at Lac d'Allos. The park's headquarters are in Nice (see the Nice to Menton chapter).

VALLÉE DE L'UBAYE

The Ubaye river, a tributary of the Durance, skirts Provence's northern tip between Lac de Serre-Poncon and Barcelonnette. Along with the Verdon, it offers some top white

water rafting. The Ubaye valley, a desolate place shielded by the southern Alps, is sandwiched between the Parc Régional du Queyras to the north and the Mercantour to the south. It is crossed by the D900 which closely follows the river banks.

Barcelonnette (pop 3000; postcode 04400; alt 1135m), founded by the Count of Barcelona in 1231, is the only town in the valley and is a good base for expeditions up the surrounding ski slopes and down the Ubaye river. From the start of the 18th century until WWII, some 5000 Barcelonnetais followed in the footsteps of the enterprising Arnaud brothers who had emigrated to Mexico in 1805 to seek their fortunes in the silk and wool weaving industry. Their colourful history, and that of the valley, unfolds in the **Musée de la Vallée** (☎ 04 92 81 27 15), in a sumptuous Mexican-inspired villa (1878-80) built by a returned emigré at 10 ave de la Libération.

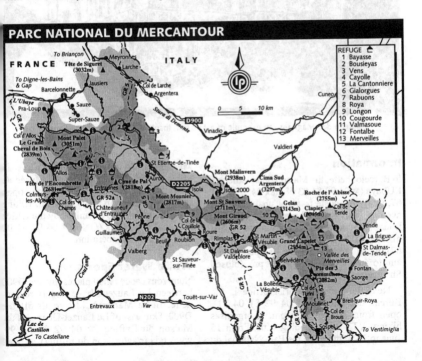

PARC NATIONAL DU MERCANTOUR

Chateau des Magnans, an example of a Mexican inspired chateau in Barcelonnette.

Information

In Barcelonnette, the Maison de la Vallée de l'Ubaye (☎ 04 92 81 03 68, fax 04 92 81 51 67, ubaye@laposte.fr, www.ubaye.com), 4 ave des Trois Frères Arnaud, has information on the valley. Barcelonnette tourist office (☎ 04 92 81 04 71, fax 04 92 81 22 67), place Frédéric Mistral, is open from 9 am to noon and 2 to 6.30 pm (closed Sunday).

Next door to the tourist office is the Bureau des Guides (☎ 04 92 81 04 71), open from 3.30 to 7.30 pm. It organises hiking, VTT and canoeing trips. From 15 June to 15 September, the Parc National du Mercantour (☎ 04 92 81 21 31) has an office on the ground floor of the Musée de la Vallée, 10 ave de la Libération, open from 10 am to noon and 3 to 7 pm. Hiking expeditions are also organised by the Office National des Forêts (ONF; ☎ 04 92 81 00 32), 9 ave de la Libération.

White Water Sports

Numerous canoe rental places line the D900 between Le Lauzet-Ubaye and Barcelonnette. In Le Martinet, just south off the D900, 8km east of Le Lauzet-Ubaye, is the Maison du Rafting (☎ 04 92 85 53 99, www.oda.fr/aa/maison.du.rafting) as well as AN Rafting (☎ 04 92 85 54 90, an-rafting @anrafting.com). Both are open from April to October and arrange rafting (200FF for 1½ hours), canyoning (370FF a day) and other water sports.

In **Méolans-Revel**, 12km west of Barcelonnette, Adventure Rio Raft (☎ 04 92 81 91 15, ☎/fax 04 75 35 52 59), next to Camping du Rioclar, runs rafting (180FF; 1½ hours) and body boarding (200FF; 1¼ hours) expeditions.

Cycling

The Vallée de l'Ubaye is linked to the outside world by seven *cols* (mountain passes). Cyclists tough enough to conquer them all, including Col de Restefond la Bonette (2802m) – the highest road in Europe – are given a medal; the Maison de la Vallée de l'Ubaye in Barcelonnette has details.

Hire a mountain bike in Le Lauzet-Ubaye from Le Relais du Lac (☎ 04 92 85 51 07) for 30/100FF an hour/day. In Le Martinet, both bases rent wheels (40FF an hour) and offer guided trips (180FF).

In Méolans-Revel, hire a bicycle from Camping du Rioclar or at the Domaine Loisirs de l'Ubaye (☎ 04 92 81 01 96), a camping ground 1km east. Both charge 100FF a day. In Barcelonnette, try Plein Air Sport (☎ 04 92 81 23 69), 51 ave de Trois Frères Arnaud.

Skiing

Pra-Loup This is the main resort, 8.5km south-west of Barcelonnette, connected by a lift system across the Vallon des Agneliers with La Foux d'Allos ski resort in the Vallée du Haut-Verdon (see next section). Pra-Loup (1500m) has 160km of runs, served by 58 lifts best suited for intermediate and advanced skiers. Neighbouring **Sauze-Super Sauze** (1400m) has 65km of pistes, three *télésièges* (chairlifts) and 21 *téléskis* (drag lifts).

A six day Ski Pass Vallée covering the above resorts plus **Sainte Anne La Condamine** (1800m) costs 675/820FF in the low/high season. The École du Ski Français (ESF; ☎ 04 92 84 11 05 in Pra-Loup, and

04 92 81 05 20 in Sauze) charges around 500FF for six group lessons. Skis, boots and poles cost from 100FF a day to hire.

The Pra-Loup tourist office (☎ 04 92 84 10 04, fax 04 92 84 02 93, praloup@ karatel.com, www.praloup.com), Maison de Pra-Loup, is open from 9 am to 7 pm (until 6 pm with a midday break in the off-season). The Sauze-Super Sauze tourist office (☎ 04 92 81 05 61, fax 04 92 81 21 60, sauze@laposte.fr) is only open during the ski season (December to April).

Places to Stay & Eat

Camping You can pitch your tent by the river next to the Maison du Rafting in Le Martinet for 30FF per person. Hot showers are free.

In Méolans-Revel, *Camping du Rioclar (☎ 04 92 31 20 30, ave Georges Pompidou)* is open in summer only; check in between 8.30 am to noon and 2.30 to 7 pm. The *Domaine Loisirs de l'Ubaye (☎ 04 92 81 01 96, 04 92 81 92 53)* has four-person chalets to rent starting at 1480/1580FF a week in summer/winter. A chalet room for two with shower costs 190FF the first night, 140FF the second night, and 45FF a night thereafter.

Hotels The tourist offices have accommodation lists for the ski resorts. Two person, self-catering studios start at 1090FF a week. Hotels in Barcelonnette include the *Hôtel du Cheval Blanc (☎ 04 92 81 00 19, fax 04 92 81 15 39, 12 rue Grenette)* which has comfortable doubles for 270FF; and the cheaper *Grand Hôtel (☎ 04 92 81 03 14, 6 place Manuel)* where rock-bottom singles/ doubles with washbasin cost 140/160FF.

Getting There & Away

The nearest train station is Gap (outside Provence), 60km north, from where there are a couple of buses a day to Pra-Loup (48FF; 1½ hours) via Barcelonnette. SCAL (☎ 04 92 81 00 20 or 04 92 51 06 05 in Gap) runs buses from Barcelonnette to Gap, Marseille and Digne-les-Bains.

Buses in the Vallée de l'Ubaye are operated by Autocars Maurel (☎ 04 92 81 20 09).

HAUTE-PROVENCE

There are three Barcelonnette-La Martinet buses a day, and four shuttle buses a day to/from Barcelonnette and Sauze (10FF one-way). *Navettes* (shuttle buses) between Sauze (3.5km south of Barcelonnette) and Super Sauze (5km farther south) are free.

VALLÉE DU HAUT VERDON

The breathtaking **Col d'Allos** (2250m) links Vallée de l'Ubaye with its southern neighbour, the Vallée du Haut Verdon which penetrates the **Parc National du Mercantour**. The mighty Verdon river has its source here at La Tête de la Sestrière (2572m).

Immediately after crossing the pass (snow blocked in winter), you arrive at the rather unattractive ski resort of **La Foux d'Allos** (1800m), 23.5km south of Pra-Loup and connected by *télécabine* (cable car). The tourist office (π 04 92 83 80 70, fax 04 92 83 86 27) is in the Maison de la Foux, on the main square. In the upper part of the village near the main lift stations, there is an *Auberge de Jeunesse* (π 04 92 83 81 08, fax 04 92 83 83 70) which charges 80FF for a dorm bed in summer and from 1900FF for a one week winter skiing package.

Allos (π 04 92 83 02 81 for the tourist office), 8km farther south on the D908, bears the same architectural stamp as its ugly sister and is as equally deserted outside of the ski season, with the exception of July and August when hotels reopen their doors to hikers for two months.

Lac d'Allos, 12km east of Allos along the D226, is the valley's main draw in summer. From Parking du Laus, the car park at the end of the road on Plateau du Laus, trails lead to Lac d'Allos (2226m) which, at 62 hectares, is the largest Alpine lake in Europe. Smaller **Lac de la Petite Cayolle** and **Lac des Garrets** are also accessible on foot. Route maps and hiking information are available from the Parc National du Mercantour office that operates from the car park in July and August. The park also organises guided nature walks (65/100FF for a half/full day). Book through the tourist office in Allos or La Foux d'Allos.

Lower down the valley, the villages of **Colmars** and **Beauvezer** are ideal retreats for hikers or skiers keen to escape the crowds. Colmars, 24km south of Allos and 28km north of Saint André les Alpes (see the Lacs du Verdon section earlier), is a pretty fortified village graced by high thick walls built by Vauban.

In Beauvezer (1179m), *Le Bellevue* (π/fax 04 92 83 51 60, place du Village) overlooking the village square is an appealing option. Charming rooms for two inside the former Café de la Poste – now painted pink – start at 235FF. The open-air swimming pool in the village is open in July and August from 10 am to 6 pm. *Camping Les Relarguiers* (π 04 92 83 47 73 or 04 92 83 57 60) in Beauvezer on the D908 charges 19/18FF per tent/person. Reception is open from 9 to 10.30 am.

For information on the region, go to the Maison de Pays de Haut Verdon (π 04 92 83 47 84, fax 04 92 83 50 43) in Beauvezer.

Getting There & Away

Autocars Girieud (π 04 92 83 40 27 in Colmar-les-Alpes) runs buses from Digne-les-Bains to La Foux d'Allos (two hours; two a day), 9km south-east of the actual resort, stopping at Saint André, Thorame-Haute Gare, Colmars and Allos.

From Nice, you can take the Chemin de Fer railway to Thorame-Haute Gare (see the boxed text Mountain Railway), from where you can get a bus. In addition to the two Digne-La Foux buses, there are three buses a day from Thorame-Haute Gare to Allos.

VALLÉE DE LA TINÉE

Europe's highest mountain pass, the **Col de Restefond la Bonette** which peaks at 2802m, links Barcelonnette and the Vallée de l'Ubaye with the tamer, more southern Vallée de la Tinée. In winter when the snowy pass is closed (November to June most years), the 149km Tinée valley can only be accessed up its southern leg from Nice. The narrow road (D2205) is laced with lacets and wiggles along the French-Italian border for the duration of its journey from the col to **Isola** (875m), where it plummets sharply south towards the coast.

The steep D97 makes an eastbound climb to **Isola 2000** (2000m), a horrible purpose-built ski resort from where the **Col de la Lombarde** (2350m) crosses into Italy. It offers good skiing but the snow can be heavy due to the Mediterranean's proximity. Isola 2000, 15km of hairpins from Isola and 93km north of Nice, is open from December to May and in summer, between mid-June and 1 September. Its 120km of pistes are served by 24 lifts and suitable for skiers/snow boarders of all levels. In March it hosts a Snow Carnival.

Saint Étienne-de-Tinée (pop 1780), a lovely Alpine village offering endless hiking opportunities around the Cime de la Bonette in summer, is 15km north of Isola village on the D2205. Southbound, the road twists through the beautiful Gorges de Valabres to **Saint Sauveur-sur-Tinée** (pop 340; alt 490m), a gateway to the Mercantour park. Three kilometres south on the D2205 is the **Ouvrage de la Frassinea**, a WWI military bunker cut in the rock to control the entrance to the valley.

West from Saint Sauveur along the torturous D30, you can access the spectacular **Gorges du Cians** and parallel **Gorges de Dalius**. Both gorges are carved from a deep burgundy coloured rock. The Gardienne des Gorges, a giant red rock naturally shaped to form a woman's head, guards the northern entrance to the Dalius gorges. Near by thrill-seekers **bungee jump** from the Pont du la Mariée, an 80m high stone footbridge across the gorges. In April, May, June and September, jumps have to be booked in advance (☎ 04 93 73 50 29). In July and August, jumpers can jump daily between 9 am and 5 pm; just turn up at the bridge.

Information

In Isola 2000, the tourist office (☎ 04 93 23 15 15, fax 04 93 23 14 25, isola@nicematin .fr, www.skifrance.fr/isola2000) is inside the Galerie Marchande high rise complex which also houses the ESF (☎ 04 93 23 11 78) in winter and a Parc National du Mercantour bureau in summer. The ESF organises ski touring in the park and heli-skiing. Internet access is available at the Cyber Châlet (☎ 04 93 23 90 40). In summer, the Mercantour has an office in Saint Sauveur-sur-Tinée (☎ 04 93 02 01 63), on the banks of the Tinée at 11 ave des Blavets.

Places to Stay

The nine *gîtes ruraux* around Isola can be booked through Gîtes de France des Alpes-Maritimes (☎ 04 92 15 21 30, fax 04 93 86 01 06), 55 Promenade des Anglais, Nice.

Isola 2000 has a host of unappealing concrete blocks. Down the valley in Isola village, one star *Hôtel de France (☎ 04 93 02 17 04)* has rooms from 215FF per person (half board).

In Saint Sauveur-sur-Tinée, *Au Relais d'Auron (☎ 04 93 02 00 03)* above the village tabac at 18 ave des Blavets (D2205) has rooms for 160FF. Guillaumes, 54km west at the northern mouth of the Gorges de Dalius, has rooms for 200FF at *Hôtel La Renaissance (☎ 04 93 05 12, fax 04 93 05 59 60)*. The hotel has a prime view of the sheep folds where the weekly village sheep fair takes place.

Getting There & Away

Year round, there are four buses between Nice and Isola (90FF; 2¼ hours).

VALLÉE DE LA VÉSUBIE

The Vésubie, a dead-end valley that has to be accessed from the south, is less wild that its north-western neighbours, primarily due to its proximity to Nice and the Côte d'Azur. Its calming lack of life still comes as a breath of fresh air after the touristic circus on the coast however.

The lacet laced **Gorges de la Vésubie** weaves its way from the Vésubie's southern foot which kicks off at Plan-du-Var, 20km north of Nice on the busy N202. For a stunning aerial view of the gorge and surrounding valley, head for **La Madone d'Utelle** (1181m), a pilgrimage site settled by Spanish sailors in the 9th century which, since 1806, has been crowned with a chapel. Sunday Mass is held here at 3 pm. Pilgrims come here each year on 15 August

(Assumption) and 8 September (Nativité de la Vierge). From the mountain village of **Saint Jean la Rivière** (D2565), a stone bridge crosses the Var river from where a steep, curvacious mountain pass (D32) leads west to **Utelle**, 6km north of La Madone.

Small old **Saint Martin-Vésubie** (pop 1041; postcode 06450; alt 964m), 24km north of Saint Jean, is the valley's main hiking base. The village's *vieux moulin* (old mill), at the foot of the village in the Quartier des Moulins, houses an interesting **Musée des Traditions Vésubiennes** (☎ 04 93 03 32 72), open daily from 2 to 6 pm. The Parc National du Mercantour office (☎ 04 93 03 23 15 or 04 93 16 78 88), inside the Maison du Parc at 8 rue Kellermann Sérurier, is open year round. For guided hikes and ski tours in the park, go to the Bureau des Guides (☎ 04 93 03 26 60 or 04 93 03 44 30), rue Cagnoli. Saint Martin tourist office (☎ 04 93 03 21 28), place Félix Faure, has details on other mountain guides that operate from here.

A good map for walks in the area is the Didier-Richard No 9 or IGN's Série Bleue maps Nos 3741OT *(Vallée de la Vésubie, Parc National du Mercantour)*

Activities

The small **skiing** station of La Colmiane, 7km west of Saint Martin across the Col de Saint Martin, is a friendly and unpretentious spot. Its only télésiège (☎ 04 93 02 83 54) is open from 10 am to 6 pm. (23/60FF single ticket/day pass). It whisks skiers and hikers to Pic de la Colmiane (1795m), from where 30km of pistes and many kilometres more of **hiking** trails can be accessed.

La Colmiane is graced with a **via ferrata** which takes intrepid want-to-be climbers on a breathtaking journey up sheer rock faces and over mind-blowing high rope-bridges. Anyone (with guts) can do it. You can hire all the necessary equipment (harness, ropes and karabiners, helmet) from Igloo Sports (☎ 04 93 02 83 43) for 30/60FF for a half/full day. The latter also rents skis and mountain bikes (30/120FF an hour/day). The via ferrata is 3km from the ski station

along an unpaved track; access costs 20FF. The Bureau des Guides (☎ 04 93 02 84 16) in La Colmiane, which arranges guided climbs (250FF for half a day), or the tourist office (☎ 04 93 02 88 59), has details.

Saint-Dalmas-Valdeblore (1350m), 5km farther west, is a leading **hang-gliding** *(parapente)* centre. The tourist office (☎ 04 93 23 25 90) in La Roche Valdeblore has a list of schools.

Places to Stay

On La Madone d'Utelle, the *Refuge Agapé* *(☎ 04 93 03 19 44)* next to the ochre-painted chapel is open year round. Full board costs 180-240FF per person and six nights is the maximum stay. Wild camping (for free) is allowed. Snow cuts off the gîte most winters for about 10 days.

In Saint Martin, *La Rouguière (☎ 04 93 03 29 19, rue Kellermann Sérurier)*, next to the Maison du Parc, is open year round and charges 62FF per person (no heating in winter). The lakeside *Gîte d'Étape du Mercantour (☎ 04 93 03 27 27 or 04 93 03 34 82)* in Le Boréon, 5km north-west of Saint Martin on the D89, overlooks Lac du Boréon and offers half board for 180FF. En route, buy honey from the *miellerie (☎ 04 93 03 20 97, route du Lac)*.

Camping Saint Dalmas (☎ 04 93 02 83 30) in Saint Dalmas is open year round. Rates are 10/22FF per tent/adult. The *gîte d'étape (☎ 04 93 02 83 96)* here has beds for 45FF.

Saint Martin and Saint Dalmas each have a handful of hotels. About 500m north of Utelle village is *Hôtel Bellevue (☎/fax 04 93 03 17 19)*, a Logis de France place with rooms from 190FF and a pool. It is open Easter to mid-September.

Places to Eat

Two kilometres west of Saint Jean la Rivière on the D32 is the *Auberge del Campo (☎ 04 93 03 13 12)*, a charming farmhouse inn run by a very humorous patron. The stone *mas* dates from 1785 and offers sweeping views of the gorges and village from its hillside terrace. A roaring fire warms the place in winter. *Menus* oozing local fresh produce cost 105, 140 and 160FF. The final *addition* (bill) is delivered to the table by Hubert, the alsatian dog. The auberge is open year round.

Don't miss sampling the *vin du lavande*, a potent lavender wine that is sold in the small shop adjoining the church on top of La Madone d'Utelle.

Getting There & Away
TRAM (☎ 04 93 03 20 23 in Saint Martin or 04 93 89 47 14 in Nice) operates one or two buses a day from Nice to Saint Martin (1¼ hours), stopping in Saint Jean la Rivière (45 minutes) en route. There are also a couple of buses to Saint Dalmas (2¼ hours) and La Colmiane (two hours).

VALLÉE DES MERVEILLES
Sandwiched between the Vésubie valley to the west and the Roya valley to the east, is the Valley of Wonders. It lies at the heart of the Parc National du Mercantour and protects one of world's most precious collections of Bronze Age petroglyphs. The rock engravings of human figures, bulls and other animals spread over 30 sq km around Mont Bégo (2872m) date from 1800 and 1500 BC and are thought to have been done by a Ligurian cult. The area is sprinkled with lakes.

The moonscape valley is snowcovered much of the year and the best time to visit is between July and September. Access is restricted. Hikers are only allowed to walk on authorised footpaths and are strongly encouraged by park authorities to only enter the valley with a guide. Guideless walkers have little chance of uncovering the wondrous petroglyphs. The Bureau des Guides in Saint Martin-Vésubie organises weekly guided hikes in the valley (150FF per person).

The main access routes into the valley are the eastbound D91 which can be picked up in Saint Dalmas-de-Tende (see later) in the Vallée de la Roya, or the dead-end D171 which leads north in to the valley from Roquebillière in the Vallée de la Vésubie. Half way along the 15km track you pass Cascade du Ray, a waterfall. From the car park at the end of the road, it is an easy 1km hike along the left bank of the river (signposted 'Refuge de Nice via L'Éstrech') to the Cascade de L'Éstrech. The GR52 links the Refuge de Nice (2232m) with the rest of the Vallée des Merveilles. The Club Alpin Français (☎ 04 93 62 59 99), 14 ave Mirabeau, 06000 Nice, takes bookings for Refuge de Nice (check-in before 6 pm) and other valley refuges.

IGN's Série Bleue maps and 3841OT *(Vallée de la Roya, Vallée des Merveilles)* covers the area in a scale of 1:25,000.

VALLÉE DE LA ROYA
The Roya Valley once served as a hunting ground for King Victor Emmanuel II of Italy and only became part of France in 1947. In this valley is the pretty village of Breil-sur-Roya (pop 2000; postcode 06540; alt 280m), just 62km north-east of Nice. There are good views of the village from the Col de Brouis (879m) which links Sospel, 21km south, with the Roya valley.

The dramatic Gorges de Saorge, 9km north of Breil, lead to the fortified village of Saorge (520m), overlooking the valley and set in a natural amphitheatre. The village is a maze of narrow, stepped streets and 15th to 17th century houses.

Immediately north of here, the Gorges de Bergue goes to Saint Dalmas-de-Tende, the main gateway into the Vallée des Merveilles. From St Dalmas, the D91 wiggles 10km west to Lac des Mesches (1390m), from where trails lead in to the valley past the Refuge des Merveilles (2111m). Alternatively, continue for 5km to Casterino at the end of the D91 where more northern trails start.

In neighbouring Tende (pop 2000; postcode 06430; alt 815m), 4km north of Saint Dalmas, the modern Musée des Merveilles (☎ 04 93 04 32 50), ave du 16 Septembre 1947, is a good place to go before embarking on a trek into the Merveilles. The museum unravels the natural history of the valley and exhibits numerous archaeological finds. It is open from 10.30 am to 6.30 pm; until 9 pm on Saturday; closed Tuesday (30/15FF for adult/student).

Activities

Breil-sur-Roya is a leading water sports base. Roya Évasion (☎/fax 04 93 04 91 46), 1 rue Pasteur, organises **kayaking** (80FF initiation), **canyoning** (290FF) and **rafting** (250FF) trips on the Roya river, as well as one-day hikes (130FF) and VTT expeditions (220-280FF). Bookings have to be made in advance. AET Nature (☎/fax 04 93 04 47 64), overlooking central place Biancheri, is run by knowledgeable mountain guides who run white water trips and one-day **guided hikes** (130/90FF for adult/child). Breil-sur-Roya tourist office (☎ 04 93 04 99 76), place Biancheri, sells local maps and guides.

Guides for the Vallée des Merveilles can be hired at Saint Dalmas and Tende. Tende tourist office (☎ 04 93 04 73 71), ave du 16 Septembre 1947; and the Bureau des Guides du Val des Merveilles (☎ 04 93 04 77 73), 18 rue de France, have details on guided jeep and hiking expeditions. The latter also rents equipment and sells tickets for the **via ferrata des Comtes Lascaris** in Tende (see Facts for the Visitor chapter).

In Sospel, the tourist office (☎ 04 93 04 15 80, fax 04 93 04 19 96), tucked inside the old city gate on *Le Pont Vieux* (the old bridge) is open year round and has reams of information on hiking and canoeing around Sospel and the Vallée de la Roya.

Places to Stay & Eat

The *USBTP Municipal Azur & Merveilles* (☎ 04 93 04 46 66, fax 04 93 04 92 22) is a large ground signposted from Breil-sur-Roya train station. It is open year round and

rates start at 28/17/10FF for a tent/adult/car. It has caravan rental and a swimming pool.

The *Refuge des Merveilles* (☎ 04 93 04 64 64) has 40 beds and is open from mid June to the end of September. Half board costs 158FF. *Neige & Merveilles* (☎ 04 93 04 62 40, fax 04 93 04 88 58) in Saint Dalmas-de-Tende is a mountain activity centre, open from 1 April to 31 October. It charges 105/80/65FF for a bed in a double/dormitory/refuge. In Tende, *Gîte d'Étape Les Carlines* (☎/fax 04 93 04 62 74) charges similar rates.

Hotel-wise, the valley boasts a couple of lovely places. In Breil-sur-Roya *Hôtel Le Roya* (☎ 04 93 04 48 10, fax 04 93 04 92 70, place Biancheri) is housed in a 16th century mill, the old mill stone and grinding mechanisms of which adorn the basement restaurant. Half board starts at 270FF per person and *menus* in the mill are 98, 128 and 230FF. It has seven types of trout (still happily swimming around when you arrive) to choose from.

In Saint Dalmas-de-Tende, the lakeside *Hôtel-Restaurant Le Prieuré* is housed in a majestic priory (☎ 04 93 04 75 70, fax 04 93 04 71 58). It hosts organ recitals and prides itself on its gastronomy.

Getting There & Away

There are SNCF train station in Sospel (☎ 04 93 04 00 17), Breil-sur-Roya (☎ 04 93 04 40 15), Saint Dalmas-de-Tende and Tende (☎ 04 93 04 65 60). They are all served by the Nice-Turin line which runs several times a day from the coast, along the Roya valley and into Italy.

Nice to Menton

Nice and Menton (and the 30km of towns in between) are linked by three *corniches* (coastal roads), each one higher and more hazardous than the last. They are particularly celebrated for their breathtaking sea views and, in July and August, hellish traffic which moves at a snail's pace in the searing heat. In the 1920s, motorists tried to race the coastal *Train Bleu* (Blue Train) from Paris along these roads. Speed fiends today should opt for the inland A8 which continues east to Ventimiglia (Vintimille in French) in Italy.

Luxurious seaside villas, medieval *villages perchés* (hilltop villages), breathtaking *belvédères* (view-points) and body-packed beaches abound along this stretch of the coast. Inland is the *arrière-pays Niçois* (Niçois hinterland), a remote maze of hilltop villages and hairpin mountain passes guaranteed to send a chill through the raciest of drivers.

Nice makes an ideal base for exploring the rest of the Côte d'Azur. The city has plenty of relatively cheap places to stay and is only a short train or bus ride from Monaco (see the Monaco chapter), Cannes and other Riviera hot spots.

Nice

• pop 400,000   ✉ 06000, 06300

Nice is nice. So it's apt that Nice (Nissa in Niçois, Niço in Provençal, Nizza in Italian) – the fifth largest town in France – should be dubbed the Côte d'Azur's capital. This fashionable but relaxed city is fun fun fun, and never more so than in the height of summer when backpackers flock here in their droves to dip their toes in its sparkling waters and sample the best of southern France's 'sky-blue coast'.

The city's grey pebble beach may not be worthy of a postcard home, but the city's fantastic architecture from the turn-of-the-century *belle époque*, its fine ensemble of

HIGHLIGHTS

- Feel romantic, looking at wedding cake mansions of belle époque Nice
- Discover what made Matisse tick in Cimiez; see his modern friends at MAMAC
- Follow in Le Corbusier's footsteps in Cap Martin-Roquebrune
- See how the rich live: visit Cap Ferrat's Villa Rothschild and the Villa Grecque Kérylos in Beaulieu-sur-Mer
- Take the coastal path from Cap Martin to Monte Carlo (three hours)
- Eat *socca*, *pan bagnat* and other nice treats in and around Nice

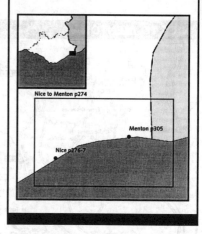

Nice to Menton p274

Menton p305

Nice p276-7

art museums, and its buzzing cultural scene most certainly are. The famous Nice Carnival sets the streets ablaze each year around Mardi Gras with a merry-go-round of masked parades, colourful floats and fireworks.

Nice was founded by the seafaring Greeks who named the colony Nikaia, to commemorate a victory *(nike* in Greek) over a nearby town. The Romans who followed in 154 BC settled farther uphill in Cemenelum (now Cimiez). The city only become part of France in 1860.

Plans are afoot to grace nice Nice with a tramway in the next century.

Orientation

Ave Jean Médecin runs south from near the train station to place Masséna. The modern city centre, the area north and west of place Masséna, includes the upmarket pedestrianised streets of rue de France and rue Masséna. The Station Centrale (bus terminal on square Général Leclerc) and Intercity bus station are three and five blocks east of place Masséna.

The famous promenade des Anglais follows the gently curved beachfront westwards from the port area, past the city centre to the airport, 6km to the west. Vieux

Nice (Old Nice) is delineated by blvd Jean Jaurès, quai des États-Unis and, to the east, the hill known as Le Château. Place Garibaldi is at the north-eastern tip of Vieux Nice.

The wealthy residential neighbourhood of Cimiez, home to several outstanding museums, is just north of the city centre.

Information

Tourist Offices The most convenient tourist office (☎ 04 93 87 07 07, fax 04 93 16 85 16, otc@nice-coteazur.org, www .nice-coteazur.org) is next to the train station on ave Thiers. It's open from 8 am to 7 pm (8 pm from July to September). The less crowded annexe (☎ 04 92 14 48 00, fax 04 92 14 49 03), 5 promenade des Anglais, is open from 8 am to 6 pm (8 pm from May to September; closed Sunday).

Near the airport, there is the Nice Ferber branch office (☎ 04 93 83 32 64, fax 04 93

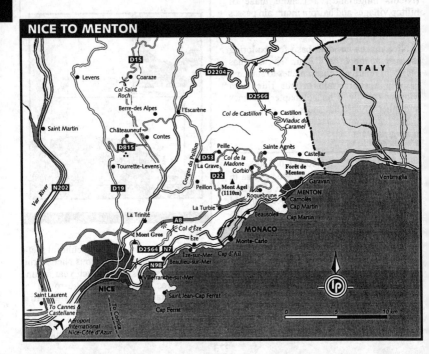

72 08 27), promenade des Anglais (towards town from the airport terminal). Inside the airport, there is an information desk (☎ 04 93 21 44 11, fax 04 93 21 44 50), situated at Terminal 1.

The Centre Information Jeunesse (☎ 04 93 80 93 93), 19 rue Gioffredo, is open from 8.45 am to 6.45 pm (closed on weekends).

For departmental information, go to the Comité Régional du Tourisme Côte d'Azur (☎ 04 93 37 78 78, fax 04 93 86 01 06, crt06@nicematin.fr, www.crt-riviera.fr), 55 promenade des Anglais. It's open from 8.30 am to noon and 2 to 6 pm (closed on weekends).

National Park Office The headquarters of the Parc National du Mercantour (☎ 04 93 16 78 88, fax 04 93 88 79 05), 23 rue d'Italie, is open from 9 am to 6 pm (closed on weekends). It stocks numerous guides including the free *Les Guides Randoxygène* series which detail 25 canyoning routes, 40 VTT trails and hiking trails in the national park.

Money The Banque de France, 14 ave Félix Faure, is open from 8.45 am to 12.15 pm and 1.30 to 3.30 pm (closed on weekends).

American Express (☎ 04 93 16 53 53), 11 promenade des Anglais, is open from 9 am to noon and 2 to 6 pm (Saturday until noon; closed Sunday). Daily hours from May to September are 9 am to 9 pm. Barclays Bank, rue Alphonse Karr, is open from 8.40 to 11.45 am and 1.30 to 4.45 pm (closed on weekends).

Opposite the train station, Change (☎ 04 93 88 56 80), 17 ave Thiers (to the right as you exit the terminal building), offers decent rates and is open from 7 am to midnight. Its opening hours are the same at its other branches: 64 ave Jean Médecin (☎ 04 93 13 45 44), and 10 rue de France (☎ 04 93 82 16 55).

The Banque Populaire de la Côte d'Azur, 17 ave Jean Médecin, has a 24-hour currency exchange machine, as does its branch,

just north of Vieux Nice, at 20 blvd Jean Jaurès.

Post The main post office – a fantastic red-brick building near the main train station at 23 ave Thiers – exchanges foreign currency and is open from 8 am to 7 pm (Saturday until noon; closed Sunday). Hours at the place Grimaldi branch, 20 rue du Maréchal Joffre, and at the branch on the corner of rue de Russie and rue Clémenceau, are 8 am to 6.30 pm (Saturday until noon; closed Sunday).

In Vieux Nice, the post office, 2 rue Louis Gassin, off cours Saleya, is open from 8.30 am to 6.30 pm (Wednesday from 9 am; Saturday from 8.30 am to noon; closed Sunday). Poste restante services are available at American Express too (see Money).

The postcode for central Nice north and west of blvd Jean Jaurès and ave Galliéni is 06000. The postcode for Vieux Nice and the ferry port is 06300.

Email & Internet Access The Web Store (☎ 04 93 87 87 99, info@webstore.fr, www.webstore.fr), 12 rue de Russie, charges 30/50FF for half/one hour online. It's open from 10 am to noon and 2 to 7 pm (closed Sunday).

For a drink while you surf, log in at La Douche Cybercafé (☎ 04 93 62 81 31), 32 cours Saleya. It is open from 6 pm to 12.30 am. Half/one hour online is 25/45FF.

Travel Agencies USIT Voyages (☎ 04 93 87 34 96), the Irish student travel outfit, has branches at 10 rue de Belgique, and 17 rue de France. Both are open from 9.30 am to 6 pm (Saturday from 10 am to 1 pm; closed Sunday).

Bookshops New and second-hand English-language novels and guides are available at The Cat's Whiskers (☎/fax 04 93 80 02 66), 26 rue Lamartine, open from 9.30 am to 12.15 pm and 2 to 6.45 pm (Saturday from 9.30 am to 12.15 pm and 3 to 6 pm; closed Sunday).

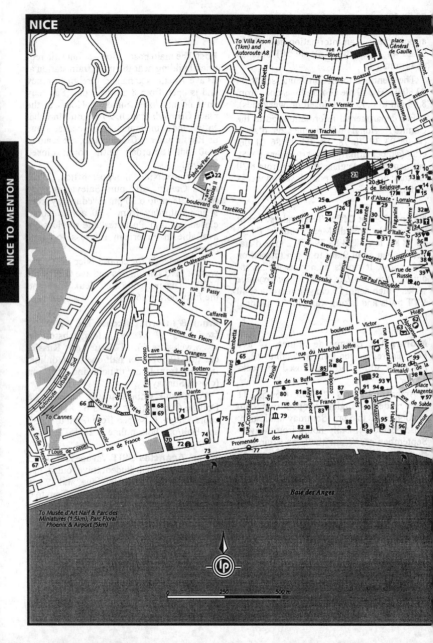

NICE

To Villa Arson
(1km) and
Autoroute A8

place
Général
de Gaulle

rue A
Binet

rue Clément - Roassal

rue Vernier

rue Trachel

boulevard Gambetta

avenue Malausséna

avenue Villermont

rue

boulevard du Tzaréwich

avenue Thiers

de Belgique

d'Alsace - Lorraine

avenue Durante

rue Paganini

rue d'Angleterre

rue d'Italie

rue Clémenceau

rue de
Russie

rue Berlioz

avenue Gounod

rue Aubert

avenue Georges

rue Paul Déroulède

rue Hugo

rue de Châteauneuf

rue Guiglia

rue Rossini

rue Verdi

boulevard Victor

rue Maccarani

rue Alphonse Karr

rue F Passy

Caffarelli

avenue des Fleurs

boulevard Gambetta

rue du Maréchal Joffre

place
Grimaldi

place
Magenta

des Orangers

boulevard François Grosso

rue Bottero

rue Rivoli

rue de la Buffa

rue Dalpozzo

rue Meyerbeer

rue de France

avenue du Congrès

rue de Suède

rue Masséna

rue Halévy

avenue

ave des Baumettes

rue Dante

avenue de Verdun

rue de France

rue de la Buffa

Promenade

des

Anglais

To Cannes

avenue Emile Henriot

rue Saint Louis de Coppet

avenue Renoir

Autoroute Urbaine Sud

Baie des Anges

To Musée d'Art Naïf & Parc des
Miniatures (1.5km), Parc Floral
Phoenix & Airport (5km)

0   250   500 m

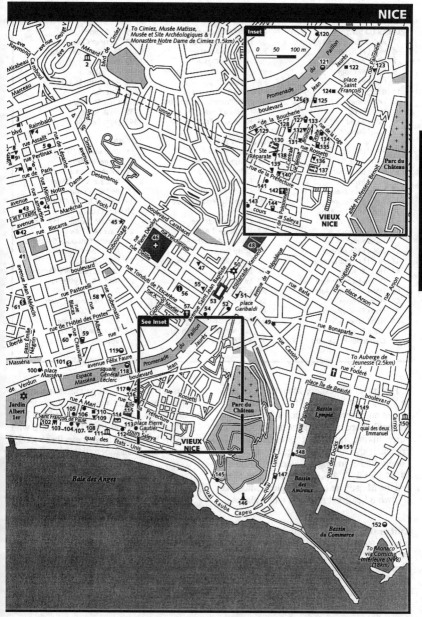

NICE

PLACES TO STAY

3 Pado Tourisme Hostel
6 Hôtel Plaisance
7 Hôtel Alexandra
9 Hôtel Regency
10 Hôtel Pastoral
11 Backpackers' Hôtel &
Le Faubourg Montmartre
Restaurant;
Hôtel Astrid
13 Hôtel Darcy & Restaurant
de Paris
15 Hôtel Novelty
16 Hôtel de la Gare
17 Hôtel Idéal Bristol
23 Hôtel Bamby
28 Hôtel Belle Meunière
29 Hôtel du Piemont
30 Hôtel Les Orangers
32 Hôtel du Centre
36 Hôtel Lyonnais &
Hôtel Notre Dame
37 Hôtel Clémenceau
43 Hôtel Le Petit Louvre
49 Hotel Genève
67 Centre Hébergement Jeunes
68 Hôtel Résidence Astoria
69 Hôtel Carlone
70 Melia Elysée Palace
76 Hôtel Cronstadt
78 Hôtel Négresco &
Chantecler Restaurant

81 Hôtel Meyerbeer
82 Hôtel Westminster Concorde
85 Hôtel Les Mimosas
86 Hôtel Les Cigales
96 Hôtel Méridien; L'Absolute
98 Hôtel Little Masséna
102 Hôtel Beau Rivage
110 Hôtel Meublé Le Genevois
122 Hôtel au Picardy
124 Hôtel Saint François

PLACES TO EAT

4 Chez Mireille
8 L'Ange Gourmand
12 China Fast Food
14 Restaurant Le Toscan
18 Casino Cafétéria
35 L'Allegria; Restaurant au
Soleil
39 Crêperie Bretonne
47 L'Auberge d'Acropolis
51 L'Olivier & 4 Wheels
Skate Shop
55 Lou Balico - Chez Adrienne
58 La Nissarda
60 Le Bistrot Saint Germain
83 La Trattoria
84 Manoir Café
87 Le Moulin à Poivre
93 Aux Spécialités Belges;
La Ferme (Cheese Shop)
97 Scotch Tea House

103 Le Comptoir
107 Mexican Café
109 La Divina Commedia
123 Escalinada
129 À L'Écurie
131 Restaurant La Fanny
132 Calexico
136 Chez Thérèsa
139 Nissa Socca
140 Nissa La Bella

OTHER

1 Gare du Sud (Trains to
Digne-les-Bains)
2 Musée National Message
Biblique Marc Chagall
5 Best One Laundrette
19 Central Tourist Office
20 Nicea Location Rent
(Bicycle/Motorcycle Rental)
21 Gare Nice Ville
22 Russian Orthodox Cathedral
24 Main Post Office
25 Sports Évasion
26 Change (Currency Exchange)
27 Rent a Car Système;
Budget (Car Rental)
31 Parc National du Mercantour
Headquarters
33 Église Notre Dame
34 Magellan Librairie de
Voyages

The travel bookshop, Magellan Librairie de Voyages (☎ 04 93 82 31 81), 3 rue d'Italie, has an excellent selection of IGN maps, Didier-Richard hiking maps, topoguides and other hiking information, most of it in French. It also stocks travel guides, including Lonely Planet in English. Papéterie Rontani (☎ 04 93 62 32 43), 5 rue Alexandre Mari, and the Maison de la Presse, place Masséna, are two other great map and guide places.

Cultural Centres The ornate Église Anglicane, Holy Trinity Anglican Church (☎ 04 93 87 19 83), 11 rue de la Buffa, has a mixed American and British membership and functions as an Anglophone cultural centre. Sunday Mass is at 11 am. Adjoining the church is a cemetery containing the graves of 'pioneer' expatriates from the 19th and early 20th centuries. Among the tombs is that of Henri Francis Lyte (1793-1847), a British vicar from Devonshire who wrote the hymn, *Abide with me*, three weeks before dying from tuberculosis in Nice.

A list of church services celebrated in other languages (12 in total, including Croat, Filipino, Polish, Spanish and Italian) is pinned outside the Église du Vœu (☎ 04 93 85 35 63), 2 rue Alfred Mortier.

The English-American library, 12 rue de France, is open from 10 to 11 am and 3 to 5 pm (closed Monday, Friday and on weekends). Short-term memberships are welcomed. Cut through the passageway opposite 17 rue de France and walk straight ahead down the steps.

38 Web Store (Cybercafé)	77 Airport Buses	119 Sunbus Information Office
40 Anglo-American Bridge Club	79 Musée Masséna	120 Motor Vespa Centre
41 Nice Étoile Shopping Mall &	80 Cave de la Buffa	121 Intercity Bus Station
FNAC Store	(Wine Cellar)	125 William's Pub
42 Prisunic (Supermarket)	88 Palais de la Méditerranée	126 Banque Populaire de la
44 The Cat's Whiskers	89 American Express	Côte d'Azur
(English Books)	90 USIT Voyages	127 Jonathan's Live Music Pub
45 Police Headquarters	91 English-American Library	128 Pub Oxford
46 Hôpital Saint Roch	92 Église Anglicane	130 Cathédrale Sainte Réparate
48 Acropolis (Congress Palace)	94 Ducs de Gascogne	133 Palais Lascaris
50 Jardin Maréchal Juin	(Luxury Food Shop)	134 Espace Photographique
52 Prisunic (Supermarket)	95 Tourist Office Annexe	Quinto-Albicocco
53 Musée d'Art Moderne	99 Cycles Arnaud	135 Scarlett O'Hara Irish Pub
et d'Art Contemporain	(Bicycle Rental)	137 Église Saint Jacques le Majeur
54 Théâtre de Nice	100 Maison de la Presse	138 Gelati Azzurro (Ice-Creams)
56 Centre Information Jeunesse	101 Banque de France	141 La Poulette (Chicken Shop)
57 Église du Voeu	104 Moulin à Huile d'Olive	142 Église Saint Giaume
59 Le Pub Giofreddo	Alziari (Olive Oil)	143 Fruit & Vegetable Market
61 24-Hour Currency Exchange	105 Hôtel de Ville	144 La Douche Cybercafé;
62 UK Consulate	106 Papéterie Rontani	Thor Pub
63 Post Office	108 Opéra de Nice	145 Tour Bellanda; Lift;
64 US Consulate	111 Galérie des Ponchettes;	Musée Naval
65 Casino (Supermarket)	Galerie Musée Alexis et	146 WWI Memorial
66 Musée des Beaux-Arts	Gustav Adolf Mossa	147 Factory
Jules Chéret	112 Flower Market	148 Trans Côte d'Azur
71 Le Capitole (Boulangerie)	113 Chapelle de la Miséricorde	(Boat Excursions);
72 Comité Régional du Tourisme	114 Vieux Nice Post Office	Poiseïdon (Diving School)
Côte d'Azur & Gîtes de	115 Palais de Justice;	149 PH + Plongée (Diving Shop)
France Office	Palais de la Préfecture	150 Musée Terra Amata
73 Public Showers & Toilets	116 Chez Waynes	151 L'Odyssée (Diving Shop)
74 Airport Buses	117 No-Name Boulangerie	152 Ferry Terminal & SNCM
75 Intermarché (Supermarket)	118 Station Centrale (Bus Station)	Office

Laundry Self-service laundrettes are plentiful. Near the train station, head for 8 rue de Belgique (open 7 am to 11 pm), 14 rue de Suisse or 16 rue d'Angleterre (both open 7 am to 9 pm). Nearer to the beach, try 39 rue de la Buffa (open 7 am to 9 pm) or Top Speed, 12 rue de la Buffa (open 8 am to 8 pm). Taxi Lav, corner of rue Pertinax and rue Lamartine, is handy for backpackers staying at Hôtel Le Petit Louvre. Best One, 26 rue Pertinax, is open from 6 am to 10 pm.

Medical Services Hôpital Saint Roch (☎ 04 92 03 33 75), 5 rue Pierre Dévoluy, has a 24-hour emergency service.

There is a 24-hour pharmacy at 7 rue Massé (☎ 04 93 87 78 94) and at 66 ave Jean Médecin (☎ 04 93 62 54 44).

Emergency The police headquarters (☎ 04 92 17 22 22), 1 ave Maréchal Foch, has a special *cellule touristes étrangers* (foreign tourist department; ☎ 04 92 17 20 31), open daily from 8 to 11 am and 2 to 5.45 pm. Be prepared to queue.

Promenade des Anglais

The palm-lined 'English Promenade', paid for by Nice's English colony in 1822 as a shoreside walking path, provides a fine stage for a stroll along the beach and the Baie des Anges (Bay of Angels). Don't miss the façade of the art deco **Palais de la Méditerranée**, crumbling in all its magnificence at 13-17 promenade des Anglais. The 1930s casino was the prize property of American millionaire Frank Jay Gould whose seafront enterprise was France's top-earning casino until the 1970s when his luck turned and he had to shut up shop. Plans to turn it into a commercial centre appear to have likewise taken a tailspin.

Heading east towards Vieux Nice and the port, promenade des Anglais becomes **quai des États-Unis**, named after the United States in honour of President Wilson's decision in 1917 for the USA to join WWI. A colossal memorial commemorating the 4000 Niçois who died in the war is carved in the rock at the eastern end of the quay.

At 77 quai des États-Unis is the **Galérie des Ponchettes**, known also as the Galérie-Musée Raoul Dufy (☎ 04 93 62 31 24), dedicated to fauvist Raoul Dufy (1877-1953) who spent many years in Nice and is buried in the cemetery of Cimiez Monastery. The 19th century, vaulted hall houses a dull natural history museum but some good temporary exhibitions. The building served as an arsenal for the Sardinian navy, then as a fish market until 1950, when Matisse persuaded the council to revamp it.

Locally-produced works of art can be seen at the **Galerie Musée Alexis et Gustav Adolf Mossa** (☎ 04 93 62 37 11), 59 quai des États-Unis. Alexis Mossa (1844-1926) is best known, not for his watercolours, but for introducing wildly-decorated floats to the Nice Carnival.

Other pleasant places for a walk include **Cimiez** (see later), Nice's most exclusive quarter; and the **Jardin Maréchal Juin**, a modernist red concrete garden on the eastern side of the Musée d'Art Moderne et d'Art Contemporain (see later), opposite the **Acropolis** (☎ 04 93 92 83 00), a congress and exhibition palace.

At the south end of **ave Jean Médecin**, Nice's main commercial street, sits **place Masséna**, whose early 19th century, neoclassical arcaded buildings are painted in various shades of ochre and red. This is Nice's largest public square. Its western end is dominated by the 19th century **Jardin Albert 1er**, in which a giant arc

which was designed by sculptor Bernar Venet elegantly reclines. The sculpture, entitled *Arc 115°5*, commemorates the centenary of the appellation 'Côte d'Azur', the brainchild of French poet Stéphane Liégeard (1830-1925) who published a guidebook on the southern French coast in 1887 entitled *La Côte d'Azur* (The Azure Coast). The name stuck.

Espace Masséna, a public square enlivened by fountains, a rollerblading dome and ornamental gardens, straddles the eastern side of place Masséna.

Absolutely Fabulous

Belle époque Nice was absolutely fabulous. The wedding cake mansions, palaces and pastel-painted concrete gâteaux that sprung up in abundance at this time were not just fabulous; they were absolutely fantastical.

The Cimiez quarter remains the pearl of this lavish, turn-of-the-century legacy. The Haussmann-style **Conservatoire de Music**, 8 blvd de Cimiez, dates from 1902. Continuing north along blvd Cimiez to No 46 is **L'Alhambra** (1901), an opulent private mansion set on a small, palm tree-studded mound and surrounded by a high wall – but not high enough to hide the Moorish minarets that rise from the sparkling white building. The **Villa Raphaeli-Surany** (1900), opposite at No 35, is adorned with intricate mosaic reliefs. The boulevard's crowning jewel is the **Hôtel Excelsior Régina** Palace, 71 ave Régina, at the north end of blvd de Cimiez. It was built in 1896 to welcome Queen Victoria to Nice (a statue of her stands in front) and was later home to Henri Matisse.

The pink wedding cake you see from Nice ferry port, atop Mont Boron, is the **Château des Anglais**, built in 1859 by an English engineer for a Scot. He was renowned at the time as being the only foreigner to live in Nice year round.

Vieux Nice

This area of narrow, winding streets between quai des États-Unis and the Musée d'Art Moderne et d'Art Contemporain has looked pretty much the same since the 1700s. Arcade-lined **place Garibaldi**, built during the latter half of the 18th century, is named after one of the great heroes of Italian unification, Giuseppe Garibaldi (1807-82), born and buried in Nice (in the cemetery in Parc du Château).

Cours Saleya and rue de la Préfecture, the old city's main artery, are dominated by the imposing **Palais de la Préfecture**, built at the beginning of the 17th century for the Princes of Savoy.

Interesting churches in Vieux Nice include the baroque **Cathédrale Sainte Réparate** built in honour of the city's patron saint on place Rossetti around 1650; the blue-grey and yellow **Église Saint Jacques Le Majeur**, place du Gésu (close to rue Rossetti), whose baroque ornamentation dates from the mid-17th century; the **Église Saint Giaume**, 1 rue de la Poissonnerie; and the **Chapelle de la Miséricorde** (1740), next to place Pierre Gautier on cours Saleya.

Rue Benoît Bunico, which runs perpendicular to rue Rossetti, served as Nice's Jewish ghetto after a 1430 law restricted where Jews could live. Gates at each end were locked at sunset. The parallel street, rue Droite, is home to the contemporary **Espace Photographique Quinto-Albicocco** (☎ 04 93 85 94 36), 14 rue Droite, which hosts a variety of photographic exhibitions, usually featuring the much-photographed Côte d'Azur. The gallery is open from 10.30 am to 1 pm and from 2 to 6 pm. It is closed Sunday and Monday; admission is free.

Continuing south along the same street you come to the 17th century, baroque **Palais Lascaris** (☎ 04 93 62 05 54) at No 15. The arms and motto of the Lascaris-Ventimiglia family who owned the house can still be seen above the entrance hall. The motto between the two-headed eagles reads 'Not even lightning shall strike me'. The monumental staircase leads up to state apartments, the ceilings of which are richly decorated with elaborate frescoes depicting ancient mythology. Fine Flemish tapestries line the walls. Traditional occupations such as weaving and pottery are brought to life in the 3rd floor exhibition. The 18th century pharmacy on the ground floor originates from the Jura region. The Palais Lascaris is open from 10 am to noon and 2 to 6 pm; closed Monday (25/15FF for adult/student). Open-house children's workshops take place on Wednesday between 2 and 4 pm. Guided tours of the palace (for adults) depart on Wednesday, Friday and Saturday at 3 pm.

Parc du Château

At the eastern end of quai des États-Unis, atop a 92m hill, is this shady public park, where local families come to stroll, admire the panoramic views of Nice and the sparkling Baie des Anges, or visit the **Cascade Donjon**, an artificial waterfall crowned with a spacious viewing platform. It's a great place to escape the heat on a summer afternoon (open 7 am to 8 pm). Open-air concerts are held here on summer evenings.

The 12th century chateau after which the hill and park are named was razed by Louis XIV in 1706. In the one remaining tower, the 16th century **Tour Bellanda**, above the eastern end of quai des États-Unis, is the **Musée Naval**, also known as the Musée de la Marine (☎ 04 93 80 47 61), with exhibits for dyed-in-the-wool Sinbads. It's open from 10 am to noon and 2 to 5 pm (7 pm in summer; closed Monday and Tuesday). The cemetery where Garibaldi (see Vieux Nice) is buried covers the north-west area of the park.

To get to the top of Le Château, take the lift, the **ascenseur du château** (3.80/5.40FF single/return; 1.90/3.80FF for children) from under the Tour Bellanda, rue des Ponchettes. It operates from 9 am to 5.50 pm (7.50 pm in summer). Alternatively, trudge up the staircase on montée Lesage or at the east end of rue Rossetti.

Passport to Nice

Museums in Nice are free every first Sunday of the month. Beyond that, you have to pay to view Matisse's *Blue Nude*, Warhol's *Dollar Sign* or Christo's wrapped shopping trolley (unless you're seven years old or younger).

The Promenade des Anglais tourist office sells a one week *passe musée* costing 40FF which allows one visit to each of Nice's museums during seven consecutive days. If you intend straying farther afield, invest in a *Carte Musée Côte d'Azur* (see the Facts for the Visitor chapter for details).

Musée d'Art Moderne et d'Art Contemporain

The Museum of Modern and Contemporary Art, MAMAC (☎ 04 93 62 61 62) is Nice's pride and joy in the architectural stakes. It specialises in European and American avant-garde works from the 1960s to the present. Glass walkways connect the four marble-coated towers, on top of which is a rooftop garden and gallery featuring pieces by Nice-born Yves Klein (1928-62). The sweeping views of Nice are equally attractive.

Highlights include Andy Warhol's *Campbell's Soup Can* (1965), a shopping trolley wrapped by Christo, *Entablature* (1971) by pop artist Roy Lichtenstein, and a pea-green model-T Ford compressed to a 1.60m-tall block by French sculptor César.

The hall, dedicated to the 1960s new realism movement, features works by Romanian Daniel Spoerri (1930-) and Arman (1928-). Spoerri's *La Table Bleue* (The Blue Table) features the remnants from a table in a Parisian restaurant – unwashed cutlery and crockery stuck behind glass. Arman is best known for encasing mountains of mundane objects like kitchen trash, letters or children's toys in monumental perspex containers, some of which are on display in the museum. Arman, born in Nice as Armand Fernandez in 1928, studied at the

city's École Nationale d'Art Décoratif. A printer's mistake inspired him to drop the 'd' from his name in 1958.

MAMAC, ave Saint Jean Baptiste, is open from 10 am to 6 pm; closed Tuesday (25/15FF for adult/student). Art films and cult movies are screened twice a month (usually on Thursday) at 3 and 8.30 pm in the auditorium. Take bus No 17 from the train station to the Station Centrale from where the museum is a three minute walk north-east.

Musée National Message Biblique Marc Chagall

The Marc Chagall Biblical Message Museum (☎ 04 93 53 87 20) is close to blvd de Cimiez across the street from 4 ave Docteur Ménard. It houses the largest public collection of works by Russian painter Marc Chagall (1887-1985) who lived in Saint Paul de Vence from 1950 until his death at the age of 98.

Floating humans, goats and green-headed violins characterise Chagall's work. His *Biblical Message Cycle*, displayed in the severe, purpose-built museum, includes 12 canvases illustrating scenes from the Old Testament. Don't miss a second version of the *Blue Rose* mosaic (1958) of the rose window at Metz Cathedral viewed through a plate-glass window and reflected in a small pond.

The museum is open from 10 am to 5 pm; to 6 pm from July to October; closed Tuesday year round (30/20FF for adult/student). Take bus No 15 from place Masséna to the stop in front of the museum; or walk (signposted from ave de L'Olivetto).

Musée Masséna

The Masséna Museum (☎ 04 93 88 11 34), also known as the Musée d'Art et d'Histoire, is in the Palais Masséna, 65 rue de France. The eclectic collection of paintings, furniture, icons, ceramics and religious art – housed in an Italian-style villa dating from 1898 – can be viewed between 10 am and noon and from 2 to 6 pm. It is closed Monday (25/15FF for adult/student).

The palm tree-studded gardens behind the museum (off promenade des Anglais) are equipped with the same blue chairs as promenade des Anglais, making for a shady, pleasantly popular hideaway from the posing crowds on the packed prom. The gardens close at 7 pm in summer.

Musée des Beaux-Arts Jules Chéret

The Jules Chéret Fine Arts Museum (☎ 04 93 44 50 72), 33 ave des Baumettes, just off rue de France, is housed in a fantastic, cream and apricot 19th century villa built for Ukrainian Princess Elisabeth Vassilievna Kotschoubey in 1878. Its decorative stucco friezes and six-column rear terrace overlooking luxuriant gardens are typical of houses dating from Nice's *belle époque*.

The collection includes works by Dutch artist Kees van Dongen (1877-1968) and Dufy; several Flemish tapestries; Pierre Bonnard's 20th century *Window Opening onto the Seine at Vernonnet*; some late impressionist pieces by Monet and Sisley; and a large number of works by Jules Chéret (1836-1932), the creator of modern poster art.

Museum opening hours and admission fees are the same as at the Musée Masséna. The one-hour guided tour on Wednesday at 3 pm (in French only) costs an extra 20FF. Bus No 38 from the Station Centrale stops outside.

Cimiez & the Musée Matisse

The Matisse Museum (☎ 04 93 81 08 08), 164 ave des Arènes de Cimiez, which houses a fine collection of works by Henri Matisse, is 2.5km north-east of the train station in the bourgeois district of Cimiez. The museum's permanent collection is displayed in a red-ochre, 17th century Genoese villa overlooking an ancient olive grove and the **Parc des Arènes**. Temporary exhibitions are hosted in the futuristic basement building which leads through to the stucco-decorated villa. The reception hall of the museum is dominated by a colourful, 4.10 x 8.70m, paper cut-out frieze entitled *Flowers and Fruits* and designed by Matisse for the inner courtyard of a Californian villa in 1953.

Well known pieces in the permanent collection include Matisse's blue paper cutouts of *Blue Nude IV* (1952) and *Woman with Amphora* (1953). Among the many Indian ink drawings on display are Matisse's *Reclining Nude* (1935) and his lesser-known *La Blouse Roumaine* series (1939). Exhibited in a small room on the ground floor is *Fleur* (1945), a simple but enchanting line drawing of a flower drawn *sans lunettes le 21 October à deux heures de l'après minuit* (without glasses on 21 October, two hours after midnight!). Two further rooms are devoted to the sombre oil paintings representative of Matisse's early career from 1890 until 1905.

The Musée Matisse is open from 10 am to 6 pm; until 5 pm between September and April; closed Tuesday year round (25/15FF for adult/student). There are guided tours (in French) on Wednesday at 3 pm; you can arrange tours in English (☎ 04 93 26 31 77 or 04 93 46 49 14). Take bus No 15, 17, 20, 22 or 25 from the Station Centrale to the Arènes stop.

Matisse is buried in the cemetery of the 16th century **Monastère Notre Dame de Cimiez** (Cimiez Monastery). The artist's grave is signposted *sépulture Henri Matisse* from the graveyard's main entrance (next to the monastery's Église Notre Dame on ave Bellanda). Dufy's grave is also here. Stairs leads from the eastern end of the olive grove (on allées Miles Davis) to ave Bellanda.

Inside the monastery is the **Musée Franciscain** (☎ 04 93 81 00 04) a small museum run by, and unravelling the history of the monastery's Franciscan monks. Three pieces of precious medieval art by Nice artist Louis Bréa hang in the adjoining Église Notre Dame. The monumental baroque altar, carved in wood and decorated with gold leaf, dates from the 17th century. The beautifully-landscaped **Jardin du Monastère** surrounding the monastery offers a sweeping panorama of the Baie des Anges. The garden, studded with cypress trees and an abundance of sweet-smelling roses, is open until 8 pm (7 pm in April and May; 6 pm in winter). Museum opening hours are 10 am to noon and 3 to 6 pm (closed Sunday); the church art can be viewed between 3 and 7 pm. Both are free.

Matisse – the Essential Elements

Henri Matisse (1869-1954) was passionate about pure colour. His paintings epitomised the radical use of violent colour, heavy outlines and simplified forms characteristic of fauvism. Fauvism – which rose to prominence around 1905 – was a short-lived movement, but Matisse clung to the method of setting striking complementary colours against one another throughout his career.

Matisse was a latecomer compared to other influential painters, not becoming interested in painting until he was 20. By the time he was 22 however he had given up his law career in his home region, Picardy, and had gone to Paris.

Matisse studied art for many years under the symbolist painter Gustave Moreau. While visiting Brittany, he met an Australian artist, John Russell, who introduced him to the works of Van Gogh, Monet and other impressionists, prompting (so it is believed) Matisse's change from a rather sombre palette to brighter colours. He also spent time in Corsica, whose clear and rich Mediterranean light was to have a lasting influence on his work. By the early 1900s he was well known in Paris among followers of modern art and his paintings were being exhibited, but he was still struggling financially. It wasn't until the first fauvist exhibition in 1905, which followed a summer of innovative painting in the fishing village of Collioure in Roussillon, that his financial situation improved. By 1913 he had paintings on display in London and New York.

In the 1920s Matisse moved to the Côte d'Azur but still spent much time travelling – to Étretat in Normandy and abroad to Italy and Tahiti. During these years he painted prolifically but was less radical; his work's characteristic sensuality and optimism, however, were always present. The 1930s saw him return to more experimental techniques and a renewed search for simplicity, in which the subject matter was reduced to essential elements. In 1948 he began working on a set of stained-glass windows for the Chapelle du Rosaire in Vence, run by Dominican nuns. He ended up designing not just the windows but the entire chapel, altar *et al* – a project which took several years. He died in Nice, and was buried there, three years later.

Musée et Site Archéologiques

Behind the Matisse museum, on the east side of the Parc des Arènes, lie ruins of the Roman city of Cemenelum, the focus of the Archaeology Museum (☎ 04 93 81 59 57), 160 ave des Arènes de Cimiez. The public baths and the amphitheatre – the venue for outdoor concerts during the Nice Jazz festival – can both be visited.

Opening hours and admission fees for the Musée et Site Archéologiques are the same as the Musée Matisse. To get here from the latter, turn left out of the main park entrance on ave des Arènes de Cimiez, walk 100m, then turn left again onto ave Monte Croce where the main entrance to the archaeological site is.

Villa Arson

Some wonderful temporary contemporary art and photographic exhibitions can be enjoyed at the Centre National d'Art Contemporain (☎ 04 92 07 73 73 or 04 92 07 73 80), 20 ave Stéphane Liégeard, housed in the 18th century Villa Arson.

Opening hours are from 1 to 6 pm (7 pm from July to September). Between October and June it is closed on Monday. Take bus No 36 to the Villa Arson stop, or bus No 4, 7 or 26 to the Fanny stop on blvd de Cessole.

Cathédrale Orthodoxe Russe Saint Nicolas

The multicoloured Russian Orthodox Cathedral of Saint Nicolas (☎ 04 93 96 88 02), crowned by six onion domes, was built between 1902 and 1912 in early 17th century style and is an easy 15 minute walk from the train station. Step inside and you're transported to Imperial Russia. The cathedral, on ave Nicolas II opposite 17 blvd du Tzaréwich, is open from 9 or 9.30 am to noon and 2.30 to 5.30 pm. It is closed Sunday morning (12/10FF for adult/student). Shorts, miniskirts and sleeveless shirts are forbidden.

Musée International d'Art Naïf Anatole Jakovsky

A collection of naive art from all over the world can be seen at the Anatole Jakovsky International Naive Art Museum (☎ 04 93 71 78 33), ave du Val Marie, less than 2km west of the city centre. The very pink Château Sainte-Héléne, in which the museum is housed, was built in the 19th century atop Mont Fabron by François Blanc who founded the casino in Monte Carlo; it later served as the country home of a perfume manufacturer. The collection – which includes the works of 200 artists from 27 countries – was donated to the museum by Romanian art critic, Anatole Jakovsky (1909-83), who lived in southern France with his wife Renée, from 1932. The museum is open from 10 am to noon and 2 to 6 pm; 5 pm from September to May; closed Tuesday year round (25/15FF for adult/student).

To get to the museum, take bus No 10, 12 or 24 from the Station Centrale to the Fabron stop, then walk or take bus No 34 to the Musée Art Naïf stop.

Parc des Miniatures

Continuing west along promenade des Anglais, the city takes on new dimensions in the city's Miniature Park (☎ 04 93 44 57 74), ave Impératrice Eugénie, in the Magnan-L'Arrchet quarter of town. Both historic and contemporary Nice are cut down to size, the model buildings ranging in size from one to 2m tall.

In the park, the **Musée des Trains Miniatures** (☎ 04 93 97 41 40), among Europe's largest, vividly illustrates the history of train travel to and from the Côte d'Azur. The miniature models range from tiny steam trains dating from the end of the 19th century to contemporary models of today's speedy TGV. Both park and museum are open from 9.30 am to 7 pm; to 5 pm in the low season (30/20FF for adult/child).

Parc Floral Phoenix

At 7000 sq metres, the greenhouse in Nice's floral Phoenix Park (☎ 04 93 18 03 33), 405 promenade des Anglais (near the airport), is said to be Europe's largest. Seven different climates are reproduced inside the gigantic glass house, known as *le diamant vert* (the green diamond), which contains everything from an exotic orchid garden to an insectarium, Australian garden, 25m-tall palmier and butterfly house. Some 1500 different plant species are represented in the seven-hectare park which sports a small lake, zoo, Maya temple and tacky theme park. It is open between April and September from 9 am to 7 pm; until 5 pm the rest of the year (a hefty 40/25FF for adult/child).

Since October 1998, Phoenix Park has been endowed with the equally colourful **Musée des Arts Asiatiques** (☎ 04 92 29 37 00), home to a large collection of Oriental Art. The white marble building, a 65 million FF investment, was designed by Japanese architect Kenzo Tange. It is open from 10 am to 5 pm; to 6 pm from May to mid-October. It is closed Tuesday (35/15FF for adult/student).

Musée Terra Amata

Just east of Bassin Lympia (the port), this museum (☎ 04 93 55 59 93), 25 blvd Carnot, displays objects from a site inhabited some 400,000 years ago by the predecessors of *Homo sapiens*. It reopened in January 1999 after extensive renovations. Opening hours are from 9 am to noon and 2 to 6 pm (closed on Monday).

Activities

If you don't like the feel of sand between your toes, Nice's **beach** is for you. It's covered with smooth round pebbles. Sections of beach open to the public without charge alternate with 15 *plages concédées* (private beaches) which you have to pay for by renting a chair (around 60FF a day) or mattress (around 55FF).

Along the beach you can hire catamaran paddleboats (80-90FF an hour) or sailboards and jet skis (300FF for 30 minutes), take a parachute ride (220FF for 15 minutes) or go water-skiing (100-130FF for 10 minutes). There are public indoor showers (15FF) and toilets (2FF) opposite 50 promenade des Anglais.

Water World (☎ 06 11 33 42 53), in the private sector of Castel Plage opposite the Tour Bellanda at the east end of quai des États-Unis, is the most central **diving** school. Around the port, PH + Plongée (☎ 04 93 26 09 03), 3 quai des deux Emmanuel, Poseïdon (☎ 04 92 00 43 86), quai Lunel, and L'Odyssée (☎ 04 93 89 42 44, fax 04 93 89 12 69), inside the Exploration Sous-Marine shop, 14 quai des Docks, all offer **diving** courses, diving expeditions and rent equipment. A baptism dive costs 160FF (excluding equipment).

Trans Côte d'Azur (☎ 04 92 00 42 30), quai Lunel, organises **glass-bottomed boat trips** around the Baie des Anges (60/35FF for adult/child). Between April and September, a boat departs on the hour from 9 am to 7 pm; only four or five boats a day sail between October and March (closed Monday and Thursday). The same company also offers trips to the Îles de Lérins (see the Cannes Region chapter), Saint Tropez, Monaco and San Remo in neighbouring Italy. Its ticket office is open from 8 am to 7 pm (Saturday until 11.45 pm; closed Sunday).

For detailed **hiking** and **mountain-biking** trails in the region, go to the headquarters of the Parc National du Mercantour (see Information) in Nice or to the Club Alpin Français (☎ 04 93 62 59 99), 14 ave Mirabeau. Nice-based Destination Merveilles (☎/fax 04 93 16 08 72), 34 corniche Frère Marc, specialises in guided hiking expeditions in the national park. Trips range from a day (290FF) to two/five days (485/1950FF).

Pétanque enthusiasts can try their hand at the local sport at the pétanque pitch, place Arson; alternatively contact the Comité Bouliste Départemental des Alpes-Maritimes (☎ 04 93 85 96 06), 22 ave Jean Médecin. For a hand of **bridge**, head for the Anglo-American Bridge Club (☎ 04 93 82 12 82), 20 rue Paul Déroulède, housed in a turn-of-the-century building with ornate balconies covered in creeping vines.

Rollerblading Promenade des Anglais is *the* hot spot to blade. City Sport, inside the Nice Étoile shopping centre, ave Jean Médecin, rents roller blades (and protective elbow/knee pads for those not too proud to don something so un-chic) for 30/50/80FF for half a day/day/two days. Super Sports (☎ 04 93 62 28 92), 9 rue Saint François de Paule, and the Roller Station (☎ 04 93 26 63 35), 10 rue Cassini, both have roller rental too.

The latest trends in roller fashion are sold at the 4 Wheels Skate Shop, 4 place Garibaldi.

Organised Tours

Between April and October, Santa Azur (☎ 04 93 85 46 81, fax 04 93 87 90 08), 11 ave Jean Médecin, organise one day coach tours (with an English commentary) to Monaco and Èze (135FF), the Vallée des Merveilles (280FF), San Remo in Italy (130FF), the Gorges du Verdon (150FF), the Golfe de Saint Tropez (130FF). Half-day trips include Grasse (100FF) and Saint Paul de Vence (100FF). Book 24 hours in advance.

Riviera Bus Service (☎ 04 93 16 00 09), 45 rue Rossini, also offers English-language day trips by bus. Its house speciality is a Monte Carlo Panoramic Tour (590-995FF) which takes in the Basse Corniche road, the Monte Carlo skyline, dinner, casino and a glitzy cabaret show.

Special Events

The celebrated Carnaval de Nice (Nice Carnival), which dates from 1294, is held every spring around Mardi Gras (Shrove Tuesday), filling the streets with floats and musicians. The highlight of the two-week festival is the *bataille de fleurs* (battle of the flowers) when hundreds upon thousands of fresh flowers are tossed into the crowds from processing floats. A mock carnival king is subsequently burned and fireworks lit on promenade des Anglais.

The week-long Nice Jazz Festival sets the town jiving in July; the main venue (fabulous!) is the olive grove behind the Musée Matisse in the Cimiez district. A one-day/week pass costs 170/600FF; 40FF a day for children aged 6-12; available from FNAC (see Entertainment section) or the Bureau du Festival (☎ 04 93 87 19 18, fax 04 93 88 00 77, www.club-internet.fr/nice-jazz) inside the promenade des Anglais tourist office.

Equally atmospheric is the two day Fête au Château, an open-air music festival held in mid-June in Parc du Château. A touch more sober is Nice's moving Festival de Musique Sacrée (Festival of Sacred Music) when Russian sacred chants meet with Mozart's *Requiem* for two weeks in late June. Concerts take place in the Cathédrale Sainte Réparate and other churches in Vieux Nice.

Between mid-June and mid-September during the annual Nice – Un Été d'Or (Nice – a Golden Summer), concerts are held every Wednesday and Saturday evening. The tourist office on promenade des Anglais lists what's on where. During the three-week Les Nuits Musicales de Nice in mid-July/early August, open-air classical musical concerts are held in the cloisters of Cimiez Monastery, the olive grove in Cimiez and around the Musée d'Art Moderne et d'Art Contemporain. Contact the Académie Internationale d'Été de Nice (☎ 04 93 81 01 23) or FNAC for details.

Places to Stay

Nice has a surfeit of reasonably priced places to stay. During the Easter university holidays, lots of American students descend on Nice for a transatlantic 'College Week', making cheap accommodation hard to find after 10 am. Nice is crowded with budget travellers during July and August, too. Inexpensive places are filled by late morning.

In summer, many young people sleep on the beach. This is theoretically illegal and public beaches are supposed to be closed between midnight and 6 am, but Nice (and nice) police usually look the other way. Watch out for thieves.

The information desk at the bus station (see Getting There & Away section) has information on Logis de France hotels and other idyllic properties in the region. For information on gîtes in and around Nice, contact Gîtes de France des Alpes-Maritimes (☎ 04 92 15 21 30, fax 04 93 86 01 06), 55 promenade des Anglais.

Places to Stay – Budget

Hostels Touting a great tree-studded garden decked out with tables and chairs for guests to lounge on is the busy *Hôtel Belle Meunière*, (☎ 04 93 88 66 15, 21 ave Durante), which has non-bunk dorm beds for 76FF (96/101FF with shower/shower and toilet), including breakfast.

Almost opposite is the equally popular rambling *Hôtel Les Orangers* (☎ 04 93 87 51 41, fax 04 93 87 51 41, 10bis ave Durante) in a turn-of-the-century town house. A bed in a snug 4-6 bed room with shower and fantastically huge windows, costs 85FF. The cheerful owner speaks excellent English, the result of dealing with Anglophone backpackers for the past 17 years! Nearby, the *Hôtel Darcy* (see Hotels – train station area) has dorm beds for 92FF.

Along ave Jean Médecin, you have the popular 20-bed *Backpackers' Hotel* (☎ 04 93 80 30 72, 32 rue Pertinax). A dorm bed is 70FF a night, there's no curfew or lockout, and cheery Patrick, who runs the place, is said to be an absolute darling (and great at directing party-mad backpackers to the hot spot of the moment). The hotel is above the Faubourg Montmartre restaurant.

The *Pado Tourisme Hostel* (☎ 04 93 80 98 00, 26 blvd Raimbaldi) charges 60FF for a bed in a mixed dorm. Reception is open from 8 am to noon and 6 to 9 pm; there is a lock-out between noon and 6 pm.

Nice's *Auberge de Jeunesse* (☎ 04 93 89 23 64, fax 04 92 04 03 10, route Forestière de Mont Alban) is 5km east of the train station. B&B is 66FF. Curfew is at midnight and rooms are locked from 10 am to 5 pm. Take bus No 14 (last one at 8.20 pm) from the Station Centrale, linked to the train station by bus Nos 15 and 17, and get off at L'Auberge stop.

The *Centre Hébergement Jeunes* (☎ 04 93 86 28 75, fax 04 93 44 93 22, 31 rue Louis de Coppet) is open from mid-June to mid-September. A bed in a six-person room costs only 50FF. Rooms are locked from 10 am to 6 pm, there's a midnight curfew and by day, bags must be stored in the luggage room.

Hotels – Train Station Area The quickest way to get to all these hotels is to walk straight down the steps opposite the train station onto ave Durante. The first place you hit is the clean, warm and welcoming *Hôtel Belle Meunière* (see Hostels, earlier), always packed with backpackers. As well as dorms, it has doubles/triples with high ceilings from 182/243FF (with shower and toilet). There's private parking in the front courtyard. This hotel is closed in December and January.

The highly-recommended *Hôtel Les Orangers* (see Hostels) has great doubles and triples with shower and a balcony overlooking palm-tree gardens, for 210FF. Rooms are gloriously sunlit thanks to their great century-old windows and come with fridge (and hotplate upon request).

Hard cash and nothing else is accepted at the dreary *Hôtel Idéal Bristol* (☎ 04 93 88 60 72, 22 rue Paganini) which has basic doubles from 145FF (180FF with shower and toilet). Rooms for four people with shower and toilet are 425FF. It also has a 5th-floor terrace where guests can sunbathe and picnic. More dubiously, the Bristol has 130FF rooms to rent during the day for 'passengers waiting for a train'.

The *Hôtel Les Cigales* (☎ 04 93 88 33 75, 15 rue Dalpozzo) warrants no complaints. Simple but satisfying singles/doubles with

shower cost 165/185FF. Triples/quads with bath and toilet weigh in at 300/345FF.

On rue d'Angleterre the *Hôtel Darcy* (☎ 04 93 88 67 06) at No 28 has singles/doubles/triples for 125/150/195FF (210/255/300FF with shower and toilet). At No 38, the new, clean and attractive *Hôtel de la Gare* (☎ 04 93 88 75 07, fax 04 93 88 75 07) has modern singles for 115/175FF with washbasin/shower and toilet. Doubles/triples/quads cost 155/240/320FF. The less-exciting *Hôtel Novelty* (☎ 04 93 87 51 73, fax 04 93 87 04 01), at No 26, has singles/doubles with shower and toilet for 160/230FF.

The *Hôtel Pastoral* (☎ 04 93 85 17 22, 27 rue Assalit, 1st floor), just off ave Jean Médecin, has large, old-fashioned and clean singles/doubles with fridge from 100/120FF. Doubles with shower/shower and toilet are 150/170FF. Kitchenettes cost 15FF extra per person a day. Reception is open daily from 8 am to 3 pm and 6 to 8 pm.

The *Hôtel Regency* (☎ 04 93 62 17 44, fax 04 93 92 23 26, 2 rue Saint Siagre, 2nd floor) has split-level studios with shower, toilet, kitchenette and fridge for two/three people for 220/270FF. Ring the bell to enter. Nearby the rundown *Hôtel Astrid* (☎ 04 93 62 14 64, 26 rue Pertinax) has singles/doubles/triples with shower for 120/180/240FF.

Rue d'Alsace-Lorraine is dotted with more upmarket two-star hotels. One of the cheapest is the *Hôtel du Piemont* (☎ 04 93 88 25 15), No 19, which has bargain singles/doubles/triples with washbasin from 110/130/190FF. Singles/doubles with shower start at 130/160FF, while rooms with shower and toilet cost from 180/200FF. Triples/quads are 225/300FF. It rents rooms on a long-term basis too.

Tucked away from the action is the tiny *Hôtel Bamby* (☎ 04 93 88 10 30, 55 rue Berlioz). Singles/doubles start at 160/200FF with shower. Exit the train station, turn right onto ave Thiers, then turn left after the post office onto rue Berlioz.

Hotels – City Centre The reception of the friendly *Hôtel Little Masséna* (☎ 04 93 87

The tiered village of Gordes, on the southern face of the Vaucluse plateau

The perfume of Provence – lavender fields blooming in July

Lavender fields

72 34, 22 rue Masséna) is on the 5th floor (open until 8 pm). Doubles with washbasin/shower are 140/180FF; with shower and toilet 220FF. Most rooms have a hotplate and fridge.

The relaxed, family-style *Hôtel Les Mimosas* (☎ 04 93 88 05 59, 26 rue de la Buffa, 2nd floor) is two blocks north-east of the Musée Masséna. Good-sized, utilitarian rooms for one/two people cost 120/190FF. Showers cost 10FF.

Midway between the sea and the station, off ave Jean Médecin, is the colourful *Hôtel Le Petit Louvre* (☎ 04 93 80 15 54, fax 04 93 62 45 08, 10 rue Emma Tiranty), run by a humorous musician and his wife for 17 years. A faceless Mona Lisa greets guests as they enter and corridors are adorned with an eclectic bunch of paintings. Singles/doubles with shower, washbasin, fridge and hotplate are 171/205FF, singles/doubles with shower and toilet are 191/230FF and triples cost 249FF. Breakfast (25FF) comprises cereal and fruit as well as the usual baguette, croissant and coffee.

On a side street off the opposite side of ave Jean Médecin is the one-star *Hôtel Lyonnais* (☎ 04 93 88 70 74, fax 04 93 16 25 56, 20 rue de Russie) which has unrenovated singles/doubles with washbasin for 110/140FF. Nightly rates increase by about 30FF in the high season. Triples/quads start at 210/240FF.

The cool and friendly *Hôtel Clémenceau* (☎ 04 93 88 61 19, fax 04 93 16 88 96, 3 ave Georges Clémenceau) has singles/doubles with shared bath for 150/200FF. Singles/doubles with shower and toilet cost 300/350; triples/quads are 450/550FF.

Hotels – Vieux Nice The *Hôtel Saint François* (☎ 04 93 85 88 69, fax 04 93 85 10 67, 3 rue Saint François) has singles/doubles/triples for 130/168/237FF. Showers cost 15FF. Reception is open until 10 pm.

The *Hôtel au Picardy* (☎ 04 93 85 75 51, 10 blvd Jean Jaurès) has singles/doubles from 120/140FF; pricier rooms include toilet and shower. Hall showers are 10FF.

The *Hôtel Meublé Le Genevois* (☎ 04 93 85 00 58, 11 rue Alexandre Mari, 3rd floor) has 1950s-style singles/doubles with kitchenette from 130/180FF. Huge studios with shower and toilet are 180-240FF for two people. If no one answers the *sonnerie* (bell) push the little red button.

By the port, the one-star *Hôtel Genève* (☎ 04 93 56 73 73, 1 rue Cassini) has singles/doubles/triples for 180/200/300FF.

Hotel – Gay The *Hôtel Meyerbeer* (☎ 04 93 88 95 65, 15 rue Meyerbeer, 1st floor) markets itself as a gay and lesbian hotel. Rooms for one or two people with shower are 250FF. Identify yourself as homosexual and you get a 10% discount.

Places to Stay – Mid-Range

Near the train station, there are lots of two-star hotels along rue d'Angleterre, rue d'Alsace-Lorraine, rue de Suisse, rue de Russie and ave Durante.

In the centre, the *Hôtel Plaisance* (☎ 04 93 85 11 90, fax 04 93 80 88 92, 20 rue de Paris) is a pleasing old two-star pile with air-conditioned doubles from 320FF.

Named after its location near the Église Notre Dame is the very clean and modern *Hôtel Notre Dame* (☎ 04 93 88 70 44, fax 04 93 82 20 38, 22 rue de Russie), which has spacious doubles/triples with shower and toilet for 240/300FF. Its 17 rooms fill quickly, so get there early. Another good-value place on the other side of Église Notre Dame and little publicised, is the modest, 28-room *Hôtel du Centre* (☎ 04 93 88 83 85, fax 04 93 82 29 80, 2 rue de Suisse), which has rooms with shared/private shower for 144/174FF. After 11.30 pm guests need a door code to enter.

A stone's throw from the sea and from the Musée des Beaux-Arts is the good-value *Hôtel Carlone* (☎/fax 04 93 44 71 61, 2 blvd François Grosso). Light and airy rooms for one or two with washbasin/shower and toilet start at 170/250FF and it has triples/quads from 340/400FF. The *Hôtel Résidence Astoria* (☎ 04 95 15 25 45), next door, has rooms with bathroom, fridge, hotplate etc to let on a nightly/weekly/monthly or longer basis. Rates depend on the season, starting from 190/1000/2800FF in the low season and peaking at 250/1650FF a night/week (no monthly rentals) in August. The Astoria has a pretty garden too.

Wonderfully like home and equally close to the sea is the welcoming *Hôtel Cronstadt* (☎ 04 93 82 00 30, 3 rue Cronstadt). Exceptionally quiet and graceful rooms cost 280/320/410/590FF for singles/doubles/ triples/rooms for four or five people. Prices include breakfast.

The *Hôtel Alexandra* (☎ 04 93 62 14 43, fax 04 93 62 30 34, 41 rue Lamartine) is everything you would expect of a hotel managed by the Best Western group. Singles/doubles cost 465/560FF.

There are a couple of small, family-run options in upmarket Cimiez. The two-star *Hôtel Le Floride* (☎ 04 93 53 11 02, fax 04 93 81 57 46, 52 blvd de Cimiez) has comfortable singles/doubles with shower, toilet and great views of Cimiez' opulent mansions from 190/215FF. Next door at No 54, the *Hôtel Helios* (☎ 04 93 53 04 55, fax 04 93 81 41 40), towering over the absolutely fabulous L'Alhambra mansion, charges 200/220FF for singles/doubles with shower.

Places to Stay – Top End

The legendary pink-domed, green-shuttered, four-starred *Hôtel Négresco* (☎ 04 93 16 64 00 or 04 93 88 00 58, fax 04 93 88 35 68, negresco@nicematin.fr, 37 promenade des Anglais), built in the *belle époque* style, is Nice's fanciest hotel. Rooms with a sea view start at 1300/1700FF in the low/high season. A continental/American breakfast is a mere 130/190FF. The Négresco's restaurant is considered the best in town.

The stylish four-star *Hôtel Méridien* (☎ 04 93 82 25 25, fax 04 93 16 08 90, 106001.1250@compuserve.com, 1 promenade des Anglais) is known for its very comfortable rooms and rooftop pool. Rooms cost 1450-3300FF. For a touch of class for less cash, try the *Hôtel Westminster Concorde* (☎ 04 93 88 29 44, fax 04 93

82 45 35, 27 promenade des Anglais). Rooms start at 750FF.

Matisse stayed at the *Hôtel Beau Rivage* (☎ 04 93 80 80 70, fax 04 93 80 55 77, info@new-hotel.com, 24 rue Saint François de Paule) when he was in town in 1916. Before that, in 1891, the Russian playwright Anton Chekhov (1860-1904) graced the place with his presence. Sea views from the hotel, which today touts four stars, remain superb. The cheapest rooms cost 650/850FF in the low/high season.

The modern face of Nice is reflected in the black glass walls of the *Melia Elysée Palace* (☎ 04 93 86 06 06, fax 04 93 97 03 36, 59 promenade des Anglais). The building's concrete rear is adorned with a giant statue of Venus baring a breast to passersby on rue de France. Finely-tuned singles with a town/garden/sea view cost 650/ 750/850FF in the low season and 800/ 950/1100FF between July and September. Doubles cost 800/900/1000FF and 950/ 1100/11250FF respectively.

Places to Eat

Restaurants – Train Station Area
Restaurant Le Toscan (☎ 04 93 88 40 54, 1 rue de Belgique) is a family-run Italian place offering large portions of tripe or homemade pasta from noon to 2 pm and 6.45 to 10 pm (closed Sunday).

Corsican chants and energetic guitar duets are some of the Île de Beauté delights performed every Thursday, Friday and Saturday evening at the Corsican *L'Allegria* (☎ 04 93 87 42 00, 7 rue d'Italie). Next door is the unpretentious and very friendly *Restaurant au Soleil* which offers good local cuisine at unbeatable prices, including an all day omelette breakfast for 33FF. Another cheap favourite is the bustling *Restaurant de Paris* (☎ 04 93 88 99 88), adjoining the Hôtel Darcy at 28 rue d'Angleterre, which has a bargain 38FF menu.

Adorned with fat contented cherubs on its outside walls is the atmospheric *L'Ange Gourmand* (47 rue Lamartine). Its *carte* (menu), which changes daily and is handwritten, includes an 85FF menu. Close by, on the corner of rue Raimbaldi and rue Miron is the handsome *Chez Mireille (☎ 04 93 85 27 23)*, which specialises in paella, paella and more paella. It is closed Monday, Tuesday, during June and early July.

Bursting with hungry backpackers is cheap and cheerful *Le Faubourg Montmartre (☎ 04 93 62 55 03, 32 rue Pertinax)*. The house speciality is bouillabaisse (120FF for two) and there's a 68FF *menu*. It's open for lunch from noon and in the evening from 5.30 pm.

There are over a dozen Vietnamese and Chinese restaurants on rue Paganini, rue d'Italie and rue d'Alsace-Lorraine. Don't expect miracles – except maybe at *China Fast Food*, a spanking-clean fast food place, conveniently near the train station on the corner of ave Thiers and ave Jean Médecin. Choose from beautifully presented meat dishes for 27-38FF and various rice variations for 14-20FF. It's open from 9 am to midnight.

Restaurants – City Centre The rue Masséna pedestrian mall and nearby streets and squares, including rue de France and place Magenta, are crammed with touristy outdoor cafés and restaurants. Most don't offer particularly good value.

One worth sampling is *La Trattoria (☎ 04 93 88 20 07, 37 rue de France)* whose terrace restaurant fills the entire southern stretch of rue Dalpozzo. It specialises in pizza *au feu de bois* (cooked over a wood fire). Nearby is small and homely *Le Moulin à Poivre (☎ 04 93 87 65 02, 22 rue de France)*, a couple of doors west of the Manoir Café (see Cafés). The Pepper Mill has a *plat du jour* for 50FF, a 120FF *menu* and plenty of homemade pasta dishes.

Near the port, *L'Olivier (☎ 04 93 26 89 09, 2 place Garibaldi)* is a small, simple and very local place. A meal guaranteed to stuff you costs around 100FF; it is closed Wednesday evening, Sunday and in August.

La Nissarda (☎ 04 93 85 26 29, 17 rue Gubernatis) serves specialities of Nice and Normandy. The *menus* are reasonably priced at 60 (lunch only), 78, 98 and 138FF

(closed on Sunday and in August). Nearby, *Le Bistrot Saint Germain (☎ 04 93 13 45 12, 9 rue Chauvain)* brings a touch of Paris to Nice, with walls decorated with photos of Parisian scenes (closed Sunday).

Graceful and very local is *Le Comptoir (☎ 04 93 92 08 80, 20 rue Saint François de Paule)*, close to the seashore. The restaurant, which has an adjoining nightclub, is decked out in Art Deco style and has a terrace too. Pasta/fish dishes start at 52/90FF.

For a mind-blowing traditional French meal in a luxurious setting, try the Michelin two-star *Chantecler (☎ 04 93 88 39 51)* inside the Hôtel Négresco. Impeccable service and tantalising cuisine add up to a hefty 500FF per head (at least) bill!

Restaurants – Vieux Nice Many of the narrow streets of Vieux Nice are lined with restaurants, cafés, pizzerias and so on that draw locals and visitors alike. There are dozens of cafés and restaurants on cours Saleya, place Pierre Gautier and place Rossetti, many of which buzz until well past midnight (later during the summer).

A perennial favourite with locals is *Nissa Socca (☎ 04 93 80 18 35, 5 rue Sainte Réparate)* which specialises in delicious Niçois dishes such as *socca* (a chickpea flour and olive oil batter fried in a thin layer on a griddle), *salade niçoise* (green salad with tuna, egg and anchovies), *farcis* (stuffed vegetables) and ratatouille. Nissa Socca is open daily (closed in January and June). If you don't want to stand in line (inevitable) try *Nissa La Bella (☎ 04 93 62 10 20)* opposite, which serves similar (but not as good) dishes. *Chez Thérèsa (☎ 04 93 85 00 04)* has homemade socca served from a little hole in the wall at 28 rue Droite from 8 am to 1 pm (closed Monday).

Homemade pasta and local snails are just some of the delights served with a flourish at busy *À L'Écurie (☎ 04 93 62 32 62, 4 rue du Marché)* which has been run by the same family since 1945. Tucked away off the beaten track, is the absolutely charming *Braconnier (☎ 04 93 80 85 45)* whose tables, chairs and twittering bird cages spill out – and fill – tiny place Vieille.

Of particular appeal to those on a budget is the colourful, Mexican *Calexico* (☎ *04 93 80 36 72, 16 rue Benoît Bunico)* which offers a cut-price student Tex-Mex *menu* for 65FF and an equally enticing *menu touristique* for 98FF. Both include wine, complimentary salsa and tortilla chips. Calexico is open for dinner only, from 7 pm to midnight (closed Monday).

A short distance north of Vieux Nice *Lou Balico – Chez Adrienne* (☎ *04 93 85 93 71, 20 ave Saint Jean Baptiste)* serves excellent Niçois specialities, as well as bouillabaisse (250FF). Mains range from 80-125FF, and it's open daily. Nearby is the equally local *L'Auberge d'Acropolis* (9 rue Penchienatti) which has a regional plat du jour for 45FF, a wholesome lunch *menu* for 60FF, and evening ones for 95 and 120FF.

Small, select and decked out with colourful furnishings is *La Divina Commedia* (☎ *04 93 80 71 84, 7 rue de la Terrasse)* off cours Salaya. Its plat du jour costs 62FF and it has a 48FF lunchtime *menu*.

Restaurant La Fanny (☎ *04 93 80 70 63, 2 rue Rossetti)* is a blue and white place on the corner of rue Benoît Bunico which serves a tantalising *assiette Fanny* (Fanny plate) comprising a mixture of Niçois specialities, for 50FF. The house special at the enchanting (smiling staff, candlelit terrace etc) *Escalinada* (☎ *04 93 62 11 71, 22 rue Pairolière)* is *testicules de mouton panés* (sheep testicles in batter).

Cafés For homemade cakes and hearty tarts like grandma bakes, look no further than the cosy *Scotch Tea House* (☎ *04 93 87 75 62)*, tucked between designer clothes shops at 4 ave de Suède. It's open from 9 am to 7 pm and is *the* place to go for good old-fashioned afternoon tea.

Cool, chic and always packed is the refined *Manoir Café* (☎ *04 93 16 36 16, 32 rue de France)*. Jazz bands play here on Wednesday evenings. Reserve a table in advance if you want to dine here (serves full meals too).

Aux Spécialités Belges, 3 rue Maccarani, is a small *salon de thé* (tea room) which serves delicious cakes, pastries and other naughty-but-nice treats.

Sweet crêpes, savoury galettes, punchy ciders and a great range of ice creams are beautifully presented at the packed *Crêperie Bretonne* (☎ *04 93 16 02 98, 3 rue de Russie)*. It is closed on Monday.

Guess what type of cuisine the dynamic *Mexican Café* (14 rue Saint François de Paule) specialises in. Wild salsa nights are held here on weekends.

Cafeterias Dirt cheap places near the train station include the *Flunch Cafétéria* (☎ *04 93 88 41 35)*, to the left as you exit the station building; open from 11 am to 10 pm.

The *Casino Cafétéria* (☎ *04 93 82 44 44, 7 ave Thiers)* serves breakfast (10-17FF) from 8 to 11 am and other meals until 9.30 pm. Its good-value 29FF *formule* comprises its plat du jour plus entrée, cheese or dessert.

Self-Catering There's a fruit and vegetable *market* in front of the prefecture, cours Saleya, from 6 am to 5.30 pm (closed Sunday afternoon and Monday), and a fresh fish market every morning on place Saint François. The no-name *boulangerie* at the south end of rue du Marché is the best place for cheap sandwiches, pizza slices, traditional *michettes* (savoury bread stuffed with cheese, olives, anchovies and onions) and other local breads. Otherwise take a mouth-watering stroll along rue du Collet and its continuation, rue Pairolière, which is lined with *fromageries*, *boulangeries* and *fruit shops*. Cooked chickens, hot from the spit, are sold at *La Poulette* on the corner of rue de la Préfecture and rue Gaétan. *Gelati Azzurro*, 1 rue Sainte Réparate, is the place for homemade Italian icecream; two scoops in a crunchy cone cost 16FF.

The *Ducs de Gascogne*, 4 rue de France, sells foie gras, fine wines and other pricey culinary delights. *La Ferme*, 3 rue Maccarani, sells fantastic cheeses.

For a mind-boggling array of different breads, head for *Le Capitole* (☎ *04 93 44 67*

77, 78 rue de France). Just around the corner on the south end of big blvd Gambetta is the *Intermarché* supermarket, open from 8.45 am to 8 pm (closed Sunday).

There is a *Prisunic* supermarket opposite No 33 ave Jean Médecin; another branch on place Garibaldi; and a *Casino* at 27 blvd Gambetta.

Entertainment

The tourist office has detailed information on Nice's abundant cultural activities, many of which are listed in its free monthly brochure, *Le Mois à Nice*. More useful is the weekly *L'Officiel des Loisirs Côte d'Azur* (2FF) published Wednesday and sold at newsstands. Tickets to cultural events of all sorts can be purchased at FNAC (☎ 04 92 17 77 72/4/7), 30 ave Jean Médecin (inside the Nice Étoile shopping mall); open from 10 am to 7 pm (until 7.30 pm in July and August; closed Sunday year round).

Late or all-night clubbers should pick up a copy of the free *L'Exes* magazine, published fortnightly and featuring hot pics from, and schedules for, the city's numerous nightclubs, bars and discos. Listings for gay clubbers are in the gay mags, *LX* (published fortnightly), and *Le Zoom* (monthly).

Bars Bars and terraced cafés – just made for beer quaffing and pastis sipping – abound in Nice. For a taste of an excellent Belgian brew or any of its 70-plus types of beer, try *Le Pub Gioffredo*, corner of rue Chauvain and rue Gioffredo. For a hearty pint of Guinness head straight for the *Scarlett O'Hara Irish Pub*, corner of rue Rossetti and rue Droite, Vieux Nice.

Nightclubs Strictly house belts out at *L'Absolute* (☎ 04 93 87 92 00), behind the Hôtel Méridien on rue Halévy. *Blue Boy* (☎ 04 93 44 68 24, 9 rue Spinetta) just off blvd François Grosso (open 11 pm to 6 am), is a gay club close to the centre.

Live Music Nice boasts a rash of pubs, run by Anglophones, sporting a happy hour, and serving as a venue for live music concerts.

Pub Oxford (☎ 04 93 92 24 54, 4 rue Masscoïnat) sells itself as a traditional English pub. It has live music every night from 10 pm (open from 6 pm to 4 am).

Best known however is *Chez Wayne's* (☎ 04 93 13 46 99, www.waynes.fr, 15 rue de la Préfecture) which hosts a bi-lingual quiz on Tuesday, ladies' night on Wednesday, karaoke on Sunday and live bands on Friday and Saturday. In summer it holds beach parties (admission 50FF). Wayne's is open from 3 pm to midnight (later on weekends). Happy Hour is until 9 pm.

Another hot spot is *Jonathan's Live Music Pub* (☎ 04 93 62 57 62, 1 rue de la Loge), also a *bar à musique*. Live bands (country, boogie-woogie, Irish folk etc) play every night in summer. Tuesday is student night, meaning beer costs a mere 10FF and happy hour kicks off daily between 5 and 9.30 pm (18/30FF for a pint/pichet of beer).

William's (☎ 04 93 85 84 66, 4 rue Centrale) has live music from around 9 pm (not Sunday); the pub is open from 6 pm to 2.30 am. There's pool, darts and chess in the basement. Still bored? Head for the *Thor Pub* (☎ 04 93 62 49 90, 32 cours Saleya).

The *Hole-in-the-Wall* (☎ 04 93 80 40 16, 3 rue de l'Abbaye) is both a restaurant and a venue for live music; open from 8 pm to midnight (closed Monday).

Classical Music Operas and orchestral concerts are held at the ornate *Opéra de Nice* (☎ 04 92 17 40 40), built in 1885 and undergoing a three-year facelift in 1998, estimated to cost 50 million FF (US$8.3 million). The box office is open from 10 am to 6 pm (closed Sunday). The best tickets for operas/concerts and ballets cost 50/20FF. The opera house is at 4-6 rue Saint François de Paule (around the corner from quai des États-Unis). It is closed from mid-June to September.

Cinemas Nice has two cinemas offering original-language films, many of them in English. The *Cinéma Nouveau Mercury* (☎ 04 93 55 32 31 for a recorded message in French, 16 place Garibaldi), and the

Cinéma Rialto (☎ *04 93 88 08 41, 4 rue de Rivoli*).

Art films (usually in French or with French subtitles) are screened in the cinema inside the auditorium at the Museum of Modern & Contemporary Art (see that section).

Theatre The superbly modern **Théâtre de Nice** (☎ *04 93 80 52 60)*, whose entrance on promenade des Arts faces the Musée d'Art Moderne et d'Art Contemporain, is one block west of place Garibaldi. The two halls host a wide variety of first-rate theatre performances and concerts. Ticket prices range from 60-170FF. The information desk is open from 1 to 7 pm (closed Sunday and Monday) and one hour before each performance. A new, 6850-seat theatre, estimated to cost 100 million FF, has been planned for the year 2001.

Shopping

Cours Saleya hosts a wonderful flower market Tuesday to Saturday from 6 am to 5.30 pm and on Sunday morning. There are a number of vendors selling *fruits glacés* (glazed or candied fruits), a speciality of the region. The figs, tangerine slices and pears have to be tasted to be believed. To tour, taste and buy chocolate-coated orange slices, cocoa-covered almonds and the like, visit the Confiserie Florian (☎ 04 93 55 43 50), 14 quai Papacino; free factory tours run between 9 am and noon and 2 to 6 pm.

The best place for wine tasting and buying is the traditional wine cellar, the Cave de la Buffa (☎ 04 93 88 10 26), 49 rue de la Buffa. Olive oil is sold at the Moulin à Huile d'Olive Alziari, 14 rue Saint François de Paule.

In Vieux Nice, rue du Collet and rue Pairolière offer bargains galore for shoppers in search of cheap clothes, hats and trinkets. Designer names abound above the beautiful fashion boutiques which languish the length of rue Paradis, rue de Suède, rue Alphonse Karr, and rue du Maréchal Joffre.

Shop for unusual hand-made art, crafts and jewellery at the *marché nocturne* (night market), held from 6.30 pm to midnight on cours Saleya between July and September. By day, rue Gaétan, off cours Saleya, is the street for leather sandals and perfumes from Grasse.

Close to the train station, Sports Évasion (☎ 04 93 16 88 44), 16 ave Thiers, is a top-rate hiking and climbing shop which sells all the gear, including maps, compasses etc.

Getting There & Away

Air Nice's international airport (see the Getting There & Away chapter), Aéroport International Nice-Côte d'Azur (☎ 04 93 21 30 30, www.nice.aeroport.fr), is 6km west of the city centre.

Bus Lines operated by some two dozen bus companies stop at the intercity bus station (☎ 04 93 85 61 81), 5 blvd Jean Jaurès. The busy information counter (☎ 04 93 85 03 90) is open from 8 am to 6.30 pm (closed Sunday).

There are slow but frequent services daily until about 7.30 pm to Antibes (25FF; 1¼ hours), Cannes (32FF; 1½ hours), Grasse (37FF; 1¼ hours), Menton (28FF return; 1¼ hours); Monaco (17FF return; 45 minutes) and Saint Raphaël (50FF; two hours). Hourly buses run to Vence (21FF; 45 minutes).

To Castellane, the gateway to the Gorges du Verdon, there's one bus a day at 7.30 am (97FF; 1½ hours). There are four buses a day to the ski resort of Isola 2000 (87FF; 2¼ hours).

For long-haul travel, Intercars (☎ 04 93 80 08 70) at the bus station, takes you to various European destinations; it also sells Eurolines tickets for buses to London, Brussels and Amsterdam.

Train Nice's main train station, Gare Nice Ville, also called Gare Thiers (☎ 08 36 35 35 35), ave Thiers, is 1200m north of the beach. The information office is open from 8 am to 6.30 pm (closed Sunday).

There is a fast, frequent service (up to 40 trains a day in each direction) to towns along the coast between Saint Raphaël and Ventimiglia across the Italian border, including

Antibes (17FF; 25 minutes), Cannes (32FF; 40 minutes), Menton (28FF; 35 minutes), Monaco (40FF; 20 minutes) and Saint Raphaël (57FF; 45 minutes).

The two or three TGVs that link Nice with Paris' Gare de Lyon (530FF; seven hours) are infrequent, so you may find it more convenient to go via Marseille.

The left luggage lockers, in the ticket hall, can be accessed between 7 am and 10 pm (15/20/30FF for a small/medium/large locker; maximum deposit 72 hours). Lost luggage and other problems are handled by SOS Voyageurs (☎ 04 93 82 62 11), open from 9 am to noon and 3 to 6 pm (closed on weekends).

The ever-popular two-car diesel trains operated by Les Chemins de Fer de la Provence (☎ 04 93 88 34 72 in Nice; 04 92 31 01 58 in Digne-les-Bains) make the scenic trip four times daily from Nice's Gare du Sud (☎ 04 93 82 10 17), 4bis rue Alfred Binet.

destination	FF	hours
Villars-sur-Var	39	1
Puget-Théniers	52	1¼
Entrevaux	55	1½
Annot	63	1¾
Saint André	91	2½
Digne-les-Bains	109	3¼

Seniors over 55 get 25% discount; children under 12 are half-price.

Boat The fastest SNCM ferries from mainland France to Corsica depart from Nice (see the Getting There & Away chapter).

The SNCM office (☎ 04 93 13 66 99 or 04 93 13 66 66), ferry terminal, quai du Commerce, issues tickets (otherwise try a travel agency in town). It is open from 8 am to 7 pm (until 11.45 am on Saturday; open two hours before a scheduled departure on Sunday). From ave Jean Médecin take bus No 1 or 2 to the Port stop.

Getting Around
To/From the Airport Sunbus bus No 23 (8FF), which runs every 20 or 30 minutes from around 6 am to 8 pm, can be picked up

at the train station or on blvd Gambetta, rue de France or rue de la Californie. From the intercity bus station or promenade des Anglais (near the Hôtel Négresco) you can also take the yellow ANT bus (21FF; ☎ 04 93 56 35 40) which bears a symbol of an aeroplane pointing upward (every 20 minutes; 30 minutes on Sunday). Buses also make the run from the train station.

A taxi from the airport to the centre of Nice will cost between 120-140FF, depending on the time of day and whether you're at Terminal 1 or 2.

Bus The Station Centrale, Sunbus' main hub, takes up three sides of square Général Leclerc, which is between ave Félix Faure and blvd Jean Jaurès (near Vieux Nice and the intercity bus station). Tickets (8/68FF for a single/10 rides) and passes for local buses – run by Sunbus – are sold at the Sunbus information office (☎ 04 93 16 52 10), 10 ave Félix Faure. After you time-stamp your ticket, it's valid for one hour and can be used for one transfer. The Nice by Bus pass, valid for one/five/seven days costs 22/85/110FF and includes a return trip to the airport. The Sunbus office is open from 7.15 am to 7 pm (Saturday until 6 pm; closed Sunday). Bus information and route maps are available here too.

Bus No 12 links the train station with promenade des Anglais and the beach. To get from the train station to Vieux Nice and the intercity bus station, take bus No 2, 5 or 17. At night, four Noctambuses run north, east and west from place Masséna.

Car & Motorcycle Rent a Car Système (☎ 04 93 88 69 69, fax 04 93 88 43 36, www.rentacar.fr), in the same building as Budget (☎ 04 97 03 35 03) opposite the train station at 38 ave Aubert, offers the best car rental rates. Around the corner, JML (☎ 04 93 16 07 00, fax 04 93 16 07 48), 36 ave Aubert, is another cheapie.

Nicea Location Rent (☎ 04 93 82 42 71, fax 04 93 87 76 36), 9 ave Thiers, rents mopeds from 250FF a day (extra for petrol and a helmet), 50cc scooters for 390FF a day and 125cc motorcycles for 465FF a day. The office is open from 9 am to 6 pm (closed Sunday).

The Motor Vespa Centre (☎ 04 93 85 34 04), 1 rue Alfred Mortier, does not rent two-wheel contraptions but sells all the spare parts, flashy gear and accessories two-wheelers could possibly need.

Taxi There are taxi stands outside the train station and on ave Félix Faure near place Masséna; otherwise order a taxi (☎ 04 93 13 78 78).

Bicycle Cycles Arnaud (☎ 04 93 87 88 55), 4 place Grimaldi, has mountain bikes for 100/180FF a day/weekend (with a deposit of 2000FF). The shop is open from 9 am to noon and 2 to 4 pm (closed Monday morning and Sunday). Nicea Location Rent (see Car & Motorcycle) rents mountain bikes for 80FF a day.

The Three Corniches

The Corniche Inférieure (also known as the Basse Corniche or Lower Corniche; the N98) sticks pretty close to the nearby train line and villa-lined waterfront. The Moyenne Corniche, the middle and least exciting coastal road (N7), clings to the hillside, affording great views if you can find somewhere to pull over. The Grande Corniche, whose panoramas are by far the most spectacular, leaves Nice as the D2564 and passes the **Col d'Èze** (512m), where there's great views; La Turbie; and **Le Vistaëro**, which offers a breathtaking view of the entire coastline.

Accommodation here is generally pricey and limited. The cheapest option is to stay in Nice from where easy day or half-day trips can be made. The Corniche Inférieure, the lowest of the trio, is well served by train from Nice; the higher two roads, and the entire Niçois hinterland, are practically in-accessible without private transport or a sturdy set of hiking boots.

CORNICHE INFÉRIEURE

Heading eastward from Nice to Menton, the Corniche Inférieure passes through Ville-franche-sur-Mer, Saint Jean-Cap Ferrat, Beaulieu-sur-Mer, Èze-sur-Mer, Cap d'Ail and Monaco (see the Monaco chapter).

It was built in the 1860s. Look out for the pretty pink Château des Anglais (see the Absolutely Fabulous boxed text), 176 blvd Carnot, on Mont Boron, on the right as you flash past leaving Nice.

Getting There & Away The lower coastal road is well served by bus and train. Bus No 100 runs the length of the Corniche Inférieure (19 daily between 6.45 am and 7.45 pm) from Nice to Menton, stopping at all the villages along the way. From Nice, Bus No 111 (10 daily) serves Saint Jean-Cap Ferrat.

Trains run from Nice along the coast to Ventimiglia, Italy, every 10-20 minutes between 6 am and 6 pm (every 30-50 minutes from 6 pm to 1 am). Most trains stop at:

destination	FF	minutes
Villefranche-sur-Mer	9	8
Beaulieu-sur-Mer	9	14
Èze	10	17
Cap d'Ail	13	21
Monaco	17	25
Cap Martin-Roquebrune	20	32
Carnolès	22	36
Menton	23	38

Between July and September, if you intend making several train trips along the coast in one day, buy a Carte Isabelle (see Train Passes in the Getting Around chapter).

Villefranche-sur-Mer
• pop 8000   ✉ 06230

Set in one of the Côte d'Azur's most charm-ing – and unspoilt – harbours, this little port village overlooks the Cap Ferrat peninsula. It has a well preserved, 14th century *vieille ville* (old town). Steps break up the tiny streets, the most interesting and evocatively named of which is the arcaded rue Obscure.

Keep a lookout for occasional glimpses of the sea as you wander through the streets that lead down to quai Courbet, the **fishing port** where weathered fishermen tending their nets remain a common sight. The crooked houses overlooking the harbour through wooden shutters are painted in a rainbow of muted colours, ranging from bedtime pink to sea blues and peppermint greens. On Sunday, the weekly *marchés artisanal* (artisans' market) adds another splash of colour to the old town streets and squares.

From the fishing port a narrow **coastal path** runs around the citadel to the modern pleasure port, Port de la Darse. From the path, there are good views of Cap Ferrat and the wooded slopes of the *rade* (gulf) of Villefranche which served as a naval base for the Russians during their conflicts with the Turks in the 19th century. **Plage de Villefranche-sur-Mer**, north-west of the vieille ville, is a shallow shingle beach.

Citadelle The imposing Fort Saint Elme (1557), place Emmanuel Philibert, was built by the Duke of Savoy at the end of the 16th century to defend the rade. Its thick walls today shelter Villefranche's Hôtel de Ville; the open-air Théâtre de la Citadelle where films are screened every evening at 9.30 pm (35FF) in July and August; public gardens sporting a purple-carpeted path; and two art museums. The more interesting of the two, the Musée Volti (☎ 04 93 76 33 27), specialises in bronze sculptures of women and has voluptuous female forms in all shapes, sizes and postures on display. Most are the work of Villefranche-born sculptor Antoniucci Volti (1915-89).

The contemporary works by husband-and-wife-team, Henri Goetz (1909-89) and Christine Boumeester (1904-71), in the Musée Goetz-Boumeester draw less of a crowd. Gifts to the American couple from Picasso and Miró are also on display. Both museums are open from 9 or 10 am to noon and 2 or 3 pm to 5, 6 or 7 pm. They are closed Tuesday, Sunday morning, and in November (both free).

Chapelle de Saint Pierre Villefranche was a particular favourite of Jean Cocteau (1889-1963) who sought solace here in 1924 following the death of his close companion, Raymond Radiguet. In 1957, Cocteau decorated the inside of the Chapelle de Saint Pierre, a derelict 14th century Romanesque chapel used by local fishermen to store their nets until the 68-year-old artist got his hands on it. The engraving above the entrance to the waterfront chapel reads 'Enter this building as if it were made of living stone'. The interior, pastel-coloured frescoes, the altar – carved out of a rock from nearby La Turbie – and its cloths, crucifix and candelabra inside the waterfront chapel were all designed by Cocteau.

Mass is celebrated in the chapel (☎ 04 93 76 90 70) once a year – on 29 June, the feast day of Saint Peter, the patron saint of fishermen. Between June and September, it is open from 10 am to noon and 4 to 8.30 pm (closed Monday). Hours the rest of the year are 9.30 am to noon and 2 or 3 pm to 6 or 7 pm (12.50FF).

When in town, Cocteau stayed at the Hôtel Welcome, a restored 17th century convent opposite the chapel on quai Courbet. He wrote the play *Orphée* (Orpheus), and the libretto for Stravinsky's *Oedipus Rex* here.

Places to Stay & Eat The cheapest place in town is the *Hôtel de la Darse* (☎ 04 93 01 72 54, fax 04 93 01 84 37), overlooking the pleasure port on ave Général de Gaulle. Rooms with shower start at 270FF.

Double rooms at Cocteau's *Hôtel Welcome* (☎ 04 93 76 27 62, fax 04 93 76 27 66, welcome@riviera.fr, 1 quai Courbet) start at 560/720FF in the low/high season. *Le Saint Pierre*, the restaurant below, serves succulent fish dishes at reasonable prices.

Saint Jean-Cap Ferrat

- **pop 2250**   ✉ 06230

Once a fishing village, the seaside resort of Saint Jean-Cap Ferrat lies on the spectacular wooded peninsula of Cap Ferrat, which conceals a bounty of millionaires' villas and a star-studded past.

Charlie Chaplin, Churchill and Cocteau all holidayed here. King Leopold II of Belgium and *Pink Panther* actor David Niven (1910-83) retired here. Writer Somerset Maugham lived – never without house guests – and died at the luxurious Villa Mauresque; Noël Coward, Ian Fleming, TS Elliot and Evelyn Waugh were among his regular guests. British film director Michael Powell ran a hotel at the port.

In 1938 Murray Burnett wrote the play *Everybody Comes to Rick's* here, which was the basis for the classic film *Casablanca*.

Several coastal *sentiers pédestres* wend their way around Cap Ferrat; a coastal path leads from the sandy **Plage de Passable** on the cape's western shore to the café-lined port on the eastern side of the cape. All the routes are marked on a map outside the tourist office (☎ 04 93 76 08 90, fax 04 93 76 16 67), 59 ave Denis Séméria. On clear days scale the 164 steps of the *phare* (lighthouse) on the cape's most southern tip for a stunning panorama of the coast from Italy to the Esterel.

Villa Ephrussi de Rothschild On the narrow isthmus of Cap Ferrat is the Musée de Béatrice Ephrussi de Rothschild (☎ 04 93 01 33 09), housed in a *belle époque* villa built for the Baroness de Rothschild in 1912. Her house was designed in the style of the great Renaissance houses of Tuscany and took 40 architects seven years to build. It abounds with paintings, tapestries, porcelain and antique furniture and is surrounded by seven hectares of beautiful gardens, each manicured in a different style. The central garden was landscaped like a ship's deck so that the baroness could imagine herself aboard the *Île de France* ship after which she named the villa. On her ship's prow, stands an enchanting temple of love, behind which sprawl Spanish, Japanese, Florentine, cactus and oriental gardens. Different herbs, laurier roses and an olive grove adorn the Jardin Provençal.

Between 15 February and 1 November, the villa is open from 10 am to 6 pm (7 pm in July and August); its hours are 2 to 6 pm (10 am to 6 pm on weekends) the rest of the year. Admission to the gardens and collections on the *rez-de-chaussée* (ground floor) costs 46/35FF for adult/student under 18. A ticket to the collections on the 1st floor is an extra 15FF. Guided tours depart daily at 11.30 am and 3.30, 4.30 and 5.30 pm.

Places to Stay The cheapest is the one-star *La Bastide* (☎ 04 93 76 06 78, fax 04 93 76 19 10, 3 ave Albert 1er) which has singles/doubles from 280/310FF. Similar rates are charged at *La Flégate* (☎ 04 93 76 04 51, fax 04 93 76 14 93, 11 ave Denis Séméria).

Michael Powell's former joint, *Hôtel La Voile d'Or* (☎ 04 93 01 13 13, fax 04 93 76 11 17, 27 ave Mermoz), overlooks the port. Today it touts four stars with sky-high prices to match. An equally dreamy paradise is the *Grand Hôtel du Cap Ferrat* (☎ 04 93 76 50 50, fax 04 93 76 04 52, 71 blvd Général de Gaulle) where guests pay 950-5500FF a room.

Beaulieu-sur-Mer
• pop 4000   ✉ 06310

Upmarket Beaulieu-sur-Mer never witnessed such a grand old time as during the turn-of-the-century's flamboyant *belle époque* when Europe's wealthy and aristocratic bequeathed their presence upon the resort.

French architect Gustave Eiffel lived at the waterfront Villa Durandy in Beaulieu-sur-Mer from 1896 until his death in 1923; the Florentine-style villa was consequently converted into luxury holiday apartments (see Places to Stay). Next door is the Villa Grecque Kérylos, Beaulieu's main draw today.

Tamer remnants of the resort's golden age include the **Grand Casino**, 4 ave Fernand Dunan, dating from 1928; and the domed La Rotonde (1899), ave des Hellènes, a former hotel restaurant and today a conference centre. Just across from the harbour are the **Jardins de L'Olivaie**, the venue for a two-week, international Jazz Parade (☎ 04 93 88 41 50; www.beaulieu-jazz-parade.org), held each year in August.

Beaulieu's shingle beach overlooks Baie des Fourmis (Bay of Ants). From here, narrow **promenade Maurice Rouvier** leads south-west beneath a hedgerow of laurier roses to Saint Jean-Cap Ferrat, making for a pleasant 45 minute stroll.

The tourist office (☎ 04 93 01 44 04, fax 04 93 01 02 21), place Georges Clémenceau, is next to the train station. From here, turn right along rue Georges Clémenceau, then right along rue du Marché and its continuation rue Gallieni, to get to central ave Général Leclerc and the seafront. Villa Kérylos is a 15 minute walk south-west from here.

Villa Grecque Kérylos This luxurious villa, perched on the rocky Baie des Fourmis peninsula, is a unique reconstruction of an ancient Greek dwelling built in 1902 for scholar and archaeologist Théodore Reinach (1860-1928). The villa took seven years to complete and is a near-perfect reproduction of an Athenian villa from the 1st and 2nd centuries BC.

The rooms retain their original Hellenic name and purpose. From the marble bath tub decorated with mosaics of splashing dolphins in the *balanéion* (bathroom), Reinach's male guests retired to the *triklinos* (dining room) and afterwards to the *andron*, a large parlour clad in yellow marble from Siena. Reinach saw no need to invite women to the villa where he lived for some 20 years, given it has no *gynaeceum*, the parlour women retired to after dinner in ancient Greece. In the gardens, a botanical trail highlights the ancient uses of plants typical to Greece and the French coast.

The Villa Kérylos (☎ 04 93 01 01 44), ave Gustave Eiffel, is open from 10.30 am to 6 pm (until 7 pm in July and August). Weekday hours from mid-December to mid-February are 2 to 6 pm (40/20FF for adult/student). In summer, classical music concerts are held here (☎ 04 93 01 61 70 for reservations).

Places to Stay & Eat Beaulieu's bargain-basement hotel is the one-star *Hôtel Rivièra (☎ 04 93 01 04 92, fax 04 93 01 19 31, 6 rue Paul Dommer)*, north off the main street blvd Général Leclerc. Singles/doubles with washbasin are 180/190FF and doubles/triples/quads with shower and toilet cost 280/360/440FF.

The four-star and very pink *La Réserve (☎ 04 93 01 00 01, fax 04 93 01 28 99, 5 blvd Général Leclerc)* has been Beaulieu's decadent hang-out since its grand opening in the 1870s. Eccentric American, Gordon Bennet of the *New York Herald*, was a frequent diner here.

Weekly rates for a four-person self-catering studio at Gustave Eiffel's former family home, the *Résidence Eiffel (☎ 04 93 76 46 46, fax 04 93 76 46 00, rue Gustave Eiffel)*, start at 3696/5551FF in the low/high season.

Cap d'Ail
✉ 06320
There is little to do on unpoetically-named Cape Garlic, a lush, heavily-vegetated headland of palm trees, pines and paradisiac villas, except stroll or swim.

Greta Garbo and Valentina Schlee both hung out on Cap d'Ail in the 1960s. Cocteau's spectacular **amphithéâtre** is today used as a *théâtre de la jeunesse* (youth theatre), by the Centre Méditerranéen d'Études Françaises (☎ 04 93 78 21 59), chemin des Oliviers.

As part of the cape's *Opération Plage Propre* (Operation Clean Beach) campaign, smoking and dogs are banned on **Plage La Réserve de La Mala**, Cap d'Ail's shingle beach tucked in a small cove. To get here from Cap d'Ail train station, walk down the steps to ave Raymond Gramaglia, a promenade from where the coastal path can be accessed. Bear west (right) for a pleasant, 20 minute stroll around rocks to the beach, or east (left) for a more strenuous 3.5km hike to Monaco. The tourist office (☎ 04 93 78 02 33, fax 04 92 10 74 36), 104 ave du 3 Septembre, at the east end of the village on the N98, has details on more walks in the area.

Cap d'Ail's other attraction is its seaside youth hostel, the *Relais International de la Jeunesse (☎ 04 93 78 18 58, 26 ave Scuderi)*, signposted from ave Raymond

NICE TO MENTON

Gramaglia. A bed in a four, six or 10-bed dorm costs 72FF a night, including breakfast (135/170FF half/full-board). Travellers have to vacate their rooms between 9.30 am and 5 pm (curfew from 11 pm).

Cap Martin

Cap Martin is the coastal quarter of Cap Martin-Roquebrune (see the Grande Corniche section). This green headland is best known for its sumptuous villas, presumptuous collection of royal honorary citizens and famous past residents – among them, Winston Churchill, Coco Chanel, Marlène Dietrich, the architect Le Corbusier and the Irish poet WB Yeats.

The Cap Martin-Roquebrune tourist office (☎ 04 93 35 62 87, fax 04 93 28 57 00), 20 ave Paul Doumer, is at the north end of the cape, midway between Carnolès and Cap Martin-Roquebrune train stations. Its hours are 9.30 am to 12.30 pm and 3 to 7 pm (closed Sunday). It stocks information on the medieval hilltop village of Roquebrune (see Grande Corniche section) and arranges guided tours to its 10th century chateau (30/10FF for adult/child).

Things to See & Do Exploring on foot is one of the most pleasurable pastimes on Cap Martin. The closest beach to Cap Martin-Roquebrune train station, ave de la Gare, is **Plage du Buse**, a two minute walk from the station and accessible from ave Le Corbusier.

Ave Le Corbusier follows the coast eastwards, around Baie de Roquebrune to the north end of the cape where it turns into promenade Le Corbusier. It runs past the **Cabanon Le Corbusier**, an unassuming wooden chalet used by Le Corbusier as his studio in summer. In 1965 the architect suffered a heart attack while diving off Cap Martin and died. He is buried in Roquebrune cemetery. The tourist office runs a once-weekly visit (advance reservations only) to the cabanon.

Another fine walk is from Cap Martin to Monte Carlo (three hours). Inland, Roquebrune hilltop village is a one-hour walk (up

numerous staircases) from Cap Martin-Roquebrune train station (1½ hours from Carnolès).

Places to Stay The most affordable place on Cap Martin is *Hôtel Europe Village* (☎ 04 93 35 62 45 or 04 92 10 13 10, fax 04 93 57 72 59, ave Virginie Hériot) which has simple singles/doubles from 270/370FF. It is closed from mid-November to mid-February. Similar prices are charged at *Hôtel Westminister* (☎ 04 93 35 00 68, fax 04 93 28 88 50, 14 ave Louis Laurens), about 500m west of Cap Martin-Roquebrune train station.

MOYENNE CORNICHE

Cut through rock in the 1920s, the Moyenne Corniche takes you from Nice past the Col de Villefranche (149m), Èze and Beausoleil, the French town up the hill from Monte Carlo in Monaco.

Getting There & Away From Nice, bus No 112 serves the Moyenne Corniche, stopping at Èze and Beausoleil (seven daily).

By train from Nice, get off at Èze-sur-Mer train station on the Corniche Inférieure, from where it is a 3km uphill walk to Èze village.

Èze

• pop 2450   ✉ 06360   alt 390m

Perched on a rocky peak is the picturesque village of Èze, once occupied by Ligurians and Phoenicians and today grossly overrun with tourists. Below is its modern coastal counterpart, Èze-sur-Mer, accessible by road or train from the Corniche Inférieure.

The German philosopher Friedrich Nietzsche (1844-1900) spent some time here, during which he started to write *Thus Spoke Zarathustra*; the path that links Èze-sur-Mer and Èze is named after him. Walt Disney also holidayed here once.

The tourist office (☎ 04 93 41 26 00, fax 04 93 41 04 80), place Général de Gaulle, in the car park at the foot of the village perché, is open from 9 am to 7 pm (10 am to 1 pm and 2 to 7 pm on Sunday). Ask for information on summer cultural activities; the old town church, rue d'Église, is a popular venue for classical concerts.

Vieille Ville The steep narrow streets leading up to the top of the old village perché are crammed with art galleries, souvenir shops and pricey cafés. The chateau ruins crowning medieval Èze are surrounded by a cactus-laden **jardin exotique** (☎ 04 93 41 10 30), open from 9 am to noon and 2 pm to dusk. Those keen to savour the marvellous panorama of Cap Ferrat to the Massif de l'Ésterel have no choice but pay the cheeky 12FF admission fee.

Perfumeries Perfumery Fragonard (see Grasse in the Cannes Region chapter), has an outlet in Èze where the subtleties of its sweet-smelling products can be discovered. The Fragonard factory (☎ 04 93 41 05 05), on the eastern edge of Èze on the Moyenne Corniche, is open for tours from 8.30 am to 6.30 pm (closed between 12 and 2 pm in the low season). Admission is free. Rival perfumery Galimard (☎ 04 93 41 10 70), place de Gaulle, also has an outlet here.

Places to Stay & Eat In Èze village the cheapest option, always fully booked months in advance, is the 11-room *Hôtel du Golf* (☎ 04 93 41 18 50, fax 04 93 41 29 93, place de la Colette), which has rooms for one or two for 150FF, or 220/250FF with shower/shower and toilet. Equally booked out, although definitely not by the budget-conscious is the fabulous, four-star *Chèvre d'Or* (☎ 04 92 10 66 66, rue du Barri) which has a wonderful terrace, fine restaurant and nine cosy rooms from 1400FF.

There is a camping ground and a good-value auberge above Èze village on the Col d'Èze (see Observatoire de Nice section later).

GRANDE CORNICHE
The Grande Corniche was built by Napoléon along part of the Roman via Julia Augusta. Its entire length is shot through with spectacular (read: dangerous) tunnels slicing through rock and blinding *lacets*

(hairpin bends) – all of which proved sufficiently cliff-hanging in the 1950s to act as a backdrop to Hitchcock's film *To Catch a Thief* (1956), starring Cary Grant and Grace Kelly. The Hollywood actress, who met her Monégasque prince charming while shooting the film, died in 1982 after crashing her car on this same road.

Getting There & Away This road is practically impossible to explore without your own wheels. From Nice (☎ 04 93 85 64 44 or 04 93 85 61 81), bus No 74 runs sporadically to the Observatoire de Nice. Bus No 116 stops at La Trinité and La Turbie en route to Peille (three times daily; no Sunday service).

Observatoire de Nice
This 19th century, classical-domed observatory, 5km east of Nice centre atop Mont Gros (375m), was designed by French architects Gustave Eiffel and Charles Garnier. It sits amid 35 hectares of landscaped parkland. When the observatory opened in 1887, its telescope – 76cm in diameter – was among the largest in Europe.

Guided 1½ hour tours of the observatory (☎ 04 92 00 31 45 or 04 93 85 85 58, www.obs-nice.fr) and its grounds are available on Saturday at 3 pm; at other times, you have to call in advance to make an appointment. Star gazers keen to observe the skies should head instead to **Astrorama** (☎ 04 93 41 23 04), a planetarium and astronomy centre 8km farther east along the Grande Corniche in La Trinité. On the Col d'Èze, turn left along a small road signposted 'Parc Départemental de la Grande Corniche-Astrorama'. Astrorama is open Tuesday and Friday from 5.30 to 11 pm. Between June and August it is open daily, except Sunday, from 6.30 pm (40FF).

Places to Stay & Eat The Col d'Èze offers a couple of excellent value places to stay. Pitch your tent at *Camping les Romarins* (☎ 04 93 01 81 64), west end of the Col d'Èze. Nightly rates are 78/92FF for one/two people, including tent site and car. It is closed from October to April.

From Les Romarins, it is a short hike to the *Hermitage du Col d'Èze (☎ 04 93 41 00 68, fax 04 93 41 21 11)*, an old-style inn spectacularly set at the top of the Col d'Èze and touting unbeatable views from its terrace restaurant. A night's sleep in one of its 13 rooms costs 170/310FF for one/two people.

La Turbie
• pop 2600   ✉ 06320

La Turbie teeters on a promontory directly above Monaco and offers a stunning night-time vista of the principality. By day, an unparalleled aerial view can be had from the gardens of the **Trophée des Alpes**, a trophy monument on the highest point of the old Roman road. It was built by the Roman emperor Augustus in 6BC to celebrate his victory over the Alps. The 45 different Alpine tribes he successfully conquered are listed on the nine-line, 9m-wide inscription carved on the west side of the monument.

Restoration work started on the trophy in the 1920s. Steps lead up to the top of the shoddily reconstructed monument and there is a small museum (☎ 04 93 41 10 11) at its base recounting its history. The site (entrance on place Théodore de Banville) is open from 9.30 am to 5 pm; until 6 pm between April and June; until 7 pm from July to September (25/15FF for adult/ student and child over 12). The last ticket is sold 30 minutes before closing.

La Turbie village is unexciting bar its small but intact vieille ville, neatly packed around the baroque-style **Église Saint Michael** (1777), at the foot of the Trophée des Alpes. From the village, a perilously-steep mountain road leads to the top of **Mont Agel** (1110m), the slopes of which are graced with the greens of Monte Carlo Golf Club (☎ 04 93 41 09 11), a members-only club at a heady height of 810m.

Places to Stay In La Turbie, the simple *Hôtel Le Cesarée (☎ 04 93 41 16 08, fax 04 93 41 19 49)*, opposite the entrance to the Trophée des Alpes at 16 cours Albert 1er,

has basic singles/doubles for 230/270FF, triples/quads for 370/425FF. Rooms at the *Hôtel Napoléon (☎ 04 93 41 00 54, fax 04 93 41 28 93, 7 ave de la Victoire)* are a touch more upmarket; singles/doubles start at 250/350FF.

Cap Martin-Roquebrune
• pop 12,300   ✉ 06190   alt 70m

Cap Martin-Roquebrune, sandwiched between Monaco and Menton, became part of France in 1861; prior to that it was a free town following its revolt against Grimaldi rule in 1848. The town is neatly divided into four quarters, stretching northwards from the exclusive suburb of Cap Martin on the coast (accessible from the Corniche Inférieure – see that section) to the medieval hilltop town of Roquebrune (300m) which straddles the Grande Corniche. The less touristy quarters of Saint-Roman and Carnolès border Monaco and Menton respectively.

Medieval Roquebrune is a donjon complete with a re-created feudal castle dating from the 10th century. The mock-medieval *tour anglaise* (English tower) near the entrance was built by wealthy British lord, William Ingram, who bought the chateau in 1911. His fairytale tower caused such an outrage in the village that the state almost immediately classified the chateau as a historical monument to protect it from further fantastical modifications. The castle is open from 10 am to noon and 2 to 5 pm (7 pm in summer). The tortuous little streets leading up to it are lined with souvenir shops and overrun with tourists in summer. Don't miss the impressive rue Moncollet, with arcaded passages and stairways carved out of the rock.

Cemetery The Swiss architect Le Corbusier (see the Corniche Inférieure section) is buried with his wife in the old cemetery at the top of the village. The grave – designed by Corbusier before his death – is adorned with nothing more than a cactus and the simple epitaph, *ici repose Charles Édouard Jeannet (1887-1965)*, painted in Corbusier's cursive hand on a small yellow, red and blue ceramic tile. Until 1948, William Butler Yeats (1865-1938) was also buried in Roquebrune cemetery. The writer died in Cap Martin-Roquebrune in 1938 while wintering on Cap Martin. His remains were moved to his native Ireland in 1948.

To get to the cemetery from central place des 2 Frères, walk east to the end of rue Grimaldi, turn left onto rue d'Église, right onto rue de la Fontaine, then left onto chemin de Gorbio from where 160 steps lead to Le Corbusier's grave (section J).

The Cap Martin-Roquebrune tourist office (see Corniche Inférieure section) arranges visits to the architect's summer house on Cap Martin.

Arrière-Pays Niçois

The Niçois hinterland stretches inland from Nice to Menton. It's studded with medieval villages perchés, aloft rocky crags as a safeguard and lookout point, and is practically impossible to explore without your own transport.

Contes & Coaraze

Roman Contes (pop 5800; postcode 06390) sits on a ship-shaped rocked above the Paillon de Contes river. On the river's left bank, close to the *moulin à huile communal* (communal olive press), is a preserved **moulin à fer**, forge (☎ 04 93 79 00 01 at the Mairie), open Saturday between 9 am and noon and 2.30 to 5.30 pm. South-west by 6km is **Châteauneuf-de-Contes**, a small hamlet at the foot of the overgrown ruins of an older village, abandoned prior to WWI. A scraggy path' occasionally barred by a territorial pack of goats' leads from the road to the crumbling ruins which can – goats allowing – be freely explored.

To get to the **ruines de Châteauneuf** from Châteauneuf-de-Contes, follow the route de Châteauneuf (D815) through the village then bear left at the wrought-iron roadside cross along route des Chevaliers de Malte. The ruins are 2km from here. Continuing west along the D815, you come to **Tourrette Levens**, a particularly dramatic village

perché topped with a chateau which houses a collection of exotic butterflies.

Coaraze (pop 540; postcode 06390; alt 640m), 9km north of Contes on the Col Saint Roch (D15), is known as the *village du soleil* (village of the sun) after the ceramic **sun dials** that adorn its cobble streets. The Provençal poem engraved in stone next to the green lizard mosaic on place Félix-Giordan tells the tale of how villagers trapped the devil then demanded he sacrifice his tail like a lizard to be set free. Coaraze is derived from the Provençal words '*coa raza*' meaning 'cut tail'.

The village celebrates its Fête de L'Olivier (Olive Festival) on 15 August. The Syndicat d'Initiative (☎ 04 93 79 37 47), off place Alexandre Mari, has information on hiking and *gîtes ruraux*.

Places to Stay & Eat In Berre-des-Alpes (675m), 7km north-east of Contes, rooms with shower, toilet and mountain view for one or two people at the one-star *Hôtel-Restaurant des Alpes* (☎ 04 93 91 80 05, fax 04 93 91 85 69) cost 250FF. Up the hill on central place Bellevue, the *Hôtel Beauséjour* (☎ 04 93 91 80 08) has doubles from 200FF.

In Coaraze, the hotel-restaurant *Auberge du Soleil* (☎ 04 93 79 08 11, fax 04 93 79 37 79), tucked in the village's heart, has doubles with shower/toilet for 360FF. *Menus* on its terrace are 137FF. The auberge is closed from mid-November to mid-March.

Peille & Peillon

Quaintly restored Peille (pop 1830; postcode 06440; alt 630m) is quite untouched by tourism tack despite the raving reports it gets as among the hinterland's most intact village perché. Its eastern entrance is guarded by the 12th century **Chapelle Saint Roch**, place Jean Mioul.

Captions are written in Pelhasc in the village **Musée du Terroir** (open summer weekends from 2 to 6 pm). This is a dialect specific to Peille and distinguishable from the Niçois dialect by its absent R's and silent L's – the Peillasques say *carriea* instead of *carriera* (Niçois for *rue*, meaning street). Peille celebrates a **Fête du Blé et de la Lavande** (Wheat & Lavender Festival) in August. There are three buses daily (none on Sunday) from Nice to Peille (one hour).

Six kilometres of hairpins south-west of Peille on the D53 towards Peillon, is **La Grave**, a giant, blot-on-the-landscape cement works where the hinterland's limestone is turned into cement. The best aerial view of Peille and La Grave is from the **Col de la Madone** (927m; D22), a beautiful, stone tunnelled mountain pass that runs east from Peille to Sainte Agnès (see later).

Peillon (pop 1140; postcode 06440; alt 456m), 14km east of Nice, is known for its precarious *nid d'aigle* (eagle's nest) location. From the village car park, a footpath leads to the **Chapelle des Pénitents Blancs**, noteworthy for its set of macabre 15th century frescoes. Longer trails lead to Peille (two hours on an old Roman road), La Turbie (two hours) and the Chapelle Saint Martin (1½ hours). North of Peillon, the **Gorges du Peillon** (D21) cuts through the Peillon valley to **L'Escarène**, an important mule stop in the 17th and 18th centuries for traders working the Route du Sel (salt road) from Nice to Turin.

Places to Stay & Eat In Peille, the *Hôtel Belvédère* (☎ 04 93 79 90 45, place Jean Mioul) has doubles from 190FF and a half-board option for 230-250FF per person.

In Peillon, the upmarket *Auberge de la Madone* (☎ 04 93 79 91 17) touts three stars and has pricey rooms for 450-820FF in the low season and 550-920FF in the high season. Its restaurant, specialising in local Peillonnais cuisine, is closed Wednesday. Book in advance.

Gorbio & Sainte Agnès

The flowery village perché of **Gorbio** (pop 930; postcode 06920; alt 360m), 10km north-west of Menton and 2km west of Sainte Agnès as the crow flies, is best known for its annual Fête Dieu in June. On this feast day, during a traditional Procession aux Limaces, villagers light up Gorbio's medieval cobble streets with snail shells set in pots of sand and filled with burning olive oil.

A trail leads from Gorbio to neighbouring **Sainte Agnès** which commands a bird's eye view from its 780m perch and claims to be Europe's highest seaside village. Steps lead from Montée du Souvenir to the scanty 12th century chateau ruins that crown the village. Beneath, is the **Fort Sainte Agnès**, a 2500 sq metre underground fort built after WWI. It was designed by the André Maginot when Defence Minister in 1931-38 as part of a series of fortifications built to defend Nice and its coastline. Today the fort is a museum (☎ 04 93 35 87 35 or 04 93 35 84 58 at the Mairie). Close to the drawbridge, the reinforced concrete bunkers of one of four artillery blocks are clearly visible. The fort-museum is open on weekends from 2.30 to 5.30 pm; daily from 3 to 6 pm between July and September (20/10FF for adult/child under 16).

Places to Stay & Eat Close to the fort, *Le Saint Yves* (☎ 04 93 35 91 45) has doubles from 190FF; its terrace restaurant is especially appealing. Lower down the village, *La Vieille Auberge* (☎ 04 93 35 92 02) on the D22, offers half-board deals only for 230FF per person. Both places are closed for a couple of months in winter; year round it is best to book in advance.

Getting There & Away There are three buses daily (bus No 902) in each direction between Sainte Agnès and Menton (44FF return; 45 minutes).

Menton

• pop 29,000   ✉ 06500

Menton, reputed to be the warmest spot on the Côte d'Azur (particularly in winter), is only a few kilometres from the Italian border. In part because of the weather, Menton is popular with older holiday-makers, whose way of life and preferences have made the town's after-dark a tad tranquil compared to other hot spots along the coast.

Gustave Flaubert, Guy de Maupassant, Katherine Mansfield, and Robert Louis Stevenson who wrote his essay *Ordered South* here in 1874, all found solace in Menton in the past. Today, the town mainly draws Italians from across the border and retains a magnetic charm free of the airs, graces and pretensions so painfully obvious elsewhere on the coast.

Historically, Menton, along with neighbouring Cap Martin-Roquebrune, found itself under Grimaldi rule until 1848, when its people rebelled and declared a new in-

dependent republic under the protection of Sardinia. In 1861, the two towns voted to become part of France forcing Charles III of Monaco to sell Menton to Napoléon III for four million FF.

Above all, Menton is famed for its cultivation of lemons. Giant, larger-than-life sculptures made from lemons, lemons and more lemons (about 130 tonnes) take over the town for two weeks during Menton's fabulous Fête des Citrons (Lemon Festival) in February. The 1997 theme was comic-strip character, Tintin. The festival kicks off

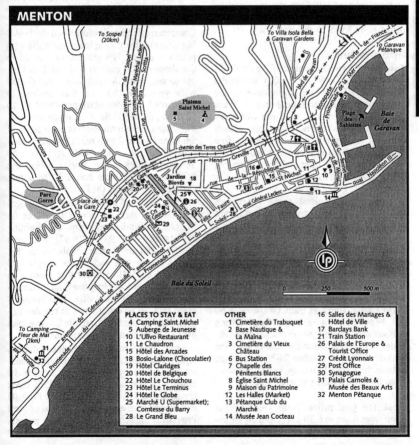

MENTON

PLACES TO STAY & EAT
4 Camping Saint Michel
5 Auberge de Jeunesse
10 L'Ulivo Restaurant
11 Le Chaudron
15 Hôtel des Arcades
18 Bosio-Lalone (Chocolatier)
19 Hôtel Claridges
20 Hôtel de Belgique
22 Hôtel Le Chouchou
23 Hôtel Le Terminus
24 Hôtel le Globe
25 Marché U (Supermarket);
   Comtesse du Barry
28 Le Grand Bleu

OTHER
1 Cimetière du Trabuquet
2 Base Nautique &
   La Maïna
3 Cimetière du Vieux
   Château
6 Bus Station
7 Chapelle des
   Pénitents Blancs
8 Église Saint Michel
9 Maison du Patrimoine
12 Les Halles (Market)
13 Pétanque Club du
   Marché
14 Musée Jean Cocteau

16 Salles des Mariages &
   Hôtel de Ville
17 Barclays Bank
21 Train Station
26 Palais de l'Europe &
   Tourist Office
27 Crédit Lyonnais
29 Post Office
30 Synagogue
31 Palais Carnolès &
   Musée des Beaux Arts
32 Menton Pétanque

around the ornamental Jardins Biovès on Mardi Gras.

Orientation

The old town and port are wedged around a small hill between Baie de Garavan to the east and Baie du Soleil which stretches 3km west to Cap Martin-Roquebrune.

Promenade du Soleil and its continuations quai Général Leclerc and quai de Monléon run west to east along Menton's shingle beach in the Baie du Soleil; the train line runs approximately parallel about 500m inland.

Ave Édouard VII links the train station with the beach; ave Boyer, where the tourist office is, is 350m to the east.

Information

Tourist Office The tourist office (☎ 04 93 57 57 00, fax 04 93 57 51 00), inside the Palais de l'Europe, a contemporary art gallery at 8 ave Boyer, is open from 8.30 am to 12.30 pm and 1.30 to 6 pm (Saturday from 9 am to noon and 2 to 6 pm; closed Sunday). In summer, you can pick up a free city map and information brochures from the open-air stall operated by the tourist office opposite Les Halles, quai de Monléon.

Thematic organised tours (Menton's *belle ʾpoque*, artists, gardens etc) are arranged by the Maison du Patrimoine (☎ 04 92 10 33 66, fax 04 93 28 46 85), 5 rue Ciapetta; it has a more central information point (☎ 04 92 10 97 10) at 24 rue Saint Michel. Tours cost 30FF per person.

Money There are plenty of banks along rue Partouneaux. Barclays Bank (☎ 04 93 28 60 00), 39 ave Félix Faure, is open from 8.30 am to noon and 1.50 to 4.30 pm (closed on weekends). It has an automatic exchange machine outside. There is another 24-hour machine outside the Crédit Lyonnais, two doors down from the tourist office on ave Boyer.

Post The post office, cours George V, is open from 8 am to 6.30 pm (6 pm on Thursday; until noon on Saturday; closed Sunday).

Bookshops A fine range of guides, travel books and foreign-language newspapers are available at the Maison de la Presse, 25 ave Félix Faure.

Things to See & Do

Walking Tour Down by the port, a small **17th century fort** crowns the tip of land wedged between Menton's two bays behind which the old town sprawls. It was built in 1636 to defend Menton and later used as a salt cellar, prison and lighthouse. Today, the seafront bastion houses the **Musée Jean Cocteau** (☎ 04 93 57 72 30), square Jean Cocteau, in which drawings, tapestries and ceramics by the French artist are displayed. Cocteau restored and refurbished the building himself, decorating the outer walls with pebble mosaics. His gravestone, tucked in the shade of the bastion walls and looking out to sea, reads *Je reste avec vous* (I stay with you). In 1957 he was invited to Menton's **Salles des Mariages** (☎ 04 92 10 50 00) in the Hôtel de Ville, place Ardoïno. The Jean Cocteau museum is open from 10 am to noon and 2 to 6 pm; closed Tuesday (20/15FF for adult/student; free on Sunday). Hours at the Marriage Hall are 8.30 am to 12.30 pm and 1.30 to 5 pm; closed on weekends (5FF).

From the bastion, walk west along quai de Monléon then cut across the place du Marché, an outdoor marketplace adjoining **Les Halles** (☎ 04 93 35 75 93), Menton's bustling indoor market. Walk under the arches at the east end of the square and cross the café-filled **place aux Herbes** to get to rue Saint Michel, the main pedestrian street in the **vieille ville**. This becomes place du Cap where it leads to rue des Logettes and its continuation, rue Longue, part of the old Roman Via Julia Augusta.

From here a ramp leads to the Italianate **Église Saint Michel**, considered the grandest baroque church in southern France. Its creamy façade is flanked by a 35m clock tower and a 53m steeple, built in 1701-03 and topped with a campanile typical of most Provençal churches. Sunday Mass is celebrated at 11 am. The *parvis* (square in front of the church) is paved with a grey and white pebble mosaic featuring the Grimaldi coat of arms. Perched above the Church of Saint Michael on place de la Conception is the ornate, apricot **Chapelle des Pénitents Blancs** (1689).

Farther up the hill via the Montée du Souvenir is the cypress-shaded **Cimetière du Vieux Château** (☎ 04 93 35 87 21), open from 7 am to 6 pm (8 pm from May to September). The graves of English, Irish, Americans, New Zealanders and other foreigners who died here during the 19th century – including the inventor of rugby, the Reverend William Webb Ellis (1805-72) – can be seen in the cemetery's south-west corner. The view alone is worth the climb.

From here, you can continue north along the steep chemin du Trabuquet to the **Cimetière du Trabuquet**, a much larger, multilevel and landscaped cemetery with stunning panoramic views over Menton and the sea and into Italy. The sign reading 'Commonwealth War Graves' seems a tad imprecise; you soon ascend into clearly marked sections set aside for those who 'died for France' *(mort pour la France)* in campaigns in both Asia and Africa. Even in the 'Commonwealth' section there's something for everyone, with tombstones dating from the late 19th to the mid-20th century in English, French, Flemish and even Russian.

Blvd de Garavan, which runs north parallel with chemin du Trabuquet, leads to the upmarket neighbourhood of **Garavan**, best known for its luxurious villas and imaginative public gardens. In 1920-21, the sick novelist Katherine Mansfield (1888-1923) stayed at the **Villa Isola Bella**, ave Katherine Mansfield, to try to ease her worsening tuberculosis. Her short story, *The Doves' Nest*, published the year she died, is about a group of lonely women living in a villa on the French Riviera.

Gardens Garavan gardens include the **Jardin Fontana Rosa**, ave Blasco Ibañez, a garden created by Spanish novelist Blasco Ibañez in the 1920s and featuring fanciful benches, pergolas, pools and columns made from ceramic. Opposite, the **Jardin Exotique**, ave Saint-Jacques, was laid out for Lord Radcliffe in 1905. In France's most temperate garden, the **Jardin de Maria Serena**, 21 promenade Reine-Astrid, the temperature never falls below 5°C; the Villa Maria Serena was built by Charles Garnier in 1866 and is a venue for musical recitals in summer. The **Jardins des Colombières**, route des Colombières Garavan, was designed by Ferdinand Bac (1859-1952), comic-writer and the illegitimate son of Napoléon III, between 1918 and 1927. Visits to all these gardens (30FF each) have to be arranged through the Maison du Patrimoine (see Information – Tourist Office).

At the far south-western end of promenade du Soleil, overlooking the Baie du Soleil, is the early 18th century **Palais Carnolès**, a former summer residence of Monaco's royal family which today houses Menton's **Musée des Beaux Arts** (☎ 04 93 35 49 71), 3 ave de la Madone. Works dating from the 13th to 19th centuries are displayed here although one room is devoted to contemporary art. The palace's surrounding **Jardin de Sculptures** (sculpture garden), set amidst a lemon and orange grove, makes for a delightful afternoon stroll. The palace is open from 10 am to noon and 2 to 6 pm (closed Tuesday).

Boules & Beaches Menton has a plethora of **pétanque clubs** (boules clubs). The most central is the Pétanque Club du Marché (☎ 04 93 57 17 13), opposite Les Halles on quai de Monléon. Alternatively, head for Garavan Pétanque (☎ 04 93 28 08 34), square Baden-Baden, east of the old town; or Menton Pétanque (☎ 04 93 35 47 58), ave Florette, next to the Palais Carnolès.

The beach along promenade du Soleil is public but, like its counterpart in Nice, it's covered with smooth little rocks. There are more beaches directly north-east of the Vieux Port, including **Plages des Sablettes** with fine sand and clean water, and east of Port de Garavan the main pleasure-boat harbour.

The Base Nautique (☎ 04 93 35 49 70, fax 04 93 35 77 05), promenade de la Mer, rents laser boats/catamarans/kayaks for 100/120/50FF an hour. The **sailing** school also runs two-hour courses and arranges water skiing (120FF). La Maïna (☎ 04 93 35 95 83), 3 promenade de la Mer, is a **diving** club.

The Compagnie de Navigation et de Tourisme de Menton (☎ 04 93 35 51 72), Vieux Port, organises **boat trips** to Monaco (60FF) and the Italian Riviera (90FF).

Places to Stay

Camping The two-star *Camping Saint Michel (☎ 04 93 35 81 23, route des Ciappes de Castellar)*, open from April to mid-October, is 1km north-east of the train station up plateau Saint Michel. It costs 19/18/19FF per person/tent site/car. The two-star *Camping Fleur de Mai (☎ 04 93 57 22 36, 67 route de Gorbio)*, just 2km north-west of the train station, is open from late March or early April to September. Rates here are 60FF for a tent and two people plus 16FF for a car.

Hostels The *Auberge de Jeunesse (☎ 04 93 35 93 14, fax 04 93 35 93 07, plateau Saint Michel)* is a short distance from Camping Saint Michel. Bed & breakfast is 66FF. It's closed from 10 am to 5 pm; curfew is at midnight. The walk from the train station is quite a hike uphill and there are lots of steps.

Hotels Next door to the train station, the *Hôtel Le Chouchou (☎/fax 04 93 57 69 87, place de la Gare)* has basic singles/doubles above the bar for 180/250FF. Opposite, the *Hôtel Le Terminus (☎ 04 93 35 77 00)*, on the same square, has a few singles/doubles starting at 140/160FF. Hall showers are free. Reception is closed after 11 am on Saturday and after 5 pm on Sunday, but you can always find someone in the bar/restaurant areas during opening times. Half a block down the road, the *Hôtel de Belgique (☎ 04 93 35 72 66, 1 ave de la Gare)* has singles/doubles from 145/195FF; rooms

with a shower start at 260FF. The hotel is closed in November.

Heading towards the sea, *Hôtel Claridges (☎ 04 93 35 72 53)*, corner of ave de la Gare and ave de Verdun, has comfortable singles/doubles starting at 160/220FF. The *Hôtel le Globe (☎ 04 92 10 59 70, fax 04 92 10 59 71, 21 ave de Verdun)*, opposite the tourist office, is part of the recommended Logis de France chain; rooms are around 350FF.

In town, the *Hôtel des Arcades (☎ 04 93 35 70 62, fax 04 93 35 35 97)*, under the arches at 41 ave Félix Faures, is one of Menton's most picturesque options. Singles/doubles with washbasin cost 180/220FF in the low season, rising to 260FF in the high season. The best sea views are to be found at *Le Grand Bleu (☎ 04 93 57 46 33, 1684 promenade du Soleil)*. Singles/doubles are 250/350FF in summer.

Places to Eat

Restaurants There are places to eat galore – at any time of day – along ave Félix Faure and its pedestrianised continuation, rue Saint Michel. Place Clémenceau and place aux Herbes in the Vieille Ville are equally table-packed. There are more pricey restaurants with terraces fanned by cool breezes along promenade du Soleil.

Notable places include *Le Chaudron (☎ 04 93 35 90 25, 28 rue Saint Michel)* which has filling salads for 38 to 63FF and *menus* for 89 and 115FF; and *L'Ulivo (☎ 04 93 35 45 65, place du Cap)* which is run by Italians and specialises in *moule* (mussel) dishes. Ten different types – all for 45FF – are on offer. Pasta dishes start at 42FF and giant salads kick off at 25FF.

Slightly cheaper places, including *pizzerias*, line quai de Monléon in the old town. Along pedestrianised rue Saint Michel, delicious takeaway crêpes or *gauffres* (waffles) are available for between 10 and 25FF, depending on the topping.

Self-Catering In the old town, the *Marché Municipal* inside Les Halles, quai de

Monléon, sells food. It's open from 5 am to 1 pm (closed Monday morning).

The *Marché U* supermarket, 38 rue Partouneaux, is open from 8.30 am to 7.15 pm (Saturday until 7 pm; closed Sunday). The *Comtesse du Barry* shop, next door, serves luxury foie gras products. Chocolate chessboards and a game of draughts made from almond-flavoured *calissons* from Aix-en-Provence are sold at *Bosio-Lalone* (☎ 04 93 35 70 95), a chocolatier/pâtissier at No 19 on the same street. Wonderful lemon curds and other sweet treats are sold at *L'Arche des Confitures*, 2 rue du Vieux Collège.

Getting There & Away

Bus The bus station (☎ 04 93 28 43 27), is next to 12 promenade Maréchal Leclerc, the northern continuation of ave Boyer. The information office (☎ 04 93 35 93 60; international services ☎ 04 93 28 43 27) is open from 8 am to noon and 2 to 6 pm (closed Saturday afternoon and Sunday).

There are buses to Monaco (12FF return; 30 minutes), Nice (28FF return; 1¼ hours), Sainte Agnès (44FF return; 45 minutes), Sospel (50FF return; 45 minutes) and, just across the border in Italy, Ventimiglia (12FF; 30 minutes). There are also buses to the Aéroport International Nice-Côte d'Azur (95FF; 1½ hours) via Monaco run by Bus RCA (☎ 04 93 21 30 83).

Train The information office (☎ 08 36 35 35 35) at the train station is open from 8.45 am to noon and 2 to 6 pm (Saturday from 8.30 am to noon and 2 to 6 pm; closed Sunday). Trains to Ventimiglia across the border cost 12FF and take 10 minutes. For more information on rail services along the Côte d'Azur see Getting There & Away earlier in this chapter.

Getting Around

Car & Motorcycle ADA (☎ 04 92 10 20 25), 7 cours George V, rents scooters for 189/359FF a day/weekend.

AROUND MENTON

A string of mountain villages peer down on Menton from the **Col de Castillon** (707m), a hair-raising pass (D2566) that wends its way up the Vallée du Carei from the coast to **Sospel**, 21km north of Menton and gateway to the Parc National du Mercantour (see the Haute-Provence chapter).

The road cuts through the **Fôret de Menton**, a thick forest traversed with walking trails, following which you pass the **Viaduc du Caramel**, a viaduct formerly used by the old Menton-Sospel tramway which trundled its way through the valley in former times. **Castillon**, just south of the top of the col, is considered a model of modern rural planning; the village was destroyed by an earthquake in 1887 then heavily bombed in 1944. The village was built anew, perched on the mountain slopes in true Provençal fashion.

Cannes Region

Cannes is famous for its cultural activities, the most renowned being the 10 day International Film Festival in mid-May which sees the city's population triple overnight. Cannes has just one museum and, since its speciality is ethnography, the only art you're likely to come across is in the many rather chichi galleries scattered around town. The town's adopted slogan may well be 'life is a festival', but the main tourist season only runs from May to October.

Offshore from Cannes lie the two Lérins islands. Continuing south along the coast, you arrive at Antibes and its singing cape, Vallauris and Golfe-Juan (Picasso territory). Then there's a cluster of arty, inland villages crowned with Renoir's Cagnes-sur-Mer, Chagall's Saint Paul de Vence, and Matisse's Vence. Farther inland is smelly Grasse.

The most stunning natural feature of the entire Côte d'Azur – apart from the azure-blue sea, of course – is the lump of red porphyry rock known as the Massif de l'Estérel. At its foot is Saint Raphaël, a beachside resort town a couple of kilometres south-east of Roman Fréjus.

Cannes

- **pop 68,670**   ✉ **06400**

It's the money of the affluent, spent with fashionable nonchalance, that keeps Cannes' expensive hotels, restaurants and exorbitant boutiques in business and ocean liner-sized yachts afloat. But the harbour, the bay, the old quarter of Le Suquet, the beachside promenade, the beaches and the sunworshippers laid out on them, provide more than enough natural beauty to make at least a day trip here well worth the effort.

From Cannes, the route Napoléon (see Facts about Provence chapter) winds northwards, passing Grasse and Castellane on its way to Digne-les-Bains and beyond.

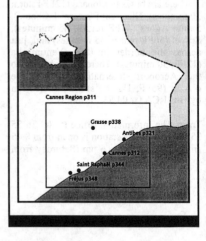

Orientation

Don't expect to be struck down by glitz 'n glamour the minute you step foot in Cannes. Seedy sex shops and peep shows abound around the train station and bus stop on rue Jean Jaurès. Things glam up along rue d'Antibes, the main shop-till-you-drop street a couple of blocks south of here. Several blocks farther south still is the huge Palais des Festivals et des Congrès, just east of the Vieux Port (old port).

Cannes' famous promenade, the magnificent, hotel-lined blvd de la Croisette, begins at the Palais des Festivals and continues eastward along Baie de Cannes to Pointe de la Croisette. Place Bernard Cornut Gentille, home to the main bus station, is on the north-west corner of the Vieux Port. Perched on a hill west of the Vieux Port is the less crowded quarter of Le Suquet.

Information

Tourist Offices The tourist office (☎ 04 93 39 24 53 or 04 93 39 01 01, fax 04 92 99 84 23, www.cannes-on-line.com), on the ground floor of the Palais des Festivals, is open from 9 am to 6.30 pm (closed Sunday). Daily hours in July and August are 9 am to 7.30 pm.

The tourist office annexe (☎ 04 93 99 19 77) adjoining the train station is open from 9 am to 7 pm (Saturday until 1 pm; closed Sunday). The office is signposted 'Syndicat

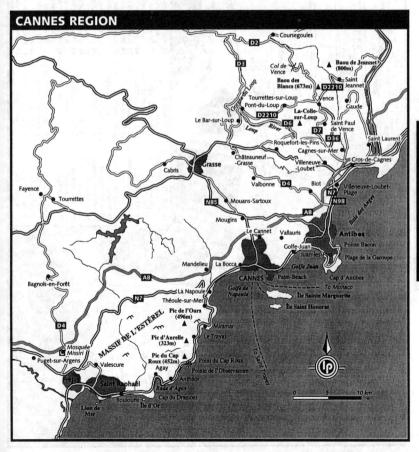

CANNES REGION

CANNES REGION

CANNES

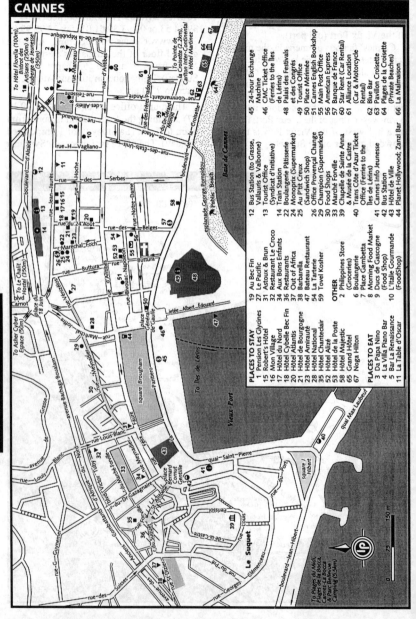

PLACES TO STAY
1 Pension Les Glycines
15 Robert's Hotel
16 Hôtel du Nord
17 Mon Village
18 Hôtel Cybèle Bec Fin
20 Hôtel Atlantis
21 Hôtel de Provence
23 Hôtel Amirauté
28 Hôtel National
35 Hôtel Chanteclair
52 Hôtel Alizé
53 Hôtel de la Poste
58 Hôtel Majestic
65 Grand Hôtel
67 Noga Hilton

PLACES TO EAT
3 Da Papa Nino
4 La Villa Piano Bar
5 Bar La Renaissance
11 La Table d'Oscar
19 Au Bec Fin
27 Le Pacific
31 Astoux & Brun
32 Restaurant Le Croco
36 Aux Bons Enfants
37 Restaurants
38 Out of Africa
38 Barbarella
47 Bateau Restaurant
54 La Tarterie
59 Tovel Kosher

OTHER
2 Philippines Store
   (Groceries)
6 Boulangerie
7 Place Gambetta
8 Morning Food Market
9 Ducs de Gascogne
   (Food Shop)
10 L'Italie Gourmande
   (FoodShop)

12 Bus Station (to Grasse,
   Vallauris & Valbonne)
13 Tourist Office
   (Syndicat d'Initiative)
14 Train Station
24 Boulangerie Pâtisserie
24 Monoprix (Supermarket)
25 Au P'tit Creux
   (Sandwich Shop)
26 Office Provençal Change
29 Champion (Supermarket)
30 Food Shops
33 Marché Forville
39 Chapelle de Sainte Anna
   & Musée de la Castre
40 Trans Côte d'Azur Ticket
   Office (Ferries to the
   Îles de Lérins)
41 Cannes Info Jeunesse
42 Bus Station
43 Hôtel de Ville
44 Planet Hollywood; Zanzi Bar

45 24-hour Exchange
   Machine
46 CMC Ticket Office
   (Ferries to the Îles
   de Lérins)
48 Palais des Festivals
   et des Congrés
49 Tourist Office
50 Place Mérimée
51 Cannes English Bookshop
55 Main Post Office
56 American Express
57 Banque de France
60 Star Rent (Car Rental)
61 Alliance Location
   (Car & Motorcycle
   Rental)
62 Blue Bar
63 Pavillon Croisette
64 Plages de la Croisette
   (Private Beaches)
66 La Malmaison

d'Initiative'; exit the train station, turn left and walk up the flight of stairs.

The Cannes Info Jeunesse office (☎ 04 93 06 31 51, fax 04 93 06 31 39), 2 quai Saint Pierre, is open from 9 am to noon and 2 to 6 pm (closed on weekends). The Bureau de Jeunesse (☎ 04 94 19 47 38, fax 04 94 83 15 08), 25 place Gallieni, is open from 8 am to noon and 1.30 to 5 pm (Friday until 4.30 pm, closed on weekends).

Money The Banque de France, 8 blvd de la Croisette, is open from 8.30 am to noon and 1.30 to 3.30 pm (closed on weekends). There are banks on rue d'Antibes and rue Buttura.

American Express (☎ 04 93 38 15 87), 8 rue des Belges, is open from 9 am to noon and 2 to 6 pm (Saturday until noon; closed Sunday). Thomas Cook has a bureau at 8 rue d'Antibes. Office Provençal Change (☎ 04 93 39 34 37) is inside the Maison de la Chance, corner of rue Maréchal Foch and rue Jean Jaurès. There is a 24-hour bank-note exchange machine behind the port building on La Pantiero.

Post The main post office, 22 rue Bivouac Napoléon, is open from 8 am to 7 pm (Saturday until noon; closed Sunday). It offers foreign currency exchange.

Email & Internet Access Asher Cyber Espace (☎ 04 92 99 03 01, asher@riviera .net), 44 blvd Carnot, is open from 9 am to 7 pm (Friday and Sunday from 9 am to noon; closed Saturday).

Bookshops English-language novels are available at the Cannes English Bookshop (☎ 04 93 99 40 08), 11 rue Bivouac Napoléon, open from 9.30 am to 1 pm and 2 to 7 pm (closed Sunday).

Walking Tour

Since people-watching is the main reason to come to Cannes, and since people are best watched while strolling, and strolling is one of the few activities in Cannes that doesn't cost anything, taking a leisurely walk is

highly recommended. You can even stop and pay to get your shoes polished by hand afterwards.

The best spots to walk (and be seen) are not far from the water. The pine and palm-shaded walkway along **blvd de la Croisette**, known locally as La Croisette, is considered the classiest promenade on the Riviera. **La Malmaison** (1863) at No 47, tucked between the awesome Grand Hôtel and the flashy Noga Hilton hotel, hosts various art exhibitions. The 19th century seafront villa is open from 10.30 am to 12.30 pm and 4 to 8 pm. It is closed Tuesday (10FF).

Continuing east along the prom is **John Taylor & Son** (☎ 04 93 38 00 66), 55 blvd de la Croisette. The sparkling windows of this real estate agent – founded in 1864 and an agent for Christie's auction house – is ideal for window-shopping. The snaps of the absolutely fabulous properties displayed is the closest glimpse you'll get of where the rich and famous languish.

When it all gets too much, pop into the **Carlton**, 58 blvd de la Croisette, for tea on the terrace; this is what the stars (who want to be seen) do. The hotel's twin cupolas, erected in 1912, were modelled on the breasts of La Belle Otéro, infamous for the string of lovers – Spain's Alphonso XIII, Tsar Nicholas II and Leopold II of Belgium – she picked up at Monte Carlo's gambling tables.

The French writer, Prosper Mérimée (1803-70), who penned the 1845 novella *Carmen* which Bizet turned into an opera, died in a house on place Mérimée, the small square on the corner of blvd de la Croisette and rue du Mai Joffre, north side of the Vieux Port.

Just west of the Vieux Port, hilly **Le Suquet** affords spectacular views of Cannes. Lord Brougham, the first foreigner to live in Cannes, built himself the **Villa Eleanore** (1862) here. The locals thought the former Lord Chancellor of England completely nutty when he insisted on laying a large green lawn around his mansion. The hill is topped by a **12th century chateau** and adjoining **Chapelle de Sainte Anne**, in which is housed the **Musée de la Castre**

CANNES REGION

(☎ 04 93 38 55 26). A diverse collection of Mediterranean and Middle Eastern antiquities, as well as objects of ethnographic interest from all over the world, are displayed inside the museum. Its opening hours are 10 am to noon and 2 to 5 pm (closed Tuesday). From April to June afternoon hours are from 2 to 6 pm; from 3 to 7 pm in July and August (10FF, students and children free).

Beaches & Boat Excursions

Unlike Nice, Cannes is endowed with sandy beaches. Unfortunately most of **Plages de la Croisette** are sectioned off for guests of the fancy hotels lining blvd de la Croisette. Here, sunworshippers pay for a cushioned sunlounger and lap up the beachside equivalent of room service (65FF for a less-than-generous tomato salad delivered to your deck chair; strips of carpet leading to the water's edge etc). This arrangement leaves only a relatively small strip of sand near the Palais des Festivals for the bathing pleasure of the picnicking hoi polloi. However, free public beaches, **Plages du Midi** and **Plages de la Bocca**, stretch for several kilometres westward from the Vieux Port along blvd Jean Hibert and blvd du Midi.

Trans Côte d'Azur (see Îles de Lérins later in this chapter) runs day trips by boat from Cannes to Saint Tropez (120FF), Monaco (120FF), Île de Port-Cros (250FF), Île de Porquerolles (250FF) and San Remo (Italy, 220FF).

Places to Stay

Don't even consider staying in Cannes during the film festival in May unless you have booked months in advance (a year in advance at the budget places). Most upmarket places only accept 12-day bookings during this period.

Places to Stay – Budget

Camping *Parc Bellevue* (☎ 04 93 47 28 97, fax 04 93 48 66 25, 67 ave Maurice Chevalier), Cannes-La Bocca, about 5.5km west of the centre of town, is open from April to October. It charges 102FF for two

people with a tent and car. Bus No 9 from the bus station, place Bernard Cornut Gentille, stops 400m from the site.

Hostels Cannes' modern *Auberge de Jeunesse* (☎/fax 04 93 99 26 79, 35 ave de Vallauris) is about 400m north-east of the train station. A bed in a four or six-person dorm is 80FF, including one free breakfast. If you don't have an HI card (available for 70/100FF for those under/over 26) you can buy a 10FF one-night stamp. Each floor has a kitchen and there's a laundry room. Reception is open from 8 am to 12.30 pm and 2.30 to 10.30 pm (3 to 10 pm on weekends). Curfew is at midnight (1 am on weekends).

The very pleasant private hostel, *Le Chalit* (☎ 04 93 99 22 11, fax 04 93 39 00 28, 27 ave du Maréchal Galliéni), is some 300m north-west of the station. It charges 80FF for a bed in rooms for four to eight people. Sheets are extra. There are two kitchens. Le Chalit is open year round and there is no curfew, but you must leave a deposit to get a key.

Hotels Cannes has a handful of handy hotels for budget travellers which won't break the bank. Directly opposite the train station is the uninspiring but cheap *Hôtel du Nord* (☎ 04 93 38 48 79, fax 04 92 99 28 20, 6 rue Jean Jaurès). Basic one-star singles/doubles with washbasin are 140/180FF. On the same street at No 10, there are 110FF rooms in the small makeshift hotel above the *Mon Village* bar (☎ 04 93 38 57 70).

Close by, *Hôtel Cybelle Bec Fin* (☎ 04 93 38 31 33, fax 04 93 38 43 47, 14 rue du 24 Août) has single/double rooms with washbasin for 120/150FF, doubles with shower for 170FF, and doubles with shower and toilet from 200FF.

Heading towards the Auberge de Jeunesse, you pass the excellent value but little known *Hôtel Florella* (☎ 04 93 38 48 11, 55 blvd République). Rooms like home for one/two people with washbasin cost 140/170FF; doubles with shower and TV are 190FF.

Starring at Cannes

The Festival International du Film is a closed shop. Unless you're John Travolta, Brigitte Bardot or rich, beautiful and worth a tabloid splash, you have absolutely no chance of scoring a ticket to the legendary Cannes film festival.

The 10 day festival revolves around the 60,000 sq metre Palais des Festivals, likened to an Egyptian tomb by Liza Minnelli and called 'the bunker' by the local population. Either way, it's ugly. Its stark concrete base is adorned with hand prints and autographs of celebrities: Timothy Dalton (007), Brooke Shields, BB, David Lynch, Johnny Hallyday and the like. The largest of the Film Palace's 12 theatres seats an audience of 2300. A 170 million FF project, which kicked off in August 1998, will see the bunker capable of bundling in a further 5000 people. Project completion is already a race against time, given the place is booked out until 2003.

At the centre of the competition is the prestigious Palme d'Or, awarded by the jury and its president to the winning film – generally not a box office hit. Notable exceptions include Coppola's *Apocalypse Now* (1979), *Sex, Lies & Video Tapes* (1989), David Lynch's *Wild at Heart* (1990), and Tarentino's *Pulp Fiction* (1994).

An equally integral part of the annual festival is the Marché du Film (Film Market) where an estimated US$200 million worth of business takes place.

Around 7000 'names', trailed by 3000 journalists, attend the star-studded spectacle. Most stay at the Carlton, Majestic or Noga Hilton hotels. They eat at Eden Roc on the Cap, Alain Ducasse's Le Louis XV in Monaco or Roger Vergé's Moulin de Mougins, 8km north of Cannes. The festival's annual US$2000 a head Cinema Against AIDS dinner is often held at the latter. In 1997 Hollywood star Sharon Stone auctioned off her belly-button ring over dinner.

Starlets have always stripped off at Cannes. In the early days dropping your top shocked. The 1954 festival, for example, saw the unknown Simone Sylva drop her top in front of actor Robert Mitchum who, being a gentleman and all that, had his hands covering her boobs within seconds to hide them from the public eye. The cameras clicked, it hit the headlines, Mitchum's wife was mortified – and Simone Sylva committed suicide six months later. The line of glamour girls who pose topless on the beach today (snapped mainly by tourists) is passé.

The Festival International du Film was created in 1939 to counter Mussolini's fascist propaganda film festival in Venice. It was not until after WWII however that the first festival starred at Cannes. Tickets to be pitched for no later than March) are issued by the Bureau du Festival International du Film (☎ 01 45 61 66 00, fax 01 45 61 97 60, festival@cannes.bull.net, www.festival-cannes.fr), 99 blvd Malesherbes, 75008 Paris.

The friendly 17-room *Hôtel Chanteclair* (☎/fax 04 93 39 68 88, 12 rue Forville) has simple singles/doubles for 130/150FF (mid-October to mid-April) and 160/190FF (peak periods).

The *Hôtel National* (☎ 04 93 39 91 92, fax 04 92 98 44 06, 8 rue Maréchal Joffre) has singles/doubles from 150/220FF. Doubles/triples with shower and toilet are 250/350FF.

The large *Hôtel Atlantis* (☎ 04 93 39 18 72, fax 04 93 68 37 65, 4 rue du 24 Août) may have a two-star rating, but its cheapest singles/doubles with TV cost only 145/180FF during the low season. The price jumps to 340/395FF during festival periods and in July and August.

The *Hôtel de Bourgogne* (☎ 04 93 38 36 73, fax 04 92 99 28 41, 13 rue du 24 Août) has singles/doubles with washbasin for

150/180FF and doubles with shower/shower and toilet for 220/250FF.

The *Pension Les Glycines* (☎ 04 93 38 41 28, 32 blvd d'Alsace), in an old villa east of the train station, has basic singles/doubles from 130/150FF (150/200FF in summer). A huge room for three or four people costs 190/200FF in winter/summer. Close by, the *Hôtel Amirauté* (☎ 04 93 39 10 53, fax 04 93 38 98 54, 15 rue Maréchal Foch) has singles with washbasin and bidet for 154FF and doubles with shower for 190FF. Book well ahead in summer.

Places to Stay – Mid-Range

Opposite the main post office, the rule-happy *Hôtel de la Poste* (☎ 04 93 39 22 58, fax 04 93 39 52 58, 31 rue Bivouac Napoléon) has singles/doubles with shower for 220/240FF (280/340FF in summer). Next door at No 29, the *Hôtel Alizé* (☎ 04 93 39 62 17, fax 04 93 39 64 32) has singles/doubles with all mod-cons for 300/350FF.

Opposite the train station, *Robert's Hôtel* (☎ 04 93 38 06 07, 16 rue Jean Jaurès) has singles/doubles with shower and toilet from 240/300FF.

Places to Stay – Top End

During the film festival, Cannes' horribly expensive hotels buzz with the frantic comings and goings of journalists, paparazzi and stars. Fortunately for their fans – who can only dream of ever staying in such a place during Cannes' most precious days of May – all of the top end hotels are along blvd de la Croisette. The best known ones include the *Carlton Inter-Continental* (☎ 04 93 06 40 06, fax 04 93 06 40 25, cannes@interconti.com) at No 58; the Art Deco *Hôtel Martinez* (☎ 04 92 98 73 00, fax 04 93 39 67 82, martinez@concorde-hotels.com) at No 73; the *Grand Hôtel* (☎ 04 93 38 15 45, fax 04 93 68 97 45) at No 45; and the *Noga Hilton* (☎ 04 92 99 70 00, fax 04 92 99 70 11) at No 50. Guests pay at least 2000FF a night for a double.

Places to Eat

Restaurants There are a few inexpensive restaurants around rue du Marché Forville and lots of little, though not necessarily cheap, restaurants along rue Saint Antoine and rue du Suquet. Up in Le Suquet itself, try the beautifully furnished, African-inspired *Out of Africa* (☎ 04 93 68 98 06, 6-8 rue Saint Dizier); or the less tame *Barbarella* (☎ 04 92 99 17 33, 12-14 rue Saint Dizier).

Near the train station, *La Table d'Oscar* (☎ 04 93 38 42 46, 26 rue Jean Jaurès) has daily specialities – *aïoli garni* (poached fish with garlic mayonnaise), rabbit, *farcis* (stuffed vegetables) for 50-75FF and a 98FF *menu* in summer. It is closed on Sunday night and Monday. Nearby, *Au Bec Fin* (☎ 04 93 38 35 86, 12 rue du 24 Août) is often filled with regulars. You can choose from two excellent *plats du jour* for 45-60FF or a 79, 85 or 99FF *menu*. Try the *daube de bœuf* (beef stew) à la Provençale. This place is closed Saturday evening and Sunday.

Close by is the atmospheric *La Villa Piano Bar* (☎ 04 93 38 79 73, 7 rue Marceau), housed in a fine 19th century villa. Main dishes start at around 100FF and it has live music most evenings. The terrace, tucked beneath rambling plants in the shade of deep ochre walls, is particularly enchanting. La Villa is open from 8 pm to 2.30 am.

For something fishy, dine at *Astoux & Brun* (☎ 04 93 39 21 87, 21 rue Félix Faure). Every type and size of oyster is available by the dozen here as well as elaborate fish platters, mussels stuffed with garlic and parsley, scallops etc. In summer, chefs draw a crowd by preparing their shellfish on the pavement outside. It's open from 10 am to 1 am. For dinner afloat, try the *Bateau Restaurant* (☎ 04 93 68 98 88) moored on the jetée Albert Édouard.

In the centre of town, *Le Pacific* (☎ 04 93 39 46 71, 14 rue Vénizélos) is a favourite with local Cannois – its generous three-course 60FF *menu* being the major draw card. It is closed Friday evening and all day Saturday.

Another good choice is the popular *Aux Bons Enfants (80 rue Meynadier)*. It offers regional dishes like aïoli garni and *mesclun* (a rather bitter salad of dandelion greens and other roughage) in a convivial atmosphere. It has a 94FF *menu* and is open for lunch and dinner weekdays and for lunch on Saturday (open Saturday evenings in June and July). There are several other small restaurants at this end of rue Meynadier.

One of the cheapest restaurants in Cannes is *Restaurant Le Croco* (☎ 04 93 68 60 55, 11 rue Louis Blanc), just south of blvd Victor Tuby. Pizzas, grilled meat and fish and shish kebabs are the main items on the menu. The plat du jour is 49FF and lunch/evening *menus* are 59/89FF.

The Sicilian restaurant *Da Papa Nino* (☎ 04 93 38 48 08, 16 blvd de la République), south-east of the station, has many varieties of pizza (from 40FF), pasta (from 46FF) and a good value three-course *menu* for 67FF (closed Wednesday). North of the train tracks, *Bistrot des Artisans* (☎ 04 93 68 33 88, 67 blvd de la République) is an unpretentious restaurant serving starters (around 40FF), hearty main dishes (60-100FF) and a variety of salads from 45FF (closed Sunday).

Tovel Kosher (☎ 04 93 39 24 53, 3 rue du Docteur Gérard Monod) is a kosher spot.

Cafés Cafés and *salons de thé* (tea rooms) abound in upmarket Cannes. One very down-to-earth place worth a bite (or at least a pastis before dining) is the small and cosy *Bar La Renaissance*, overlooking the bustling place Gambetta market from the corner of rue Teisseire and rue Marceau. Black and white photos of yesterday's stars and glamour queens line the walls – a pleasant contrast to the simple wooden tables and chairs.

La Tarterie (☎ 04 93 39 67 43, 33 rue Bivouac Napoléon) has a range of salads from 30FF, but it's the house specialities – sweet/savoury tarts costing no more than 15/35FF a slice – that are the most tasty.

Self-Catering A *food market* is held on place Gambetta every morning (except Monday in winter). The *Marché Forville*, a fruit and vegetable market on rue du Marché Forville, two blocks north of place Bernard Cornut Gentille, is open every morning except Monday (when a flea market takes pride of place).

Entertainment

Ask the tourist office for a copy of the monthly *Le Mois à Cannes* which lists what's on where. Non-dubbed films are occasionally screened at the cinemas on rue Félix Faure and rue d'Antibes.

Hot spots guaranteed to draw a crowd (and various stars when they roll into town) include the *Blue Bar* opposite Christian Dior on the corner of blvd de la Croisette and rue Commandant André; the *Pavillon Croisette, (42 blvd de la Croisette)*, which has oyster platters for 135FF; *Planet Hollywood* (☎ 04 93 06 78 27, 1 allée de la Liberté) where super-waif Kate Moss and actor Johnny Depp were caught stuffing burgers after doing a runner from some official function during the 1998 film festival; and *Le Bar des Célébrités*, Carlton Hotel, named after the people sufficiently rich to afford its 2000FF bottles of champagne. Drag queens hang out in and around the gay *Zanzi Bar* (☎ 04 93 39 30 75, 85 rue Félix Faure).

Getting There & Away

Bus Buses leave from place Bernard Cornut Gentille, next to the Hôtel de Ville in Cannes centre to these and other destinations: Nice (32FF; 1½ hours; every 20 minutes from 6 am to 7.40 pm) and Nice airport (70FF for the 40 minute trip via the autoroute and 47FF for the 1-1½ hour trip via the regular road; hourly from 8 am to 7 pm).

Most are operated by Rapides Côte d'Azur. The information office (☎ 04 93 39 11 39) at the bus station is open from 7 am to 7 pm (closed Sunday).

Buses to Grasse (line No 600 or No 605; 19.50FF; 45 minutes) via Mougins and Mouans-Sartoux, Vallauris (line No 640), and Valbonne (line No 630) depart from the bus station to the left as you exit the train station.

CANNES REGION

Train The information desk at the train station (☎ 04 93 99 50 50 or 08 36 35 35 35), rue Jean Jaurès, is open from 8.30 am to 6 pm (8.30 am to 7 pm from mid-July to mid-September).

Destinations within easy reach include: Saint Raphaël (31FF; 25 minutes; two an hour) from where you can get buses to Saint Tropez and Toulon; Nice (32FF; 40 minutes) and Marseille (150FF; two hours).

Getting Around
Bus Bus Azur serves Cannes and destinations up to 7km from town. Its office (☎ 04 93 39 18 71), place Bernard Cornut Gentille (same building as Rapides Côte d'Azur), at the bus station, is open from 7 am to 7 pm.

A single/10-tickets cost 7.50/49FF. A weekly Carte Palm'Hebdo/monthly Carte Croisette is 54/190FF. Bus No 8 runs along the coast from place Bernard Cornut Gentille (Hôtel de Ville) to the port and Palm Beach Casino on La Pointe de la Croisette. All bus routes are listed on the *Plan du Réseau* distributed free at the ticket office.

Car & Motorcycle Star Rent (☎ 04 93 38 13 48), 92 rue d'Antibes, and Excellence (☎ 04 93 94 67 67, sales@excellence.fr), 66 blvd de la Croisette, rent cars fit for a star (Ferraris from 13,900FF a day, Bentleys for 20,900FF a day etc). The thriftier should try Thrifty (☎ 04 93 94 61 00), 16 rue du 14 Juillet, which has simple Fiat Cinquecentos from 250FF a day. Access Rent A Car (☎ 04 93 94 06 05), 5 rue Latour Maubourg, is another cheapie.

Alliance Location (☎ 04 93 38 62 62, all iance.location@wanadoo.fr), 19 rue des Frères, rents motorcycles (from 260FF a day) and scooters (160/200FF for one/two people) as well as mobile phones (70FF plus calls). The shop is open from 9 am to 7 pm. Aventure Scooter (☎ 06 60 06 16 16), 12 blvd Carnot, is another outlet to try.

Parking can be a nightmare in Cannes; city car parks charge at least 10FF an hour. Tell your chauffeur there's usually free spaces north of the old city across ave des Anciens Combattants d'Afrique du Nord!

Bicycle Alliance Location (see Car & Motorcycle) rents mountain bikes for 80FF a day. Thrifty (☎ 04 93 94 61 00), 16 rue du 14 Juillet, rents bicycles too.

Îles de Lérins

The two islands of Lérins – Île Sainte Marguerite and Île Saint Honorat – lie within a 20 minute boat ride of Cannes. Known as Lero and Lerina in ancient times, these tiny, traffic free oases of peace and tranquillity remain a world away from the glitz, glamour and hanky-panky of cocky Cannes.

Wild camping, bicycling and smoking (theoretically at least; visitors still light up) are forbidden on both islands. There are no hotels, *gîtes* or camp sites on either island and Saint Honorat, the smaller of the two, sports no restaurants or cafés either; take a picnic and good supply of drinking water with you.

Neither island has fantastic beaches. There are some pretty coves on the south side of Sainte Marguerite (a 45 minute walk from the harbour), but on the north side bathers lie on rocks and mounds of dried seaweed.

ÎLE SAINTE MARGUERITE
The eucalyptus and pine-covered Île Sainte Marguerite lies 1km from the mainland. The island is famed as the place where the enigmatic Man in the Iron Mask – immortalised by Alexandre Dumas (1802-70) in his novel *Le Viscomte de Bragelonne* (1847) and in the 1998 Hollywood release starring Leonardo DiCaprio – was held in the late 17th century (see the boxed text The Man in the Iron Mask).

The island, today home to 20 families and measuring just 3.25km by 1km, is encircled and criss-crossed by walking trails and paths. Its centrepiece is the 17th century **Fort Royal**, constructed by Richelieu to defend the islands from the Spanish (who still succeeded in occupying the fort in 1635-37), with later additions by Vauban.

The oldest part of the fort houses the **Musée de la Mer** (☎ 04 93 43 18 17), a well put together museum with interesting

The Man in the Iron Mask

"More than 68 names have been suggested for this prisoner whose name no one knows, whose face no one has seen: a living mystery, shadow, enigma, problem."

Victor Hugo.

The man in the iron mask was imprisoned by Louis XIV (1661-1715) in the fortress on Île Sainte Marguerite from around 1660 until 1690 when he was transferred to the Bastille in Paris. Only the king knew the identity of the man behind the mask, prompting a rich pageant of myth and legend to be woven around the mysterious, ill-fated inmate.

Political and social satirist Voltaire (1694-1778) claimed the prisoner was the king's brother – a twin or an illegitimate older brother. In 1751 he published *Le Siècle de Louis XIV* which attested that Louis XIV's usurped brother, face shrouded in iron, arrived on the island in 1661, was personally escorted to the Bastille by its new governor in 1690, and died in 1703 aged around 60. His featureless mask was lined with silk and fitted with a spring mechanism at the chin to allow him to eat. Prison guards had orders to kill if the man with no name dared remove his iron face.

Voltaire's masked prince theory was sparked off by two factors. The face was one that Louis XIV feared was easily recognisable by the masses, hence the need to shield it in iron. This, coupled with the fact that no leading public figure disappeared at this time, convinced Voltaire that the man in the iron mask was a potentially important national figure, the existence of whom had never been made public.

Countless other identities were showered on the masked prisoner, among them the Duke of Monmouth (actually beheaded under James II), the Comte de Vermandois (son of Louis XIV said to have died from smallpox in 1683), the Duc de Beaufort (killed by the Turks in 1669) and Moliére (put forward as an iron mask candidate in 1883). Some theorists claimed the man in the iron mask was actually a woman.

The storming of the Bastille in 1789 fuelled yet more stories. Revolutionaries claimed to have discovered a skeleton, the skull of which was locked in an iron mask, when plundering the prison; while others focused on a supposed entry found in the prison register which read *détenu 64389000: l'homme au masque de fer* (prisoner 64389000: the man in the iron mask). To the contrary, others provoked a storm with their allegations that there was *no* iron mask entry in the prison register – just a missing page. In 1855, an iron mask was found in a scrap heap in Langres, north of Dijon, consequently displayed in the town museum as the feted mask.

Voltaire's tragic tale of a usurped heir sentenced to a life behind iron fired the imagination of playwrights and a flurry of theatrical tragedies followed. With the 1850 publication of Alexandre Dumas' novel *Le Vicomte de Bragelonne*, the last of his musketeers trilogy, the royal crime became written in stone: in 1638 Anne of Austria, wife of Louis XIII (1617-43) and mother of Louis XIV, gives birth to twins, one is taken away from her, leaving her to bear the secret alone until an old friend uncovers the terrible truth. The rest is history.

Dozens of iron mask films have been made this century. Richard Chamberlain starred as the masked prince/evil king in 1976 and in 1998, Leonardo DiCaprio took on board the dual role of Louis and brother Philippe in the box office hit *The Man in the Iron Mask*. The Hollywood film adapted to screen by Randall Wallace saw Dumas' three musketeers – John Malkovich, Gérard Depardieu and Jeremy Irons – embark on the perilous mission of solving the riddle of the man in the iron mask. Unmasked or not, his identity remains a mystery.

exhibits on the fort's history and ship-wrecks. A door to the left in the reception hall of the museum leads to the **old state prisons**, built under Louis XIV. In 1685 six Huguenot pastors who refused to renounce their Protestant faith following the revoca-tion of the Edit of Nantes were kept here. The steam boat inventor, Claude François Dorothée, allegedly came up with his idea while watching slaves row to the island during his imprisonment here in 1773-74.

The prison's most famous inmate, the Man in the Iron Mask, has his story unfold in the *cellule du masque de fer* (Man in the Iron Mask's cell), open from 10.30 am to 12.15 pm and 2 to 5.40 pm (6.30 pm from July to September). It's closed Tuesday. Entry to the Musée de la Mer is 10FF.

ÎLE SAINT HONORAT

The forested island of Saint Honorat, 1.5km by 400m, is the smallest and most southern of the Îles de Lérins. It was the site of a powerful monastery in the 5th century. Today, it is home to Cistercian monks who own the island but welcome people to visit their monastery and the seven small chapels dotted around the island which have at-tracted pilgrims since the Middle Ages.

The small **monastère fortifié** (fortified monastery) which stands guard on the island's southern shores is all that remains of the original monastery. The donjon was built in 1073 to protect the monks from pirate attacks; the entrance stood 4m above ground level and was accessible only by ladder (later replaced by the stone staircase evident today). The elegant arches of the vaulted **cloître de la prière** (cloister of prayer) on the 1st floor date from the 15th century. A magnificent panorama of the Côte d'Azur from the Estérel to Cap d'An-tibes can be enjoyed from the terrace.

In front of the donjon is the walled, 19th century **Abbaye de Lérins** (☎ 04 93 48 68 68), inhabited by 31 monks today. A collection of Roman archaeological finds are displayed in the small museum, to the left of the main cloister. It is also possible to visit the adjoin-ing 19th century church and souvenir shop where the 50% alcohol *Lérina* liqueur manu-factured by the monks in their spare time is sold. The pea-green liqueur, concocted from 44 different herbs, is the local version of the Chartreuse made by Carthusian monks in the Alps. The shop is open from 11.30 am to 12.15 pm and 2 to 4.30 pm. Hours at the donjon are 9 am to 4.30 pm. The abbey door is closed from 1.30 to 2 pm.

Getting There & Away

From Cannes, the Compagnie Maritime Can-noise (CMC; ☎ 04 93 38 66 33, fax 04 93 38 66 44) runs ferries to Île Saint Honorat (45FF return; 20 minutes) and Île Sainte Marguerite (40FF return; 15 minutes); both islands can be visited for 60FF. The ticket office (☎ 04 92 98 71 36) at the Vieux Port, across jetée Albert Édouard from the Palais des Festivals, is open from 8.30 am to 12.30 pm and 1.30 to 6.30 pm (later in July and August).

Trans Côte d'Azur (☎ 04 92 98 71 30, fax 04 93 38 69 02) charges the same price for trips to/from both islands. Its office is op-posite the Hôtel Sofitel on quai Luberf.

Both companies run boats year round. There are also seasonal boats from Juan-les-Pins and Golfe Juan – see those sections for details.

North of Cannes

ANTIBES
• **pop 71,000**

Antibes, the next coastal hot spot north-east of Cannes and directly across the Baie des Anges from Nice, has as many attractions as its larger neighbours but is not as crowded. It has beautiful sandy beaches, 16th century ramparts that run right along the shore, an attractive pleasure-boat harbour (Port Vauban) and an old city with narrow, winding streets and flower-bedecked houses. Picasso, Max Ernst and Nicolas de Staël all found an appealing charm in Antibes. Between 1966 and 1990, acclaimed globetrotter and writer Grahame Green chose Antibes as his base.

Greater Antibes (postcode 06600) em-braces the modern beach resort of

Rocks of ochre near Roussillon

Bories, archaic shepherds' huts, near Apt

Château des Baux, the Grimaldi's feudal castle

How much is that doggy in the window? Arrière-Pays Niçois

Juan-les-Pins and Cap d'Antibes (postcode 06160), the exclusive green cape on which Antibes and Juan-les-Pins sit.

Juan-les-Pins sprung up west of Antibes in the 1880s. It is known for its beautiful 2km sandy beach backed by pine trees, and outrageous nightlife – a legacy of the 1920s when Americans swung into town with their jazz music and oh-so-brief swimsuits. Party madness peaks in late July when the resort hosts Jazz à Juan, a week-long jazz festival attracting musicians and music lovers from around the world.

Cheap accommodation here is particularly scarce; try the hardly-a-hardship hostel on Cap d'Antibes or hike to one of many camping grounds in Biot (see that section).

Orientation

Antibes is made up of three parts: the commercial centre around place du Général de Gaulle; Vieil Antibes (Old Antibes) south of Port Vauban and the Vieux Port; and, to the south-west, Cap d'Antibes and the contiguous community of Juan-les-Pins.

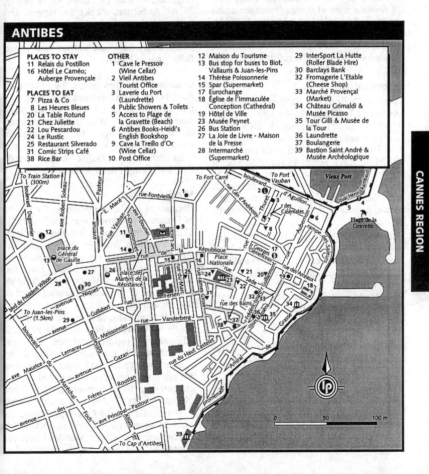

ANTIBES

PLACES TO STAY
11 Relais du Postillon
16 Hôtel Le Caméo;
   Auberge Provençale

PLACES TO EAT
7 Pizza & Co
8 Les Heures Bleues
20 La Table Rotund
21 Chez Juliette
22 Lou Pescardou
24 Le Rustic
25 Restaurant Silverado
31 Comic Strips Café
38 Rice Bar

OTHER
1 Cave le Pressoir
   (Wine Cellar)
2 Vieil Antibes
   Tourist Office
3 Laverie du Port
   (Laundrette)
4 Public Showers & Toilets
5 Access to Plage de
   la Gravette (Beach)
6 Antibes Books-Heidi's
   English Bookshop
9 Cave la Treillo d'Or
   (Wine Cellar)
10 Post Office

12 Maison du Tourisme
13 Bus stop for buses to Biot,
   Vallauris & Juan-les-Pins
14 Thérèse Poissonnerie
15 Spar (Supermarket)
17 Eurochange
18 Église de l'Immaculée
   Conception (Cathedral)
19 Hôtel de Ville
23 Musée Peynet
26 Bus Station
27 La Joie de Livre - Maison
   de la Presse
28 Intermarché
   (Supermarket)

29 InterSport La Hutte
   (Roller Blade Hire)
30 Barclays Bank
32 Fromagerie L'Etable
   (Cheese Shop)
33 Marché Provençal
   (Market)
34 Château Grimaldi &
   Musée Picasso
35 Tour Gilli & Musée de
   la Tour
36 Laundrette
37 Boulangerie
39 Bastion Saint André &
   Musée Archéologique

CANNES REGION

The principal streets in Antibes centre are blvd Albert 1er and rue de la République, which leads eastward from place du Général de Gaulle to place des Martyrs de la Résistance (touting a kiddies' playground) and the tree-lined place Nationale. Ave Robert Soleau links Antibes train station with place du Général de Gaulle. The narrow promenade Amiral de Grasse hugs the waterfront east of the old city.

From place du Général de Gaulle, Juan-les-Pins is a straight 1.5km walk along blvd du Président Wilson which runs south-west off Antibes' central square. From the south end of blvd du Président Wilson in Juan-les-Pins, ave Guy de Maupassant and its continuation, blvd Charles Guillaumont, runs westward along the resort's seafront.

Information

Tourist Offices In Antibes centre, the Maison du Tourisme (☎ 04 92 90 53 00, fax 04 92 90 53 01), 11 place du Général de Gaulle, is open from 9 am to 12.30 pm and 2 to 7 pm (Saturday until noon and 6 pm; closed Sunday). Hours in July and August are 8.45 am to 7.30 pm (Sunday from 9.30 am to 12.30 pm). Tickets for cultural events are sold at La Billetterie inside the tourist office; it shuts 30 minutes before the tourist office.

In Vieil Antibes, there is a small tourist office (☎ 04 93 34 65 65) inside the Porte Marine on the corner of rue Thuret and blvd d'Aguillon. It arranges two-hour guided tours (30FF) of Vieil Antibes in English from Monday to Thursday at 5 pm; advance reservations are obligatory.

The tourist office in Juan-les-Pins (☎ 04 92 90 53 05), 51 blvd Charles Guillaumont, overlooking the seafront, keeps the same hours as its big sister in Antibes centre.

Money In Antibes centre, Eurochange (☎ 04 93 34 48 30), 4 rue Georges Clémenceau, changes money and cashes travellers cheques. It is open from 9 am to 7 pm (10 am to 12.30 pm on Sunday). Barclays Bank is at 11 blvd Albert 1er;

branches of all French commercial banks are spread the length of ave Robert Soleau.

Post The main post office in Antibes centre, east of the tourist office on place des Martyrs de la Résistance (entrance on ave P Doumer), is open from 8 am to 7 pm (Saturday until noon; closed Sunday). In Juan-les-Pins the post office is opposite the train station on square Pablo Picasso.

Bookshops Antibes Books-Heidi's English Bookshop (☎/fax 04 93 34 74 11), 24 rue Aubernon, stocks the biggest and best selection of new and second-hand English-language books on the Riviera. Heidi works hard; she's open year round from 7 am to 10 pm.

Laundry In Antibes centre, the Laverie du Port, 14 rue Thuret, is open from 7 am to 9 pm. There is another laundrette, less busy, near the Musée de la Tour at the west end of rue des Bains; open from 9 am to noon and 2.30 to 7 pm (closed Sunday).

In Juan-les-Pins, Quick Wash, 4 ave de l'Estérel, is open from 7 am to 9 pm.

Vieil Antibes

Because of Antibes' position on the border of France and Savoy, it was fortified in the 17th and 18th centuries, but these fortifications were torn down in 1896 to give the city room to expand. From the tourist office on place du Général de Gaulle, bear east along rue de la République to the **Porte de France**, one of the few remaining parts of the original city walls.

On the south side of café-filled place Nationale is the **Musée Peynet** (☎ 04 92 90 54 32). Over 300 pictures, cartoons, sculptures and theatrical costumes designed by Antibes-born cartoonist Peynet, best known for his *Lovers* series, are displayed here. It is open from 10 am to noon and 2 to 6 pm; closed Monday (20/10FF for adult/student).

A splendid **Marché Provençal** (Provençal market) sprawls the length of cours Masséna every morning (except Monday) between September and May. At the south end of cours Masséna, the 19th century **Tour Gilli**, 2 rue de l'Orme, is home to the **Musée de la Tour** (☎ 04 93 34 50 91), a small popular arts and traditions museum. It is open on Wednesday, Thursday and Saturday from 4 to 7 pm; 3 to 5 pm in winter (10/5FF).

East of cours Masséna on rue Saint Esprit (entrance on montée de la Souchère), is Antibes' **cathedral**, known as the **Église de L'Immaculée Conception**. It was built on the site of an ancient Greek temple and has an ochre neoclassical façade. The tall, square Romanesque bell tower dates from the 12th century.

South-west of the cathedral on promenade Amiral de Grasse is the **Musée Archéologique** (☎ 04 92 90 54 35), inside the Vauban-built **Bastion Saint André**. Its displays are devoted to Antibes' Greek history. Its opening hours are 10 am to noon and 2 to 6 pm; closed Monday (10/5FF for adult/child).

Musée Picasso

From the cathedral, steps lead up to the **Château Grimaldi**, set on a spectacular site overlooking the sea. This 12th century castle served as Picasso's studio between July and December 1946. Today it houses the Picasso Museum (☎ 04 92 90 54 20) which boasts an excellent collection of Picasso's paintings, lithographs, drawings and ceramics as well as interesting displays about his life. A collection of contemporary art by other artists graces the sculpture-lined terrace facing the Mediterranean.

Particularly poignant is Picasso's *La Joie de Vivre (The Joy of Life)*, one in a series of 25 paintings which form *The Antipolis Suite*. The young flower girl, happily surrounded by mountain goats and flute playing fauns, symbolises Françoise Gilot, the 23-year-old love of Picasso (1881-1973) who he lived with at the time in neighbouring Golfe-Juan. The entire series, along with its preparatory drawings and sketches, are displayed in the museum. Some of the ceramic pieces he created in Vallauris (see that section) in 1947-49 can be seen on the 1st and 2nd floors.

Pablo Picasso worked in Antibes while living in Golfe-Juan with his muse, Françoise Gilot.

The Musée Picasso is open from 10 am to noon and 2 to 6 pm (no midday break from June to September). It is closed Monday year round (30/18FF for adult/child under 7). Guided tours are available on Sunday (at 2.45 pm) and Tuesday (at 2.30 pm) in July and August.

Fort Carré & Port Vauban

The impregnable 16th century Fort Carré, enlarged by Vauban in the 17th century, dominates the approach to Antibes from Nice. Port Vauban, one of the first pleasure ports to be established on the Mediterranean, languishes between the fort and Antibes old town.

Since 1998 the fortress has been open to visitors (by guided tour only). A pedestrian walkway twists its way around the stadium inside the star-shaped walls. The fort is open from 10 am to noon and 1.30 to 7 pm (closed Monday) except between mid-September and the end of October when its hours are 10 am to 12.30 pm and 1.30 to 4.30 pm and from November to May, when it is open on Wednesday, Saturday and Sunday from 10 am to 12.30 pm and 1.30 to 4 pm. Guided tours depart every 15 minutes.

CANNES REGION

Cap d'Antibes

Nowhere do you feel more like a very shrunken Alice in Wonderland than on this select peninsula where larger-than-life villas, security fences and pine trees loom above you at every turn. The sense of wonder at the sheer luxury is further exacerbated by the constant buzz of *cigales* (cicadas) whose frenzied chants reach a shrilling crescendo in the midday sun.

The south-western tip of the cape is crowned by the legendary **Hôtel du Cap Eden Roc**, Côte d'Azur's most exclusive hotel dating from 1870. It made a name for itself in 1923 when its Italian owner, Antoine Sella, kept his doors open in July and August, heralding the start of a summer season on the coast. The Hôtel du Cap Eden Roc was consequently immortalised in F Scott Fitzgerald's novel *Tender is the Night* (1934) under the guise of the fictional Hôtel des Étrangers. By 1925 the luxury complex, which sported the first open-air swimming pool on the Riviera (actually built in 1914 for WWI servicemen), was known as Eden Roc.

Other notable names on Cap d'Antibes' guestbook include Cole Porter who rented the **Château de la Garoupe** in 1922; novelist Jules Verne (1828-1905) who lived at Les Chênes Verts, 152 blvd John F Kennedy; and more recently, supermodel Kate Moss who succeeded in getting herself barred from the Hôtel du Cap for her wild partying during the 1998 Cannes film festival.

Immediately north-west of the hotel is the **Musée Naval et Napoléonien** (☎ 04 93 61 45 32), housed in the Tour Sella off blvd John F Kennedy. The museum, which documents Napoléon's return from exile in 1815 particularly well, is open from 9.30 am to noon and 2.15 to 6 pm. It is closed Saturday afternoon, Sunday, and October (20/10FF for adult/student).

The centre of the cape is dominated by the beautiful **Jardin Botanique de la Villa Thuret** (☎ 04 93 67 88 00), 41 blvd du Cap. The botanical gardens dating from 1857 are open from 8 am to 6 pm; 5.30 pm in winter; closed on weekends year round (free). The lovely gardens surrounding the

Villa Eilenroc (☎ 04 93 67 74 33), right on the tip of Cap d'Antibes, can also be visited on Wednesday from 1.30 to 5 pm (9 am to 5 pm in summer). Eilenroc was designed by Garnier for a Dutchman who scrambled the name of his wife Cornélie to come up with the villa's name.

Sweeping views of the coastline stretching from Saint Tropez to the Italian border can be enjoyed from the **Chapelle de la Garoupe**, atop a hillock off route du Phare. The neighbouring **phare** (lighthouse) cannot be visited. The chapel is open from 9.30 or 10 am to noon and 2.30 to 7 pm (5 pm in winter). Sunday Mass is celebrated at 11 am, with an additional service at 9 am in July and August. Steps lead from the side of the chapel down the hill to ave Aimé Bourreau; bear right then turn left along ave Guide to get to the sandy **Plage de la Garoupe**. A coastal path leads from here to **Cap Gros**, the most south-eastern tip of the cape.

Beach Activities

Antibes has a small beach, the sandy **Plage de la Gravette**, accessible from quai Henri

---

Love Song

The frenzied buzz that serenades sunny days in Provence's hot south is, in fact, *cigales* (cicadas) on the pull.

The cicada (cicadidae) is a transparent-winged insect, most common in tropical or temperate climes. The male cicada courts when the temperatures is above 25°C in the shade. Its shrill love song is produced with tymbals, vibrating music-making plates attached to the abdomen. Female cicadas do not sing.

The life span of a cicada is three to 17 years, all but four to six weeks of which is spent underground. Upon emerging from the soil to embark on its adult life, the cicada attaches itself to a tree where it immediately begins its mating rituals. It dies just weeks later.

Rambaud at the Vieux Port. Public showers, open from 8 am to 8 pm, are tucked in the arches of Vauban's 17th century ramparts which run the length of quai Henri Rambaud (17/13FF for a five minute rinse with/without soap and towel).

The long, golden-sand beaches fronting Juan-les-Pins buzz with business from sunrise to sunset. You can water ski (140FF for 15 minutes), sail (350FF for 30 minutes), parasail (250/400/550FF for one/two/three jumps), ride rubber rings from the back of a motorboat (100FF for 15 minutes) and partake in a host of other, expensive cheapthrill **water sports** at Activities Nautique (☎ 04 93 67 05 11 or 06 11 12 68 48), at the end of the wooden jetty off Plage du Columbier. Dry off afterwards with a snappy game of **table tennis** at Ping Pong (30/50FF for half/one hour) or a quick race around the **karting** circuit (40/100FF for one/three sessions), next to each other on blvd Charles Guillaumont. Both are open from 2 pm until sunset.

Rollerblading fans can hire a set of blades for 25/40/80FF an hour/half day/day from InterSport La Hutte (☎ 04 93 34 20 14), 10 ave Guillabert, in Antibes centre. It is open from 9 am to 12.15 and 2.30 to 7.15 pm.

Boat Excursions
From Juan-les-Pins between April and September, eight daily ferries (☎ 04 92 93 02 36) sail to the **Îles de Lérins** (see that section earlier) from the Embarcadère Courbet (☎ 04 93 68 98 98), directly opposite the tourist office on blvd Charles Guillaumont. A return ticket to Île Sainte Marguerite/Île Sainte Honorat is 50/60FF. A combination ticket good for both islands costs 80/40FF for adult/child under 7.

The same company also arranges summer day trips by boat to **Saint-Tropez** (120FF), departing daily, except Sunday and Monday, from the Embarcadère Courbet at 9.30 am.

Special Events
Antibes' premier occassion is Jazz à Juan, also known as the Festival de Jazz d'Antibes Juan-les-Pins, which kicks off with a

flourish in the third week in July. Juan-les-Pins' Eden Casino (☎ 04 92 93 71 71), blvd Édouard Baudoin, and the gardens fronting the beach on square Gould, are leading venues. Festival programs and tickets are available from FNAC in Nice or from the Antibes or Juan-les-Pins tourist office.

Places to Stay
Antibes Those on a tight budget should immediately head out of town to the hostel, idyllically placed by the sea on Cap d'Antibes (see later), or to one of the many camp sites around Biot (see Biot – Places to Stay section).

The large *Hôtel Le Caméo* (☎ 04 93 34 24 17, fax 04 93 34 35 80, 62 rue de la République)*, overlooking place Nationale, has singles/doubles with shower from 200/250FF. Nearby, the small and welcoming, one-star *Auberge Provençale* (☎ 04 93 34 13 24, fax 04 93 34 89 88, 61 place Nationale)*, charges 240/250FF for a single/double with all *conforts* (mod-cons).

A notch up on the price scale but well priced for the comforts it offers is the cosy, 15-room *Relais du Postillon* (☎ 04 93 34 29 77, fax 04 93 34 61 24, 8 rue Championnet)*. Rooms for one or two, all named after beautiful cities, islands or villages (Florence, Malta, Vallauris etc) to reflect their worth, cost between 248 and 428FF. Breakfast is an extra 38FF; the pretty terraced restaurant is good for a nibble by night.

Juan-les-Pins Juan-les-Pins' two best value hotels are both a five minute walk from Juan-les-Pins train station on ave de l'Estérel. The one-star *Hôtel Trianon* (☎ 04 93 61 18 11) at No 14 has rooms for one or two people with washbasin/shower for 230/285FF. Next door at No 16, the *Hôtel Parisiana* (☎ 04 93 61 27 03, fax 04 93 67 97 21) has singles/doubles/triples with shower for 177/245/287FF in the low season, rising in the high season to 197/285/347FF.

F Scott and Zelda Fitzgerald stayed at the Villa Saint Louis when they rolled into town – then an untouched spot of unfamed paradise – in 1926. Three years later, their humble abode reopened as the *Hôtel Belles Rives* (☎ 04 93 61 02 79, fax 04 93 67 43 51, www.french-riviera.fr, blvd Edouard Baudoin). A private jetty, beach and swimming pool are just some of the little perks thrown in for today's guests who pay from 780/1570FF to stay in a single/double at this 1930s seashore palace. Dogs cost an extra 100FF a day.

Cap d'Antibes The best choice is the *Relais International de la Jeunesse* (☎ 04 93 61 63 54, ☎/fax 04 93 61 34 40), open from mid-March to mid-November and beautifully set on blvd de la Garoupe, south of the centre. Bed and breakfast costs 72FF; sheets are 10FF and an evening meal is 40FF. You can pitch your tent in the garden for 42FF per person. Reception is only open from 8 to 11 am and 5.30 to 11 pm and guests have to evacuate their rooms between 10 am and 5.30 pm. From Antibes' bus station, take bus No 2A (direction Eden Roc) to L'Antiquité stop. The hostel is open from March to October.

At the other end of the scale is the extortionately expensive *Hôtel du Cap Eden Roc* (☎ 04 93 61 39 01, fax 04 93 67 76 04, blvd Kennedy). Rooms cost a startling 2050-2600FF from mid-October to April, and 2500-3000FF in the high season.

Places to Eat

Restaurants The catch of the day can be had at Vieil Antibes' *Lou Pescardou* (☎ 04 93 34 59 11, 13 rue Sade). Highlights on its *poisson frais* (fresh fish) menu include bouillabaisse for 210FF or a more luxurious 330FF *royal* (royal) option which includes half a lobster. Its regular house *menu* – solely fish dishes – is 99FF.

Chez Juliette (☎ 04 93 34 67 37), almost opposite at 18 rue Sade, is another popular spot, mainly because of Juliette's staggering choice of reasonably priced dishes. Fresh pasta starts at 45FF, salads at 40FF, meat dishes at 60FF and *menus* at 80FF. Advanced reservations are recommended.

Slavic specialities are served with a flourish at the small *Restaurant Silverado*

(☎ 04 93 34 99 34, 18 rue du Marc). Lunch/ evening *menus* start at 59/79FF and it has an exotic *menu slave* for 160FF. Silverado is closed on Wednesday.

La Table Rotund (☎ 04 93 34 31 61, 5 rue Frédéric Isnard), markets itself as a typically Provençal place, despite touting bison, ostrich and kangaroo steaks on its lengthy, tri-lingual menus. Buffalo ribs cost 150FF and a duck fillet with peach and honey sauce is 90FF. A less meaty kid's *menu* costs 38FF.

Set up with vegetarians in mind, is the unusual *Rice Bar* (☎ 04 93 34 12 84, 1 rue des Bains). Its numerous rice-based dishes are served on a pretty little terrace in a quiet and calm old town backstreet.

Cafés Café hot spots in Antibes centre include place Nationale, the fountain-clad corner of rue Thuret and rue Georges Clémenceau, and most old town streets.

Les Heures Bleues (☎ 04 93 34 50 61), tucked away in the old city at 2 rue des Casemates, is a lively café-theatre. Stroll home afterwards munching a slice of fire-baked pizza from *Pizza & Co* opposite.

Equally playful is the young and fun *Comic Strips Café* (☎ 04 93 34 91 40, 4 rue James Close). Smiling punters are free to flick through their childhood greats, ranging from Tintin and Astérix to the more sophisticated Sempé.

Self-Catering Self-caterers with a passion for fresh fish should head for *Thérèse Poissonnerie*, next to the Relais du Postillon hotel on rue Championnet. It is open from 7.30 am to 1.30 pm (closed Sunday and Monday). Wine is sold at the *Cave le Pressoir*, which dates from 1846, on rue Fontvieille; or from the equally well stocked *Cave la Treillo d'Or* (☎ 04 93 34 33 87, 12 rue Lacan). The latter makes home/boat deliveries too.

The *Fromagerie L'Etable*, corner of rue Sade and rue Guillaumont, is the place for cheese. Delicious breads are sold in the heart of the old town at the *Boulangerie*, corner of rue de la Pompe and rue des Bains.

Mundane groceries are sold in Antibes centre at the *Spar* supermarket, place des Martyrs de la Résistance; or *Intermarché*, rue Albert 1er.

Getting There & Away

Bus Antibes bus station (☎ 04 93 34 37 60) is just off rue de la République, a short distance south-east of place du Général de Gaulle. The STGA information office (Syndicat des Transports Grasse-Antibes, www.stga.com) is open from 8 am (9 am on Saturday) to 12.30 pm and 2 to 6.30 pm (Saturday until 5 pm; closed Sunday). It distributes free timetables and transport maps.

STGA buses serve Nice (25FF), Cannes and Cagnes-sur-Mer (both 13FF), Biot (7FF) and Vallauris (14FF). Most stop outside the Maison du Tourisme on place du Général de Gaulle too. Pay the bus driver.

Train Antibes train station, place Pierre Semard, is north of place du Général de Gaulle at the end of ave Robert Soleau, close to Port Vauban. There are frequent trains to/from Nice (22FF; 25 minutes) and Cannes (17FF; 15 minutes). The left luggage counter, on the right as you exit the station, is open from 8.10 am to 12.30 pm and 2 to 5 pm (9 to noon and 2 to 6 pm on Sunday). It costs 20FF per bag.

Unlike Antibes train where many TGVs stop, Juan-les-Pins train station on ave de l'Estérel is only served by local trains.

Getting Around

Bus Summer long, a *minibus gratuit* (free minibus) shuttles travellers between Antibes centre and Vieil Antibes. The Centre Ville line (shaded blue on the route maps displayed at bus stops) links the train station with place du Général de Gaulle and the bus station. The Vieil Antibes line (shaded red) links the train station with Fort Carré. The bus stop is immediately on the right as you exit the train station on ave Robert Soleau. Minibuses run every 15 minutes between 7.30 am and 7.30 pm.

A single ticket/carnet of 10 for other city buses cost 7/65FF. Bus Nos 1a, 3a and 8a link Antibes bus station and place du Général de Gaulle with square du Lys in Juan-les-Pins. Buses run every 10-20 minutes.

Bus No 2a to Eden Roc on Cap d'Antibes departs every 30 minutes from Antibes bus station. Between 15 June and 15 September, bus No 2abis circles the Cap, continuing along the coast from Eden Roc to Juan-les-Pins before returning to Antibes.

Car & Motorcycle FRL Location (☎ 04 93 67 65 67), midway between Antibes centre and Juan-les-Pins at 43 blvd du Président Wilson, and JML Location (☎ 04 92 93 05 06), 93 blvd du Président Wilson, offer competitive car rental rates. They both hire scooters/125cc motorcycles for around 170/270FF a day.

Bicycle FRL Location and JML Location rent bicycles for around 75FF a day. Holiday Bikes (☎ 04 93 61 51 51), 122 blvd du Président Wilson, has good two-wheel rates.

VALLAURIS & GOLFE-JUAN
• pop 8,000   ✉ 06220

The traditional potters' town of Vallauris is as closely associated with Picasso as Antibes, 7km east. The town itself has little charm beyond three memorable museums, one of which is dedicated to the eccentric artist who lived in Vallauris with Françoise Gilot from 1948 until 1955.

Clay pots have been churned out in Vallauris since Roman times. A declining trade in the 16th century was given a major boost by a group of Genoese potters who moved their studios to Vallauris in order to exploit its clay-rich soil. An artistic revival, spearheaded by Picasso, in the 1940s ensured the trade's survival. Today, it is tourism that Vallauris potters rely on, as visitors flock into town to visit the museums and buy one of its signature *marmites* (giant pots, usually only glazed on the inside and traditionally used for cooking Provençal stew).

The satellite resort of Golfe-Juan, 2km south on the coast, is unmonumental beyond its historic claim to fame as the spot where Napoléon I landed following his return from exile in 1815. From here, boats sail to the Îles des Lérins in summer.

Orientation & Information

Vallauris bus station adjoins place de la Libération, the central square in the northern part of town. From here, ave George Clémenceau, the main street, leads south to the tourist office (☎ 04 93 63 82 58); at the roundabout continue south along the D135 to Parking Sud. The tourist office is in this car park.

The closest train station is in Golfe-Juan. From Vallauris tourist office continue south along the D135 to Golfe-Juan's central square Nabonnand. The Golfe-Juan tourist office (☎ 04 93 63 95 01, fax 04 93 63 95 01), 84 ave de la Liberté, overlooks this square.

Château Musée de Vaullaris

The Castle Museum of Vallauris (☎ 04 93 64 16 05 or 04 93 64 98 05), place de la Libération, houses three museums. The **Musée National Picasso** (National Picasso Museum) based around the Picasso-decorated Chapelle La Guerre et La Paix (War and Peace Chapel); the **Musée Magnelli** devoted to the works of Italian artist Albert Magnelli (1899-1971); and a **Musée de la Céramique** (Ceramic Museum) in which the history of Vallauris' age-old craft is unravelled.

Picasso (1881-1973) was 71 years old when he started work on what he dubbed his *temple de la paix* (temple of peace), a 12th century chapel built on the site of an abbey dating from the Middle Ages. He painted his dramatic murals on plywood panels secured to the church's stone walls.

Ceramics cast by Picasso in Vallauris are displayed in the room adjoining the tiny vaulted chapel. A handful of licensed copies are on sale at the Galerie Madoura (☎ 04 93 64 66 39, fax 04 93 64 93 14, info@madoura.com, www.madoura.com), the pottery where Picasso first dabbled in the clay medium in 1946 under the guidance of local potters Georges and Suzanne Ramié. He consequently granted the Ramiés the exclusive right to reproduce his work, resulting in a limited edition – between 25 and 500 in number – of 633 different Picasso pieces being cast between 1947 and 1971. These much sought after ceramic *œuvres* (works of art) today fetch anything from 1250 to 50,000FF. The Galerie Madoura on ave Suzanne Ramié, off ave des Anciens Combattants d'Afrique du Nord, in the Quartier du Plan, is open from 10 am to 12.30 pm and 2.30 to 6.30 pm (closed on weekends). From the bus station, walk south along ave George Clémenceau then turn right (west) along ave des Anciens Combattants d'Afrique du Nord.

The ungainly statue of a life-size, bronze stick figure clutching a sheep by its hind legs, entitled *L'Homme au Mouton*, on place Paul Isnard, the tree-filled square adjoining place de la Libération, was a gift from Picasso to the town.

The Château Musée de Vaullaris is next to Vaullaris bus station; steps lead from the station to place de la Libération. Its opening hours are from 10 am to noon and 2 to 6 pm; 10 am to 12.30 pm and 2 to 6.30 pm in July and August. It's closed Tuesday year round (25/16.50FF for adult/student).

Chapelle de la Miséricorde

The **Centre Européen d'Art Contemporain** (☎ 04 93 63 24 85, fax 04 93 63 56 91), place Jules Isnard, is a contemporary arts centre housed in an old chapel. Temporary exhibitions are held here. Its opening hours are 10 am to noon and 2 to 6 pm; closed Tuesday (free).

From place de la Libération, cross place Paul Isnard and continue west along rue Clement Bel to place Jules Isnard.

Maison de la Pétanque

Everything from its invention to its contemporary champions can be discovered in this quaint museum, dedicated to the region's most popular sport. Enthusiasts can get their own set of boules made to measure. (See Spectator Sports in Facts for the Visitor for more detail.)

The Maison de la Pétanque (☎ 04 93 64 11 36, fax 04 93 64 38 41), 11931 chemin de Saint-Bernard, is open from 9 am to noon and 2 to 6.30 pm (closed Sunday). The museum is 2km north of Vallauris bus station. From the station, head north along ave de Grasse and at the roundabout bear east (right) along chemin Saint Bernard.

Places to Stay

In Vallauris centre there is one cheap hotel. The *Bar-Hôtel du Stade* (☎ 04 93 64 91 27, *48 ave Georges Clémenceau*), above a local bar, has nine simply equipped rooms for one or two people for 150FF a night. Shared showers and toilet are in the corridor.

The 15-room *Le Provence* (☎ 04 93 63 71 19, fax 04 93 63 35 53, *15-17 ave de la Gare*), close to Golfe-Juan train station, is another cheapie. No frill single/double rooms cost 140/200FF.

Getting There & Away

Bus Arriving by bus is the most convenient way of getting to Vallauris if you only intend to visit its museums. The Golfe-Juan train station, from where there are trains in both directions along the coast, is 3km south of Vallauris town in Golfe-Juan.

From the bus station (☎ 04 93 39 11 39), corner of ave de la Grasse and ave Aimé Berger, bus No 6v goes to Cannes train station (every 30 minutes between 7.15 am and 7 pm), and bus No 5v serves Antibes bus station (14FF; hourly from 7.10 am to 6 pm). Buses are less frequent on Sunday.

Boat In summer, ferries (☎ 04 93 63 45 94) sail daily from quai Saint Pierre at the Vieux Port in Golfe-Juan to the Îles des Lérins (see that section). From May to October, ferries sail hourly between 9 am and noon and 2 to 4 pm (30 minutes; 50FF return).

To get to the port from Golfe-Juan train station, turn right (east) along ave de Belgique, then turn right (south) onto ave de la Gare which cuts underneath the railway track towards the sea. At the end of the street, bear south onto blvd des Frères Roustan, the promenade fronting the Vieux Port.

Getting Around

There is a regular STGA bus (No 4v) between Vallauris bus station and Golfe-Juan train station (every 15 minutes between 6 am and 7.40 pm). Journey time is 15 minutes.

MOUGINS & MOUANS-SARTOUX

Haughty **Mougins** (pop 13,014; postcode 06250; alt 260m), 9km north-west of Vallauris and 7km from Cannes, prides itself on two things: art and gastronomy. Picasso, who first visited the then-undiscovered spot in 1935 with lover Dora Marr and surrealist photographer Man Ray (1890-1976), lived in Mougins with his final love, Jacqueline Roque, from 1961 until his death.

Today the village is known for the culinary wonders cooked up by French chef Roger Vergé in his Mougins restaurant housed in a 16th century mill, and for its innovative photography museum. Five kilometres south of the village is the colourful **Musée de l'Automobiliste** (Motorist Museum; ☎ 04 93 69 27 80), 772 chemin de Font-de-Currault, just off the D3.

Neighbouring **Mouans-Sartoux** (pop 7989; postcode 06370; alt 120m), 4km farther north off the route Napoléon (N85), sports a centre of concrete art.

Musée de la Photographie

Celebrated Riviera photographer Jacques Henri Lartigue (1894-1986) is among the wealth of known photographers represented in the Photography Museum (☎ 04 93 75 85 67), inside the medieval Porte Sarrazine, behind the church bell tower. The museum was set up in 1989 by André Villers, best known for photographing Picasso to whom the 3rd floor of the museum is dedicated.

A collection of antique cameras and a series of aerial photographs of Mougins in the early 1900s are displayed on the 2nd floor. Temporary, contemporary photographic exhibitions are housed on the ground floor. Its opening hours are 1 to 6 pm (closed Tuesday and November). Daily hours in July and August are 2 to 11 pm (5FF).

L'Espace de l'Art Concret

Open since 1990, this Centre of Concrete Art (☎ 04 93 75 71 50) hosts the collections of Sybil Albers-Barrier and Gottfried Honegger. Concrete art, which focuses on the intellectual (as opposed to emotional or aesthetic) aspect of art, was coined by Theo van Doesburg in the 1930s.

Bold, gigantic geometric shapes, the use of industrial materials, and mischievous tampering with natural light and space, typical of concrete art and most of works exhibited, create a grandiose juxtaposition with the museum's unfabricated setting – the 16th century **Château de Mouans**, built on the site of Mouans' former castle, destroyed by the Duke of Savoie's troops in 1588 during the Wars of Religion.

Museum opening hours are 11 am to 7 pm; until 6 pm from October to May; closed Tuesday year round (15/7.50FF for adult/student).

Places to Stay & Eat

Mouans tourist office (☎ 04 93 75 87 67, fax 04 92 92 04 03, www.mougins-coteazur.org), 15 ave Jean-Charles Mallet, and the tourist office in Mouans-Sartoux (☎ 04 93 75 75 16, fax 04 92 92 09 16), 258 ave de Cannes, both stock accommodation lists.

The only camping ground is *L'Eau Vive (☎ 04 93 75 36 35, 713 chemin des Cabrières)*, about 1.5km south of Mougins. From place Commandant Lamy in the village centre, bear south-west along ave de la Victoire and its continuations, chemin des Moines and chemin du Fassun. At the end of chemin du Fassun, turn right (west) onto ave Maréchal Foch (N85), and after some 400m turn right again onto chemin des Cabrières. The nightly rate is 70FF for two people with a tent and car; the ground is open year round.

Four-star hotels easily outnumber two-star places in Mougins. The cheapest option is to stay elsewhere (eg in Nice). Those lucky enough to have the cash should not miss wining, dining and sleeping at Roger Vergé's old *Moulins de Mougins (☎ 04 93 75 78 24, fax 04 93 90 18 55, ave Notre Dame de Vie)*, housed in a 16th century oil

mill near the Ermitage Notre Dame de Vie, 2.5km south-east of the Mougins village off the D3. Both tables *(menus* from 250FF) and rooms (three rooms, 800-900FF; two apartments, 1500FF) have to be booked well in advance. The place is closed on Monday (open Monday evenings from mid-July to the end of August), the first two weeks of December, and from mid-February to mid-March. Those who'd rather save a few bob can always invest in Vergé's cookbook, *The Cuisine of the Sun*.

Getting There & Away

Mougins and Mouans-Sartoux are on the Cannes-Grasse bus route (bus No 600 or No 605) operated by Rapides Côte d'Azur (☎ 04 93 39 11 39 in Cannes, ☎ 04 93 36 08 43 in Grasse).

From the bus station next to Cannes train station, buses depart every half-hour between 6.30 am and 7.30 pm to Mougins (17 minutes) and Mouans-Sartoux (20 minutes). On Sunday, the service is hourly between 8.30 am and 7.30 pm on Sunday. Grasse is a 20 minute bus journey from Mougins.

BIOT

• pop 5575   ✉ 06410   alt 80m

This charming *village perché* (perched village) was once an important pottery-manufacturing centre specialising in large earthenware oil and wine containers. Metal containers brought an end to this industry, but Biot is still active in handicraft production. The village streets are pleasant to stroll; get there early to beat the hordes. On tiny **rue des Bachettes**, there is an out-of-the-norm art gallery and unusual jewellery boutique, both worth a browse. The attractive **place des Arcades** dates from the 13th and 14th centuries.

The history of the old Templar village is explained in the **Musée de Biot** (☎ 04 93 65 54 54), 9 rue Saint Sébastien. At the foot of the village is **La Verrerie de Biot** (☎ 04 93 65 03 00, www.biotverre.fr), chemin des Combes, a glass factory where you can watch glass-blowers at work and visit its glass eco-museum and modern glass art galleries.

The tourist office (☎ 04 93 65 05 85, fax 04 93 65 70 96), 9 rue Saint Sébastien, is next to the Musée de Biot.

Musée National Fernand Léger

This museum (☎ 04 92 91 50 30), 2km from the centre of Biot on chemin du Val de Pôme, dedicated to the artist Fernand Léger (1881-1955) contains some 350 of his works, including paintings, mosaics, ceramics and stained-glass windows. The museum, dating from 1960, was built by Léger's wife following his death. Léger had bought the land one month earlier to build himself a studio.

Colourful Léger mosaics decorate the façade of the museum. The predominant mosaic above the entrance was intended for a sports stadium. In the grounds are several Léger sculptures.

The National Fernand Léger Museum is open from 10 am to 12.30 pm and 2 to 5.30 pm; until 6 pm from May to September; closed Tuesday year round (30/20FF).

Marineland

Well distanced from the hilltop village is the Disneyland-style **Parc de la Mer** (Sea Park; ☎ 04 93 33 49 49), a giant amusement complex offering a mind-boggling spectacle of games, shows, and activities to amuse kids and adults alike. Waterworld **Marineland**, open from 10 am to midnight in July and August, is the park's main draw. Acrobatic killer whale/dolphin shows are held three/five times daily in summer. Sharks can be viewed through a transparent, underwater tunnel. Admission for an adult/child is a staggering 116/78FF.

To get to the park, turn right out of Biot train station, walk 50m along route de Nice (N7), then turn right along the D4 signposted 'Marineland & Biot'.

Places to Stay

Camping Biot's abundant camping sites attract backpackers like bees to a honeypot

in summer. All the sites listed are within easy walking distance of Biot train station.

Les Embruns (☎ 04 93 33 33 35, fax 04 93 74 46 70, 63 route de Biot), charges 80-100FF for two people and a tent. The site is open from June to October. Close by is the *Logis de la Brayne* (☎ 04 93 33 54 72, 1221 route de Nice), opposite Biot train station. At No 991, 50m south on the same busy road, is *Ideal Camping* (☎ 04 93 74 27 07); nightly rates per person start at 50FF.

Bus No 10a linking Antibes with Biot village stops outside *Camping du Pylone* (☎ 04 93 33 52 86, fax 04 93 33 30 54, ave du Pylone). It charges 25/35/25FF for a tent site/person/car per night.

Hotels In Biot village, the best value bet is the rambling, one-star *Hôtel des Arcades* (☎ 04 93 65 01 04, 16 place des Arcades). A very small double with shower is 280FF; larger rooms with shower and toilet are 450FF. At the tourist office, at the end of rue Saint Sébastian, turn right onto place des Arcades.

Getting There & Away

Biot village is a good 4km hike from Biot train station. From Antibes, take bus No 10a from the bus station or place du Général de Gaulle to Biot village (7FF; 20 minutes; 11 buses daily).

To get to Marineland take bus No 10a from Antibes bus station to the Biot-Marineland stop. By train, alight at Biot train station from where it is a 300m walk.

CAGNES-SUR-MER

• **pop 41,000**   ✉ **06800**

Cagnes-sur-Mer comprises **Haut de Cagnes**, the old hilltop town; **Le Cros de Cagnes**, the former fishing village by the beach; and **Cagnes Ville**, a fast-growing modern quarter. The old city with its ramparts is dominated by the 14th century Château Grimaldi.

Near Cagnes Ville, is the Musée Renoir, dedicated to the artist who spent his last 16 years in Cagnes-sur-Mer. The magnificent olive and orange groves around the Provençal

Pierre-Auguste Renoir lived in Cagnes-sur-Mer where he captured the light in his work.

mas (farmhouse; today the ticket office) and bourgeois house (the museum) are as much a draw as the museum itself.

Cagnes-sur-Mer tourist office (☎ 04 93 20 61 64, fax 04 93 20 52 63), 6 blvd Maréchal Juin, in Cagnes Ville, is just off the A8.

Château Grimaldi

Home to the Grimaldi family until the French Revolution, the Château Grimaldi (☎ 04 93 20 85 57), 9 place Grimaldi, at the top of the village, houses an eclectic selection of museums: a **Musée de l'Olivier** (Olive Tree Museum) featuring paintings of olive groves as well as the predictable ethnographic collection; a **Musée de l'Histoire** focusing on local history; and a **Musée d'Art Méditerranéen Moderne** (Museum of Modern Mediterranean Art) dedicated to the host of 20th century artists inspired by the Côte d'Azur. Between June and September,

the permanent art collection is replaced by the Festival International de la Peinture.

The castle was restored in the early 1900s. Its grandiose banquet hall is dominated by a 17th century ceiling fresco depicting the Greek mythological fall of Phaeton. The Marquise of Grimaldi's old boudoir is filled with a bizarre collection of portraits featuring **Suzy Solidor** (1900-85), a cabaret singer who spent the last 25 years of her life living in Cagnes-sur-Mer. When not starring in Parisian cabarets, sexy Suzy starred on the canvases of Europe's leading artists. Among the 40 portraits she donated to the chateau-museum before her death (out of the 224 she possessed) are pieces by Brayer, Cocteau, Dufy, Kisling and Van Dongen.

Opening hours at the Château Grimaldi (signposted 'Château-Musée' from the foot of the village) are 10 am to noon and 2.30 to 5 pm (between May and September, 10.30 am to 12.30 pm and 1.30 to 6 pm). It is closed on Tuesday year round, and for three weeks in October-November.

Musée Renoir

La Domaine des Collettes, today the Renoir Museum (☎ 04 93 20 61 07), chemin des Collettes, served as home and studio to an arthritis-crippled Renoir (1841-1919) from 1903 until his death.

It has retained its original décor. The north-facing, 2nd-floor studios are where the wheelchair-bound artist painted with a brush bandaged to his fingers. The chicken wire covering the window protected Renoir from his children's mis-hit tennis balls.

Several of the artist's works are on display, including *Les Grandes Baigneuses* (The Women Bathers; 1892), a reworking of the 1887 original. Photographs documenting his life are dotted around the house. Outside is *Vénus Victrix* (Venus Victorious), a Renoir statue of a fashionably rounded, nude Venus.

The Renoir museum is open the same hours as the Château Grimaldi (20/10FF for adult/child). From the place Bourdet bus stop, bear east (up the hill) along ave Auguste Renoir.

Getting There & Away

Cagnes-sur-Mer is served by two train stations, Gare Cagnes-sur-Mer (☎ 08 36 35 35 35) and Gare Le Cros de Cagnes. Most trains running the length of the coast from Cannes to Ventimiglia stop at both (two to three minutes apart by train).

Buses from Cannes to Nice (every 20 minutes between 6 am and 7.40 pm) stop outside Cagnes-sur-Mer (52 minutes) and Le Cros de Cagnes train stations (one hour), and at the central place Bourdet bus stop at the west end of ave Auguste Renoir. The Grasse-Nice bus (No 500) only stops outside Cagnes-sur-Mer train station (35 minutes; 10 daily between 6.20 am and 7.30 pm).

From Vence (bus No 400), there is a bus every 30 minutes between 6.15 am and 6.45 pm to Cagnes-sur-Mer (20 minutes) via Saint Paul de Vence. Cheap day passes are available on this route (see under Saint Paul de Vence).

SAINT PAUL DE VENCE

• pop 2900   ✉ 06570   alt 125m

This picturesque and very, *very* touristy medieval hilltop village 10km north of Cagnes-sur-Mer, has been a haven to a great many artists and writers over the centuries and is a must for any art lover following in the footsteps of the great masters of the 20th century. Some of their works are exhibited at the extraordinary Fondation Maeght and, for those into fine dining, at La Colombe d'Or.

Saint Paul de Vence was home to Russian artist Marc Chagall (1887-1985) who is buried in the village cemetery. The African-American novelist James Baldwin (1924-85) also spent the last years of his life in Saint Paul.

Yves Montand (1921-91) was a frequent visitor here for many years. The French singer/actor was best known for his roles in the 1986 film adaptations of Pagnol's novels *Jean de Florette* and *Manon des Sources* (and more recently for the controversial exhumation of his corpse for DNA testing in 1998 as part of a 10-year paternity suit filed against him). He met his wife, the actress Simone Signoret, for the first time in Saint Paul in 1949. They held their wedding reception at La Colombe d'Or.

The tourist office (☎ 04 93 32 86 95, fax 04 93 32 60 27, info@provence-prestige .com, www.saint-paul-de-vence.com, www .competences.com/stpaul), rue Grande, on your right as you enter the old village through its northern gate, is open from 10 am to noon and 2 to 6 pm (10 am to 7 pm in July and August).

The Village

Strolling the narrow shaded cobble streets packaged within **15th century ramparts** is how most visitors while away a trip to Saint Paul. No less than 38 of Saint Paul's **68 art galleries and studios**, are on rue Grande. The tourist office has a complete list.

Steps from rue Grande lead eastwards to Saint Paul's crowning glory, the **Église Collégiale et son Trésor** and adjoining **Chapelle des Pénitents**, place de l'Église. Organ recitals (free) are occasionally held here in July and August.

The **point de vue** (viewpoint) at the south end of the village offers a panorama. Marc Chagall and his wife, Vava, are buried in the **cemetery** here. Small beach pebbles are scattered on top of their plain tombs. From the main cemetery entrance, turn right, then immediately left; the Chagall graves are the third on the left.

Fernand Léger's mosaic mural, *Les Femmes au Perroquet* (Women with a Parrot) is among a handful of pieces of modern art that can be viewed at **La Colombe d'Or** (The Golden Dove; ☎ 04 93 32 80 02, fax 04 93 32 77 78), on place des Ormeaux, overlooking the Rond Point St Claire. This upmarket restaurant is where Braque, Chagall, Dufy, Picasso and other then-impoverished artists dined in the post WWI years in exchange for one of their humble creations which today form one of the largest private art collections in France. Viewing is strictly for diners; book well in advance (closed November). During the Cannes film festival, stars frequently throw parties here.

CANNES REGION

Fondation Maeght

The Maeght Foundation (☎ 04 93 32 81 63) is one of France's foremost centres for contemporary art. It hosts an exceptional permanent collection of 20th century works featuring Braque, Bonnard, Chagall, Matisse, Miró and Léger.

The gallery dates from 1964 and is set on a hill in beautiful Provençal countryside amidst gardens embellished with sculptures and fountains. Next to the main entrance of the futuristic building, a pair of sculpted *ondines* (water sprites) languish on a stone slab amid a pool of water lilies.

In the gardens behind the museum, visitors can stroll through the **Miró Labyrinth**, a terraced area laid out by Catalan architect José Luis Sert, a pupil of Le Corbusier. The *parcours* (route) is studded with gigantic sculptures and mosaics – some spouting water – by Spanish surrealist Joan Miró (1893-1983) who frequently visited the Côte d'Azur to see Picasso and other artists living on the coast.

The façade of the **Chapelle de Saint Bernard** is adorned with a Léger mosaic. Its interior is illuminated with stained glass windows by Braque. The crucifix dates from the 15th century.

The Fondation Maeght is open from 10 am to 12.30 pm and 2.30 to 6 pm; 10 am to 7 pm from July to September (50/40FF for adult/student). The centre, signposted from Rond Point St Claire, is 800m from the central bus stop. A steep driveway leads up to the Fondation. Approaching Saint Paul by car, turn left off the D7 from La-Colle-sur-Loup.

Places to Stay & Eat

Saint Paul de Vence is strictly for the rich and wealthy. The tourist office stocks a list of hotels (nothing under 400FF a night), as well as studios and houses to rent in the area on a long-term basis. The Relais & Château *Hôtel Le Saint Paul* (☎ 04 93 32 65 25, fax 04 93 32 52 94, 86 rue Grande) is famed as one of the Riviera's most exclusive places to stay; rooms fit for a queen cost 800-1500FF. Equally pricey is *La Colombe*

d'Or (see The Village section earlier) where double rooms start at 1350FF (half-board for two 1750FF). Count at least 400FF (excluding wine) to dine in the à la carte restaurant.

Getting There & Away

Saint Paul de Vence, listed simply as Saint Paul on bus timetables and road signs, is served by the Nice-Vence bus service (bus No 400). Buses run approximately every 30 minutes between 7 am and 6 pm (until 7 or 8 pm in July and August). A single fare from Nice to Saint Paul de Vence is 20FF. If you intend stopping at Cagnes-sur-Mer en route or continuing to Vence, buy a one day *billet circulaire* (35FF) which allows one stop in Nice, Cagnes-sur-Mer, Saint Paul and Vence.

VENCE

• pop 15,300   ✉ 06140   alt 325m

Vence is a beautiful but touristy inland town 4km north of Saint Paul de Vence. The area is typically built up with holiday homes and villas, but the medieval centre is perfect for a stroll past the town's art galleries and down-to-earth street markets.

Exceptional is Vence's Chapelle du Rosaire, designed and decorated by Matisse, and lovingly tended today by the small community of Dominican nuns for whom the 77-year-old Matisse created the chapel in 1947-51.

Music fills the streets during the annual music festival, Nuits du Sud, which takes place during the last two weeks of July and the first week of August. A fruit and vegetable market is held every morning, except Monday, on place du Grand Jardin.

Orientation

Large place du Grand Jardin is the central square in Vence. To get to the old city, turn left onto ave Marcellin Maurel which skirts the medieval city's southern wall. Port du Peyra, the main entrance to the city, is at the west end of ave Marcellin Maurel. Place Clémenceau lies at the heart of the medieval city.

Information
Vence tourist office (☎ 04 93 58 06 38, fax 04 93 58 91 81), place du Grand Jardin, is open from 9 am to 1 pm and 2 to 7 pm (closed Sunday). It issues free maps enabling visitors, with the aid of 25 numbered, bilingual signs in English and French displayed at pertinent points in the old city, to lead themselves on a 45 minute self-guided tour.

The post office, place Clémenceau, is open from 9 am to noon and 2 to 5 pm (Saturday from 8.30 to 11 am; closed Sunday). Banks line place du Grand Jardin.

Medieval Vence
Porte du Peyra The main gate of the 13th century wall that encircles the old city leads to pretty little place du Peyra with a **fountain** (1578). Gate and square are named after the execution block which used to adorn the square.

The western edge of place du Peyra is dominated by the imposing **Château de Villeneuve**, 3 place du Frêne, and adjoining, 12th century **watchtower**. It houses the **Fondation Émile Hughes** (☎ 04 93 24 24 23), a cultural centre specialising in various temporary 20th century art exhibitions. The centre is open from 10 am to 12.30 pm and 2 to 6 pm; 10 am to 6 pm between July and October (25/10FF for adult/student). A 400-year-old ash tree stands in front.

From place du Peyra, narrow **rue du Marché** – crammed with delectable food shops selling homemade pasta, bouillabaisse, fresh fish – leads east. Cut along rue Alsace-Lorraine to reach **place Clémenceau**, the city's central square and market place. The **Romanesque cathedral** on the east side of the square was built in the 11th century on the site of an old Roman temple.

The best panorama of medieval Vence can be had from Matisse's chapel at the foot of the Col de Vence (see Around Vence). The watchtower provides a ready landmark.

Matisse's Chapelle du Rosaire
Matisse moved from war-torn Nice to Vence in June 1943. Upon his arrival he was reunited with Monique Bourgeois, his former nurse and model who had since become a Dominican nun under the name Sœur Jacques-Marie. She persuaded the artist to design a chapel for her community, the result being the striking **Chapelle du Rosaire** (Chapel of the Rosary; ☎ 04 93 58 03 26), 468 ave Henri Matisse. Matisse was 81 when he completed the project in 1951.

The chapel is still used by the *Dominicaines du Rosaire* (Dominican nuns of the Rosary) today. Blue and white ceramic tiles coat the low roof, which is topped by a 13m-tall wrought-iron cross and bell tower. Inside, stark white walls provide a dramatic contrast to the stained glass windows, through which the sun's rays throw a wash of colour. A line image of the Virgin Mary and child is painted on white ceramic tiles on the northern interior wall. The western wall is dominated by the bolder *Chemin de Croix* (Stations of the Cross), numbered in Matisse's frenzied handwriting. Saint Dominic overlooks the altar.

Matisse also designed the chapel's stone altar, candlesticks, cross, and colourful priests' vestments displayed in an adjoining hall. Many of his preparatory sketches and models for the four-year project are here too, as is a photograph of the artist with Sœur Jacques-Marie, arms linked in friendly companionship.

The chapel is about 800m north of Vence on the route de Saint Jeannet (D2210). From place du Grand Jardin, head east along ave de la Résistance then turn right (north) along ave Tuby. At the next junction, bear right (north-east) along ave de Provence then left (north) onto ave Henri Matisse. It is open on Tuesday and Thursday from 10 to 11.30 am and 2.30 to 5.30 pm; during holidays it is also open on Wednesday, Friday and Saturday from 2.30 pm to 5.30 pm (10/5FF). Sunday Mass (open to everyone) is celebrated at 10 am.

Villa Le Rêve
Matisse lived in Vence for six years, accomplishing such works as *Lemons and mimosas against a black background* (1943), *Yellow and blue interior* (1946) and

CANNES REGION

Still life with pomegranates (1947) while he was here. His home and studio was **Le Rêve** (The Dream), a delightfully rambling old villa 200m from the Chapelle du Rosaire on the left as you approach the chapel from Vence (opposite 320 ave Henri Matisse).

Today, art workshops are held here (see the Facts for the Visitor chapter). The entrance to the villa is on the right along a small lane, off ave Henri Matisse, signposted 'Residence Altitude 350'.

Pétanque

When not filled with market stalls, place du Grand Jardin's wide open spaces shaded by plane trees double as a free-for-all pétanque court. Staff at the tourist office are happy to lend their balls (and a set of rules) to those keen to give it a try; its Journées Provençales (130FF) includes a game of pétanque.

Places to Stay & Eat

The Dominican nuns offer beds for the night in the *Maison Lacordaire* (☎ 04 93 58 03 26, fax 04 93 58 21 10, 466 ave Henri Matisse), adjoining the Chapelle du Rosaire. A night's accommodation is 195FF. Rooms *have* to be reserved in advance.

More mundane options include the *Hôtel la Lubane* (☎ 04 93 58 01 10, fax 04 93 58 84 44), midway between place du Grand Jardin and Matisse's chapel at 10 ave Joffre, which has singles/doubles with washbasin and fine views of the Col de Vence for 178/210FF. Rooms with shower are 265FF.

The *Hôtel Victoire* (☎ 04 93 58 61 30, fax 04 93 58 74 68, place du Grand Jardin), is above a busy bar. Rooms for one or two with shower/bath are 150/180FF.

Le P'tit Provençal (☎ 04 93 58 50 64), tucked beside the Hôtel de Ville on place Clémenceau, serves deliciously local cuisine on its small, pavement terrace. It has a lunchtime 60FF *menu* which usually includes a fresh fish dish, a children's *menu* for 50FF and adult-sized evening ones for 90 and 140FF. Its blood-red fruity soup with Muscat de Beaumes de Venise is truly delightful.

Getting There & Away

Bus No 400 to/from Nice (50 minutes), Cagnes-sur-Mer (20 minutes) and Saint Paul de Vence (10 minutes) drops passengers opposite the tourist office on place du Grand Jardin. Southbound, the bus stop is on the north side of place du Grand Jardin, in front of the TAM Voyages Excursions office, 14 place du Grand Jardin. There are also four direct Nice-Vence buses (No 410; 40 minutes; 21.50FF).

If you arrive by car, there is large car park underneath place du Grand Jardin.

AROUND VENCE

Varied **hiking, biking & driving** terrain surrounds Vence. The northbound D2 from Vence leads to the **Col de Vence** (963m), a mountain pass 10km north offering good views of the *baous* (rocky promontories), typical to this region. At the foot of the col is the **Baou des Blancs** (673m), crowned by the stony remains of the **Bastide Saint-Laurent**, inhabited by the Templars in the 13th century. Destination Nature (☎ 04 93 32 06 93 or ☎/fax 04 92 13 24 02), 6 rue Maréchal Juin in Cagnes-sur-Mer (office on the col in summer), organises full and half day hikes and mountain-bike trips around the col, some of which follow part of the GR51.

Coursegoules, 6km further north along the D2, is a typical Provençal village perché with 11th century castle ruins and fortifications. From here follow the D3 back south, bearing east along the D6 to cut through the dramatic **Gorges du Loup**. Between mid-June and mid-September, Destination Nature organise **canyoning & rafting** expeditions along the Loup.

At **Pont du Loup**, follow the eastbound D2210 towards Tourrettes-sur-Loup. Some 5km before the village is the Ferme des Courmettes (☎ 04 93 59 31 93), a 600 hectare farm where *chèvre* (goats cheese) is made. Guided tours of the *fromagerie* and *dégustation* (tasting) sessions are available; Vence tourist office has details. **Tourrettes-sur-Loup**, known as the city of violets after its production of the purple flower, is a picturesque, 15th century perched village crammed with art galleries and craft shops.

Six kilometres north-east of Vence, at the foot of the **Baou de Jeannet** (800m), is the village of **Saint Jeannet** (the setting for Peter Mayle's fictional *Chasing Cézanne)*. A marked trail (45 minutes) leads from central place Sainte Barbe to the baou summit. Wine enthusiasts can taste (and buy) Cabernet from the **vineyards** of La Bastide du Collet de Mourre (☎ 04 93 24 96 01), 800 chemin des Sausses. Top off the trip with a visit to **Gaude**, a less touristy perched village 1.5km south of Saint Jeannet.

Grasse

• pop 42,000   ✉ 06130   alt 250m

If it weren't for the scents around Grasse, just 17km north of Cannes and the Mediterranean, you might detect a sea breeze. But for centuries, Grasse, with its distinct red and orange tile roofs rising up the slopes of the pre-Alps, has been one of France's most important centres of perfume production.

These days there are five famous master perfumers – or *nez* (noses), as they're called – in the world. Combining their natural gift with seven years of study, they are able to identify, from no more than a whiff, about 6000 scents. Somewhere between 200 and 500 of these fragrances are used to make just one perfume. Compelling reading associated with Grasse is *Perfume*, a novel by Patrick Süskind about the fantastic life and amazing nose of Jean-Baptiste Grenouille.

Grasse and the surrounding region also produce some of France's most highly prized flowers, including lavender (which you'll see growing in profusion in the countryside), jasmine, centifolia roses, mimosa, orange blossom and violets. Cut flowers are sold at the *marché Provençal* (Provençal market) which brings a splash of colour to cours Honoré Cresp on the first and third Saturdays of the month.

History

Founded by the Romans, Grasse became a small republic by the early Middle Ages,

exporting tanned skins and oil (from which it may have earned its name since *gras* or *matière grasse* means 'fat' in French). It was taken over by the counts of Provence in 1226 and became part of France in the 16th century. Already a strong trading centre, Grasse grew even richer with the advent of perfumed gloves in the 1500s. Once established, the glove-makers split from the tanners, setting up a separate industry that eventually led to the creation of perfumeries. These in turn flourished in the 18th century, when perfume became fashionable, and members of high society never went anywhere without leaving a distinct aroma in their wake. Of course, it was a fashion necessity, not accessory; people seldom – if ever – took a bath in the 18th century.

Orientation

While the town of Grasse and its suburbs sprawl over a wide area of hill and valley, the old city is small, densely packed into the hillside like so many of the towns across the border in Italy. Its steep, cobbled stairways and roads (some with impossibly tight hairpin bends) are best explored on foot. The N85, better known as the route Napoléon, which leads north to Castellane and Digne-les-Bains and south to Cannes, runs into Grasse, where it becomes the town's main (and often congested) thoroughfare, blvd du Jeu de Ballon.

Information

Tourist Offices The tourist office, marked Grasse Espace Accueil (☎ 04 93 40 13 13, fax 04 93 40 12 82), a two minute walk from the bus station at place de la Foux, is open from 9 am to 12.30 pm and 1.30 to 6 pm (closed Sunday).

Farther in town, the tiny tourist office (☎ 04 93 36 66 66, fax 04 93 36 86 36), inside the Palais de Congrès, 22 cours Honoré Cresp, is open from 9 am to 12.30 pm and 1.30 to 6 pm (closed on weekends). Daily hours between July and mid-September are 9 am to 7 pm.

Money Banks abound on blvd du Jeu de Ballon. You can also change money at the Change du Casino (☎ 04 93 36 48 48), Palais de Congrès.

Post The post office, blvd Fragonard, is open from 8 am to 6.30 pm (Monday from 9 am, Saturday until noon; closed Sunday).

Laundry The laundrette, 1bis rue Gazan, is open from 6 am to 9 pm. Hours at 10 blvd Fragonard, opposite the post office, are 7 am to 9 pm.

Perfumeries

Follow your nose along rue Jean Ossola to the archway at the beginning of rue Tracastel, where several perfumeries have been conjuring up new scents for many years. The air around the alley entrance is saturated with aromas. Seasoned (as it were) travellers will be reminded of visits to Old Delhi, Cairo or Istanbul.

While more than 40 perfumeries exist in Grasse, only three are open to the public. It's unlikely that you'll know any by name,

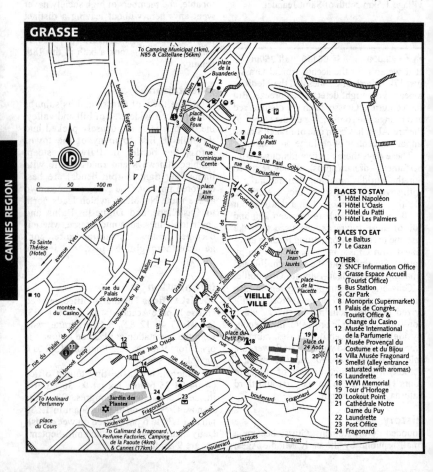

GRASSE

To Camping Municipal (1km), N85 & Castellane (56km)

CANNES REGION

place de la Buanderie

place de la Foux

place du Patti

place aux Aires

rue Paul Goby

rue du Rouachier

Place Jean Jaurès

place de la Placette

VIEILLE VILLE

place du Petit Puy

place du 24 Août

To Sainte Thérèse (Hotel)

To Molinard Perfumery

place du Cours

Jardin des Plantes

To Galimard & Fragonard Perfume Factories, Camping de la Paoute (4km) & Cannes (17km)

PLACES TO STAY
1 Hôtel Napoléon
4 Hôtel L'Oasis
7 Hôtel du Patti
10 Hôtel Les Palmiers

PLACES TO EAT
9 Le Baltus
17 Le Gazan

OTHER
2 SNCF Information Office
3 Grasse Espace Accueil (Tourist Office)
5 Bus Station
6 Car Park
8 Monoprix (Supermarket)
11 Palais de Congrès, Tourist Office & Change du Casino
12 Musée International de la Parfumerie
13 Musée Provençal du Costume et du Bijou
14 Villa Musée Fragonard
15 Smells! (alley entrance saturated with aromas)
16 Laundrette
18 WWI Memorial
19 Tour d'Horloge
20 Lookout Point
21 Cathédrale Notre Dame du Puy
22 Laundrette
23 Post Office
24 Fragonard

as the perfumes are sold only from their factories or by mail order. The names the world knows are the big brands who buy the perfumers' essence and reap considerable profit from it.

During a tour, you'll be taken through every stage of perfume production, from extraction and distillation to the work of the 'noses'. The guides will explain the differences between perfume, which contains 20% pure essence, and its weaker partners, eau de toilette and eau de Cologne, which contain 2% to 6% concentrate. You'll also hear about the extraordinary quantity of flowers needed to make one litre of essence. At the end you'll be squirted with a few of the house scents, invited to purchase as many as you'd like, and leave reeking.

Fragonard If you're on foot the most convenient perfumery is Fragonard (☎ 04 93 36 44 65), 20 blvd Fragonard. Among Grasse's oldest perfumeries, it is named after one of the town's original perfume-making families and is housed in a 16th century tannery.

The factory gives a brief introduction to perfume, but these days it's more a tourist showcase than a working factory; the real production factory (also open for free visits) is out of town on the N85 to Cannes. From October to May the Fragonard perfumery is open from 9 am to 12.30 pm and 2 to 6 pm. The rest of the year it is open daily from 9 am to 6.30 pm.

Galimard Galimard (☎ 04 93 09 20 00, fax 04 93 70 36 22), 73 route de Cannes, is 3km out of town towards Mouans-Sartoux (not far from Fragonard's factory). Unless you have wheels it's not a feasible option. The factory is open from 9 am to noon and 2 to 5.30 pm (9 am to 6 pm in summer).

Close by is the Galimard Studio des Fragrances (same ☎/fax), route de Pégomas, where you can create your own fragrance from 126 different scents under the guidance of a professional nez (two hours; 200FF). The Galimard perfumery has a second outlet in Èze (see Corniche Inférieure in the Nice to Menton chapter).

Molinard Housed in a turreted, Provençal-style villa surrounded by immaculate lawns and a blaze of flowers, Molinard (☎ 04 93 36 01 62, fax 04 93 36 03 91), 60 blvd Victor Hugo, is a ritzier affair than Fragonard. Molinard also offers 'create your own perfume' sessions (1¼ hours; 200FF) as well as seminars to unravel the history of perfume (one hour; 150FF). Molinard, which dates from 1849, is open from 9 am to 12.30 pm and 2 to 6 pm (closed Sunday); from July to September daily hours are 9 am to 6.30 pm.

Museums

Villa Musée Fragonard Named after the artist Jean-Honoré Fragonard, who was born in Grasse in 1732, this villa (☎ 04 93 40 32 64), 23 blvd Fragonard, now a museum, is where the artist lived for a year in 1790. The artist's paintings, famous for their licentious scenes, are on display in the museum. It is open from 10 am to noon and 2 to 5 pm (closed Monday and Tuesday). From June to September it's open daily from 10 am to 1 pm and 2 to 7 pm (free).

Musée Provençal du Costume et du Bijou Visiting Grasse's colourful costume and jewellery museum comes as a breath of fresh air after touring the town's perfumeries. The museum (☎ 04 93 36 44 65), 2 rue Jean Ossola, is housed inside the stately Hôtel de Clapiers Cabris, the private mansion of the sister of revolutionary Mirabeau, the Marquise de Cabris, who lived in Grasse from 1769. It is open from 10 am to 1 pm and 2 to 6 pm (free).

Musée International de la Parfumerie Opened in 1989, the International Perfume Museum (☎ 04 93 36 80 20), 8 blvd Fragonard, examines every detail of perfume production – from extraction techniques to sales and publicity – and traces its 400 years of history in Grasse. One of the most appealing sections of the museum is the rooftop conservatory, where lavender, mint, thyme and jasmine are grown in a heady mix of aromatic scents. It is open from 10 am to noon and 2 to 5 pm (closed Monday and Tuesday). Daily hours from June to September are 10 am to 7 pm (25/12.50FF for adult/student).

Cathédrale Notre Dame du Puy

Although rather uninteresting in itself, the former cathedral, built in Provençal Romanesque style in the 12th and 13th centuries and reworked in the 18th century, contains a painting by Fragonard entitled *Washing of the Feet* and several early paintings by Rubens, including *The Crown of Thorns* and *Christ Crucified*. The cathedral is open from 9.30 am (8.30 am on Saturday) to 11.30 am and 2.30 to 6 pm (3 to 7 on Saturday). Summer concerts are occasionally held here.

Special Events

Grasse's two main events – related to flowers and scents *naturellement* – are Exporose in May and La Jasminade, held during the first weekend in August.

Places to Stay

Camping The two-star *Camping Municipal* (☎ 04 93 36 28 69), blvd Alice de Rothschild (continuation of ave Thiers), is 1km north-east of the bus station. It charges 57FF for one person with tent and car. It is closed in January. Bus No 8, marked 'Piscine', leaves from the bus station and stops at the front of the camping ground. Another site is *Camping de la Paoute* (☎ 04 93 09 11 42, fax 04 93 40 06 40, 160 route de Cannes), 4km south of Grasse signposted off the N567 towards Cannes.

Hotels The cheapest option in town is the one-star *Hôtel Napoléon* (☎ 04 93 36 05 87, fax 04 93 36 41 09, 6 ave Thiers). Singles/doubles with washbasin start at 130/160FF, triples/quads are 200/350FF. The hotel is closed from the end of December to the end of January.

Opposite is the small, rather run-down *Hôtel L'Oasis* (☎ 04 93 36 02 72, fax 04 93 36 03 16, place de la Buanderie), which has rooms with washbasin for 170/180FF and singles/ doubles/triples with shower for 190/225/ 270FF.

If you have a car or don't mind an uphill amble, *Sainte Thérèse* (☎ 04 93 36 10 29, fax 04 93 36 11 73, 39 ave Yves Emmanuel Baudoin), just over 1km from the tourist office, is a good choice. From the hotel you get a panoramic view of the valley and the dusty, orange-roofed town. Singles/doubles start at 180/200FF; private parking is available. The hotel is closed from October to mid-November. Another option on the same road is *Hôtel Les Palmiers* (☎ 04 93 36 07 24) at No 17. Prices in winter/summer start at 160/240FF.

For something more upmarket, try the modern, rather unattractive *Hôtel du Patti* (☎ 04 93 36 01 00, fax 04 93 36 36 40, place du Patti), in the heart of the old city. It has pleasant singles/doubles/triples with bath and toilet from 330/420/520FF. Parking is available.

Places to Eat

Very charming and very small is Provençal *Le Baltus* (☎ 04 93 36 32 90), in the old town at 15 rue de la Fontette. It has a *menu* for 90FF, a plat du jour for 60FF, bouillabaisse for 280FF per person and, upon special request, *langouste* (crayfish) for 450FF per person. Le Baltus is open from 12.15 to 2 pm and 7.30 to 9.30 pm (closed the first two weeks of July). Close by, *Le Gazan* (☎ 04 93 36 22 88, rue Gazan), offers good value 65FF lunchtime *menus*.

Getting There & Away

Bus The ticket office at the bus station (☎ 04 93 36 08 43), place de la Buanderie, closes at 5.15 pm. Several companies operate from here. Rapides Côte d'Azur (☎ 04 92 96 88 88 in Vallauris, ☎ 04 93 39 11 39 in Cannes) operates bus No 500 to Nice (37FF; 1¼ hours) via Cannes (19.50FF; 45 minutes) every half-hour (hourly on Sunday) between 6.20 am and 7.30 pm. In addition, buses No 600 or No 605 link Grasse with Cannes, stopping at Mouans-Sartoux and Mougins (see those sections for details) en route.

STGA, Syndicat des Transports Grasse-Antibes (☎ 04 93 36 37 37, www.stga.com) operates buses from Grasse to Valbonne and Mouans-Sartoux.

VFD has a morning bus to Grenoble (six hours) which stops in Castellane (near the Gorges du Verdon) and Digne-les-Bains.

Train The train line does not reach Grasse but SNCF has an information office (☎ 04 93 36 06 13) at the bus station, open from 8.30 am to 5.30 pm (closed Sunday).

Massif de l'Estérel

Covered by pine, oak and eucalyptus trees until the devastating fires of 1985 and 1986 and now beginning to return to life, this spectacular range sprawls immediately south-west of Cannes. It is roughly marked by Mandelieu-La Napoule to the north and Saint Raphaël to the south. The latter, together with its Roman neighbour, Fréjus, serves as the main gateway to the Massif de l'Estérel and Saint Tropez.

There are all sorts of walks you can go on in the Massif de l'Estérel, but for the more difficult trails you will need to come equipped with a good map, such as IGN's *Série Bleue* (1:25,000) No 3544ET. Indispensable, providing you can read French, is the Didier-Richard walking guide entitled *Au Pays d'Azur – de l'Estérel à la Roya* (79FF; No 126 in Les Tracés Grand Air hiking series) which maps out 165 walks in the region. Those not keen to go it alone can link up with an organised hike; the tourist office in Saint Raphaël has details.

CORNICHE DE L'ESTÉREL

The coastal road that runs along the base of the massif is called the Corniche de l'Estérel (also known as the Corniche d'Or and the N98). A drive or walk along this winding road is not to be missed as the views are spectacular. Small summer resorts and inlets where you can swim are dotted the length of the 40km-odd coastal stretch, all of which is easily accessible by bus or train (see the Getting There & Away section later).

If the snail-paced traffic amid the searing heat gets too much in summer, opt for the inland N7. This quieter road runs through the hills and transports you into an entirely different world.

La Napoule

'Once upon a time' is an apt label for the turreted, 14th century **Château de la Napoule** (☎ 04 93 49 95 05), ave Henry Clews, that dominates this small seaside village. The fanciful castle was the creation of Henry and Marie Clews, an American couple, who arrived on the coast in 1918 and spent 17 years rebuilding the sea-facing Saracen tower. Above the main entrance to the chateau, considered a folly by many, are carved the words 'Once upon a time'.

The interior and the gardens overlooking the sandy **Plage du Château** are adorned with equally fantastical sculptures created by Henry Clews (1876-1937). The monumental statue, *The God of Humormystics*, which stands in the courtyard, was the sculptor's wedding present to his wife. Château de la Napoule was occupied during WWII (forcing the widowed Marie to move into the gatehouse). In 1951, Marie Clews established the **Fondation d'Art de la Napoule** (La Napoule Art Foundation) in commemoration of her husband's eccentric art. The epitaph on his gravestone in the castle grounds reads 'Poet, Sculptor, Actor, Grand Knight of La Mancha, Supreme Master humormystic, Castelan of Once upon a time, Chevalier de Marie'.

The chateau, which remains privately owned, can only be visited with a guide. Tours depart from the main entrance between March and October at 3 and 4 pm. In July and August there is an additional tour at 5 pm. It's closed Tuesday year round and from November to February (25/20FF for adult/child).

The neighbouring resort of **Théoule-sur-Mer**, 2.5km farther south along the coast, is dominated by the **Château de la Théoule**, also privately owned and built in the same architectural style as its better-known sister.

During the 18th century, it served as a *savonnerie* (soap factory).

Le Trayas

Seven kilometres south of Théoule-sur-Mer is Le Trayas, the highest point of the corniche from where the road gets more dramatic as it twists and turns its way past the **Fôret Domaine de l'Estérel** along the jagged coastline. Needles of red rock strike out amid the splashing sea, hugging small sheltered *anses* (coves). There is a largish beach at **Anse de la Figueirette**, a cove at the north end of Le Trayas which, in the 17th century, was a leading tuna fishing centre.

There are several small parking areas along this stretch of the corniche where you can stop to picnic and photograph the red rocks. There are good views of the spectacular **Rocher de Saint Barthélemy** (Saint Bartholomew's Rock) and Cap Roux from the **Pointe de l'Observatoire**, about 2km south of Le Trayas.

Agay

The village resort of Agay, 10km or so south of Le Trayas, is celebrated for its fine views of the **Rade d'Agay**, a perfectly horseshoe-shaped bay embraced by sandy beaches and abundant pine trees. Numerous watersport activities and boat excursions are on offer at the busy central Plage d'Agay. Agay tourist office (☎ 04 94 82 01 85, fax 04 94 82 74 20), directly opposite the beach at 577 blvd de la Plage, has details.

From Agay, the route de Valescure leads inland into the massif, from where various hiking trails are signposted, including up to the **Pic de l'Ours** (496m), the **Pic du Cap Roux** (452m) and the **Pic d'Aurelle** (323m). All three *pics* (peaks) offer stunning panoramas of the Massif de l'Estérel.

Le Dramont

Cap du Dramont This cape, also called Cap Estérel, is crowned by a military semaphore and sits at the south end of the Rade d'Agay. From the semaphore there are unbeatable views of the Golfe de Fréjus flanked by the **Lion de Terre** and the **Lion de Mer** – two red porphyry rocks jutting out of the sea – to the west. *Circuits touristiques* (tourist paths) lead to the semaphore from Plage du Débarquement in Le Dramont on the west side of the cape. In Agay, a path starts from the car park near Plage du Camp Long, at the eastern foot of the cape. Both beaches are accessible from the N98.

From the **Plage du Débarquement** you can sail (15 minutes) to the **Île d'Or** (Golden Island), a pinprick island, uninhabited bar a small stone fort which is someone's summer house. You can hire catamarans (180/800FF for one/five hours) and sailboards (70/300FF for one/five hours) from the Accueil Base Nautique (☎ 04 94 82 76 57 or 06 14 02 44 18), a wooden hut on the beach.

Overlooking Plage du Débarquement, 1km west of Boulouris on the Corniche de l'Estérel (N98), is a large **memorial park**, blvd de la 36ème DI du Texas, which commemorates the landing of the 36th US Infantry Division on the beach here on 15 August 1944. A monumental landing craft faces out to sea. Steps lead from here down to the beach.

Places to Stay

Camping Camping grounds are most plentiful in and around Agay. In Agay centre overlooking the bay, is *Camping Agay Soleil* (☎ 04 94 82 00 79), close to the tourist office on blvd de la Plage (N98). The nightly rate is 97/124FF for a tent, two people and car on a small/large site. The ground is open from mid-March to mid-November.

Royal Camping (☎ 04 94 82 00 20), a two minute walk from Plage du Camp Long on the N98, charges 92FF for a tent, two people and car. It is open from mid-March to mid-October.

Equally convenient is *Camping International du Dramont* (☎ 04 94 82 07 68), next to Plage du Débarquement on the western side of Cap du Dramont. The site is open between April and mid-October and charges 116FF for two people with a tent and car. It also has caravans to let (minimum three nights) for up to five people costing 580FF for three nights.

Hostels In Le Trayas, the 110-bed *Auberge de Jeunesse* (☎ 04 93 75 40 23, fax 04 93 75 43 45), is on a beautiful site overlooking the sea. The hostel, 9 ave de la Véronèse, is 1.5km up the hill from the Auberge Blanche bus stop. Reception is open from 8 to 10 am and 6.30 to 9.30 pm. Bed & breakfast is 66FF (an additional 19FF a night for non HI card holders). Telephone reservations are not accepted. You can camp for 44FF (including breakfast).

Hotels In La Napoule, the two-star *Hôtel La Calanque* (☎ 04 93 49 95 11, fax 04 93 49 67 44, ave Henry Clews), directly oppos-ite the Château de la Napoule, is one of the cheapest places to stay. It has singles/ doubles for 195/330FF. The north end of the resort, which touts a concrete skyline, is dominated by the eyesore, four-star *Hôtel Royal Casino* (☎ 04 92 97 70 00, fax 04 93 49 51 50, 605 ave du Général de Gaulle) where rooms for one or two people cost 690-1650FF a night.

At the south end of Le Trayas on the N98, *Le Relais des Calanques* (☎ 04 94 44 14 06, fax 04 94 44 10 93) offers striking views of the red-rocked sea. The hotel charges from 350/480FF for comfortable doubles/ triples with shower and toilet. It is closed from November to 1 April.

Agay has numerous hotels to choose from. In Le Dramont close to the Plage du Débarquement, the *Hôtel du Débarque-ment* (☎ 04 94 82 02 51) has doubles with shower and toilet for 250/300FF. It is one of the few places along the Corniche de l'Estérel to stay open year round.

Getting There & Away
Bus Beltram (☎ 04 94 83 87 63) runs fre-quent daily buses along the Corniche d'Estérel from Cannes to Saint Raphaël. From Cannes, buses on this route, labelled 'Ligne de la Corniche d'Or' on timetables, stop at La Napoule (10FF; 10 minutes), Théoule-sur-Mer (11FF; 15 minutes), Le Trayas (16FF; 30 minutes), Agay (26.50FF; 45 minutes), Cap du Dramont and Le Dramont (28FF; 55 minutes) and Boulouris (30.50FF; one hour).

There are seven Cannes-Saint Raphaël buses between 8 am and 7 pm (three on Sunday) and an additional four buses from Agay to Saint Raphaël.

Train There are train stations (☎ 08 36 35 35 35) at Mandelieu-la-Napoule (4km north of La Napoule), Théoule-sur-Mer, Le Trayas, Agay, Le Dramont and Boulouris.

They are served by the Nice-Saint Raphaël-Les Arcs Draguignan coastal rail route (9-11 trains daily between 7 am and 6 pm; less frequently on Sunday and in winter). There are plenty more trains from Cannes to Saint Raphaël (see the Saint Raphaël – Getting There & Away section later) from where there are regular buses.

SAINT RAPHAËL
• pop 26,500   ✉ 83700
Saint Raphaël port was where Napoléon Bonaparte landed in 1799 upon his return from Egypt, and from where he set sail for exile in Elba in 1814. During WWII, the resort was one of the main landing bases of US and French troops in August 1944.

The resort of Saint Raphaël was created by Félix Martin (1842-99), who, as mayor of the then small fishing commune, decided to build on the Plateau de Veillat. By the 1920s Saint Raphaël was a fashionable place to be seen at.

The resort is 2km south-east of Fréjus, once an important port. The suburbs of the two places have now become so intertwined that they seem almost to form a single town. From Saint Raphaël, it is a pleasant 20 minute walk westwards along blvd de la Libération past the Gare Maritime and Vieux Port, to Fréjus beach.

Orientation
The new centre of Saint Raphaël is neatly packed between rue Waldeck Rousseau and the promenade; the old town is immediate-ly north of rue Waldeck Rousseau off rue de la Liberté. Saint Raphaël's beach activ-ities sprawl as far east as Port Santa Lucia, some 2km east along the coast from the centre.

Maps The Maison de la Presse, opposite Saint Raphaël Mairie, rue de la Liberté, stocks a good range of city, regional and hiking maps and guides.

Information

Tourist Offices The tourist office (☎ 04 94 19 52 52, fax 04 94 83 85 40, touroff@ clubinternet.fr, www.saint-raphael.com), rue Waldeck Rousseau, opposite the train station, is open from 8.15 am to noon and 1.30 to 6 pm (closed Sunday). Hours in July and August are 8.30 am to 7 pm.

The tourist office annexe (☎ 04 94 95 42 44), Port Santa Lucia, is open the same hours. Details of day trips organised by the tourist office are listed in its free, quad-lingual newsletter, *InfoVacances*.

Post The post office is east of the tourist office on ave Victor Hugo.

Email & Internet Access Send emails home from the Blue Jibe Cybercafé (☎ 04 94 19 84 58, blue-jibe@blue-jibe.pacman.net),

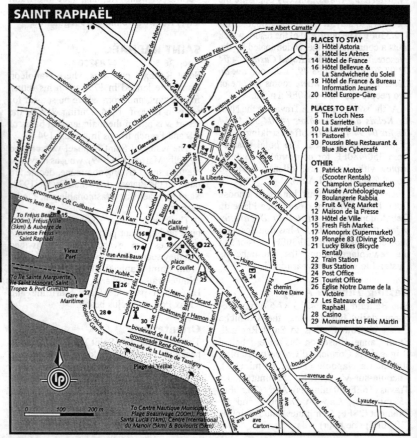

SAINT RAPHAËL

PLACES TO STAY
3 Hôtel Astoria
4 Hôtel les Arènes
14 Hôtel de France
16 Hôtel Bellevue & La Sandwicherie du Soleil
18 Hôtel de France & Bureau Information Jeunes
20 Hôtel Europe-Gare

PLACES TO EAT
5 The Loch Ness
8 La Sarriette
10 La Laverie Lincoln
11 Pastorel
20 Poussin Bleu Restaurant & Blue Jibe Cybercafé

OTHER
1 Patrick Motos (Scooter Rentals)
2 Champion (Supermarket)
6 Musée Archéologique
7 Boulangerie Rabbia
9 Fruit & Veg Market
12 Maison de la Presse
13 Hôtel de Ville
15 Fresh Fish Market
17 Monoprix (Supermarket)
19 Plongée 83 (Diving Shop)
21 Lucky Bikes (Bicycle Rental)
22 Train Station
23 Bus Station
24 Post Office
25 Tourist Office
26 Église Notre Dame de la Victoire
27 Les Bateaux de Saint Raphaël
28 Casino
29 Monument to Félix Martin

41 blvd de La Libération, inside the seafront Poussin Bleu restaurant in Saint Raphaël. Online rates are 35/60/230FF for 30 minutes/one hour/five hours. The cybercafé is open from 1 pm to midnight.

Laundry Wash your dirty linen at La Laverie Lincoln, 5 rue Jules Ferry, open from 7 am to 9 pm (8 am to 8 pm between October and March).

Beach Activities

Saint Raphaël has excellent sandy beaches including **Plage du Veillat,** the main beach; eastwards, **Plage Beaurivage** is covered in small pebbles. You can parachute (200/550FF for one/two people) and ride the waves in a rubber tyre (60FF per person) from all the beaches along this stretch of coast.

Port Santa Lucia, farther east still, is a watersports hub; the tourist office here sells a 50FF Pass Nautique Découverte entitling cardholders to try one of eight different water activities, and a 90FF Ticket Nautique valid for three hours. Sailing and kayaking lessons and guided expeditions are available at the Centre Nautique Municipal (☎ 04 94 83 84 50, cnsr@comx.fr), blvd Général de Gaulle.

Saint Raphaël is a leading **diving** centre, thanks in part to the **WWII shipwrecks** off the coast. Most diving clubs in town organise dives to the wrecks which range from a 42m-long US minesweeper to a landing craft destroyed by a rocket in 1944 during the Allied landings. Plongée 83 (☎ 04 94 95 27 18), 29 rue Waldeck Rousseau (also called ave de la Gare), and CIP Saint Raphaël Odyssée (☎ 04 94 83 66 65), Vieux Port, organise night, day and maiden dives. A baptism dive for beginners costs around 160FF (plus 60FF for equipment hire).

Les Bateaux de Saint Raphaël (☎ 04 94 95 17 46, fax 04 94 82 71 45), Gare Maritime, organises daily **boat excursions** in summer from Saint Raphaël to the Îles de Lérins (160FF return), the Fréjus and Saint Tropez gulfs (60FF return). It also runs daily

boats to Saint Tropez and Port Grimaud (see the Saint Tropez to Toulon chapter).

Special Events

Saint Raphaël's strong fishing community continues to honour its patron saint, Saint Peter, every August with a two day Fête de la Saint Pierre des Pêcheurs. Local fishermen, dressed in traditional costume, joust Provençal-style from flat-bottomed boats moored in the harbour. Later a fleet of fishing boats proceeds to the Lion de Mer.

Each year, Saint Raphaël hosts numerous Provençal jousting competitions; in summer watch out for the Société des Joutes Raphaëloises (Raphaëloises Jousting Society; ☎ 06 09 77 89 67) practising in boats around the Vieux Port.

Places to Stay

Accommodation options are not cheap; see the Fréjus section for camping options.

Hostels The *Auberge de Jeunesse Fréjus-Saint Raphaël (International Youth Hostel & Camp Site;* ☎ *04 94 53 18 75, fax 04 94 53 25 86, chemin du Counillier),* near Fréjus Ville, is set in a 7 hectare park. Dorm beds cost 66FF including breakfast; sheets are an extra 17FF and an evening meal is available for 49FF. Camp here for 32FF a night (19FF extra for breakfast). Hostelling cards (114FF) are obligatory; non cardholders pay 19FF a night (free hostelling card after six nights). The hostel also has family rooms for up to five people with washbasin and toilet for 81FF per person, including breakfast. The bad news? Guests are evacuated and the hostel closed between 10 am and 6 pm, so you have to check in between 8 and 10 am or 6 and 8 pm.

If you arrive by train, get off at Saint Raphaël, take bus No 7 to Les Chênes stop from where it is a 1km uphill walk. In July and August, bus No 6 (departing from Saint Raphaël bus station at 8.30 am and 6 pm) goes directly to the hostel. From Fréjus' train station or from place Paul Vernet bus No 3 is the best option.

CANNES REGION

The very comfortable *Centre International du Manoir (☎ 04 94 95 20 58, fax 04 94 83 85 06, chemin de l'Escale)* is 5km south-east of Saint Raphaël in Boulouris. Prices start at 110/119FF for a dorm bed/bed in a double or triple room with shower and toilet in the low season and 115/145FF in summer.

Hotels Zero-star *Hôtel les Arènes (☎ 04 94 95 06 34, fax 04 94 83 18 97, 31 ave du Général Leclerc)* is the cheapest joint in town, and has rooms for one or two people with washbasin/shower/shower and TV costing 150/190/250FF. Ranking second is *Hôtel Astoria (☎ 04 94 95 42 79)* at No 77 on the same street, which has grotty rooms with shower/shower, toilet and TV starting at 150/190FF.

The two-star *Hôtel Bellevue (☎ 04 94 19 90 10, fax 04 94 19 90 11, 24 blvd Félix Martin)* has good value singles/doubles from 150/180FF and rooms for three to five people for 190-360FF. Close by, two-star *Hôtel de France (☎ 04 94 95 19 20, fax 04 94 95 61 84, 25 place Galliéni)* has doubles/triples with shower and toilet for 249/299FF.

Places to Eat
Restaurants *The Loch Ness*, 15 ave de Valescure, is a Scottish tavern, which despite its traditional claims, serves a variety of Tex-Mex dishes (75FF), Texas ribs (55F) and Mexican steaks (59FF). Live bands play at this pub-cum-brasserie.

Tucked under the shade of a tree in the heart of the old town is small but sweet *La Sarriette (☎ 04 94 19 28 13, 45 rue de la République)*. It has 69 and 88FF *menus*, both featuring lots of local herbs and spices (closed Wednesday).

Very tempting cooking smells waft from the canary-yellow walls of *Pastorel (☎ 04 94 95 02 36, 54 rue de la Liberté)*, dating from 1922. It has a luxury 160FF *menu du marché*, well worth every centime. The restaurant is closed Sunday evening and all day Monday.

Self-Catering Self-caterers can cook up their own market menu at the succulent

fruit and vegetable market which fills the old town square every morning at the crossroads of rue de la République and rue du Peyron. There is a morning *fresh fish market* next to the jetée Pêcheurs Professionnels (Professional Fishermens' Jetty) at the Vieux Port.

Stock up on a local *tarte au fromage blanc* (fromage blanc pie), *tarte Tropézienne* (a creamy, sponge cake sandwich topped with sugar and almonds), *farinette Niçois* (Niçois bread) and *pain blanc bio* (organic white bread) at the superb *Boulangerie Rabbia (☎ 04 94 95 07 82, 29 rue Allongue)*, a family-run bakery founded in 1885.

There is a *Monoprix* supermarket at 58 blvd Félix Martin, and *Champion*, opposite Hôtel Astoria on ave du Général Leclerc. *La Sandwicherie du Soleil*, adjoining Hôtel Bellevue at 22 blvd Félix Martin, stocks a good selection of sandwiches and other lunchtime snacks.

Getting There & Away
Bus Saint Raphaël bus station (☎ 04 94 95 16 71), behind the train station on ave Victor Hugo, serves as Fréjus' main bus station too. For information on buses to/from Fréjus (☎ 04 94 53 78 46 in Fréjus) see Fréjus – Getting There & Away section.

The ticket office at Saint Raphaël bus station is open from 8.35 am to 12.30 pm and 2 to 8.35 pm (Saturday until noon; closed Sunday). It has a left luggage counter (5FF).

From Saint Raphaël, FORUM cars (☎ 04 94 95 16 71) operates daily buses to Draguignan (32FF) via Fréjus (8 FF; 1¼ hours; 9-12 daily). Beltram runs buses along the Corniche de l'Estérel (see that section earlier) to Cannes. SODETRAV (☎ 04 94 12 55 12 in Hyères runs buses to Saint Tropez (49FF; 1¼ hours; 8-10 daily) via Port Grimaud or Grimaud (43.50FF; 55 minutes) and Sainte Maxime (31FF; 35 minutes).

None of the above bus services run as frequently in winter.

Train There is a very frequent service from Nice to Gare de Saint Raphaël-Valescure (every 30 minutes), on rue Waldeck Rousseau. The information office here is open from 9.15 am to 1 pm and 2.30 to 6 pm. Some trains stop at the small, village train stations along the Corniche d'Estérel (see that section for details).

Getting Around

Lucky Bikes (☎ 04 94 95 86 35), 20 rue Waldeck Rousseau, opposite Saint Raphaël-Valescure train station, rents mountain bikes for 50/70/330FF a half-day/day/five days; it also stores bicycles. Its opening hours are 8 am to 9 pm. To hire a scooter (180FF a day), try Patrick Motos (☎ 04 94 53 65 99), 199 ave du Général Leclerc.

FRÉJUS

• pop 41,000   ✉ 83600   alt 250m

Fréjus, first settled by Massiliots (the Greek colonists from Marseille) and then colonised by Julius Caesar around 49 BC as Forum Julii, is known for its Roman ruins. Once an important port, the town was sacked by various invaders, including Muslims, from the 10th century on. Much of the town's commercial activity ceased after its harbour silted up in the 16th century.

Fréjus' golden-sand beach, known as Fréjus Plage, is lined with buildings from the 1950s. Its chic ultramodern port, full of expensive places to eat offering every shellfish imaginable at unimaginable prices, was built in the 1980s.

Fréjus Ville, the old heart of the town, hosts a colourful food market on central place Paul Albert Février on Wednesday and Saturday morning (Monday morning too between July and October). On the first and third Friday of the month a *marché brocante* (flea market) rolls into town.

Orientation & Information

Fréjus comprises the hillside Fréjus Ville, 3km from the seafront, and Fréjus Plage, on the Gulf of Fréjus. Fréjus' modern port is at the west end of blvd de la Libération and its continuation, blvd d'Alger. The Roman remains are almost all in Fréjus Ville.

Tourist Offices Fréjus tourist office (☎ 04 94 17 19 19, fax 04 91 51 00 26), 325 rue Jean Jaurès, is open from 9.30 am to noon and 3 to 7 pm (Sunday from 10 am to noon and 3 to 6 pm). Staff make hotel reservations and distribute a good map of Fréjus locating its archaeological treasures. It also organises two-hour guided city tours (25/15FF for adult/student) on Tuesday and Thursday.

From June to mid-September the tourist office kiosk (☎ 04 94 51 48 42) by the beach (opposite 11 blvd de la Libération) is open from 10 am to noon and 3 to 7 pm (until 6 pm on Sunday).

Money The Banque National de Paris, just west of the Fréjus Ville tourist office on rue Jean Jaurès, is open from 8.30 am to noon and 1.45 to 5 pm (closed on weekends).

Post The post office, rue Aristide Briand, is open from 8.30 am to 7 pm (Saturday until noon; closed Sunday). The branch at 75 rue de la Juiverie is open on Monday from 2 to 4.30 pm, Tuesday to Thursday from 9.30 am to 12.15 pm and 2 to 6.30 pm, and on Saturday from 8.30 to 11.30 am. There's another on blvd de la Libération opposite the tourist office kiosk.

Laundry Le Lavoir, 43 rue Paulin, is open from 8 am to 7 pm.

Roman Ruins

West of Fréjus' old city on rue Henri Vadon, past the ancient **Porte des Gaules**, is the mostly rebuilt 1st and 2nd century **Arènes** (amphitheatre; ☎ 04 94 17 19 19). It once sat an audience of 10,000 and is today used for rock concerts and bullfights. Its opening hours are 9 am to noon and 2 to 4.30 pm (9.30 am to noon and 2 to 6 pm between April and November). It is closed on Tuesday year round.

At the south-eastern edge of the old city is the 3rd century **Porte d'Orée**, rue des Moulins, the only arcade of the monumental Roman thermal baths still standing today. North of the old town on rue du

Théâtre Romain are the remains of a **Théâtre Romain** (Roman theatre, ☎ 04 94 17 19 19), open from 9.30 am to 5 pm (9 am to 6.30 pm between April and November; closed Tuesday year round). Part of the stage and the outer walls are all that can be seen today.

North-east, on ave du Quinzième Corps d'Armée towards La Tour de Mare, you pass the remaining section of a 40km **aqueduc** (aqueduct) which once carried water to Roman Fréjus.

Le Groupe Épiscopal

In the centre of town on place Formigé, on the site of a Roman temple, is an episcopal ensemble comprising an 11th and 12th century **cathédrale** (☎ 04 94 51 26 30), 58 rue de Fleury, one of the first Gothic buildings in the region, though it retains certain Roman features. The carved wood doors at the main entrance were added during the Renaissance.

To the left of the cathedral is the octagonal 5th century **baptistère** (baptistry), with a Roman column at each of its eight corners.

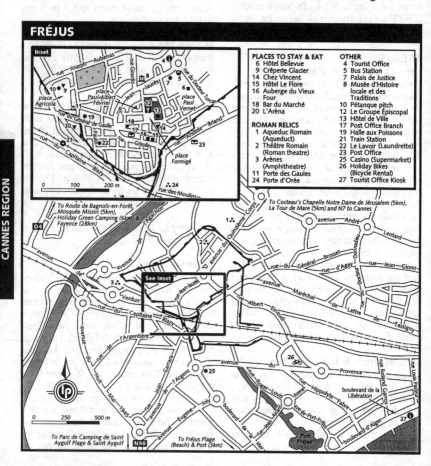

FRÉJUS

PLACES TO STAY & EAT
6 Hôtel Bellevue
9 Crêperie Glacier
14 Chez Vincent
15 Hôtel Le Flore
16 Auberge du Vieux Four
18 Bar du Marché
20 L'Arèna

ROMAN RELICS
1 Aqueduc Romain (Aqueduct)
2 Théâtre Romain (Roman theatre)
3 Arènes (Amphitheatre)
11 Porte des Gaules
24 Porte d'Orée

OTHER
4 Tourist Office
5 Bus Station
7 Palais de Justice
8 Musée d'Histoire locale et des Traditions
10 Pétanque pitch
12 Le Groupe Épiscopal
13 Hôtel de Ville
17 Post Office Branch
19 Halle aux Poissons
21 Train Station
22 Le Lavoir (Laundrette)
23 Post Office
25 Casino (Supermarket)
26 Holiday Bikes (Bicycle Rental)
27 Tourist Office Kiosk

CANNES REGION

Stairs from the narthex lead up to the stunning 11th and 13th century **cloître** (cloister) whose features include some of the columns of the Roman temple and painted wooden ceilings from the 14th and 15th centuries. It looks onto a beautiful courtyard with a well tended garden and a well.

In the cathedral's cloister is the **Musée Archéologique**, which has a marble statue of Hermes, a head of Jupiter and a magnificent 3rd century mosaic depicting a leopard. The museum is open from 9 am to noon and 2 to 5 pm (closed Tuesday); from April to October, daily hours are 9 am to 7 pm (25/15FF for adult/student which includes entry to the baptistry and cloister).

The town's history is illustrated in the **Musée d'Histoire locale et des Traditions du Pays de Fréjus** (Local History and Fréjus Traditions Museum; ☎ 04 94 51 64 01), 153 rue Jean Jaurès. Its opening hours are 9 am to noon and 2 to 6.45 pm (closed Sunday and Tuesday).

Chapelle Notre Dame de Jérusalem

This small chapel (☎ 04 94 40 76 30) was one of the last pieces of work embarked upon by Jean Cocteau (1889-1963). Cocteau, best known for the fishermen's Chapelle de Saint Pierre he decorated farther up the coast in Villefranche-sur-Mer (see the Nice to Menton chapter), started work on the chapel in 1961. The Chapelle Notre Dame in Fréjus was not completed until 1988 when Cocteau's legal heir, Édouard Dermit, completed his former companion's work. The altar is made from a millstone.

The chapel, ave François Nicolaï, is about 5km north-east of the old city in the quarter of La Tour de Mare, on the N7 towards Cannes. Its opening hours are 2 to 5 pm; until 6 pm between April and November; closed Tuesday year round (free).

Some 5km north of Fréjus on the route de Bagnols-en-Forêt (D4 towards Fayence) is the **Mosquée Missiri**, rue des Combattants d'Afrique du Nord, a mosque built in the 1920s for Sudanese troops serving at the marine base in Fréjus. It is a concrete replica of a mosque in Djenné, Mali.

Places to Stay

Hostellers note: it is equally feasible to stay in one of the two hostels in Saint Raphaël (see Saint Raphaël – Places to Stay section).

Camping Fréjus has more than a dozen camping grounds, one of the best being the four-star *Holiday Green* (☎ 04 94 19 88 30, fax 04 94 40 78 59), on the road to Bagnols, open from April to mid-October. It's 6km from the beach but has its own large pool. Nightly rates are 38/24FF per adult/child and 42/60FF per tent site in the low/high season.

Closest to the beach is the *Parc de Camping de Saint Aygulf Plage* (☎ 04 94 17 62 49, 270 ave Salvarelli) in Saint Aygulf south of Fréjus. This huge camp site, with space for more than 1600 tents, is open from April to October.

Hotels In Fréjus Ville, the 11-room, no-star *Hôtel Bellevue* (☎ 04 94 51 39 04, fax 04 94 51 35 20, place Paul Vernet) has basic singles/doubles from 149/170FF; doubles with shower 280FF. The two-star *Auberge du Vieux Four* (☎ 04 94 51 56 38, 49 rue Grisolle) has well kept singles/doubles with shower and toilet for 200/250FF, and a good restaurant too! Next door at No 35, two-star *Hôtel Le Flore* (☎ 04 94 51 38 35, fax 04 94 52 28 20) has rooms from 180FF.

At Fréjus Plage, the 27-room *Hôtel L'Oasis* (☎ 04 94 51 50 44, impasse Jean-Baptiste Charcot), set amidst pine trees, has comfortable room with TV for 350FF. It is closed from November to mid-February. Also at Fréjus Plage is the *Hôtel Sable et Soleil* (☎ 04 94 51 08 70, fax 04 94 53 49 12, 158 ave Paul Arène) facing an ugly car park, where doubles cost 240/350FF in the low/high season. The Sand and Sun has facilities for disabled people.

Places to Eat

Bar du Marché (place de la Liberté) has a busy outside terrace and serves giant pizzas from 38FF. *L'Arèna*, a Logis de France inn at the west end of rue Général de Gaulle, is a more upmarket choice. The *Crêperie Glacier* (☎ 04 94 53 36 92, place Agricola) is the best bet for sweet treats – crêpes start at 21FF and savoury pizzas at 30FF (open from 11 am to 6 pm). Alternatively, try *Chez Vincent (15 rue Desaugiers)* behind the cathedral.

Self-caterers can buy fresh fish at the *Halle aux Poissons*, 122 rue du Général de Gaulle, There is a *Casino* supermarket south of the centre on the Rond Point de la Mougrano.

Getting There & Away
Bus Fréjus bus station (☎ 04 94 53 78 46), place Paul Vernet, is only served by local buses to/from Saint Raphaël (10.50FF; 20-27 minutes). The information kiosk here is open from 9 am to 12.15 pm and 1.35 to 5.40 pm (Saturday until noon; closed Sunday).

Bus No 5, run by Estérel Buses (☎ 04 94 53 78 46), links Fréjus' train station and place Paul Vernet with Saint Raphaël. Buses No 6 and 7 runs between place Paul Vernet and Saint Raphaël; bus No 6 follows the coastal road while No 7 follows inland ave de Provence.

Train Fréjus train station (information ☎ 08 36 35 35 35) is on the Nice-Marseille rail route, but few trains stop here (some three a day). However, there is a very frequent service to/from Saint Raphaël.

Getting Around
Bus Bus No 6 links the beaches of Fréjus-Plage with place Paul Vernet in Fréjus-Ville.

Bicycle Cycles Patrick Bèraud (☎ 04 94 51 20 20), 337 rue de Triberg, Fréjus-Ville rents mountain bikes. Holiday Bikes (☎ 04 94 52 30 65), on the corner of rue de Triberg and ave de Provence, rents bicycles from 70FF and scooters/motorcycles from 215/320FF a day. Daily hours are 9 am to noon and 2.30 to 7 pm.

Saint Tropez to Toulon

In 1956 Saint Tropez was the setting for the film *Et Dieu Créa la Femme* (And God Created Woman), starring Brigitte Bardot. Its stunning success brought about Saint Tropez's rise to stardom – or destruction – depending on your viewpoint. But one thing is clear: the peaceful little fishing village of Saint Tropez, somewhat isolated from the rest of the Côte d'Azur at the end of its own peninsula, suddenly became the favourite of the jet set. Ever since, Saint Tropez has lived on its sexy image.

Inland from Saint Tropez, medieval Les Arcs-sur-Argens is equidistant (31km) between the coastal towns of Saint Raphaël and Sainte Maxime. Ten kilometres further north is Pays Dracénois (literally 'country of the Dracénois) with Draguignan at its heart.

West from Saint Tropez sprawls a wild, remote and heavily forested massif smothered with fine pine, chestnut and cork oak trees. Its vegetation makes it appear almost black and gives rise to the name Massif des Maures, which is derived from the Provençal word *mauro* (dark pine wood).

The arc-shaped massif stretches from Fréjus in the north-east to Hyères in the south-west. Its inland northern boundary is roughly marked by the A8 autoroute, which splits into the A57 at Le-Cannet-des-Maures before making its descent towards Hyères and Toulon on the coast.

Pretty, palm tree lined Hyères lies 20km east of Toulon and 22km west of Le Lavandou. While the town is mainly used as a launch pad for day trips to the golden islands of Hyères, the medieval streets in its Vieille Ville (Old Town) are worth a wander.

The alluring Îles d'Hyères, each about 15km off the coast between Le Lavandou and Hyères, are a delight to explore and easily accessible by boat year round.

Toulon is France's most important naval port, serving as a base for the French navy's Mediterranean fleet. As a result of heavy bombing in WWII, the city's run-down

HIGHLIGHTS

- See works by the world's great pointillists, fauvists and cubists at Saint Tropez's Musée de l'Annonciade
- Go island hopping around the golden Îles d'Hyères
- Hike around the Chartreuse de la Verne monastery in the Massif des Maures
- Go window-shopping in Saint Tropez and sip pastis at the Vieux Port
- Sample a dozen different Côtes de Provence wines in Les Arcs-sur-Argens, then lunch at the Domaine de la Maurette

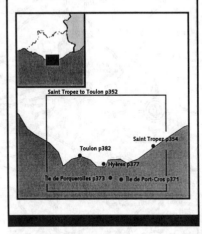

Saint Tropez to Toulon p352
Saint Tropez p354
Toulon p382
Hyères p377
Île de Porquerolles p373
Île de Port-Cros p371

centre looks very grim when compared to Nice, Cannes or even Marseille – some would say downright ugly, in fact.

Farther west, the islands off Toulon's shores, dubbed the Îles du Fun (Islands of Fun), were acquired by French industrialist Paul Ricard in the 1950s and rapidly transformed into concrete playgrounds.

SAINT TROPEZ TO TOULON

351

Saint Tropez

• pop 5700   ✉ 83990

Attempts to keep Saint Tropez small and exclusive have created at least one tangible result: huge traffic queues into town. Yachts, way out of proportion to the size of the old harbour and irritatingly blocking the view, chased away the simple fishing boats a long time ago. Painters jostle each other for easel space along the quay, and in summer there's little of the intimate village air that artists such as the pointillist Paul Signac found so alluring.

Still, sitting in a café on place des Lices in late May, watching the locals playing pétanque in the shade of the age-old plane trees, is pleasant enough – as is that seductive image of Saint Tropez from out at sea. Arriving by boat, the yellow and orange-painted church tower crowned with a typically Provençal campanile stands beautifully aloft amid the sloping roofs and sprawling citadel.

Once seen, never forgotten is the fantastic food, flower and clothing market which is

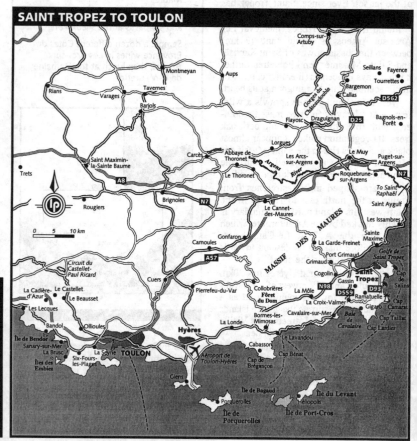

SAINT TROPEZ TO TOULON

ernand Lèger mosaic, Biot

Villefranche-sur-Mer harbour

a Bastide de Moustiers, chef Alain Ducasse' hotel in Moustiers Sainte Marie

View over Monaco

also an antique fair and fills place des Lices on Tuesday and Saturday morning. Equally memorable is the spectacle of stupidly rich people dining aboard their floating palaces within spitting distance of the crowds gathered on the prom to gawk at them eating dinner.

Tropeziens call Saint Tropez 'Saint Trop' (literally, Saint Too Much). Rather apt, really.

History

The Greeks founded Athenopolis here and were followed by the Romans in 31 BC who called it Heraclea. Saint Tropez gained its contemporary name in 68 AD when a boat landed on its shores bearing the decapitated body of the Roman officer, Torpes, whom Nero had beheaded in Pisa for his conversion to Christianity. The village adopted the headless Torpes as their saint.

A syphilis-ridden Maupassant (1850-93) arrived in Saint Tropez in 1887. Signac (1863-1935) followed five years later, exclaiming upon arrival in his boat *L'Olympia*, 'Je ne fais pas escale. Je me fixe!' ('I'm not just stopping here. I'm staying!'). Sexy Saint Trop has not looked back since – Colette, Pagnol, Matisse, Marlène Dietrich, Bardot, Johnny Hallyday, Pink Floyd (As I reach for a peach/Slide a line down behind a sofa in San Tropez) George Michael, Joan Collins, Mohammad Al-Fayed ...

Torpedoes have been manufactured at the Usine de Gassin in Saint Tropez since 1912.

Orientation

Saint Tropez lies at the southern end of the narrow Bay of Saint Tropez, opposite the Massif des Maures. The old city is packed between quai Jean Jaurès, the main quay of the Vieux Port (Old Port); place des Lices, a shady rectangular 'square' a few blocks inland; and what's left of the 16th century citadel overlooking the town from the north-east.

Saint Tropez's flashy visiting floating palaces are moored alongside quai Suffren. There are public toilets and showers for the less fortunate inside the Bureau du Port

building, quai de l'Épi, the continuation of quai Bouchard.

Information

Tourist Offices The tourist office (☎ 04 94 97 45 21, fax 04 94 97 82 66, tourisme@ nova.fr, www.nova.fr/saint-tropez), quai Jean Jaurès, is open from 9.30 am to 1 pm and 3.30 to 8.30 pm. Winter hours are shorter. Between April and October, it organises guided tours (☎ 04 94 55 98 56, fax 04 94 55 98 59) of Saint Tropez, Gassin and Ramatuelle in English (20/10FF for adult/child).

Money At the port, Crédit Lyonnais, 21 quai Suffren, is open from 8 am to noon and 1.30 to 4.45 pm (closed on weekends). It has a 24-hour exchange machine. The Thomas Cook branch (☎ 04 94 97 88 00), 10 rue Allard, one street from the port, is open from 9 am to 4.30 pm (8.30 am to 9.30 pm from June to September; closed on weekends).

Overlooking place des Lices, Cambio Change, corner of rue Joseph Quaranta and rue des Charrons, is open from 9 am to noon and 4 to 10 pm. It has a second outlet, 9 ave du Général Leclerc, close to the bus station.

Post The post office, place Celli, is open from 9 am to 5.30 pm (Saturday until noon; closed Sunday). It has an exchange service.

Bookshop Buy English-language newspapers, magazines and guides to the region from the Maison de la Presse on quai Suffren.

Laundry C'est Wash, 19 ave du Général Leclerc, is open from 8 am to 11 pm. La Bugade, 5 rue Quaranta, is open from 7 am to 10 pm.

Walking Tour

The **Vieux Port** – the heart of the *vie Tropézienne* (Tropezien life) – is as good a place as any to take a stroll and watch the antics of the rich and not so famous. From the south-east side of the port, on quai Suffren, a **statue of** the **Bailli de Suffren** cast from a 19th century cannon peers out to sea. The Bailiff of Suffren (1729-88), a sailor, fought with a Tropezien crew against Britain and Prussia during the Seven Years' War. The west side of the port is dominated by the Musée de l'Annonciade (see that section later).

In a backstreet one block south-west of quai Péri is **La Maison des Papillons** (House of Butterflies; ☎ 04 94 97 63 45), 9 rue Étienne Berny. Some 4500 of the colourful winged creatures are pinned to the wall. The 1st floor collection of European species is the collection of Dany Lartigue, son of Riviera photographer, Jacques Henri Lartigue (1894-1986). The cottage in which the museum is housed was the Lartigue home until 1993 when Dany donated it to the town. Family photos taken by his father line the staircase. Between April and September the museum is open from 10 am to noon and 3 to 7 pm daily except Tuesday; from October to March the daily hours are 3 to 6 pm (20FF).

The old fishermen's quarter of **La Ponche** lies north-east of the Vieux Port. To get to

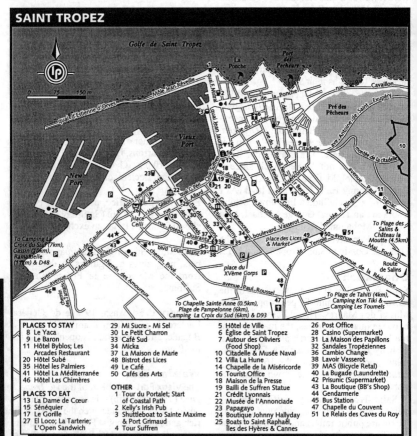

SAINT TROPEZ

PLACES TO STAY	29 Mi Sucre - Mi Sel	5 Hôtel de Ville	26 Post Office
8 Le Yaca	30 Le Petit Charron	6 Église de Saint Tropez	28 Casino (Supermarket)
9 Le Baron	33 Café Sud	7 Autour des Oliviers	31 La Maison des Papillons
11 Hôtel Byblos; Les	34 Micka	(Food Shop)	32 Sandales Tropéziennes
Arcades Restaurant	37 La Maison de Marie	10 Citadelle & Musée Naval	36 Cambio Change
20 Hôtel Subé	48 Bistrot des Lices	12 Villa La Hune	38 Lavoir Vasserot
35 Hôtel les Palmiers	49 Le Café	14 Chapelle de la Miséricorde	39 MAS (Bicycle Retal)
41 Hôtel La Méditerranée	50 Cafés des Arts	16 Tourist Office	40 La Bugade (Laundrette)
46 Hôtel Les Chimères		18 Maison de la Presse	42 Prisunic (Supermarket)
	OTHER	19 Bailli de Suffren Statue	43 La Boutique (BB's Shop)
PLACES TO EAT	1 Tour du Portalet; Start	21 Crédit Lyonnais	44 Gendarmerie
13 La Dame de Cœur	of Coastal Path	22 Musée de l'Annonciade	45 Bus Station
15 Sénéquier	2 Kelly's Irish Pub	23 Papagayo	47 Chapelle du Couvent
17 Le Gorille	3 Shuttleboat to Sainte Maxime	24 Boutique Johnny Hallyday	51 Le Relais des Caves du Roy
27 El Loco; La Tarterie;	& Port Grimaud	25 Boats to Saint Raphaël,	
L'Open Sandwich	4 Tour Suffren	Îles des Hyères & Cannes	

the original fishing harbour (where Signac and company docked) from quai Suffren, walk to the northern end of its continuations, quai Jean Jaurès and quai Frédéric Mistral. At the 15th century **Tour du Portalet** (Portalet Tower), turn right (east) to the sandy fishing cove. From here a coastal path snakes its way around the Saint Tropez peninsula (see Coastal Walks later).

From the south end of quai Frédéric Mistral, place Garrezio sprawls east from the 10th century **Tour Suffren** to place de l'Hôtel de Ville. From here, rue Guichard leads south-east to the early 19th century **Église de Saint Tropez**, built in an Italian baroque style on place de l'Ormeau. Inside, in one of the side chapels, is a bust of Saint Tropez which is carried through the streets during Les Bravades (see Special Events later).

A 16th century **citadelle** dominates the hillside overlooking Saint Tropez to the east. A **Musée Naval** (☎ 04 94 97 59 43) occupies its former dungeon. The museum houses an exhibition on the town's maritime history and displays on the Allied landings here in August 1944. It is open daily except Tuesday from 10 am to 5 or 6 pm (25/15FF for adult/ student).

Steps lead from the east end of rue de la Citadelle, up montée de la Citadelle, to the citadel. Good photographs of Saint Tropez can be had from the citadel grounds. Ave Paul Signac, the road that runs along the southern edge of the grounds, is named after the painter who lived on this street in **Villa La Hune** from 1897.

South of rue de la Citadelle on rue Miséricorde is the 17th century **Chapelle de la Miséricorde** (1645) with its pretty bell tower and dome, decorated with green, yellow and brown ceramic tiles. One block farther south is **place des Lices** whose 200m length is lined with plane trees and pétanque players. The **Chapelle du Couvent** (1757) and **Chapelle Sainte Anne** (1618) lie about 0.7km and 1.5km south of here respectively along ave Augustin Grangeon. Inside Saint Anne's Chapel, there is an impressive collection of ex-voto paintings and centuries-old miniature boats given by Tropezien fishermen. They can be viewed once a year – on 26 July, the feast day of Saint Anne.

Musée de l'Annonciade

The graceful Musée de l'Annonciade (☎ 04 94 97 04 01), in an early 16th century chapel on place Grammont, Vieux Port, contains an impressive collection of modern art, with works by Matisse, Bonnard, Dufy, Derain, Rouault and Signac.

The pointilist collection in the first room on the 2nd floor includes Signac's *Saint Tropez, l'oragé* (1895), *Saint Tropez, le quai* (1899) and *Saint Tropez – le sentier côtier* (1901). The second room, dedicated to the fauvist period, boasts Matisse's *La Gitane* (The Gypsy; 1905-06). Matisse spent the summer of 1904 in Saint Tropez, starting preliminary studies for *Luxe, Calme et Volupté* while he was here. The cubists are also represented.

The museum is open between December and May from 10 am to noon and 2 to 6 pm; between June and September from 10 am to noon and 3 to 7 pm; closed on Tuesday year round and during November (30/15FF for adult/ student).

Interesting summer art exhibitions are held in the early 19th century **Lavoir Vasserot**, rue Quaranta, the former public wash-house.

Beaches

About 4km south-east of the town is the start of a magnificent sandy beach, **Plage de Tahiti**, and its continuation, **Plage de Pampelonne**, overlooking the Baie de Pampelonne (Pampelonne Bay). It runs for about 9km between Cap du Pinet and the rocky Cap Camarat which is dominated by France's second-tallest *phare* (lighthouse), dating from the 19th century and standing 130m tall. To get to the beach on foot, head out of town along ave de la Résistance (south of place des Lices) to route de la Belle Isnarde and then route de Tahiti. Otherwise, the bus to Ramatuelle, a village south of Saint Tropez, stops at points along a road that runs about 1km inland from the beach.

On the southern side of Cap Camarat is a secluded *naturiste* (nudist) beach, **Plage de l'Escalet**. Several streams also attract bathers in the buff. To get there take the bus to Ramatuelle, but you'll have to walk or, if lucky, hitch the 4km south-east to the beach.

Closer to Saint Tropez is **Plage des Salins**, a long and wide sandy beach 4.5km east of town at the southern foot of Cap des Salins. To get here, follow route des Salins to its end. En route you pass **La Treille Muscate** (The Wine Trellis), a rambling villa framed with red-ochre columns wrapped in honeysuckle. In 1927 Colette wrote *La Naissance du Jour*, which evokes a 1920s unspoilt Saint Tropez, here. After she left the town in 1938, two further villas, named after her novels, were built on the grounds.

At the north end of Plage des Salins, on a rock jutting out to sea, is the **tomb of Émile Olivier** (1825-1913), who served as first minister to Napoléon III until his exile in 1870. Olivier's 17-volume *L'Empire Libéral* is preserved in the library of the **Château La Moutte**, his former home on Cap des Salins overlooking the beach. Musical soirées are held in summer in the chateau. The unmarked entrance to the chateau is on chemin de la Moutte, the road running parallel (to the north) with route des Salins. A sand track leads from the car park at the end of chemin de la Moutte to the beach.

Olivier's sea-facing tomb looks out towards **La Tête de Chien** (The Dog's Head), a rocky islet named after the legendary dog who was flung in the boat, along with a cock, to eat the decapitated remains of St Torpes. Thankfully for the Tropeziens, neither did. The ultramodern seaside villa at the south end of Plage des Salins was built for a princess of Greece. Farther south, **Pointe du Capon** is a beautiful cape crisscrossed with walking trails. BB – Brigitte Bardot – lives here. She donated her 1960s home, the celebrated **Villa La Madrague** overlooking Baie des Cannebiers, in 1991 to the Fondation Brigitte Bardot, an animal activist campaign group which the actress set up in Saint Trop in 1986 (today headquartered in Paris).

Coastal Walks

A *sentier littoral* (coastal path) leads 35km south from Saint Tropez to the beach of Cavalaire, and around the Saint Tropez peninsula as far west as Le Lavandou (60km). The picturesque path, challenging at points, takes you around splendid rocky outcrops and hidden bays. In parts the setting is reminiscent of the tropics, minus the coconut palms.

In Saint Tropez, the coastal path, flagged with *un balisage jaune* (a yellow marker), starts at **La Ponche**, immediately east of the Tour du Portalet at the north end of quai Frédéric Mistral. From here, trails lead to Baie des Cannebiers (2.7km; 50 minutes), La Moutte (7.4km; two hours), Plage des Salins (8.5km; 2½ hours) and Plage de Tahiti (12km; 3½ hours). If the distance is too great, walk one way and return by bus (see Getting Around for bus details). Alternatively, drive to the end of route des Salins, from where it is a shorter walk along the coastal path to Plage de Tahiti (2.7km; 45 minutes) and the naturiste Plage de la Moutte (1.7km; 30 minutes) on the north side of Cap des Salins.

Cap Lardier, the peninsula's southernmost cape, falls under the protection of the Parc National de Port-Cros (see later). Motorised vehicles are forbidden on the rocky headland which is frequented by large colonies of birds and smaller schools of dolphins. The Maison du Cap Lardier in **Gigaro** has information on the park.

The pocket-size *Promenez-vous à pied – Le Golfe de Saint Tropez* (45FF) details 26 hikes around Saint Tropez.

Boat Excursions

The regular daily boats that sail from Saint Tropez to Saint Raphaël, and the summer boats to Sainte Maxime, Port Grimaud, Les Issambres and around the Baie des Cannebiers, make for a jolly day out. See Getting There & Away later.

Special Events

Guns blaze and flags flutter in Saint Tropez on 15 June during the *Bravades des Espagnols*, a festival held to mark Saint Tropez's victory over 22 Spanish galleons that attacked the port on 15 June 1637. The militaristic street processions are led by a nominated *Capitaine de Ville* who, between 1481 and 1672 when Saint Tropez enjoyed a special autonomy, served as captain of the town.

On 16 May, Saint Torpes' day, another bravade has been celebrated since 1558. During this festival the town captain, followed by an army of 140 musket-firing *bravadeurs*, move through the street bearing a bust of the saint.

Places to Stay – Budget & Mid-Range

Surprise, surprise! There's not a cheap hotel, let alone a hostel, to be found in Saint Tropez. However, the beach is free and, though it's technically illegal to sleep there, backpackers making Zs are occasionally tolerated.

Camping To the south-east of Saint Tropez, along Plage de Pampelonne, there are plenty of multi-starred camping grounds. Overlooking the north end of Plage de Pampelonne is *Camping Kon Tiki* (☎ 04 94 55 96 96, fax 04 94 55 96 95, 100776.3460@compuserve.com, route des Tamaris), which charges 114FF a night for two people with a tent and car. It is open from mid-March to October.

Rates at the four-star *Camping Les Tournels* (☎ 04 94 55 90 90, fax 04 94 55 90 99, route de Camarat), on Cap Camarat, are 103FF for a two person tent and car site. In July and August the nightly rate is 142FF. Les Tournels is open from mid-February to December.

Camping La Croix du Sud (☎ 04 94 79 80 84, fax 04 94 79 89 21, route des Plages) is 7km south of Saint Tropez on the road to Ramatuelle (D93). Nightly rates here for two campers with car and tent is 122/135FF in the low/high season. The site is open from 1 April to mid-October.

Hotels Cheapest is the dingy, 13-room *Hôtel La Méditerranée* (☎ 04 94 97 00 44, fax 04 94 97 47 83, 21 blvd Louis Blanc). Doubles

start at 200FF. One notch up the price ladder is the *Hôtel Les Chimères* (☎ 04 94 97 02 90, fax 04 94 97 63 57), Port du Pilon, at the south-western end of ave du Général Leclerc. Singles/doubles with shower and breakfast cost 328/358FF. This hotel is closed from mid-November to mid-December and from January to mid-February.

Well worth the cash is the calm and quiet, three-star *Le Baron* (☎ 04 94 97 06 57, fax 04 94 97 58 72, 23 rue de l'Aïoli) at the foot of the citadel. Rooms with TV and bath cost 350-450FF. The 10-room Baron is open year round.

The *Hôtel les Palmiers* (☎ 04 94 97 01 61, fax 04 94 97 10 02, 26 blvd Vasserot) offers a star view of place des Lices' pétanque players from its square-facing rooms. Fully equipped doubles cost from 300/520FF in the low/high season.

Places to Stay – Top End

Saint Tropez's top end hotels are open from around Easter to mid-October.

The town's most choice, and among the Côte d'Azur's most sumptuous, is the four-star *Hôtel Byblos* (☎ 04 94 97 00 04, fax 04 94 56 68 01, saint-tropez@byblos.com, ave Paul Signac), near the citadel. Outside, it is painted in muted colours of the rainbow, from terracotta to lavender-blue. Inside, luxurious rooms warranting no complaints cost 1500-3070FF depending on the season. Its restaurant, Les Arcades, is equally worthy of a postcard home.

Rooms with a seaview at delightful, four-star *Le Yaca* (☎ 04 94 55 81 00, fax 04 94 97 58 50, nova@nova.fr, 1 blvd d'Aumale), in the heart of the old town, start at 1250/1650FF in the low/high season. Rooms with sea view and terrace are 2000/2300FF and suites are even more! Breakfast is an awe-inspiring 90FF.

The 32-room, *Hôtel Subé* (☎ 04 94 54 89 08, fax 04 94 54 89 08, sube@nova.fr), behind the Bailli de Suffren statue on quai Suffren, has plush rooms with a port view for 990/1500FF in the low/high season and rooms with a garden view from 390/590FF. The reception resembles the deck of a sailing boat; the hotel entrance is in the passage du Port. The Subé is open all year.

Places to Eat

Don't leave Saint Trop without sampling a sweet and creamy *tarte Tropézienne*, a sponge cake sandwich filled with custard-cream and topped with sugar and almonds.

Restaurants Quai Jean Jaurès is lined with restaurants, most with *menus* from 100 or 150FF and a strategic view of the silverware and crystal of those dining on the decks of their yachts.

Extremely tasteful and not *too* expensive by Tropezien standards is the informal *Café Sud* (☎ 04 94 97 42 52), tucked down a narrow street off places des Lices at 12 rue Étienne Berny. It has a 140FF *menu* and tables are outside in a star-topped courtyard. House specialities include *beignets de langouste* (crayfish fritters) served with an apple and mango julienne for 95FF. The 'South Café' has a second outlet, *La Plage des Jumeaux* (☎ 04 94 79 84 21, route de l'Épi) on the beach overlooking the legendary Baie de Pampelonne. Don't miss its deliciously stuffed *petits farcis Provençaux* (Provençal filled vegetables). The *courgette* (zucchini) flowers are delicious.

Close by, the *Bistrot des Lices* (☎ 04 94 97 29 00, 3 places des Lices) serves traditional Provençal cuisine, including wonderful ratatouille. *La Maison de Marie* (☎ 04 94 97 09 99, 2 rue Quaranta) is a large garden restaurant shaded by trees (entrance at 26 rue des Charrons).

Le Petit Charron (☎ 04 94 97 73 78, 5 rue Charrons) is another inviting bet with an enticing *menu* for 150 or 180FF. Don't miss the *crème brûlée à la fleur de lavande* (crème brûlée scented with sweet lavender). Reservations are recommended. Cheap by Saint Trop standards is *La Dame de Cœur* (☎ 04 94 97 23 16, 2 rue de la Miséricorde). No name is signposted outside; look for the Queen of Hearts playing card sign.

Cafés Saint Tropez's most famous café is the Café des Arts, next to the cinema on place des Lices (corner of traverse des Lices), where artists and intellectuals have been meeting for years. The historic café is called *Le Café* today, not to be confused with the newer, red-canopied *Café des Arts* on the corner of place des Lices and ave du Mai Foch. Despite its copycat name, it has no connection with the former haunt of BB and her glam friends (and foe).

Another good people-watching spot, also with a large terrace filled with red tables and chairs, is the buzzing *Sénéquier* (☎ 04 94 97 00 90 or 04 94 97 08 98) on quai Jean Jaurès overlooking the Vieux Port (closed from mid-November to mid-December). Sartre is said to have written parts of *Les Chemins de la Liberté* here. *Le Gorille*, on the same quai, is open 24 hours and is a perfect place for breakfast after dancing the night away.

El Loco (☎ 04 94 97 52 82, 1 place Celli) is a trendy Mexican-style joint adjoining *La Tarterie*, a good value hole-in-the-wall place serving sweet and savoury tarts. Freshly-made sandwiches are stylishly doled out from *L'Open Sandwich* next door. Substantially more down to earth is *Mi Sucre – Mi Sel* (☎ 04 94 97 18 76, 20 rue Allard) which serves well filled sandwiches for around 18FF. Its hours are 7 am to 8 pm.

Self-Catering The place des Lices *market* is held on Tuesday and Saturday mornings; the one on place aux Herbes behind quai Jean Jaurès is open daily until about noon. Supermarket *Prisunic* (9 ave du Général Leclerc) is open from 8 am to 8 pm (closed Sunday). Opening hours at *Casino* (37 rue Allard) are 7.30 am to 2.30 pm and 4 to 9 pm (8 am to 1 pm and 5 to 8 pm on Sunday).

Micka (36 rue Georges Clémenceau) sells tartes Tropéziennes – which the boulanger first cooked up in neighbouring Cogolin. *Autour des Oliviers* (☎ 04 94 97 64 31, 2 place de l'Ormeau) is the place to go for Provençal olive oil.

Tropezien wines can be tried and tested at *La Cave de Saint Tropez* (☎ 04 94 97 01 60), opposite Parc des Lices.

SAINT TROPEZ TO TOULON

Entertainment

The top spot to dance the night away, and maybe rub shoulders with a star or two, is *Le Relais des Caves du Roy (☎ 04 94 56 68 20, ave Foch)*, a bistro-style place with an Italian inspired menu and an extravagantly flood-lit terrace. *Papagayo (Résidence du Port)*, a restaurant, nightclub and terrace bar overlooking the port from quai Bouchard, is another favourite.

Kelly's Irish Pub (☎ 04 94 54 89 11, quai Frédéric Mistral) is as un-Irish as most Irish pubs along the French coast come. Its opening hours are 10.30 to 1 am in the low season and 10.30 to 3 am in the high season.

Shopping

Saint Tropez is loaded with expensive designer boutiques, gourmet food shops and galleries overflowing with bad art.

La Boutique, place Croix de Fer, is a small gift shop supporting the animal welfare charity, Fondation Brigitte Bardot. Postcards on sale portray BB sitting among her furry friends, looking like the Virgin Mary herself as she calls on the faithful. La Boutique is open from 10 am to 1 pm and 4 to 7 pm (closed Sunday).

Boutique Johnny Hallyday (☎ 04 94 97 87 56), Résidence du Port, overlooking ave du 11 Novembre 1918, sells overpriced T-shirts, shirts and jeans embossed with the Hallyday logo.

Traditional Tropezien sandals, said to have been inspired by a pair of simple leather sandals bought by Colette from Greece to show her local cobbler, are sold at Sandales Tropéziennes (☎ 04 94 97 19 55), 16 rue Georges Clémenceau.

Getting There & Away

Bus St Tropez bus station (☎ 04 94 97 88 51), ave du Général de Gaulle, is on the main road out of town on the south-western edge. The information office (☎ 04 94 54 62 36) is open from 8.20 am to 12.40 pm and 1.50 to 8 pm (until noon Saturday; closed Sunday).

Buses to Ramatuelle (16.50FF; 40 minutes; five daily) and Gassin (16.50FF; 50 minutes; three daily), two villages in the middle of the

peninsula, leave from the bus station and run parallel to the coast about 1km inland.

SODETRAV (☎ 04 94 12 55 00 or 04 94 12 55 12 in Hyères) also runs buses to Saint Raphaël bus station (49FF; 1¼ hours; 8-10 daily), via Grimaud or Port Grimaud (19FF; 20 minutes), Sainte Maxime (24FF; 40 minutes) and Fréjus (48FF; one hour). Buses to Toulon (95FF; 2¼ hours) go inland before joining the coast at Cavalaire; they also stop at Le Lavandou (70FF; one hour) and Hyères (77FF; 1¼ hours).

There are daily buses to Aéroport de Hyères-Toulon (100FF; one hour). See the Getting Around chapter for details.

Boat Between April and July, Les Bateaux de Saint Raphaël (☎ 04 94 95 17 46, fax 04 94 83 88 55 in Saint Raphaël) runs two boats daily from Saint Tropez to Saint Raphaël (50FF; 50 minutes). Boats depart from the new harbour, from the jetty off ave du 8 Mai 1945 opposite the bus station.

Between July and September, Compagnie CR Navigation (☎ 04 94 62 41 14, or 04 92 98 71 30) operates three boats a week to Port-Cros (1¼ hours) and Porquerolles (1¾ hours), two of the three Îles d'Hyères. Boats depart from Saint Tropez at 10.15 am on Thursday, Friday and Sunday. A round-trip ticket costs 160FF. The same company also runs seasonal boats to Cannes (three times a week) and Nice (twice weekly).

In July and August only, MMG (☎ 04 94 96 51 00, fax 04 94 96 25 41 in Sainte Maxime, www.nova.fr/mmg) operates a *navette regulière* (regular shuttleboat) service from Saint Tropez to Sainte Maxime (32FF; 30 minutes; 26 daily), Port Grimaud (26FF; 20 minutes; 11 daily) and Les Issambres (34FF; 20 minutes; nine daily). It also organises boat excursions around the Baie des Cannebiers. Boats depart from the *embarcadère* (pier) off quai Jean Jaurès, Vieux Port. Tickets are sold five minutes before departure from the kiosk here.

Getting Around

Bus In July and August a free minibus shuttles lazy tourists from the car park opposite the bus station to/from ave du Général Leclerc, ave Gambetta (place des Lices) and quai Suffren (Vieux Port). In July and August, it runs between 9 am and midnight (from 8 am on Tuesday and Saturday). Hours in September are 9 am to 12.45 pm and 3 to 7 pm (9 am to midnight on weekends).

The Ramatuelle bus (five daily) stops at Plage de Pampelonne.

Taxi To order a taxi, ring ☎ 04 94 97 05 27.

Bicycle MAS (☎/fax 04 94 97 00 60), 3-5 rue Joseph Quaranta, rents mountain bikes/scooters for 80/190-290FF a day (plus 2000/2500FF deposit). The shop is open from 9 am to 7 pm (until 3 pm on Sunday).

There are several hire places along ave du Général Leclerc. Location Espace 83 (☎ 04 94 55 80 00), 2 ave du Général Leclerc (entrance in the bus station), rents bicycles for 100/600FF a day/week (deposit 3500FF). Scooters 80/125cc start at 295/330FF a day and 600/1200cc motorcycles cost from 660/1200FF a day. Its opening hours are 9 am to 12.30 pm and 2 to 8 pm.

Boat To order a taxi boat call Taxi de Mer (☎ 06 09 53 15 47), 5 Quartier Neuf. It sails between Easter and October from 10 to 2 am.

GASSIN & RAMATUELLE
The sparsely populated interior of the **Presqu'île de Saint Tropez** (Saint Tropez peninsula) is crossed by sprawling vineyards and a handful of narrow roads which link the medieval *villages perchés* (perched villages) of Gassin and Ramatuelle to the coast.

Gassin (pop 2600; postcode 83580; alt 200m), 11km south-west of Saint Tropez, is classified as one of France's *plus beau* (most beautiful) villages. Its narrow streets, which wend their way up to the 16th century **église** (1558) topping the rocky promontory, are a delight to stroll. In summer, the village hosts a colourful array of cultural events, including contemporary art exhibitions in the Foyer des Campagnes (☎ 04 94 56 28 89), rue Longue.

From Gassin, the route des Moulins de Paillas snakes 3km south-east, past the ruins of ancient **windmills**, to **Ramatuelle** (pop 1945; postcode 83350; alt 136m), 10km south of Saint Tropez via the D61. The fruits of the peninsula's lush vineyards – Côtes de Provence wines – can be tested at Les Celliers de Ramatuelle (☎ 04 94 79 23 60), about 1km east of the village on the D93 towards La Croix Valmer. The two-week Festival de Ramatuelle (☎ 04 94 79 20 50), held at the beginning of August, brings live jazz and theatre to the streets.

Between Easter and September, the tourist office in Saint Tropez and the Ramatuelle tourist office (☎ 04 94 79 26 04, fax 04 94 79 12 66), place de l'Ormeau, organise guided tours of both villages (20/10FF for adult/teenager).

GOLFE DE SAINT TROPEZ
The Gulf of Saint Tropez, north-west of Saint Tropez, is dominated by the brash resort of **Sainte Maxime** at the north end of the bay, and the more pleasing, architectural wonder of **Port Grimaud**, 8km south-west along the coast. In summer, shuttle boats plough their way back and forth across the gulf between Saint Tropez and the two resorts.

Accommodation can be booked through the Maison du Tourisme – Golfe de Saint Tropez (☎ 04 94 43 42 10 or 04 94 43 40 70, fax 04 94 43 42 78 or 04 94 43 42 77, semgst@franceplus.com, www.franceplus.com/golfe.de.st-tropez), overlooking the busy roundabout in Carrefour de la Foux, 2km south of Port Grimaud, on the N98. The centre is open from 9 am to 7 pm (on Saturday from 10 am to 6 pm; closed Sunday). Hours in July and August are 9 am to 8 pm (on weekends from 10 am to 7 pm).

Sainte Maxime
• pop 12,000   ✉ 83120

Sandy-beached Sainte Maxime, 24km south of Saint Raphaël and 14km north-west of Saint Tropez, is a crowded, modern ugly resort with few thrills greater than those on offer at the countless watersports clubs that line the beachfront.

Maxime's Vieille Ville, centred around rue Gambetta, is crammed with touristy cafés, craft stalls and souvenir shops. Giant pans of paella royale, fruit stalls and pastry shops line rue Courbet, a narrow cobbled street which aptly leads to the town's main market square, place du Marché. Fresh flowers, fish, olives, olive oil, wine and other culinary goodies are sold in the nearby *marché couvert* (covered market), 4 rue Bessy. West of here is the **Musée de la Tour Carrée** (☎ 04 94 96 70 30), a popular arts museum housed in a 16th century tower overlooking the port on ave du Général Leclerc.

The tourist office (☎ 04 94 96 19 24, fax 04 94 49 17 97), promenade Simon Lorière, is open from 9 am to noon and 2 to 6.30 pm (closed Sunday). In July and August it's open from 9 am to 8 pm (10 am to noon and 4 to 7 pm on Sunday). It sells the handy *Circuits VTT* brochure (7FF), compiled by the local cycling club, Association Sportive Maximoise (ASM; ☎ 04 94 43 77 55 or 04 94 43 82 80).

Getting There & Away There are regular buses between Saint Tropez and Sainte Maxime (see the Saint Tropez section).

The MMG shuttle boat to/from Saint Tropez departs from quai Léon Condroyer at the port. From here, Les Bateaux Verts (☎/fax 04 94 49 29 39) also runs regular boats to Saint Tropez and organises fishing expeditions.

Port Grimaud

Dubbed the Venice of Provence, it is hard to believe that pretty little Port Grimaud was built in the 1960s on top of a 100 hectare swamp. Within the high wall barricading the town, Provençal cottages, painted every colour of the rainbow, stand gracefully alongside yacht-laden waterways. Frescoes reminiscent of Italy decorate the outer walls of the public buildings on place du Marché, the central square where Sunday markets are held. Across a small wooden bridge, in Port Grimaud's modernist church on place de L'Église, sunbeams sparkle through a stained glass window designed by Vasarely.

A panorama of gently sloping red rooftops spreads out from the top of the bell tower (5FF).

Alsatian architect Francis Spoerry, who conceived the entire *cité lacustre* (lake city) project, fought for four years (1962-66) to get the authorities to agree to his water-world proposal. Pictures of prehistoric lagoon towns displayed in Zurich's Landesmuseum were apparently Spoerry's inspiration. He went on to design Port Liberty in New York.

Cars are forbidden to enter the floating village. Bronzed residents either walk, row, or cruise around in speedboats. Port Grimaud is endowed with 12km of quays, 7km of canals and mooring space for 3000 luxury yachts – gaped at by 400,000 visitors a year. *Tenue correcte* (correct dress) is insisted upon, except on the beach. In summer, a small tourist office (☎ 04 94 56 28 87 or 04 94 43 26 98 in Grimaud) operates on the roadside (N98) in Saint Pons les Mûres, opposite the main entrance to Port Grimaud. Its hours are from 9 am to 12.30 pm and 3 to 7 pm (10 am to 12.30 pm and 4 to 7 pm on Sunday).

Places to Stay There are a couple of handy camping grounds immediately north of Port Grimaud on the N98. The three-star *Camping des Mûres* (☎ 04 94 56 16 97, fax 04 94 56 37 91) is a large site which charges 115FF for two people with a tent and car (open from mid-March until the end of September). The nightly rate at the adjacent *Camping de la Plage* (☎ 04 94 56 31 15, fax 04 94 56 49 61) is 105FF (open from mid-March to mid-October). Buses from Saint Raphaël and Sainte Maxime stop in front of both grounds.

About 500m farther south along the N98, overlooking the busy roundabout in Saint Pons les Mûres, is *Camping Les Prairies de la Mer* (☎ 04 94 79 09 09, fax 04 94 79 09 10). The rate is 115FF for two people with tent and car and the ground is open between April and early October. Similar rates are charged at *Camping Holiday Marina* (☎ 04 94 56 08 43, fax 04 94 56 41 39), 200m south again on the N98. The Marina is open until the end of October. There are more camp sites in and around medieval Grimaud (see later).

Port Grimaud has one hotel, *Le Giraglia* (☎ *04 94 56 31 33, fax 04 94 56 33 77, place du 14 Juin)* at the foot of the jetty where boats from Saint Tropez arrive and depart. Unfortunately, this four-star joint is extortionately expensive and always booked months in advance.

Getting There & Away There are six buses daily between Port Grimaud and Grimaud (5-10 minutes). In summer a small tourist train (☎ 04 94 56 30 60 or 06 81 35 77 90) shunts visitors between Port Grimaud and Grimaud (30/15FF for adult/child). In Port Grimaud, the stop is next to the tourist office.

There are regular buses and boats from Port Grimaud to Saint Tropez.

Getting Around Les Coches d'Eau (☎ 04 94 56 21 13) runs boat tours of Port Grimaud, departing every 10 minutes from central place du Marché. The 20 minute tour costs 18/9FF for adult/child.

Across the bridge on place de L'Église, you can hire a *barque électrique* (electric boat) costing 80/90/100FF per 30 minutes for 2/3/4 people. Nautic Location (☎ 04 94 43 47 27), 22 place du Sud, rents boats with speed (60cv without a permit).

To beckon a water taxi in Port Grimaud, call La Royale (☎ 06 09 53 15 47). It operates from 10 to 2 am.

Medieval Grimaud
• pop 3322   ✉ 83310   alt 105m
Port Grimaud's popular medieval sibling lies 3km inland. The typically Provençal hilltop village is most notable for the ruins of its **Château du Grimaud**, originally built in the 11th century and fortified four centuries later. In summer, look out for posters advertising musical concerts here.

The tourist office (☎ 04 94 43 26 98, fax 04 94 43 32 40), 1 blvd des Aliziers, is open year round. It has accommodation details.

Off the D14, *Camping à la Ferme*

Ferraro Janine (☎ *04 94 56 08 68)*, 1.5km from the sea in the Hameau des Cagnignons, charges 55FF for a tent site for two people with a car. It is open from June to October. *Camping La Pinède* (☎ *04 94 56 04 36* or *04 94 56 08 61, fax 04 94 56 30 86)*, 2km east of Grimaud on the D14 towards Port Grimaud, is open from April to mid-October and charges 85/98FF in summer/autumn. Grimaud has few hotels.

Getting There & Away There are five direct buses from Saint Tropez to Grimaud (19FF; 25 minutes). Alternatively take a Port Grimaud bus as far as La Foux, from where there are connecting buses up to the medieval village. From Saint Raphaël, there are five direct buses (fewer in the low season) to Grimaud (43.50FF; one hour).

Pays Dracénois

The dramatic **Gorges de Châteaudouble** slice their way northwards from Draguignan, 40km north of Saint Tropez. Eastwards, a cluster of unspoilt villages serve as an alternative accommodation base to Draguignan for visitors to Pays Dracénois. To the south lies medieval Les Arcs-sur-Argens.

LES ARCS-SUR-ARGENS
• pop 4744   ✉ 83460
The two drawcards to Les Arcs are its perfectly restored old town perched on a hillock and its **Maison des Vins Côtes de Provence** where you can buy, taste and learn everything you ever wanted to know about local Côtes de Provence wines.

The tourist office (☎ 04 94 73 37 30, fax 04 94 47 47 94), place de Général de Gaulle, is at the foot of the medieval village. A markets fills the square on Tuesday morning. The 11th century castle crowning the old town houses the elegant *Logis du Guetteur* (☎ *04 94 73 30 82, fax 04 94 73 39 95, place du Château)* which has doubles from 600FF and succulent 150, 230 and 320FF *menus*.

Wine Tasting

The *vinothèque* inside the Maison des Vins (☎ 04 94 99 50 20, fax 04 94 99 50 29), 2.5km south of the village on the N7, is the obvious place to start. Twelve different Côtes de Provence wines are available for tasting each week, while a staggering 650 different Côtes de Provence wines are displayed for sale. Bottles, all sold at producers' prices, range from 14.50-110FF. The Centre de Dégustation is open from 10 am to 1 pm and 1.30 to 7 pm (6 pm on Saturday; closed Sunday). The adjoining restaurant *Le Bacchus Gourmand* (☎ 04 94 47 48 47), where you can sample local wines and culinary creations together, is closed Sunday and Monday. For more details see the special section Food & Wine of Provence.

Beautifully placed among sprawling vineyards is the centuries-old **Château Sainte-Roseline** (☎ 04 94 99 50 30, fax 04 94 47 53 06), 4.5km east of Les Arcs-sur-Argens on the D91 towards La Motte. Its prestigious *cru classé* wines, produced here since the 14th century, can be sampled in the caveau de dégustation between 9 am and noon and 2 to 7 pm Monday to Friday; from 10 am to noon and 2 to 6 pm on Saturday; closed Sunday. A 1975 mosaic by Marc Chagall illuminates the 13th century Romanesque **Chapelle de Sainte Roseline**, home to the corpse of Saint Roseline since 1329. Nearby in an old *bergerie* (sheepfold) is *Le Relais des Moines* (☎ 04 94 47 40 93, fax 04 94 47 52 51), an upmarket bistro (closed Sunday and Monday).

A further 3km east along the D91 (across the N555) is **La Motte**, the first village in Provence to be liberated after the August 1944 Allied landings. For the ultimate Provençal feast, head east out of La Motte along the D47 to the **Domaine de la Maurette** (☎ 04 94 45 92 82) on the intersection of the D47 and the D25. Here you can taste and buy wine (open from 8 am to noon and 2.30 to 6.30 pm), and dine in its *ferme auberge*, open for lunch from 12.30 pm and dinner (summer only) from 7.30 pm. There is a choice of two menus (100 or 130FF) and the atmosphere of chattering people

dining on good, wholesome, homemade food is electric. The place is packed by 1 pm; book to guarantee a table.

Getting There & Away

The train station is 2km south of the tourist office off ave Jean Jaurès. Exit the train station, turn left, then turn right (north) at the end of the street onto ave Jean Jaurès from where it is a straight 2km walk to place de Général de Gaulle.

Les Arcs-sur-Argens is on the rail line between Saint Raphaël and Toulon and is well served by trains to most stops along the entire coast, including Nice (92FF; 1½ hours), Toulon (78FF; 45 minutes) and Marseille (119FF; 1½ hours).

Les Arcs also serves as the train station for Draguignan: Les Rapides Varois (☎ 04 94 47 05 05 in Draguignan) operates buses every 30 minutes between 6.30 am and 8.30 pm between Les Arcs train station and Draguignan.

DRAGUIGNAN

• pop 30,183   ✉ 83300   alt 187m

Dull Draguignan is home to the French army whose *camp militaire* (military base) occupies the Plateau de Canjuers. It has had an artillery school in Draguignan since 1976 – a sign at the entrance to the town welcomes visitors to France's 'Capital d'Artillerie' (artillery capital). In Draguignan's **cimitière Américain** (American cemetery), on the corner of ave Lazare Carnot and ave Patrick Rosso, a monument pays homage to the heavy combat that occurred around Draguignan during WWII – 9000 American and British soldiers were dropped here by parachute on 15 August 1944.

Draguignan tourist office (☎ 04 94 68 63 30, fax 04 94 47 10 76, officedetourisme@ ville-draguignan.fr, www.ville-draguignan .fr), 9 blvd Clémenceau, is open from 9 am to 1 pm and 2 to 7 pm Monday to Friday; and until noon on Saturday. It is closed Sunday.

Traditional Provençal costumes, musical instruments and other ethnographic finds are displayed in the **Musée des Traditions**

Provençales (☎ 04 94 47 05 72), 15 rue Roumanille. In the tiny remaining patch of Draguignan's old town, the 18m **tour d'horloge** (clock tower), topped with an ornate, wrought-iron campanile, is worth a visit too.

The tourist office has a comprehensive list of hotels in the region. A cheapie is the zero-star *Touring (☎/fax 04 94 68 15 46, rue Frédéric Mireur, off place Claude Gay)* which has singles/doubles/triples with shared toilet for 110/130/210FF.

Pays Dracénois

People from Draguignan are known as Les Dracénois. Their town lies at the heart of this magnificent country. From Draguignan head east along the D562 which skirts the military camp, then follow the D225 and its continuation, the D25, north to Callas. As the D25 climbs up to Callas a stunning panorama of the red rock Massif de l'Ésterel unfolds. In **Callas** the good value *Hôtel de France (☎ 04 94 76 61 02, place Georges Clémenceau)* is a typical Provençal village hotel with a pink façade and cheap rooms. Stock up on locally milled olive oil (75FF a litre) from the restored *Moulin de Callas (☎ 04 94 76 68 05)* at the south end of the village.

Six kilometres further north is **Bargemon** (☎/fax 04 94 47 81 73 for the tourist office). You can sleep at the *Auberge des Arcades (☎ 04 94 76 60 36, fax 04 94 47 83 37, ave Pasteur)*, which has creaking floorboards and charming doubles from 250FF with shower; and eat at the excellent *La Taverne (☎ 04 94 76 62 19)*, uphill from the auberge on the central village square, place Chauvier. It has truly scrumptious *menus* packed with local culinary delights for 90, 130 and 160FF (closed mid-October to mid-November).

Big spenders or honeymooning couples should head straight for the heavenly *Hostellerie Les Gorges de Pennafort (☎ 04 94 76 66 51, fax 04 94 76 67 23)*, 8km south of Callas on the vineyard clad D25. The grand old hostellerie, in the middle of nowhere, has its own lake and overlooks the stunning red rock **Gorges de Pennafort** – ideal for gentle strolls hand in hand.

Doubles fit for a queen start at 700FF; *menus* in the restaurant start at 200FF.

Getting There & Away

The Pays Dracénois is pretty much inaccessible without your own private transport. Draguignan is served by regular daily buses to/from Les Arcs-sur-Argens where the closest train station is. Advance train tickets are sold at the SNCF office (open 9 am to 5.30 pm; closed Sunday) at Draguignan bus station on blvd des Martyrs de la Résistance.

Les Rapides Varois (☎ 04 94 42 05 05) operates buses from Draguignan to Nice (three daily) and Les Arcs (every 30 minutes). Estérel Cars (☎ 04 94 52 00 50 in Fréjus) runs 16 buses daily to Saint Raphaël. There are less frequent services to Grasse, Marseille and Toulon.

ABBAYE DE THORONET

The Romanesque abbey at Le Thoronet is the third in a trio of great abbeys built by the Cistercian order in Provence in the 12th and 13th centuries. The Abbaye de Thoronet (☎ 04 94 60 43 90) was built between 1160 and 1190, housing some 20 monks and several dozen lay brothers by the early 13th century. By 1790 just a handful of elderly monks remained. The church, the monks' cells and cloisters were all built with dry stone. The chapter house, where the monks met each morning to discuss any community problems – or to elect a new abbot – is noticeably more ornate than the rest of the austere abbey. This was because it was the only secular room, where prayers were never held. Early gothic influences are evident in the *ogival* (pointed) arches which rest on two columns.

The abbey is open from April to September from 9 am to 7 pm (9 am to noon and 2 to 7 pm on Sunday). Daily hours from October to March are 10 am to 1 pm and 2 to 5 pm (35/23FF for adult/student). Self-guides in several languages are available. Occasional musical soirées are held here in summer.

Massif des Maures

Much of the heavily forested Massif des Maures is inaccessible by car but there are five roads you can take through the hills. The lowest, straightest, southernmost road (N98) cuts eastwards, through vineyards and cork oak tree plantations, from Saint Tropez to **Bormes-les-Mimosas** and onto Hyères. Parallel to this road is the D14 which runs through **Collobrières**, the largest town in the massif known for its chestnut produce. This road, very popular with cyclists, is among the prettiest in the Maures and offers good panoramas of the rolling hills.

The mountainous, hairpin-laced D39 which leads north from the D14, just east of Collobrières, snakes between **La Sauvette** (779m) and **Notre Dame des Anges** (780m), the massif's highest peaks. The Massif des Maures, not surprisingly, offers superb walking and cycling opportunities too. The GR9 penetrates the massif at its northern edge, near **Carnoules**, and wends its way past Notre Dame des Anges (which is topped by a small chapel) and La Sauvette to the unspoilt village of **La Garde Freinet**, a perfect getaway spot. From here it runs south to Port Grimaud on the coast. From Collobrières, the southbound GR90 loops its way 12km east to the wonderfully isolated monastery, **La Chartreuse de la Verne**. Northbound, it hooks up with the GR9 at Notre Dame des Anges.

The Saint Tropez tourist office distributes a map-guide called *Tours in the Golfe of St Tropez – Pays des Maures* which describes four driving, cycling or walking itineraries. The detailed hiking guide entitled *Var: de la Sainte Baume au Massif des Maures* (Didier-Richard; No 245 in the Les Tracés Grand Air hiking series; 69FF) maps out 103 walks and is a must for any committed hiker. The walking guide, *Massif des Maures – Randonées pédestres* (Édisud; No 33 (1996); 68FF) is another useful tool, as is the hiking map, *Maures Haut-Pays Varois* (Didier-Richard; No 25 in the Les Tracés Grand Air hiking series; 74FF).

COLLOBRIÈRES
• pop 1600   ✉ 83610

If you like chestnuts, then Collobrières – a small town renowned for its chestnut purée and *marrons glacés* (candied chestnuts) – is the place to go. It lies 24km west of Grimaud and is considered the 'capital' of the Maures. Most days in summer, a small village market fills the square in front of the tourist office, straddling the Collobrier river, on blvd Charles Caminat where local artisans sell slabs of cork, homemade chestnut purée and other local delights.

Walk across the 12th century **vieux pont** (old bridge) to the other side of the river to get to the **Confiserie Azuréenne** (✆ 04 94 48 07 20, fax 04 94 48 07 20, www.franceplus .com/confiserie) where an irresistable array of nutty products are sold. Sample *crème de marrons* (chestnut cream), *marrons au sirop* (chestnuts in syrup) or maybe have a shot of the *liqueur de châtaignes* (chestnut liqueur).

In August, Collobrières marks its annual Grande Fête des Fontaines by cooking up a monstrous-sized *aïoli*. It celebrates its Fête de la Châtaigne (Chestnut Festival) on the last three Sundays in October.

Almost 12,000 hectares of protected forest surround the town.

Information
The tourist office (✆ 04 94 48 08 00, fax 04 94 48 04 10, collotour@compuserve.com), at the east end of the village on blvd Charles Caminat, is open from 10 am to 12.30 pm and from 3.30 to 6.30 pm (closed Sunday).

Opening hours at the village post office, cours Mirabeau, are 9 am to noon and 2 to 5 pm (closed Saturday afternoon and all day Sunday). There are a couple of banks where you can change money on blvd Carnot.

Places to Stay & Eat
Collobrières offers good value accommodation options and serves as the ideal base for exploring the Massif des Maures. *Camping Municipal Saint Roch* (✆ 04 94 48 00 00, fax 04 94 13 83 80), 200m from the village centre, signposted off place

Général de Gaulle, charges 5/12FF a night for a car and tent or a caravan site under the trees, plus 8/5FF per adult/child under 8 years. Reception is open from 8 to 11 am and 5 to 10 pm and the ground is open between April and December.

Twelve kilometres east of Collobrières on route de Grimaud (D14), is *La Ferme de Capelude* (☎ 04 94 56 80 35, capelude@ club-internet.fr, www.chez.com /capelude), a gîte d'étape offering a bed in an eight or 10-person dorm for 80FF a night. Half board costs 180FF per person, and a picnic is 40FF per person. The 16th century farm also has a shop where you can buy *miel de châtaigne* (chestnut honey), and *miel de lavande* (lavender honey) as well as fruity *confitures* (jams) including fig, melon, peach, apricot, cherry and plum. It arranges guided farm tours for groups of eight or more (25FF per person).

In the centre of the village, the cosy 10-room *Hôtel-Restaurant des Maures* (☎ 04 94 48 07 10, fax 04 94 48 02 73), above a little bar at 19 blvd Lazare Carnot (the continuation of blvd Charles Caminat), has adequate rooms for one or two people for 120FF; breakfast is 21FF and half board is a bargain at 150FF per person. The only other alternative is the 16-room *Hôtel-Restaurant Notre Dame* (☎ 04 94 48 07 13, fax 04 94 48 05 93, 15 ave de la Libération) which has doubles with shower and toilet for 180FF.

Sample local Côtes de Provence wines at the *Caves des Vignerons de Collobrières* (☎ 04 94 48 07 26, fax 04 94 48 02 07), west of the village on route de Pierrefeu. The wine cellars are open from 8 am to noon and 2 to 6 pm (closed Monday morning and Sunday).

LA CHARTREUSE DE LA VERNE

The majestic, 12th to 13th century monastery of La Chartreuse de la Verne (420m) is tucked in a forest, 12km southeast of Collobrières. It was founded in 1190 by Pierre Isnard, Bishop of Toulon, for the Carthusian monks who had settled in the massif from 1170 onwards. Much of the original charterhouse was destroyed by Huguenots in 1577.

The solitary monastic complex, which has been slowly renovated since the 1960s, is home to 15 Carthusian nuns today. One of the old monks' cells has been fully restored, complete with the small garden and covered corridor where the monk would pray as he paced its length. The 70m grand cloister, bakery and mill can all be visited. Don't miss the nuns' homemade *pain à la farine de châtaignes* (chestnut flour bread) or *pain aux olives* (olive bread), available most days at reception for 15FF a loaf.

Various **hiking paths** lead from the monastery into its forested surrounds. Trails are marked from the *châtaigneraie du Monastère* (monastery chestnut grove) to La Môle, to the Barrage de la Verne, and the neighbouring hamlet of Capelude (12km).

The monastery, signposted 'Monastère de la Verne' (☎ 04 94 43 45 51) is open from 11 am to 6 pm; until 5 pm in winter; closed in January and on Tuesday year round (30/20/15FF for adult/student/child aged 8-14 years). Smoking and revealing clothes are forbidden. To get there from Collobrières, follow the route de Grimaud (D14) eastwards for 6km, then turn right (south) onto the narrow D214. Follow this road for a farther 6km to the monastery; the final section of the single-track road is unpaved.

LE VILLAGE DES TORTUES

About 20km north of Collobrières on the northern tip of the massif is a Tortoise Village where one of France's rarest and most endangered species can be viewed in close quarters. The *testudo hermanni* (Hermann tortoise), once common along the Mediterranean coastal strip, is today found only in the Massif des Maures and Corsica. Forest fires in 1990 destroyed 250,000 hectares of forest in the massif, reducing the tortoise population further still.

The Station d'Observation et de Protection des Tortues des Maures (Maures Tortoise Observation and Protection Station; SOPTOM) was set up in 1985 by French writer and filmmaker Bernaud Devaux and an English biologist to ensure the Hermann's survival. Since 1988 some 8000 tortoises have been returned to the wild.

A well documented marked trail (captions in English, French and German) leads visitors around the centre, from the quarantine quarter and reproduction enclosures to the tropical conservatory, egg hatcheries (home to pregnant females from mid-May to end of June), and nurseries where the young tortoises (a delicacy for preying magpies, rats, foxes and wild boars) spend the first three of their 60 to 100 years. The tortoise mating season runs from March to May and August to September. In the tortoise clinic, wounded animals – usually wild tortoises kept as domestic pets – are treated. Dog bites and lawnmower injuries are the most common wounds. Following their rehabilitation in the centre, most are repatriated into the Maures forest.

The Village des Tortues (☎ 04 94 78 26 41, fax 04 94 78 24 27, soptom@compuserve.com) is open from 9 am to 7 pm; closed during the hibernation season from the end of November to beginning of March (40/25FF for adult/child aged 6-16). It costs 100FF to sponsor a tortoise. The village, about 6km east of Gonfaron, is only accessible by private transport; follow the signs from Gonfaron.

In **Gonfaron** (N97), there is a small **Écomusée du Liège** (Cork Ecomuseum; ☎ 04 94 78 25 65), housed in an old *bouchonnerie* (bottle-stopper factory) at 5 rue de la République. Its opening hours are from 2 to 6 pm (closed Sunday, Monday and from October to March).

LA GARDE FREINET
• pop 1465   ✉ 83310   alt 380m

This village is a delight to explore in late summer when its streets are quiet and empty. A fantastic panorama of its red roof tops can be had from the **ruins of Fort Freinet** (450m). The fort was built in the 13th century but abandoned 200 years later when the villagers moved their homes down to the plateau. Below the ruins stands a large stone **croix** (cross) where pilgrims pay their respects on May 1 each year.

The cross and fort is a 20 minute uphill walk from the village centre. From central place Neuve, walk south along rue Longue, turn left onto rue des Aires, cross place des Aires, then turn right (west) onto rue de la Planette. A track signposted 'direction de la croix' leads from the Aire de la Planette at the end of this street to the cross. By car, follow the N558 towards Grimaud and turn right (south) immediately after the pétanque court.

La Garde Freinet celebrates its traditional Fête de la Transhumance, marking the seasonal moving of the flocks in mid-April, and hosts a Fête de la Châtaigne in mid October. Markets fill the old town squares on Wednesday and Sunday morning.

The Maison du Tourisme (☎ 04 94 43 67 41, fax 04 94 43 08 69), 1 place Neuve, has details on hiking, arranges wine-tasting tours in the region and has a list of local *chambres d'hôtes*. The *Camping Municipal Saint Éloi* (☎ 04 94 43 62 40), next to the pétanque court (N558) charges 16/16/17FF per person/tent/car. The tiny, eight-room *Hôtel Le Fraxinois* (☎ 04 94 43 62 84, fax 04 94 43 69 65, place Neuve) has doubles for 220-300FF.

COGOLIN & LA MÔLE
Industrious **Cogolin** (pop 8500; postcode 83310), 15km south of La Garde Freinet, is known for its wooden pipes, cork products and carpets, the latter being woven in the village since the 1920s when Armenian refugees settled here. The sweet, succulent *tarte Tropézienne*, a creamy sandwich cake, was created at the Micka pâtisserie (☎ 04 94 54 42 59), 2 rue Beausoleil, in 1955.

The tourist office (☎ 04 94 55 01 50, fax 04 94 55 01 11, www.nova.fr/cogolin), place de la République, has a list of local artisans to visit and arranges guided tours of the old town and its pipe makers. In July and August SODETRAV runs a shuttle bus (8.50FF) from Cogolin bus station (☎ 04 94 54 62 36), ave George Clémenceau, to Cogolin's sandy **beach & pleasure port**, 5km north-east.

Equally inviting to the tastebuds is the neighbouring village of **La Môle**, 9km west along the vineyard-laden N98. Tourist information is available from the Mairie (☎ 04 94 49 57 17, fax 04 94 49 55 24) in the village centre.

This charming spot is best known for the pain aux olives produced in its large boulangerie; and for the superb culinary delights served with a Provençal flourish at the blue-canopied *Auberge de La Môle (☎ 04 94 49 57 01)* on the right as you enter the village from the east. Specialities in-season include *pommes de terre aux truffes* (truffled potatoes). Lunch/dinner *menus* are 150/300FF (closed January and February). Local wines can be sampled here or at one of the neighbouring **châteaux** on the westbound N98.

Private jets can land at the Aérodrome International du Golfe de Saint Tropez (☎ 04 94 49 57 29), just east of La Môle on the N98. See the Getting There & Away chapter for details.

FÔRET DU DOM & BORMES-LES-MIMOSAS

Vineyards melt into a rich patchwork of cork oak, pine and chestnut trees as the N98 continues its westward path into the **Fôret du Dom**, 12km west of La Môle. The best place to explore on foot is at the **Arboretum de Gratteloup**, 1km north of the Col de Gratteloup on the N98. The three hectare 'tree garden', established in 1935, is divided into zones each dedicated to the cultivation of a different tree species. Guided hikes through the forest (2½ hours; 35FF per person) are organised by the Maison Forestière de Gratteloup (☎ 04 94 71 06 07), near the arboretum entrance. Opposite, on the N98, is the very charming, eight-room *Hôtel de la Reine Jeanne (☎ 04 94 15 00 83, fax 04 94 64 77 89)*.

From the top of the **Col de Gratteloup** (199m), the steep D41 climbs northwards over the **Col de Babaou** (415m) towards Collobrières. This road is a major cycling route; views across the wooded slopes are splendid. Southbound, the D41 wiggles its way over the **Col de Caguo-Ven** (237m),

offering good coastal views to **Bormes-les-Mimosas** (pop 5000; postcode 83230; alt 180m). The attractive, 12th century village is famous for its great diversity of flora and draws lots of artists and craftspeople, many of whom you will see at work as you wander through the tiny streets. The tourist office (☎ 04 94 71 15 17, fax 04 94 64 79 57) is at 1 place Gambetta.

CORNICHE DES MAURES

From La Môle, the breathtaking 267m **Col de Canadel** (D27) plummets down to the Corniche des Maures, a 26km coastal road (D559) that stretches south-west from La Croix-Valmer to Le Lavandou. The mountain pass offers unbeatable views of the Massif des Maures, the coastline and the islands off its rugged shores. Fine sandy beaches made for swimming, sunbathing and windsurfing line the coastal road. Village resorts it passes through include Cavalaire-sur-Mer (tourist office ☎ 04 94 01 92 10), Le Rayol and Pramousquier.

From Le Rayol, a narrow road leads south to the **Domaine du Rayol** (☎ 04 94 05 32 50), ave des Belges. The fabulous 20 hectare gardens date from 1910 when a Parisian banker built himself a seaside villa here. In July and August, you can dive in the underwater **Jardin Marin** (Marine Garden; bookings required). The Domaine du Rayol is open from 9.30 am to 12.30 pm and 2.30 to 6.30 pm; in July and August from 9.30 am to 12.30 pm and 4.30 to 8 pm; closed December and January. Guided tours are available (40/20FF for adult/child aged 6-16; 70/50FF for the marine garden).

In July and August, the Domaine hosts open-air musical *soirées*. Reserve a ticket (120FF) in advance (☎ 04 94 05 32 50, fax 04 94 05 33 99).

LE LAVANDOU
• pop 5200   ✉ 83980

Once a fishing village, Le Lavandou is approximately 5km east of Bormes-les-Mimosas. The name derives from the Provençal 'Lou Lavandou', meaning 'wash-house'. It has become a popular resort, thanks mainly to its 12km sandy beach, good value accommodation, and proximity to the idyllic Îles d'Hyères which can easily be reached by boat from here.

While the south-west end of the resort is dominated by concrete blocks and should be avoided, the Vieille Ville at its north-east end is beautifully intact. Here, the large pétanque pitch, under the shade of the trees on quai Gabriel Péri, remains abuzz with activity; while an age-old *lavoir* (communal wash-house) sits serenely on square des Héros, at the east end of ave du Général de Gaulle. Dramatist Bertolt Brecht and composer Kurt Weill wrote parts of *The Threepenny Opera* while holidaying here in 1928.

Le Lavandou sits north-east of **Cap de Brégançon**, a small rocky cape embraced by a really beautiful sandy beach in **Cabasson**, on its west side, and crowned with the 16th to 18th century Fort de Brégançon. Since 1968 the heavily guarded fortress (good views from Cabasson beach) has served as a summer residence of the French President.

Orientation & Information

Quai Gabriel Péri and its continuation, quai Baptistin Pins, runs north-east along the beach front. The port (Gare Maritime), quai des Îles d'Or, sits at its easternmost end, opposite the Vieille Ville.

The bus station is two bus shelters either side of the D559. Walk south past the tourist office annexe, then turn left (east) onto ave des Martyrs de la Résistance to get to the centre. Its continuation, ave du Général de Gaulle, traverses the old town.

Le Lavandou's tourist office (☎ 04 94 71 00 61, fax 04 94 64 73 79, www.provence web.fr/83/lavandou), quai Gabriel Péri, is opposite the port. It runs a small annexe at the bus station too.

Boat Excursions

Year round, the Compagnie de Transports Maritimes Vedettes Îles d'Or (☎ 04 94 71 01 02, fax 04 94 71 78 95), 15 quai Gabriel Péri and at the port, operates boats to the Îles d'Hyères. Boats sail daily (between two and seven return boats a day depending on the season) to **Île du Levant** (30 minutes; 122/80FF return for adult/child) and **Port-Cros** (40 minutes; 125.50/82FF), except in November when boats only sail on Thursday, Saturday and Sunday (twice daily). If you intend visiting both islands, buy a cheaper *billet circulaire* (104/147.50FF).

Boats to **Porquerolles**, the last of the Îles d'Hyères trio, sail daily in July and August (one return a day; 55 minutes; 143/105FF return for adult/child). In April, May and September, the boat only runs on Monday, Wednesday and Saturday (no boats from October to March).

Also seasonal, is the Compagnie de Transports Maritimes' boat trips to **Saint Tropez**. A boat departs every Saturday from Le Lavandou to Saint Tropez in July and August (163/102FF). There is one weekly boat on Tuesday during the second half of June and the first half of September. Boat excursions along the coast, or in a glass-bottomed boat (69/45FF) are also available in summer.

All boats depart from the port (Gare Maritime; ☎ 04 94 71 13 09) on quai des Îles d'Or. Tickets are sold at the ticket office, open 30 minutes before departure (except in July and August when never-ending queues ensure it remains open all day).

Places to Stay

Camping The tourist office has a complete list of camping grounds in the region. There is a cluster along route Benat, a couple of kilometres south of Le Lavandou in the suburb of La Favière.

Heading towards Cap de Brégançon is **Camping La Griotte** *(☎ 04 94 15 20 72, 2168 route de Cabasson)*, open from May to October.

Hotels The cheap, two-star *Hôtel Terminus (☎ 04 94 71 00 62, fax 04 94 15 17 51, place des Joyeuses Vacances)*, behind the tourist office annexe at the bus station, has rooms for one or two with shower/shower and toilet for 200/250FF. Close by, the 16-room *Hôtel Côte d'Azur (☎ 04 94 71 01 79, fax 04 94 15 13 07, 17 ave des Martyrs de* *la Résistance)* has singles/doubles from 305/410F. Reception is on the 1st floor. The hotel is closed from November to April.

Overlooking the port on quai Gabriel Péri is the delightful *Hôtel Le Rabelais (☎ 04 94 71 00 56, fax 04 94 71 82 55, 2 rue Rabelais)*, a rambling old building offering particularly good-value rooms for 310/350FF without/with a seaview. All rooms have shower, toilet and TV. It is closed from mid-November to January.

Another oozing-charm type of place is the two-star *La Ramade (☎ 04 94 71 20 40, 16 rue Patron Ravello)*, which has rooms for two people with kitchenette from 280/350FF in the low/high season. Opposite, on the same busy little street at No 11, is the amazingly good value, one-star *Auberge Provençale (☎ 04 94 71 00 44, fax 04 94 15 02 25)*. Very comfortable rooms for one or two people with bidet and washbasin cost 170FF and rooms with shower are 220FF.

One-star *Hôtel Neptune (☎ 04 94 71 01 01, fax 04 94 64 91 61, 26 ave du Général de Gaulle)* is a touch run down and grotty, but at 220FF for a double with shower, it warrants no complaints.

Places to Eat

The pedestrian streets in the Vielle Ville overflow with terrace restaurants. Most tout *menus* at around 100FF.

One little spot that comes highly recommended is *La Pignato (☎ 04 94 71 13 02, rue de L'Église)* which specialises in *cuisine Provençale*. As part of its 85FF *menu*, start off with some grilled sardines or a Roquefort and nut salad, followed by sliced duck breast in a mustard sauce, or battered squid laced with spices.

Slightly more expensive but guaranteed to please is *La Fanouille (☎ 04 94 71 34 29)*, occupying a small square on the corner of ave Patron Ravello and Abbé Helin. It has a 98 and 128FF *menu* and the service is impeccable. Note the sloping tables!

Nearby, *La Ramade* (see Places to Stay earlier) serves huge bowls of *moules* (mussels) for 58FF and a giant *aïoli*

Provençale complet for 118FF. It has *menus* for 79 and 120FF and is always packed.

Getting There & Away

Le Lavandou is on the main SODETRAV (☎ 04 94 12 55 00 in Hyères) bus route between Saint Tropez (70FF; 1 hour) and Toulon (58FF; 1¼ hours). Buses follow the coastal road, stopping en route in Le Rayol, Le Lavandou, Bormes-les-Mimosas, La Londe and Hyères. In July and August there are about eight Saint Tropez-Toulon buses daily (fewer in the low season).

In the high season there are additional buses from Le Lavandou to Toulon, stopping en route in Hyères (30 minutes).

Getting Around

Hire a set of wheels from Holiday Bikes (☎ 04 94 15 19 99, fax 04 94 71 63 44), L'Albatros, ave Vincent Auriol. Daily rates for a pair of roller blades/mountain bike/scooter/motorcycle start at 50/70/200/290FF. It's open from 9 am to 12.30 pm and 3 to 7 pm.

Near the port, Bleu Marin (☎ 04 94 71 42 48), quai Baptistin Pins, hires roller blades for 45/60/250FF for a half-day/day/week. Next door, Star Bike (☎ 04 94 01 03 82), open from 9 am to 7 pm, has mountain bikes to rent for 50FF a day and scooters/motorcycles for 200/250FF a day.

The Islands

The alluring Îles d'Hyères are also known as the Îles d'Or (Islands of Gold). According to legend, the islands in this archipelago were created from beautiful princesses who, upon being chased by pirates while swimming, were turned by the gods into golden islands.

Porquerolles, 7km long and 3km wide, is the westernmost and largest. Port-Cros – the middle island – is a national park; while its eastern sister, Île du Levant, is a nudist colony. Wild camping is forbidden throughout the archipelago.

Rather less magical are the Îles du Fun, the overdeveloped islands of Bendor and Embiez, farther west off Toulon's shores.

ÎLE DE PORT-CROS

• pop 40   ✉ **83400**

Created in 1963 to protect at least one small part of the Côte d'Azur's natural beauty from overdevelopment, the **Parc National de Port-Cros** is France's smallest national park. It encompasses the 675 hectares of the island of Port-Cros (4km long and 2.5km wide) and an 1800 hectare zone of water around it. Until the end of the 19th century, the islanders' vineyards and olive groves ensured their self-sufficiency. Today, tourism is their sustenance.

The island can be visited all year, but hikers must stick to the marked paths. Fishing, fires, camping, smoking outside of the village, motorised vehicles and bicycles are not allowed.

Port-Cros, the smallest of the Îles d'Hyères, is primarily a marine reserve but is also known for its rich variety of insects, butterflies and birds. Keeping the water around it clean (compared with the rest of the coast) is one of the national reserve's big problems.

A **sentier sous-marin** (underwater trail), marked off the island's northern shore, allows snorkellers to discover some of the marine flora and fauna typical to the national park. The miniscule **Îlot de la Gabinière**, an islet off Port-Cros' southern shore, is popular with experienced divers.

The Parc National de Port-Cros also manages neighbouring **Île de Bagaud** (40 hectares), the fourth of the Îles d'Hyères due west of Port-Cros. The densely vegetated island is used for scientific research and is off-limits for tourists. Plans in 1998 included eradicating its large rat population and developing a sanctuary for the ash-gray and yelkouan shearwater.

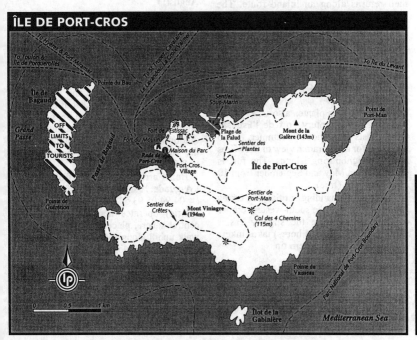

ÎLE DE PORT-CROS

Orientation & Information

Boats dock at the port in the village on the island's north-western shores.

The Maison du Parc (☎ 04 94 01 40 72, fax 04 94 01 40 71), at the port, sells maps of the island (25FF) and stocks the plastic-covered *Guide de Sentier Sous-Marin* (70FF), a guide used underwater by snorkellers to identify species. The office has information on hiking and diving too. It's open from 9.30 am to 12.15 pm and 3.30 to 6.45 pm (no break in July and August; closed from October to March). The park's headquarters is in Hyères.

Things to See & Do

From the post office at the port, a track leads inland, from where 30km of marked hiking trails criss-cross the island.

From the 15th century Fort du Moulin, a circular sentier des plantes (botany trail; 1½-2 hours) leads to the Plage de la Palud then returns along an inland route. The beach itself, on the north of the island, is only a 30 minute walk from the Fort du Moulin. Between mid-June and mid-September, snorkellers can follow the 30 minute sentier sous-marin, accessible daily from 10 am to 4.30 pm. Sun Plongée, inside the Sun Bistrot (☎ 04 94 05 90 16) at the port hires gear.

The sentier des plantes also takes in the imposing, 16th century **Fort de l'Estissac** which hosts exhibitions in summer. Climb the tower for a panoramic view of Port-Cros and its neighbouring islands. The fort is open between May and September from 10 am to 5.30 pm (free).

The more demanding **sentier des crêtes** (3 hours) explores the south-western corner of the island, while the slightly easier **sentier de Port-Man** (4 hours) takes hikers to Port-Cros' north-eastern tip.

Places to Stay

Next door to the Maison du Parc, at the port, there are quaint self-catering *studios* (☎ 04 94 05 92 72) to rent. A four-person apartment costs 800/1000FF a day in the low/high season, and a two-person apartment costs

450/550FF. The same place also has rooms in the low season for 250/300FF without/with a bathroom, and in the high season for 300/350FF. Book well in advance.

The only other option is the exclusive, 23-room *Hôtel Le Manoir* (☎ 04 94 05 90 52, fax 04 94 05 90 89), at the port, which has singles/doubles for 920/1440FF in the low season and 1070/1620FF in the high season. Triples and quads are also available. Le Manoir is closed between October and April.

Getting There & Away

Le Lavandou (see that section – Boat Excursions) is the main stepping stone to Port-Cros. There are also frequent boats year round from Hyères.

There are seasonal boats – several times a week – from Toulon and Saint Tropez (June to September); and Port Miramar, La Croix Valmer and Cavalaire (July and August).

ÎLE DU LEVANT
- **pop 120**   ✉ **83400**

Nowhere is the quest for natural beauty more explicit than on oddball Île du Levant, a narrow 8km strip of an island, of which 90% is a military camp and strictly off-limits. The remaining pocket of **Héliopolis**, on the island's north-eastern tip, has been a nudist colony since the 1930s. Its tiny population increases ten fold in summer when the village is overrun with bathers in the buff.

Boats arrive and depart from **Port de L'Ayguade**. A small tourist information hut (☎ 04 94 05 93 52 or 04 94 05 91 65 at the Mairie) operates here in summer. The central square, place du Village, is a 1km walk uphill along route de L'Ayguade, the street running along Héliopolis' southern boundary. The post office, cafés and several hotels are clustered around this square. The island's only camping ground, *Le Colombero* (☎ 04 94 05 90 29), is 500m from the port on route de l'Ayguade. It charges 33FF per person and is open from April to October.

The eastern part of the colony is covered by the **Domaine des Arbousiers**, a nature reservation with rare island plants such as the Eryngium tricuspidatum (a type of thistle). A *sentier-nature* (nature trail) leads from place du Village east into the protected area. Contact the tourist office for information on guided tours.

Baring all is not obligatory – except on the sandy **Plage Les Grottes**, the main nudist beach east of Port de L'Ayguade. From the port, walk in the direction of 'Plage de Sable Levant' along the **sentier Georges Rousseau**, a rocky coastal path. Bold signs reading *Nudisme Intégral Obligatoire* mark the moment you are obliged to strip.

Getting There & Away

The Île du Levant is 10 minutes by boat from Port-Cros. There are regular boats year round from Le Lavandou and Hyères (see those sections), and in July and August from Port Miramar (La Londe), La Croix Valmer and Cavalaire.

ÎLE DE PORQUEROLLES
- **pop 30** ✉ 83400

Despite being the most developed of the Îles d'Hyères, Porquerolles is home to a wide variety of indigenous and tropical flora, including the requien larkspur which grows nowhere else in the world. In winter, blossoming mimosas bring a splash of colour to the green island. April and May are the best months to spot some of its 114 bird species. Sadly, the monk seal, which used to be a regular visitor to Porquerolles, is rarely seen around its shores today.

Most of the island is protected under the Parc National de Port-Cros which manages 1000 of its 1254 richly vegetated hectares. Exploring by foot or by bicycle is as good a reason as any to visit. Avoid July and August when the happy owners of Porquerolles' numerous *résidences secondaires* return to the island, increasing the population six fold. Smoking is forbidden outside the village.

Orientation & Information

Boats dock at the port on the island's northern coast. Walk to the tourist office at the

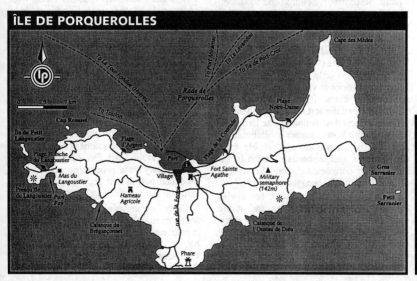

ÎLE DE PORQUEROLLES

end of the jetty, then bear right along rue de la Ferme to get to place d'Armes, the central village square.

The tourist office (☎ 04 94 58 33 76, fax 04 94 58 36 39) is open from 9 am to 5.30 pm (9 am to 1 pm and 2.30 to 5 pm on Tuesday and Thursday). It sells a map of the island (10FF) with *pistes cyclables* (cycling paths) and *sentiers pédestres* (footpaths) marked on it. Various walks and bicycle rides are also detailed in the excellent *Short History of the Island of Porquerolles*; the tourist office has a reference copy you can consult.

The Société Marseillaise du Crédit, 3 rue de la Ferme, has an ATM and currency exchange (open on Monday only out of season). The post office, next to Église Sainte Anne on the south side of place d'Armes, is open from 9 am to 4 pm (Saturday until noon; closed Sunday). There is a laundrette on rue de la Douane.

Things to See & Do

Central **place d'Armes** is dominated by a giant, tree-shaded pétanque pitch. In summer, music concerts are held in **Église Sainte Anne**, on the south side of the square. Festivities fill church and square on 25 July when islanders celebrate their patron saint's day.

From the square, head south along chemin Sainte Agathe to the 16th century **Fort Sainte Agathe** (☎ 04 94 58 36 45), built in 1518 and the only one of Porquerolles' fortifications open to visitors today. Much of the edifice dates from 1812-14 when Napoléon I had the fort rebuilt following its plundering and destruction by the British in 1739. The fort hosts summer exhibitions. An awesome island panorama is visible from the tower. Its opening hours are from 10 am to 5.30 pm between May and September (25/15FF for adult/teenager under 18).

From place d'Armes, walk (or cycle) south along rue de la Ferme and at the crossroads turn right. The **Hameau Agricole**, home to the Conservatoire Botanique National Méditerranéen (☎ 04 94 12 30 32, cbn@www.see.it, www.see.it/cbn) is 700m along this trail. Inside the laboratories a

well documented history of the island's flora is presented. A *promenade botanique* (botanical walk) leads visitors through gardens featuring plants typical to the island: 20 types of almond trees, 150 fig types, 83 lauriers rose types, and numerous olive trees. The centre is open from 9.30 am to 12.30 pm and 1 to 5 pm; closed between October and April (free).

The island's 82m **phare** (lighthouse), built in 1837 to tip the island's southernmost cape, is 2km farther along rue de la Ferme. In summer the keeper allows visitors to climb to the top of his tower which, on clear days, offers a stunning panorama. A military semaphore (142m) north-east of here marks the highest point of the island; it can't be visited.

Porquerolles' **vineyards**, covering around 195 hectares on the western part of the island, are tended by three wine producers. They each offer *dégustation* (wine tasting) sessions of their predominantly rosé wines; the tourist office has a list.

Beaches

The island's northern coast is laced with white sandy beaches, including **Plage de la Courtade** signposted 800m east from the port, and **Plage de Notre-Dame**, a farther 2.5km east. To get to **Plage d'Argent**, 2km west of the village, walk along rue de la Ferme and turn right at the crossroads.

More secluded is the **Plage Blanche du Langoustier**, a former lobster farm 4.5km from the village on the northern shores of the Presqu'île du Langoustier. It is known as the 'white' beach in contrast to the black sand that darkens the southern shores of this peninsula around Port Fay – the legacy of a 19th century soda processing plant which produced potash and soda from sulphuric acid and sea salt from 1828-76.

Cliffs line the island's more dangerous, southern coast where swimming and diving is restricted to the **Calanque du Brégançonnet** to the east and, to the west, the **Calanque de l'Oustau de Dieu** (literally 'House of God').

Places to Stay & Eat

Porquerolles is expensive. It has no camping ground and wild camping is forbidden.

Reception staff at the two-star *Hôtel Sainte Anne* (☎ 04 94 58 30 04, fax 04 94 58 32 92, place d'Armes) lend boules to guests keen to have a spin on the pétanque pitch. Next door, on the corner of place d'Armes and chemin Sainte Agathe, is the charming *Auberge des Glycines* (☎ 04 94 58 30 36, fax 04 94 58 35 22) which has comfortable doubles for 450FF including breakfast. Between April and September, half-board (650FF per person) is compulsory. Its restaurant specialises in tasty *cuisine Porquerollaise* – lots of fish dishes.

Nightly rates at the cranky but cool *Relais de la Poste* (☎ 04 94 58 30 26, fax 04 94 58 33 57, place d'Armes, east) start at 490FF. The more modern *Hôtel Résidence Les Mèdes* (☎ 04 94 12 41 24, fax 04 94 58 32 49, rue de la Douane) has studios to rent from 2219/5110FF a week for two people in the low/high season. Both are closed in winter.

The four-star *Mas du Langoustier* (☎ 04 94 58 30 09, fax 04 94 58 36 02, www.langoustier.com), offering fantastic seaviews from its perch on the south-west corner of the island, is Porquerolles' top hotel. Doubles start at 700FF.

Getting There & Away

On Tuesday and Thursday in July and August, Le Pélican (☎ 04 94 58 31 19), based at the port, operates a morning and evening boat between Porquerolles and Port-Cros.

Year round, there are regular boats from Le Lavandou and Hyères (see those sections for details) to Porquerolles. Between June and September, there is one boat daily to/from Toulon, and three boats a week to/from Saint Tropez (see Boat Excursions in those sections).

Boats operated by Vedettes Îles d'Or (☎ 04 94 64 08 04, fax 04 94 71 78 95) sail from Port Miramar at La Londe, a small port town midway between Le Lavandou and Hyères, daily (except Sunday) in July and August. An adult/child return costs 55/35FF (119/55FFF for all three islands). The same company operates boats in July and August from La Croix Valmer and Cavalaire too.

Getting Around

Two options: feet or wheels (motorised tourist vehicles forbidden). Le Cycle Porquerollais (☎ 04 94 58 30 32), 1 rue de la Ferme, hires mountain bikes for 50/75FF a half day/day and tandems for 120/180FF. Around the corner, Le Team (☎ 04 94 58 36 00), 1 rue de la Douane, rents mountain bikes/tandems from 50/150FF a day. At the port, try Locavélo (☎ 04 94 58 33 03).

Le Pelican (☎ 04 94 58 31 19), opposite the tourist office, runs a 24-hour boat taxi service.

ÎLE DE BENDOR

The pinprick island of Bendor lies 300m off the shore from Bandol, 19km east of Toulon. The 7 hectare rocky islet was uninhabited until 1951 when Paul Ricard – best known for his pastis production – bought it and dramatically transformed it into one big *centre de loisirs* (leisure centre). The rock served as a place of exile during the 17th century.

Ricard's larger-than-life creations dominating the island include the **Espace Culturel Paul Ricard** (☎ 04 94 29 48 37) where art exhibitions are held; a **Palais des Congrès** (Congress Centre); and the **Exposition Universelle des Vins et Spiritueux** (☎ 04 94 29 44 34) in which the history and production of wine and spirits is unravelled. More than 8000 bottles from 52 countries are represented in the exhibition contained within the wildly painted, frescoed walls. Opening hours from April to the end of September are 10 am to noon and 2 to 6 pm; closed Wednesday, and from October to March (free).

Getting There & Away

Boats to Île de Bendor (☎ 04 94 29 44 34) depart year round from Bandol (see the Toulon section later) every half hour between 7 and 2 am. Return boats from Île de Bendor leave every 30 minutes between

6.45 am to 1.45 am. A return ticket is 26/16FF for adult/child and dog. Journey time is seven minutes. There is a reduced service in winter.

ÎLES DES EMBIEZ

Bendor's big sister, the Embiez archipelago, sits less than a kilometre off the Presqu'île du Cap Sicié, between Sanary-sur-Mer and Toulon.

The largest of the islet cluster, officially Île de la Tour Fondue but better known as Île des Embiez, is also home to a Ricard creation: the **Institut Océanographique Paul Ricard** (☎ 04 94 34 02 49), housed in an old fort, where over 100 Mediterranean species can be viewed at close quarters in its 27 seawater aquariums and marine museum. Opening hours from May to September are 10 am to 12.30 pm and 1.30 to 5.45 pm; to 6.30 pm in July and August; closed Wednesday and Saturday morning from October to April (16/10FF).

The rest of Ricard's 95 hectare island, purchased in 1958, is occupied by a vast **pleasure port** (☎ 04 94 34 07 51), a **centre de plongée** (diving centre; ☎ 04 94 34 12 78), patches of pine forest and maquis scrubland, some apartment blocks, and a couple of expensive hotels.

Getting There & Away

Boats to the island leave year round from the embarcadère (☎ 04 94 74 97 00) or capitainerie (☎ 04 94 34 05 51) at **Le Brusc**, a small beach resort adjoining Six-Fours-les-Plages, 5km south of Sanary-sur-Mer. In summer boats run approximately every 40 minutes between 6.40 am and midnight. From mid-November until mid-March, boats only run after 9.30 pm on Friday, Saturday and Sunday. From mid-March to mid-June and from mid-September to mid-November, daily boats stop running at 11.30 pm. A single/return fare is 24/33FF (18/24FF for a child aged 3-12). It costs an additional 320/16/165FF to transport a car/bicycle/motorcycle to the island, and 16FF to take your dog. Journey time is 12 minutes.

To call a water taxi, dial ☎ 04 94 34 07 51. A single fare for up to four people from Le Brusc is 450/520FF by day/night.

Between June and September, there are also boats to the island from the port at **Sanary-sur-Mer**. See the Sanary-sur-Mer section below for details.

Hyères

• pop 48,000   ✉ 83400

Relatively unspoilt coastline becomes increasingly urban as you continue westwards to Toulon and on to Marseille. The exception is Hyères which, with its age-old palm trees, succeeds in retaining a charm of its own.

Hyères was settled by the Greeks from Marseille in 350 BC who named their colony Olbia (later renamed Pomponiana by the Romans). Tolstoy in the 1860s was followed by Robert Louis Stevenson in the 1880s who lived in Hyères from 1883 and starting work on *Kidnapped* (1886) in the town.

Four kilometres south of Hyères centre is La Capte, two narrow sand bars supporting salt pans known as Les Salins des Presquiers and a lake (Étang des Presquiers). In mid-September pink flamingos add a splash of colour to the otherwise barren landscape. The spectacular, western sand bar – the route du Sel (Salt Road) – is only accessible in summer. Buses use the eastern-bar road.

At the foot of La Capte sits the beach clad Presqu'île de Giens. French poet and 1960 Nobel Literature prize winner, Saint-John Perse (1887-1975) is buried in the tiny cemetery off route Madrague, on the presqu'île's north-western shore.

Orientation

Hyères' medieval Vieille Ville is perched on a hillside north of the new town. The nearest beach is 4km south on La Capte. The main pleasure port, Port de la Gavine, from where boats to Le Levant and Port-Cros depart, is on La Capte's eastern shore. Boats to Porquerolles depart from La Tour Fondue – the port on the south-eastern corner of Presqu'île de Giens.

Hyères train station, place de l'Europe, is 1.5km south of the old town centre. If you are travelling by foot, walk north-east from the station along ave Edith Cavelland to place du 11 Novembre, then head north along palm tree lined ave Gambetta, the main street in the new town.

Buses to the centre depart from rue de la Gare, opposite the train station. Buses to Port de la Gavine and La Tour Fondue leave from the place de l'Europe stop, immediately in front of the station.

Maps In the new town, the Maison de la Presse, 5 ave Gambetta, stocks an excellent range of maps and guides, many in English.

Information

Tourist Office The tourist office (☎ 04 94 65 18 55, fax 04 94 35 85 05, tourisme@ provence-azur.com, www.provence-azur .com), inside the Rotunde Jean Salusse building on the corner of ave Joseph Clotis and ave Mai Foch, stocks numerous free brochures and sells local walking guides. It

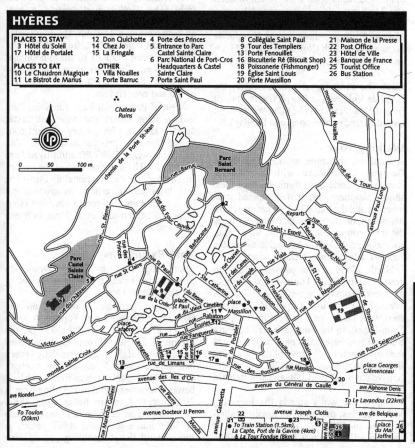

HYÈRES

PLACES TO STAY
3 Hôtel du Soleil
17 Hôtel de Portalet

PLACES TO EAT
10 Le Chaudron Magique
11 Le Bistrot de Marius

12 Don Quichotte
14 Chez Jo
15 La Fringale

OTHER
1 Villa Noailles
2 Porte Barruc

4 Porte des Princes
5 Entrance to Parc
   Castel Sainte Claire
6 Parc National de Port-Cros
   Headquarters & Castel
   Sainte Claire
7 Porte Saint Paul

8 Collégiale Saint Paul
9 Tour des Templiers
13 Porte Fenouillet
16 Biscuiterie Ré (Biscuit Shop)
18 Poissonerie (Fishmonger)
19 Église Saint Louis
20 Porte Massillon

21 Maison de la Presse
22 Post Office
23 Hôtel de Ville
24 Banque de France
25 Tourist Office
26 Bus Station

SAINT TROPEZ TO TOULON

also arranges weekly guided tours (30FF; free for under 12s) of the old town and the Villa Noailles; reserve in advance. It's open from 9 am to noon and 2 to 5.45 pm (closed Sunday); the SNCF counter, inside the office, shares the same hours.

In summer a small tourist office operates inside the train station.

National Park Office The administration (☎ 04 94 12 82 30, fax 04 94 12 82 31, pnpc@wanadoo.fr) of the Parc National de Port-Cros, Castel Sainte Claire, 50 rue Sainte Claire, is open from 10 am to noon and 2 to 6 pm (closed on weekends).

Money Exchange hours at the Banque de France, ave Joseph Clotis, are 8.30 to 11 am and 3 to 5.30 pm (closed on weekends).

Post The central post office, next to the Hôtel de Ville on ave Joseph Clotis, is open from 8.30 am to 6 pm (5 pm on Wednesday; closed Saturday afternoon and Sunday).

Walking Tour

A Saturday morning market fills **place Georges Clémenceau** with a colourful jumble of second-hand furniture, floor tiles, shoes, handbags, marmalade spiced with lavender and the like. The 13th century **Porte Massillon**, on the west side of the square, is the main entrance to the Vieille Ville. Walk west along cobbled rue Massillon to **rue des Porches**, a beautifully arcaded street.

North of the market square is the 13th century **Église Saint Louis**, a fine example of sober, Romanesque-style architecture. Weave your way uphill to rue Bourg Neuf, then walk west along its continuation, rue Saint-Esprit, to the limestone arch of **Porte Barruc**. From here, steps pass an iron gate to the rambling hillside grove of the **Parc Saint Bernard**. Remnants of the 12th century defensive city wall and **Château Saint Bernard** are visible.

Below the walls stands the imposing **Villa Noailles**, designed by Robert Mallet-Stevens in 1923 for devoted patron of modern art, Vicomte Charles de Noailles.

The architect's mission: to build a winter residence 'interesting to inhabit'. The result: a cubist maze of concrete and glass, set within a Mediterranean park designed by Noailles and featuring a cubist garden designed by Gabriel Guevrekian in 1925. Contemporary design exhibitions are held here in summer (free).

Heading back downhill along rue Barbacane, you come to the 12th century **Porte Saint Paul**, the first city gate to be built. It frames the **Collégiale Saint Paul**, comprising two churches dating from the 12th and 14th centuries joined together perpendicularly. The Gothic part houses a vast collection of predominantly 18th century, ex-voto paintings. The oldest painting dates from 1613, the newest from 1997. The church is open from 10.30 am to noon and 3.30 to 6 pm. From the terrace in front of the church there is a marvellous panorama of old and new Hyères.

West of Porte Saint Paul, rue Saint Paul and rue Sainte Claire lead to the **Parc Castel Sainte Claire**, a 17th century convent converted into a private residence. The American writer Edith Wharton lived here from 1927. The mansion houses the administration of the Parc National de Port-Cros (see Information earlier). Its grounds are open from 8 am to 6 pm (5 pm from November to March and until 7 pm between June and August).

Boat Excursions

Boats, operated by TLV (www.oda.fr/aa/tlv), sail year round from Hyères to the three Îles d'Hyères.

Boats to Porquerolles depart from the Gare Maritime de La Tour Fondue (☎ 04 94 58 21 81, fax 04 94 58 91 73) on the Presqu'île de Giens. From May to September there are eight to 21 boats daily (every half hour between 5 July and 30 August). Six to 10 boats daily run to/from the island between October and April. Sailing time is 20 minutes. A return ticket costs 78FF. Transporting an adult/child's bicycle costs 50/38FF and a surfboard 100FF return. A three-island ticket, enabling you to visit

SAINT TROPEZ TO TOULON

Port-Cros and Le Levant from Porquerolles, costs 145/83FF for adult/child.

Boats to Île du Levant and Port-Cros leave Hyères from Port de la Gavine (☎ 04 94 57 44 07) on La Capte. Between mid-March and June, and in September and October, there are two return sailings daily from Hyères to Île du Levant (1½ hours) stopping at Port-Cros (one hour) en route. In July and August, five boats sail daily. Between January and mid-March, one boat only sails on Monday, Wednesday, Friday and Saturday. Tickets and timetables are available from the port's capitainerie. A return ticket to one of the two islands costs 112/73FF for adult/child aged 4-11 years; a combined ticket allowing passage to Le Levant and Port-Cros is 130/83FF.

Places to Stay

Hyères has some good value places to stay. The tourist office has a list of places on La Capte and Presqu'île de Giens.

Camping Close to Port de la Gavine, *Camping Saint-Pierre des Horts* (☎ 04 94 57 65 31, fax 04 94 38 93 38, 2503 chemin de la Font de Horts), 4km from the Hyères town centre, is a large site open all year.

There are no less than nine campings on Presqu'île de Giens, all within walking distance of the beach. In Giens, *Camping Le Clair de Lune* (☎ 04 94 58 20 19, fax 04 94 58 15 90, 27 ave du Clair de Lune) charges 67-92FF for two people with car and tent. The site is open from February to November. *Camping La Bergerie* (☎ 04 94 58 91 75, fax 04 94 58 14 28, 4231 route de Giens) is open from mid-February to the end of December and charges 80FF for two people with a tent and car; buses to La Tour Fondue stop almost directly outside.

Similar rates are charged at *Camping Les Îles d'Or* (☎ 04 94 58 20 55, blvd Alsace Lorraine), open June to September; and *Camping Les Cigales* (☎ 04 94 58 21 06), 150m from the beach at the south end of blvd Alsace Lorraine, open between March and October.

Hotels – New Town Opposite the train station, *Centrôtel* (☎ 04 93 38 38 10, fax 04 94 38 37 73, 45 ave Edith Cavelle) has uninspiring singles for 260-330FF and doubles from 330-360FF. Doubles with a large terrace cost 420FF.

Cheapies include the one-star *Hôtel de la Poste* (☎ 04 94 65 02 00, 7 ave Lyautey) which charges 160/180FF in the low/high season for a respectable double. Also touting one star is the five room *Hôtel Régina* (☎ 04 94 65 03 90, ave Alphonse Denis) which charges 160FF for a room with shower and washbasin (toilet in the corridor) for one or two people.

The pretty *Hôtel du Lion d'Or* (☎ 04 94 65 25 55, 2 rue de la République) has rooms for one or two people with washbasin for 150/170FF in the low/high season. The zero-star *Hôtel Acropole* (☎ 04 94 35 42 22, fax 04 94 35 51 98, 45 ave Victoria) has more upmarket rooms with shower and toilet for 202/255FF for a single/double.

Top notch in style and decadence is the plush, glass-topped, 15-room *Casino des Palmiers* (☎ 04 94 12 80 80, fax 04 94 65 01 99, 1 rue Ambroise Thomas). Doubles overlooking the sea/town start at 590/490FF.

Hotels – Vieille Ville Medieval Hyères' best hotel is the two-star *Hôtel du Soleil* (☎ 04 94 65 18 26, fax 04 94 35 46 00), an ivy-clad building at the top of very, *very* steep (read: not for the unfit) rue du Rampart. Singles/doubles/triples start at 170/200/280FF.

At the bottom of the hill is *Hôtel de Portalet* (☎ 04 94 65 39 40, 4 rue de Limans) which has large airy rooms with appealing age-old furnishings. In the low season, singles/doubles with washbasin and bidet cost 155/165FF, with shower 185/195FF while triples are 275FF (170/180FF; 205/230FF and 345FF in July and August).

Places to Eat

Restaurants Rue de Limans, rue Portalet and rue Massillon in the lower part of the Vieille Ville are lined with touristy places to

SAINT TROPEZ TO TOULON

eat. Particularly tasty is *Chez Jo* (☎ *04 94 65 31 13, 22 rue de Limans)*, a rustic place where you can eat well for around 70FF. Another that stands out from the crowd is colourful *La Fringale* (☎ *04 94 35 42 52, 12 rue de Limans)*. The small bistro sports a blue ceiling and its walls are adorned with large modern paintings. It has a *plat du jour* for 45FF and a lunchtime *formule* for 60FF (closed on Sunday).

Place Massillon is one big restaurant in summer. *Le Bistrot de Marius* (☎ *04 94 35 88 38)*, at No 1 on the square, specialises in fish dishes including bouillabaisse du pêcheur, *poissons grillés* (grilled fish) and *saumon fumé* (smoked salmon). *Menus* are 90, 140 and 190FF.

For a hearty plate of aïoli Provençal complet (75FF), comprising a boiled egg, boiled potatoes, a mound of boiled vegetables, shellfish and a bowl of garlicky aïoli, head for *Le Chaudron Magique* (☎ *04 94 35 38 45, 8 place Massillon)*. It also has a (substantially) lighter 58FF *menu* and various grilled fish. The Magic Cauldron is open from 11 am to 11 pm in summer.

The house speciality at *Don Quichotte* (☎ *04 94 35 63 25, rue Rabaton)*, off place Massillon, is Spanish tapas and *moules* (mussels). Among the 10 varieties on offer are moules au pastis and moules au whisky (mussels marinated in pastis or in whisky), both costing 60FF a bowl. *Menus* here are 65, 85 and 125FF.

In the new town close to the bus station, *Le Jardin de Saradam* (☎ *04 94 65 97 53, 35 ave de Belgique)* dishes up Mediterranean and oriental cuisine. Its couscous is reputed to be the best in town.

Self-Catering A *fruit and veg market* spills across the north end of ave Gambetta on Saturday morning. Ave Edith Cavell is lined with small grocery stores. In the old town, there are a couple of well stocked *poissonneries* (fishmongers) on rue Massillon (closed afternoons).

The *Boulangerie-Pâtisserie Micka*, corner of ave 8 Mai and ave Gambetta, sells tartes Tropéziennes and a good selection of breads and pastries. In the old town, delicious homemade biscuits and meringues are baked at the *Biscuiterie Ré*, 8 rue de Limans.

Fill up your water bottle with wine from the *Vinothèque Hyèroise* (☎ *04 94 57 55 97)*, spitting distance from the train station at 38bis ave Edith Cavell; or from the *Cave des Îles d'Or* (☎ *04 94 65 70 47)*, 5 place du 11 Novembre, on the corner of ave Gambetta.

Getting There & Away

Air The Aéroport de Toulon-Hyères (☎ 04 94 00 83 83) is 3km from the centre towards La Capte.

Bus The bus station, place du Mal Joffre, is in the modern centre between ave de Belgique and ave Jean Jaurès. The ticket office is open various hours; buy tickets from the driver when it is closed.

Regular buses, operated by SODETRAV (☎ 04 94 12 55 00), serve Toulon (35-50 minutes; 25 daily), Le Lavandou (30 minutes; 14 daily), Cavalaire (one hour; 6 daily) and Saint Tropez (1½ hours, 6 daily).

Train Hyères train station (☎ 04 94 09 51 32), place de l'Europe, is open from 5.30 am to 8.35 pm (6.30 am on weekends).

There are plenty of local trains between Hyères and Toulon (17 minutes). The Marseille-Hyères train (70FF; 1¼ hours; four daily) stops at Cassis, La Ciotat, Bandol, Ollioules-Sanary and Toulon en route.

Getting Around

To/From the Airport SODETRAV operates a regular shuttle bus from Aéroport de Hyères-Toulon to Hyères bus station (25.50FF; 10 minutes). Buses coincide with flight arrivals/departures.

Bus Every 30 minutes, a bus links Hyères bus station with the train station (5 minutes), Port de la Gavine (15 minutes), La Capte (20 minutes), Giens (30 minutes) and La Tour Fondue (35 minutes). A single ticket costs 10.50FF. Buses run between 6.25 am and 10 pm.

For the Port de la Gavine (boats to Îles du Levant and Port-Cros), get off at Le Port stop, ave de la Meditérranée. For Tour Fondue (boats to Porquerolles), get off at the Tour Fondue stop.

Bicycle Near the bus station, Cycles Cad (☎ 04 94 65 07 69), 59 ave Alphonse Denis, has road and mountain bikes for hire.

Holiday Bikes (☎ 04 94 38 79 45, fax 04 94 57 39 11), Centre Commercial Nautique at Port de la Gavine, rents mountain bikes/scooters from 70/200FF a day. It also has roller blades/motorcycles/motor boats for 50/290/800FF a day. It's open from 9 am to noon and 3 to 7 pm.

Also in the Port de la Gavine area, L'Horizon (☎ 04 94 58 03 78), 14 ave de la Meditérranée, rents road/mountain bikes for 25/30FF an hour or 55/70FF a day.

Toulon

• **pop 168,000**   ✉ **83000**

Originally a Roman colony, Toulon only became part of France in 1481; the city grew in importance after Henri IV established an arsenal here. In the 17th century the port was enlarged by Vauban. The young Napoléon Bonaparte first made a name for himself in 1793 during a siege in which the English, who had taken over Toulon, were expelled.

As in any large port, there's a lively quarter with heaps of bars where locals and sailors spill out of every door. Women travelling on their own should avoid some of the old city streets at night, particularly around rue Chevalier Paul and the western end of rue Pierre Sémard.

All in all, it's a city like no other on the Côte d'Azur, though it's unclear why anyone would want to spend much time here when pulsating Marseille, fine beaches and the tranquil Îles d'Hyères are so close. Toulon moreover holds the dubious distinction of having elected a mayor, Jean-Marie Le Chevallier, from the extreme right National Front in 1995. What better reason to avoid this unfortunate city?

Orientation

Toulon is built around a *rade*, a sheltered bay lined with quays. To the west is the naval base and to the east the ferry terminal, from where boats set sail for Corsica. The city is at its liveliest along quai de la Sinse and quai Stalingrad – from where ferries depart for the Îles d'Hyères – and in the old city. Northwest of the old city is the train station.

Separating the old city from the northern section is a multilane, multinamed thoroughfare (known as ave du Maréchal Leclerc and blvd de Strasbourg as it runs through the centre), which teems with traffic. It continues west to Marseille and east to the French Riviera. Immediately north-west of here, off rue Chalucet, is a pleasant city park. Toulon's central square is the enormous place de la Liberté; the giant Palais de la Liberté under construction on the east side of the square will house a 9500 sq metre commercial centre when it opens for the year 2000.

Raimu, the great Provençal actor (see Facts for the Visitor chapter), was born in a house at 6 rue Anatole France, off place d'Armes, immediately north of the arsenal building.

Information

Tourist Offices The main tourist office (☎ 04 94 18 53 00, fax 04 94 18 53 09, tourisme@wanadoo.fr, www.toulon.com), place Raimu, is open from 9 am to 6 pm (Sunday from 10 am to noon). It arranges guided tours of the city on Saturday and Wednesday (20/15/10FF for adult/student/teenager). Book in advance.

The Maison de l'Étudiant (☎ 04 94 93 14 21), rue de la Glaoière, is a handy information source. The Club Alpin Français (CAF; ☎ 04 94 46 26 63) is at 55 rue Frédéric Mineur.

Money The Banque de France, ave Vauban, is open from 8.30 am to noon and 1.30 to 5.30 pm (closed on weekends). Commercial banks line blvd de Strasbourg.

Post The post office, rue Dr Jean Bertholet (second entrance on rue Ferrero) is open from 8 am to 7 pm (Tuesday until 6 pm, Saturday until noon; closed Sunday).

SAINT TROPEZ TO TOULON

TOULON

PLACES TO STAY
3 Hôtel Terminus
8 Hôtel La Résidence
10 Hôtel Maritima
15 Hôtel d'Europe
23 Hôtel de Provence
25 Hôtel Molière
29 Hôtel Little Palace

PLACES TO EAT
5 La Muraille de Chine
6 Al Dente
11 Le Maharajah
14 Cafétéria du Centre
   (Two Entrances)
26 Le Petit Prince
27 Les Enfants Gâtés
34 Le Constantinois

OTHER
1 Train Station
2 SODEVTRAV (Bus Office)
4 Scubazur (Diving Shop)
7 Boulangerie
9 Entrance to City Park
12 Laundrette
13 Banque de France
16 RMTT (Bus) Kiosk
17 Palais de la Liberté
   (Under Construction)
18 Casino (Supermarket)
19 Musée de Toulon
20 8 à Huit (Grocery)
21 Cinéma Le Royal
22 Post Office
24 Théâtre Municipal
28 Place des Trois Dauphins
30 Place Puget
31 Covered Food Market
32 Laundrette
33 Maison de l'Étudiant
35 Tourist Office; Place Raimu
36 Place Gustave Lambert
37 Cathédrale Sainte
   Marie Majeure
38 Food Market
39 Hôtel de Ville
40 Musée de la Marine
41 Maritime Préfecture
42 Rade Boat Trips
43 Ferries to Îles d'Hyères
44 Sitcat RMTT Boats
45 Statue
46 Rade Boat Trips
47 Place Pasteur; Cyber Espace

Email & Internet Access For an Internet connection, contact Cyber Espace (☎ 04 94 41 06 05, cyberespace@terranet.fr), 10 place Pasteur. It is open from 10 am to 8 pm (42FF an hour).

Laundry There are several laundrettes in the old city, including one at 25 rue Baudin (open from 7 am to 9 pm); another at 16 rue Peiresc (open from 7 am to 8.30 am; Sunday until 8 pm).

Musée de Toulon

The Toulon Museum (☎ 04 94 93 15 54), 113 ave du Maréchal Leclerc, houses an unexceptional **Musée d'Art** (Art Museum; open from 1 to 6 pm) and a moth-eaten **Musée d'Histoire Naturelle** in a Renaissance-style building. The Natural History Museum is open from 9.30 am to noon and 2 to 6 pm; from 1 to 6 pm on Sunday (both free).

Musée de la Marine

The Marine Museum (☎ 04 94 02 02 01) in the lovely old arsenal building, place Monsenergue, is open from 9.30 am to noon and 2 to 6 pm (closed Tuesday). In July and August daily hours are 9.30 am to noon and 3 to 7 pm (29/19FF for adult/student).

Musée Naval de la Tour Royale & La Dives

The sturdy **Tour Royale** (Royal Tower) on the Pointe de la Mître in the suburb of Le Mourillon, just south of Toulon centre and the ferry terminal, was constructed under Louis XII at the beginning of the 16th century. Serving as a prison in the past, it today houses a small naval museum (☎ 04 94 02 17 99), open from 9.30 am to noon and 2 to 6 pm; closed Monday and Tuesday (12/7FF for adult/child). The views of the rade, Toulon and Mont Faron, from the tower are quite majestic.

Next to the tower is moored the cumbersome **La Dives** (☎ 04 94 02 06 96), a 102m landing craft in service between 1961 and 1986, and today used as a naval museum. A permanent exhibition of military vehicles from the WWII is displayed inside. You can visit the boat, by guided tour only, on Wednesday, Saturday and Sunday from 10 am to noon and 1 to 6.30 pm. Daily hours from June to October are 10 am to noon and 1.30 to 6.30 or 7 pm (25/12.50FF for adult/child).

Mont Faron

Overlooking the old city from the north is Mont Faron (580m), from which you can see Toulon's port in its true magnificence. Near the hill's summit rises the **Tour Beaumont Mémorial du Débarquement** (☎ 04 94 88 08 09), which commemorates the Allied landings that took place along the coast here in August 1944. Closed Monday, it can be visited between 9.30 and 11.30 am and 2 to 4.30 pm (25/10FF for adult/child aged 5-16).

A *téléphérique* (☎ 04 94 92 68 25) climbs the mountain from blvd Amiral Vence. It runs from 9 am to noon and 2 to 5.30 pm; closed Monday (37/25FF return for adult/child aged 4-10). If you are visiting the **zoo** (☎ 04 94 88 07 89) on Mont Faron, then buy a combination ticket which costs 55/35FF for adult/child and covers the téléphérique and zoo admission (40/30FF without a téléphérique ticket). The zoo is open from 10 am to 6.30 pm (closed on rainy days).

To get to the téléphérique, take bus No 40 from place de la Liberté to the téléphérique stop. It does not operate on windy days.

Boat Excursions

Excursions around the rade, with a commentary (French only) on the events that took place here during WWII, leave from quai Stalingrad or its continuation, quai de la Sinse. Trips cost an average of 45FF for one hour.

Between June and September, Le Batelier de la Rade (☎ 04 94 46 24 65), quai de la Sinse, runs a daily boat to the Îles d'Hyères (100FF return to Porquerolles; 150FF to Port-Cros; 160FF to Porquerolles, Port-Cros and Le Levant). The trip to Porquerolles takes one hour. It's another 40 minutes to Port-Cros, from where it is only a 20 minute hop to Île du Levant.

SAINT TROPEZ TO TOULON

Between May and September, Compagnie de Navigation SNRTM (☎ 04 94 93 07 56), 1247 route du Faron and at the port, operates a boat to the three Îles d'Hyères on Wednesday (170FF return) and a boat to the Îles des Embiez and the Calanques near Marseille on Tuesday (160FF return).

Sitcat boats (☎ 04 94 46 35 46) run by RMTT, the local transport company, link quai Stalingrad with the towns on the peninsula across the harbour, including La Seyne (line 8M), Saint Mandrier-sur-Mer (line 28M) and Sablettes (line 18M). The 20 minute ride costs the same as a bus ticket: 8FF (10FF if you buy your ticket aboard). The ticket office at the port is open from 8.45 am to 12.10 pm and 1.30 to 6.15 pm. Boats run from around 6 am to 8 pm.

Scubazur (☎ 04 94 92 19 29, fax 04 94 92 24 13), 26 rue Mirabeau, is a first-class diving shop which has a plentitude of information on all the **diving clubs and schools** along the Côte d'Azur.

Special Events
For nigh on 50 years, Toulon has held an International Festival of Music (mainly classical) in various locations around town, including the Théâtre Municipal on place Victor Hugo, from June to early July.

Places to Stay
Camping The closest camping ground to Toulon, *Camping Le Beauregard (☎ 04 94 20 56 35)*, is on the coast some 6km east in Quartier Sainte Marguerite. It costs 22.50/11FF per adult/child and 19.50FF for a tent. Take bus No 7 from the train station to the 'La Terre Promise' stop.

Hotels There are plenty of cheap options in the old city, though some (particularly those at the western end of rue Jean Jaurès) are said to double as brothels.

Immediately opposite the train station is the cheap and unsmiling *Hôtel Terminus (☎ 04 94 89 23 54, 7 blvd de Tessé)* which has singles/doubles from 115/185FF. It flogs 59FF *menus* in its adjoining restaurant.

Another one, conveniently close to the bus and train stations is *Hôtel La Résidence (☎ 04 94 92 92 81, 18 rue Gimelli)*. The rooms are not as impressive as the lobby, with its enormous gilt mirror and balding Oriental carpets, but they're a bargain. Simple singles/doubles are 120/130FF and those with shower are 190FF. Showers costs 15FF – and the *patron* guards the key as if it opened the very gates of heaven. It's easy to park around here.

Heading into town, the *Hôtel Maritima (☎ 04 94 92 39 33, 9 rue Gimelli)* has equally simple single/double rooms for 125/140FF. Rooms with a shower/shower and toilet are 180/220FF. The pleasant *Hôtel Little Palace (☎ 04 94 92 26 62, fax 04 94 89 13 77, 6 rue Berthelot)* has simple rooms from 80/125FF and from 150FF with shower. Beside the opera house, the one-star *Hôtel Molière (☎ 04 94 92 78 35, fax 04 94 62 85 82, 12 rue Molière)* has doubles from 110FF.

Hôtel de Provence (☎ 04 94 93 19 00, 53 rue Jean Jaurès) is welcoming but often full. Basic rooms start around 115/125FF for singles/doubles and 150/190FF with shower.

East of the train station, *Hôtel d'Europe (☎ 04 94 92 37 44, fax 04 94 62 37 50, 7 rue de Chabannes)* has rooms for one or two people for 198, 230, and 310FF. Photographs of each room category accompany the price list displayed in reception. Some rooms have little balconies.

Places to Eat
Pricey restaurants, terraces and bars with occasional live music are abundant along the quays; *menus* start at 100FF and a tiny bouillabaisse or aïoli garni will set you back 80-100FF. Another lively area is place Victor Hugo and neighbouring place Puget. Cheaper fare can be found in the old city's more dilapidated streets around rue Chevalier Paul where plenty of prostitutes ply their trade.

Restaurants In rue Pierre Sémard you can have a hearty meal in the humble Algerian restaurant *Le Constantinois*. It is mainly frequented by local men, but a friendly outsider, particularly in these tense times in Toulon, is more than welcome. A generous serving of couscous with salad costs as little as 30FF and the coffee is black, thick and sweet.

Another very popular and modern place is **Les Enfants Gâtés** (☎ 04 94 09 14 67, 7 rue Corneille). The Spoilt Children is run by a young crowd and is one of the most pleasant places in town to dine without breaking the bank. The plat du jour is 60FF. Close by is the equally charming **Le Petit Prince** (10 rue de l'Humilité), poetically named after Antoine de Saint Exupéry's children's book.

There are some decent restaurants on rue Gimelli near the train station: **La Muraille de Chine** (☎ 04 94 92 04 21) at No 32 has Chinese menus for 58 and 85FF. Closed on Sunday. Nearby at No 30 is **Al Dente** (☎ 04 94 93 02 50), a cool and elegant Italian place serving eight types of homemade pasta for about 40FF and salads for 38-46FF. The lunch/evening menu is 59/100FF. Al Dente is open for lunch (except Sunday) and dinner to 10.30 or 11 pm. **Le Maharajah** (☎ 04 94 91 93 46), an Indian eatery at 15 rue Gimelli, has lunch/dinner menus for 59/129FF and thalis (trays with an assortment of dishes) for 145FF. It is closed on Monday.

Cafétéria du Centre (☎ 04 94 92 68 57, 27-29 rue Gimelli and 4-8 rue de Chabannes) has cheap three-course menus for around 30FF. It is open from 11 am to 2.30 pm and 6.30 to 10 pm (closed Sunday).

Self-Catering The southern half of cours Lafayette is one long open-air *food market* held, in typical Provençal style, under the plane trees. There's a covered *food market* on place Vincent Raspail. Both are open daily except Monday.

Near the train station, the *boulangerie*, 21 rue Mirabeau, serves sandwiches, pizza and quiche. It is open daily from 5 am to 7 pm. Close by there is a small *Casino* supermarket, 7 ave Vauban, and an *8 à Huit* grocery directly opposite.

Getting There & Away

Air The Aéroport de Toulon-Hyères (☎ 04 94 00 83 83) is 25km east of Toulon, near Hyères.

Bus Intercity buses leave from the bus terminal on place de l'Europe, to the right as you exit the train station. Information and bus tickets for the several companies that service the region are available from SODETRAV (☎ 04 94 28 93 40), 4 blvd Pierre Toesca (opposite the terminal).

The buses to Hyères (35FF; 40 minutes; seven a day) continue eastward along the coast, stopping at Le Lavandou (58FF; 1¼ hours) and other towns, before arriving in Saint Tropez (92FF; 2¼ hours). Francelignes Comett (☎ 04 91 61 83 00 in Marseille) has buses to Aix-en-Provence (84/134FF single/return; 1¼ hours). There are four daily (two on Sunday in July and August). Phocéens Cars (☎ 04 93 85 66 61 in Nice) goes to Nice (132FF; 2½ hours) via Hyères and Cannes (120FF; two hours) twice daily (except Sunday).

Train The train station (☎ 08 36 35 35 35), place Albert 1er, is near blvd Pierre Toesca. The information office is open from 8 am to 7 pm (closed Sunday). There are frequent connections to cities along the coast, including Marseille (55FF; 40 minutes), Saint Raphaël (94FF; 50 minutes; hourly) and Nice (129FF; 1½ hours; hourly). Trains to Paris' Gare de Lyon (464FF; 5¾ hours) go via Marseille.

Boat Ferries to Corsica and Sardinia are run by the SNCM (☎ 04 94 16 66 66), which has an office at 49 ave de l'Infanterie de Marine (opposite the ferry terminal). It is open from 8.30 am to noon (11.30 am on Saturday) and 2 to 5.45 pm (closed Sunday). Car ferries to Porto Torres in Sardinia operate four to six times a month from mid-April to September. For more information see the Getting There & Away chapter.

For information on boats to the Îles d'Hyères see Boat Excursions earlier.

Getting Around

To/From the Airport SODETRAV (☎ 04
94 12 55 12 in Hyères) operates a regular
shuttle bus from Aéroport de Hyères-
Toulon to Toulon train station (56FF; 35
minutes). Buses coincide with flight arrivals and departures.

Bus Local buses are run by RMTT (☎ 04 94
03 87 03) which has an information kiosk at
the main local bus hub on place de la
Liberté. It is open from 7.30 am to noon and
1.30 to 6.30 pm (closed on weekends).
Single/10 tickets cost 8/56FF. Buses generally run until around 7.30 or 8.30 pm.
Sunday service is limited.

Bus Nos 7 and 13 link the train station
with quai Stalingrad.

Towards Marseille

Heading towards Marseille from Toulon,
there are a couple of spots worth a stop.
Sanary-sur-Mer is as serene as its name
suggests; Bandol is best known for its
wines; while inland, the Circuit du Castellet is strictly for wannabe Schumachers.

Sanary-sur-Mer

This quiet seaside resort, 15km east of
Toulon, was home to novelist Aldous
Huxley (1894-1963) in the early 1930s, his
biographer Sybille Bedford (1911-) in the
late 1930s, and to a host of German
refugees very soon after. Thomas Mann and
his brother, Heinrich, both sought refuge
here, as did the German painter Feucht-
wanger.

Its sandy beaches today are packed in
summer. Sanary-sur-Mer is just 6km north
of La Brusc, from where boats depart year
round to Paul Ricard's Îles des Embiez (see
The Islands section earlier). Between June
and September SMS (☎ 04 94 07 69 89) operates direct boats from Sanary to Île des
Embiez (15 minutes; 45/25FF return for
adult/child; three boats a day). The Maison
du Tourisme in Sanary-sur-Mer (☎ 04 94 74
01 04), Jardin de la Ville, has details.

Bandol

In the 1900s, Bandol, 8km west of Sanary-
sur-Mer (pop 14,730, postcode 83110) was
a refuge for ailing foreigners such as novel-
ists DH Lawrence and Katherine Mansfield.
Today it is better known for its viticulture,
an industry that is far from ailing. The terraced vineyards stretching for about 15km
inland from the coast (as far north as Saint
Anne du Castellet) are managed by 50 wine
producers who, since 1941, have sold their
wine under their own coveted AOC.

The Association Les Vins de Bandol (☎ 04
94 90 29 59, fax 04 94 98 50 24), Espace
Mistral, 2 ave Saint Louis, in Le Beausset,
10km north of Bandol, has a complete list of
all the producers. Most allow you to visit their
caves (wine cellars) and taste their wines. Alternatively contact the Bandol tourist office
(☎ 04 94 29 41 35, fax 04 94 32 50 39, bando
lot@riviera-on-line.fr, www.bandol.org), opposite the port on allées Vivien.

From Bandol port, there are boats year
round to the Île de Bendor. In July and
August, Atlantide (☎ 04 94 32 51 41) at the
port, organises boat excursions along the
coast; as does Bandolaise II (☎ 04 94 29 65
91), Port de Bandol.

Circuit du Castellet Paul Ricard

The calm and tranquility which caresses the
northern realms of the Bandol vineyards
around the perched village of **Le Castellet**
(252m) is smashed with racy aplomb at the
Circuit du Castellet, a motorsports race
track built by Paul Ricard in 1970. The
5.8km circuit hosts the Grand Prix de France
Moto in July and the Bol d'Or in mid-September (see Facts for the Visitor chapter).

Aspiring Schumachers can pay 250FF for
a lap – in the passenger seat – in the *bâpteme
de piste* (fast lane) with a 1950s Caterham
Super Seven (Lotus). The track (☎ 04 94 98
24 49 or 06 08 51 54 42) is open from 6 to
8 pm on weekdays (by appointment only
between September and June). Miniature
cars, trains, planes and other fast machines
are displayed in the **Musée du Modélisme**
(☎ 04 94 90 61 90), next to the entrance of
the 1000 hectare racetrack complex.

Monaco

• pop 30,000 ☎ 377 ✉ 98000

The tiny Principality of Monaco (Principauté de Monaco) has been under the rule of the Grimaldi family for most of the period since 1297. It is a sovereign state whose territory, surrounded by France, covers just 1.95 sq km. Since 1949 it has been ruled by Prince Rainier III (born in 1923), whose sweeping constitutional powers make him much more then a mere figurehead. For decades, the family has been featured on the front pages of the tabloids, though since the death in 1982 of the much-loved Princess Grace (best remembered from her Hollywood days as the actress Grace Kelly) the media has concentrated on the love lives of the couple's two daughters, Caroline and Stephanie, and their ageing bachelor son, Albert.

Glamorous Monte Carlo – Monaco's capital – is famed for its casino and its role as host to the annual Formula One Grand Prix. Since 1911, every May, drivers from around the world tear round a track that winds through the town and around the port. Unsurpassable views of the race, the principality and its legendary Monte Carlo scraper skyline can be enjoyed from the Musée Océanographique's terrace restaurant or the Trophée des Alpes' gardens in French La Turbie (see the Nice to Menton chapter).

Citizens of Monaco (known as Monégasques), of whom there are only about 5000, pay no taxes. They have their own flag (red and white); own national anthem and national holiday (19 November); own country telephone code (377); and own traditional dialect, Monégasque – broadly speaking a mixture of French and Italian – which is taught in schools alongside French, the official language. Many street signs are bi-lingual. The official religion is Roman Catholicism. There are no border formalities upon entering Monaco from France. The principality was admitted to the UN as a full member in 1993.

HIGHLIGHTS

• See the changing of the guard at Monaco palace
• Gape at the glamorous yachts moored in the port
• Have a flutter at Monte Carlo Casino
• Make a date for a night at the opera
• Discover the underworld at the Musée Océanographique

By law, it is forbidden to walk around town barechested, barefooted or bikini-clad.

History

Monoïkos (Monaco) was settled by the Greeks in the 4th century and later on by the Romans who incorporated 'the rock' into their province. In 1297, François Grimaldi penetrated the town disguised as a monk, marking the start of Grimaldi rule – solidified in 1346 when the family purchased Menton and Roquebrune to add to their territory.

Monégasque independence was first recognised in 1489 by Charles VIII, king of France. Monaco fell under Spanish protectorship from 1525 until 1641 when the French drove out the Spanish and established their own alliance with the principality instead. The French Revolution is the black period in its history. Monaco was seized by France, the Monégasque royal family was arrested, their palace was turned into a warehouse and their land was renamed Fort Hercule.

Under the 1814 Treaty of Paris the Grimaldi family was restored to the throne.

In 1860 Monégasque independence was recognised for a second time by France and consolidated the following year when Monaco relinquished all claims over its former territories of Menton and Roquebrune which it had lost in 1848. A customs and monetary union agreement was signed with France in 1865, sealing future cooperation between the two countries.

Monaco's absolute monarchy was replaced in 1911 by a constitution, reformed by Rainier III in 1962. The ruling prince is assisted by a *conseil national* (national

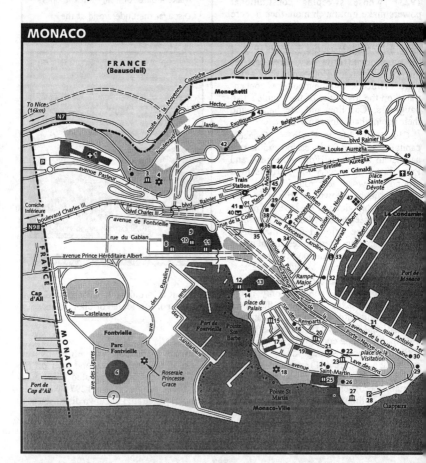

MONACO

council) comprising 18 democratically elected members. Only Monégasques aged 21 or over can vote in the council elections held every five years; Monégasque nationality is granted to people born in Monaco or of Monégasque parentage.

Radio

French and Italian language, Radio Monte Carlo (RMC; ☎ 377-93 15 16 17) transmits from antennas on the Plateau de Fontbonne and the Col de la Madone and attracts a nationwide audience (0.9 million listeners).

It can be picked up in Monaco on 98.8 MHz FM.

Orientation

Monaco consists of five principal areas: Monaco Ville (also known as the old city or Le Rocher), a 60m-high outcrop of rock 800m long on the south side of the Port de Monaco where the Palais du Prince (Prince's Palace) is; Monte Carlo, famous for its casino and annual Grand Prix, which is north of the port; La Condamine, the flat area south-west of the port; Fontvieille, the

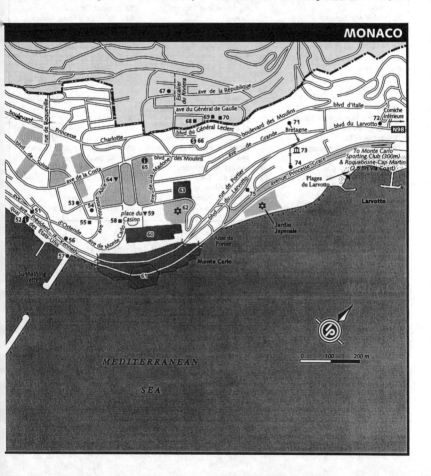

MONACO

MONACO

PLACES TO STAY	9 Centre Commercial de	34 Public Lift Entrance
36 Hôtel Helvetia	Fontvieille	35 Place d'Armes; Food Market
38 Hôtel Cosmopolite; Hôtel de	10 Collection de Voitures	37 Scruples Bookshop
France	Anciennes	39 Galerie Riccadonna
41 Hôtel Terminus	11 Musée des Timbres et des	40 Post Office
44 Centre de la Jeunesse	Monnaies	42 Public Lift Entrance
Princesse Stéphanie	12 Musée des Souvenirs	43 Public Lift Entrance
55 Hôtel Hermitage	Napoléoniens	47 Casino (Supermarket)
58 Hôtel de Paris; Le Louis XV	13 Palais du Prince	48 Public Lift Entrance
(Restaurant)	14 Entrance to State Apartments	49 Public Lift Entrance
68 Hôtel Diana (Beausoleil)	15 Musée de Vieux Monaco	50 Église Sainte Dévote
69 Hôtel Olympia (Beausoleil)	16 Princess Grace Irish Library	51 CAM (Local Bus Company)
70 Hôtel Cosmopolite (Beau-	17 Cathédrale De Monaco	Office
soleil)	(Burial Place of Princess	52 Tourist Office Kiosk
75 Hôtel Mirabeau	Grace)	53 Palais de la Scala; Main Post
	18 Jardins Saint-Martin	Office
PLACES TO EAT	19 Hôtel de Ville	54 Square Beaumarchais
31 Stars 'n' Bars	20 Musée de Cire	56 Théâtre Princesse Grace
45 Restaurant de Trende	21 Post Office	57 Les Bateaux de La French
46 Le Texan	22 Ministère d'Etat (State	Riviera (Boat Excursions)
59 Café de Paris	Ministry)	60 Casino de Monte Carlo; Salle
64 Haagen-Däz	23 Musée de la Chapelle de la	Garnier
	Visitation	61 Centre de Congrès Auditori-
OTHER	24 Azur Express Tourist Train	um
1 Centre Hospitalier Princess	Station	62 Jardins du Casino
Grace (Hospital)	25 Musée Océanographique	63 FNAC; Centre Commercial Le
2 Public Lift	26 Escalator to Monte Carlo	Métropole; Parking
3 Musée d'Anthropologie	Story; Parking des Pêcheurs	65 Office National de Tourisme
Préhistorique	27 Monte Carlo Story	66 American Express
4 Jardin Exotique	28 Parking des Pêcheurs	67 Laundrette
5 Stade Louis II (Stadium)	29 Théâtre du Fort Antoine	71 Public Lift Entrance
6 Espace Fontvieille	30 Yacht Club de Monaco	72 Public Lift
7 Helipad	32 Public Lift Entrance	73 Musée National
8 Musée Naval	33 Tourist Office Kiosk	74 Public Lift Entrance

industrial area south of Monaco Ville; and Larvotto, the beach area east of Monte Carlo. The French town of Beausoleil is just three streets up the hill from Monte Carlo.

Information

Tourist Offices The Office National de Tourisme (☎ 377-92 16 61 66, fax 377-92 16 60 00, mgto@monaco1.org, www .monaco.mc), 2a blvd des Moulins, is across the public gardens from Monte Carlo Casino. It's open from 9 am to 7 pm (Sunday from 10 am to noon). From mid-June to mid-September there are several tourist office kiosks open around the principality, including one at the train station, another next to the Jardin Exotique, one on

blvd Albert 1er, one on quai des États-Unis (the street that runs along the north side of the port) and another north of the Palais du France between place du Canton and place d'Armes.

Money Monaco uses the French franc. Both French and Monégasque franc coins are in circulation, but the latter are hard to find inside the principality and not accepted outside of it. Monaco will trade in its Monégasque franc for the euro from 2002 onwards (see Money in the Facts for the Visitor chapter).

In Monte Carlo there are numerous banks in the vicinity of the casino. In La Condamine, try blvd Albert 1er. American

Express (☎ 377-93 25 74 45), 35 blvd Princesse Charlotte, is open from 9 am to noon and 2 to 6 pm (Saturday until noon; closed Sunday). Barclays Bank (☎ 377-93 15 35 35) has a branch at 31 ave de la Costa in Monte Carlo.

Post Monégasque stamps are only valid for letters sent within Monaco. Postal rates are the same as those in France.

The main post office is in Monte Carlo, inside the Palais de la Scala at 1 ave Henri Dunant. It's open from 8 am to 7 pm (Saturday until noon; closed Sunday), but it does not exchange foreign currency. There are post offices in each of the other four principal areas, including at place de la Visitation (near the Musée Océanographique) in Monaco Ville; and across the road from the train station (look for the sign to the Hôtel Terminus) in La Condamine (open from 8 am to 7 pm; Saturday until noon; closed Sunday).

Telephone Telephone numbers in Monaco only have eight digits. Calls between Monaco and the rest of France are treated as international calls. Dial ☎ 00 followed by Monaco's country code, 377, when calling Monaco from the rest of France or abroad. To call France from Monaco, dial ☎ 00 and France's country code, 33. This applies even if you are only making a call from the east side of blvd de France (in Monaco) to its west side (in France)!

Monaco's public telephones accept Monégasque or French *télécartes* (telephone cards).

Email & Internet Access There is a cybercorner inside Stars 'n' Bars (☎ 93 50 95 95, info@starsnbars.com, www.isp-riviera .com/starsnbars), 6 quai Antoine 1er, open from 11 am to midnight (40FF for 30 minutes online).

Bookshops Scruples (☎ 93 50 43 52), 9 rue Princesse Caroline, is an English-language bookshop open from 9.30 am to noon

and 2.30 to 7 pm (6.30 pm on Saturday; closed Sunday).

Libraries The Princess Grace Irish Library (☎ 93 50 12 25), 9 rue Princesse Marie de Lorraine, is open from 9 am to 4 pm (closed on weekends). Grace Kelly's grandparents hailed from Drimurla in county Mayo, Ireland, a remote spot visited by Kelly and Rainier in 1961.

Laundry In Beausoleil, there is a laundrette at 1 Escalier de la Riviéra, open from 7 am to 9 pm.

Monaco Ville

Poetically named Le Rocher (The Rock) to reflect its geographical location, Monaco Ville is home to the state's most alluring sights.

Musée Océanographique The world-renowned Musée Océanographique de Monaco (☎ 93 15 36 00), ave Saint Martin, has to be seen to be believed. It was founded in 1910 by Prince Albert I (1848-1922) who had set up an oceanographic institute for marine science here in 1906. An exhibition hall was added to display his collection of oceanographic finds acquired during his seafaring career. Today, it houses 90 tanks and 6000 fishes in an underground aquarium, a zoological hall dominated by a 20m whale skeleton, and all sorts of exhibits on ocean exploration. Even if aquariums are not really your thing, Monaco's *is* worth a visit, if only for its ornate interior which features fanciful seabird-shaped chandeliers, monumental staircases, mosaic floors, and oak door frames carved into marine-inspired shapes such as the effigy of Neptune. Beautiful views of Monaco and the French and Italian Rivieras are on offer from the terrace restaurant.

The museum is open from 9 am to 7 pm; 8 pm in July and August (a stiff 60/30FF for adult/student). Bus Nos 1 and 2 from place d'Armes are the alternatives to a relatively long walk up the hill. The train stop for the slightly tacky **Azur Express tourist train**

(☎ 92 05 64 38, azurtrain@imcn.mc), ave Saint Martin, is opposite the museum entrance. The city tour (35 minutes) costs 35FF (free to children under five).

Monte Carlo Story Horribly ticky-tacky is the underground Monte Carlo Story (☎ 93 25 32 33), reached by an escalator opposite the Musée Océanographique. The 45 minute soap-opera style film, screened in seven languages, recalls the history of the Grimaldi dynasty. Admission, which includes entrance to a display of cinematic posters featuring Monte Carlo through the ages, costs 38/30/20FF for adult/student/child aged 6-14. A cassette-recording of the Monégasque national anthem (20FF) is sold at the ticket booth. The museum is open from 11 am to 5 pm (6 pm in July and August; from 2 to 5 pm only between November and February).

Reclining gracefully next to both museums are the coastal **Jardins Saint-Martin**, statue-studded gardens open from 7 am to 6 pm (until 8 pm from April to September).

Palais du Prince The changing of the guard at the Prince's Palace takes place daily, on place du Palais at the southern end of rue des Remparts, at precisely 11.55 am. The guards of the Compagnie des Carabiniers, who carry out their state duties in spiffy dress uniform (white in summer, black in winter), appear resigned to the comic-opera nature of their duties. Even more comic is the pushing, shoving and acrobatic antics among the huge crowd that gathers each day to watch the whole affair. If the Grimaldi standard is flying from the top of the palace tower, it means Prince Rainier is at home.

The palace (☎ 93 25 18 31), with its Renaissance façade, was built on the site of a 13th century Genoese fortress, later fortified by Vauban. A tour of the **state apartments** allows visitors a glimpse of its interior grandeur, including the 16th and 17th century frescoes depicting mythological scenes in the Galerie d'Hercule. From June to October only, you can visit the **palace apartments** between 9.30 am and 6.30 pm (10 am to 5 pm in October). Obligatory guided tours (35 to 40 minutes) in English begin every 15 or 20 minutes; but be prepared for a long wait, 30 minutes in July and August, just to get in (30/15FF for adult/child aged 8-14).

The palace's south wing houses the **Musée des Souvenirs Napoléoniens**. Its displays include some of Napoléon I's personal effects (handkerchiefs, a sock etc) and a fascinating collection of the sort of bric-a-brac (medals, coins, swords, uniforms) that princely dynasties collect over the centuries. It has the same opening hours as the Palais du Prince; closed mid-November to mid-December (20/10FF). If you intend visiting the apartments and museum, invest in a combined 40/20FF ticket.

Cathédrale de Monaco The unspectacular Romanesque-Byzantine cathedral (1875), 4 rue Colonel, has one draw: tourists do a quick march around the cathedral to see the grave of the legendary Hollywood star Grace Patricia Kelly (1929-82). Her plain, modest tombstone lies on the west side of the cathedral choir. It is inscribed with the Latin words *Gratia Patricia Principis Rainerii III* and is heavily adorned with flowers. The remains of other members of the royal family, buried in the church crypt since 1885, today rest behind Princess Grace's grave.

Between September and June, Sunday Mass in the cathedral (☎ 93 30 87 70) is held at 10 am. The Mass is sung by Les Petits Chanteurs de Monaco – Monaco's boys choir. Between July and October free evening organ recitals are occasionally held here.

Other Museums Life-size wax figures capture 24 snapshots from the history of the Grimaldi dynasty in the Musée de Cire (Wax Museum; ☎ 93 30 39 05), 27 rue Basse, open from 9.30 am to 6 pm; 11 am to 4 pm between October and March (26/10FF for adult/child aged 6-12).

The Grimaldi Dynasty

The House of Grimaldi has ruled the Rock with a golden fist since 1297 when François Grimaldi, frocked as a monk, sneaked through the city gates and seized it as his own. The dynasty almost died in 1731 when Antoine I failed to produce a male heir. His daughter stepped in as queen, retaining her Grimaldi name to ensure the dynasty's survival.

Two centuries on, the pioneering Prince Charles III (1818-89) gave the poverty-stricken state independence, followed in 1865 by the casino and its accompanying million dollar fortune. His successor, seafaring Prince Albert I (1848-1922), preferred marine biology to money-making playgrounds and devoted his life to oceanographic research. In 1873 he sailed around the Mediterranean and the Atlantic to the Azores in a 200-tonne sailing boat.

Reigning monarch, Rainier III (1923), son of Princess Charlotte and Prince Pierre de Polignac, succeeded his grandfather Prince Louis II to the throne in 1949. Monaco's longest ruling monarch won the heart of a nation with his fairytale marriage to Grace Kelly in 1956. The legendary Philadelphia-born actress made 11 films in the 1950s, including Hitchcock's *Dial M for Murder* (1954), *Rear Window* (1954), and *To Catch a Thief* (1955) in which she starred as the quintessential cool blonde on the coast. The movie took Kelly to Cannes, then to the Monégasque palace to attend a *Paris Match* photo shoot with Rainier. One year later Monaco's prince charming wed Hollywood's movie queen. The princess made no more films. She died in a car crash in 1982.

The far-from-fairytale love lives of the couple's three children – Caroline (1957), ageing bachelor Albert (1958) and Stephanie (1965) – take centre stage today. Princess Caroline was widowed in 1990 when her second husband (her marriage to the first was annulled), and father of her three children, was killed in a speedboat accident. In January 1999, on her 42nd birthday, she wed Prince Ernst of Hannover, a cousin to Britain's Queen Elizabeth. Eight lone guests attended the civil ceremony which took place secretly.

In 1995 Princess Stephanie wed her bodyguard and divorced him a year later after photographs of him frolicking by a pool with a Belgian stripper were published in Italian magazines. In July 1998, she gave birth to baby Camille Grimaldi, her third child (father unnamed). During the 1980s and early 1990s the entrepreneurial princess launched her own swimwear label – ironically called Pool Position – and released three albums and a flurry of pop singles, including *Ouragan* (Hurricane), *I am waiting for you* and *How can it be?*.

The *Bal de la Rose* (Rose Ball in May), the *Bal de l'Été* (Summer Ball) organised for Europe's jet-setting uppercrust, fundraising *Gala de la Croix Rouge* (Red Cross Ball) and the Gala Ball, hosted by the charitable Princess Grace Foundation, are Monaco's key society events. They afford a rare glimpse of the House of Grimaldi in a fairytale spotlight. Tickets cost around US$1000 a head.

Spitting distance from these wax creatures is the small Musée de Vieux Monaco (☎ 93 50 57 28), rue Emile de Loth. The history of the rock is illustrated in this old Monaco museum; open by appointment only (free). From here, bear east along rue Emile de Loth to place de la Mairie, and farther east still to place de la Visitation. The enchanting Musée de la Chapelle de la Visitation (☎ 93 50 07 00) overlooks this large square. The Baroque chapel houses the private art collection of Pia Secka Johnson (20/10FF for adult/student and child aged 6-14).

Monte Carlo

In the 1850s, Monaco was the poorest state in Europe. Its luck changed with the opening of Monte Carlo Casino in 1865. The rather dull-sounding Plateau des Sélugues on which it stood was renamed Monte Carlo in 1866 and within months it ranked as one of Europe's most glamorous playgrounds.

The colourful geometrical mosaic entitled *Hexa Grace* (1975) that adorns the roof of the Centre de Congrès Auditorium is a Vasarely creation – best viewed from the skies. From Monte Carlo a coastal path (2-3 hours) leads to Roquebrune-Cap Martin.

Casino The drama of watching people risk all (or, at the very least, *a lotta lotta* money) in Monte Carlo's spectacularly ornate casino (☎ 92 96 21 21) makes visiting the gaming rooms almost worth the stiff entry fees. These are 50/120/250/350FF for a day/week/month/year pass into the Salon Ordinaire, which has European roulette and trente et quarante, and 100FF for the Salons Privés, which offer baccarat, chemin de fer, craps, English roulette etc. Flutterers accustomed to different rules should ask for a copy of the English language brochure entitled *European Games*.

The decor of the casino is as extravagant as those who play in it. It was built in two phases, the earliest of which dates to 1878 and was created by French architect Charles Garnier who did Paris' opera house. The second section was completed in 1910. The casino today remains in the hands of its founding owners, the Société des Bains de Mer (SBM) established by French entrepreneur François Blanc in 1863. Original shareholders included Monaco's Prince Charles III who held a 10% stake – the state remains the leading shareholder today. In 1875, when the Prince and Princess of Wales visited, around 150,000 players a day were frequenting the drinks.

Despite an initial drop in revenue in 1933 following the legalisation of the roulette wheel in neighbouring France, Monte Carlo Casino continues to rake it in today. The SBM is Monaco's largest corporation, owning all the principality's upmarket hotels and restaurants. Annual sales in 1997 totalled 1.78 billion FF. Income from gambling accounts for 4.31% of Monaco's total state revenue (it used to account for most of the government's budget).

To enter the casino, you must be aged at least 21 (you usually have to show a piece of ID regardless of age). Short shorts (but not short skirts) are forbidden in the Salon Ordinaire. For the Salons Privés, men must wear a tie and jacket.

The Salon Ordinaire/Salons Privés are open from noon. The *appareils automatiques* (one-armed bandits and other cheap-thrill devices; open from 2 pm), which are tucked in a small room to the right as you enter the main reception, do not command an entrance fee or dress code.

Jardin Japonais Sandwiched between the built-up quarters of Monte Carlo, Larvotto and the Mediterranean, this Japanese garden is intended as an enchanting spot of paradise. It was blessed by a Shinto high priest; quiet contemplation and meditation is encouraged in the peaceful jardin Zen. The gardens (entrance on ave Princesse Grace) are open from 9 am to dusk.

Musée National Housed in a sumptuous, Garnier-designed villa, the National Museum (☎ 93 30 91 26), 17 ave Princesse Grace, at the east end of Monte Carlo, contains a fascinating collection of 18th and 19th century *poupées* (dolls) and mechanical toys made in Paris. Some 250 figurines nestle in the 18th century *crèche* (crib scene), originating from Naples.

The museum is open from 10 am to 12.15 pm and 2.30 to 6.30 pm; no midday closure from Easter to September (26/15FF for adult/student).

Fontvieille

Adjoining Cap d'Ail in neighbouring France, Fontvieille covers the westernmost part of Monaco. From here a 3.5km *sentier touristique* (coastal path) leads west to Cap d'Ail. The lush gardens of the **Parc Fontvieille** are equally pleasant for a summer stroll; over 4000 rose bushes adorn the **Roseraie Princesse Grace**, planted in her memory in 1984. Swans swim on the small lake. Contemporary sculptures – including *Le Poing* (The Fist) by César – stud the length of the park's **Chemin des Sculptures**. Museum-wise, Fontvieille is Monaco's 'collector's corner'.

Collection de Voitures Anciennes

Over 100 vehicles are on display in this vintage car museum housing the private collection of Rainier III. Highlights in the colourful collection include the Rolls Royce Silver Cloud that was given by local shop keepers to Prince Rainier to mark his marriage to Grace Kelly in 1956. Also on display is a black London cab (Austin 1952) that was fitted out especially for the Hollywood actress. The first Formula One racing car to win the Monaco Grand Prix – the Bugatti 1929 – can be seen in the *salon d'honneur* (room of honour), as can a helmet belonging to the late Brazilian racing driver Ayrton Senna (1960-94).

Monaco's Vintage Cars Collection (☎ 92 05 28 56), inside the Centre Commerical de Fontvieille, is open from 10 am to 6 pm; closed November (30/15FF for adult/child aged 8-14).

Musée Naval An impressive collection of model ships constructed by Grimaldi princes are displayed in Monaco's Naval Museum (☎ 92 05 28 48), inside the Centre Commercial de Fontvieille. The oldest ship in the 200-odd piece collection was stuck together by Albert I in 1874. Other pieces include an imperial gondola built in 15 days for Napoléon I to admire, the *Fiorentino Emigrato* sailing ship built in the 17th century, a miniature of the *Missouri* where the armistice with Japan was signed in 1945, and a 5m model of the US aircraft carrier *Nimitz*. Museum opening hours are 10 am to 6 pm; closed Friday in winter, and all of November (25/15FF for adult/child).

Musée des Timbres et des Monnaies

Prince Rainier also has a stamp and coin collection – displayed in the Stamp and Money Museum (☎ 93 15 41 50) in the Centre Commerical de Fontvieille. Monégasque stamps dating from 1885 and numismatic wonders dating from 1640 are exhibited. Museum opening hours are from 10 am to 6 pm; 5 pm in winter (20/10FF for adult/senior or student).

Moneghetti

The steep slopes of the Moneghetti district, immediately north of Fontvieille, are home to the wonderful **Jardin Exotique** (☎ 93 15 29 80, jardin-exotique@monte-carlo.mc), 62 blvd du Jardin Exotique. The exotic garden boasts some 7000 varieties of cacti and succulents from all over the world – including a 100-year-old South American cacti and 10m-tall African candelabras. The spectacular view alone is worth at least half the entrance fee of 39/18FF for adult/student, which also gets you into the on-site **Musée d'Anthropologie Préhistorique** (☎ 93 15 80 06) and includes a 30 minute guided visit to the **Grottes de l'Observatoire**. The prehistoric Observatory Caves comprise a fantastical network of stalactite and stalagmite caves 279 steps down the hillside. Prehistoric rock scratchings found here are among the oldest of their kind in the world.

The Jardin Exotique is open from mid-September to mid-May from 9 am until 6 pm (or dusk) and until 7 pm the rest of the year. From the tourist office, take bus No 2 to the Jardin Exotique terminus.

Boats & Beaches

The central quarter of **La Condamine** is mainly boats and water – namely the **Port de Monaco** where palatial pleasure crafts of all (exceedingly large) shapes and sizes can be found languishing. Overlooking the port, at the east end of quai Antoine 1er, is the exclusive members-only **Yacht Club de Monaco** (☎ 93 10 63 00, fax 93 50 80 88, ycm@yacht-club-monaco, www.yacht-club -monaco), 16 quai Antoine 1er. Lesser mortals can sail the waters in a glass-bottomed boat (55 minutes; 70/50FF for adult/student) operated by Les Bateaux de la French Riviera (☎ 92 16 15 12), at the east end of quai des États-Unis. These **boat excursions** depart at 1, 2.30 and 4 pm.

The nearest **beaches**, Plage du Larvotto and Plage de Monte Carlo, are a couple of kilometres east of Monte Carlo in the easternmost **Larvotto quarter**. In Monte Carlo, sun worshippers lie their oiled bodies out to bake on giant concrete slabs on the eastern side of the jetty, at the north end of quai des États-Unis.

Special Events

The Fête de la Sainte-Dévote on 27 January is among the most special days on the Monégasque calendar. It is the feast day of Monaco's patron saint, Dévote, whose corpse was flung in a boat and left to drift at sea following her death at the hands of a Roman general in Corsica. Thanks to a dove who blew the boat in the right direction, Dévote's corpse landed on the shores of Monaco in 312 AD. Each year, a traditional Mass in Monégasque is held in Église Sainte-Dévote, place Sainte-Dévote. In the evening a torchlit procession, blessing and symbolic burning of a boat take place on the square.

Dancers in traditional Monégasque folk costume dance around a big bonfire on place du Palais on 23 June, the eve of Saint John's Day. The beginning of August brings a glittering International Fireworks Festival to the port area, while a carnival spirit fills the streets with the Fête Nationale Monégasque – Monaco's National Holiday – on 19 November.

Places to Stay

Cheap accommodation is almost nonexistent in Monaco. Mid-range rooms are equally scarce and often full. Indeed, over three-quarters of Monaco's hotel rooms are classified as 'four-star deluxe'. Fortunately, Nice is not too far away.

Places to Stay – Budget & Mid-Range

Hostel The *Centre de la Jeunesse Princesse Stéphanie* (☎ 93 50 83 20, fax 93 25 29 82, 24 ave Prince Pierre), is 120m up the hill from the train station. Only travellers aged between 16 and 31 can stay here – for 70FF per person, including breakfast, shower and sheets. Stays are usually limited to three nights during the summer. Beds are given out each morning on a first-come, first-served basis; numbered tickets are distributed from 9 am or even earlier near the front gate. Registration begins at 11 am.

Hotels In La Condamine, the clean and pleasant, one-star *Hôtel Cosmopolite* (☎ 93 30 16 95, 4 rue de la Turbie) has decent singles/doubles with shower for 288/322FF and doubles without shower for 240FF. The *Hôtel de France* (☎ 93 30 24 64, 6 rue de la Turbie) has singles/doubles with shower, toilet and TV starting at 350/460FF, including breakfast.

Two-star *Hôtel Terminus* (☎ 92 05 63 00, fax 92 05 20 10, 9 ave Prince Pierre) and *Hôtel Helvetia* (☎ 93 30 21 71, fax 92 16 70 51, 1bis rue Grimaldi) at the train station are cheapies by Monaco standards. Rooms are 350-450FF.

In French Beausoleil, there are three hotels virtually in a row on blvd du Général Leclerc, three streets up from the casino and close to the Beausoleil market. At No 17, the *Hôtel Diana* (☎ 04 93 78 47 58, fax 04 93 41 88 94) has rooms for one or two with shower/bath for 280/380FF. At No 19, the *Hôtel Cosmopolite* (☎ 04 93 78 36 00), unrelated to the hotel of the same name in La Condamine, has rooms with shower and TV for 195FF (270/290FF with toilet for one/two people). Between them at No 17bis is the *Hôtel Olympia* (☎ 04 93 78 12 70) which has rooms with shower, TV and toilet for 265/300FF. All offer breakfast for an extra 30FF and there is a Beausoleil tourist tax of 5FF per person. Remember to call the country code for France when dialling these numbers from Monaco (eg from the train station).

The even-numbered side of blvd du Général Leclerc is in Monaco and is called blvd de France. The nearest bus stop is named Crémaillère and is served by bus Nos 2 and 4. For those who are more visual, the Beausoleil side (ie blvd du Général Leclerc) begins with a pavement tiled with smiling faces of the *beau soleil* (beautiful sun).

Places to Stay – Top End

World-famous pads include the magnificent *Hôtel de Paris* (π 92 16 30 00, fax 92 16 38 50, hp@sbm.mc, www.sbm.mc, place du Casino) where writer Colette spent the last years of her life. The hotel dates from 1864 and hosts a gastronomic temple (see Places to Eat). The four-star *Hôtel Hermitage* (π 92 16 40 00, fax 93 16 38 52, hh@sbm.mc, square Beaumarchais) has a beautiful Italian-inspired façade and a pink-marbled restaurant. Prices reflect the luxurious *belle époque* ambience of both hotels. Expect to pay a minimum of 2100FF for a double room fit for a queen.

Slightly less expensive is the *Hôtel Mirabeau* (π 92 16 65 65, fax 93 50 84 85, mi@sbm.mc, 1 ave Princesse Grace), which has extremely comfortable singles/doubles from 1400/2000FF.

Places to Eat

In Monte Carlo, the place to people-watch is from the sprawling terrace of the *Café de Paris* (π 92 16 20 20, place du Casino).

Restaurants There are a few cheap restaurants in La Condamine along rue de la Turbie. Farther down the hill overlooking the port and yacht club is the flashy *Stars 'n' Bars* (π 93 50 95 95, 6 quai Antoine 1er), open from noon to 3 am (closed Monday). Billed as a blues bar and restaurant, it is more like a huge country and western barn. Here you can eat main dishes of American-sized portions and excellent-quality salads (60-70FF), listen to live music and watch the multilingual staff strut their stuff in starred-and-striped leather shorts and boots. There's live music on Thursday, Friday and Saturday nights in the

upstairs nightclub until 3 am; the restaurant closes at midnight. The same Texan businessman runs *Le Texan* (π 93 30 34 54, 4 rue Suffren Reymond).

Very traditional and cosy is the small *Restaurant de Trende* (π 93 30 37 72, 19 rue de la Turbie). The decor is totally 1930s and the food, absolutely Provençal.

On a totally different plain is *Le Louis XV* (π 92 16 30 01), sporting three Michelin stars and in the Hôtel de Paris (see Places to Stay); some say it's the best restaurant on the Riviera. It offers high-quality dishes (prices to match) prepared by top French chef Alain Ducasse who flits between Monaco and Paris' 16th arrondissement where he runs his second three-star restaurant. *Menus* start at 780FF; an à la carte meal will cost around 1000FF.

Self-Catering *Haagen-Däz* has a great little ice cream outlet in the pavilion in the public gardens in front of the casino.

In La Condamine, there's a *food market*, place d'Armes, and a *Casino* supermarket, blvd Albert 1er, open from 8.30 am to 8 pm (closed Sunday).

Entertainment

In addition to the box offices listed below, tickets for many cultural events are available at FNAC (π 93 10 81 81, www.fnac.fr), Centre Commercial Le Métropole, 17 ave Spélugues.

Bars & Nightclubs The Irish pub, *McCarthy's Pub* (π 93 25 87 67, mccarthy's@monte-carlo.mc, 7 rue du Portier) hosts live music. Its hours are 6 pm to dawn.

Among Monaco's best-known clubs are *Jimmy'z* (π 92 16 22 77 or 92 16 36 36, 26 ave Princesse Grace), inside the Monte Carlo Sporting Club; the *L'X Club* (π 93 30 70 55, 13 ave des Spélugues); and *The Living Room* (π 93 50 80 31, 13 ave des Spélugues).

Cinemas Between June and September, films are screened at the open-air *Cinéma d'Été* (π 93 25 86 80) in the Monte Carlo

Sporting Club, 26 ave Princesse Grace, Larvotto. Non-dubbed films with French subtitles are shown daily at 9.30 pm (50-90FF). *Cinéma Le Sporting (☎ 08 36 68 00 72, place du Casino)* also shows films in their original language.

Theatre A charming spot to while away a summer evening is a fortress built between 1709 and 1713, today housing the open-air *Théâtre du Fort Antoine (☎ 93 50 80 00, fax 93 50 66 94, ave de la Quarantaine)*. In July and August, plays are staged here on Monday at 9.30 pm (50-70FF); tickets are sold 45 minutes before performances.

The decor of the *Théâtre Princesse Grace (☎ 93 50 03 45 or 93 25 32 27, 12 ave d'Ostende)* was designed by Princess Grace. The box office is open from 10 am to 12.30 pm and 3 to 6.30 pm (closed Sunday).

Ballet, Opera & Classical Music The *Salle Garnier* (Garnier Hall, 1892) adjoining the casino on place du Casino is home to the Opéra de Monte Carlo and ballet company. Ticket bookings can be made at the *Atrium du Casino (☎ 92 16 22 99 or 92 16 24 14, place du Casino)*, open from 10 am to 12.30 pm and from 2 to 5 pm (closed Monday).

Performances by the Monte Carlo Philharmonic Orchestra, dating from 1863, are held in the Rainier III auditorium inside the *Centre de Congrès Auditorium (☎ 93 10 84 00, blvd Louis II)*. In July and August its venue shifts to the beautiful Cour d'Honneur (Courtyard of Honour) inside the Palais du Prince. Predictably, tickets (available from the Atrium du Casino) are like gold dust.

Spectator Sports

The sporting calendar kicks off with the legendary Rallye Automobile Monte Carlo (Monte Carlo Rally, www.acm.mc) in January. The four-day event is a series of timed stages. The rally starts and finishes at the Monégasque port using part of the Grand Prix circuit and, in between, rips through Haute-Provence. The traditional night stage and the concentration run where drivers set off from various European cities to meet in Monte Carlo – such as Disney's Herbie did on screen in the 1970s – were both scrapped in 1997.

The Monte Carlo International Tennis Championships, held at the Monte Carlo Country Club (☎ 04 93 41 30 15), ave Princesse Grace, opens the hard-court season in April.

Soccer team AS Monaco and world champion goalie Fabian Barthez can be seen in action on their home ground, the Stade Louis II (☎ 92 05 40 00 for the stadium or 92 05 74 73 for ASM), ave des Castelans, Fontvieille. Guided tours in English (☎ 92 05 40 20) are available most weekdays at 2.30 pm. The official AS Monaco boutique (☎ 93 50 55 21), rue de la Turbie, sells all the gear. Opening hours are 9 am to 12.30 pm and 2 to 7 pm (closed on weekends).

Shopping

The 155-page, pocket-size *Monaco Shopping* guide, published annually and distributed free by the tourist office, is indispensable to committed shoppers.

The Galerie Riccadonna (☎ 93 50 84 46, fax 92 16 06 78), 7 rue Grimaldi, sells seriously funky designer furniture for very serious amounts of money. Ave des Beaux Arts, which runs immediately west off place du Casino, is laced with Cartier, Dior and Givenchy boutiques and is Monaco's most expensive street. Blvd des Moulins is another fancy shopping street.

Getting There & Away

Air Héli-Air Monaco (☎ 92 05 00 50) will twirl you anywhere along the coast your heart desires, for a not-so-small fee, including to/from Nice airport (see the Getting Around chapter).

Bus There is no bus station in Monaco. Inter-city buses leave from various stops around the city.

Train Trains to/from Monaco are run by the French SNCF. The information desk at Monaco train station, ave Prince Pierre, is

The Formula One Grand Prix

The Grand Prix Automobile de Monaco is the world's most glamorous race. It screams round the streets each year in May, lapping a 3.28km circuit highly revered in the racing world for its narrow, unrelenting *virages* (bends) and awkward chicanes.

Few succeed in completing the required 78 laps which takes drivers from the port, through a right-hand bend, and uphill along ave d'Ostende to place du Casino where the track bombs downhill around a hairpin and two sharp rights into the tunnel and back to the port along ave Président JF Kennedy and quai Albert 1er. Schumacher smashed all records in 1994 when he screeched past the finishing line in just 1h49'55"372, clocking up an average speed of 141.690km/h. The German racing driver with his Benetton Ford also scooped the fastest lap speed – 147.772km/h – yet to be beaten.

The race is watched by 150,000 thrilled spectators from *tribunes* (stands) around the port and on place du Casino. The cheapest spot is on ave de la Porte Neuve. The wealthy survey the spectacle from the terrace restaurant of the Hôtel Hermitage or from the deck of a yacht moored in the harbour. The Grimaldis watch the start and finish from the royal box at the port, retiring during the event for a champagne brunch on the 13th floor at an undisclosed address overlooking the circuit. Mechanics, girlfriends, driver support teams etc hobnob at Stars 'n Bars near the paddock area on quai Antoine 1er.

Time trials and various races including the Grand Prix de Monaco 3000 take place during the three days leading up to the Formula One Grand Prix, which is always held on Sunday afternoon. Tickets for all races, including the Grand Prix, are available from the Comité d'Organisation Grand Prix Automobile de Monaco, Automobile Club de Monaco (☎ 93 15 26 00, fax 92 25 80 08, www.monaco.mc/monaco/gprix), 23 blvd Albert 1er, BP 464, 98012 Monaco. Grand Prix tickets in 1998 cost 200FF in the Secteur Rocher on ave de la Porte Neuve, 600FF on place du Casino, and 1100 to 1800FF around the port. The best/most expensive seats are in the stands opposite the starting line, on the north side of the swimming pool on quai Albert 1er. Tickets go on sale in January and are snapped up in hours.

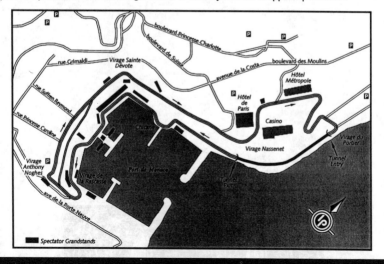

MONACO

open from 9.30 am to noon and 2.30 to 6.30 pm. The automatic luggage lockers (20FF for 72 hours) are accessible round the clock.

Taking the train along this coast is highly recommended – the sea and the mountains provide a truly magnificent sight. There are frequent trains eastward to Menton (12FF; 10 minutes) and the first town across the border in Italy, Ventimiglia (Vintimille in French; 19FF; 25 minutes). For trains to Nice (17FF; 25 minutes) and for connections to other towns, see Getting There & Away in the Nice to Menton chapter.

Car & Motorcycle If you are driving out of Monaco, either eastward toward Italy or westward to Nice, and you want to go via the A8, you first have to join the Corniche Moyenne (N7). For Italy, look for signs indicating Gênes (Genoa in English; Genova in Italian). Blvd du Jardin Exotique leads to the N7 in the direction of Nice.

Getting Around

Some 15 *ascenseurs publics* (public lifts) run up and down the hillside, all marked on the free brochure distributed by the tourist office entitled *Monaco: Getting There &*

Getting About. Most operate 24 hours; some run between 6 am and midnight or 1 am.

Bus Monaco's urban bus system has six lines. Line No 2 links Monaco Ville with Monte Carlo and then loops back to the Jardin Exotique. Line No 4 links the train station with the tourist office, the casino and the Larvotto district. A ticket costs 8.50FF. Much better value are the four/eight-ride magnetic cards (19/30FF) on sale from bus drivers and vending machines at all stops, or the one-day tourist pass (21FF). Buses run until 7 or 9 pm.

The local bus company, Compagnie des Autobus de Monaco (CAM; ☎ 93 50 62 41), 3 ave du Président John F Kennedy, on the north side of the port, is open from 8.30 am to noon and 2 to 6 pm (Friday until 5 pm; closed on weekends).

Taxi To order a taxi, call ☎ 93 15 01 01 or 93 50 56 28.

Bicycle Hire two wheels from the Auto-Moto Garage (☎ 93 50 10 80), 7 rue de Milo.

Appendix – Provençal Place Names

Aigo-Morto – Aigues-Mortes
Ais – Aix-en-Provence
Antibou – Antibes
Arenjo – Orange
Arle – Arles
Ate – Apt
Avignoun – Avignon
Bandòu – Bandol
Bèucaire – Beaucaire
Cano – Cannes
Camargo – Camargue
Castelano – Castellane
Cavaioun – Cavaillon
Cavalairo – Cavalaire
Cougoulin – Cogolin
Couloubriero – Collobrières
Digno – Digne-les-Bains
Durènço – Durance (river)
Ezo – Éze
Gordo – Gordes
Goulfe-Jouan – Golfe-Juan
Grasso – Grasse
Iero – Hyères
La Ciéutat – La Ciotat
Leberoun – Lubéron
Lis Isclo d'or – Les Îles d'Or
Li Santo – Saintes-Maries-de-la-Mer
Lou Lavandou – Le Lavandou
Manosco – Manosque

Marsihès/Marsiho – Marseille
Mentan – Menton
Mieterrano – Mediterranean
Móunegue – Monaco
Moustié Santo Mario – Moustiers Sainte Marie
Nime – Nîmes
Niço – Nice
Prouvènço – Provence
Rose – Rhône (river)
Sanari – Sanary-sur-Mer
Sant Jouan Cau Ferrat – Saint Jean-Cap Ferrat
Sant Martin Vesubio – Saint Martin Vésubie
Sant Rafèu – Saint Raphaël
Santo Massimo – Saint Maxime
Sant Troupez – Saint Tropez
Seloun – Salon-de-Provence
Sousper – Sospel
Tarascoun – Tarascon
Tèndo – Tende
Touloun – Toulon
Van Cluso – Vaucluse
Venço – Vence
Vervoudon – Verdon (river)
Vilo-Novo-Avignoun – Villeneuve-lès-Avignon

Language

Standard French is taught and spoken in Provence. However, travellers accustomed to schoolbook French, or the unaccented, strait-laced French spoken in cities and larger towns, will find the lyrical, flamboyant French spoken in Provence's rural heart (and by most in Marseille) absolutely incomprehensible. Here, words caressed by the heavy southern accent end with a flourish: vowels are sung; the traditional rolling 'r' is turned into a mighty long trill. So *douze* (the number 12) becomes 'douz-eh' with an emphasised 'e' and *pain* (bread) becomes 'peng'. Take time to tune in and you'll quickly pick up the beat

PROVENÇAL

Despite the bi-lingual signs that greet tourists when they enter most towns and villages, the region's mother tongue – Provençal – is scarcely heard on the street or in the home. Just a handful of older people in rural Provence (Prouvènço) keep alive the rich lyrics and poetic language of their ancestors.

Provençal (*prouvençau* in Provençal) is a dialect of *langue d'oc* (Occitan), the traditional language of southern France. Its grammar is closer to Catalan and Spanish than to French. In the grand age of courtly love between the 12th and 14th centuries, Provençal was the literary language of France and northern Spain and even used as far afield as Italy. Medieval troubadours and poets created melodies and elegant poems motivated by the ideal of courtly love, and Provençal blossomed.

The 19th century witnessed a revival of Provençal after its rapid displacement by *langue d'oïl*, the language of northern France which originated from the vernacular Latin spoken by the Gallo-Romans and which gave birth to modern French (*francés* in Provençal). The revival was spearheaded by Vaucluse poet Frédéric Mistral (1830-

1914), whose works in Provençal landed him the Nobel Prize for Literature in 1904.

Mistral was the backbone of Le Félibrige, a literary society created in 1854 to safeguard Provençal literature, culture and identity. A wealth of literature in Provençal was published by Le Félibrige which, from its contemporary base at Aix-Marseille University (☎ 04 42 26 23 41, fax 04 42 27 52 89, info@felibrige.com, www.felibrige.com, Parc Jourdan), 8bis ave Jules Ferry, 13100 Aix-en-Provence, remains as vocal today as it was yesterday.

FRENCH

While the French rightly or wrongly have a reputation for assuming that all human beings should speak French – until WWI it was the international language of culture and diplomacy – you'll find that any attempt to communicate in French will be much appreciated. Probably your best bet is always to approach people politely in French, even if the only sentence you know is *Pardon, madame/monsieur/mademoiselle, parlez-vous anglais?* (Excuse me, madam/sir/miss, do you speak English?).

Basic French words and phrases are listed below. Food and wine-related words and phrases are included in the Culinary Lexicon at the front of this book. For a more comprehensive guide to the French language get hold of Lonely Planet's *French phrasebook*.

Grammar

An important distinction is made in French between *tu* and *vous*, which both mean 'you'. *Tu* is only used when addressing people you know well, children or animals. When addressing an adult who is not a personal friend, *vous* should be used unless the person invites you to use *tu*. In general, younger people insist less on this distinction, and you may find that they use *tu* from the beginning of an acquaintance.

All nouns in French are either masculine or feminine and adjectives reflect the gender of the noun they modify. The feminine form of many nouns and adjectives is indicated by a silent 'e' added to the masculine form, as in *étudiant* and *étudiante*, the masculine and feminine for 'student'. In the following phrases we have indicated both masculine and feminine forms where necessary; the masculine form comes first, separated from the feminine by a slash. The gender of a noun is also often indicated by a preceding article: *le/un/du* (m), *la/une/de la* (f) (the/a/some); or a possessive adjective, *mon/ton/son* (m), *ma/ta/sa* (f) (my/your/his/her). With French, unlike English, the possessive adjective agrees in number and gender with the thing possessed: *sa mère* (his/her mother).

Pronunciation

Most letters in French are pronounced more or less the same as their English equivalents. A few which may cause confusion are:

j   as the 's' in 'leisure', eg *jour* (day)
c   before **e** and **i**, as the 's' in 'sit'; before **a**, **o** and **u** it's pronounced as English 'k'. When undescored with a 'cedilla' (ç) it's always pronounced as the 's' in 'sit'.

French has a number of sounds that are difficult for Anglophones to produce. These include:

- The distinction between the 'u' sound (as in *tu*) and 'oo' sound (as in *tout*). For both sounds, the lips are rounded and projected forward, but for the 'u' the tongue is towards the front of the mouth, its tip against the lower front teeth, whereas for the 'oo' the tongue is towards the back of the mouth, its tip behind the gums of the lower front teeth.
- The nasal vowels. With nasal vowels the breath escapes partly through the nose and partly through the mouth. There are no nasal vowels in English; in French there are three, as in *bon vin blanc*, (good white wine). These sounds occur where a

syllable ends in a single **n** or **m**; the **n** or **m** is silent but indicates the nasalisation of the preceding vowel.
- The **r**. The standard French **r** is produced by moving the bulk of the tongue backwards to constrict the air flow in the pharynx while the tip of the tongue rests behind the lower front teeth. It's similar to the noise made by some people before spitting, but with much less friction.

Basics

Yes.	*Oui.*
No.	*Non.*
Maybe.	*Peut-être.*
Please.	*S'il vous plaît.*
Thank you.	*Merci.*
You're welcome.	*Je vous en prie.*
Excuse me.	*Excusez-moi.*
Sorry/Forgive me.	*Pardon.*

Greetings

Hello/Good morning.	*Bonjour.*
Good evening.	*Bonsoir.*
Good night.	*Bonne nuit.*
Goodbye.	*Au revoir.*

Language Difficulties

I understand.	*Je comprends.*
I don't understand.	*Je ne comprends pas.*
Do you speak English?	*Parlez-vous anglais?*
Could you please write it down?	*Est-ce que vous pouvez l'écrire?*

Small Talk

How are you?	*Comment allez-vous?* (polite) *Comment vas-tu?*/ *Comment ça va?* (informal)
Fine, thanks.	*Bien, merci.*
What's your name?	*Comment vous appelez-vous?*
My name is ...	*Je m'appelle ...*
I'm pleased to meet you.	*Enchanté* (m)/ *Enchantée* (f).
How old are you?	*Quel âge avez-vous?*
I'm ... years old.	*J'ai ... ans.*
Do you like ...?	*Aimez-vous ...?*

Where are you from?	De quel pays êtes-vous?

I'm from ...	Je viens ...
Australia	d'Australie
Canada	du Canada
England	d'Angleterre
Germany	d'Allemagne
Ireland	d'Irlande
New Zealand	de Nouvelle Zélande
Scotland	d'Écosse
Wales	du Pays de Galle
the USA	des États-Unis

Getting Around

I want to go to ...	Je voudrais aller à ...
I'd like to book a seat to ...	Je voudrais réserver une place pour ...

What time does the ... leave/arrive?	À quelle heure part/arrive ...?
aeroplane	l'avion
bus (city)	l'autobus
bus (intercity)	l'autocar
ferry	le ferry(-boat)
train	le train
tram	le tramway

Where is (the) ...?	Où est ...?
bus stop?	l'arrêt d'autobus
metro station	la station de métro
train station	la gare
tram stop	l'arrêt de tramway
ticket office	le guichet

Signs

ENTRÉE	ENTRANCE
SORTIE	EXIT
COMPLET	NO VACANCIES
RENSEIGNEMENTS	INFORMATION
OUVERT/FERMÉ	OPEN/CLOSED
INTERDIT	PROHIBITED
(COMMISSARIAT DE) POLICE	POLICE STATION
CHAMBRES LIBRES	ROOMS AVAILABLE
TOILETTES, WC	TOILETS
HOMMES	MEN
FEMMES	WOMEN

I'd like a ... ticket.	Je voudrais un billet ...
one-way	aller-simple
return	aller-retour
1st class	première classe
2nd class	deuxième classe

How long does the trip take?	Combien de temps dure le trajet?

The train is ...	Le train est ...
delayed	en retard
on time	à l'heure
early	en avance

Do I need to ...?	Est-ce que je dois ...?
change trains	changer de train
change platform	changer de quai

left-luggage locker	consigne automatique
platform	quai
timetable	horaire

I'd like to hire ...	Je voudrais louer ...
a bicycle	un vélo
a car	une voiture
a guide	un guide

Around Town

I'm looking for ...	Je cherche ...
a bank/ exchange office	une banque/ un bureau de change
the city centre	le centre-ville
the ... embassy	l'ambassade de ...
the hospital	l'hôpital
my hotel	mon hôtel
the market	le marché
the police	la police
the post office	le bureau de poste/ la poste
a public phone	une cabine téléphonique
a public toilet	les toilettes
the tourist office	l'office de tourisme

Where is (the) ...?	Où est ...?
beach	la plage
bridge	le pont
castle/mansion	le château
cathedral	la cathédrale

church	*l'église*
island	*l'île*
lake	*le lac*
main square	*la place centrale*
mosque	*la mosquée*
old city (town)	*la vieille ville*
the palace	*le palais*
quay/bank	*le quai/la rive*
ruins	*les ruines*
sea	*la mer*
square	*la place*
tower	*la tour*

What time does it open/close?	*Quelle est l'heure d'ouverture/ de fermeture?*
I'd like to make a telephone call.	*Je voudrais téléphoner.*

I'd like to change ...	*Je voudrais changer ...*
some money	*de l'argent*
travellers cheques	*chèques de voyage*

Directions

How do I get to ...?	*Comment dois-je faire pour arriver à ...?*
Is it near/far?	*Est-ce près/loin?*
Can you show me on the map/ city map?	*Est-ce que vous pouvez me le montrer sur la carte/le plan?*
Go straight ahead.	*Continuez tout droit.*
Turn left.	*Tournez à gauche.*
Turn right.	*Tournez à droite.*

at the traffic lights	*aux feux*
at the next corner	*au prochain coin*
behind	*derrière*
in front of	*devant*
opposite	*en face de*
north	*nord*
south	*sud*
east	*est*
west	*ouest*

Accommodation

I'm looking for ...	*Je cherche ...*
the youth hostel	*l'auberge de jeunesse*
the campground	*le camping*
a hotel	*un hôtel*

Where can I find a cheap hotel?	*Où est-ce que je peux trouver un hôtel bon marché?*
What's the address?	*Quelle est l'adresse?*
Could you write it down, please?	*Est-ce vous pourriez l'écrire, s'il vous plaît?*
Do you have any rooms available?	*Est-ce que vous avez des chambres libres?*

I'd like to book ...	*Je voudrais réserver ...*
a bed	*un lit*
a single room	*une chambre pour une personne*
a double room	*une chambre double*
a room with a shower and toilet	*une chambre avec douche et WC*

I'd like to stay in a dormitory.	*Je voudrais coucher dans un dortoir.*

How much is it ...?	*Quel est le prix ...?*
per night	*par nuit*
per person	*par personne*

Is breakfast included?	*Est-ce que le petit dé-jeuner est compris?*
Can I see the room?	*Est-ce que je peux voir la chambre?*

Where is ...?	*Où est ...?*
the bathroom	*la salle de bains*
the shower	*la douche*

Where is the toilet?	*Où sont les toilettes?*

I'm going to stay ...	*Je resterai ...*
one day	*un jour*
a week	*une semaine*

Time & Dates

What time is it?	*Quelle heure est-il?*
It's (two) o'clock.	*Il est (deux) heures.*
When?	*Quand?*
today	*aujourd'hui*
tonight	*ce soir*
tomorrow	*demain*
day after tomorrow	*après-demain*
yesterday	*hier*
all day	*toute la journée*

in the morning	du matin
in the afternoon	de l'après-midi
in the evening	du soir

Monday	lundi
Tuesday	mardi
Wednesday	mercredi
Thursday	jeudi
Friday	vendredi
Saturday	samedi
Sunday	dimanche

January	janvier
February	février
March	mars
April	avril
May	mai
June	juin
July	juillet
August	août
September	septembre
October	octobre
November	novembre
December	décembre

Numbers

1	un
2	deux
3	trois
4	quatre
5	cinq
6	six
7	sept
8	huit
9	neuf
10	dix
11	onze
12	douze
13	treize
14	quatorze
15	quinze
16	dix-sept
20	vingt
100	cent
1000	mille
one million	un million

Emergencies

Help!	Au secours!
Call a doctor!	Appelez un médecin!
Call the police!	Appelez la police!
Leave me alone!	Fichez-moi la paix!
I've been robbed.	On m'a volé.
I've been raped.	On m'a violée.
I'm lost.	Je me suis égaré/ égarée. (m/f)

Health

I'm sick.	Je suis malade.
I need a doctor.	Il me faut un médecin.
Where is the hospital?	Où est l'hôpital?
I have diarrhoea.	J'ai la diarrhée.
I'm pregnant.	Je suis enceinte.

I'm ...	Je suis ...
diabetic	diabétique
epileptic	épileptique
asthmatic	asthmatique
anaemic	anémique

I'm allergic ...	Je suis allergique ...
to antibiotics	aux antibiotiques
to penicillin	à la pénicilline
to bees	aux abeilles

antihistamines	l'antihistaminique
antiseptic	l'antiseptique
aspirin	l'aspirine
condoms	les préservatifs
contraceptive	un contraceptif
insect repellant	l'anti-insecte
medicine	le médicament
nausea	la nausée
painkillers	des analgésiques
sunblock cream	la crème solaire haute protection
tampons	les tampons hygiéniques

Glossary

Word gender is indicated as (m) masculine, (f) feminine. Food and wine terms are in the Culinary Lexicon.

anse (f) – cove
arène (f) – amphitheatre
arrière-pays (m) – hinterland
atelier (m) – artisan's workshop
baie (f) – bay
bastide (f) – country house
belle époque (f) – pre-WWI period
boulangerie (f) – bread shop
bravade (f) – Tropézian festival with cannons and gun fire; literally 'act of bravado'
calanque (f) – rocky inlet
cap (m) – cape
capitainerie (f) – harbour master's office
cave (f) – wine or cheese cellar
charcuterie (f) – pork butcher & delicatessen
chemin de terre (m) – unpaved road
cime (f) – mountain summit or peak
cluse (f) – transverse valley
col (m) – mountain pass
corniche (f) – coastal or cliff road
corso (m) – procession of floral floats
corso nautique (m) – procession of floral boats
cour (f) – courtyard
crèche vivante (f) – nativity scene with real people; literally 'living crib'
défilé (m) – procession or cortege
dégustation (f) – tasting
défense forestière contre l'incendie (DFCI) – fire road (public access forbidden)
député (m) – member of Parliament
digue (f) – dyke or sea wall
douane (f) – customs
eau potable (f) – drinking water
embarcadère (m) – pier or jetty
escalier (m) – stairs or staircase
étang (m) – lagoon, pond or lake
faïence (f) – earthenware
féria (f) – bullfighting festival
ferme auberge (f) – family-run inn attached to a farm or chateau.
flamant rose (m) – pink flamingo
fromagerie (f) – cheese shop
gardian (m) – Camargue horseman
garrigue (f) – cover of aromatic plants
gîte d'étape (m) – hiker's accommodation, usually in a village
gîte rural (m) – country cottage
golfe (m) – gulf

goût (m) – taste
hôtel particulier (m) – private mansion
jardin botanique (m) – botanical garden
jetée (f) – pier
joute Provençale (f) – nautical jousting tournament
lacet (m) – hairpin bend
laiterie (f) – dairy
lait de vache (m) – cow's milk
lait cru (m) – unpasteurised milk
mairie (f) – town hall
manade (f) – herd of bulls or horses
manadier (m) – herdsman
marais (m) – marsh or swamp
marais salant (m) – salt pan
marché aux puces (m) – flea market
marché couvert (m) – covered market
marché Provençal (m) – open air market
mas (m) – farmhouse
méduse (f) – jellyfish
menu (m) – meal at a fixed price with two or more courses
mistral (m) – incessant north wind
moulin à vent (m) – windmill
moulin à huile (m) – oil mill
œuvre (f) – work (of art, literature)
parvis (m) – square in front of a church
pâtisserie (f) – cake & pastry shop
pétanque (f) – a game not unlike lawn bowls
phare (m) – lighthouse
pic (m) – mountain peak
pied noir (m) – Algerian born French person
place (f) – square
plage (f) – beach
planche à voile (f) – surfboard
pont (m) – bridge
pourboire (m) – tip
presqu'île (f) – peninsula
prieuré (m) – priory
produit du terroir (m) – local food product
rade (f) – gulf or harbour
ravin (m) – gully or ravine
refuge (m) – hikers' shelter in a mountain hut
salin (m) – salt marsh
sentier (m) – trail
sentier sous-marin (m) – underwater trail
sur rendez-vous (SRV) – by appointment only
tabac (m) – tobacconist selling newspapers, bus tickets, *télécartes* etc
table d'orientation (f) – viewpoint indicator
vendange (f) – harvest
vente en détaxe (f) – duty-free sales

LONELY PLANET

Phrasebooks

L onely Planet phrasebooks are packed with essential words and phrases to help travellers communicate with the locals. With colour tabs for quick reference, an extensive vocabulary and use of script, these handy pocket-sized language guides cover day-to-day travel situations.

- handy pocket-sized books
- easy to understand Pronunciation chapter
- clear & comprehensive Grammar chapter
- romanisation alongside script to allow ease of pronunciation
- script throughout so users can point to phrases for every situation
- full of cultural information and tips for the traveller

'...vital for a real DIY spirit and attitude in language learning'
  – *Backpacker*

'the phrasebooks have good cultural backgrounders and offer solid advice for challenging situations in remote locations'
  – *San Francisco Examiner*

Arabic (Egyptian) • Arabic (Moroccan) • Australian *(Australian English, Aboriginal and Torres Strait languages)* • Baltic States *(Estonian, Latvian, Lithuanian)* • Bengali • Brazilian • Burmese • Cantonese • Central Asia • Central Europe *(Czech, French, German, Hungarian, Italian, Slovak)* • Eastern Europe *(Bulgarian, Czech, Hungarian, Polish, Romanian, Slovak)* • Ethiopian (Amharic) • Fijian • French • German • Greek • Hill Tribes • Hindi/Urdu • Indonesian • Italian • Japanese • Korean • Lao • Latin American Spanish • Malay • Mandarin • Mediterranean Europe *(Albanian, Croatian, Greek, Italian, Macedonian, Maltese, Serbian, Slovene)* • Mongolian • Nepali • Papua New Guinea • Pilipino (Tagalog) • Quechua • Russian • Scandinavian Europe *(Danish, Finnish, Icelandic, Norwegian, Swedish)* • South-East Asia *(Burmese, Indonesian, Khmer, Lao, Malay, Tagalog Pilipino, Thai, Vietnamese)* • Spanish (Castilian) *(also includes Catalan, Galician and Basque)* • Sri Lanka • Swahili • Thai • Tibetan • Turkish • Ukrainian • USA *(US English, Vernacular, Native American languages, Hawaiian)* • Vietnamese • Western Europe *(Basque, Catalan, Dutch, French, German, Greek, Irish)*

LONELY PLANET

Lonely Planet Journeys

JOURNEYS is a unique collection of travel writing – published by the company that understands travel better than anyone else. It is a series for anyone who has ever experienced – or dreamed of – the magical moment when they encountered a strange culture or saw a place for the first time. They are tales to read while you're planning a trip, while you're on the road or while you're in an armchair in front of a fire.

These outstanding titles explore our planet through the eyes of a diverse group of international writers. JOURNEYS books catch the spirit of a place, illuminate a culture, recount a crazy adventure or introduce a fascinating way of life. They always entertain, and always enrich the experience of travel.

MALI BLUES
Traveling to an African Beat
Lieve Joris (translated by Sam Garrett)

Drought, rebel uprisings, ethnic conflict: these are the predominant images of West Africa. But as Lieve Joris travels in Senegal, Mauritania and Mali, she meets survivors, fascinating individuals charting new ways of living between tradition and modernity. With her remarkable gift for drawing out people's stories, Joris brilliantly captures the rhythms of a world that refuses to give in.

THE GATES OF DAMASCUS
Lieve Joris (translated by Sam Garrett)

This best-selling book is a beautifully drawn portrait of day-to-day life in modern Syria. Through her intimate contact with local people, Lieve Joris draws us into the fascinating world that lies behind the gates of Damascus. Hala's husband is a political prisoner, jailed for his opposition to the Assad regime; through the author's friendship with Hala we see how Syrian politics impacts on the lives of ordinary people.

THE OLIVE GROVE
Travels in Greece
Katherine Kizilos

Katherine Kizilos travels to fabled islands, troubled border zones and her family's village deep in the mountains. She vividly evokes breathtaking landscapes, generous people and passionate politics, capturing the complexities of a country she loves.

'beautifully captures the real tensions of Greece' – *Sunday Times*

KINGDOM OF THE FILM STARS
Journey into Jordan
Annie Caulfield

Kingdom of the Film Stars is a travel book and a love story. With honesty and humour, Annie Caulfield writes of travelling in Jordan and falling in love with a Bedouin with film-star looks.

She offers fascinating insights into the country – from the tent life of traditional women to the hustle of downtown Amman – and unpicks tight-woven western myths about the Arab world.

LONELY PLANET

Lonely Planet Travel Atlases

Lonely Planet has long been famous for the number and quality of its guidebook maps. Now we've gone one step further and produced a handy companion series: Lonely Planet travel atlases – maps of a country produced in book form.

Unlike other maps, which look good but lead travellers astray, our travel atlases have been researched on the road by Lonely Planet's experienced team of writers. All details are carefully checked to ensure the atlas corresponds with the equivalent Lonely Planet guidebook.

- full-colour throughout
- maps researched and checked by Lonely Planet authors
- place names correspond with Lonely Planet guidebooks
- no confusing spelling differences
- legend and travelling information in English, French, German, Japanese and Spanish
- size: 230 x 160 mm

Available now: Chile & Easter Island • Egypt • India & Bangladesh • Israel & the Palestinian Territories • Jordan, Syria & Lebanon • Kenya • Laos • Portugal • South Africa, Lesotho & Swaziland • Thailand • Turkey • Vietnam • Zimbabwe, Botswana & Namibia

Lonely Planet TV Series & Videos

Lonely Planet travel guides have been brought to life on television screens around the world. Like our guides, the programs are based on the joy of independent travel, and look honestly at some of the most exciting, picturesque and frustrating places in the world. Each show is presented by one of three travellers from Australia, England or the USA and combines an innovative mixture of video, Super-8 film, atmospheric soundscapes and original music.

Videos of each episode – containing additional footage not shown on television – are available from good book and video shops, but the availability of individual videos varies with regional screening schedules.

Video destinations include: Alaska • American Rockies • Australia – The South-East • Baja California & the Copper Canyon • Brazil • Central Asia • Chile & Easter Island • Corsica, Sicily & Sardinia – The Mediterranean Islands • East Africa (Tanzania & Zanzibar) • Ecuador & the Galapagos Islands • Greenland & Iceland • Indonesia • Israel & the Sinai Desert • Jamaica • Japan • La Ruta Maya • Morocco • New York • North India • Pacific Islands (Fiji, Solomon Islands & Vanuatu) • South India • South West China • Turkey • Vietnam • West Africa • Zimbabwe, Botswana & Namibia

The Lonely Planet TV series is produced by: Pilot Productions
The Old Studio
18 Middle Row
London W10 5AT, UK

LONELY PLANET

Lonely Planet On-line
www.lonelyplanet.com *or* **AOL keyword: lp**

Whether you've just begun planning your next trip, or you're chasing down specific info on currency regulations or visa requirements, check out Lonely Planet On-line for up-to-the minute travel information.

As well as mini guides to more than 250 destinations, you'll find maps, photos, travel news, health and visa updates, travel advisories, and discussion of the ecological and political issues you need to be aware of as you travel. You'll also find timely upgrades to popular guidebooks which you can print out and stick in the back of your book.

There's also an on-line travellers' forum where you can share your experience of life on the road, meet travel companions and ask other travellers for their recommendations and advice.

And of course we have a complete and up-to-date list of all Lonely Planet travel products including travel guides, diving and snorkeling guides, phrasebooks, atlases, travel literature and videos, and a simple on-line ordering facility if you can't find the book you want elsewhere.

Lonely Planet Diving & Snorkeling Guides

Known for indispensible guidebooks to destinations all over the world, Lonely Planet's Pisces Books are the most popular series of diving and snorkeling titles available.

There are three series: **Diving & Snorkeling Guides**, **Shipwreck Diving** series and **Dive Into History**. Full colour throughout, the **Diving & Snorkeling Guides** combine quality photographs with detailed descriptions of the best dive sites for each location, giving divers a glimpse of what they can expect both on land and in water. The **Dive Into History** series is perfect for the adventure diver or armchair traveller. The **Shipwreck Diving** series provides all the details for exploring the most interesting wrecks in the Atlantic and Pacific oceans. The list also includes underwater nature and technical guides.

LONELY PLANET

Guides by Region

L onely Planet is known worldwide for publishing practical, reliable and no-nonsense travel information in our guides and on our Web site. The Lonely Planet list covers just about every accessible part of the world. Currently there are nine series: travel guides, shoestring guides, walking guides, city guides, phrasebooks, audio packs, travel atlases, diving and snorkeling guides and travel literature.

AFRICA Africa – the South • Africa on a shoestring • Arabic (Egyptian) phrasebook • Arabic (Moroccan) phrasebook • Cairo • Cape Town • Central Africa • East Africa • Egypt • Egypt travel atlas • Ethiopian (Amharic) phrasebook • The Gambia & Senegal • Kenya • Kenya travel atlas • Malawi, Mozambique & Zambia • Morocco • North Africa • South Africa, Lesotho & Swaziland • South Africa, Lesotho & Swaziland travel atlas • Swahili phrasebook • Trekking in East Africa • Tunisia • West Africa • Zimbabwe, Botswana & Namibia • Zimbabwe, Botswana & Namibia travel atlas
Travel Literature: The Rainbird: A Central African Journey • Songs to an African Sunset: A Zimbabwean Story • Mali Blues: Traveling to an African Beat

AUSTRALIA & THE PACIFIC Australia • Australian phrasebook • Bushwalking in Australia • Bushwalking in Papua New Guinea • Fiji • Fijian phrasebook • Islands of Australia's Great Barrier Reef • Melbourne • Micronesia • New Caledonia • New South Wales & the ACT • New Zealand • Northern Territory • Outback Australia • Papua New Guinea • Papua New Guinea (Pidgin) phrasebook • Queensland • Rarotonga & the Cook Islands • Samoa • Solomon Islands • South Australia • Sydney • Tahiti & French Polynesia • Tasmania • Tonga • Tramping in New Zealand • Vanuatu • Victoria • Western Australia
Travel Literature: Islands in the Clouds • Sean & David's Long Drive

CENTRAL AMERICA & THE CARIBBEAN Bahamas and Turks & Caicos • Bermuda • Central America on a shoestring • Costa Rica • Cuba • Eastern Caribbean • Guatemala, Belize & Yucatán: La Ruta Maya • Jamaica • Mexico • Mexico City • Panama
Travel Literature: Green Dreams: Travels in Central America

EUROPE Amsterdam • Andalucía • Austria • Baltic States phrasebook • Berlin • Britain • Central Europe • Central Europe phrasebook • Czech & Slovak Republics • Denmark • Dublin • Eastern Europe • Eastern Europe phrasebook • Edinburgh • Estonia, Latvia & Lithuania • Europe • Finland • France • French phrasebook • Germany • German phrasebook • Greece • Greek phrasebook • Hungary • Iceland, Greenland & the Faroe Islands • Ireland • Italian phrasebook • Italy • Lisbon • London • Mediterranean Europe • Mediterranean Europe phrasebook • Paris • Poland • Portugal • Portugal travel atlas • Prague • Romania & Moldova • Russia, Ukraine & Belarus • Russian phrasebook • Scandinavian & Baltic Europe • Scandinavian Europe phrasebook • Scotland • Slovenia • Spain • Spanish phrasebook • St Petersburg • Switzerland • Trekking in Spain • Ukrainian phrasebook • Vienna • Walking in Britain • Walking in Italy • Walking in Switzerland • Western Europe • Western Europe phrasebook
Travel Literature: The Olive Grove: Travels in Greece

INDIAN SUBCONTINENT Bangladesh • Bengali phrasebook • Bhutan • Delhi • Goa • Hindi/Urdu phrasebook • India • India & Bangladesh travel atlas • Indian Himalaya • Karakoram Highway • Nepal • Nepali phrasebook • Pakistan • Rajasthan • South India • Sri Lanka • Sri Lanka phrasebook • Trekking in the Indian Himalaya • Trekking in the Karakoram & Hindukush • Trekking in the Nepal Himalaya
Travel Literature: In Rajasthan • Shopping for Buddhas

LONELY PLANET

Mail Order

Lonely Planet products are distributed worldwide. They are also available by mail order from Lonely Planet, so if you have difficulty finding a title please write to us. North and South American residents should write to 150 Linden St, Oakland, CA 94607, USA; European and African residents should write to 10a Spring Place, London NW5 3BH, UK; and residents of other countries to PO Box 617, Hawthorn, Victoria 3122, Australia.

ISLANDS OF THE INDIAN OCEAN Madagascar & Comoros • Maldives • Mauritius, Réunion & Seychelles

MIDDLE EAST & CENTRAL ASIA Arab Gulf States • Central Asia • Central Asia phrasebook • Iran • Israel & the Palestinian Territories • Israel & the Palestinian Territories travel atlas • Istanbul • Jerusalem • Jordan & Syria • Jordan, Syria & Lebanon travel atlas • Lebanon • Middle East on a shoestring • Turkey • Turkish phrasebook • Turkey travel atlas • Yemen
Travel Literature: The Gates of Damascus • Kingdom of the Film Stars: Journey into Jordan

NORTH AMERICA Alaska • Backpacking in Alaska • Baja California • California & Nevada • Canada • Florida • Hawaii • Honolulu • Los Angeles • Miami • New England USA • New Orleans • New York City • New York, New Jersey & Pennsylvania • Pacific Northwest USA • Rocky Mountain States • San Francisco • Seattle • Southwest USA • USA phrasebook • Washington, DC & the Capital Region
Travel Literature: Drive Thru America

NORTH-EAST ASIA Beijing • Cantonese phrasebook • China • Hong Kong • Hong Kong, Macau & Guangzhou • Japan • Japanese phrasebook • Japanese audio pack • Korea • Korean phrasebook • Kyoto • Mandarin phrasebook • Mongolia • Mongolian phrasebook • North-East Asia on a shoestring • Seoul • South-West China • Taiwan • Tibet • Tibetan phrasebook • Tokyo
Travel Literature: Lost Japan

SOUTH AMERICA Argentina, Uruguay & Paraguay • Bolivia • Brazil • Brazilian phrasebook • Buenos Aires • Chile & Easter Island • Chile & Easter Island travel atlas • Colombia • Ecuador & the Galapagos Islands • Latin American Spanish phrasebook • Peru • Quechua phrasebook • Rio de Janeiro • South America on a shoestring • Trekking in the Patagonian Andes • Venezuela
Travel Literature: Full Circle: A South American Journey

SOUTH-EAST ASIA Bali & Lombok • Bangkok • Burmese phrasebook • Cambodia • Hill Tribes phrasebook • Ho Chi Minh City • Indonesia • Indonesian phrasebook • Indonesian audio pack • Jakarta • Java • Laos • Lao phrasebook • Laos travel atlas • Malay phrasebook • Malaysia, Singapore & Brunei • Myanmar (Burma) • Philippines • Pilipino (Tagalog) phrasebook • Singapore • South-East Asia on a shoestring • South-East Asia phrasebook • Thailand • Thailand's Islands & Beaches • Thailand travel atlas • Thai phrasebook • Thai audio pack • Vietnam • Vietnamese phrasebook • Vietnam travel atlas

ALSO AVAILABLE: Antarctica • Brief Encounters: Stories of Love, Sex & Travel • Chasing Rickshaws • Not the Only Planet: Travel Stories from Science Fiction • Travel with Children • Traveller's Tales

LONELY PLANET

FREE Lonely Planet Newsletters

We love hearing from you and think you'd like to hear from us.

Planet Talk

Our FREE quarterly printed newsletter is full of tips from travellers and anecdotes from Lonely Planet guidebook authors. Every issue is packed with up-to-date travel news and advice, and includes:

- a postcard from Lonely Planet co-founder Tony Wheeler
- a swag of mail from travellers
- a look at life on the road through the eyes of a Lonely Planet author
- topical health advice
- prizes for the best travel yarn
- news about forthcoming Lonely Planet events
- a complete list of Lonely Planet books and other titles

To join our mailing list, residents of the UK, Europe and Africa can email us at go@lonelyplanet.co.uk; residents of North and South America can email us at info@lonelyplanet.com; the rest of the world can email us at talk2us@lonelyplanet.com.au, or contact any Lonely Planet office.

Comet

Our FREE monthly email newsletter brings you all the latest travel news, features, interviews, competitions, destination ideas, travellers' tips & tales, Q&As, raging debates and related links. Find out what's new on the Lonely Planet Web site and which books are about to hit the shelves.

Subscribe from your desktop: www.lonelyplanet.com/comet

Index

Text

Bold indicates maps.
Italics indicates boxed text.

Boxed Text

MAP LEGEND

BOUNDARIES

.............International
.............State
.............Disputed
.............Arrondissement

HYDROGRAPHY

.............Coastline
.............River, Creek
.............Lake
.............Intermittent Lake
.............Canal
.............Rapids
.............Waterfalls
.............Swamp

ROUTES & TRANSPORT

.............Freeway
.............Highway
.............Major Road
.............Minor Road
.............Unsealed Road
.............City Freeway
.............City Highway
.............City Road
.............City Street, Lane

.............Pedestrian Mall
.............Tunnel
.............Train Route & Station
.............Metro & Station
.............Tramway
.............Cable Car or Chairlift
.............Walking Track
.............Walking Tour
.............Ferry Route

AREA FEATURES

.............Building
.............Park, Gardens
.............Cemetery

.............Market
.............Beach, Desert
.............Urban Area

MAP SYMBOLS

✪ CAPITAL	National Capital	✈	Airport	←	One-Way Street
◉ CAPITAL	State Capital		Ancient or City Wall	P	Parking
● CITY	City	⁘	Archaeological Site	)(	Pass
● Town	Town	⑤	Bank	★	Police Station
● Village	Village	🏖	Beach	✉	Post Office
○	Point of Interest	🚲	Bicycle Rental	❖	Shopping Centre
		◪	Castle or Fort		Ski Field
■	Place to Stay	🏰 ✚	Church	🏛	Stately Home
▲	Camping Ground		Cliff or Escarpment	☎	Telephone
⌂	Caravan Park	◎	Embassy	⬛	Temple
⌂	Hut or Chalet	✚	Hospital	⊙	Toilet
		⚐	Monument	❶	Tourist Information
▼	Place to Eat	▲	Mountain or Hill	●	Transport
⊟	Pub or Bar	🏛	Museum	🐘	Zoo

Note: not all symbols displayed above appear in this book

LONELY PLANET OFFICES

Australia
PO Box 617, Hawthorn 3122, Victoria
tel: (03) 9819 1877 fax: (03) 9819 6459
e-mail: talk2us@lonelyplanet.com.au

USA
150 Linden St, Oakland, CA 94607
tel: (510) 893 8555 TOLL FREE: 800 275-8555
fax: (510) 893 8572
e-mail: info@lonelyplanet.com

UK
10a Spring Place, London, NW5 3BH
tel: (0171) 428 4800 fax: (0170) 428 4828
e-mail: go@lonelyplanet.co.uk

France
1 rue du Dahomey, 75011 Paris
tel: 01 55 25 33 00 fax: 01 55 25 33 01
e-mail: bip@lonelyplanet.fr

World Wide Web: www.lonelyplanet.com *or* AOL keyword: lp
Lonely Planet Images: lpi@lonelyplanet.com.au